MANETHO

WITH AN ENGLISH TRANSLATION BY

W. G. WADDELL

PROFESSOR OF CLASSICS IN FUAD EL AWAL UNIVERSITY,
CAIRO, EGYPT

ISBN: 978-1-63923-938-2

All Rights reserved. No part of this book maybe reproduced without written permission from the publishers, except by a reviewer who may quote brief passages in a review to be printed in a newspaper or magazine.

Printed: March 2023

Published and Distributed By:
Lushena Books
607 Country Club Drive, Unit E
Bensenville, IL 60106
www.lushenabks.com

ISBN: 978-1-63923-938-2

CONTENTS

	PAGE
INTRODUCTION	vii
The Life of Manetho: Traditions and Conjectures	ix
Manetho's Works	xiv
The History of Egypt	xv
Possible Sources of the Αἰγυπτιακά . .	xx
Other Works attributed to Manetho . .	xxvi
The Book of Sôthis	xxvii
BIBLIOGRAPHY	xxix
LIST OF ABBREVIATED TITLES . . .	xxxi
EDITOR'S NOTE	xxxii
THE HISTORY OF EGYPT	1-187
THE SACRED BOOK	188
AN EPITOME OF PHYSICAL DOCTRINES . .	196
ON FESTIVALS	198
ON ANCIENT RITUAL AND RELIGION . .	198
ON THE MAKING OF KYPHI	202
[CRITICISMS OF HERODOTUS] . . .	204
APPENDIX I., PSEUDO-MANETHO . . .	208
„ II., ERATOSTHENES (?) . . .	212
„ III., THE OLD *Chronicle* . .	226
„ IV., THE BOOK OF SÔTHIS . .	234
MAP OF EGYPT	250
ILLUSTRATIONS: PLATES I-IV . . .	*facing* 250
INDEX	251

Hermes Trismegistus speaks:

O Aegypte, Aegypte, religionum tuarum solac supererunt fabulae, eaeque incredibiles posteris tuis; solaque supererunt verba lapidibus incisa, tua pia facta narrantibus. ["O Egypt, Egypt, of thy religious rites nought will survive but idle tales which thy children's children will not believe; nought will survive but words graven upon stones that tell of thy piety."]
> The Latin Asclepius III. 25, in W. Scott, *Hermetica*, i. 1924, p. 342.

* * * * * * *

"Never has there arisen a more complicated problem than that of Manetho."
> —BOECKH, *Manetho und die Hundssternperiode*, 1845, p. 10.

INTRODUCTION

AMONG the Egyptians who wrote in Greek, Manetho the priest holds a unique place because of his comparatively early date (the third century B.C.) and the interest of his subject-matter—the history and religion of Ancient Egypt. His works in their original form would possess the highest importance and value for us now, if only we could recover them; but until the fortunate discovery of a papyrus,[1] which will transmit the authentic Manetho, we can know his writings only from fragmentary and often distorted quotations preserved chiefly by Josephus and by the Christian chronographers, Africanus and Eusebius, with isolated passages in Plutarch, Theophilus, Aelian, Porphyrius, Diogenes Laertius, Theodoretus, Lydus, Malalas, the Scholia to Plato, and the *Etymologicum Magnum*.

Like Bêrôssos, who is of slightly earlier date, Manetho testifies to the growth of an international

[1] F. Bilabel (in P. Baden 4. 1924, No. 59: see also *Die Kleine Historiker*, Fragm. 11) published a papyrus of the fifth century after Christ containing a list of Persian kings with the years of their reigns (see further Fr. 70, note 1), and holds it to be, not part of the original *Epitome*, but a version made from it before the time of Africanus. It certainly proves that Egyptians were interested in Greek versions of the Kings' Lists, and much more so, presumably, in the unabridged Manetho. See Fr. 2 for Panodôrus and Annianus, who were monks in Egypt about the date of this papyrus. *Cf.* also P. Hibeh, i. 27, the Calendar of Saïs, translated into Greek in the reign of Ptolemy Sôter, *i.e.* early in the lifetime of Manetho.

MANETHO

spirit in the Alexandrine age: each of these "barbarians" wrote in Greek an account of his native country; and it stirs the imagination to think of their endeavour to bridge the gulf and instruct all Greek-speaking people (that is to say the whole civilized world of their time) in the history of Egypt and Chaldaea. But these two writers stand alone:[1] the Greeks indeed wrote from time to time of the wonders of Egypt (works no longer extant), but it was long before an Egyptian successor of Manetho appeared—Ptolemy of Mendês,[2] probably under Augustus.

The writings of Manetho, however, continued to

[1] *Cf.* W. W. Tarn on Ptolemy II. in the *Journal of Egyptian Archaeology*, 1928, xiv. p. 254: (Activity at Alexandria had no effect at all on Egyptians) "Ptolemy Sôter had thought for a moment that Egyptians might participate in the intellectual activities of Alexandria: . . . but, though Manetho dedicated his work to Ptolemy II., in this reign all interest in native Egypt was dropped, and a little later Alexandria appears as merely an object of hatred to many Egyptians. (Its destruction is prophesied in the Potter's Oracle.)" (See p. 123 n. 1.)

The complete isolation of Manetho and Bêrôssos is the chief argument of Ernest Havet against the authenticity of these writers (*Mémoire sur les écrits qui portent les noms de Bérose et de Manéthon*, Paris, 1873). He regards the double tradition as curious and extraordinary—there is no other name to set beside these two Oriental priests; and he suspects the symmetry of the tradition—each wrote three books for a king. *Cf.* Croiset, *Histoire de la Littérature Grecque*, v. p. 99; *Abridged History of Greek Literature*, English translation, p. 429 (Manetho's works were probably written by a Hellenized Oriental at the end of the second century B.C.); and F. A. Wright, *Later Greek Literature*, p. 60.

[2] See p. x.

INTRODUCTION

be read with interest; and his *Egyptian History* was used for special purposes, *e.g.* by the Jews when they engaged in polemic against Egyptians in order to prove their extreme antiquity. (See further pp. xvi ff.) Manetho's religious writings are known to us mainly through references in Plutarch's treatise *On Isis and Osiris*.

The Life of Manetho : Traditions and Conjectures.

Our knowledge of Manetho is for the most part meagre and uncertain; but three statements of great probability may be made. They concern his native place, his priesthood at Hêliopolis, and his activity in the introduction of the cult of Serapis.

The name Manetho ($Μανεθώς$, often written $Μανέθων$) has been explained as meaning " Truth of Thôth ", and a certain priest under Dynasty XIX. is described as " First Priest of the Truth of Thôth ".[1] According to Dr. Černý [2] " Manetho " is from the Coptic ⲘⲀⲚⲈϨⲦⲞ " groom " (ⲘⲀⲚⲈ " herdsman ", and ϨⲦⲞ " horse "); but the word does not seem to occur elsewhere as a proper name. In regard to the date of Manetho, Syncellus in one passage [3] gives us the information that he lived later than Bêrôssos: elsewhere [4] he puts Manetho as " almost contemporary with Bêrôssos, or a little later ". Bêrôssos, who

---

[1] W. Spiegelberg, *Orient. Literaturz.* xxxi. 1928, col. 145 ff., xxxii. 1929, col. 321 f. Older explanations of the name Manetho were " Gift of Thôth," " Beloved of Thôth," and " Beloved of Neith ".

[2] In the centenary volume of the Vatican Museum : I owe this reference to the kindness of Dr. Alan H. Gardiner.

[3] Manetho, Fr. 3.   [4] Syncellus, p. 26.

MANETHO

was priest of Marduk at Babylon, lived under, and wrote for, Antiochus I. whose reign lasted from 285 to 261 B.C.; and Bêrôssos dedicated his Χαλδαϊκά to this king after he became sole monarch in 281 B.C. The works of Manetho and Bêrôssos may be interpreted as an expression of the rivalry of the two kings, Ptolemy and Antiochus, each seeking to proclaim the great antiquity of his land.

Under the name of Manetho, Suidas seems to distinguish two writers: (1) Manetho of Mendês in Egypt, a chief priest who wrote on the making of *kyphi* (*i.e.* Fr. 87): (2) Manetho of Diospolis or Sebennytus. (Works): *A Treatise on Physical Doctrines* (*i.e.* Fr. 82, 83). *Apotelesmatica* (or *Astrological Influences*), in hexameter verses, and other astrological works. (See p. xiv, note 3.) Nowhere else is Manetho connected with Mendês; but as Mendês was distant only about 17 miles from Sebennytus across the Damietta arm of the Nile, the attribution is not impossible. Müller suspects confusion with Ptolemy of Mendês, an Egyptian priest (probably in the time of Augustus), who, like Manetho, wrote a work on Egyptian Chronology in three books. In the second note of Suidas Diospolis may be identified, not with Diospolis Magna (the famous Thebes) nor with Diospolis Parva, but with Diospolis Inferior, in the Delta (now Tell el-Balamûn), the capital of the Diospolite or 17th nome[1] to the north of the Sebennyte nome and contiguous with

---

[1] The Greek word νομός means a division of Egypt, called in Ancient Egyptian *sp.t*,—a district corresponding roughly to a county in England. Pliny (*Hist. Nat.* 5, 9) refers to nomes as *praefecturae oppidorum*.

INTRODUCTION

it. Diospolis Inferior lay near Damietta, some 30 miles from Sebennytus. (See Strabo, 17. 1, 19, and Baedeker, *Egypt and the Sûdân*, 8th ed. (1929), p. 185.) We may therefore accept the usual description of Manetho (Fr. 3, 77, 80 : Syncellus, 72, 16), and hold that he was a native of Sebennytus (now Samannûd)[1] in the Delta, on the west bank of the Damietta branch of the Nile. Manetho was a priest, and doubtless held office at one time in the temple at Sebennytus ; but in the letter (App. I.) which he is said to have written to Ptolemy II. Philadelphus, he describes himself as " high-priest and scribe of the sacred shrines of Egypt, born at Sebennytus and dwelling at Hêliopolis ". Although the letter, as we have it, is not genuine in all its details, this description may have been borrowed from a good source ; and while his precise rank as a priest remains in doubt, it is reasonable to believe that Manetho rose to be high-priest in the temple at Hêliopolis.[2] This eminent position agrees with the important part he played in the introduction of the cult of Serapis. As a Heliopolitan priest, Manetho (to quote from Laqueur, Pauly-Wissowa-Kroll, *R.-E.* xiv. 1, 1061) " was, without doubt, acquainted with

[1] See Baedeker[8], p. 185. Sebennytus was the seat of Dynasty **XXX.**, and therefore a place of great importance shortly before the time of Manetho. In Ancient Egyptian, Sebennytus is *Tjeb-nuter*, " city of the sacred calf " : it is tempting to connect with Sebennytus the worship of the Golden Calf in *O.T. Exodus* xxxii., *1 Kings* xii. 28 ff. (P. E. Newberry).

[2] See Strabo, 17. 1, 29 for the " large houses in which the priests had lived ". According to Herodotus (ii. 3, 1), " the Heliopolitans are said to be the most learned of the Egyptians ".

MANETHO

the sacred tree in the great Hall of Hêliopolis,—the tree on which the goddess Seshat, the Lady of Letters, the Mistress of the Library, wrote down with her own hand the names and deeds of the rulers.[1] He did nothing more than communicate to the Greek world what the goddess had noted down.[2] But he did so with a full sense of the superiority which relied on the sacred records of the Egyptians in opposition to Herodotus whom he was contradicting" (Fr. 43, § 73 : Fr. 88). His native town, Sebennytus, was visited as a place of learning by Solon when Ethêmôn was a priest in residence there (see Proclus *in Plat. Tim.* i. 101, 22, Diehl); and the Greek culture of the place must have been a formative influence upon Manetho at an early age.

In the introduction of the statue of Serapis to Alexandria as described by Plutarch (Manetho, Fr. 80), Manetho the Egyptian was associated with the Greek Timotheus as a priestly adviser of King Ptolemy Sôter. It is natural to suppose that the cult of Serapis itself, which was a conflation of

---

[1] See Erman-Ranke, *Ägypten*, 1923, pp. 396 f.; or Erman, *Die Religion der Ägypter*, 1934, pp. 56 f.; or the original drawing in Lepsius, *Denkmäler*, iii. 169. This illustration shows the goddess, along with Thôth and Atûm, making inscriptions upon the leaves (or fruit) of the venerable tree.

[2] It may be added that the Egyptians are surpassed by no nation in their strong and ever-present desire to leave upon stone or papyrus permanent records of their history, their motive being to glorify the ruling king. *Cf.* Herodotus, ii. 77, 1 (of the Egyptians who live in the cultivated country), " the most diligent of all men in preserving the memory of the past, and far better skilled in chronicles than any others whom I have questioned ".

INTRODUCTION

Egyptian and Greek ideas intended to be acceptable to both nationalities, had already been organized [1] with the help of the two priests, and the magnificent temple in Rhakôtis, the Egyptian quarter in the west of Alexandria, had doubtless been built. The date is not certain : according to Jerome (Fotheringham, p. 211, Helm, p. 129) " Sarapis entered Alexandria " in 286 B.C., while the Armenian Version of the *Chronicle* of Eusebius says that in 278 B.C. " Sarapis came to Alexandria, and became resident there " (Karst, 200). Perhaps the two statements refer to different stages in the development of the cult : if the former describes the entry of the statue by Bryaxis, the latter may possibly refer to the final establishment of the whole theology. As a proof that the work of Manetho in building up the cult of Serapis must not be belittled, it may suffice to refer to the inscription of the name $Μανέθων$ on the base of a marble bust found in the ruins of the Temple of Serapis at Carthage (*Corpus Inscr. Lat.* viii. 1007). The name is so uncommon that the probability is that the bust which originally stood on this base represented the Egyptian Manetho, and was erected in his honour because of his effective contribution to the organization of the cult of

---

[1] The earliest date for Serapis is given by Macrobius, *Sat.* i. 20, 16, a questioning of Serapis by Nicocreon of Cyprus, c. 311-310 B.C. For Dittenberger, *O.G.I.S.* 16 (an inscription from Halicarnassus on the founding of a temple to Serapis-Isis under (the satrap) Ptolemy Sôter), the date is uncertain, probably c. 308-306 B.C. Already in Menander's drama, $Ἐγχειρίδιον$ (before 291 B.C. when Menander died), Serapis is a " holy god " (P. Oxy. XV. 1803).

MANETHO

Serapis.[1] Hence it is not impossible also that the following reference in a papyrus of 241 B.C. may be to Manetho of Sebennytus. It occurs in a document containing correspondence about a Temple Seal (P. Hibeh, i. 72, vv. 6, 7, γράφειν Μανεθῶι). The person named was evidently a well-known man in priestly circles: he was probably our Manetho, the writer on Egyptian history and religion, if he lived to a considerable age.[2]

Manetho's Works.

Eight works [3] have been attributed to Manetho: (1) *Αἰγυπτιακά*, or *The History of Egypt*, (2) *The Book of Sôthis*, (3) *The Sacred Book*, (4) *An Epitome of Physical Doctrines*, (5) *On Festivals*, (6) *On Ancient Ritual and Religion*, (7) *On the Making of Kyphi* [a kind of incense], (8) *Criticisms of Herodotus*.

Of these, (2) *The Book of Sôthis* (App. IV. and

---

[1] *Cf.* Lafaye, *Histoire du Culte des Divinités d'Alexandrie* (1884), p. 16 n. 1: "At all events, there is no doubt that the adepts of the Alexandrine cult had great veneration for Manetho, and considered him in some measure as their patriarch".

[2] Bouché-Leclercq (*Histoire des Lagides*, iv. p. 269 n. 4) holds a different opinion: "the reference is not necessarily to the celebrated Manetho, whose very existence is problematical".

[3] A work wrongly attributed in antiquity (*e.g.* by Suidas, see p. x) to Manetho of Sebennytus is *Ἀποτελεσματικά*, in 6 books, an astrological poem in hexameters on the influence of the stars. See W. Kroll (*R.-E. s.v.* Manethon (2)), who with Köchly recognizes in the 6 books 4 sections of different dates from about A.D. 120 to the fourth century after Christ. Books I. and V. open with dedications to King Ptolemy: *cf.* Pseudo-Manetho, Appendix I.

INTRODUCTION

pp. xxvii. ff.) is certainly not by Manetho; and there is no reason to believe that (8) *Criticisms of Herodotus* formed a separate work, although we know from Josephus, *C. Apion.* i. 73 (Fr. 42), that Manetho did convict Herodotus of error. Six titles remain, but it has long been thought that some of these are " ghost " titles. Fruin (*Manetho*, p. lxxvii) supposed that Manetho wrote only two works—one on Egyptian history, the other on Egyptian mythology and antiquities. Susemihl (*Alex. Lit.-Gesch.* i. 609, n. 431) and W. Otto (*Priester und Tempel in Hellenistischen Ägypten*, ii. 215, n. 4) modified this extreme view : they recognized three distinct works of Manetho (*The History of Egypt, The Sacred Book*, and *An Epitome of Physical Doctrines*), and assumed that the titles *On Festivals, On Ancient Ritual and Religion*, and *On the Making of Kyphi* referred to passages in *The Sacred Book*. In the paucity of our data, no definite judgement seems possible as to whether Manetho wrote six works or only three; but in support of the former theory we may refer to Eusebius (Man. Fr. 76).

The History of Egypt.

The *Egyptian History* [1] of Manetho is preserved in extracts of two kinds. (1) Excerpts from the original work are preserved by Josephus, along with other passages which can only be pseudo-

[1] Or *Notes about Egypt*. There are two variants of the Greek title : Αἰγυπτιακά (Josephus in Fr. 42), and Αἰγυπτιακὰ ὑπομνήματα (*Aegyptiaca monumenta*, Eus. in Fr. 1), with a possible third form Αἰγυπτίων ὑπομνήματα (*Aegyptiorum monumenta*, Eus., p. 359).

MANETHO

Manethonian. The Jews of the three centuries following the time of Manetho were naturally keenly interested in his *History* because of the connexion of their ancestors with Egypt—Abraham, Joseph, and Moses the leader of the Exodus; and they sought to base their theories of the origin and antiquity of the Jews securely upon the authentic traditions of Egypt. In Manetho indeed they found an unwelcome statement of the descent of the Jews from lepers; but they were able to identify their ancestors with the Hyksôs, and the Exodus with the expulsion of these invaders. The efforts of Jewish apologists account for much re-handling, enlargement, and corruption of Manetho's text, and the result may be seen in the treatise of Josephus, *Contra Apionem*, i.

(2) An *Epitome* of Manetho's history had been made at an early date,—not by Manetho himself, there is reason to believe,—in the form of Lists of Dynasties with short notes on outstanding kings or important events. The remains of this *Epitome* are preserved by Christian chronographers, especially by Africanus and Eusebius. Their aim was to compare the chronologies of the Oriental nations with the Bible, and for this purpose the *Epitome* gave an ideal conspectus of the whole *History*, omitting, as it does, narratives such as the account of the Hyksôs preserved by Josephus. Of the two chronographers, the founder of Christian chronography, Sextus Julius Africanus, whose *Chronicle*[1] came down to

[1] For a later miscellaneous work, the Κεστοί, see P. Oxy. iii. 412 (between A.D. 225 and 265); and Jules Africain, *Fragments des Cestes*, ed. J.-R. Vieillefond, Paris, 1932.

INTRODUCTION

A.D. 217 or A.D. 221, transmits the *Epitome* in a more accurate form ; while Eusebius, whose work extends to A.D. 326, is responsible for unwarranted alterations of the original text of Manetho. About A.D. 800 George the Monk, who is known as Syncellus from his religious office (as " attendant " of Tarasius, Patriarch of Constantinople), made use of Manetho's work in various forms in his Ἐκλογὴ Χρονογραφίας, a history of the world from Adam to Diocletian. Syncellus sought to prove that the incarnation took place in Anno Mundi 5500 ; and in his survey of the thirty-one Egyptian dynasties which reigned from the Flood to Darius, he relied on the authoritative work of Manetho as transmitted by Africanus and Eusebius, and as handed down in a corrupt form in the *Old Chronicle* (App. III.) and the *Book of Sôthis* (App. IV.) which had been used by the chronographer Panodôrus (c. A.D. 400).

Even from the above brief statement of the transmission of Manetho's text, it will be seen that many problems are involved, and that it is extremely difficult to reach certainty in regard to what is authentic Manetho and what is spurious or corrupt. The problems are discussed in detail by Richard Laqueur in his valuable and exhaustive article in Pauly-Wissowa-Kroll, *R.-E. s.v.* Manethon ; and it may be sufficient here to quote his summary of the results of his researches in regard to Manetho (1) in Josephus, and (2) in the Christian Chronographers.

(1) Manetho in Josephus, *Contra Apionem*, i. (see Fr. 42, 50, 54.)

" (a) Extracts from the genuine Manetho appear in §§ 75-82, 84-90, 94-102a, 232-249, 251. Of these

passages, §§ 75-82, 94-102a, 237-249 are quoted *verbatim*, the others are given in Indirect Speech.

"(b) A rationalistic critique of the genuine Manetho was written by a Hellenist, and was used by Josephus for his work. The remains of this critique appear in §§ 254-261, 267-269, 271-274, 276-277. Perhaps §§ 102b-103 is connected with these.

"(c) The authoritative work of Manetho was further exploited by Jews and Egyptians in their mutual polemic, in the course of which additions to Manetho's works were made: these additions were partly favourable to the Jews (§§ 83, 91), partly hostile to the Jews (§ 250). These passages, like those mentioned in (b), were collected before the time of Josephus into a single treatise, so that one could no longer clearly recognize what had belonged to Manetho and what was based upon additions.

"(d) Josephus originally knew only the genuine Manetho (*cf.* (a)), and used him throughout as a witness against the aggressors of Judaism. In this it was of importance for Josephus to show that the Hyksôs had come to Egypt from abroad, that their expulsion took place long before the beginning of Greek history, and that they, in their expedition to aid the Lepers, remained untainted by them.

"(e) After Josephus had completed this elaboration, he came later to know the material mentioned in (b) and (c): so far as it was favourable to the Jews or helpful in interpretation, it led only to short expansions of the older presentation; so far, however, as it was hostile to the Jews, Josephus found himself induced to make a radical change in his attitude towards Manetho. He attacked Manetho

INTRODUCTION

sharply for his alleged statement (§ 250), and at the same time used the polemic mentioned in (*b*) in order to overthrow Manetho's authority in general.

" (*f*) From the facts adduced it follows that Manetho's work was already before the time of Josephus the object of numerous literary analyses."[1]

Cf. the following summary.

(2) Manetho in the Christian Chronographers.

" (*a*) Not long after the appearance of Manetho's work, an *Epitome* was made, giving excerpts from the Dynasty-Lists and increasing these from 30 to 31. The possibility that other additions were made is not excluded.

" (*b*) The *Epitome* was remodelled by a Hellenistic Jew in such a way that the Jewish chronology became compatible with that of Manetho.

" (*c*) A descendant of version (*a*) is extant in Julius Africanus: a descendant of version (*b*), in Eusebius."

The *Chronicle* of Africanus in five books is lost except for what is preserved in the extracts made by Eusebius, and the many fragments contained in the works of Syncellus and Cedrenus, and in the *Paschale Chronicon*. For Eusebius we have several lines of transmission. The Greek text of Eusebius has come down to us in part, as quoted by Syncellus; but the whole work is known through (1) the Armenian Version, which was composed in v./A.D.[2]

---

[1] A further study of the transmission of Manetho in Josephus is made by A. Momigliano, " Intorno al *Contro Apione*," in *Rivista di Filologia*, 59 (1931), pp. 485-503.

[2] The Armenian MS. G (*Codex Hierosolymitanus*) printed by Aucher (1818) is dated by him between A.D.

MANETHO

from a revision of the first Greek text,[1] and is, of course, quite independent of Syncellus; and (2) the Latin Version made by Jerome towards the end of the fourth century.

Possible Sources of the Αἰγυπτιακά.

An Egyptian high priest, learned in Greek literature, had an unrivalled opportunity, in early Ptolemaic times, of writing an excellent and accurate history of Egypt. He had open access to records of all kinds—papyri[2] in the temple archives (annals, sacred books containing liturgies and poems), hieroglyphic tablets, wall sculptures, and innumerable inscriptions.[3] These records no one but an Egyptian priest could consult and read; and only a scholar who had assimilated the works of Greek historians could make a judicious and scientific use of the abundant material. It is hardly to be expected,

---

1065 and 1306. Karst quotes readings from this and two other Armenian MSS., but the variations are comparatively unimportant.

[1] See A. Puech, H*ist. de la Litt. grecque chrétienne*, iii. p. 177.

[2] Herodotus (ii. 100: *cf.* 142) mentions a papyrus roll (βύβλος) containing a list of 331 kings. Diodorus (i. 44, 4) tells of " records (ἀναγραφαί) handed down in the sacred books " (ἐν ταῖς ἱεραῖς βίβλοις), giving each king's stature, character, and deeds, as well as the length of his reign.

[3] *Cf.* the Annals of the Reign of Tuthmôsis III. (Breasted, *Ancient Records*, ii. §§ 391-540): this important historical document of 223 lines is inscribed on the walls of a corridor in the Temple of Amon at Karnak, and " demonstrates the injustice of the criticism that the Egyptians were incapable of giving a clear and succinct account of a military campaign ".

INTRODUCTION

however, that Manetho's *History* should possess more worth than that of his sources ; and the material at his disposal included a certain proportion of unhistorical traditions and popular legends.[1]

There is no possibility of identifying the particular records from which Manetho compiled his *History*: the following are the kinds of monuments which he may have consulted and from which we derive a means of controlling his statements.

(1) *The Royal List of Abydos*, on the wall of a corridor of the Temple of Sethôs I. at Abydos, gives in chronological order a series of seventy-six kings from Mênês to Sethôs I. Dynasties XIII. to XVII. are lacking. A mutilated duplicate of this list was found in the Temple of Ramessês II. at Abydos (now in the British Museum: see *Guide*, p. 245): it arranges the kings in three rows, while the more complete list has them in two rows.

(2) *The Royal List of Karnak* (now in the Louvre) has a list of kings, originally sixty-one, from Mênês down to Tuthmôsis III., Dynasty XVIII., with many names belonging to the Second Intermediate Period (Dynasties XIII.-XVII.).

The Royal Lists of Abydos and Karnak give the tradition of Upper Egypt.

(3) *The Royal List of Sakkâra* (found in a tomb at Sakkâra, and now in the Cairo Museum) preserves the cartouches of forty-seven (originally fifty-eight) kings previous to, and including, Ramessês II. It begins with Miebis, the sixth king of Dynasty I. ; and like

---

[1] The popular tales introduced kings as their heroes, without regard to chronological order: see G. Maspero, *Bibliothèque Egyptologique*, vol. vii. (1898), pp. 419 ff.

MANETHO

the *Royal List of Abydos*, it omits Dynasties XIII.-XVII. Like (4) the *Turin Papyrus*, the *Royal List of Sakkâra* gives the tradition of Lower Egypt.

(4) More important than any of the preceding is the *Turin Papyrus*, written in hieratic on the *verso* of the papyrus, with accounts of the time of Ramessês II. on the *recto* (which gives the approximate date, c. 1200 B.C.). In its original state the papyrus must have been an artistically beautiful exemplar, as the script is an exceptionally fine one. It contains the names of kings in order, over 300 when complete, with the length of each reign in years, months, and days; and as the definitive edition of the papyrus has not yet been issued, further study is expected to yield additional results.[1] The papyrus begins, like Manetho, with the dynasties of gods, followed by mortal kings also in dynasties. The change of dynasty is noted, and the sum of the reigns is given: also, as in Manetho, several dynasties are added together, *e.g.* " Sum of the Kings from Mênês to [Unas] " at the end of Dynasty V. The arrangement in the papyrus is very similar to that in the *Epitome* of Manetho.

(5) *The Palermo Stone*[2] takes us back to a much greater antiquity: it dates from the Fifth Dynasty, c. 2600 B.C., and therefore contains Old Egyptian annals of the kings. The Stone or Stele was origin-

---

[1] See Sir J. G. Wilkinson, *Fragments of the Hieratic Papyrus at Turin*, London, 1851 : E. Meyer, *Aeg. Chron.* pp. 105 ff., and *Die Ältere Chronologie Babyloniens, Assyriens, und Ägyptens*, revised by Stier (1931), pp. 55 ff.

[2] Plate II. See H. Schäfer, *Abhandl. Akad. Berl.* 1902 : Breasted, *Ancient Records*, i. §§ 76-167: Sethe, *Urkunden des Alten Reichs*, pp. 235-249; and *cf.* Petrie, *The Making of Egypt*, 1939, pp. 98 f.

INTRODUCTION

ally a large slab [1] of black diorite, about 7 feet long and over 2 feet high; but only a fragment of the middle of the slab is preserved in the Museum of Palermo, while smaller pieces of this, or of a similar monument, have been identified in the Cairo Museum and in University College, London. Although the text is unfortunately fragmentary, this early document is clearly seen to be more closely related to the genuine Manetho than are the Kings' Lists of later date (1, 2, 3, 4 above).[2] In a space marked off on each side by a year-sign and therefore denoting one year, notable events are given in an upper section of the space and records of the Nile-levels in a lower. A change of reign is denoted by a vertical line prolonging the year-sign above, on each side of which a certain number of months and days is recorded—on one side those belonging to the deceased king, and on the other to his successor. In the earliest Dynasties the years were not numbered, but were named after some important event or events, *e.g.* "the year of the smiting of the *'Inw*," "the year of the sixth time of numbering". Religious and military events were particularly common, just as they are in Manetho. A year-name of King Snefru (Dynasty IV.) states that he conquered the Nehesi, and captured 7000 prisoners and 200,000 head of cattle: *cf.* Manetho, Fr. 7, on the foreign expedition of Mênês. So, too, under

[1] More plausibly, according to Petrie (*The Making of Egypt*, 1939, p. 98), the text of the annals was divided among six slabs each 16 inches wide, both sides being equally visible.
[2] Borchardt, in *Die Annalen* (1917), quoted in *Ancient Egypt*, 1920, p. 124, says, "Manetho had really good sources, and his copyists have not altogether spoiled him".

MANETHO

Shepseskaf, the last king of Dynasty IV., the building of a pyramid is recorded, and under Dynasties I., IV., and VI. Manetho makes mention of pyramid-building. It is especially noteworthy that the first line of the Palermo Stone gives a list of kings before Mênês: *cf.* the *Turin Papyrus*, as quoted on Fr. 1. (For the Cairo fragments see Sethe, *op. cit.*)

* * * * * * *

In regard to Manetho's relation to his Greek predecessors in the field of Egyptian history, we know that he criticized Herodotus, not, as far as we can tell, in a separate work, but merely in passages of his H*istory*. In none of the extant fragments does Manetho mention by name Hecataeus of Abdera, but it is interesting to speculate upon Manetho's relation to this Greek historian. The *floruit* of Hecataeus fell in the time of Alexander and Ptolemy son of Lagus (Gutschmid gives 320 B.C. as an approximate estimate); and it is very doubtful whether he lived to see the reign of Philadelphus, who came to the throne in 285 B.C. (Jacoby in *R.-E.* vii. 2, 2750). His *Aegyptiaca* was " a philosophical romance," describing " an ethnographical Utopia ": it was no history of Egypt, but a work with a philosophical tendency. Manetho and Hecataeus are quoted together, *e.g.* by Plutarch, *Isis and Osiris*, chap. 9, perhaps from an intermediary writer who used the works of both Manetho and Hecataeus. If we assume that Hecataeus wrote his " romance " before Manetho composed his *History*, perhaps one of the purposes of Manetho was to correct the errors of his predecessor. No

INTRODUCTION

criticism of Hecataeus, however, has been attributed to Manetho; and it is natural that similarities are found in their accounts (*cf.* p. 131, n. 2). Be that as it may, Hecataeus enjoyed greater popularity among the Greeks than Manetho: they preferred his " romance " to Manetho's more reliable annals. Yet Manetho's *Aegyptiaca* has no claim to be regarded as a critical history: its value lies in the dynastic skeletons which serve as a framework for the evidence of the monuments, and it has provided in its essentials the accepted scheme of Egyptian chronology.[1] But there were many errors in Manetho's work from the very beginning: all are not due to the perversions of scribes and revisers. Many of the lengths of reigns have been found impossible: in some cases the names and the sequence of kings as given by Manetho have proved untenable in the light of monumental evidence. If one may depend upon the extracts preserved in Josephus, Manetho's work was not an authentic history of Egypt, exact in its details, as the *Chaldaïca* of Bêrôssos was, at least for later times. Manetho introduced into an already corrupted series of dynastic lists a number of popular traditions written

[1] *Cf.* H. R. Hall, *Cambridge Ancient History*, i. p. 260: " So far as we are able to check Manetho from the contemporary monuments, his division into dynasties is entirely justified. His authorities evidently were good. But unhappily his work has come down to us only in copies of copies; and, although the framework of the dynasties remains, most of his royal names, originally Graecized, have been so mutilated by non-Egyptian scribes, who did not understand their form, as often to be unrecognizable, and the regnal years given by him have been so corrupted as to be of little value unless confirmed by the Turin Papyrus or the monuments."

MANETHO

in the characteristic Egyptian style. No genuine historical sense had been developed among the Egyptians, although Manetho's work does illustrate the influence of Greek culture upon an Egyptian priest. He wrote to correct the errors of Greek historians, especially of Herodotus (see Fr. 88); but from the paucity of information about certain periods, it seems clear that in ancient times, as for us at the present day, there were obscure eras in Egyptian history.[1] Before the Saïte Dynasty (XXVI.) there were three outstanding periods—in Dynasties IV.-VI., XI.-XII., and XVIII.-XX., or roughly the Old Kingdom, the Middle Kingdom, and the New Kingdom (sometimes called the Empire); and these are the periods upon which the light falls in all histories.

The significance of Manetho's writings is that for the first time an Egyptian was seeking to instruct foreigners in the history and religion of his native land.

Other Works attributed to Manetho.

To judge by the frequency of quotation, the religious treatises of Manetho were much more popular in Greek circles than the *History of Egypt* was; yet the fragments surviving from these works (Fr. 76-88) are so meagre that no distinct impression of their nature can be gained. The *Sacred Book* (Fr. 76-81)

---

[1] *Cf.* H. R. Hall, *Ancient History of the Near East*[8], p. 14: "In fact, Manetho did what he could: where the native annals were good and complete, his abstract is good: where they were broken and incomplete, his record is incomplete also and confused. . . ."

INTRODUCTION

was doubtless a valuable exposition of the details of Egyptian religion, as well as of the mythological elements of Egyptian theology. It testifies to the importance of the part played by Manetho in support of Ptolemy Sôter's vigorous policy of religious syncretism. It seems probable that the *Sacred Book* was Manetho's main contribution in aid of this policy: it may have been the result of a definite commission by the king, in order to spread a knowledge of Egyptian religion among the Greeks. That an Egyptian priest should seek to instruct the Greek-speaking world of his time in the history of Egypt and in the religious beliefs of the Egyptians, including festivals, ancient rites and piety in general, and the preparation of *kyphi*, is not at all surprising; but it seems strange that Manetho should feel called upon, in the third century B.C., to compose an *Epitome of Physical Doctrines* (Fr. 82, 83) with the apparent object of familiarizing the Greeks with Egyptian science. One may conjecture that his special purpose was to give instruction to students of his own.

The Book of Sôthis (Appendix IV.).

The Book of Sôthis[1] or *The Sôthic Cycle* is transmitted through Syncellus alone. In the opinion of Syncellus, this *Sôthis-Book* was dedicated by Manetho

[1] Sôthis is the Greek form of *Sopdet*, the Egyptian name for the Dog-star, Sirius, the heliacal rising of which was noted at an early date: on the great importance of the Sôthic period in Egyptian chronology, see Breasted, *Ancient Records*, i. §§ 40 ff., and H. R. Hall, *Encyclopaedia Britannica*[14], s.v. Chronology. *Cf. infra*, Appendix III., p. 226, and Appendix IV., p. 234.

MANETHO

to Ptolemy Philadelphus (see App. I.). The king wished to learn the future of the universe, and Manetho accordingly sent to him " sacred books " based upon inscriptions which had been written down by Thôth, the first Hermês, in hieratic script, had been interpreted after the Flood by Agathodaemôn, son of the second Hermês and father of Tat, and had been deposited in the sanctuaries of the temples of Egypt. The letter which purports to have accompanied the " sacred books " is undoubtedly a forgery; but the *Sôthis-Book* is significant for the textual transmission of Manetho. According to the LXX the Flood took place in Anno Mundi 2242 (see Frags. 2, 6 : App. III., p. 232). This date must close the prehistoric period in Egypt and in Chaldea : the 11,985 years of the Egyptian gods are therefore regarded as months and reduced to 969 years. Similarly, the 858 years of the demigods are treated as quarter-years or periods of three months, thus becoming $214\frac{1}{2}$ years: total, $969 + 214\frac{1}{2} = 1183\frac{1}{2}$ years (Fr. 2). In Chaldean prehistory, by fixing the saros at 3600 days, 120 saroi become 1183 years $6\frac{5}{6}$ months. Accordingly, the beginning of Egyptian and Babylonian history is placed at $2242 - 1184$, or 1058 Anno Mundi : in that year (or in 1000, Fr. 2) falls the coming of the Egregori, who finally by their sins brought on the Flood. The *Book of Sôthis* begins with the reign of Mestraïm, Anno Mundi 2776 (App. IV., p. 234 : App. III., p. 232), *i.e.* 534 years after the Flood, and continues to the year 4986, which gives 2210 years of Egyptian rule—almost the same number as Manetho has in either Book I. or Book II. of his *History of Egypt*.

BIBLIOGRAPHY

Greek text of Manetho in
1. C. Müller, *Fragmenta Historicorum Graecorum*, ii. (1848), pp. 512-616.
2. *Manethonis Sebennytae Reliquiae*, R. Fruin, 1847.

Greek text of the *Epitome* in
3. G. F. Unger, *Chronologie des Manetho*, Berlin, 1867.

Greek text of Kings' Lists summarized in parallel columns:
4. R. Lepsius, *Königsbuch der alten Ägypter*, Berlin, 1858.

Greek text of religious writings in
5. *Fontes Historiae Religionis Aegyptiacae*, Th. Hopfner, 1922-25.

Accounts of Manetho and his work.

1. Richard Laqueur in Pauly-Wissowa-Kroll, *R.-E.* xiv. 1 (1928), *s.v.* Manethon (1).
2. F. Susemihl, *Alex. Lit.-Geschichte*, i., 1891, pp. 608-616.
3. W. Otto, *Priester und Tempel im hellenist. Aegypten* (1908), ii. pp. 215 f., 228 f.

Subsidiary Works.

Josephus
　ed. Niese, Vol. v., 1889.
　ed. Thackeray (L.C.L., Vol. i., 1926).
　ed. Reinach and Blum (Budé, 1930).
Arnaldo Momigliano, *Rivista di Filologia*, 59 (1931), pp. 485-503.
Syncellus or George the Monk, in *Corpus Scriptorum Historicorum Byzantinorum*, W. Dindorf, 1829.
Heinrich Gelzer, *Sextus Julius Africanus*, 1880-89.
Eusebius, *Praeparatio Evangelica*, E. H. Gifford, 1903.
Eusebii chronicorum lib. I., A. Schöne, 1875.
Eusebius, *Chronica* (in Armenian Version):
　(a) Latin translation by Zohrab-Mai, 1818 (in Müller's *F.H.G.* ii.).

BIBLIOGRAPHY

(b) Latin translation by Ancher, 1818 (partly quoted in R. Lepsius, *Königsbuch*—see above).
(c) Latin translation by H. Petermann, in Schöne (above).
(d) German translation by Josef Karst in *Eusebius, Werke V. Die Chronik*, 1911.

Ed. Meyer, *Aegyptische Chronologie*, 1904 (Nachträge, 1907: Neue Nachträge, 1907). French translation by Alexandre Moret, 1912.
Ed. Meyer, *Geschichte des Altertums* [5], I. ii., II. i., ii.
James H. Breasted, *Ancient Records*, 1906.
T. E. Peet, H. R. Hall, J. H. Breasted, in the *Cambridge Ancient History*, Vols. i.-vi.
A. von Gutschmid, *Kleine Schriften*, iv., 1893.

For further works and articles relating to Manetho, see the article by Laqueur, Pauly-Wissowa-Kroll, *R.-E.*

MSS.

SYNCELLUS

A = 1711 of Paris (dated A.D. 1021), used by Scaliger and Goar, the first two editors. Editions: Paris, 1652; Venice, 1729.
B = 1764 of Paris—a much better MS. than A.
G signifies readings of Goar.
m signifies conjectures and notes in the margin of Goar's edition.

EUSEBIUS, *Chronica* (Armenian Version)
G = Codex Hierosolymitanus (see Intro., p. xix n. 2).

JOSEPHUS, *Contra Apionem*, i.
L = Codex Laurentianus plut. lxix. 22 of eleventh century.
Hafniensis, No. 1570, at Copenhagen, fifteenth century.
Bigotianus, known from readings transmitted by Emericus Bigotius.
Quotations by Eusebius (A.D. 264-340), sometimes best preserved in the Armenian version.
Lat. = Latin version made by order of Cassiodorus, the minister of Theodoric, c. A.D. 540.
Editio princeps of Greek text (Basel, 1544).

LIST OF ABBREVIATED TITLES USED IN REFERENCE

Ann. Serv. Antiq. = *Annales du Service des Antiquités de l'Égypte*, Le Caire, 1900– .

Baedeker [8] = *Egypt and the Sûdân*, by Karl Baedeker (English translation, 8th edition, 1929).

Karst = Joseph Karst's German translation *Die Chronik*, in *Eusebius, Werke*, v., 1911.

P. Baden = F. Bilabel, *Griechische Papyri (Veröffentlichungen aus den badischen Papyrus-Sammlungen)*, Heidelberg, 1923-24.

P. Hibeh = Grenfell and Hunt, *The Hibeh Papyri*, I., 1906.

P. Mich. Zen. = C. C. Edgar, *Zenon Papyri in the University of Michigan Collection*, 1931.

P. Oxy. = Grenfell, Hunt, and Bell, *The Oxyrhynchus Papyri*, 1898-1927.

Petermann = H. Petermann's Latin translation in Schöne (below).

Schöne = *Eusebii Chronicorum lib. I.*, A. Schöne, 1875.

Syncellus = Syncellus or George the Monk, in *Corpus Scriptorum Historicorum Byzantinorum*, W. Dindorf, 1829.

NOTE

THE editor wishes to acknowledge with gratitude the valuable help ungrudgingly given to him in all Egyptological matters by Professor Percy E. Newberry (Liverpool and Cairo) and by Professor Battiscombe Gunn (Oxford); but neither of these Egyptologists must be held responsible for the final form in which their contributions appear, except where their names or initials are appended. Thanks are also due to Professor D. S. Margoliouth (Oxford), who very kindly revised the Latin translation of the Armenian Version of Eusebius, *Chronica*, by comparing it with the original Armenian as given in Aucher's edition: the footnotes show how much the text here printed has benefited from his revision.

In a work which brings before the mind's eye a long series of Kings of Egypt, the editor would have liked to refer interested readers to some book containing a collection of portraits of these kings; but it seems that, in spite of the convenience and interest which such a book would possess, no complete series of royal portraits has yet been published.[1] For a certain number of portrait-sketches (25 in all), skilfully created from existing mummies and ancient representations, see Winifred Brunton, *Kings and Queens of Ancient Egypt* (1924), and *Great Ones of Ancient Egypt* (1929).

[1] For portraits of some kings, see Petrie, *The Making of Egypt*, 1939, *passim*.

THE *AEGYPTIACA* OF MANETHO:
MANETHO'S *HISTORY OF EGYPT*

B

ΑΙΓΥΠΤΙΑΚΑ

ΤΟΜΟΣ ΠΡΩΤΟΣ

Fr. 1. Eusebius, *Chronica* I. (Armenian Version), p. 93 (Mai).

Ex Aegyptiacis Manethonis monumentis, qui in tres libros historiam suam tribuit,—de diis et de heroibus, de manibus et de mortalibus regibus qui Aegypto praefuerunt usque ad regem Persarum Darium.

1. Primus homo (deus) Aegyptiis Vulcanus [1] est, qui etiam ignis repertor apud eos celebratur. Ex eo Sol; [postea Sôsis [2];] deinde Saturnus; tum

---

[1] *Cf.* Joannes Lydus, *De Mensibus*, iv. 86 (Wünsch). On *Maius*, after speaking of Hephaestus, Lydus adds: κατὰ δὲ ἱστορίαν Μανέθων Αἰγυπτιακῶν ὑπομνημάτων ἐν τόμῳ τρίτῳ φησίν, ὅτι πρῶτος ἀνθρώπων * παρ' Αἰγυπτίοις ἐβασίλευσεν Ἥφαιστος ὁ καὶ εὑρέτης τοῦ πυρὸς αὐτοῖς γενόμενος· ἐξ οὗ Ἥλιος, οὗ Κρόνος, μεθ' ὃν Ὄσιρις, ἔπειτα Τυφών, ἀδελφὸς Ὀσίρεως. From this passage we see that Lydus gives the sequence "Hêphaestus, Hêlios (the Sun), Cronos, Osiris, Typhôn," omitting Sôsis as Eusebius does. After this passage in Lydus comes Fr. 84 Ἰστέον δὲ . . .

[2] From Joannes Antiochenus (Malalas), *Chron.*, 24 (Migne, *Patrologia*, Vol. 97).

* Bracketed by Hopfner, *Fontes Historiae Religionis*, Bonn, 1922-3, p. 65.

THE *AEGYPTIACA* OF MANETHO: MANETHO'S *HISTORY OF EGYPT*

BOOK I.

Fr. 1 (*from the Armenian Version of Eusebius, Chronica*). DYNASTIES OF GODS, DEMIGODS, AND SPIRITS OF THE DEAD.

FROM the *Egyptian History* of Manetho, who composed his account in three books. These deal with the Gods, the Demigods, the Spirits of the Dead, and the mortal kings who ruled Egypt down to Darius, king of the Persians.

1. The first man (or god) in Egypt is Hephaestus,[1] who is also renowned among the Egyptians as the discoverer of fire. His son, Helios (the Sun), was succeeded by Sôsis: then follow, in turn, Cronos,

---

[1] The Pre-dynastic Period begins with a group of gods, "consisting of the Great Ennead of Heliopolis in the form in which it was worshipped at Memphis" (T. E. Peet, *Cambridge Ancient History*, i. p. 250). After summarizing §§ 1-3 Peet adds: "From the historical point of view there is little to be made of this". See Meyer, *Geschichte des Altertums* [5], I. ii. p. 102 f. for the Egyptian traditions of the Pre-dynastic Period. In the Turin Papyrus the Gods are given in the same order: (Ptah), Rê, (Shu), Geb, Osiris, Sêth (200 years), Horus (300 years), Thoth (3126 years), Ma'at, Har, . . . Total . . . . See Meyer, *Aeg. Chron.* p. 116, and *cf.* Fr. 3.

Fr. 1 MANETHO

Osiris; exin Osiridis frater Typhon; ad extremum Orus, Osiridis et Isidis filius. Hi primi inter Aegyptios rerum potiti sunt. Deinceps continuata successione delapsa est regia auctoritas usque ad Bydin (Bitem) per annorum tredecim milia ac nongentos. Lunarem tamen annum intelligo, videlicet xxx diebus constantem : quem enim nunc mensem dicimus, Aegyptii olim anni nomine indigitabant.

2. Post deos regnarunt heroes annis MCCLV : rursusque alii reges dominati sunt annis MDCCCXVII : tum alii triginta reges Memphitae annis MDCCXC : deinde alii Thinitae decem reges annis CCCL.

3. Secuta est manium heroumque dominatio annis MMMMMDCCCXIII.

4. Summa temporis in mille et myriadem¹ consurgit annorum, qui tamen lunares, nempe menstrui,

¹ Müller : mille myriadas Mai.

---

¹ The name Bydis (or Bites) seems to be the Egyptian *bity* " king " (from *bit* " bee "), the title of the kings of Lower Egypt : see the Palermo Stone, and *cf.* Herodotus, iv. 155, " the Libyans call their king ' Battos ' " (P. E. Newberry). Bitys appears in late times as a translator or interpreter of Hermetical writings : see Iamblich. *De Mysteriis*, viii. 5 (= Scott, *Hermetica*, iv. p. 34) where the prophet Bitys is said to have translated [for King Ammôn] a book (*The Way to Higher Things, i.e.* a treatise on the theurgic or supernatural means of attaining to union with the Demiurgus) which he found inscribed in hieroglyphs in a shrine at Saïs in Egypt. *Cf.* the pseudo-Manetho, App. I.

² There is no evidence that the Egyptian year was ever equal to a month : there were short years (each of 360 days) and long years (see Fr. 49).

³ See *Excerpta Latina Barbari* (Fr. 4) for the beginning of this dynasty : " First, Anubis . . . ".

AEGYPTIACA (EPITOME) FR. 1

Osiris, Typhon, brother of Osiris, and lastly Orus, son of Osiris and Isis. These were the first to hold sway in Egypt. Thereafter, the kingship passed from one to another in unbroken succession down to Bydis (Bites)[1] through 13,900 years. The year I take, however, to be a lunar one, consisting, that is, of 30 days: what we now call a month the Egyptians used formerly to style a year.[2]

2. After the Gods, Demigods reigned for 1255 years,[3] and again another line of kings held sway for 1817 years: then came thirty more kings of Memphis,[4] reigning for 1790 years; and then again ten kings of This, reigning for 350 years.

3. There followed the rule of Spirits of the Dead and Demigods,[5] for 5813 years.

4. The total [of the last five groups] amounts to 11,000 years,[6] these however being lunar periods, or

---

[4] Corroborated by the Turin Papyrus, Col. ii.: "of Memphis".

[5] "Demigods" should be in apposition to "Spirits of the Dead" (νέκυες ἡμίθεοι), as in *Excerpta Latina Barbari* (Fr. 4) and Africanus (Fr. 6. 1). These are perhaps the *Shemsu Hor*, the Followers or Worshippers of Horus, of the Turin Papyrus: see H. R. Hall, *Cambridge Ancient History*, i. p. 265. Before King Mênês (Fr. 6), the king of Upper Egypt who imposed his sway upon the fertile Delta and founded the First Dynasty,—the *Shemsu Hor*, the men of the Falcon Clan whose original home was in the West Delta, had formed an earlier united kingdom by conquering Upper Egypt: see V. Gordon Childe, *New Light on the Most Ancient East*, 1934, p. 8, based upon Breasted, *Bull. Instit. Franç. Arch. Or.* xxx. (Cairo, 1930), pp. 710 ff., and Schäfer's criticism, *Orient. Literaturz.* 1932, p. 704.

[6] The exact total of the items given is 11,025 years. So also 24,900 *infra* is a round number for 24,925.

Fr. 1 MANETHO

sunt. Sed revera dominatio, quam narrant Aegyptii, deorum, heroum, et manium tenuisse putatur lunarium annorum omnino viginti quattuor milia et nongentos,¹ ex quibus fiunt solares anni MMCCVI.

5. Atque haec si cum Hebraeorum chronologia conferre volueris, in eandem plane sententiam conspirare videbis. Namque Aegyptus ab Hebraeis Mestraïmus appellatur: Mestraïmus autem ⟨haud ²⟩ multo post diluvium tempore exstitit. Quippe ex Chamo, Noachi filio, post diluvium ortus est Aegyptus sive Mestraïmus, qui primus ad Aegypti incolatum profectus est, qua tempestate gentes hac illac spargi coeperunt. Erat autem summa temporis ab Adamo ad diluvium secundum Hebraeos annorum MMCCXLII.

6. Ceterum³ quum Aegyptii praerogativa antiquitatis quadam seriem ante diluvium tenere se iactent Deorum, Heroum, et Manium annorum plus viginti milia regnantium, plane aequum est ut hi anni in

---

[1] Aucher's version runs: duae myriades quatuor millia et DOCCO.

[2] haud: conj. approved by Karst.

[3] Petermann's version of the first sentence of this section runs as follows: Itaque placet (licet) Egiptiis, priscis (primis) temporibus quae praecesserunt diluvium, se iactare ob antiquitatem. Deos quosdam fuisse dicunt suos, semideosque et manes. In menses redactis annis apud Hebraeos enarratis, lunarium annorum myriades duas et amplius etiam computant (computarunt), ita ut tot fere menses fiant, quot anni apud Hebraeos comprehenduntur; scilicet (id est) a protoplasto homine usque ad Mezrajim tempora nostra computando ("And so, for the early times which preceded the Flood, the Egyptians may well boast of their antiquity. They say that certain Gods were theirs, as well as Demigods and Spirits of the Dead. Having reduced to

AEGYPTIACA (EPITOME) FR. 1

months. But, in truth, the whole rule of which the Egyptians tell — the rule of Gods, Demigods, and Spirits of the Dead—is reckoned to have comprised in all 24,900 lunar years, which make 2206[1] solar years.

5. Now, if you care to compare these figures with Hebrew chronology, you will find that they are in perfect harmony. Egypt is called Mestraïm[2] by the Hebrews; and Mestraïm lived ⟨not⟩ long after the Flood. For after the Flood, Cham (or Ham), son of Noah, begat Aegyptus or Mestraïm, who was the first to set out to establish himself in Egypt, at the time when the tribes began to disperse this way and that. Now the whole time from Adam to the Flood was, according to the Hebrews, 2242 years.

6. But, since the Egyptians claim by a sort of prerogative of antiquity that they have, before the Flood, a line of Gods, Demigods, and Spirits of the Dead, who reigned for more than 20,000 years, it clearly follows that these years should be reckoned

---

[1] Boeckh, *Manetho und die Hundssternperiode*, p. 85, corrects this to 2046.

[2] Mestraïm: the Mizraïm of *O.T. Genesis* x. 6: Arabic *Miṣrun*, Cuneiform *Muṣri*, *Miṣri* (Egypt). Mizraïm is a dual name-form, perhaps to be explained in reference to the two great native divisions of Egypt, Upper and Lower.

---

months the years recorded by the Hebrews, they reckon 20,000 lunar years and even more than that number, so that it comes to practically as many months as the years of Hebrew chronology, *i.e.* reckoning our times * from the creation of man to Mezraïm.")

* Karst emends this to "Biblical times".

FR. 1   MANETHO

menses tot convertantur quot ab Hebraeis memorantur anni: nempe ut qui menses continentur in memoratis apud Hebraeos annis, ii totidem intelligantur Aegyptiorum lunares anni, pro ea temporum summa, quae a primo condito homine ad Mestraïmum usque colligitur. Sane Mestraïmus generis Aegyptiaci auctor fuit, ab eoque prima Aegyptiorum dynastia manare credenda est.

7. Quodsi temporum copia adhuc exuberet, reputandum est plures fortasse Aegyptiorum reges una eademque aetate exstitisse; namque et Thinitas regnavisse aiunt et Memphitas et Saïtas et Aethiopes eodemque tempore alios.¹ Videntur praeterea alii quoque alibi imperium tenuisse: atque hae dynastiae suo quaeque in nomo² semet continuisse: ita ut haud singuli reges successivam potestatem acceperint, sed alius alio loco eadem aetate regnaverit. Atque hinc contigit, ut tantus numerus annorum confieret. Nos vero, his omissis, persequamur singillatim Aegyptiorum chronologiam.

(Continued in Fr. 7(b).)

¹ Petermann renders: ac interim (iuxta eosdem) alios quoque, "and others too, besides these".
² The Armenian version here confuses νόμος "law" and νομός "nome": the Latin translation corrects this blunder.

---

¹ For the contemporaneous existence of a number of petty kingdoms in Egypt, see the Piankhi *stele*, Breasted, *Ancient Records*, iv. §§ 830, 878, and the passage from Artapanus, *Concerning the Jews*, quoted on p. 73 n. 3. T. Nicklin (in his *Studies in Egyptian Chronology*, 1928-29,

AEGYPTIACA (EPITOME) Fr. 1

as the same number of months as the years recorded by the Hebrews: that is, that all the months contained in the Hebrew record of years, should be reckoned as so many lunar years of the Egyptian calculation, in accordance with the total length of time reckoned from the creation of man in the beginning down to Mestraïm. Mestraïm was indeed the founder of the Egyptian race; and from him the first Egyptian dynasty must be held to spring.

7. But if the number of years is still in excess, it must be supposed that perhaps several Egyptian kings ruled at one and the same time; for they say that the rulers were kings of This, of Memphis, of Saïs, of Ethiopia, and of other places at the same time. It seems, moreover, that different kings held sway in different regions, and that each dynasty was confined to its own nome: thus it was not a succession of kings occupying the throne one after the other, but several kings reigning at the same time in different regions.[1] Hence arose the great total number of years. But let us leave this question and take up in detail the chronology of Egyptian history.

(Continued in Fr. 7(*b*).)

p. 39) says: " The Manethonian Dynasties are not lists of rulers over all Egypt, but lists partly of more or less independent princes, partly of princely lines from which later sprang rulers over all Egypt. (*Cf.* the Scottish Stuarts, or the Electors of Hanover.) Some were mere Mayors of the Palace or princelets maintaining a precarious independence, or even more subordinate Governors of nomes, from whom, however, descended subsequent monarchs. (*Cf.* the Heptarchy in England.) "

Fr. 2. *Syncellus*, p. 73.

1. Μετὰ δὲ ταῦτα καὶ περὶ ἐθνῶν Αἰγυπτιακῶν πέντε ἐν τριάκοντα δυναστείαις ἱστορεῖ τῶν λεγομένων παρ' αὐτοῖς θεῶν καὶ ἡμιθέων καὶ νεκύων καὶ θνητῶν, ὧν καὶ Εὐσέβιος ὁ Παμφίλου μνησθεὶς ἐν τοῖς Χρονικοῖς αὐτοῦ φησὶν οὕτως·

2. "Αἰγύπτιοι δὲ θεῶν καὶ ἡμιθέων καὶ παρὰ τούτοις νεκύων καὶ θνητῶν ἑτέρων βασιλέων πολλὴν καὶ φλύαρον συνείρουσι μυθολογίαν· οἱ γὰρ παρ' αὐτοῖς παλαιότατοι σεληναίους ἔφασκον εἶναι τοὺς[1] ἐνιαυτοὺς ἐξ ἡμερῶν τριάκοντα συνεστῶτας, οἱ δὲ μετὰ τούτους ἡμίθεοι ὥρους ἐκάλουν τοὺς ἐνιαυτοὺς τοὺς[2] τριμηνιαίους."

3. Καὶ ταῦτα μὲν ὁ Εὐσέβιος μεμφόμενος αὐτοῖς τῆς φλυαρίας εὐλόγως συνέγραψεν, ὃν ὁ Πανόδωρος οὐ καλῶς, ὡς οἶμαι, ἐν τούτῳ μέμφεται, λέγων ὅτι ἠπόρησε διαλύσασθαι τὴν ἔννοιαν τῶν συγγραφέων, ἣν αὐτὸς καινότερόν τι δοκῶν κατορθοῦν λέγει·

4. "'Επειδὴ ἀπὸ τῆς τοῦ Ἀδὰμ πλάσεως ἕως[3] τοῦ Ἐνώχ, ἤτοι τοῦ καθολικοῦ κοσμικοῦ ͵ασπβ' ἔτους, οὔτε μηνὸς οὔτε ἐνιαυτοῦ ἀριθμὸς ἡμερῶν ἐγνωρίζετο, οἱ δὲ ἐγρήγοροι, κατελθόντες ἐπὶ τοῦ καθολικοῦ

---

[1] MSS. εἶναι τοὺς ͵τψ' μηνιαίους τοὺς ἐνιαυτοὺς : ͵τψ' μηνιαίους τοὺς seel. Scaliger.
[2] MSS. τοὺς ψ' τριμηνιαίους : ψ' delet m.
[3] ἕως add. m.

AEGYPTIACA (EPITOME)   Fr. 2

Fr. 2 (*from Syncellus*).

Thereafter [1] Manetho tells also of five Egyptian tribes which formed thirty dynasties, comprising those whom they call Gods, Demigods, Spirits of the Dead, and mortal men. Of these Eusebius, " son " of Pamphilus, gives the following account in his *Chronica* : " Concerning Gods, Demigods, Spirits of the Dead, and mortal kings, the Egyptians have a long series of foolish myths. The most ancient Egyptian kings, indeed, alleged that their years were lunar years consisting of thirty days, whereas the Demigods who succeeded them gave the name *hôroi* to years which were three months long." So Eusebius wrote with good reason, criticizing the Egyptians for their foolish talk ; and in my opinion Panodôrus [2] is wrong in finding fault with Eusebius here, on the ground that Eusebius failed to explain the meaning of the historians, while Panodôrus thinks he himself succeeds by a somewhat novel method, as follows :

" From the creation of Adam, indeed, down to Enoch, *i.e.* to the general cosmic year 1282, the number of days was known in neither month nor year ; but the Egregori (or ' Watchers '),[3] who had

---

[1] This passage follows after Appendix I., p. 210.

[2] Panodôrus (*fl. c.* 395-408 A.D.) and his contemporary Annianus were Egyptian monks who wrote on *Chronology* with the purpose of harmonizing Chaldean and Egyptian systems with that of the Jews. Panodôrus used (and perhaps composed) the *Book of Sôthis* (App. IV.).

[3] Ἐγρήγοροι, " Watchers, Angels "—in *Enoch*, 179, of the angels who fell in love with the daughters of men. The Greek word Ἐγρήγοροι is a mispronunciation of the Aramaic word used in *Enoch*, 179.

Fr. 2 MANETHO

κοσμικοῦ χιλιοστοῦ ἔτους, συναναστραφέντες τοῖς ἀνθρώποις ἐδίδαξαν αὐτοὺς τοὺς κύκλους τῶν δύο φωστήρων δωδεκαζῳδίους εἶναι ἐκ μοιρῶν τριακοσίων ἑξήκοντα, οἱ δὲ ἀποβλέψαντες εἰς τὸν περιγειότερον, μικρότερον καὶ εὐδηλότερον τριακονθήμερον σεληνιακὸν κύκλον ἐθέσπισαν εἰς ἐνιαυτὸν ἀριθμεῖσθαι, διὰ τὸ καὶ τὸν τοῦ ἡλίου κύκλον ἐν τοῖς αὐτοῖς δώδεκα ζῳδίοις πληροῦσθαι ἐν ἰσαρίθμοις μοίραις τξ'. ὅθεν συνέβη τὰς βασιλείας τῶν παρ' αὐτοῖς βασιλευσάντων θεῶν γενεῶν ἕξ, ἐν δυναστείαις ἕξ, κατ' ἔτη[1] ἐν σεληνιακοῖς τριακονθημέροις κύκλοις παρ' αὐτοῖς ἀριθμεῖσθαι· ἃ καὶ συνῆξαν σελήνια α΄ ͵απε΄ ἔτη, ἡλιακὰ ͵αξθ΄· ταῦτα δὲ συναριθμούμενα τοῖς πρὸ τῆς τούτων βασιλείας ἡλιακοῖς ͵ανη΄ ἔτεσι συνάγουσιν ὁμάδα ἐτῶν ͵βκζ΄." ὁμοίως δὲ κατὰ τὰς δύο δυναστείας τῶν ἐννέα ἡμιθέων τῶν μηδέποτε γεγονότων ὡς γεγονότων ἔτη σιδ΄ καὶ ἥμισυ σπουδάζει συνιστᾶν ἀπὸ τῶν ωνη΄ ὡρῶν,[2] ἤτοι τρόπων, ὡς γίνεσθαί φησι, σὺν ͵αξθ΄, ͵αρπγ΄[3] καὶ ἥμισυ ἔτη, καὶ συναπτόμενα τοῖς ἀπὸ Ἀδὰμ μέχρι τῆς τῶν θεῶν βασιλείας ͵ανη΄ ἔτεσι συνάγειν ἔτη ͵βρμβ΄ ἕως τοῦ κατακλυσμοῦ.

5. Καὶ ταῦτα μὲν ὁ Πανόδωρος τὰς κατὰ θεοῦ καὶ τῶν θεοπνεύστων γραφῶν Αἰγυπτιακὰς συγγραφὰς συμφωνεῖν αὐταῖς ἀγωνίζεται δεικνύναι, μεμφόμενος τὸν Εὐσέβιον, μὴ εἰδὼς ὅτι καθ' ἑαυτοῦ καὶ τῆς ἀληθείας ἀποδέδεικται ταῦτα αὐτοῦ τὰ

---
[1] MSS. ἔτη alone: κατ' ἔτη m.
[2] ωνή ὡρῶν or ὅρων m.: ὠνιώρων MSS.: ἐνιαυσίων ὡρῶν Scaliger.
[3] ͵αρπγ΄ m.: ͵αρυγ΄ MSS.

descended to earth in the general cosmic year 1000, held converse with men, and taught them that the orbits of the two luminaries, being marked by the twelve signs of the Zodiac, are composed of 360 parts. Observing the moon's orbit which is nearer the earth, smaller, and more conspicuous, as it has a period of thirty days, men decided that it should be reckoned as a year, since the orbit of the sun also was filled by the same twelve signs of the Zodiac with an equal number of parts, 360. So it came to pass that the reigns of the Gods who ruled among them for six generations in six dynasties were reckoned in years each consisting of a lunar cycle of thirty days. The total in lunar years is 11,985, or 969 solar years. By adding these to the 1058 [1] solar years of the period before their reign, they reach the sum total of 2027 years." Similarly, in the two dynasties of nine Demigods,—these being regarded as real, although they never existed,—Panodôrus strives to make up $214\frac{1}{2}$ years out of 858 *hôroi* (periods of three months) or *tropoi*, so that with the 969 years they make, he says, $1183\frac{1}{2}$, and these, when added to the 1058 years from the time of Adam to the reign of the Gods, complete a total of 2242 years down to the Flood.

Thus Panodôrus exerts himself to show that the Egyptian writings against God and against our divinely inspired Scriptures are really in agreement with them. In this he criticizes Eusebius, not understanding that these arguments of his, which are incapable of proof or of reasoning, have been proved

[1] See Intro. p. xxx.

Fr. 2, 3   MANETHO

ἀναπόδεικτά τε καὶ ἀσυλλόγιστα, εἴ γε... οὔτε Βαβυλὼν ἢ Χαλδαϊκὴ πρὸ τοῦ κατακλυσμοῦ οὔτε ἡ Αἴγυπτος πρὸ τοῦ Μεστρὲμ ἐβασιλεύθη, οἶμαι δ' ὅτι οὐδ' ᾠκίσθη ...

Fr. 3.   Syncellus, p. 32.

Περὶ τῆς τῶν Αἰγυπτίων ἀρχαιολογίας.

Μανεθῶ ὁ Σεβεννύτης ἀρχιερεὺς τῶν ἐν Αἰγύπτῳ μιαρῶν ἱερῶν μετὰ Βήρωσσον γενόμενος ἐπὶ Πτολεμαίου τοῦ Φιλαδέλφου γράφει τῷ αὐτῷ Πτολεμαίῳ, ψευδηγορῶν καὶ αὐτὸς ὡς ὁ Βήρωσσος, περὶ δυναστειῶν ς΄, ἤτοι θεῶν τῶν μηδέποτε γεγονότων ς΄,[1] οἵ, φησί, διαγεγόνασιν ἐπὶ ἔτη α΄ ͵αϡπε΄. ὧν πρῶτος, φησί, θεὸς Ἥφαιστος ἔτη ͵θ ἐβασίλευσε. ταῦτα τὰ ͵θ ἔτη πάλιν τινὲς τῶν καθ' ἡμᾶς ἱστορικῶν ἀντὶ μηνῶν σεληνιακῶν λογισάμενοι καὶ μερίσαντες τὸ τῶν ἡμερῶν πλῆθος τῶν αὐτῶν ͵θ σεληνίων παρὰ τὰς τριακοσίας ἑξήκοντα πέντε ἡμέρας τοῦ ἐνιαυτοῦ συνῆξαν ἔτη ψκζ΄ ⌣δ΄, ξένον τι δοκοῦντες κατωρθωκέναι, γελοίων δὲ μᾶλλον εἰπεῖν ἄξιον τὸ ψεῦδος τῇ ἀληθείᾳ συμβιβάζοντες.

Πρώτη δυναστεία[2] Αἰγυπτίων.

α΄   ἐβασίλευσεν Ἥφαιστος ἔτη ψκζ΄ ⌣δ΄.[3]
β΄   Ἥλιος Ἡφαίστου, ἔτη π΄ ς΄.
γ΄   Ἀγαθοδαίμων, ἔτη νς΄ ⌣ιβ΄.

[1] MS. A ζ΄.
[2] MS. A has πρώτη δυναστεία after Ἥφαιστος.
[3] Müller: MSS. ψκδ΄ ⌣δ΄ (724½).

AEGYPTIACA (EPITOME) Fr. 2, 3

against himself and against truth, since indeed . . . neither Babylon nor Chaldea was ruled by kings before the Flood, nor was Egypt before Mestrem, and in my opinion it was not even inhabited before that time. . . .

Fr. 3 (*from Syncellus*).

On the Antiquity of Egypt.

Manetho of Sebennytus, chief priest of the accursed temples of Egypt, who lived later than Bêrôssos in the time of Ptolemy Philadelphus, writes to this Ptolemy, with the same utterance of lies as Bêrôssos, concerning six dynasties or six gods who never existed: these, he says, reigned for 11,985 years. The first of them, the god Hêphaestus, was king for 9000 years. Now some of our historians, reckoning these 9000 years as so many lunar months, and dividing the number of days in these 9000 lunar months by the 365 days in a year, find a total of $727\frac{3}{4}$ years. They imagine that they have attained a striking result, but one must rather say that it is a ludicrous falsehood which they have tried to pit against Truth.

The First Dynasty of Egypt.

1. Hêphaestus reigned for $727\frac{3}{4}$ years.
2. Hêlios (the Sun), son of Hêphaestus, for $80\frac{1}{6}$ years.
3. Agathodaemôn, for $56\frac{7}{12}$ years.

Fr. 3, 4   MANETHO

δ'   Κρόνος, ἔτη μ'υ.
ε'   Ὄσιρις καὶ Ἶσις, ἔτη λε'.
ϛ'   Τύφων, ἔτη κθ'.

ζ'   Ὧρος ἡμίθεος, ἔτη κε'.
η'   Ἄρης ἡμίθεος, ἔτη κγ'.
θ'   Ἄνουβις ἡμίθεος, ἔτη ιζ'.
ι'   Ἡρακλῆς ἡμίθεος, ἔτη ιε'.
ια' Ἀπόλλων ἡμίθεος, ἔτη κε'.
ιβ' Ἄμμων ἡμίθεος, ἔτη λ'.
ιγ' Τιθοῆς ἡμίθεος, ἔτη κζ'.
ιδ' Σῶσος ἡμίθεος, ἔτη λβ'.
ιε' Ζεὺς ἡμίθεος, ἔτη κ'.

Fr. 4. *Excerpta Latina Barbari* (Schöne, p. 215).

Egyptiorum regnum invenimus vetustissimum omnium regnorum; cuius initium sub Manethono[1] dicitur memoramus scribere. Primum[2] deorum qui ab ipsis scribuntur faciam regna sic:

Ifestum [*i.e.* Hephaestum] dicunt quidam deum regnare in Aegypto annos sexcentos LXXX: post hunc Solem Iphesti annos LXXVII: post istum

[1] ὑπὸ Μανέθωνος Scaliger.
[2] Frick (*Chronica Minora*, i., 1893, p. 286) restores the original Greek as follows: πρῶτον θεῶν τῶν παρ' αὐτοῖς γραφομένων ποιήσω βασιλείας οὕτως. α' Ἥφαιστόν φασί τινες θεὸν βασιλεῦσαι ἐν Αἰγύπτῳ ἔτη χπ'.

---
[1] Total, 969 years.
[2] Total, 214 years. Total for Gods and Demigods, 1183 years. See Fr. 2.

AEGYPTIACA (EPITOME) Fr. 3, 4

4. Cronos, for 40½ years.
5. Osiris and Isis, for 35 years.
6. Typhôn, for 29 years.¹

Demigods :

7. Ôrus, for 25 years.
8. Arês, for 23 years.
9. Anubis, for 17 years.
10. Hêraclês, for 15 years.
11. Apollô, for 25 years.
12. Ammôn, for 30 years.
13. Tithoês,* for 27 years.
14. Sôsus, for 32 years.
15. Zeus, for 20 years.²

Fr. 4 ³ (*from Excerpta Latina Barbari*).

In the kingdom of Egypt we have the oldest of all kingdoms, and we are minded to record its beginning, as it is given by Manetho. First, I shall put down as follows the reigns of the Gods, as recorded by the Egyptians. Some say that the god Hêphaestus reigned in Egypt for 680 years: after him, Sol [Hêlios, the Sun], son of Hêphaestus, for 77

---

³ This extract made by an anonymous and ignorant scribe depends chiefly upon Africanus. See Weill, *La fin du moyen empire égyptien*, pp. 640, 642 f., 655 f. Gelzer and Bauer have inferred that the Greek account translated by Barbarus was either the work of the Egyptian monk Annianus (see Fr. 2, p. 11 n. 2) or at least a source derived from him (Laqueur, *R.-E.* xiv. 1, 1081).

* For the divinity Tithoês in two inscriptions of *Coptos*, see O. Guéraud in *Ann. Serv. Antiq.*, 35 (1935), pp. 5 f.

FR. 4 MANETHO

Sosinosirim[1] annos CCCXX: post hunc Oron ptoliarchum annos XXVIII: post hunc Tyfona annos XLV.[2] Colliguntur deorum regna anni mille DL.

Deinceps Mitheorum[3] regna sic:

Prota[4] Anube S[amusim, qui etiam Aegyptiorum scripturas conposuit] annos LXXXIII.

[Post hunc Apiona grammaticus qui secundum Inachum interpraetatur annos LXVII quem sub Argios initio regnaverunt.]

[1] Corrected by the first hand from Sisinosirim: Sosin, Osirim Scaliger. Barbarus probably intended: post istum Sosin, post hunc Osirim. Cf. Cedren., i. p. 36, 2: καὶ μετ' αὐτὸν Σῶσις, εἶτα Ὄσιρις.
[2] After XLV the digit I or II seems to have been erased.
[3] Frick restores: Ἑξῆς Ἡμιθέων βασιλεῖαι οὕτως· α΄ πρῶτα Ἄνουβις ἔτη πγ΄. β΄ μετὰ τοῦτον Ἀμουσίν ⟨φασί τινες βασιλεῦσαι, ὃν⟩ Ἀπίων ὁ γραμματικὸς ὁ καὶ τὰς Αἰγυπτίων γραφὰς συνθεὶς κατὰ Ἴναχον ἑρμηνεύει τὸν ἐπ' Ἀργείων ἀρχῆς βασιλεύσαντα ἔτη ξζ΄.

μετὰ ταῦτα τοὺς Νεκύων βασιλέας ἡρμήνευσεν Ἡμιθέους καλῶν καὶ αὐτούς . . . κρατίστους καλῶν ἔτη ͵βρ΄.
[4] πρῶτα. Along with the reign of the demigod Anubis, Barbarus has preserved a note by Africanus referring to Amôsis: see Fr. 52. This note was, for some reason, transferred from its original place between Potestas XVI. and XVII. See Unger, *Manetho*, pp. 163 f. This mangled sentence, as interpreted by Unger, Gelzer, and Frick, attests the value of the tradition preserved by Barbarus.

---

[1] The actual total of the items given is 1150 years.
[2] The translation follows the restored Greek original: see note 3 on the text.

AEGYPTIACA (EPITOME)   FR. 4

years : next, Sosinosiris [Sôsis and Osiris], for 320 years : then Orus the Ruler, for 28 years ; and after him, Typhon, for 45 years. Total for the reigns of the Gods, 1550 years.[1]

Next come the reigns of the Demigods, as follows: first, Anubes[2] for 83 years; then after him, Amusis, some say, was king. About him, Apiôn the grammarian,[3] who composed a history of Egypt, explained that he lived in the time of Inachus[4] who was king at the founding of Argos . . . for 67 years.[5]

[3] Apiôn the grammarian, born in Upper Egypt, lived at Rome in the time of Tiberius, Gaius, and Claudius: Tiberius called him by the nickname of "cymbalum mundi". As leader of the anti-Jewish movement, Apiôn was later attacked by Josephus in his *Contra Apionem*.

The quotation from Apiôn appears to derive in part from the H*istory* of Ptolemy of Mendês : see Tatian, *Or. adversus Graecos*, § 38, in Migne, *Patrologia Graeca*, vi. 880-882, and in Müller, *F.H.G.* iv. p. 485 (quoted in *F.H.G.* ii. p. 533). (Ptolemy of Mendês dated the Exodus to the reign of Amôsis, who was contemporary with Inachus. Apiôn in the fourth volume of his *Aegyptiaca* (in five volumes) stated that Auaris was destroyed by Amôsis.) Much matter must have been common to the works of Ptolemy of Mendês and Apiôn : *cf.* Africanus in Eusebius, *Praepar. Evang.* x. 10, " Apiôn says that in the time of Inachus Moses led out the Jews ". *Cf.* Fr. 52, 1 ; 53, 9.

[4] The founder of the First Dynasty of kings of Argos, Inachus is said to have died twenty generations before the Fall of Troy, *i.e. circa* 1850 B.C. Aegyptus and Danaus were fifth in descent from Inachus : *cf.* Fr. 50, § 102.

[5] This appears to be the length of the reign of Amôsis, not of Inachus. *Cf.* Fr. 52, 1, where Africanus as recorded by Syncellus omits the number of years.

Fr. 4   MANETHO

  I. Post hec¹ Ecyniorum² reges interpraetavit,
     Imitheus² vocans et ipsos³ . . . annos duo
     milia C, fortissimos vocans.
 II. Mineus et pronepotes ipsius VII regnaverunt
     annos CCLIII.⁴
III. Bochus et aliorum octo annos CCCII.
 IV. Necherocheus et aliorum VII annos CCXIV.
  V. Similiter aliorum XVII annos CCLXXVII.
 VI. Similiter aliorum XXI annos CCLVIII.
VII. Othoi et aliorum VII annos CCIII.
VIII. Similiter et aliorum XIV annos CXL.
 IX. Similiter et aliorum XX annos CCCCIX.
  X. Similiter et aliorum VII annos CCIV.

Hec⁵ finis de primo tomo Manethoni habens tempora annorum duo milia C.

 XI. Potestas Diopolitanorum annos LX.
XII. Potestas Bubastanorum annos CLIII.

¹ For *haec*.
² These words are perversions of Νεκύων and Ἡμιθέους respectively: see p. 18 n. 3.
³ In the lacuna here, there would be an account of the mortal kings to whom the number 2100 (2300) belongs.
⁴ *Cf.* Fr. 6, Dynasty I.   ⁵ For *haec*.

---

¹ The totals given by Barbarus are generally those of Africanus. Barbarus omits Manetho's Dynasty VII.; and Potestas X. is explained by Gelzer (*Sextus Julius Africanus*, p. 199) as being Manetho's X. + XI. + Ammenemes (16 years) = 244 years. Total, 2300.
² The actual total of the items given is 2260 years.
³ Potestas XI. is Manetho's Dynasty XII. Barbarus therefore gives Dynasties XII.-XVIII.: the totals (corrected by Meyer, *Aeg. Chron.* 99, n. 2) are—XII. 160, XIII. 453, XIV. 184, XV. 284, XVI. 518, XVII. 151,

AEGYPTIACA (EPITOME) FR. 4

I. Thereafter he [Manetho] gave an account of the kings who were Spirits of the Dead, calling them also Demigods, . . . who reigned for 2100 years: he called them " very brave " (Heroes).
  II. Mineus and seven of his descendants reigned for 253 years.[1]
  III. Bochus and eight other kings reigned for 302 years.
  IV. Necherocheus and seven other kings for 214 years.
  V. Similarly seventeen other kings for 277 years.
  VI. Similarly twenty-one other kings for 258 years.
  VII. Othoi and seven other kings for 203 years.
  VIII. Similarly fourteen other kings for 140 years.
  IX. Similarly twenty other kings for 409 years.
  X. Similarly seven other kings for 204 years.

Here ends the First Book of Manetho, which contains a period of 2100 years.[2]

XI.[3] A dynasty of kings of Diospolis, for 60 years.
XII. A dynasty of kings of Bubastus, for 153 years.

XVIII. 262 (+ XIX. 209). Sum total for Book II. 2221 years: cf. Fr. 55 Africanus, 56 Eus. (Arm.), 2121 years.

The names of Potestates XII.-XVII., or Dynasties XIII.-XVIII., come from some other source than Manetho: the Tanites of Potestas XIII. or Dynasty XIV. appear to correspond with the Hyksôs, just as in the *Book of Sôthis* (App. IV.); while others may be local dynasties of the Hyksôs age. The kings of Hermupolis (Potestas XVII.) apparently denote the kings of the Eighteenth Dynasty, whose names indicate the cult of the Moon-deities 'Ioh and Thôth of Hermupolis (Meyer, *Gesch.*[5] I. ii. p. 326).

Fr. 4, 5 MANETHO

XIII. Potestas Tanitorum annos CLXXXIV.
XIV. Potestas Sebennitorum annos CCXXIV.
XV. Potestas Memfitorum annos CCCXVIII.
XVI. Potestas Iliopolitorum annos CCXXI.
XVII. Potestas Ermupolitorum annos CCLX.

Usque ad septimam decimam potestatem secundum scribitur tomum,[1] ut docet numerum habentem annos mille quingentos XX. Haec sunt potestates Aegyptiorum.

Fr. 5. MALALAS, *Chronographia*, p. 25 (MIGNE, *Patrologia Graeca*, Vol. 97).

Ταῦτα δὲ τὰ παλαιὰ καὶ ἀρχαῖα βασίλεια τῶν Αἰγυπτίων Μανέθων συνεγράψατο· ἐν οἷς συγγράμμασιν αὐτοῦ ἐμφέρεται ἄλλως λέγεσθαι τὰς ἐπωνυμίας τῶν πέντε πλανητῶν ἀστέρων. Τὸν γὰρ λεγόμενον Κρόνον ἀστέρα ἐκάλουν τὸν λάμποντα, τὸν δὲ Διὸς τὸν φαέθοντα, τὸν δὲ Ἄρεος τὸν πυρώδη, τὸν δὲ Ἀφροδίτης τὸν κάλλιστον, τὸν δὲ Ἑρμοῦ τὸν στίλβοντα· ἅτινα μετὰ ταῦτα Σωτάτης ὁ σοφώτατος ἡρμήνευσε. Cf. id., p. 59: Αἰγυπτίων δὲ ἐβασίλευσε πρῶτος βασιλεὺς τῆς φυλῆς τοῦ Χάμ, υἱοῦ Νῶε, Φαραὼ ὁ καὶ Ναραχὼ

---

[1] MS. totum. Frick restores the original Greek as follows: μέχρι τῆς ιζ' δυναστείας ὁ δεύτερος γράφεται τόμος, ὡς δηλοῖ ὁ ἀριθμός, ἔχων ἔτη ,αφκ'.

---

[1] The actual total of the items given is 1420 years.
[2] 4407 codd.

AEGYPTIACA (EPITOME)   Fr. 4, 5

XIII. A dynasty of kings of Tanis, for 184 years.
XIV. A dynasty of kings of Sebennytus, for 224 years.
XV. A dynasty of kings of Memphis, for 318 years.
XVI. A dynasty of kings of Hêliopolis, for 221 years.
XVII. A dynasty of kings of Hermupolis, for 260 years.

The Second Book continues the record down to the Seventeenth Dynasty, and comprises 1520 years.[1] These are the Egyptian dynasties.

Fr. 5 (*from the Chronicle of Malalas*).

[After recording the reigns of Hêphaestus (1680 days), Hêlios (4477 [2] days), Sôsis, Osiris, Hôrus, and Thulis, Malalas adds :]

These ancient reigns of early Egyptian kings are recorded by Manetho, and in his writings it is stated that the names of the five planets are given in other forms : Cronos [Saturn] they used to call the shining star ; Zeus [Jupiter], the radiant star [Phaethôn] ; Arês [Mars], the fiery star ; Aphroditê [Venus], the fairest ; Hermês [Mercury], the glittering star. These names were later explained by the wise Sôtatês [? Sôtadês or Palaephatus [3]].

The first king of Egypt belonged to the tribe of Cham [Ham], Noah's son ; he was **Pharaôh**, who was also called **Narachô**.

[3] Palaephatus of Egypt, or Athens, wrote on Egyptian theology and mythology, c. 200 B.C.,—more than seven centuries earlier than Malalas himself (c. A.D. 491-578).

Fr. 5, 6   MANETHO

καλούμενος. Τὰ οὖν πρὸ τούτου παλαιὰ βασίλεια Αἰγυπτίων ἐξέθετο Μανέθων ὁ σοφώτατος, ὡς προείρηται.

Fr. 6. *Syncellus*, p. 99.

Ἐπειδὴ δὲ τῶν ἀπὸ Μεστραὶμ Αἰγυπτιακῶν δυναστειῶν[1] οἱ χρόνοι ἕως Νεκταναβῶ χρειώδεις τυγχάνουσιν ἐν πολλοῖς τοῖς περὶ τὰς χρονικὰς καταγινομένοις ζητήσεις, αὗται δὲ παρὰ Μανεθῶ ληφθεῖσαι τοῖς ἐκκλησιαστικοῖς ἱστορικοῖς διαπεφωνημένως κατά τε τὰς αὐτῶν προσηγορίας καὶ τὴν ποσότητα τῶν χρόνων τῆς βασιλείας ἐκδέδονται, ἐπὶ τίνος τε αὐτῶν Ἰωσὴφ ἡγεμόνευσε τῆς Αἰγύπτου καὶ μετ' αὐτὸν ὁ θεόπτης Μωϋσῆς τῆς τοῦ Ἰσραὴλ ἐξ Αἰγύπτου πορείας ἡγήσατο, ἀναγκαῖον ἡγησάμην δύο τῶν ἐπισημοτάτων ἐκδόσεις ἐκλέξασθαι καὶ ταύτας ἀλλήλαις παραθέσθαι, Ἀφρικανοῦ τέ φημι καὶ τοῦ μετ' αὐτὸν Εὐσεβίου τοῦ Παμφίλου καλουμένου, ὡς ἂν τὴν ἐγγίζουσαν τῇ γραφικῇ ἀληθείᾳ δόξαν ὀρθῶς ἐπιβάλλων τις[2] καταμάθοι, τοῦτο πρό γε πάντων εἰδὼς ἀκριβῶς, ὅτι Ἀφρικανὸς μὲν εἴκοσιν ἔτη προστίθησιν ἐν τοῖς ἀπὸ Ἀδὰμ ἕως τοῦ κατακλυσμοῦ χρόνοις, καὶ ἀντὶ ‚βσμβ' ‚βσξβ' ἔτη βούλεται εἶναι, ὅπερ οὐ δοκεῖ καλῶς ἔχειν. Εὐσέβιος δὲ ‚βσμβ' ὑγιῶς ἔθετο καὶ ὁμοφώνως τῇ γραφῇ. ἐν δὲ τοῖς ἀπὸ τοῦ κατακλυσμοῦ ἀμφότεροι διήμαρτον ἕως τοῦ Ἀβραὰμ

---

[1] δυναστειῶν Bunsen: ἐτῶν MSS.   [2] τις add. m.

AEGYPTIACA (EPITOME) FR. 5, 6

Now, the ancient reigns in Egypt before King Narachô were set forth by the wise Manetho, as has already been mentioned.

Fr. 6 (*from Syncellus*).

Since a knowledge of the periods of the Egyptian dynasties from Mestraïm [1] down to Nectanabô [2] is on many occasions needful to those who occupy themselves with chronological investigations, and since the dynasties taken from Manetho's *History* are set forth by ecclesiastical historians with discrepancies in respect both to the names of the kings and the length of their reigns, and also as to who was king when Joseph was governor of Egypt, and in whose reign thereafter Moses,—he who saw God,—led the Hebrews in their exodus from Egypt, I have judged it necessary to select two of the most famous recensions and to set them side by side—I mean the accounts of Africanus and of the later Eusebius, the so-called " son " of Pamphilus,—so that with proper application one may apprehend the opinion which approaches nearest to Scriptural truth. It must, above all, be strictly understood that Africanus increases by 20 years the period from Adam to the Flood, and instead of 2242 years he makes it out to be 2262 years, which appears to be incorrect. On the other hand, Eusebius keeps to the sound reckoning of 2242 years in agreement with Scripture. In regard to the period from the Flood down to Abraham and Moses, both have gone astray by 130

---

[1] See p. 7 n. 2.
[2] Nectanabô or Nectanebus, the last king of Dynasty XXX.

FR. 6 MANETHO

καὶ Μωϋσέως ἔτεσι ρλ' τοῦ δευτέρου Καϊνᾶν υἱοῦ
Ἀρφαξὰδ καὶ γενεᾷ μιᾷ, τῇ ιγ', παρὰ τῷ θείῳ
εὐαγγελιστῇ Λουκᾷ, ἀπὸ Ἀδὰμ κειμένῃ. ἀλλ' ὁ
μὲν Ἀφρικανὸς ἐν τοῖς ἀπὸ Ἀδὰμ προστεθεῖσιν
αὐτῷ καὶ ἐπὶ τὸν κατακλυσμὸν ἔτεσιν κ' προαφῄρ-
παξε ταῦτα, καὶ ἐν τοῖς τοῦ Καϊνᾶν καὶ τῶν μετέ-
πειτα ρι' μόνα λείπεται. διὸ καὶ ἕως Ἀβραὰμ
πρώτου ἔτους ͵γσβ' ἔτη ἐστοιχείωσεν. ὁ δὲ
Εὐσέβιος ὁλοκλήρως τὰ ρλ' ὑφελών, ͵γρπδ' ἕως
πρώτου ἔτους Ἀβραὰμ ἐξέδωκε.

ΚΑΤΑ ΑΦΡΙΚΑΝΟΝ.

Περὶ τῶν [μετὰ τὸν κατακλυσμὸν]¹
Αἰγύπτου δυναστειῶν, ὡς ὁ Ἀφρικανός.

α' Μετὰ νέκυας τοὺς ἡμιθέους πρώτη βασιλεία²
καταριθμεῖται βασιλέων ὀκτώ, ὧν πρῶτος

¹ Bracketed by Müller.   ² δυναστεία Boeckh.

---

[1] Arphaxad, son of Shem : *O.T. Genesis* x. 22. "Arphaxad" is probably a Mesopotamian name (W. F. Albright, *The Archaeology of Palestine and the Bible*³, 1932-3, p. 139).
[2] *N.T. Luke* iii. 36.
[3] Eusebius reckoned 2242 years from Adam to the Flood, and 942 years from the Flood to Abraham.
[4] Dynasties I. and II., the Thinites : c. 3200–c. 2780 B.C.

Note.—The dates which have been adopted throughout this book are those of Eduard Meyer, except where another authority is specified. Meyer's revised dates (as in *Die Ältere Chronologie* . . ., 1931) may conveniently be found in G. Steindorff's chapter on Ancient History in Baedeker⁸, pp. ci. ff. In the *Cambridge Ancient History*, vol. i., H. R. Hall gives for the dynasties a series of dates

AEGYPTIACA (EPITOME)

years belonging to the second Caïnan, son of Arphaxad,[1] even one generation, the thirteenth, from Adam, as it is recorded by the divine evangelist Luke.[2] But Africanus, in the 20 years which he added between Adam and the Flood, anticipated this; and in the period of Caïnan and his successors, only 110 years remain. Hence, down to the first year of Abraham he reckoned 3202 years; but Eusebius, completely omitting those 130 years, gave 3184 years [3] as far as Abraham's first year.

DYNASTY I.

ACCORDING TO AFRICANUS.

Here is the account which Africanus gives of the dynasties of Egypt [after the Flood].

1. In succession to the spirits of the Dead, the Demigods,—the first royal house [4] numbers eight kings, the first of whom Mênês [5] of

which differ from those of Breasted and the German School: he assigns earlier dates to the first twelve dynasties, *e.g.* Dynasty I. *c.* 3500 B.C. A. Scharff, on the other hand, dates the beginning of Dynasty I. *c.* 3000 B.C. (*Journ. of Eg. Arch.* xiv., 1928, pp. 275 f.).

Dynasty I. For the identifications of Manetho's kings with monumental and other evidence, see Meyer, *Geschichte des Altertums* [5], I. ii. p. 140: he identifies (1) Mênês, (2) Atoti I., II., III., (5) Usaphaïs, (6) Miebis.

(3) Kenkenês and (5) Usaphaïs are two names of the same king: see Newberry and Wainwright, "King Udymu (Den) and the Palermo Stone" in *Ancient Egypt*, 1914, p. 148 ff.

[5] On Mênês (*c.* 3200 B.C.) see P. E. Newberry in Winifred Brunton's *Great Ones of Ancient Egypt*, 1929: Min in Herodotus, ii. 4.

FR. 6 MANETHO

Μήνης Θινίτης ἐβασίλευσεν ἔτη ξβ'· ὃς ὑπὸ ἱπποποτάμου διαρπαγεὶς διεφθάρη.

β' Ἄθωθις υἱός, ἔτη νζ', ὁ τὰ ἐν Μέμφει βασίλεια οἰκοδομήσας· οὗ φέρονται βίβλοι ἀνατομικαί, ἰατρὸς γὰρ ἦν.

γ' Κενκένης υἱός, ἔτη λα'.

δ' Οὐενέφης υἱός, ἔτη κγ'· ἐφ' οὗ λιμὸς κατέσχε τὴν Αἴγυπτον μέγας. οὗτος τὰς περὶ Κωχώμην ἤγειρε πυραμίδας.

ε' Οὐσαφαῖδος υἱός, ἔτη κ'.

ϛ' Μιεβιδὸς υἱός, ἔτη κϛ'.

ζ' Σεμέμψης υἱός, ἔτη ιη'· ἐφ' οὗ φθορὰ μεγίστη κατέσχε τὴν Αἴγυπτον.

η' Βιηνεχὴς υἱός, ἔτη κϛ'.

Ὁμοῦ, ἔτη σνγ'.

Τὰ τῆς πρώτης δυναστείας οὕτω πως καὶ Εὐσέβιος ὡς ὁ Ἀφρικανὸς ἐξέθετο.

---

[1] This (Anc. Egyptian *Theny*), near Girga, about 310 miles S. of Cairo (Baedeker[8], p. 231), the capital of the nome of This, and the seat of the First and Second Dynasties. The cemetery of the First Dynasty kings was near Abydos: see Petrie, *Royal Tombs*, i. and ii., and Baedeker [8], p. 260.

[2] For a representation of a king fighting with a hippopotamus, see a seal-impression in Petrie, *Royal Tombs*, II. vii. 6; and for a hippopotamus-hunt, see a year-name of Udymu, Schäfer, *Palermo Stone*, p. 20, No. 8.

With the whole story, *cf.* the miraculous deliverance of Mênas by a crocodile in Diodorus Siculus, i. 89.

[3] Building of palace at Memphis—by Min or Mênês, Herodotus, ii. 99, Josephus, *Ant.* viii. 6, 2, 155; by his son Athôthis, says Manetho; by Uchoreus, Diod. i. 50.

AEGYPTIACA (EPITOME)   Fr. 6

This[1] reigned for 62 years. He was carried off by a hippopotamus[2] and perished.

2. Athôthis, his son, for 57 years. He built the palace at Memphis;[3] and his anatomical works[4] are extant, for he was a physician.
3. Kenkenês, his son, for 31 years.
4. Uenephês, his son, for 23 years. In his reign a great famine seized Egypt. He erected the pyramids near Kôchômê.[5]
5. Usaphaidos,[6] his son, for 20 years.
6. Miebidos,[6] his son, for 26 years.
7. Semempsês, his son, for 18 years. In his reign a very great calamity befell Egypt.
8. Biênechês, his son, for 26 years.

Total, 253 years.[7]

Eusebius also sets out the details of the First Dynasty in much the same way as Africanus.

---

[4] For the later study of anatomy (including, perhaps, the practice of vivisection) by kings of Ptolemaic Egypt, see G. Lumbroso, *Glossario*, s.v. Ἀνατομική.

[5] Kôchômê has been identified with Sakkâra, and excavations carried out there in the Archaic Cemetery from 1935 by W. B. Emery (assisted by Zaki Saad) have gone far to confirm Manetho. Several tombs which date from the First Dynasty were discovered at Sakkâra in 1937 and 1938. One of these, the tomb of Nebetka under the 5th king of Dynasty I., was found to contain in its interior a stepped-pyramid construction of brickwork: during the building the form of the tomb was altered to a palace-façade mastaba.

[6] These forms are really the genitives of the names Usaphaïs and Miebis.

[7] The actual total of the items given is 263 years.

Fr. 7

Fr. 7 (a). *Syncellus,* p. 102. ΚΑΤΑ ΕΥΣΕΒΙΟΝ.

Περὶ τῶν [μετὰ τὸν κατακλυσμὸν][1] Αἰγυπτίων δυναστειῶν, ὡς Εὐσέβιος.

Μετὰ νέκυας καὶ τοὺς ἡμιθέους πρώτην δυναστείαν καταριθμοῦσι βασιλέων ὀκτώ· ὧν γέγονε Μήνης, ὃς διασήμως αὐτῶν ἡγήσατο. ἀφ' οὗ τοὺς ἐξ ἑκάστου γένους βασιλεύσαντας ἀναγράψομεν ὧν[2] ἡ διαδοχὴ τοῦτον ἔχει τὸν τρόπον·

α' Μήνης Θινίτης καὶ οἱ τούτου ἀπόγονοι [ιζ', ἐν ἄλλῳ δὲ][3] ζ', ὃν Ἡρόδοτος Μῆνα ὠνόμασεν, ἐβασίλευσεν ἔτεσιν ξ'. οὗτος ὑπερόριον στρατείαν ἐποιήσατο καὶ ἔνδοξος ἐκρίθη, ὑπὸ[4] δὲ ἱπποποτάμου ἡρπάσθη.

β' Ἄθωθις ὁ τούτου υἱὸς ἦρξεν ἔτεσιν κζ', καὶ τὰ ἐν Μέμφει βασίλεια ᾠκοδόμησεν, ἰατρικήν τε ἐξήσκησε καὶ βίβλους ἀνατομικὰς συνέγραψε.

γ' Κενκένης ὁ τούτου υἱός, ἔτη λθ'.

δ' Οὐενέφης, ἔτη μβ'· ἐφ' οὗ λιμὸς κατέσχε τὴν χώραν, ὃς καὶ τὰς πυραμίδας τὰς περὶ Κωχώμην ἤγειρε.

ε' Οὐσαφάϊς,[5] ἔτη κ'.

ϛ' Νιεβάϊς,[6] ἔτη κϛ'.

---

[1] Bracketed by Müller.
[3] Bracketed by Gelzer.
[5] Οὐσαφαής A.
[2] Vulgo ἀναγραψαμένων.
[4] ἴσπου A, ἵππου B.
[6] Νιεβαής A.

AEGYPTIACA (EPITOME)   Fr. 7

Fr. 7 (a) (*from Syncellus*). ACCORDING TO EUSEBIUS.[1]

Here is the account which Eusebius gives of the Egyptian dynasties [after the Flood].

In succession to the Spirits of the Dead and the Demigods, the Egyptians reckon the First Dynasty to consist of eight kings. Among these was Mênês, whose rule in Egypt was illustrious. I shall record the rulers of each race from the time of Mênês ; their succession is as follows :

1. Mênês of This, with his [17, or in another copy] 7 descendants,—the king called Mên by Herodotus,—reigned for 60 years. He made a foreign expedition and won renown, but was carried off by a hippopotamus.
2. Athôthis, his son, ruled for 27 years. He built the palace at Memphis ; he practised medicine and wrote anatomical books.
3. Kenkenês, his son, for 39 years.
4. Uenephês, for 42 years. In his reign famine seized the land. He built the pyramids near Kôchôme.
5. Usaphaïs, for 20 years.
6. Niehaïs, for 26 years.

[1] The version (transmitted to us by Syncellus) which Eusebius gives of the *Epitome* of Manetho shows considerable differences from Africanus, both in the names of kings and in the length of their reigns. Peet (*Egypt and the Old Testament*, pp. 25 f.) says : " The astonishing variations between their figures are an eloquent testimony to what may happen to numbers in a few centuries through textual corruption." Petrie (H*istory of Egypt*, i. p. viii) compares the corruptions in such late Greek chronicles as those of the Ptolemies (C.V./A.D.).

ζ' Σεμέμψης, ἔτη ιη'· ἐφ' οὗ πολλὰ παράσημα
    ἐγένετο καὶ μεγίστη φθορά.
η' Οὐβιένθης, ἔτη κϛ'.
Οἱ πάντες ἐβασίλευσαν ἔτη σνβ'.

(b) EUSEBIUS, *Chronica* I. (Armenian Version),
pp. 94 sqq.

Post manes atque heroas primam dynastiam numerant VIII regum, quorum primus fuit Menes,[1] gloria regni administrandi praepollens: a quo exorsi singulas regnantium familias diligenter scribemus, quarum successiva series ita contexitur:

Menes Thinites eiusque posteri septem (quem Herodotus Mina nuncupavit). Hic annis XXX regnavit. Idem et extra regionis suae fines cum exercitu progressus est, et gloria rerum gestarum inclaruit. Ab hippopotamo genio[2] raptus est.

Athothis, huius filius, regno potitus est annis XXVII. Is regia sibi palatia Memphi construxit, et medicam item artem coluit, quin et libros de ratione secandorum corporum scripsit.

Cencenes eius filius, annis XXXIX.

Vavenephis, annis XLII, cuius aetate fames regionem corripuit. Is pyramidas prope Cho oppidum[3] excitavit.

---

[1] Corr. edd.: MSS. Memes.
[2] Müller conjectures the Greek original to have been: ὑπὸ δαίμονος δὲ ἱπποποτάμου. But the Armenian text, literally translated, is: "by a horse-shaped river-monster" (Karst, Margoliouth).

AEGYPTIACA (EPITOME)   Fr. 7

7. Semempsês, for 18 years. In his reign there were many portents and a very great calamity.
8. Ubienthês, for 26 years.

The total of all reigns, 252 years.[1]

(b) Armenian Version of Eusebius.

In succession to the Spirits of the Dead and the Demigods, the Egyptians reckon the First Dynasty to consist of eight kings. The first of these was Mênês, who won high renown in the government of his kingdom. Beginning with him, I shall carefully record the royal families one by one: their succession in detail is as follows:

Mênês of This (whom Herodotus named Min) and his seven descendants. He reigned for 30 years, and advanced with his army beyond the frontiers of his realm, winning renown by his exploits. He was carried off by a hippopotamus god (?).[2]

Athothis, his son, held the throne for 27 years. He built for himself a royal palace at Memphis, and also practised the art of medicine, writing books on the method of anatomy.

Cencenes, his son, for 39 years.

Vavenephis, for 42 years. In his time famine seized the land. He reared pyramids near the town of Cho.

---
[1] The actual total of the items given is 258 years.
[2] See note 2 on the text.

---
[3] Apparently = $X\hat{\omega}\ \kappa\hat{\omega}\mu\eta\nu$, for $K\omega\chi\acute{\omega}\mu\eta\nu$.

FR. 7, 8   MANETHO

Usaphaïs, annis XX.
Niebaïs, annis XXVI.
Mempses, annis XVIII. Sub hoc multa prodigia itemque maxima lues acciderunt.
Vibenthis,¹ annis XXVI.

Summa dominationis annorum CCLII.

Fr. 8. *Syncellus*, p. 101. ΚΑΤΑ ΑΦΡΙΚΑΝΟΝ.

Δευτέρα δυναστεία Θινιτῶν βασιλέων ἐννέα, ὧν πρῶτος Βοηθός, ἔτη λη´· ἐφ᾽ οὗ χάσμα κατὰ Βούβαστον ἐγένετο καὶ ἀπώλοντο πολλοί.

β´ Καιέχως, ἔτη λθ´· ἐφ᾽ οὗ οἱ βόες Ἆπις ἐν Μέμφει καὶ Μνεῦις ἐν Ἡλιουπόλει καὶ ὁ Μενδήσιος τράγος ἐνομίσθησαν εἶναι θεοί.

¹ One MS. (G) has Vibethis.

---

¹ Karst gives 270 years as the total transmitted in the Armenian version. The total of the items as given above is 228 years.
² Dynasty II.—to c. 2780 B.C. For identifications with the Monuments, etc., see Meyer, *Geschichte* ⁵, I. ii. p. 146: he identifies (1) Boêthos, (2) Kaiechôs or Kechôus, (3) Binôthris, (4) Tlas, (5) Sethenês, (7) Nephercherês, (8) Sesôchris. For (1) to (5), see G. A. Reisner, *The Development of the Egyptian Tomb*, 1936, p. 123.
³ Bubastus or Bubastis (Baedeker ⁸, p. 181), near Zagazig in the Delta: Anc. Egyptian *Per-Baste*, the *Pi-beseth* of

AEGYPTIACA (EPITOME) FR. 7, 8

Usaphaïs, for 20 years.
Niebaïs, for 26 years.
Mempses, for 18 years. In his reign many portents and a great pestilence occurred.
Vibenthis, for 26 years.
Total for the dynasty, 252 years.[1]

DYNASTY II.

Fr. 8 (*from Syncellus*).   ACCORDING TO AFRICANUS.

The Second Dynasty[2] consists of nine kings of This. The first was Boêthos, for 38 years. In his reign a chasm opened at Bubastus,[3] and many perished.

2. Kaiechôs, for 39 years. In his reign the bulls,[4] Apis at Memphis and Mnevis at Heliopolis, and the Mendesian goat were worshipped as gods.

Ezekiel xxx. 17. See also Herodotus, ii. 60, 137 f. The kings of Dynasty XXII. resided at Bubastis.

Earthquakes have always been rare in Egypt (Euseb., *Chron. Graec.* p. 42, l. 25; Pliny, *H.N.* ii. 82); but Bubastis is situated in an unstable region: see H. G. Lyons in *Cairo Scientific Journal*, i. (1907), p. 182. It stands on an earthquake line, which runs to Crete. A deep boring made at Bubastis failed to reach rock.

[4] The worship of Apis is earlier even than Dynasty II.: see Palermo Stone, Schäfer, p. 21, No. 12 (in reign of Udymu). For Apis, see Herodotus, ii. 153, and Diod. Sic. i. 84, 85 (where all three animals are mentioned). The goat was a cult animal in very early times: *cf.* Herodotus, ii. 46.

Fr. 8, 9   MANETHO

γ´ Βίνωθρις, ἔτη μζ´· ἐφ᾽ οὗ ἐκρίθη τὰς γυναῖκας βασιλείας γέρας ἔχειν.

δ´ Τλάς, ἔτη ιζ´.

ε´ Σεθένης, ἔτη μα´.

ς´ Χαίρης, ἔτη ιζ´.

ζ´ Νεφερχέρης, ἔτη κε´· ἐφ᾽ οὗ μυθεύεται τὸν Νεῖλον μέλιτι κεκραμένον ἡμέρας ἕνδεκα ῥυῆναι.

η´ Σέσωχρις, ἔτη μη´, ὃς ὕψος εἶχε πηχῶν ε´, παλαιστῶν[1] γ´.

θ´ Χενερής, ἔτη λ´.

Ὁμοῦ, ἔτη τβ´.

Ὁμοῦ πρώτης καὶ δευτέρας δυναστείας [μετὰ τὸν κατακλυσμὸν] ἔτη φνε´ κατὰ τὴν δευτέραν ἔκδοσιν Ἀφρικανοῦ.

Fr. 9.   Syncellus, p. 103.   ΚΑΤΑ ΕΥΣΕΒΙΟΝ.

Δευτέρα δυναστεία βασιλέων ἐννέα.

Πρῶτος Βῶχος, ἐφ᾽ οὗ χάσμα κατὰ Βούβαστον ἐγένετο, καὶ πολλοὶ ἀπώλοντο.

Μεθ᾽ ὃν δεύτερος Καιχῶος,[2] ὅτε καὶ ὁ Ἆπις καὶ ὁ Μνεῦις, ἀλλὰ καὶ ὁ Μενδήσιος τράγος θεοὶ ἐνομίσθησαν.

[1] Boeckh, Bunsen: MSS. πλάτος.
[2] Müller: MSS. μεθ᾽ ὃν καὶ δεύτερος Χῶος.

AEGYPTIACA (EPITOME) FR. 8, 9

3. Binôthris, for 47 years. In his reign it was decided that women [1] might hold the kingly office.
4. Tlas, for 17 years.
5. Sethenês, for 41 years.
6. Chairês, for 17 years.
7. Nephercherês, for 25 years. In his reign, the story goes, the Nile flowed blended with honey for 11 days.
8. Sesôchris, for 48 years : his stature was 5 cubits, 3 palms.[2]
9. Chenerês, for 30 years.

Total, 302 years.

Total for the First and Second Dynasties [after the Flood], 555 years, according to the second edition of Africanus.

Fr. 9 (*from* Syncellus). ACCORDING TO EUSEBIUS.

The Second Dynasty consisted of nine kings. First came Bôchos, in whose reign a chasm opened at Bubastus, and many perished.

He was succeeded by Kaichôos (or Chôos), in whose time Apis and Mnevis and also the Mendesian goat were worshipped as gods.

---

[1] No queens' names are recorded in the Royal Lists of Abydos and Karnak. Herodotus (ii. 100) records one queen : Diod. Sic. i. 44 (from Hecataeus) reckons the number of Egyptian queens as five.

[2] The stature of each king is said to be noted in the records mentioned by Diodorus Siculus, i. 44, 4. *Cf.* *infra*, Fr. 35, No. 3, App. II. No. 6 (p. 216).

Fr. 9, 10   MANETHO

γ' Βίοφις, ἐφ' οὗ ἐκρίθη καὶ τὰς γυναῖκας βασιλείας γέρας ἔχειν. καὶ μετὰ τούτους ἄλλοι τρεῖς, ἐφ' ὧν οὐδὲν παράσημον ἐγένετο.

ζ' Ἐπὶ δὲ τοῦ ἑβδόμου μυθεύεται τὸν Νεῖλον μέλιτι κεκραμένον ἡμέραις ἕνδεκα ῥυῆναι.

η' Μεθ' ὃν Σέσωχρις ⟨, ἔτη⟩ μη', ὃς λέγεται γεγονέναι ὕψος ἔχων πηχῶν ε', παλαιστῶν γ' τὸ μέγεθος.

θ' Ἐπὶ δὲ τοῦ θ' οὐδὲν ἀξιομνημόνευτον ὑπῆρχεν. Οἳ καὶ ἐβασίλευσαν ἔτεσι σϟζ'.

Ὁμοῦ πρώτης καὶ δευτέρας δυναστείας ἔτη φμθ' κατὰ τὴν ἔκδοσιν Εὐσεβίου.

Fr. 10. Eusebius, *Chronica* I. (Armenian Version), p. 96.

Secunda dynastia regum IX.
Primus Bochus: sub eo specus ingens Bubasti subsedit multosque mortales hausit.
Post eum Cechous, quo tempore [1] Apis et Mnevis atque Mendesius hircus dii esse putabantur.
Deinde Biophis, sub quo lege statutum est, ut feminae quoque regiam dignitatem obtinerent.
Tum alii tres, quorum aetate nullum insigne facinus patratum est.
Sub septimo mythici aiunt flumen Nilum melle simul et aqua fluxisse undecim diebus.

[1] Müller: MS. idemque.

3. Biophis, in whose reign it was decided that women also might hold the kingly office. In the reigns of the three succeeding kings, no notable event occurred.
7. In the seventh reign, as the story goes, the Nile flowed blended with honey for 11 days.
8. Next, Sesôchris was king for 48 years: the greatness of his stature is said to have been 5 cubits 3 palms.
9. In the ninth reign there happened no event worthy of mention. These kings ruled for 297 years.

Total for the First and Second Dynasties, 549 years, according to the recension of Eusebius.

Fr. 10. ARMENIAN VERSION OF EUSEBIUS.

The Second Dynasty consisted of nine kings.

First came Bôchus, in whose reign a huge hole opened at Bubastus, and swallowed up many persons.

He was succeeded by Cechous, in whose time Apis and Mnevis and the Mendesian goat were worshipped as gods.

Next came Biophis, in whose reign it was decreed by law that women also might hold the royal office.

In the reigns of the three succeeding kings, no notable event occurred.

Under the seventh king fabulists tell how the river Nile flowed with honey as well as water for 11 days.

FR. 10, 11   MANETHO

Postea Sesochris annis XLVIII, quem aiunt quinque cubitos altum, tres vero palmos latum fuisse.

Sub nono tandem nihil memoria dignum actum est.

Hi regnaverunt annis CCXCVII.

Fr. 11.   *Syncellus*, p. 104.   ΑΦΡΙΚΑΝΟΥ.

Τρίτη δυναστεία Μεμφιτῶν βασιλέων ἐννέα, ὧν α΄ Νεχερώφης,[1] ἔτη κη΄· ἐφ᾽ οὗ Λίβυες ἀπέστησαν Αἰγυπτίων, καὶ τῆς σελήνης παρὰ λόγον αὐξηθείσης διὰ δέος ἑαυτοὺς παρέδοσαν.

β΄ Τόσορθρος, ἔτη κθ΄, ⟨ἐφ᾽ οὗ Ἰμούθης[2]⟩. οὗτος Ἀσκληπιὸς ⟨παρὰ τοῖς[2]⟩ Αἰγυπτίοις

[1] Νεχορόφης A.   [2] Conj. Sethe.

---

[1] For this absurd perversion of the Greek words, see p. 36 n. 1: πλάτος was added, perhaps as a corruption of παλαιστῶν, and replaced μέγεθος in the Greek version of Eusebius.

[2] The Old Kingdom, Dynasties III.-V.: c. 2780–c. 2420 B.C. Dynasty III., c. 2780–c. 2720 B.C. For identifications with monumental and other evidence, see Meyer, *Geschichte*[5], I. ii. p. 174: he identifies (2) Tosorthos (Zoser I.—" the Holy "), and holds that (1) Necherôphês is one name of Kha'sekhemui, (6) Tosertasis may be Zoser II. Atoti, and (9) Kerpherês may be Neferkerê' II.

[3] Zoser was not the first builder with hewn stone: his predecessor, Kha'sekhemui, used squared blocks of limestone for building purposes; see Petrie, *Royal Tombs*, ii. p. 13. Granite blocks had already formed the floor of the tomb of Udymu (Dynasty I.).

Two tombs of Zoser are known: (1) a mastaba at Bêt Khallâf near This (Baedeker[8], p. 231), see J. Garstang, *Mahâsna and Bêt Khallâf;* and (2) the famous Step

AEGYPTIACA (EPITOME) Fr. 10, 11

Next, Sesochris ruled for 48 years : he is said to have been 5 cubits high and 3 palms broad.[1]

Finally, under the ninth king no memorable event occurred.

These kings reigned for 297 years.

Dynasty III.

Fr. 11 (*from* Syncellus). The Account of Africanus.

The Third Dynasty [2] comprised nine kings of Memphis.

1. Necherôphês, for 28 years. In his reign the Libyans revolted against Egypt, and when the moon waxed beyond reckoning, they surrendered in terror.
2. Tosorthros,[3] for 29 years. ⟨In his reign lived Imuthês,[4]⟩ who because of his medical skill has the reputation of Asclepios among the

---

Pyramid at Sakkâra, which was the work of the great architect Imhotep (Baedeker [8], p. 156 f.).

[4] If the emendation in the text be not accepted, the statement would surely be too inaccurate to be attributed to Manetho. The Egyptian Asclepios was Imouth or Imhotep of Memphis, physician and architect to King Zoser, afterwards deified : on Philae (now for the most part submerged) Ptolemy II. Philadelphus built a little temple to Imhotep. See Sethe, *Untersuchungen*, ii. 4 (1902) : J. B. Hurry, *Imhotep* (Oxford, 1926).

One of the Oxyrhynchus Papyri, edited by Grenfell and Hunt, P. Oxy. XI. 1381, of ii./A.D., has for its subject the eulogy of Imuthês-Asclepius : the fragment preserved is part of the prelude. See G. Manteuffel, *De Opusculis Graecis Aegypti e papyris, ostracis, lapidibusque collectis*, 1930, No. 3.

Fr. 11, 12   MANETHO

κατὰ τὴν ἰατρικὴν νενόμισται, καὶ τὴν διὰ ξεστῶν λίθων οἰκοδομίαν εὕρατο· ἀλλὰ καὶ γραφῆς ἐπεμελήθη.

γ´ Τύρεις,[1] ἔτη ζ´.
δ´ Μέσωχρις, ἔτη ιζ´.
ε´ Σώϋφις, ἔτη ιϛ´.
ϛ´ Τοσέρτασις, ἔτη ιθ´.
ζ´ Ἄχης, ἔτη μβ´.
η´ Σήφουρις, ⟨ἔτη⟩ λ´.
θ´ Κερφέρης, ἔτη κϛ´.

Ὁμοῦ, ἔτη σιδ´.

Ὁμοῦ τῶν τριῶν δυναστειῶν κατὰ Ἀφρικανὸν ἔτη ψξθ´.

Fr. 12 (a). *Syncellus*, p. 106. ΚΑΤΑ ΕΥΣΕΒΙΟΝ.

Τρίτη δυναστεία Μεμφιτῶν βασιλέων ὀκτώ,

α´ Νεχέρωχις, ἐφ᾽ οὗ Λίβυες ἀπέστησαν Αἰγυπτίων, καὶ τῆς σελήνης παρὰ λόγον αὐξηθείσης διὰ δέος ἑαυτοὺς παρέδοσαν.

β´ Μεθ᾽ ὃν Σέσορθος . . ., ὃς Ἀσκληπιὸς παρὰ Αἰγυπτίοις ἐκλήθη διὰ τὴν ἰατρικήν. οὗτος καὶ τὴν διὰ ξεστῶν λίθων οἰκοδομὴν εὕρατο, ἀλλὰ καὶ γραφῆς· ἐπεμελήθη.

Οἱ δὲ λοιποὶ ἓξ οὐδὲν ἀξιομνημόνευτον ἔπραξαν. Οἳ καὶ ἐβασίλευσαν ἔτεσιν ρλη´.

Ὁμοῦ τῶν τριῶν δυναστειῶν κατὰ τὸν Εὐσέβιον ἔτη ψμζ´.

[1] Τύρις A.

Egyptians, and who was the inventor of the art of building with hewn stone. He also devoted attention to writing.
3. Tyreis (or Tyris), for 7 years.
4. Mesôchris, for 17 years.
5. Sôÿphis, for 16 years.
6. Tosertasis, for 19 years.
7. Achês, for 42 years.
8. Sêphuris, for 30 years.
9. Kerpherês, for 26 years.

Total, 214 years.

Total for the first three dynasties, according to Africanus, 769 years.

Fr. 12 (a). (*from Syncellus*). ACCORDING TO EUSEBIUS.

The Third Dynasty consisted of eight kings of Memphis:
1. Necherôchis, in whose reign the Libyans revolted against Egypt, and when the moon waxed beyond reckoning, they surrendered in terror.
2. He was succeeded by Sesorthos . . . : he was styled Asclepios in Egypt because of his medical skill. He was also the inventor of the art of building with hewn stone, and devoted attention to writing as well.

The remaining six kings achieved nothing worthy of mention. These eight kings reigned for 198 years.

Total for the first three dynasties, according to Eusebius, 747 years.

FR. 12, 14   MANETHO

(b) EUSEBIUS, *Chronica* I. (Armenian Version),
p. 96.

Tertia dynastia Memphitarum regum VIII.

Necherochis, sub quo Libyes ab Aegyptiis defecerunt: mox intempestive[1] crescente luna territi ad obsequium reversi sunt.

Deinde Sosorthus . . ., qui ob medicam artem Aesculapius ab Aegyptiis vocitatus est. Is etiam sectis lapidibus aedificiorum struendorum auctor fuit: libris praeterea scribendis curam impendit.

Sex reliqui nihil commemorandum gesserunt. Regnatum est annis CXCVII.

Fr. 14. *Syncellus*, p. 105. ΚΑΤΑ ΑΦΡΙΚΑΝΟΝ.

Τετάρτη δυναστεία Μεμφιτῶν συγγενείας ἑτέρας βασιλεῖς η'.

[1] intempestive, Margoliouth; importune, Aucher; immaniter, Mai.

---

[1] Dynasty IV., c. 2720–c. 2560 B.C. For identifications with monumental and other evidence, see Meyer, *Geschichte* [5], I. ii. p. 181: he identifies (1) Sôris (Snofru), (2) Suphis I. (Cheops, Khufu), then after Dedefrê' (not mentioned by Manetho), (3) Suphis II. (Chephren), (4) Mencherês (Mycerinus), and finally (an uncertain identification), (7) Sebercherês (Shepseskaf). For (3) Chephren and

AEGYPTIACA (EPITOME) Fr. 12, 14

(b) ARMENIAN VERSION OF EUSEBIUS.

The Third Dynasty consisted of eight kings of Memphis:

Necherochis, in whose reign the Libyans revolted against Egypt: later when the moon waxed unseasonably, they were terrified and returned to their allegiance.

Next came Sosorthus . . . : he was styled Aesculapius by the Egyptians because of his medical skill. He was also the inventor of building with hewn stone; and in addition he devoted care to the writing of books.

The six remaining kings did nothing worthy of mention. The reigns of the whole dynasty amount to 197 years.

DYNASTY IV.

Fr. 14 (*from* Syncellus). ACCORDING TO AFRICANUS.

The Fourth Dynasty[1] comprised eight kings of Memphis, belonging to a different line:

(4) Mycerinus, Diodorus i. 64 gives the good variants (3) Chabryês and (4) Mencherinus. On the Chronology of Dynasty IV. see Reisner, *Mycerinus* (*cf. infra*, note 2), pp. 243 ff. Reisner reads the name Dedefrê in the form Radedef, and identifies it with Ratoisês.

The Greek tales of the oppression of Egypt by Cheops and Chephren, etc., are believed to be the inventions of dragomans. *Cf.* Herodotus, ii. 124 (contempt for the gods), 129 (Mycerinus), with How and Wells's notes. Africanus has, moreover, acquired as a treasure the " sacred book " of Cheops.

45

Fr. 14 MANETHO

α' Σῶρις, ἔτη κθ'.
β' Σοῦφις, ἔτη ξγ'· ὃς τὴν μεγίστην ἤγειρε πυραμίδα, ἥν φησιν Ἡρόδοτος[1] ὑπὸ Χέοπος γεγονέναι. οὗτος δὲ καὶ ὑπερόπτης εἰς θεοὺς ἐγένετο καὶ τὴν ἱερὰν συνέγραψε βίβλον, ἣν ὡς μέγα χρῆμα ἐν Αἰγύπτῳ γενόμενος ἐκτησάμην.
γ' Σοῦφις, ἔτη ξϛ'.
δ' Μενχέρης, ἔτη ξγ'.
ε' Ῥατοίσης, ἔτη κε'.
ϛ' Βίχερις, ἔτη κβ'.
ζ' Σεβερχέρης, ἔτη ζ'.
η' Θαμφθίς, ἔτη θ'.

Ὁμοῦ, ἔτη σοζ'.[2]

Ὁμοῦ τῶν δ' δυναστειῶν τῶν [μετὰ τὸν κατακλυσμὸν] ἔτη ‚αμϛ' κατ' Ἀφρικανόν.

[1] Hdt. ii. 124.   [2] σοδ' A.

---

[1] On the Pyramids of Giza, see Baedeker[8], pp. 133 ff.; Noel F. Wheeler, "Pyramids and their Purpose," *Antiquity*, 1935, pp. 5-21, 161-189, 292-304; and for the fourth king of Dynasty IV. see G. A. Reisner, *Mycerinus: The Temples of the Third Pyramid at Giza*, 1931. Notwithstanding their colossal dimensions and marvellous construction, the Pyramids have not escaped detraction: Frontinus (*De Aquis*, i. 16) contrasts "the

AEGYPTIACA (EPITOME) FR. 14

1. Sôris, for 29 years.
2. Suphis [I.], for 63 years. He reared the Great Pyramid,[1] which Herodotus says was built by Cheops. Suphis conceived a contempt for the gods: he also composed the Sacred Book, which I acquired in my visit to Egypt [2] because of its high renown.
3. Suphis [II.], for 66 years.
4. Mencherês, for 63 years.
5. Ratoisês, for 25 years.
6. Bicheris, for 22 years.
7. Sebercherês, for 7 years.
8. Thamphthis, for 9 years.

Total, 277 years.[3]

Total for the first four dynasties [after the Flood], 1046 years according to Africanus.

idle pyramids" with "the indispensable structures" of the several aqueducts at Rome; and Pliny (H.N. 36, 8, § 75) finds in the pyramids "an idle and foolish ostentation of royal wealth". But the pyramids have, at any rate, preserved the names of their builders, especially Cheops, to all future ages, although, as Sir Thomas Browne characteristically wrote (*Urn-Burial*, Chap. 5): "To ... be but pyramidally extant is a fallacy of duration" ... "Who can but pity the founder of the Pyramids?" The modern Egyptologist says: "The Great Pyramid is the earliest and most impressive witness ... to the final emergence of organized society from prehistoric chaos and local conflict" (J. H. Breasted, H*istory of Egypt*, p. 119).

[2] Africanus went from Palestine to Alexandria, attracted by the renown of the philosopher Heraclas, Bishop of Alexandria: see Eusebius, H*ist. Eccl.* vi. 31, 2.

[3] The MS. A gives as total 274: the items add to 284.

Fr. 15. Syncellus, p. 106. ΚΑΤΑ ΕΥΣΕΒΙΟΝ.

Τετάρτη δυναστεία βασιλέων ιζ' Μεμφιτῶν συγγενείας ἑτέρας βασιλείας.

Ὧν τρίτος Σοῦφις, ὁ τὴν μεγίστην πυραμίδα ἐγείρας, ἥν φησιν Ἡρόδοτος ὑπὸ Χέοπος γεγονέναι, ὃς καὶ ὑπερόπτης εἰς θεοὺς γέγονεν, ὡς μετανοήσαντα αὐτὸν τὴν ἱερὰν συγγράψαι βίβλον, ἣν ὡς μέγα χρῆμα Αἰγύπτιοι περιέπουσι. τῶν δὲ λοιπῶν οὐδὲν ἀξιομνημόνευτον ἀνεγράφη. οἳ καὶ ἐβασίλευσαν ἔτεσιν υμη'.

Ὁμοῦ τῶν δ' δυναστειῶν [μετὰ τὸν κατακλυσμὸν] ͵αρϟε' κατὰ Εὐσέβιον.

Fr. 16. Eusebius, *Chronica* I. (Armenian Version), p. 97.

Quarta dynastia Memphitarum regum XVII ex alia regia familia, quorum tertius, Suphis, maximae pyramidis auctor, quam quidem Herodotus a Cheope structam ait: qui in deos ipsos superbiebat; tum facti poenitens sacrum librum[1] conscribebat, quem Aegyptii instar magni thesauri habere se putant. De reliquis regibus nihil memorabile litteris mandatum est. Regnatum est annis CCCCXLVIII.

[1] libros Sacrarii (Aucher), "the sanctuary books," "books for the shrine."

AEGYPTIACA (EPITOME) FR. 15, 16

Fr. 15 (*from* Syncellus). ACCORDING TO EUSEBIUS.

The Fourth Dynasty comprised seventeen kings of Memphis belonging to a different royal line.

Of these the third was Suphis, the builder of the Great Pyramid, which Herodotus says was built by Cheops. Suphis conceived a contempt for the gods, but repenting of this, he composed the Sacred Book, which the Egyptians hold in high esteem.

Of the remaining kings no achievement worthy of mention has been recorded.

This dynasty reigned for 448 years.

Total for the first four dynasties [after the Flood], 1195 years according to Eusebius.

Fr. 16. ARMENIAN VERSION OF EUSEBIUS.

The Fourth Dynasty consisted of seventeen kings of Memphis belonging to a different royal line. The third of these kings, Suphis, was the builder of the Great Pyramid, which Herodotus declares to have been built by Cheops. Suphis behaved arrogantly towards the gods themselves: then, in penitence, he composed the Sacred Book in which the Egyptians believe they possess a great treasure. Of the remaining kings nothing worthy of mention is recorded in history. The reigns of the whole dynasty amount to 448 years.

Fr. 18. Syncellus, p. 107. ΚΑΤΑ ΑΦΡΙΚΑΝΟΝ.

Πέμπτη δυναστεία βασιλέων η' ἐξ Ἐλεφαντίνης.

α' Οὐσερχέρης, ἔτη κη'.
β' Σεφρής, ἔτη ιγ'.
γ' Νεφερχέρης, ἔτη κ'.
δ' Σισίρης, ἔτη ζ'.
ε' Χέρης, ἔτη κ'.
ϛ' Ῥαθούρης, ἔτη μδ'.
ζ' Μενχέρης, ἔτη θ'.
η' Τανχέρης,[1] ἔτη μδ'.
θ' Ὄννος,[2] ἔτη λγ'.

Ὁμοῦ, ἔτη σμη'. γίνονται σὺν τοῖς προτεταγμένοις ͵αμϛ' ἔτεσι τῶν τεσσάρων δυναστειῶν ἔτη ͵ασϟδ'.

Fr. 19 (a). Syncellus, p. 109. ΚΑΤΑ ΕΥΣΕΒΙΟΝ.

Πέμπτη δυναστεία βασιλέων τριάκοντα ἑνὸς ἐξ Ἐλεφαντίνης. ὧν πρῶτος Ὀθόης. οὗτος ὑπὸ τῶν δορυφόρων ἀνῃρέθη.

[1] Τατχέρης corr. Lepsius.   [2] Ὄβνος A.

---

[1] Dynasty V. c. 2560–c. 2420 B.C. For identifications with monumental and other evidence, see Meyer, *Geschichte*[5], I. ii. p. 203: his list runs (1) Userkaf, (2) Sahurê', (3) Nefererkerê' Kakai, (4) Nefrefrê' or Shepseskerê', (5) Kha'neferrê', (6) Neweserrê' Ini, (7) Menkeuhor (Akeuhor), (8) Dedkerê' Asosi, (9) Unas.

AEGYPTIACA (EPITOME) Fr. 18, 19

Dynasty V.

Fr. 18 (*from* Syncellus). According to Africanus.

The Fifth Dynasty [1] was composed of eight kings of Elephantine:

1. Usercherês, for 28 years.
2. Sephrês, for 13 years.
3. Nephercherês, for 20 years.
4. Sisirês, for 7 years.
5. Cherês, for 20 years.
6. Rathurês, for 44 years.
7. Mencherês, for 9 years.
8. Tancherês (? Tatcherês), for 44 years.
9. Onnus, for 33 years.
Total, 248 years.[2]

Along with the aforementioned 1046 years of the first four dynasties, this amounts to 1294 years.

Fr. 19 (a) (*from* Syncellus). According to Eusebius.

The Fifth Dynasty consisted of thirty-one kings of Elephantine. Of these the first was Othoês,[3] who was murdered by his bodyguard.

---

[2] The items total 218 years; but if the reign of Othoês, the first king of Dynasty VI. is added, the total will then be 248 years.
[3] In the chronology of Eusebius, Dynasty V. is suppressed: the kings whom he mentions belong to Dynasty VI.

Fr. 19, 20   MANETHO

Ὁ δὲ δ' Φίωψ, ἑξαέτης ἀρξάμενος, ἐβασίλευσε μέχρις ἐτῶν ἑκατόν. γίνονται οὖν σὺν τοῖς προτεταγμένοις ͵αρϟε' ἔτεσι τῶν τεσσάρων δυναστειῶν ⟨ἔτη⟩ ͵ασϟε'.

(b) Eusebius, *Chronica* I. (Armenian Version), p. 97.

Quinta dynastia regum XXXI Elephantinorum, quorum primus Othius, qui a satellitibus suis occisus est. Quartus Phiops, qui regiam dignitatem a sexto aetatis anno ad centesimum usque tenuit.

Fr. 20. Syncellus, p. 108. ΚΑΤΑ ΑΦΡΙΚΑΝΟΝ.

Ἕκτη δυναστεία βασιλέων ἐξ Μεμφιτῶν.
α' Ὀθόης,[1] ἔτη λ', ὃς ὑπὸ τῶν δορυφόρων
  ἀνηρέθη.
β' Φιός, ἔτη νγ'.
γ' Μεθουσοῦφις, ἔτη ζ'.

[1] Ὀθώης A.

---

[1] Karst translates the Armenian as referring to the sixtieth year—" began to rule at the age of 60 "; but Aucher's Armenian text has the equivalent of *sexennis*, " six years old " (Margoliouth).

AEGYPTIACA (EPITOME) FR. 19, 20

The fourth king, Phiôps, succeeding when six years old, reigned until his hundredth year. Thus, along with the aforementioned 1195 years of the first four dynasties, this amounts to 1295 years.

(b) ARMENIAN VERSION OF EUSEBIUS.

The Fifth Dynasty consisted of thirty-one kings of Elephantine. Of these the first was Othius, who was killed by his attendants. The fourth king was Phiôps, who held the royal office from his sixth [1] right down to his hundredth year.

DYNASTY VI.

Fr. 20 (*from Syncellus*). ACCORDING TO AFRICANUS.

The Sixth Dynasty [2] consisted of six kings of Memphis:

1. Othoês, for 30 years: he was murdered by his bodyguard.
2. Phius, for 53 years.
3. Methusuphis, for 7 years.

---

[2] Dynasties VI.-VIII., the last Memphites, c. 2420–c. 2240 B.C. Dynasty VI. Meyer (*Geschichte* [5], I. ii. p. 236) identifies as follows: (1) Othoês (Teti or Atoti), then after Userkerê', (2) Phius (Pepi I.), (3) Methusuphis (Merenrê' I.), (4) Phiôps (Pepi II.), (5) Menthesuphis (Merenrê' II.), (6) Nitôcris. Sethe (*Sesostris*, p. 3) draws attention to the intentional differentiation of the same family-name—Phius for Pepi I., Phiôps for Pepi II.: so also (3) Methusuphis and (5) Menthesuphis, and *cf. infra* on Psametik in Dynasty XXVI. Are these variations due to Manetho or to his source?

δ' Φίωψ, ἑξαέτης ἀρξάμενος βασιλεύειν, διεγένετο μέχρι ἐτῶν ρ'.
ε' Μενθεσοῦφις, ἔτος ἕν.
ς' Νίτωκρις, γεννικωτάτη καὶ εὐμορφοτάτη τῶν κατ' αὐτὴν γενομένη, ξανθὴ τὴν χροιάν, ἣ τὴν τρίτην ἤγειρε πυραμίδα, ἐβασίλευσεν ἔτη ιβ'.

Ὁμοῦ, ἔτη ϟγ'. γίνονται σὺν τοῖς προτεταγμένοις ͵ασϟδ' τῶν ε' δυναστειῶν ἔτη ͵αυϟζ'.

Fr. 21 (a). Syncellus, p. 109. ΚΑΤΑ ΕΥΣΕΒΙΟΝ.
Ἕκτη δυναστεία.

Γυνὴ Νίτωκρις ἐβασίλευσε, τῶν κατ' αὐτὴν γεννικωτάτη καὶ εὐμορφοτάτη, ξανθή τε τὴν χροιὰν ὑπάρξασα, ἣ καὶ λέγεται τὴν τρίτην πυραμίδα ᾠκοδομηκέναι.

---

[1] The remarkable descriptions of social disorganization and anarchy, addressed to an aged king in the Leiden Papyrus of Ipuwer and known as *The Admonitions of an Egyptian Sage*, are, according to Erman, to be associated with the end of this reign : see A. Erman, " Die Mahnworte eines ägyptischen Propheten " in *Sitz. der preuss. Akad. der Wissenschaften*, xlii., 1919, p. 813.

[2] Nitôcris is doubtless the Neit-oḳre(t) of the Turin Papyrus: the name means "Neith is Excellent" (*cf.* App. II. Eratosthenes, No. 22, Ἀθηνᾶ νικηφόρος), and was a favourite name under the Saïte Dynasty (Dyn. XXVI.), which was devoted to the worship of Neith. See Herodotus, ii. 100, 134, Diod. Sic. I. 64. 14 (if Rhodôpis is to be identified with Nitôcris), Strabo 17, 1. 33 (a Cinderella-like story), Pliny, *N.H.* 36. 12. 78, and G. A. Wainwright, *Sky-Religion*, pp. 41 ff.

A queen's reign ending the Dynasty is followed by a period of confusion, just as after Dyn. XII. when Queen

4. Phiôps, who began to reign at the age of six, and continued until his hundredth year.[1]
5. Menthesuphis, for 1 year.
6. Nitôcris,[2] the noblest and loveliest of the women of her time, of fair complexion, the builder of the third pyramid, reigned for 12 years.

Total, 203 years.[3] Along with the aforementioned 1294 years of the first five dynasties, this amounts to 1497 years.

Fr. 21 (a) (*from Syncellus*). ACCORDING TO EUSEBIUS.

The Sixth Dynasty.

There was a queen Nitôcris, the noblest and loveliest of the women of her time; she had a fair complexion, and is said to have built the third pyramid.

Scemiophris (Sebeknofrurê') closes the line: *cf.* perhaps, in Dyn. IV., Thamphthis, of whom nothing is known.

In 1932 Professor Selim Hassan discovered at Giza the tomb of Queen Khentkawes, a tomb of monumental dimensions, the so-called fourth or "false" pyramid. Khentkawes was the daughter of Mycerinus; and, disregarding the chronological difficulty, H. Junker, in *Mitteilungen des Deutschen Instituts für Ägyptische Altertumskunde in Kairo*, iii. 2 (1932), pp. 144-149, put forward the theory that the name Nitôcris is derived from Khentkawes, and that Manetho refers here to the so-called fourth pyramid, which merits the description (Fr. 21(b)),— " with the aspect of a mountain ". See further B. van de Walle in *L'Antiquité Classique*, 3 (1934), pp. 303-312.

[3] The correct total is 197 years: the reign of Phiôps is reckoned at 100, instead of 94 years (the Turin Papyrus gives $90 + x$ years).

FR. 21, 23, 24   MANETHO

Οἳ καὶ ἐβασίλευσαν¹ ἔτη τρία· ἐν ἄλλῳ σγ'.

Γίνονται σὺν τοῖς προτεταγμένοις ͵ασϟε' τῶν πέντε δυναστειῶν ἔτη ͵αυϟη'.

Σημειωτέον ὁπόσον Εὐσέβιος Ἀφρικανοῦ λείπεται ἀκριβείας ἔν τε τῇ τῶν βασιλέων ποσότητι καὶ ταῖς τῶν ὀνομάτων ὑφαιρέσεσι καὶ τοῖς χρόνοις, σχεδὸν τὰ Ἀφρικανοῦ αὐταῖς λέξεσι γράφων.

(b) EUSEBIUS, *Chronica* I. (Armenian Version), p. 97.

Sexta dynastia. Femina quaedam Nitocris regnavit, omnium aetatis suae virorum fortissima et mulierum formosissima, flava rubris genis. Ab hac tertia pyramis excitata dicitur, speciem collis prae se ferens.

Ab his quoque regnatum est annis CCIII.

Fr. 23. *Syncellus*, p. 108. ΚΑΤΑ ΑΦΡΙΚΑΝΟΝ.

Ἑβδόμη δυναστεία Μεμφιτῶν βασιλέων ο', οἳ ἐβασίλευσαν ἡμέρας ο'.

Fr. 24 (a). *Syncellus*, p. 109. ΚΑΤΑ ΕΥΣΕΒΙΟΝ.

Ἑβδόμη δυναστεία Μεμφιτῶν βασιλέων πέντε, οἳ ἐβασίλευσαν ἡμέρας οε'.

¹ ἢ καὶ ἐβασίλευσεν m.

AEGYPTIACA (EPITOME) Fr. 21, 23, 24

These rulers (or this ruler) reigned for three years: in another copy, 203 years. Along with the aforementioned 1295 years of the first five dynasties, this amounts to 1498 years.

(Syncellus adds): It must be noted how much less accurate Eusebius is than Africanus in the number of kings he gives, in the omission of names, and in dates, although he practically repeats the account of Africanus in the same words.

(b) Armenian Version of Eusebius.

The Sixth Dynasty. There was a queen Nitôcris, braver than all the men of her time, the most beautiful of all the women, fair-skinned with red cheeks. By her, it is said, the third pyramid was reared, with the aspect of a mountain.

The united reigns of all the kings amount to 203 years.

Dynasty VII.

Fr. 23 (*from Syncellus*). According to Africanus.

The Seventh Dynasty [1] consisted of seventy kings of Memphis, who reigned for 70 days.

Fr. 24 (a) (*from Syncellus*). According to Eusebius.

The Seventh Dynasty consisted of five kings of Memphis, who reigned for 75 days.

---

[1] Dynasty VII.—a mere interregnum, or period of confusion until one king gained supreme power.

Fr. 24, 25, 26   MANETHO

(b) Eusebius, *Chronica* I. (Armenian Version),
p. 97.

Septima dynastia Memphitarum regum V, qui annis LXXV dominati sunt.

Fr. 25.   *Syncellus*, p. 108.   ΚΑΤΑ ΑΦΡΙΚΑΝΟΝ.

Ὀγδόη δυναστεία Μεμφιτῶν βασιλέων κζ΄, οἳ ἐβασίλευσαν ἔτη ρμς΄. γίνονται σὺν τοῖς προτεταγμένοις ἔτη ͵αχλθ΄ τῶν ὀκτὼ δυναστειῶν.

Fr. 26 (a).   *Syncellus*, p. 110.   ΚΑΤΑ ΕΥΣΕΒΙΟΝ.

Ὀγδόη δυναστεία Μεμφιτῶν βασιλέων πέντε, οἳ ἐβασίλευσαν ἔτη ἑκατόν. γίνονται σὺν τοῖς προτεταγμένοις ἔτη ͵αφϟη΄ τῶν ὀκτὼ δυναστειῶν.

(b) Eusebius, *Chronica* I. (Armenian Version),
p. 97.

Octava dynastia Memphitarum regum V,[1] quorum dominatio annos centum occupavit.

[1] V Aucher: aliter Mai.

---

[1] Dynasty VIII., according to Barbarus (Fr. 4) fourteen kings for 140 years: according to Meyer, probably eighteen kings who reigned for 146 years.

[*Footnote continued on opposite page.*

AEGYPTIACA (EPITOME) Fr. 24, 25, 26

(b) Armenian Version of Eusebius.

The Seventh Dynasty consisted of five kings of Memphis, who held sway for 75 years.

Dynasty VIII.

Fr. 25 (*from Syncellus*). According to Africanus.

The Eighth Dynasty [1] consisted of twenty-seven kings of Memphis, who reigned for 146 years. Along with the aforementioned reigns, this amounts to 1639 years for the first eight dynasties.

Fr. 26 (a) (*from Syncellus*). According to Eusebius.

The Eighth Dynasty consisted of five kings of Memphis, who reigned for 100 years. Along with the aforementioned reigns, this amounts to 1598 years for the first eight dynasties.

(b) Armenian Version of Eusebius.

The Eighth Dynasty consisted of five [2] kings of Memphis, whose rule lasted for 100 years.

[1] "The Turin Papyrus closes the first great period of Egyptian history at the end of what appears to be Manetho's VIIIth Dynasty (the last Memphites)": it reckons 955 years from Dynasty I. to Dynasties VII. and VIII. (H. R. Hall in *C.A.H.* i. pp. 298, 170). See A. Scharff in *J. Eg. Arch.* xiv., 1928, p. 275.

[2] So Aucher, Petermann, and Karst.

Fr. 27, 28   MANETHO

Fr. 27. *Syncellus*, p. 110. ΚΑΤΑ ΑΦΡΙΚΑΝΟΝ.

Ἐνάτη δυναστεία Ἡρακλεοπολιτῶν βασιλέων ιθ΄, οἳ ἐβασίλευσαν ἔτη νθ΄· ὧν ὁ πρῶτος Ἀχθόης, δεινότατος τῶν πρὸ αὐτοῦ γενόμενος, τοῖς ἐν πάσῃ Αἰγύπτῳ κακὰ εἰργάσατο, ὕστερον δὲ μανίᾳ περιέπεσε καὶ ὑπὸ κροκοδείλου διεφθάρη.

Fr. 28 (a). *Syncellus*, p. 111. ΚΑΤΑ ΕΥΣΕΒΙΟΝ.

Ἐνάτη δυναστεία Ἡρακλεοπολιτῶν βασιλέων τεσσάρων, οἳ ἐβασίλευσαν ἔτη ἑκατόν· ὧν πρῶτος Ἀχθώης,[1] δεινότατος τῶν πρὸ αὐτοῦ γενόμενος, τοῖς ἐν πάσῃ Αἰγύπτῳ κακὰ εἰργάσατο, ὕστερον δὲ μανίᾳ περιέπεσε καὶ ὑπὸ κροκοδείλου διεφθάρη.

(b) EUSEBIUS, *Chronica* I. (Armenian Version), p. 97.

Nona dynastia Heracleopolitarum regum IV, annis C. Horum primus Ochthôis saevissimus regum fuit

[1] Ἄχθος A vulgo.

---

[1] Dynasties IX. and X. c. 2240–c. 2100 B.C.—two series of nineteen kings, both from Hêracleopolis (Baedeker [8], p. 218), near the modern village of Ahnâsia (Ancient Egyptian *Hat-nen-nesut*), 77 miles S. of Cairo, c. 9 miles S. of the entrance to the Fayûm.

The Turin Papyrus gives eighteen kings for Dynasties IX. and X. as opposed to Manetho's thirty-eight.

[*Footnote continued on opposite page.*]

AEGYPTIACA (EPITOME) Fr. 27, 28

Dynasty IX.

Fr. 27 (*from Syncellus*). According to Africanus.

The Ninth Dynasty [1] consisted of nineteen kings of Hêracleopolis, who reigned for 409 years. The first of these, King Achthoês,[2] behaving more cruelly than his predecessors, wrought woes for the people of all Egypt, but afterwards he was smitten with madness, and was killed by a crocodile.[3]

Fr. 28 (a) (*from Syncellus*). According to Eusebius.

The Ninth Dynasty consisted of four kings of Hêracleopolis, who reigned for 100 years. The first of these, King Achthôês, behaving more cruelly than his predecessors, wrought woes for the people of all Egypt, but afterwards he was smitten with madness, and was killed by a crocodile.

(b) Armenian Version of Eusebius.

The Ninth Dynasty consisted of four kings of Heracleopolis, reigning for 100 years. The first of these, King Ochthôis,[4] was more cruel than all his

---

[1] Manetho's account of Dynasty IX. is best preserved by Africanus. Barbarus has almost the same figures—twenty kings for 409 years.

[2] Achthoês: in the Turin Papyrus Akhtôi (Meyer, *Geschichte* [5], I. ii. p. 247—three kings of this name). Meyer conjectures that the "cruelty" of Achthoês may be violent or forcible oppression of the feudal nobility.

[3] *Cf.* p. 28 n. 3.

[4] Okhthovis (Petermann's translation), -ov- representing the long o.

FR. 28, 29, 30, 31   MANETHO

qui sibi praecesserant, universamque Aegyptum diris calamitatibus affecit. Idem denique vesania correptus est et a crocodilo peremptus.

Fr. 29.   Syncellus, p. 110.   ΚΑΤΑ ΑΦΡΙΚΑΝΟΝ.

Δεκάτη δυναστεία Ἡρακλεοπολιτῶν βασιλέων ιθ', οἳ ἐβασίλευσαν ἔτη ρπε'.

Fr. 30 (a).   Syncellus, p. 112.   ΚΑΤΑ ΕΥΣΕΒΙΟΝ.

Δεκάτη δυναστεία Ἡρακλεοπολιτῶν βασιλέων ιθ', οἳ ἐβασίλευσαν ἔτη ρπε'.

(b) EUSEBIUS, *Chronica* I. (Armenian Version), p. 97.

Decima dynastia Heracleopolitarum regum XIX, annis CLXXXV.

Fr. 31.   Syncellus, p. 110.   ΚΑΤΑ ΑΦΡΙΚΑΝΟΝ.

Ἑνδεκάτη δυναστεία Διοσπολιτῶν βασιλέων ιϛ', οἳ ἐβασίλευσαν ἔτη μγ'. μεθ' οὓς Ἀμμενέμης, ἔτη ιϛ'.

Μέχρι τοῦδε τὸν πρῶτον τόμον καταγήοχε Μανεθῶ.

Ὁμοῦ βασιλεῖς ρϟβ', ἔτη ͵βτ', ἡμέραι ο'.

---

[1] The Middle Kingdom, Dynasties XI.-XIII.: c. 2100–c. 1700 B.C.

[*Footnote continued on opposite page.*

predecessors, and visited the whole of Egypt with dire disasters. Finally, he was seized with madness, and devoured by a crocodile.

Dynasty X.

Fr. 29 (*from Syncellus*). According to Africanus.

The Tenth Dynasty consisted of nineteen kings of Hêracleopolis, who reigned for 185 years.

Fr. 30 (a) (*from Syncellus*). According to Eusebius.

The Tenth Dynasty consisted of nineteen kings of Hêracleopolis, who reigned for 185 years.

(b) Armenian Version of Eusebius.

The Tenth Dynasty consisted of nineteen kings of Heracleopolis, who reigned for 185 years.

Dynasty XI.

Fr. 31 (*from Syncellus*). According to Africanus.

The Eleventh Dynasty [1] consisted of sixteen kings of Diospolis [or Thebes], who reigned for 43 years. In succession to these, Ammenemês [2] ruled for 16 years.
Here ends the First Book of Manetho.
Total for the reigns of 192 kings, 2300 years 70 days.

Dynasty XI. (c. 2100–c. 2000 B.C.) with its seat at Thebes: sixteen kings of Thebes ruling for only 43 years (Manetho): Turin Papyrus gives six kings with more than 160 years.
[2] Ammenemês is Amenemhêt I.: see pp. 66 f., nn. 1, 2.

Fr. 32 (a). *Syncellus*, p. 112. ΚΑΤΑ ΕΥΣΕΒΙΟΝ.

Ἑνδεκάτη δυναστεία Διοσπολιτῶν βασιλέων ιϛ', οἳ ἐβασίλευσαν ἔτη μγ'. μεθ' οὓς Ἀμμενέμης, ἔτη ιϛ'.

Μέχρι τοῦδε τὸν πρῶτον τόμον καταγήοχεν ὁ Μανεθῶ. Ὁμοῦ βασιλεῖς ρϟβ', ἔτη ͵βτ', ἡμέραι οθ'.

(b) Eusebius, *Chronica* I. (Armenian Version), p. 97.

Undecima dynastia Diospolitarum regum XVI, annis XLIII. Post hos Ammenemes annis XVI.

Hactenus primum librum Manetho produxit. Sunt autem reges CXCII, anni MMCCC.

AEGYPTIACA (EPITOME)   FR. 32

Fr. 32 (a) (*from Syncellus*). ACCORDING TO
EUSEBIUS.

The Eleventh Dynasty consisted of sixteen kings of Diospolis [or Thebes], who reigned for 43 years. In succession to these, Ammenemês ruled for 16 years.
Here ends the First Book of Manetho.
Total for the reigns of 192 kings, 2300 years 79 days.

(b) ARMENIAN VERSION OF EUSEBIUS.

The Eleventh Dynasty consisted of sixteen kings of Diospolis [or Thebes], who reigned for 43 years. In succession to these, Ammenemes ruled for 16 years.
Here ends the First Book of Manetho.
Total for the reigns of 192 kings, 2300 years.

MANETHO

ΤΟΜΟΣ ΔΕΥΤΕΡΟΣ.

Fr. 34. *Syncellus*, p. 110. ΚΑΤΑ ΑΦΡΙΚΑΝΟΝ.

Δευτέρου τόμου Μανεθῶ.
Δωδεκάτη δυναστεία Διοσπολιτῶν βασιλέων ἑπτά.

α΄ Σεσόγχοσις,[1] Ἀμμανέμου υἱός, ἔτη μϛ΄.
β΄ Ἀμμανέμης, ἔτη λη΄, ὃς ὑπὸ τῶν ἰδίων εὐνούχων ἀνῃρέθη.
γ΄ Σέσωστρις,[2] ἔτη μη΄, ὃς ἅπασαν ἐχειρώσατο τὴν Ἀσίαν ἐν ἐνιαυτοῖς ἐννέα, καὶ τῆς Εὐρώπης τὰ μέχρι Θρᾴκης, πανταχόσε

[1] γεσονγόσις (for Σεσόγχοσις) B : Σεσόγχωρις m.
[2] A : Σέσοστρις B.

---

[1] Dynasty XII. c. 2000-1790 B.C. (Meyer, *Geschichte* [5], I. ii. p. 270). Including Ammenemês whom Manetho places between Dynasty XI. and Dynasty XII., there are eight rulers in Dynasty XII.—(1) Ammenemês (Amenemhêt I.), (2) Sesonchôsis (Senwosret or Sesôstris I.), (3) Ammanemês (Amenemhêt II.), (4) Sesôstris II. (omitted by Manetho), (5) Sesôstris (Senwosret III.), (6) Manetho's Lamarês and Amerês (Amenemhêt III., Nema'trê'), (7) Ammenemês (Amenemhêt IV.), (8) Scemiophris (Queen Sebeknofrurê'). For (5), the great Sesôstris (1887-1850 B.C.) of Herodotus, ii. 102, Diod. Sic. I. 53 ff., see Sethe, *Unters. zur Gesch.* . . . *Aeg.* ii. 1, and Meyer, *Geschichte* [5], I. ii. p. 268. The name of Amenemhêt bespeaks his Theban origin : he removed the capital further north to Dahshûr, a more central position—" Controller of the Two Lands," as its Egyptian name means. Thus the kings of Dynasty XII. are kings who came from Thebes, but ruled at Dahshûr.

[*Footnote continued on opposite page.*]

AEGYPTIACA (EPITOME)

BOOK II.

Dynasty XII.

Fr. 34 (*from Syncellus*). According to Africanus.

From the Second Book of Manetho.
The Twelfth Dynasty [1] consisted of seven kings of Diospolis.

1. Sesonchosis, son of Ammanemês, for 46 years.
2. Ammanemês, for 38 years: he was murdered by his own eunuchs.[2]
3. Sesôstris, for 48 years: in nine years he subdued the whole of Asia, and Europe as far as Thrace, everywhere erecting memorials of

---

[1] In Dynasty XII. the conquests of Dynasty VI. in the south were extended; and Sesôstris III. was the first Egyptian king to conquer Syria. Among works of peace the great irrigation schemes in the Fayûm perpetuated the name of Amenemhêt III. in " Lake Moeris ". (See G. Caton-Thompson and E. W. Gardner, *The Desert Fayûm*, 1934.) Manetho mentions his building of the Labyrinth: it is significant that after the reign of Sesôstris III. and his wide foreign conquests, his son should have built the Labyrinth. Vases of the Kamares type from Crete have been found at Kahûn, not far from the Labyrinth.

[2] See A. de Buck (*Mélanges Maspero*, vol. i., 1935, pp. 847-52) for a new interpretation of the purpose of *The Instruction of Amenemmes*: in this political pamphlet the dead king speaks from the tomb in support of his son Sesostris, now holding the throne in spite of strong opposition, and violently denounces the ungrateful ruffians who murdered him. It seems probable that Manetho's note here refers to the death of Ammenemês I. (Battiscombe Gunn).

μνημόσυνα ἐγείρας τῆς τῶν ἐθνῶν σχέσεως,¹ ἐπὶ μὲν τοῖς γενναίοις ἀνδρῶν, ἐπὶ δὲ τοῖς ἀγεννέσι γυναικῶν μόρια ταῖς στήλαις ἐγχαράσσων, ὡς ² ὑπὸ Αἰγυπτίων μετὰ Ὄσιριν πρῶτον νομισθῆναι.

δ' Λαχάρης,³ ἔτη η', ὃς τὸν ἐν Ἀρσινοΐτῃ λαβύρινθον ἑαυτῷ τάφον κατεσκεύασε.
ε' Ἀμερής,⁴ ἔτη η'.
ϛ' Ἀμμενέμης,⁵ ἔτη η'.
ζ' Σκεμίοφρις, ἀδελφή, ἔτη δ'.

Ὁμοῦ, ἔτη ρξ'.

Fr. 35. Syncellus, p. 112. ΚΑΤΑ ΕΥΣΕΒΙΟΝ.

Δευτέρου τόμου Μανεθῶ.
Δωδεκάτη δυναστεία Διοσπολιτῶν βασιλέων ἑπτά. ὧν ὁ πρῶτος Σεσόγχοσις,⁶ Ἀμμενέμου υἱός, ἔτη μϛ'.

¹ κατασχέσεως m. ² m.: ὃς MSS.
³ Λαμάρης Meyer. ⁴ Ἀμμερής A.
⁵ Ἀμενέμης B. ⁶ B: Σεσόγχωρις A.

---

¹ See *Agyptische Inschriften aus den Museen zu Berlin*, i. p. 257, for a *stele* at Semneh with an inscription in which the great Sesôstris pours contempt upon his enemies, the Nubians.

² For the sexual symbols represented upon pillars, see Hdt. ii. 102, 106, Diod. Sic. I. 55. 8: *cf.* the representation of mutilated captives on one of the walls of the Ramesseum, Diod. Sic. I. 48. 2. It has been suggested that Herodotus, who saw the pillars of Sesostris in Palestine, may possibly have mistaken an Assyrian for an Egyptian relief.

AEGYPTIACA (EPITOME) Fr. 34, 35

his conquest of the tribes.[1] Upon *stelae* [pillars] he engraved for a valiant race the secret parts of a man, for an ignoble race those of a woman.[2] Accordingly he was esteemed by the Egyptians as the next in rank to Osiris.

4. Lacharês (Lamarês),[3] for 8 years: he built the Labyrinth [4] in the Arsinoïte nome as his own tomb.
5. Amerês, for 8 years.
6. Ammenemês, for 8 years.
7. Scemiophris, his sister, for 4 years.

Total, 160 years.

Fr. 35 (*from* Syncellus).   According to Eusebius.

From the Second Book of Manetho.

The Twelfth Dynasty consisted of seven kings of Diospolis. The first of these, Sesonchosis, son of Ammenemês, reigned for 46 years.

---

[3] For other names of Amenemhêt III., see note on Marês, App. II., No. 35, p. 224.

[4] The Labyrinth is correctly attributed by Manetho to Amenemhêt III., who built it as his mortuary temple (contrast Herodotus, ii. 148, who assigns this monument to the Dodecarchy). The Fayûm was a place of great importance during this dynasty, from Amenemhêt I. onwards.

The description of the nome as "Arsinoïte" has often been suspected as a later interpolation; but if "Arsinoïte" was used by Manetho himself, it gives as a date in his life the year 256 B.C. when Ptolemy Philadelphus commemorated Queen Arsinoe (d. 270 B.C.) in the new name of the nome. (*Cf.* Intro. p. xvi for a possible reference to Manetho, the historian of Egypt, in 241 B.C.)

Fr. 35, 36 MANETHO

β' Ἀμμανέμης, ἔτη λη', ὃς ὑπὸ τῶν ἰδίων εὐνούχων ἀνῃρέθη.

γ' Σέσωστρις,[1] ἔτη μη', ὃς λέγεται γεγονέναι πηχῶν δ', παλαιστῶν γ', δακτύλων β'. ὃς πᾶσαν ἐχειρώσατο τὴν Ἀσίαν ἐν ἐνιαυτοῖς ἐννέα, καὶ τῆς Εὐρώπης τὰ μέχρι Θρᾴκης, πανταχόσε μνημόσυνα ἐγείρας τῆς τῶν ἐθνῶν κατασχέσεως, ἐπὶ μὲν τοῖς γενναίοις ἀνδρῶν, ἐπὶ δὲ τοῖς ἀγεννέσι γυναικῶν μόρια ταῖς στήλαις ἐγχαράσσων, ὡς[2] καὶ ὑπὸ τῶν Αἰγυπτίων ⟨πρῶτον⟩[3] μετὰ Ὄσιριν νομισθῆναι.

Μεθ' ὃν Λάμαρις, ἔτη η', ὃς τὸν ἐν Ἀρσενοΐτῃ[4] λαβύρινθον ἑαυτῷ τάφον κατεσκεύασεν.

Οἱ δὲ τούτου διάδοχοι ἐπὶ ἔτη μβ', οἳ πάντες ἐβασίλευσαν ἔτεσι σμέ.

Fr. 36. EUSEBIUS, *Chronica* I. (Armenian Version), p. 98.

E Manethonis secundo libro.
Duodecima dynastia Diospolitarum regum VII, quorum primus Sesonchosis Ammenemis filius annis XLVI.

Ammenemes annis XXXVIII, qui a suis eunuchis interemptus est.

Sesostris annis XLVIII, cuius mensura fertur cubitorum quattuor, palmarumque trium cum digitis

[1] A: Σέσοστρις B.   [2] m: ὃς MSS.   [3] m.

AEGYPTIACA (EPITOME) Fr. 35, 36

2. Ammanemês, for 38 years: he was murdered by his own eunuchs.
3. Sesôstris, for 48 years: he is said to have been 4 cubits 3 palms 2 fingers' breadths in stature. In nine years he subdued the whole of Asia, and Europe as far as Thrace, everywhere erecting memorials of his conquest of the tribes. Upon *stelae* [pillars] he engraved for a valiant race the secret parts of a man, for an ignoble race those of a woman. Accordingly he was esteemed by the Egyptians as the next in rank to Osiris.

Next to him Lamaris reigned for 8 years: he built the Labyrinth in the Arsinoïte nome as his own tomb.

His successors ruled for 42 years, and the reigns of the whole dynasty amounted to 245 years.[1]

Fr. 36. ARMENIAN VERSION OF EUSEBIUS.

From the Second Book of Manetho.

The Twelfth Dynasty consisted of seven kings of Diospolis. The first of these, Sesonchosis, son of Ammenemês, reigned for 46 years.

2. Ammenemês, for 38 years: he was murdered by his own eunuchs.
3. Sesôstris, for 48 years: he is said to have been 4 cubits 3 palms 2 fingers' breadth in

---

[1] The items given add to 182 years.

[4] This variant spelling with -ε- for -ι- appears to be a mere scribal error due to confusion with words beginning ἀρσεν-.

Fr. 37, 38, 39   MANETHO

duobus. Is universam Asiam annorum novem spatio sibi subdidit, itemque Europae partem usque ad Thraciam. Idem et suae in singulas gentes dominationis monumenta ubique constituit; apud gentes quidem strenuas virilia, apud vero imbelles feminea pudenda ignominiae causa columnis insculpens. Quare is ab Aegyptiis proximos post Osirin honores tulit.

Secutus est Lampares, annis VIII. Hic in Arsinoïte labyrinthum cavernosum sibi tumulum fecit.

Regnaverunt successores eius annis XLII.

Summa universae dominationis annorum CCXLV.

Fr. 38. *Syncellus*, p. 113. ΚΑΤΑ ΑΦΡΙΚΑΝΟΝ.

Τρισκαιδεκάτη δυναστεία Διοσπολιτῶν βασιλέων ξ΄, οἳ ἐβασίλευσαν ἔτη υνγ΄.¹

Fr. 39 (a). *Syncellus*, p. 114. ΚΑΤΑ ΕΥΣΕΒΙΟΝ.

Τρισκαιδεκάτη δυναστεία Διοσπολιτῶν βασιλέων ξ΄, οἳ ἐβασίλευσαν ἔτη υνγ΄.

¹ B: ρπδ΄ A.

---

[1] The Armenian has a word here for "sufferings" or "torments" (Margoliouth): Karst expresses the general meaning as—"he engraved their oppression through (or, by means of) . . ."

[2] Karst translates this word by "das höhlenwendelgangförmige".

[3] Dynasty XIII., 1790–c. 1700 B.C. In the Turin Papyrus there is a corresponding group of sixty kings: see the list in Meyer, *Geschichte* ⁵, I. ii. pp. 308 f., one of them

stature. In nine years he subdued the whole of Asia, and Europe as far as Thrace. Everywhere he set up memorials of his subjugation of each tribe: among valiant races he engraved upon pillars a man's secret parts, among unwarlike races a woman's, as a sign of disgrace.[1] Wherefore he was honoured by the Egyptians next to Osiris.

His successor, Lampares, reigned for 8 years: in the Arsinoïte nome he built the many-chambered[2] Labyrinth as his tomb.

The succeeding kings ruled for 42 years.
Total for the whole dynasty, 245 years.

Dynasty XIII.

Fr. 38 (*from Syncellus*). According to Africanus.

The Thirteenth Dynasty[3] consisted of sixty kings of Diospolis, who reigned for 453 years.

Fr. 39 (a) (*from Syncellus*). According to Eusebius.

The Thirteenth Dynasty consisted of sixty kings of Diospolis, who reigned for 453 years.

being a name ending in -mes, perhaps Dedumes, the king Τουτίμαιος of Fr. 42. The twenty-fifth king in the Turin Papyrus, Col. VII., Kha'neferrê' Sebekhotp IV., is probably the King Chenephrês of whom Artapanus (i./B.C.) says that he was " king of the regions above Memphis (for there were at that time many kings in Egypt) " in the lifetime of Moses (Artapanus, *Concerning the Jews*, quoted by Euseb., *Praepar. Evang.* ix. 27: see also Clement of Alexandria, *Strom.* i. 23, 154).

Fr. 39, 41   MANETHO

(b) Eusebius, *Chronica* I. (Armenian Version),
p. 99.

Tertia decima dynastia Diospolitarum regum LX,
qui regnarunt annis CCCCLIII.

Fr. 41 (a).   *Syncellus*, p. 113.   ΚΑΤΑ ΑΦΡΙΚΑΝΟΝ.

Τεσσαρεσκαιδεκάτη δυναστεία Ξοϊτῶν βασιλέων
ος΄, οἳ ἐβασίλευσαν ἔτη ρπδ΄.[1]

(b) *Syncellus*, p. 114.   ΚΑΤΑ ΕΥΣΕΒΙΟΝ.

Τεσσαρεσκαιδεκάτη δυναστεία Ξοϊτῶν βασιλέων
ος΄, οἳ ἐβασίλευσαν ἔτη ρπδ΄ · ἐν ἄλλῳ υπδ΄.

(c) Eusebius, *Chronica* I. (Armenian Version),
p. 99.

Quarta decima dynastia Xoïtarum [2] regum
LXXVI, qui regnarunt annis CCCCLXXXIV.

[1] B on y: a lacuna in A.
[2] Aucher: Khsojitarum (Petermann's translation).

---

[1] Dynasties XIV.-XVII., the Hyksôs Age: c. 1700-1580 B.C.

Dynasty XIV.   Nothing is known of the kings of Dynasty XIV., whose seat was at Xoïs (Sakha) in the West Delta—an island and town in the Sebennytic nome (Strabo, 17. 1. 19). They were not rulers of Upper Egypt, but probably of the West Delta only. At this period there was, it is probable, another contemporary dynasty in Upper Egypt (Dynasty XVII. of Manetho).

In the Turin Papyrus there is a long series of rulers' names corresponding to this dynasty; but the number

AEGYPTIACA (EPITOME) Fr. 39, 41

(b) ARMENIAN VERSION OF EUSEBIUS.

The Thirteenth Dynasty consisted of sixty kings of Diospolis, who reigned for 453 years.

DYNASTY XIV.

Fr. 41 (a) (*from Syncellus*). ACCORDING TO AFRICANUS.

The Fourteenth Dynasty [1] consisted of seventy-six kings of Xoïs, who reigned for 184 years.

(b) ACCORDING TO EUSEBIUS.

The Fourteenth Dynasty consisted of seventy-six kings of Xoïs, who reigned for 184 years,—in another copy, 484 years.

(c) ARMENIAN VERSION OF EUSEBIUS.

The Fourteenth Dynasty consisted of seventy-six kings of Xoïs, who reigned for 484 years.

---

given by Manetho (76) was not approximated in the Papyrus which shows between twenty and thirty names of kings. Not one of these names is preserved on the Monuments, nor on the Karnak Tablet. The kings of Dynasty XIV., and even the last kings of Dynasty XIII., reigned simultaneously with the Hyksôs kings : *cf.* the double series of kings in Dynasty XVII. In the Royal Lists of Abydos and Sakkâra the rulers of Dynasties XIII.-XVII. are altogether omitted. The Royal List of Karnak gives a selection of about thirty-five names of Dynasties XIII.-XVII., omitting Dynasty XIV. and the Hyksôs.

Fr. 42.   MANETHO

Fr. 42. Josephus, *Contra Apionem*, I. 14, §§ 73-92.[1]

73 Ἄρξομαι δὴ πρῶτον ἀπὸ τῶν παρ' Αἰγυπτίοις γραμμάτων. αὐτὰ μὲν οὖν οὐχ οἷόν τε παρατίθεσθαι τἀκείνων, Μανεθὼς[2] δ' ἦν τὸ γένος Αἰγύπτιος, ἀνὴρ τῆς Ἑλληνικῆς μετεσχηκὼς παιδείας, ὡς δῆλός ἐστιν· γέγραφεν γὰρ Ἑλλάδι φωνῇ τὴν πάτριον ἱστορίαν ἐκ δέλτων[3] ἱερῶν, ὥς φησιν

[1] For §§ 73-75, 82-90, see Eusebius, *Praepar. Evang.* x. 13: for §§ 73-105, see Eusebius, *Chron.* i. pp. 151-8, Schöne (Arm.).
[2] Eus.: Μανέθων L, Lat. (same variation elsewhere).
[3] δέλτων Gutschmid (*sacris libris* Lat.: *sacris monumentis* Eus. *Arm.*, *cf.* § 226): τε τῶν L.

---

[1] The invasion of the Hyksôs took place at some time in Dynasty XIII.: hence the succeeding anarchy in a period of foreign domination. The later Egyptians looked back upon it as the Jews did upon the Babylonian captivity, or the English upon the Danish terror. The keen desire of the Egyptians to forget about the Hyksôs usurpation accounts in part for our ignorance of what actually happened: "it is with apparent unwillingness that they chronicle any events connected with it" (Peet, *Egypt and the Old Testament*, p. 69). In Egyptian texts the "infamous" (Hyksôs) were denoted as 'Amu,—a title also given to the Hittites and their allies by Ramessês II. in the poem of the Battle of Kadesh (ed. Kuentz, § 97). Perhaps they were combined with Hittites who in 1925 B.C. brought the kingdom of Babel to an end. It is certain that with the Hyksôs numerous Semites came into Egypt: some of the Hyksôs kings have Semitic names. For the presence of an important Hurrian element among the Hyksôs, see E. A. Speiser, "Ethnic Movements," in *Ann. of Amer. Sch. of Or. Res.* xiii. (1932), p. 51. The

AEGYPTIACA FR. 42

The Hyksôs Age, c. 1700-c. 1580 b.c.[1]

Fr. 42 (*from* Josephus, *Contra Apionem*, i. 14, §§ 73-92).

[Josephus is citing the records of neighbouring nations in proof of the antiquity of the Jews.]
I will begin with Egyptian documents. These I cannot indeed set before you in their ancient form; but in Manetho we have a native Egyptian who was manifestly imbued with Greek culture. He wrote in Greek the history of his nation, translated, as he himself tells us, from sacred tablets;[2] and on many

---

Hyksôs brought with them from Asia their tribal god, which was assimilated by the Egyptians to Sêth, the god of foreign parts, of the desert, and of the enemy.
   In the first half of the second millennium b.c. the Hyksôs ruled a great kingdom in Palestine and Syria (Meyer, *Geschichte*[5], i. § 304); and when their power was broken down by the arrival of hostile tribes, King Amôsis took advantage of their plight to drive the Hyksôs out of Egypt (A. Jirku, "Aufstieg und Untergang der Hyksôs," in *Journ. of the Palestine Orient. Soc.* xii., 1932, p. 60).
   A dim tradition of Hyksôs-rule is possibly preserved in Herodotus, ii. 128. Perhaps "the shepherd Philitis" in that passage is connected with "Philistines," a tribe which may have formed part of these invaders. There is confusion between two periods of oppression of the common people,—under the pyramid-builders and under the Hyksôs. For a translation of the Egyptian records which illustrate the Hyksôs period, see Battiscombe Gunn and Alan H. Gardiner, *J. Eg. Arch.* v., 1918, pp. 36-56, "The Expulsion of the Hyksôs".
   [2] The word "tablets" is a probable emendation, since Manetho would naturally base his *History* upon temple-archives on stone as well as on papyrus: *cf.* the Palermo Stone, the Turin Papyrus, etc. (Intro. pp. xxiii ff.).

Fr. 42 MANETHO

αὐτός, μεταφράσας, ὅς[1] καὶ πολλὰ τὸν Ἡρόδοτον ἐλέγχει τῶν Αἰγυπτιακῶν ὑπ' ἀγνοίας ἐψευσμένον.
74 οὗτος δὴ τοίνυν ὁ Μανεθὼς ἐν τῇ δευτέρᾳ τῶν Αἰγυπτιακῶν ταῦτα περὶ ἡμῶν γράφει· παραθήσομαι δὲ τὴν λέξιν αὐτοῦ καθάπερ αὐτὸν ἐκεῖνον παραγαγὼν μάρτυρα·
75 "Τουτίμαιος.[2] ἐπὶ τούτου οὐκ οἶδ' ὅπως ὁ[3] θεὸς ἀντέπνευσεν, καὶ παραδόξως ἐκ τῶν πρὸς ἀνατολὴν μερῶν ἄνθρωποι τὸ γένος ἄσημοι καταθαρρήσαντες ἐπὶ τὴν χώραν ἐστράτευσαν καὶ ῥᾳδίως ἀμαχητὶ
76 ταύτην κατὰ κράτος εἷλον, καὶ τοὺς ἡγεμονεύσαντας ἐν αὐτῇ χειρωσάμενοι τὸ λοιπὸν τάς τε πόλεις ὠμῶς ἐνέπρησαν καὶ τὰ τῶν θεῶν ἱερὰ κατέσκαψαν, πᾶσι δὲ τοῖς ἐπιχωρίοις ἐχθρότατά πως ἐχρήσαντο, τοὺς μὲν σφάζοντες, τῶν δὲ καὶ τὰ
77 τέκνα καὶ γυναῖκας εἰς δουλείαν ἄγοντες. πέρας δὲ καὶ βασιλέα ἕνα ἐξ αὐτῶν ἐποίησαν, ᾧ ὄνομα

---

[1] ὅς Eus.: om. L.
[2] Gutschmid: τοῦ Τίμαιος ὄνομα L, Eus. (ὄνομα probably a gloss: ἄνεμος Gutschmid).
[3] ὁ Eus. (perhaps a survival of Ancient Egyptian usage): om. L: Meyer conj. θεός τις.

---

[1] Cf. Manetho, Fr. 88.
[2] This account of the Hyksôs invasion is obviously derived from popular Egyptian tales, the characteristics of which are deeply imprinted upon it. Meyer (Geschichte[5], I. ii. p. 313) quotes from papyri and inscriptions passages of similar style and content, e.g. Pap. Sallier I. describing the war with the Hyksôs, and mentioning "Lord Apôpi in Auaris," and an inscription of Queen Hatshepsut from the Speos Artemidos, referring to the occupation of

points of Egyptian history he convicts Herodotus [1] of having erred through ignorance. In the second book of his *History of Egypt*, this writer Manetho speaks of us as follows. I shall quote his own words, just as if I had brought forward the man himself as a witness : [2]

" Tutimaeus.[3] In his reign, for what cause I know not, a blast of God smote us ; and unexpectedly, from the regions of the East, invaders of obscure race marched in confidence of victory against our land. By main force they easily seized it without striking a blow ; [4] and having overpowered the rulers of the land, they then burned our cities ruthlessly, razed to the ground the temples of the gods, and treated all the natives with a cruel hostility, massacring some and leading into slavery the wives and children of others. Finally, they appointed as king one of their number whose name was

---

Auaris. See Breasted, *Ancient Records*, i. § 24, ii. §§ 296 ff. Meyer adds that he would not be surprised if Manetho's description reappeared word for word one day in a hieratic papyrus. *Cf.* § 75 ὁ θεός : § 76 the crimes of the Hyksôs (Fr. 54, § 249, those of the Solymites and their polluted allies) : § 77 the upper and lower lands : §§ 78, 237 religious tradition to explain the name of Auaris and its dedication to Typhôn : § 99 hollow phrases about military expeditions of Sethôs : § 237 the form of the phrase ὡς χρόνος ἱκανὸς διῆλθεν, and many other passages. See also Weill, *La fin du moyen empire égyptien*, pp. 76 ff.

[3] See Fr. 38, n. 3.

[4] The success of the Hyksôs may have been due to superior archery and to the use of horse-drawn chariots, previously unknown in Egypt (Maspero, *Hist. Anc.* ii. p. 51 ; Petrie, *Hyksos and Israelite Cities*, p. 70 ; H. R. Hall, *Anc. Hist. of Near East*[8], p. 213), as well as to superior weapons of bronze (H. R. Hall, *C.A.H.* i. p. 291 n., 312 f.).

FR. 42 MANETHO

ἦν Σάλιτις.¹ καὶ οὗτος ἐν τῇ Μέμφιδι κατεγίνετο, τήν τε ἄνω καὶ κάτω χώραν δασμολογῶν καὶ φρουρὰν ἐν τοῖς ἐπιτηδειοτάτοις καταλείπων² τόποις. μάλιστα δὲ καὶ τὰ πρὸς ἀνατολὴν ἠσφαλίσατο μέρη, προορώμενος, Ἀσσυρίων ποτὲ μεῖζον 78 ἰσχυόντων, ἐσομένην ἐπιθυμίᾳ³ τῆς αὐτοῦ βασιλείας ἔφοδον. εὑρὼν δὲ ἐν νομῷ τῷ Σαΐτῃ⁴ πόλιν ἐπικαιροτάτην, κειμένην μὲν πρὸς ἀνατολὴν τοῦ Βουβαστίτου ποταμοῦ, καλουμένην δ' ἀπό τινος ἀρχαίας θεολογίας Αὔαριν, ταύτην ἔκτισέν

---

¹ *Silitis* Eus. *Arm.*: Σαΐτης Fr. 43, 48, 49.
² *Ed. pr.*: καταλιπὼν L.   ³ Bekker: ἐπιθυμίαν L.
⁴ Conj. Σεθροΐτῃ Manetho, Fr. 43, 48, 49.

---

[1] The name may be Semitic (*cf.* Hebr. *shallīṭ*), but it has not been found on the monuments. Possibly it is not strictly a proper name, but rather a title like "prince," "general": "sultan" comes from the same root.

[2] *Cf.* § 90. Manetho regards as historically true the Greek tales of the great Assyrian Empire of Ninus and Semiramis. The period referred to here is much earlier than the time when Assyria began to harass the Mediterranean regions.

[3] If "Saïte" is correct here, it has nothing to do with the famous Saïs, but is probably used for :" Tanite ": *cf.* Herodotus, ii. 17, Strabo, 17, 1, 20 (P. Montet in *Revue Biblique*, xxxix. 1930). The Sethroïte nome (Fr. 43, 45, 49) is in the extreme E. of the Delta, adjoining the Tanite nome. For Sethroê see H. Junker, *Zeit. f. äg. Sprache* 75. 1939, p. 78.

[4] For Bubastis see Fr. 8 n. 2. The Bubastite branch is the farthest E., the next being the Tanitic.

[5] Auaris, in Ancient Egyptian *Hetwaʻret*, "town of the desert strip," but this meaning does not explain the "religious tradition". (The older interpretations, "house of the flight," "house of the leg," were attached to the Seth-Typhôn legend: *cf.* n. 3 *infra*.) Tanis was a strong-

AEGYPTIACA   Fr. 42

Salitis.[1] He had his seat at Memphis, levying tribute from Upper and Lower Egypt, and always leaving garrisons behind in the most advantageous positions. Above all, he fortified the district to the east, foreseeing that the Assyrians,[2] as they grew stronger, would one day covet and attack his kingdom. " In the Saïte [Sethroïte] nome [3] he found a city very favourably situated on the east of the Bubastite branch [4] of the Nile, and called Auaris [5] after an

hold of the Hyksôs : in *O.T. Numbers* xiii. 22, " Now Hebron (in S. Palestine) was built seven years before Zoan in Egypt," Zoan is Tanis (Dja'net), and the statement probably refers to the Hyksôs age. Sethe cautiously said, " Seth is the god of the Hyksôs cities, Tanis and Auaris ". But in *Revue Biblique*, xxxix., 1930, pp. 5-28, Pierre Montet, the excavator of Tanis, brought forward reasons to identify Auaris and Pi-Ra'messes with Tanis ; and Alan H. Gardiner (*J. Eg. Arch.* xix., 1933, pp. 122-128) gave further evidence for this view (p. 126) : " San el-Hagar marks the site of the city successively called Auaris, Pi-Ra'messe, and Tanis ". In spite of the criticism of Raymond Weill (*J. Eg. Arch.* xxi., 1935, pp. 10-25), who cited a hieroglyphic document (found in the temple of Ptah in Memphis) in which Auaris and " the field (or land) of Tanis " are separate, Pierre Montet (*Syria*, xvii., 1936, pp. 200-202) maintains the identity of Auaris, Pi-Ra'messes, and Tanis. [So does H. Junker, *Zeit. f. äg. Sprache* 75. 1939, pp. 63-84.]

Meanwhile, a new identification of Pi-Ra'messês had been suggested: by excavation M. Hamza (*Annales du Service des Antiquités de l'Égypte*, xxx. 1930, p. 65) found evidence tending to identify Pi-Ra'messês with the palace of Ramessês II. at Tell el-Yahudiya, near Kantîr, c. 25 kilometres south of Tanis; and William C. Hayes (*Glazed Tiles from a Palace of Ramessês II. at Kantîr : The Metropolitan Museum of Art Papers*, No. 3, 1937) supports this theory that Kantîr was the Delta residence of the Ramesside kings of Egypt, pointing out that there is a practically

[*Footnote continued on page* 83.

FR. 42 MANETHO

τε καὶ τοῖς τείχεσιν ὀχυρωτάτην ἐποίησεν, ἐν-
οικίσας αὐτῇ καὶ πλῆθος ὁπλιτῶν εἰς εἴκοσι καὶ
79 τέσσαρας μυριάδας ἀνδρῶν προφυλακήν. ἔνθα δὲ[1]
κατὰ θέρειαν ἤρχετο, τὰ μὲν σιτομετρῶν καὶ
μισθοφορίαν παρεχόμενος, τὰ δὲ καὶ ταῖς ἐξοπ-
λισίαις πρὸς φόβον τῶν ἔξωθεν ἐπιμελῶς γυμνάζων.
ἄρξας δ' ἐννεακαίδεκα ἔτη, τὸν βίον ἐτελεύτησε.
80 μετὰ τοῦτον δὲ ἕτερος ἐβασίλευσεν τέσσαρα καὶ
τεσσαράκοντα ἔτη καλούμενος Βνών,[2] μεθ' ὃν
ἄλλος Ἀπαχνὰν[3] ἓξ καὶ τριάκοντα ἔτη καὶ μῆνας
ἑπτά, ἔπειτα δὲ καὶ Ἄπωφις[4] ἓν καὶ ἑξήκοντα καὶ
81 Ἰαννὰς[5] πεντήκοντα καὶ μῆνα ἕνα, ἐπὶ πᾶσι δὲ
καὶ Ἄσσις[6] ἐννέα καὶ τεσσαράκοντα καὶ μῆνας δύο.
καὶ οὗτοι μὲν ἓξ ἐν αὐτοῖς ἐγενήθησαν πρῶτοι
ἄρχοντες, ποθοῦντες[7] ἀεὶ καὶ μᾶλλον[8] τῆς Αἰγύπτου
82 ἐξᾶραι τὴν ῥίζαν. ἐκαλεῖτο δὲ τὸ σύμπαν αὐτῶν[9]

[1] *Hic autem* Lat.: ἐνθάδε L.
[2] Manetho, Fr. 43, 48, 49: Βηών L.
[3] *Apakhnan* Eus.: Παχνὰν Fr. 43: *Apachnas* Lat.
[4] *Aphosis* Eus. *Arm.*: Ἄφοβις MSS., Fr. 43: Ἄφωφις Fr. 49.
[5] Ἰανίας ed. pr.: *Samnas* Lat.: *Anan* Eus. *Arm.*: Ἀννὰς or Ἀννὰν Gutschmid.
[6] *Ases* Lat.: *Aseth* Eus. (Gutschmid and Meyer hold Ἀσηθ to be the form used by Josephus).
[7] Ed. pr.: πορθοῦντες L.
[8] πολεμοῦντες ἀεὶ καὶ ποθοῦντες μᾶλλον MSS. Big. and Hafn. in Hudson.
[9] σύμπαν αὐτῶν Eus., *omne genus eorum* Lat.: om. L.

ancient religious tradition.¹ This place he rebuilt and fortified with massive walls, planting there a garrison of as many as 240,000 heavy-armed men to guard his frontier. Here he would come in summertime, partly to serve out rations and pay his troops, partly to train them carefully in manœuvres and so strike terror into foreign tribes. After reigning for 19 years, Salitis died; and a second king, named Bnôn,² succeeded and reigned for 44 years. Next to him came Apachnan, who ruled for 36 years and 7 months;³ then Apôphis for 61, and Iannas for 50 years and 1 month; then finally Assis for 49 years and 2 months. These six kings, their first rulers, were ever more and more eager to extirpate the Egyptian stock. Their race as a whole was called

unbroken series of royal Ramesside monuments which cover a period of almost 200 years.

In 1906 Petrie discovered at Kantîr a vast fortified encampment of Hyksôs date and a Hyksôs cemetery: see Petrie, *Hyksôs and Israelite Cities*, pp. 3-16 (the earthwork ramparts of the camp were intended to protect an army of chariots).

[1] See Fr. 54, § 237, for its connexion with Seth-Typhon, to whom the tribal god of the Hyksôs was assimilated.

[2] Of these Hyksôs names Bnôn and Apachnan are unexplained. Apôpi (the name of several kings—at least three), and perhaps Asêth (Assis), seem to be pure Egyptian: Iannas is presumed to be Khian, whose cartouche turned up surprisingly and significantly on the lid of an alabastron in the Palace of Minos at Knossos in Crete, as well as on a basalt lion from Baghdad. On Khian, see Griffith in *Proc. of Soc. of Bibl. Arch.* xix. (1897), pp. 294 f., 297.

[3] In his H*istory* (and for short reigns in the *Epitome*, see *e.g.* Dynasty XXVII.) Manetho reckoned by months as well as by years, like the Turin Papyrus and the Palermo Stone: see Intro. pp. xxiv f.

Fr. 42 MANETHO

ἔθνος Ὑκσώς,[1] τοῦτο δέ ἐστιν βασιλεῖς ποιμένες· τὸ γὰρ ὓκ καθ' ἱερὰν γλῶσσαν βασιλέα σημαίνει, τὸ δὲ σὼς ποιμήν ἐστι καὶ ποιμένες κατὰ τὴν κοινὴν διάλεκτον, καὶ οὕτω συντιθέμενον γίνεται Ὑκσώς. τινὲς δὲ λέγουσιν αὐτοὺς Ἄραβας εἶναι."
83 [ἐν[2] δ' ἄλλῳ ἀντιγράφῳ οὐ βασιλεῖς σημαίνεσθαι διὰ τῆς τοῦ ὓκ προσηγορίας, ἀλλὰ τοὐναντίον αἰχμαλώτους δηλοῦσθαι ποιμένας·[3] τὸ γὰρ ὓκ πάλιν Αἰγυπτιστὶ καὶ τὸ ἃκ δασυνόμενον αἰχμαλώτους ῥητῶς μηνύειν.[4]] καὶ τοῦτο μᾶλλον πιθανώτερόν μοι φαίνεται καὶ παλαιᾶς ἱστορίας ἐχόμενον.
84 Τούτους τοὺς προκατωνομασμένους βασιλέας, [καὶ][5] τοὺς τῶν Ποιμένων καλουμένων καὶ τοὺς ἐξ αὐτῶν γενομένους, κρατῆσαι τῆς Αἰγύπτου

[1] Ὑκουσσώς Eus. (*Hikkusin* Eus. *Arm.*): so also *infra*.
[2] The bracketed clause (already in Eus.) is apparently an ancient gloss, derived from § 91: *cf.* the similar marginal annotations to §§ 92, 98.
[3] ποιμένας Eus.: οὐ ποιμένας L.
[4] μηνύειν Holwerda: μηνύει L.
[5] Bracketed by Thackeray, Reinach.

---

[1] Hyksôs, "rulers of foreign lands" (Erman-Grapow, *Wörterbuch*, iii. p. 171, 29). Another form of the name, Hykussôs, is preserved by Eusebius, but it is uncertain whether the medial -u- is really authentic—the Egyptian plural (Meyer). *Hyk* = ruler of a pastoral people, a sheikh.
"The Hyksôs, like the foreign Kassite Dynasty in Babylonia, adopted the higher culture of the conquered

Hyksôs,[1] that is 'king-shepherds': for *hyk* in the sacred language means 'king,' and *sôs* in common speech is 'shepherd' or 'shepherds':[2] hence the compound word 'Hyksôs'. Some say that they were Arabs."[3] In another copy[4] the expression *hyk*, it is said, does not mean " kings ": on the contrary, the compound refers to " captive-shepherds ".[5] In Egyptian *hyk*, in fact, and *hak* when aspirated expressly denote " captives ".[6] This explanation seems to me the more convincing and more in keeping with ancient history.

These kings whom I have enumerated above, and their descendants, ruling over the so-called Shepherds, dominated Egypt, according to Manetho, for 511

country " (J. Garstang, *The Heritage of Solomon*, 1934, p. 62).

[2] This is correct: for the Egyptian word *š'sw*, " Bedouins," which in Coptic became *shôs*, " a herdsman," see Erman-Grapow, *Wörterbuch*, iv. p. 412, 10 (B.G.).

[3] In a papyrus (ii./iii. A.D.) quoted by Wilcken in *Archiv für Pap.* iii. (1906), pp. 188 ff. (*Chrestomathie*, I. ii. p. 322) ἄμμος ὑκσιωτική is mentioned—aloe [or cement (Preisigke)] from the land of the Hyksiôtae, apparently in Arabia. This gives some support to the statement in the text.

[4] Josephus, in revising this treatise just as he revised his *Antiquities*, appears to have used a second version of Manetho's *Aegyptiaca*. Did Josephus ever have before him Manetho's original work ? Laqueur thinks it more probable that Josephus consulted revisions of Manetho made from the philo- or the anti-Semitic point of view : see Intro. p. xx. Since the third century B.C. an extensive literature on the origin of the Jews had arisen.

[5] This appears to be a Jewish explanation (§ 91), to harmonize with the story of Joseph.

[6] The reference here is to the Egyptian word *h'k*, " booty," " prisoners of war " (Erman-Grapow, *Wörterbuch*, iii. p. 33) (B.G.).

FR. 42   MANETHO

85 φησὶν ἔτη πρὸς τοῖς πεντακοσίοις ἔνδεκα. μετὰ ταῦτα δὲ τῶν ἐκ τῆς Θηβαΐδος καὶ τῆς ἄλλης Αἰγύπτου βασιλέων γενέσθαι φησὶν ἐπὶ τοὺς Ποιμένας ἐπανάστασιν, καὶ πόλεμον[1] συρραγῆναι 86 μέγαν καὶ πολυχρόνιον. ἐπὶ δὲ βασιλέως, ᾧ ὄνομα εἶναι Μισφραγμούθωσις,[2] ἡττημένους[3] φησὶ τοὺς Ποιμένας[4] ἐκ μὲν τῆς ἄλλης Αἰγύπτου πάσης ἐκπεσεῖν, κατακλεισθῆναι δ' εἰς τόπον ἀρουρῶν ἔχοντα μυρίων τὴν περίμετρον· Αὔαριν[5] ὄνομα τῷ 87 τόπῳ. τοῦτόν φησιν ὁ Μανεθὼς ἅπαντα τείχει τε μεγάλῳ καὶ ἰσχυρῷ περιβαλεῖν τοὺς Ποιμένας, ὅπως τήν τε κτῆσιν ἅπασαν ἔχωσιν ἐν ὀχυρῷ 88 καὶ τὴν λείαν τὴν ἑαυτῶν. τὸν δὲ Μισφραγμουθώσεως υἱὸν Θούμμωσιν[6] ἐπιχειρῆσαι μὲν αὐτοὺς διὰ πολιορκίας ἑλεῖν κατὰ κράτος, ὀκτὼ καὶ τεσσαράκοντα μυριάσι στρατοῦ προσεδρεύσαντα τοῖς τείχεσιν· ἐπεὶ δὲ τῆς πολιορκίας[7] ἀπέγνω,

[1] + αὐτοῖς L, Lat.: om. Eus.
[2] Eus.: Ἁλισφραγμούθωσις L (Lat.): so also *infra*.
[3] Conj. Cobet: ἡττωμένους L.
[4] + ἐξ αὐτοῦ L: om. Eus.: ὑπ' αὐτοῦ *ed. pr.*
[5] Αὔαριν L (Lat.): Αὔαρις Eus.
[6] Θούμμωσιν L: Θμούθωσιν Eus.
[7] L: τὴν πολιορκίαν Eus.

---

[1] This number of years, much too high for the length of the Hyksôs sway in Egypt, may perhaps refer to the whole period of their rule in Palestine and Syria: see A. Jirku, in *Journ. of the Palestine Orient. Soc.* xii., 1932, p. 51 n. 4.

[2] Misphragmuthôsis, *i.e.* Menkheperrê' (Tuthmôsis III.) and his son Thummôsis, *i.e.* Tuthmôsis IV., are here said to have driven out the Hyksôs. In Fr. 50, § 94, Tethmôsis is named as the conqueror. In point of historical fact the

years.¹ Thereafter, he says, there came a revolt of the kings of the Thebaïd and the rest of Egypt against the Shepherds, and a fierce and prolonged war broke out between them. By a king whose name was Misphragmuthôsis,² the Shepherds, he says, were defeated, driven out of all the rest of Egypt, and confined in a region measuring within its circumference 10,000 *arûrae*,³ by name Auaris. According to Manetho, the Shepherds enclosed this whole area with a high, strong wall, in order to safeguard all their possessions and spoils. Thummôsis, the son of Misphragmuthôsis (he continues), attempted by siege to force them to surrender, blockading the fortress with an army of 480,000 men. Finally, giving up the siege in despair, he concluded

victorious king was Amôsis, and he took Auaris by main force: the genuine Manetho must surely have given this name which is preserved by Africanus and Eusebius, as also by Apiôn in Tatian, *adv. Graecos*, § 38. See p. 101 n. 2, and *cf.* Meyer, *Aeg. Chron.* pp. 73 f.

Weill, *La fin du moyen empire égyptien*, p. 95, explains the error by assuming that the exploit of the capture of Auaris was usurped by Tuthmôsis IV., as it was usurped earlier by Hatshepsut and later by Ramessês III.

Breasted (*C.A.H.* ii. p. 83) holds that, since with the catastrophic fall of Kadesh on the Orontes before the arms of Tuthmôsis III. the last vestige of the Hyksôs power disappeared, the tradition of late Greek days made Tuthmôsis III. the conqueror of the Hyksôs. He points out that the name Misphragmuthôsis is to be identified with the two cartouche-names of Tuthmôsis III.: it is a corruption of "Menkheperrê' Tuthmôsis".

³ Lit. " with a circumference of 10,000 *arûrae* ". The text (which cannot be attributed as it stands to Manetho —τὴν περίμετρον must be a later addition) implies a wrong use of *arûra* as a measure of length; it is, in reality, a measure of area, about half an acre.

Fr. 42 MANETHO

ποιήσασθαι συμβάσεις, ἵνα τὴν Αἴγυπτον ἐκλιπόντες ὅποι βούλονται πάντες ἀβλαβεῖς ἀπέλθωσι. τοὺς 89 δὲ ἐπὶ ταῖς ὁμολογίαις πανοικησίᾳ μετὰ τῶν κτήσεων οὐκ ἐλάττους μυριάδων ὄντας εἴκοσι καὶ τεσσάρων ἀπὸ τῆς Αἰγύπτου τὴν ἔρημον εἰς Συρίαν διοδοιπορῆσαι. φοβουμένους δὲ τὴν Ἀσσυρίων 90 δυναστείαν, τότε γὰρ ἐκείνους τῆς Ἀσίας κρατεῖν, ἐν τῇ νῦν Ἰουδαίᾳ καλουμένῃ πόλιν οἰκοδομησαμένους τοσαύταις μυριάσιν ἀνθρώπων ἀρκέσουσαν, Ἱεροσόλυμα ταύτην ὀνομάσαι.

91 Ἐν ἄλλῃ δέ τινι βίβλῳ τῶν Αἰγυπτιακῶν Μανεθὼς τοῦτό φησι ⟨τὸ⟩[1] ἔθνος, τοὺς καλουμένους Ποιμένας, αἰχμαλώτους ἐν ταῖς ἱεραῖς αὐτῶν βίβλοις γεγράφθαι, λέγων ὀρθῶς· καὶ γὰρ τοῖς ἀνωτάτω προγόνοις ἡμῶν τὸ ποιμαίνειν πάτριον ἦν, καὶ νομαδικὸν ἔχοντες τὸν βίον οὕτως 92 ἐκαλοῦντο Ποιμένες. αἰχμάλωτοί τε πάλιν οὐκ ἀλόγως ὑπὸ τῶν Αἰγυπτίων ἀνεγράφησαν, ἐπειδήπερ ὁ πρόγονος ἡμῶν Ἰώσηπος[2] ἑαυτὸν ἔφη πρὸς τὸν βασιλέα τῶν Αἰγυπτίων αἰχμάλωτον εἶναι,

[1] Bekker: om. L.
[2] L (in margin): ἐν ἑτέρῳ ἀντιγράφῳ εὑρέθη οὕτως· κατήχθη πραθεὶς παρὰ τῶν ἀδελφῶν εἰς Αἴγυπτον πρὸς τὸν βασιλέα τῆς Αἰγύπτου, καὶ πάλιν ὕστερον τοὺς αὐτοῦ ἀδελφοὺς μετεπέμψατο τοῦ βασιλέως ἐπιτρέψαντος.

---

[1] 240,000—the number of the garrison mentioned in § 78, where they are described as " hoplites ".

[2] On the origin of " Jeru-šalem," see A. Jirku in *Zeitschr. d. Deutsch. Morgenl. Gesellschaft*, 90 (1936), pp. * 10 * f.: the first part, Jeru-, is non-Semitic (*cf. O.T. Ezek.* xvi. 2, 45 : 2 *Sam.* xxiv. 16, and the names Jeru-baʿal, Jeru-ʾel;

a treaty by which they should all depart from Egypt and go unmolested where they pleased. On these terms the Shepherds, with their possessions and households complete, no fewer than 240,000 persons,[1] left Egypt and journeyed over the desert into Syria. There, dreading the power of the Assyrians who were at that time masters of Asia, they built in the land now called Judaea a city large enough to hold all those thousands of people, and gave it the name of Jerusalem.[2]

In another book [3] of his *History of Egypt* Manetho says that this race of so-called Shepherds is, in the sacred books of Egypt, described as " captives " ; and his statement is correct. With our remotest ancestors, indeed, it was a hereditary custom to feed sheep ; and as they lived a nomadic life, they were called Shepherds.[4] On the other hand, in the Egyptian records they were not unreasonably styled Captives, since our ancestor Joseph told the king of Egypt [5] that he was a captive, and later, with the

also, Jaru-wataš in an inscr. of Boghazköi) ; the second part, Šalem, is a Canaanitish divine name, found in the texts of Ras esh-Shamra. The name of the city occurs in the El-Amarna Letters in the form " Urusalimmu," the oldest literary mention of Jerusalem.

[3] *Cf.* § 83 for the same information, there attributed to " another copy ".

[4] *Cf. O.T. Genesis* xlvi. 32-34, xlvii. 3.

[5] In the Biblical narrative Joseph told the chief butler or cup-bearer (*Genesis* xl. 15). The margin of the Florentine MS. has a note on this passage : " In another copy (*i.e.* of the treatise *Against Apion*) the following reading was found—' he was sold by his brethren and brought down into Egypt to the king of Egypt ; and later, again, with the king's consent, summoned his brethren to Egypt '."

καὶ τοὺς ἀδελφοὺς εἰς τὴν Αἴγυπτον ὕστερον μετεπέμψατο, τοῦ βασιλέως ἐπιτρέψαντος. ἀλλὰ περὶ μὲν τούτων ἐν ἄλλοις ποιήσομαι τὴν ἐξέτασιν ἀκριβεστέραν.

Fr. 43. Syncellus, p. 113. ΚΑΤΑ ΑΦΡΙΚΑΝΟΝ.

Πεντεκαιδεκάτη δυναστεία Ποιμένων. ἦσαν δὲ Φοίνικες ξένοι βασιλεῖς ϛ′, οἳ καὶ Μέμφιν εἷλον, οἳ καὶ ἐν τῷ Σεθροΐτῃ νομῷ πόλιν ἔκτισαν, ἀφ' ἧς ὁρμώμενοι Αἰγυπτίους ἐχειρώσαντο.

Ὧν πρῶτος Σαΐτης ἐβασίλευσεν ἔτη ιθ′, ἀφ' οὗ καὶ ὁ Σαΐτης νομός.[1]

β′ Βνῶν, ἔτη μδ′.
γ′ Παχνάν, ἔτη ξα′.
δ′ Σταάν, ἔτη ν′.
ε′ Ἄρχλης, ἔτη μθ′.
ϛ′ Ἄφωφις,[2] ἔτη ξα′.
Ὁμοῦ, ἔτη σπδ′.

[1] In B the words οἳ καὶ ἐν τῷ Σεθροΐτῃ νομῷ ... ἐχειρώσαντο come after ὁ Σαΐτης νομός.
[2] m.: Ἄφοβις MSS.

---

[1] The reference seems to be to Fr. 54, § 227 ff., but ἐν ἄλλοις usually refers to a separate work.

[2] Africanus gives a less correct list than Josephus (*cf.* the transposition of Apôphis to the end): there is further corruption in Eusebius (Fr. 48) and the *Book of Sôthis* (App. IV.).

[3] This statement of the Phoenician origin of the Hyksôs kings has generally been discredited until recently: now the Ras esh-Shamra tablets, which imply a pantheon strikingly similar to that of the Hyksôs, have shown that the Hyksôs were closely related to the Phoenicians.

AEGYPTIACA (EPITOME) Fr. 42, 43

king's consent, summoned his brethren to Egypt. But I shall investigate this subject more fully in another place.[1]

Dynasty XV.

Fr. 43 (*from Syncellus*). According to Africanus.[2]

The Fifteenth Dynasty consisted of Shepherd Kings. There were six foreign kings from Phoenicia,[3] who seized Memphis: in the Sethroïte nome they founded a town, from which as a base they subdued Egypt.

The first of these kings, Saïtês, reigned for 19 years: the Saïte nome[4] is called after him.

2. Bnôn, for 44 years.
3. Pachnan [Apachnan], for 61 years.
4. Staan,[5] for 50 years.
5. Archlês,[6] for 49 years.
6. Aphôphis,[7] (Aphobis), for 61 years.

Total, 284 years.

[4] See p. 80 n. 3. The Saïte nome proper, as opposed to this "Tanite" nome, is mentioned in Egyptian texts of the Old Kingdom. For the famous Sais, the seat of Dynasty XXVI. (now Sa El-Hagar, see Baedeker,[8] p. 36 —N.W. of Tanta on the right bank of the Rosetta branch), the centre of the cult of Neith, "the metropolis of the lower country" (Strabo, 17. 1, 18), *cf.* Herodotus, ii. 62; Diod. i. 28, 4 (for its relation to Athens).

[5] For Iannas (in Josephus), the Khian of the Monuments, see p. 83 n. 2.

[6] Archlês here, and in Eusebius (Fr. 48), corresponds with Assis (or Aseth) in Josephus (Fr. 42, § 80); but the change in the form of the name is extraordinary.

[7] The length of reign (61 years, as in Josephus) leads one to believe that Africanus has transposed Apôphis from the 4th place to the 6th; but in point of fact the last Hyksôs king whom we know by name was called Apepi.

Fr. 44, 45, 46   MANETHO

Fr. 44 (a). Syncellus, p. 114. ΚΑΤΑ ΕΥΣΕΒΙΟΝ.

Πεντεκαιδεκάτη δυναστεία Διοσπολιτῶν βασιλέων, οἳ ἐβασίλευσαν ἔτη σν΄.

(b) Eusebius, Chronica I. (Armenian Version),
p. 99.

Quinta decima dynastia Diospolitarum regum, qui regnarunt annis CCL.

Fr. 45. Syncellus, p. 114. ΚΑΤΑ ΑΦΡΙΚΑΝΟΝ

Ἑκκαιδεκάτη δυναστεία Ποιμένες ἄλλοι βασιλεῖς λβ΄· ἐβασίλευσαν ἔτη φιη΄.

Fr. 46 (a). Syncellus, p. 114. ΚΑΤΑ ΕΥΣΕΒΙΟΝ.

Ἑκκαιδεκάτη δυναστεία Θηβαῖοι βασιλεῖς ε΄,[1] οἳ καὶ ἐβασίλευσαν ἔτη ρϟ΄.

(b) Eusebius, Chronica I. (Armenian Version),
p. 99.

Sexta decima dynastia Thebaeorum regum V, qui regnarunt annis CXC.

[1] η΄ Boeckh.

AEGYPTIACA (EPITOME) FR. 44, 45, 46

Fr. 44 (a) (*from Syncellus*). ACCORDING TO EUSEBIUS.

The Fifteenth Dynasty consisted of kings of Diospolis, who reigned for 250 years.

(b) ARMENIAN VERSION OF EUSEBIUS.

The Fifteenth Dynasty consisted of kings of Diospolis, who reigned for 250 years.

DYNASTY XVI.

Fr. 45 (*from Syncellus*). ACCORDING TO AFRICANUS.

The Sixteenth Dynasty were Shepherd Kings again, 32 in number: they reigned for 518 years.[1]

Fr. 46 (a) (*from Syncellus*). ACCORDING TO EUSEBIUS.

The Sixteenth Dynasty were kings of Thebes, 5 in number: they reigned for 190 years.

(b) ARMENIAN VERSION OF EUSEBIUS.

The Sixteenth Dynasty were kings of Thebes, 5 in number: they reigned for 190 years.

---

[1] Barbarus gives 318 years (p. 23, XV.); Meyer conjectures that the true number is 418 (*Aeg. Chron.* p. 99). Contrast Fr. 42, § 84 (511 years).

Fr. 47, 48   MANETHO

Fr. 47. *Syncellus*, p. 114. ΚΑΤΑ ΑΦΡΙΚΑΝΟΝ.

Ἑπτακαιδεκάτη δυναστεία Ποιμένες ἄλλοι βασιλεῖς μγ΄ καὶ Θηβαῖοι ἤ[1] Διοσπολῖται μγ΄.

Ὁμοῦ οἱ Ποιμένες καὶ οἱ Θηβαῖοι ἐβασίλευσαν ἔτη ρνα΄.

Fr. 48 (a). *Syncellus*, p. 114. ΚΑΤΑ ΕΥΣΕΒΙΟΝ.

Ἑπτακαιδεκάτη δυναστεία Ποιμένες ἦσαν ἀδελφοὶ[2] Φοίνικες ξένοι βασιλεῖς, οἳ καὶ Μέμφιν εἷλον.

Ὧν πρῶτος Σαΐτης ἐβασίλευσεν ἔτη ιθ΄, ἀφ' οὗ καὶ ὁ Σαΐτης νομὸς ἐκλήθη, οἳ καὶ ἐν τῷ Σεθροΐτῃ νομῷ πόλιν ἔκτισαν, ἀφ' ἧς ὁρμώμενοι Αἰγυπτίους ἐχειρώσαντο.

[1] Müller.
[2] A *lapsus calami* for δὲ (Meyer): Africanus (Fr. 43) preserves the true text: ἦσαν δὲ Φοίνικες . .

---

[1] See H. E. Winlock, "Tombs of the Seventeenth Dynasty at Thebes," in *J. Eg. Arch.* x. pp. 217 ff.
[2] Barbarus gives 221 years (p. 23, XVI.). According to Manetho the total length of the foreign usurpation probably was 929 years (260 in Josephus + 518 + 151). Josephus (Fr. 42, § 84) gives 511 years. These statements, even if based on actual traditions, have no weight as compared with the certain *data* of the Monuments. The almost complete lack of buildings of the Hyksôs time and the close connexion of the Thebans of Dynasty XVII.

AEGYPTIACA (EPITOME) Fr. 47, 48

Dynasty XVII

Fr. 47 (*from Syncellus*). According to Africanus.

The Seventeenth Dynasty [1] were Shepherd Kings again, 43 in number, and kings of Thebes or Diospolis, 43 in number.

Total of the reigns of the Shepherd Kings and the Theban kings, 151 years.[2]

Fr. 48 (a) (*from Syncellus*). According to Eusebius.

The Seventeenth Dynasty were Shepherds and brothers: [3] they were foreign kings from Phoenicia, who seized Memphis.

The first of these kings, Saïtês, reigned for 19 years: the Saïte nome [4] is called after him. These kings founded in the Sethroïte nome a town, from which as a base they subdued Egypt.

---

with those of Dynasty XIII. tend to show that the Hyksôs rule in the Nile Valley lasted for about a hundred and twenty years, c. 1700-1580 B.C. Under one of the Theban kings, Ta'o, who bore the epithet "The Brave," war with the Hyksôs broke out c. 1590 B.C.; Kamose, the last king of Dynasty XVII., continued the war of independence, and Amôsis (of Dynasty XVIII.) finally expelled the usurpers.

[3] This must be a mistake of transcription: see note 2 on the text.
[4] See Fr. 42, § 78, n. 3, Fr. 43, n. 4.

β' Βνῶν, ἔτη μ'.
γ'¹ Ἄφωφις, ἔτη ιδ'.
Μεθ' ὃν Ἄρχλης, ἔτη λ'.
Ὁμοῦ, ἔτη ργ'.

Κατὰ τούτους Αἰγυπτίων βασιλεὺς Ἰωσὴφ δείκνυται.

(b) Eusebius, *Chronica I.* (Armenian Version), p. 99 sq.

Septima decima dynastia Pastorum, qui fratres erant Phoenices exterique reges, et Memphin occuparunt.

Ex his primus Saïtes imperavit annis XIX, a quo Saïtarum quoque nomos nomen traxit. Eidem in Sethroïte nomo urbem condiderunt, unde incursione facta Aegyptios perdomuerunt.

Secundus Bnon, annis XL.
Deinde Archles, annis XXX.
Aphophis, annis XIV.

Summa annorum CIII.
Horum aetate regnavisse in Aegypto Josephus videtur.

¹ Om. A.

---

¹ See p. 95 n. 3.   ² See p. 80 n. 3.

AEGYPTIACA (EPITOME) FR. 48

2. Bnôn, for 40 years.
3. Aphôphis, for 14 years.
After him Archlês reigned for 30 years.
    Total, 103 years.

It was in their time that Joseph was appointed king of Egypt.

(b) ARMENIAN VERSION OF EUSEBIUS.

The Seventeenth Dynasty consisted of Shepherds, who were brothers [1] from Phoenicia and foreign kings: they seized Memphis. The first of these kings, Saïtes, reigned for 19 years: from him, too, the Saïte nome [2] derived its name. These kings founded in the Sethroïte nome a town from which they made a raid and subdued Egypt.

The second king was Bnon, for 40 years.
Next, Archles, for 30 years.
Aphophis, for 14 years.
    Total, 103 years.

It was in their time that Joseph appears to have ruled in Egypt.[3]

---

[1] The Armenian text of this sentence is rather difficult, but Professor Margoliouth, pointing out that the Armenian present infinitive is used here for the perfect, approves of this rendering. Karst translates the Armenian in the following sense: "It is under these kings that Joseph arises, to rule over Egypt".

Fr. 49. Scholia in Platonis Timaeum, 21 E (Hermann).

Σαϊτικός· ἐκ τῶν Μανεθὼ Αἰγυπτιακῶν. Ἑπτακαιδεκάτη δυναστεία Ποιμένες· ἦσαν ἀδελφοὶ[1] Φοίνικες ξένοι βασιλεῖς, οἳ καὶ Μέμφιν εἷλον.

Ὧν πρῶτος Σαΐτης ἐβασίλευσεν ἔτη ιθ', ἀφ' οὗ καὶ ὁ Σαΐτης νομὸς ἐκλήθη· οἳ καὶ ἐν τῷ Σεθρωΐτῃ νομῷ πόλιν ἔκτισαν, ἀφ' ἧς ὁρμώμενοι Αἰγυπτίους ἐχειρώσαντο.

Δεύτερος τούτων Βνῶν, ἔτη μ'.

Τρίτος Ἀρχάης, ἔτη λ'.

Τέταρτος Ἄφωφις, ἔτη ιδ'.

Ὁμοῦ, ργ'.

Ὁ δὲ Σαΐτης προσέθηκε τῷ μηνὶ ὥρας ιβ', ὡς εἶναι ἡμερῶν λ', καὶ τῷ ἐνιαυτῷ ἡμέρας ϛ', καὶ γέγονεν ἡμερῶν τξέ.

[1] δὲ conj. cf. Fr. 48 (a).

AEGYPTIACA (EPITOME) Fr. 49

Fr. 49 (*from the Scholia to Plato*).

Saïtic, of Saïs. From the *Aegyptiaca* of Manetho. The Seventeenth Dynasty consisted of Shepherds: they were brothers[1] from Phoenicia, foreign kings, who seized Memphis. The first of these kings, Saïtês, reigned for 19 years: the Saïte nome[2] is called after him. These kings founded in the Sethrôïte nome a town, from which as a base they subdued Egypt.

The second of these kings, Bnôn, reigned for 40 years; the third, Archaês, for 30 years; and the fourth, Aphôphis, for 14 years. Total, 103 years.

Saïtês added 12 hours to the month, to make its length 30 days; and he added 6 days to the year, which thus comprised 365 days.[3]

[1] See p. 95 n. 3. [2] See p. 80 n. 3.
[3] The addition of 5 days (not 6, as above) to the short year of 360 days was made long before the Hyksôs age: it goes back to at least the Pyramid Age, and probably earlier. The introduction of the calendar, making an artificial reconciliation of the lunar and solar years, perhaps as early as 4236 B.C., is believed to give the earliest fixed date in human history: see V. Gordon Childe, *New Light on the Most Ancient East*, 1934, pp. 5 f.

Fr. 50. Josephus, *Contra Apionem*, I, 15, 16, §§ 93-105.[1]

(Continued from Fr. 42.)

93 Νυνὶ δὲ τῆς ἀρχαιότητος ταύτης παρατίθεμαι τοὺς Αἰγυπτίους μάρτυρας. πάλιν οὖν τὰ τοῦ Μανεθῶ[2] πῶς ἔχει πρὸς τὴν τῶν χρόνων τάξιν 94 ὑπογράψω. φησὶ δὲ οὕτως· " μετὰ τὸ ἐξελθεῖν ἐξ Αἰγύπτου τὸν λαὸν τῶν Ποιμένων εἰς Ἱεροσόλυμα, ὁ ἐκβαλὼν αὐτοὺς ἐξ Αἰγύπτου βασιλεὺς Τέθμωσις ἐβασίλευσεν μετὰ ταῦτα ἔτη εἰκοσιπέντε καὶ μῆνας τέσσαρας καὶ ἐτελεύτησεν, καὶ παρέλαβεν τὴν ἀρχὴν ὁ αὐτοῦ υἱὸς Χέβρων ἔτη δεκατρία. 95 μεθ' ὃν Ἀμένωφις εἴκοσι καὶ μῆνας ἑπτά. τοῦ δὲ ἀδελφὴ Ἀμεσσὶς[3] εἰκοσιὲν καὶ μῆνας ἐννέα. τῆς δὲ Μήφρης δώδεκα καὶ μῆνας ἐννέα. τοῦ δὲ Μηφραμούθωσις εἰκοσιπέντε καὶ μῆνας δέκα. 96 τοῦ δὲ Θμῶσις[4] ἐννέα καὶ μῆνας ὀκτώ. τοῦ δ' Ἀμένωφις τριάκοντα καὶ μῆνας δέκα. τοῦ δὲ

---

[1] §§ 94-105 are quoted by Theophilus, *Ad Autolycum*, III, 20 f. §§ 103, 104 are quoted by Eusebius, *Praepar. Evang.*, X, 13.
[2] Niese: Μανέθωνος L.
[3] Naber: Ἀμενσὶς Fr. 52: Ἀμεσσὴς L.
[4] Τυθμώσης Manetho, Fr. 51: Τούθμωσις Fr. 52, 53.

---

[1] The New Kingdom: Dynasties XVIII.-XX.: c. 1580-c. 1100 B.C.
Dynasty XVIII. c. 1580-1310 B.C.
For identifications with the monumental evidence which is firmly established, see Meyer, *Geschichte*[2], ii. 1, p. 78: the names and order of the first nine kings are: (1) Amôsis

AEGYPTIACA

Dynasties, XVIII,[1] XIX.

Fr. 50 (*from* Josephus, *Contra Apionem*, i. 15, 16, §§ 93-105)—(*continued from* Fr. 42).

For the present I am citing the Egyptians as witnesses to this antiquity of ours. I shall therefore resume my quotations from Manetho's works in their reference to chronology. His account is as follows: " After the departure of the tribe of Shepherds from Egypt to Jerusalem, Tethmôsis,[2] the king who drove them out of Egypt, reigned for 25 years 4 months until his death, when he was succeeded by his son Chebrôn, who ruled for 13 years. After him Amenôphis reigned for 20 years 7 months ; then his sister Amessis for 21 years 9 months ; then her son Mêphrês for 12 years 9 months ; then his son Mêphramuthôsis for 25 years 10 months ; then his son Thmôsis for 9 years 8 months ; then his son Amenôphis

---

[1] (Chebrôn is unexplained), (2) Amenôphis I., (3) Tuthmôsis I., (4) Tuthmôsis II., (5) Hatshepsut (apparently Manetho's Amessis or Amensis : the same length of reign, 21 years), (6) Tuthmôsis III. (corresponding to Mêphrês, *i.e.* Menkheperrê' or Meshperê', and Misphragmuthôsis, *i.e.* Menkheperrê' Thutmose), (7) Amenôphis II., (8) Tuthmôsis IV. (the order of these two being reversed by Manetho), (9) Amenôphis III. (Hôrus, the same length of reign, 36 years).
The remaining kings of the dynasty are : Amenôphis IV. (Akhnaten, see p. 123 n. 1), Semenkhkarê' (? Acenchêrês), Tût'ankhamon (? Chebrês), Ay (? Acherrês) : see *C.A.H.* ii. p. 702. On rulers Nos. 3, 4, 5 and 6, see Wm. F. Edgerton, *The Thutmosid Succession*, 1933.
For Dynasty XIX. see p. 148 n. 1.

[2] Tethmôsis = Amôsis : see note on Misphragmuthôsis, Fr. 42, § 86. For the scarab of Amôsis see Plate 1, 3.

FR. 50   MANETHO

Ὧρος τριακονταὲξ καὶ μῆνας πέντε. τοῦ δὲ θυγάτηρ Ἀκεγχερὴς δώδεκα καὶ μῆνα ἕνα. τῆς δὲ Ῥάθωτις ἀδελφὸς ἐννέα. τοῦ δὲ Ἀκεγχήρης δώδεκα καὶ μῆνας πέντε. τοῦ δὲ Ἀκεγχήρης ἕτερος δώδεκα καὶ μῆνας τρεῖς. τοῦ δὲ Ἄρμαῖς τέσσαρα καὶ μῆνα ἕνα. τοῦ δὲ Ῥαμέσσης ἓν καὶ μῆνας τέσσαρας. τοῦ δὲ Ἁρμέσσης Μιαμοῦν ἑξηκονταὲξ καὶ μῆνας δύο. τοῦ δὲ Ἀμένωφις δεκαεννέα καὶ μῆνας ἕξ. τοῦ δὲ Σέθως ὁ καὶ Ῥαμέσσης,[1] ἱππικὴν καὶ ναυτικὴν ἔχων δύναμιν, τὸν μὲν ἀδελφὸν Ἄρμαῖν ἐπίτροπον τῆς Αἰγύπτου κατέστησεν,[2] καὶ πᾶσαν μὲν αὐτῷ τὴν ἄλλην βασιλικὴν περιέθηκεν ἐξουσίαν, μόνον δὲ ἐνετείλατο διάδημα μὴ φορεῖν μηδὲ τὴν βασιλίδα μητέρα τε τῶν τέκνων ἀδικεῖν, ἀπέχεσθαι δὲ καὶ τῶν ἄλλων βασιλικῶν παλλακίδων. αὐτὸς δὲ ἐπὶ Κύπρον καὶ Φοινίκην καὶ πάλιν Ἀσσυρίους τε καὶ Μήδους

---

[1] Eus.: Σέθωσις καὶ Ῥαμέσσης L.

[2] L (in margin): εὑρέθη ἐν ἑτέρῳ ἀντιγράφῳ οὕτως· μεθ' ὃν Σέθωσις καὶ Ῥαμέσσης δύο ἀδελφοί· ὁ μὲν ναυτικὴν ἔχων δύναμιν τοὺς κατὰ θάλατταν †ἀπαντῶντας καὶ διαχειρωμένους† (διαπειρωμένους Naber) ἐπολιόρκει· μετ' οὐ πολὺ δὲ καὶ τὸν Ῥαμέσσην ἀνελών, Ἄρμαῖν ἄλλον αὐτοῦ ἀδελφὸν ἐπίτροπον τῆς Αἰγύπτου καταστῆσαι (for κατέστησε).

---

[1] Howard Carter (*Tutankhamen*, iii. p. 3) points out that monuments of Amenôphis III. are dated to his 37th year, perhaps even to his 40th year; and he explains that Manetho has given the length of his reign as sole ruler. More commonly, the high figures assigned to the reigns of kings may be explained by the assumption that over-lapping co-regencies have been included.

[2] Miamûn = Mey-amûn, " beloved of Amûn ".

for 30 years 10 months;[1] then his son Ôrus for 36 years 5 months; then his daughter Acenchĕrês for 12 years 1 month; then her brother Rathôtis for 9 years; then his son Acenchêrês for 12 years 5 months, his son Acenchêrês II. for 12 years 3 months, his son Harmaïs for 4 years 1 month, his son Ramessês for 1 year 4 months, his son Harmessês Miamûn[2] for 66 years 2 months, his son Amenôphis for 19 years 6 months, and his son Sethôs, also called Ramessês,[3] whose power lay in his cavalry and his fleet. This king appointed his brother Harmaïs viceroy of Egypt, and invested him with all the royal prerogatives, except that he charged him not to wear a diadem, nor to wrong the queen, the mother of his children, and to refrain likewise from the royal concubines. He then set out on an expedition against Cyprus and Phoenicia and later against the Assyrians and the

[3] The margin of the Florentine MS. has a note here: "The following reading was found in another copy: 'After him Sethôsis and Ramessês, two brothers. The former, with a strong fleet, blockaded his murderous (?) adversaries by sea. Not long after, he slew Ramessês and appointed another of his brothers, Harmaïs, as viceroy of Egypt.'" This is intended as a correction of the text of Josephus, but it contains the error of the Florentine MS. in the reading Σέθωσις καὶ ʽΡαμέσσης. Sethôsis is the Sesostris of Herodotus, ii. 102, where his naval expedition in the "Red Sea" is described.

Meyer, *Aeg. Chron.* p. 91, considers the words "also called Ramesses" an addition to Manetho. See § 245.

W. Struve (see p. 148 n. 1) would here emend Sethôs into Sesôs, which was a name of Ramesês II.: according to the monuments he reigned for 67 years (*cf.* Fr. 55, 2), and his triumphant Asiatic campaigns were told by Hecataeus of Abdera (Osymandyas in Diodorus Siculus, i. 47 ff.).

Fr. 50 MANETHO

στρατεύσας, ἅπαντας τοὺς μὲν δόρατι, τοὺς δὲ ἀμαχητὶ φόβῳ δὲ τῆς πολλῆς δυνάμεως ὑποχειρίους ἔλαβε, καὶ μέγα φρονήσας ἐπὶ ταῖς εὐπραγίαις ἔτι καὶ θαρσαλεώτερον ἐπεπορεύετο τὰς πρὸς ἀνατολὰς 100 πόλεις τε καὶ χώρας καταστρεφόμενος. χρόνου τε ἱκανοῦ γεγονότος, Ἁρμαῒς ὁ καταλειφθεὶς ἐν Αἰγύπτῳ πάντα τἄμπαλιν οἷς ἀδελφὸς¹ παρῄνει μὴ ποιεῖν ἀδεῶς ἔπραττεν· καὶ γὰρ τὴν βασιλίδα βιαίως ἔσχεν καὶ ταῖς ἄλλαις παλλακίσιν ἀφειδῶς διετέλει χρώμενος, πειθόμενος δὲ² ὑπὸ τῶν φίλων 101 διάδημα ἐφόρει καὶ ἀντῆρε τῷ ἀδελφῷ. ὁ δὲ τεταγμένος ἐπὶ τῶν ἱερέων³ τῆς Αἰγύπτου γράψας βιβλίον ἔπεμψε τῷ Σεθώσει, δηλῶν αὐτῷ πάντα καὶ ὅτι ἀντῆρεν ὁ ἀδελφὸς αὐτῷ Ἁρμαῒς. παραχρῆμα οὖν ὑπέστρεψεν εἰς Πηλούσιον καὶ ἐκράτησεν 102 τῆς ἰδίας βασιλείας. ἡ δὲ χώρα ἐκλήθη ἀπὸ τοῦ αὐτοῦ ὀνόματος Αἴγυπτος· λέγεται⁴ γὰρ ὅτι ὁ μὲν Σέθως ἐκαλεῖτο Αἴγυπτος, Ἁρμαῒς δὲ ὁ ἀδελφὸς αὐτοῦ Δαναός."

¹ ἀδελφὸς Gutschmid: ἀδελφός L.   ² τε conj. Niese.
³ ἱερέων L (perhaps an Ancient Egyptian formula): ἱερῶν Hudson (*sacra* Lat., *fana* Eus.)—with this *cf. Revenue Laws of Ptolemy Philadelphus*, 51⁹ (258 B.C.) οἱ ἐπὶ τῶν ἱερῶν τεταγμένοι.   ⁴ λέγεται Gutschmid: λέγει L (*dicit* Lat.).

---

[1] A frequent title from the Old Kingdom onwards is "overseer of the priests of Upper and Lower Egypt," later applied to the high priest of Amûn. The emendation ἱερῶν (for ἱερέων) is supported by a reference in a papyrus of about the time of Manetho.

[2] See Fr. 54, § 274, n. 1 (pp. 140-141).

[3] With the return of Sethôsis to a country in revolt, *cf.* Herodotus, ii. 107 (return of Sesostris and the perilous

Medes; and he subjugated them all, some by the sword, others without a blow and merely by the menace of his mighty host. In the pride of his conquests, he continued his advance with still greater boldness, and subdued the cities and lands of the East. When a considerable time had elapsed, Harmaïs who had been left behind in Egypt, recklessly contravened all his brother's injunctions. He outraged the queen and proceeded to make free with the concubines; then, following the advice of his friends, he began to wear a diadem and rose in ievolt against his brother. The warden of the priests of Egypt [1] then wrote a letter which he sent to Sethôsis, revealing all the details, including the revolt of his brother Harmaïs. Sethôsis forthwith returned to Pêlusium [2] and took possession of his kingdom [3]; and the land was named Aegyptus after him. It is said that Sethôs was called Aegyptus, and his brother Harmaïs, Danaus." [4]

banquet), Diod. Sic. i. 57, 6-8. The tale appears to be a piece of folklore (Maspero, *Journ. des Savants*, 1901, pp. 599, 665 ff.). See Wainwright, *Sky-Religion*, p. 48.

[4] Danaus: *cf.* § 231. See Meyer, *Aeg. Chron.* p. 75, for the theory that the identification of Sethôs and Harmaïs with Aegyptus and Danaus is due, not to Manetho, but to a Jewish commentator or interpolator.

The tradition is that Danaus, a king of Egypt, was expelled by his brother and fled to Argos with his fifty daughters, and there "the sons of Aegyptus" were slain by "the daughters of Danaus." The legend appears to have existed in Egypt as well as in Greece: see Diod. Sic. i. 28. 2, 97. 2. For attempts to explain the story in terms of Aegean pre-history, see J. L. Myres, *Who Were the Greeks?* (1930), pp. 323 ff.; M. P. Nilsson, *The Mycenaean Origin of Greek Mythology* (1932), p. 64.

103 Ταῦτα μὲν ὁ Μανεθώς. δῆλον δ' ἐστὶν ἐκ τῶν εἰρημένων ἐτῶν, τοῦ χρόνου συλλογισθέντος, ὅτι οἱ καλούμενοι Ποιμένες, ἡμέτεροι δὲ¹ πρόγονοι, τρισὶ καὶ ἐνενήκοντα καὶ τριακοσίοις πρόσθεν ἔτεσιν ἐκ τῆς Αἰγύπτου ἀπαλλαγέντες τὴν χώραν ταύτην ἐπῴκησαν ἢ Δαναὸν εἰς Ἄργος ἀφικέσθαι· καίτοι
104 τοῦτον ἀρχαιότατον Ἀργεῖοι νομίζουσι. δύο τοίνυν ὁ Μανεθὼς ἡμῖν τὰ μέγιστα μεμαρτύρηκεν ἐκ τῶν παρ' Αἰγυπτίοις γραμμάτων, πρῶτον μὲν τὴν ἑτέρωθεν ἄφιξιν εἰς Αἴγυπτον, ἔπειτα δὲ τὴν ἐκεῖθεν ἀπαλλαγὴν οὕτως ἀρχαίαν τοῖς χρόνοις, ὡς ἐγγύς που προτερεῖν² αὐτὴν τῶν Ἰλιακῶν ἔτεσι χιλίοις.
105 ὑπὲρ ὧν δ' ὁ Μανεθὼς οὐκ ἐκ τῶν παρ' Αἰγυπτίοις γραμμάτων,³ ἀλλ', ὡς αὐτὸς ὡμολόγηκεν, ἐκ τῶν ἀδεσπότως μυθολογουμένων προστέθεικεν, ὕστερον ἐξελέγξω κατὰ μέρος ἀποδεικνὺς τὴν ἀπίθανον αὐτοῦ ψευδολογίαν.

Fr. 51. Theophilus, *Ad Autolycum*, III, 20 (Otto).

Ὁ δὲ Μωσῆς ὁδηγήσας⁴ τοὺς Ἰουδαίους, ὡς ἔφθημεν εἰρηκέναι, ἐκβεβλημένους ἀπὸ γῆς Αἰγύπτου

¹ δὲ Eus.: om. L, Lat.
² που προτερεῖν Eus., Lat.: τοῦ πρότερον L.
³ γραμμάτων ed. pr. (*litteris* Lat., *libris* Eus.): πραγμάτων L.
⁴ Sc. ἦν: ὡδήγησε Boeckh.

---

[1] This total is reckoned from Tethmôsis (Amôsis) to the end of the reign of Sethôsis, the latter being taken as 60 years (*cf.* § 231, where Sethôs is said to have reigned for 59 years after driving out Hermaeus).

AEGYPTIACA (EPITOME) Fr. 50, 51

Such is Manetho's account; and, if the time is reckoned according to the years mentioned, it is clear that the so-called Shepherds, our ancestors, quitted Egypt and settled in our land 393 years [1] before the coming of Danaus to Argos. Yet the Argives regard Danaus as belonging to a remote antiquity.[2] Thus Manetho has given us evidence from Egyptian records upon two very important points: first, upon our coming to Egypt from elsewhere; and secondly, upon our departure from Egypt at a date so remote that it preceded the Trojan war[3] by wellnigh a thousand years.[4] As for the additions which Manetho has made, not from the Egyptian records, but, as he has himself admitted, from anonymous legendary tales,[5] I shall later refute them in detail, and show the improbability of his lying stories.

Fr. 51 [6] (*from* Theophilus, *Ad Autolyc.* iii. 19).

Moses was the leader of the Jews, as I have already said, when they had been expelled from Egypt by

[2] The mythical King Inachus was held to be still more ancient: *cf.* Fr. 4, 1 (p. 19 n. 4).
[3] The traditional date of the Trojan war is 1192-1183 B.C.
[4] This appears to be about four times too high a figure: 250 years would be a nearer estimate.
[5] *Cf.* Fr. 54, §§ 229, 287, for Manetho's use of popular traditions.
[6] This list of Dynasties XVIII., XIX. is obviously derived wholly from Josephus, any variations from the text of Josephus being merely corruptions. Theophilus, Bishop of Antioch, wrote his apologia for the Christian faith (three books addressed to a friend Autolycus) in the second half of ii. A.D.

FR. 51　　　　MANETHO

ὑπὸ βασιλέως Φαραὼ οὗ τοὔνομα Τέθμωσις, ὅς, φασίν, μετὰ τὴν ἐκβολὴν τοῦ λαοῦ ἐβασίλευσεν ἔτη εἴκοσι πέντε καὶ μῆνας δ', ὡς ὑφήρηται Μαναιθώς.

2. Καὶ μετὰ τοῦτον Χεβρῶν, ἔτη ιγ'.
3. Μετὰ δὲ τοῦτον Ἀμένωφις, ἔτη κ', μῆνας ἑπτά.
4. Μετὰ δὲ τοῦτον ἡ ἀδελφὴ αὐτοῦ Ἀμέσση, ἔτη κα', μῆνα α'.[1]
5. Μετὰ δὲ ταύτην Μήφρης, ἔτη ιβ', μῆνας θ'.
6. Μετὰ δὲ τοῦτον Μηφραμμούθωσις, ἔτη κ',[2] μῆνας ι'.
7. Καὶ μετὰ τοῦτον Τυθμώσης, ἔτη θ', μῆνας η'.
8. Καὶ μετὰ τοῦτον Ἀμένωφις,[3] ἔτη λ', μῆνας ι'.
9. Μετὰ δὲ τοῦτον Ὧρος, ἔτη λϛ,' μῆνας ε'.
10. Τούτου δὲ θυγάτηρ,[4] ⟨Ἀκεγχερής⟩, ἔτη ι[β'], μῆνας α'.[4]
11. Μετὰ δὲ ταύτην ⟨Ῥαθῶτις, ἔτη θ'⟩.
12. ⟨Μετὰ δὲ τοῦτον Ἀκεγχήρης, ἔτη ιβ', μῆνας ε'⟩.
13. ⟨Μετὰ δὲ τοῦτον Ἀκ⟩ε[γ]χ[ή]ρης, ἔτη ιβ', μῆνας γ'.
14. Τοῦ δὲ Ἅρμαϊς, ἔτη δ', μῆνα α'.
15. Καὶ μετὰ τοῦτον Ῥαμέσσης ἐνιαυτόν, μῆνας δ'.
16. Καὶ μετὰ τοῦτον Ῥαμέσσης Μιαμμοῦ, ἔτη ξϛ'[5] καὶ μῆνας β'.

AEGYPTIACA (EPITOME) Fr. 51

King Pharaôh whose name was Tethmôsis. After the expulsion of the people, this king, it is said, reigned for 25 years 4 months, according to Manetho's reckoning.

2. After him, Chebrôn ruled for 13 years.
3. After him, Amenôphis, for 20 years 7 months.
4. After him, his sister Amessê, for 21 years 1 month [9 months in Josephus].
5. After her, Mêphrês, for 12 years 9 months.
6. After him, Mêphrammuthôsis, for 20 years [25 years in Josephus] 10 months.
7. After him, Tuthmôsês, for 9 years 8 months.
8. After him, Amenôphis, for 30 years 10 months.
9. After him, Ôrus, for 36 years 5 months.
10. Next, his daughter [Acencherês] reigned for 12 years 1 month.
11. After her, [Rathôtis, for 9 years.
12. After him, Acencherês, for 12 years 5 months.
13. After him, Ac]encherês [II.], for 12 years 3 months.
14. His son Harmaïs, for 4 years 1 month.
15. After him, Ramessês for 1 year and 4 months.
16. After him, Ramessês Miammû(n), for 66 years 2 months.

---

¹ α' i.e. ἕνα, in error for ἐννέα, Josephus, Fr. 50, § 95 (Müller).
² For κε', as in Josephus, Fr. 50, § 95.
³ Δαμενόφις Otto.
⁴ Restored from Josephus (Boeckh): MSS. θυγάτηρ ἔτη ι', μῆνας γ'. μετὰ δὲ ταύτην Μερχερής, ἔτη ιβ', μῆνας γ'.
⁵ μετὰ δὲ τοῦτον Μέσσης Μιαμμού, ἔτη [ξ]ς' Otto.

Fr. 51, 52   MANETHO

17. Καὶ μετὰ τοῦτον Ἀμένωφις, ἔτη ιθ´, μῆνας ϛ´.

Τοῦ δὲ Σέθως, ὅς¹ καὶ ʽΡαμέσσης, ἔτη ι´, ὅν² φασιν ἐσχηκέναι πολλὴν δύναμιν ἱππικῆς καὶ παράταξιν ναυτικῆς.

Fr. 52.   Syncellus, pp. 115, 130, 133.

ΚΑΤΑ ΑΦΡΙΚΑΝΟΝ.

Ὀκτωκαιδεκάτη δυναστεία Διοσπολιτῶν βασιλέων ιϛ´.

Ὧν πρῶτος Ἀμώς, ἐφ᾽ οὗ Μωϋσῆς ἐξῆλθεν ἐξ Αἰγύπτου, ὡς ἡμεῖς ἀποδεικνύομεν, ὡς δὲ ἡ παροῦσα ψῆφος ἀναγκάζει, ἐπὶ τούτου τὸν Μωϋσέα συμβαίνει νέον ἔτι εἶναι.

Δεύτερος κατὰ Ἀφρικανὸν κατὰ τὴν ιη´ δυναστείαν ἐβασίλευσε Χεβρώς, ἔτη ιγ´.
Τρίτος, Ἀμενωφθίς, ἔτη κδ´.³
Τέταρτος,⁴ Ἀμενσίς,⁵ ἔτη κβ´.

¹ τοῦ δὲ Θοῖσσος Otto.
² οὕς Otto, adding after ναυτικῆς the words κατὰ τοὺς ἰδίους χρόνους.
³ κα´ m.   ⁴ τετάρτη Müller.   ⁵ Ἀμερσίς A.

---

[1] See p. 100 n. 1.
[2] See p. 101 n. 2. On the basis of new evidence scholars now tend to conclude that the Exodus took place c. 1445 B.C. (see e.g. J. W. Jack, *The Date of the Exodus*, 1925): Jericho fell c. 1400 B.C. (J. Garstang, *The Heritage of Solomon*, 1934, p. 281).
[3] *I.e.* Africanus.

AEGYPTIACA (EPITOME) Fr. 51, 52

17. After him, Amenôphis, for 19 years 6 months.
18. Then, his son Sethôs, also called Ramessês, for 10 years. He is said to have possessed a large force of cavalry and an organized fleet.

Dynasty XVIII.

Fr. 52 (*from* Syncellus). According to Africanus.

The Eighteenth Dynasty [1] consisted of 16 kings of Diospolis.

The first of these was Amôs, in whose reign Moses went forth from Egypt,[2] as I [3] here declare; but, according to the convincing evidence of the present calculation [4] it follows that in this reign Moses was still young.

The second king of the Eighteenth Dynasty, according to Africanus, was Chebrôs, who reigned for 13 years.

The third king, Amenôphthis,[5] reigned for 24 (21) years.

The fourth king (queen), Amensis (Amersis), reigned for 22 years.

---

[4] *I.e.* by Syncellus.
[5] This Greek transcription of "Amenḥotpe," retaining both the labial and the dental, is the fullest form of the name, "Amenôthês" showing assimilation: "Amenôphis," which is regularly used to represent "Amenḥotpe," actually comes from another name, "Amen(em)ôpe" (B.G.). The month Phamenôth (February-March) is named from the "feast of Amenôthês".

FR. 52

Πέμπτος, Μίσαφρις, ἔτη ιγ'.
Ἕκτος, Μισφραγμούθωσις, ἔτη κϛ', ἐφ οὗ ὁ ἐπὶ Δευκαλίωνος κατακλυσμός.

Ὁμοῦ ἐπὶ Ἀμώσεως τοῦ καὶ Μισφραγμουθώσεως ἀρχῆς κατὰ Ἀφρικανὸν γίνονται ἔτη ξθ'. Τοῦ γὰρ Ἀμὼς οὐδ' ὅλως εἶπεν ἔτη.

ζ' Τούθμωσις, ἔτη θ'.
η' Ἀμενῶφις, ἔτη λα' Οὗτός ἐστιν ὁ Μέμνων εἶναι νομιζόμενος καὶ φθεγγόμενος λίθος.
θ' Ὧρος, ἔτη λζ'.
ι' Ἀχερρῆς, ἔτη λβ'.
ια' Ῥαθῶς, ἔτη ἕξ.
ιβ' Χεβρής, ἔτη ιβ'.
ιγ' Ἀχερρῆς, ἔτη ιβ'.
ιδ' Ἀρμεσίς,¹ ἔτη ε'.
ιε' Ῥαμεσσῆς, ἔτος α'
ιϛ' Ἀμενωφάθ,² ἔτη ιθ
Ὁμοῦ' ἔτη σξγ'.

¹ B: Ἀμεσής A.   ² B: Ἀμενώφ G.

---

[1] This note about Memnôn in both Africanus and Eusebius should be transferred to the ninth king of the dynasty, Ôrus or Amenôphis III.

[Footnote continued on opposite page.

AEGYPTIACA (EPITOME)   FR. 52

The fifth, Misaphris, for 13 years.

The sixth, Misphragmuthôsis, for 26 years: in his reign the flood of Deucalion's time occurred.

Total, according to Africanus, down to the reign of Amôsis, also called Misphragmuthôsis, 69 years. Of the length of the reign of Amôs he said nothing at all.

7. Tuthmôsis, for 9 years.
8. Amenôphis, for 31 years. This is the king who was reputed to be Memnôn and a speaking statue.[1]
9. Ôrus, for 37 years.
10. Acherrês,[2] for 32 years.
11. Rathôs, for 6 years.
12. Chebrês, for 12 years.
13. Acherrês, for 12 years.
14. Armesis, for 5 years.
15. Ramessês, for 1 year.
16. Amenôphath (Amenôph), for 19 years.

Total, 263 years.

[1] The reference is to the two monolithic colossi of Amenôphis III. (Baedeker[8], pp. 345 f.): see Pausanias, i. 42 (the Thebans say it was a statue not of Memnôn, but of Phamenôph, who dwelt in those parts) with J. G. Frazer's note (vol. ii. pp. 530 f.), and Tacitus, *Ann.* ii. 61. Amenôphis III. (Memnôn) is correctly named in Greek Amenôth and Phamenôth by the poetess Balbilla (time of Hadrian): see Werner Peek in *Mitt. des Deutsch. Inst. für äg. Alt. in Kairo,* v. 1 (1934), pp. 96, 99; *Sammelbuch,* 8211, 8213.

[2] For possible identifications of Nos. 10, 12, and 13 see p. 101 n. 1. Nos. 14, 15, and 16 should be transferred to Dynasty XIX.: see p. 148 n. 1. Armesis (Armaïs) is probably Haremhab: Ramessês, vizier of Haremhab and afterwards Ramessês I., was probably of Heliopolitan origin (P. E. Newberry).

Fr. 53 (a). Syncellus, pp. 116, 129, 133, 135.

ΚΑΤΑ ΕΥΣΕΒΙΟΝ.

Ὀκτωκαιδεκάτη δυναστεία Διοσπολιτῶν βασιλέων ιδ'.

Ὧν πρῶτος, Ἄμωσις, ἔτη κε'.
β' Χεβρὼν δεύτερος, ἔτη ιγ'.
γ' Ἀμμενῶφις, ἔτη κα'.
δ' Μίφρης, ἔτη ιβ'.
ε' Μισφραγμούθωσις, ἔτη κϛ'.

Ὁμοῦ ἀπ' Ἀμώσεως τοῦ πρώτου τῆς προκειμένης ιη' δυναστείας ἕως Μισφραγμουθώσεως ἀρχῆς κατὰ Εὐσέβιον ἔτη γίνονται οα', βασιλεῖς πέντε ἀντὶ τῶν ἕξ· τὸν γὰρ τέταρτον Ἀμένσην παραδραμών, οὗ ὁ Ἀφρικανὸς καὶ οἱ λοιποὶ μέμνηνται, ἔτη κβ' αὐτοῦ ἐκολόβωσεν.

ϛ' Τούθμωσις, ἔτη θ'.
ζ' Ἀμένωφις, ἔτη λα'. Οὗτός ἐστιν ὁ Μέμνων εἶναι νομιζόμενος καὶ φθεγγόμενος λίθος.
η' Ὧρος, ἔτη λϛ' (ἐν ἄλλῳ λη').
θ' Ἀχενχέρσης, ⟨ἔτη ιβ'⟩.
⟨Ἄθωρις, ἔτη λθ'[1]⟩.
⟨Κενχέρης⟩, ἔτη ιϛ'.[2]

Κατὰ τοῦτον Μωϋσῆς τῆς ἐξ Αἰγύπτου πορείας τῶν Ἰουδαίων ἡγήσατο. (Syncellus adds: Μόνος Εὐσέβιος ἐπὶ τούτου λέγει τὴν τοῦ Ἰσραὴλ διὰ Μωϋσέως ἔξοδον, μηδενὸς αὐτῷ λόγου μαρτυροῦντος, ἀλλὰ καὶ πάντων ἐναντιουμένων τῶν πρὸ αὐτοῦ, ὡς μαρτυρεῖ.)

AEGYPTIACA (EPITOME) Fr. 53

Fr. 53 (a) (*from Syncellus*). ACCORDING TO EUSEBIUS.

The Eighteenth Dynasty consisted of fourteen kings of Diospolis.
The first of these, Amôsis, reigned for 25 years.
2. The second, Chebrôn, for 13 years.
3. Ammenôphis, for 21 years.
4. Miphrês, for 12 years.
5. Misphragmuthôsis, for 26 years.

Total from Amôsis, the first king of this Eighteenth Dynasty, down to the reign of Misphragmuthôsis amounts, according to Eusebius, to 71 years; and there are five kings, not six. For he omitted the fourth king, Amensês, mentioned by Africanus and the others, and thus cut off the 22 years of his reign.
  6. Tuthmôsis, for 9 years.
  7. Amenôphis, for 31 years. This is the king who was reputed to be Memnôn and a speaking statue.[1]
  8. Ôrus, for 36 years (in another copy, 38 years).
  9. Achenchersês [for 12 years].
[Athôris, for 39 years (? 9).]
[Cencherês] for 16 years.

About this time Moses led the Jews in their march out of Egypt. (Syncellus adds: Eusebius alone places in this reign the exodus of Israel under Moses, although no argument supports him, but all his predecessors hold a contrary view, as he testifies.)

[1] See p. 113 n. I.

---

[1] θ′ Müller.
[2] B omits Ἄθωρις and Κενχέρης, reading θ′ ᾿Αχενχέρσης, ἔτη ιϛ′.

Fr. 53   MANETHO

ι΄ Ἀχερρῆς, ἔτη η΄.
ια΄ Χερρῆς, ἔτη ιε΄.
ιβ΄ Ἁρμαῒς ὁ καὶ Δαναός, ἔτη ε΄, μεθ' ἃ ἐκ τῆς Αἰγύπτου ἐκπεσὼν καὶ φεύγων τὸν ἀδελφὸν Αἴγυπτον εἰς τὴν Ἑλλάδα ἀφικνεῖται, κρατήσας τε τοῦ Ἄργους βασιλεύει τῶν Ἀργείων.
ιγ΄ Ῥαμεσσῆς[1] ὁ καὶ Αἴγυπτος, ἔτη ξη΄.
ιδ΄ Ἀμμένωφις, ἔτη μ΄.
Ὁμοῦ, ἔτη τμη΄.

Προσέθηκεν ὑπὲρ τὸν Ἀφρικανὸν ἔτη πε΄ Εὐσέβιος κατὰ τὴν ιη΄ δυναστείαν. (Syncellus, p. 116: Εὐσέβιος δύο βασιλεῖς περιέκρυψεν, ἔτη δὲ προσέθηκε πε΄, τμη΄ παραθεὶς ἀντὶ σξγ΄ τῶν παρ' Ἀφρικανῷ.)

(b) Eusebius, *Chronica I.* (Armenian Version), p. 99.

Octava decima dynastia Diospolitarum regum XIV, quorum primus

Amoses, annis XXV.
Chehron, annis XIII.
Amophis, annis XXI.
Memphres, annis XII.
Mispharmuthosis, annis XXVI.
Tuthmosis, annis IX.
Amenophis, annis XXXI. Hic est qui Memnon putabatur, petra loquens.
Orus, annis XXVIII.

[1] Dindorf: Ἀμεσσῆς B.

AEGYPTIACA (EPITOME)

10. Acherrês, for 8 years.
11. Cherrês, for 15 years.
12. Armaïs, also called Danaus, for 5 years: thereafter, he was banished from Egypt and, fleeing from his brother Aegyptus, he arrived in Greece, and, seizing Argos, be ruled over the Argives.
13. Ramessês, also called Aegyptus, for 68 years.
14. Ammenôphis, for 40 years.

Total, 348 years.

Eusebius assigns 85 years more than Africanus to the Eighteenth Dynasty. (Syncellus elsewhere says: Eusebius leaves out two kings, but adds 85 years, setting down 348 years instead of the 263 years of the reckoning of Africanus.)

(b) ARMENIAN VERSION OF EUSEBIUS.

The Eighteenth Dynasty consisted of fourteen kings of Diospolis. The first of these, Amoses, reigned for 25 years.

2. Chebron, for 13 years.
3. Amophis, for 21 years.
4. Memphres, for 12 years.
5. Mispharmuthosis, for 26 years.
6. Tuthmosis, for 9 years.
7. Amenophis, for 31 years. This is the king who was reputed to be Memnon, a speaking stone.
8. Orus, for 28 years.

Fr. 53, 54   MANETHO

Achencheres[1] . . . , annis XVI. Huius aetate
Moses ducem se praebuit Hebraeis ab Aegypto
excedentibus.
Acherres, annis VIII.
Cherres, annis XV.
Armaïs, qui et Danaus, annis V; quibus peractis,
Aegyptiorum regione pulsus Aegyptumque
fratrem suum fugiens, evasit in Graeciam,
Argisque captis, imperavit Argivis.
Ramesses, qui et Aegyptus, annis LXVIII.
Amenophis, annis XL.

Summa dominationis CCCXLVIII.

Fr. 54. JOSEPHUS, *Contra Apionem*, I, 26–31,
§§ 227–287.

26
227 Ἐφ' ἑνὸς δὲ πρώτου στήσω τὸν λόγον, ᾧ καὶ
μάρτυρι μικρὸν ἔμπροσθεν τῆς ἀρχαιότητος ἐχρη-
228 σάμην. ὁ γὰρ Μανεθὼς οὗτος, ὁ τὴν Αἰγυπτιακὴν
ἱστορίαν ἐκ τῶν ἱερῶν γραμμάτων μεθερμηνεύειν
ὑπεσχημένος, προειπὼν τοὺς ἡμετέρους προγόνους
πολλαῖς μυριάσιν ἐπὶ τὴν Αἴγυπτον ἐλθόντας
κρατῆσαι τῶν ἐνοικούντων, εἶτ' αὐτὸς ὁμολογῶν
χρόνῳ πάλιν ὕστερον ἐκπεσόντας τὴν νῦν Ἰουδαίαν κατασχεῖν καὶ κτίσαντας Ἱεροσόλυμα τὸν
νεὼν κατασκευάσασθαι, μέχρι μὲν τούτων ἠκολού-
229 θησε ταῖς ἀναγραφαῖς. ἔπειτα δὲ δοὺς ἐξουσίαν

[1] A lacuna here, as in the Greek version.

---

[1] According to *O.T. 1 Kings* vi. 1, the building of
Solomon's Temple was begun 480 years after the Exodus:

9. Achencheres . . . , for 16 years. In his time Moses became leader of the Hebrews in their exodus from Egypt.
10. Acherres, for 8 years.
11. Cherres, for 15 years.
12. Armaïs, also called Danaus, for 5 years : at the end of this time he was banished from the land of Egypt. Fleeing from his brother Aegyptus, he escaped to Greece, and after capturing Argos, he held sway over the Argives.
13. Ramesses, also called Aegyptus, for 68 years.
14. Amenophis, for 40 years.

Total for the dynasty, 348 years.

Fr. 54 (*from* Josephus, *Contra Apionem*, I. 26-31, §§ 227-287).

(Josephus discusses the calumnies of the Egyptians against the Jews, whom they hate.)

The first writer upon whom I shall dwell is one whom I used a little earlier as a witness to our antiquity. I refer to Manetho. This writer, who had undertaken to translate the history of Egypt from the sacred books, began by stating that our ancestors came against Egypt with many tens of thousands and gained the mastery over the inhabitants ; and then he himself admitted that at a later date again they were driven out of the country, occupied what is now Judaea, founded Jerusalem, and built the temple.[1] Up to this point he followed the chronicles : there-

---

[1] if the Exodus is dated c. 1445 B.C. (see p. 110 n. 2), the Temple was founded c. 965 B.C.

FR. 54　　MANETHO

αὐτῷ διὰ τοῦ φάναι γράψειν τὰ μυθευόμενα καὶ λεγόμενα περὶ τῶν Ἰουδαίων λόγους ἀπιθάνους παρενέβαλεν, ἀναμῖξαι βουλόμενος ἡμῖν πλῆθος Αἰγυπτίων λεπρῶν καὶ ἐπὶ ἄλλοις ἀρρωστήμασιν, ὥς φησι, φυγεῖν ἐκ τῆς Αἰγύπτου καταγνωσθέντων.
230 Ἀμένωφιν γὰρ βασιλέα προθείς,[1] ψευδὲς ὄνομα, καὶ διὰ τοῦτο χρόνον αὐτοῦ τῆς βασιλείας ὁρίσαι μὴ τολμήσας, καίτοι γε ἐπὶ τῶν ἄλλων βασιλέων ἀκριβῶς τὰ ἔτη προστιθείς, τούτῳ προσάπτει τινὰς μυθολογίας, ἐπιλαθόμενος σχεδὸν ὅτι πεντακοσίοις ἔτεσι καὶ δεκαοκτὼ πρότερον ἱστόρηκε γενέσθαι τὴν τῶν Ποιμένων ἔξοδον εἰς Ἱεροσόλυμα.
231 Τέθμωσις γὰρ ἦν βασιλεὺς ὅτε ἐξῄεσαν, ἀπὸ δὲ τούτου τῶν μεταξὺ[2] βασιλέων κατ' αὐτόν ἐστι τριακόσια ἐνενηκοντατρία ἔτη μέχρι τῶν δύο ἀδελφῶν Σέθω καὶ Ἑρμαίου, ὧν τὸν μὲν Σέθων Αἴγυπτον, τὸν δὲ Ἕρμαιον Δαναὸν μετονομασθῆναί φησιν, ὃν ἐκβαλὼν ὁ Σέθως ἐβασίλευσεν ἔτη νθ' καὶ μετ' αὐτὸν ὁ πρεσβύτερος τῶν υἱῶν
232 αὐτοῦ Ῥάμψης ξϛ'. τοσούτοις οὖν πρότερον ἔτεσιν ἀπελθεῖν ἐξ Αἰγύπτου τοὺς πατέρας ἡμῶν ὡμολογηκώς, εἶτα τὸν Ἀμένωφιν εἰσποιήσας ἐμβόλιμον βασιλέα, φησὶν τοῦτον ἐπιθυμῆσαι θεῶν γενέσθαι θεατήν, ὥσπερ Ὧρ εἷς τῶν πρὸ αὐτοῦ βεβασιλευ-

[1] προθείς Cobet : προσθείς L.
[2] τούτου τῶν μεταξὺ conj. Niese (*et ab hoc tempore regum qui postea fuerunt* Lat.) : τούτων μεταξὺ τῶν L.

---

[1] *Cf.* " the botch (or boil) of Egypt " (perhaps elephantiasis), *Deuteronomy* xxviii. 27.

after, by offering to record the legends and current talk about the Jews, he took the liberty of interpolating improbable tales in his desire to confuse with us a crowd of Egyptians, who for leprosy and other maladies [1] had been condemned, he says, to banishment from Egypt. After citing a king Amenôphis, a fictitious person,—for which reason he did not venture to define the length of his reign, although in the case of the other kings he adds their years precisely,—Manetho attaches to him certain legends, having doubtless forgotten that according to his own chronicle the exodus of the Shepherds to Jerusalem took place 518 years [2] earlier. For Tethmôsis was king when they set out; and, according to Manetho, the intervening reigns thereafter occupied 393 years down to the two brothers Sethôs and Hermaeus, the former of whom, he says, took the new name of Aegyptus, the latter that of Danaus. Sethôs drove out Hermaeus and reigned for 59 years; then Rampsês, the elder of his sons, for 66 years. Thus, after admitting that so many years had elapsed since our forefathers left Egypt, Manetho now interpolates this intruding Amenôphis. This king, he states, conceived a desire to behold the gods, as Or,[3] one of his predecessors on

[2] This number seems to be obtained by adding 393 + 59 + 66: in that case the reign of Sethôsis is counted twice, (1) as 60, (2) as 59 years (*cf.* Fr. 50, § 103).

[3] Ôr, or Hôrus, is the ninth king in Manetho's list of Dynasty XVIII. (Frs. 51, 52), in reality Amenôphis III. Reinach points out that Herodotus (ii. 42) tells the same story of the Egyptian Heracles, and conjectures that there is perhaps confusion with the god Hôrus.

Fr. 54 MANETHO

κότων, ἀνενεγκεῖν δὲ τὴν ἐπιθυμίαν ὁμωνύμῳ
μὲν αὐτῷ Ἀμενώφει, πατρὸς δὲ Παάπιος¹ ὄντι,
233 θείας δὲ δοκοῦντι μετεσχηκέναι φύσεως κατά τε
σοφίαν καὶ πρόγνωσιν τῶν ἐσομένων. εἰπεῖν οὖν
αὐτῷ τοῦτον τὸν ὁμώνυμον ὅτι δυνήσεται θεοὺς
ἰδεῖν, εἰ καθαρὰν ἀπό τε λεπρῶν καὶ τῶν ἄλλων
μιαρῶν ἀνθρώπων τὴν χώραν ἅπασαν ποιήσειεν.
234 ἡσθέντα δὲ τὸν βασιλέα πάντας τοὺς τὰ σώματα
λελωβημένους ἐκ τῆς Αἰγύπτου συναγαγεῖν· γενέ-
235 σθαι δὲ τὸ πλῆθος² μυριάδας ὀκτώ· καὶ τούτους

¹ *Ed. pr.* (*cf.* § 243): Πάπιος L
² Conj. Niese (after Lat.): τοῦ πλήθους L.

---

¹ For this Amenôphis, a historical personage, later deified (*cf.* the deification of Imhotep, Fr. 11), Amenhotpe, son of Hapu, and minister of Amenôphis III., see G. Maspero, *New Light on Ancient Egypt* (1909), pp. 189-195: Sethe, in *Aegyptiaca* (Ebers, *Festschrift*), 1897, pp. 107-116: Breasted, *Anc. Rec.* ii. §§ 911 ff.; Warren R. Dawson, *The Bridle of Pegasus*, 1930, pp. 49-79. In 1934-35 excavations by the French Institute, Cairo, revealed all that remains of the splendour of the funerary temple of Amenhotpe, son of Hapu, among a series of such temples to the N. of Medinet Habu: see Robichon and Varille, *Le Temple du Scribe Royal Amenhotep, Fils de Hapou*, i. Cairo, 1936. An inscription of iii. B.C. (and therefore contemporary with Manetho), headed Ἀμενώτου ὑποθῆκαι, " Precepts of Amenôtes or Amenôphis," was published by Wilcken in *Aegyptiaca*, 1897, pp. 142 ff. It is inscribed upon a limestone ostracon of Deir el-Bahri; and the first three injunctions run: " Practise wisdom along with justice," " Revere both the gods and your parents,"

the throne, had done; and he communicated his desire to his namesake Amenôphis,[1] Paapis' son, who, in virtue of his wisdom and knowledge of the future, was reputed to be a partaker in the divine nature. This namesake, then, replied that he would be able to see the gods if he cleansed the whole land of lepers and other polluted persons. The king was delighted, and assembled [2] all those in Egypt whose bodies were wasted by disease: they numbered 80,000 persons.

" Take counsel at leisure, but accomplish speedily whatever you do ".
An ostracon, found at Deir el-Bahri, and giving the draft of an inscription concerning the deified Amenôphis, was published by A. Bataille, *Études de Papyrologie*, IV. (1938), pp. 125-131: it celebrates the cure of a certain Polyaratos. See O. Guéraud in *Bull. Inst. Fr. d'Arch. Or.*, xxvii. (1927), pp. 121 ff., P. Jouguet, " Les Grands Dieux de la Pierre Sainte à Thèbes," *Mélanges Glotz*, II. pp. 493-500.

For the historical interpretation of this whole passage, §§ 232-251, see Meyer, *Geschichte*[2], ii. 1, pp. 421 ff. King Amenôphis is at one time Merneptah, son of Rameses II.; at another time, Amenôphis IV. (Akhnaten), some 200 years earlier. The doings of the polluted, the persecution of the gods, and the slaughter of the holy animals, clearly portray the fury of Akhnaten and his followers against Egyptian religion. For a popular Egyptian parallel to §§ 232 ff., see the Potter's Oracle, one of the Rainer Papyri (iii. A.D.) edited by Wilcken in *Hermes*, xl. 1905, pp. 544 ff. and by G. Manteuffel, *De Opusculis Graecis Aegypti e papyris, ostracis, lapidibusque collectis*, 1930, No. 7; and *cf.* the prophecy of the lamb, Manetho, Fr. 64.

For a theory about the identity of the polluted (they are the troops of Sethôs I., sent to Tanis by his father Ramessês I. during the ascendancy of Haremhab), see P. Montet, " La Stèle de l'An 400 Retrouvée," in *Kêmi*, iii. 1935, pp. 191-215.

[2] In an incredibly short time (§ 257).

FR. 54 MANETHO

εἰς τὰς λιθοτομίας τὰς ἐν τῷ πρὸς ἀνατολὴν μέρει τοῦ Νείλου ἐμβαλεῖν αὐτόν, ὅπως ἐργάζοιντο καὶ τῶν ἄλλων Αἰγυπτίων εἶεν κεχωρισμένοι.[1] εἶναι δέ τινας ἐν αὐτοῖς καὶ τῶν λογίων ἱερέων φησὶ λέπρᾳ 236 συνεσχημένους.[2] τὸν δὲ Ἀμένωφιν ἐκεῖνον, τὸν σοφὸν καὶ μαντικὸν ἄνδρα, ὑποδεῖσαι[3] πρὸς αὐτόν τε καὶ τὸν βασιλέα χόλον τῶν θεῶν, εἰ βιασθέντες ὀφθήσονται· καὶ προσθέμενον εἰπεῖν ὅτι συμμαχήσουσί τινες τοῖς μιαροῖς καὶ τῆς Αἰγύπτου κρατήσουσιν ἐπ' ἔτη δεκατρία, μὴ τολμῆσαι μὲν αὐτὸν εἰπεῖν ταῦτα τῷ βασιλεῖ, γραφὴν δὲ καταλιπόντα περὶ πάντων ἑαυτὸν ἀνελεῖν, ἐν ἀθυμίᾳ 237 δὲ εἶναι τὸν βασιλέα. κἄπειτα κατὰ λέξιν οὕτως γέγραφεν· "τῶν δ' ἐν[4] ταῖς λατομίαις ὡς χρόνος ἱκανὸς διῆλθεν ταλαιπωρούντων, ἀξιωθεὶς ὁ βασιλεὺς ἵνα πρὸς[5] κατάλυσιν αὐτοῖς καὶ σκέπην ἀπομερίσῃ τὴν τότε τῶν Ποιμένων ἐρημωθεῖσαν πόλιν Αὔαριν συνεχώρησεν· ἔστι δ' ἡ πόλις κατὰ τὴν 238 θεολογίαν ἄνωθεν Τυφώνιος. οἱ δὲ εἰς ταύτην εἰσελθόντες καὶ τὸν τόπον τοῦτον εἰς[6] ἀπόστασιν ἔχοντες, ἡγεμόνα αὐτῶν τινα τῶν Ἡλιοπολιτῶν ἱερέων Ὀσάρσηφον[7] λεγόμενον[8] ἐστήσαντο καὶ

[1] εἶεν κεχωρισμένοι conj. Holwerda : οἱ ἐγκεχωρισμένοι L.
[2] συνεσχημένους conj. Niese : συνεχομένους Dindorf : συγκεχυμένους L.
[3] ὑποδεῖσαι Dindorf : ὑποδεῖσθαι L.
[4] δ' ἐν Bekker : δὲ L.   [5] πρὸς bracketed by Niese.
[6] εἰς bracketed as apparently spurious by Niese : ⟨ὁρμητήριον⟩ εἰς ἀπ. Holwerda.
[7] L : Ὀσάρσιφον conj. Hudson.
[8] Transp. Niese (a more natural place for the participle): λεγόμενόν τινα ... Ὀσ· L.

These he cast into the stone-quarries [1] to the east of the Nile, there to work segregated from the rest of the Egyptians. Among them, Manetho adds, there were some of the learned priests, who had been attacked by leprosy. Then this wise seer Amenôphis was filled with dread of divine wrath against himself and the king if the outrage done to these persons should be discovered; and he added a prediction that certain allies would join the polluted people and would take possession of Egypt for 13 years. Not venturing to make this prophecy himself to the king, he left a full account of it in writing, and then took his own life. The king was filled with despondency. Then Manetho continues as follows (I quote his account *verbatim*): " When the men in the stone-quarries had suffered hardships for a considerable time, they begged the king to assign to them as a dwelling-place and a refuge the deserted city of the Shepherds, Auaris, and he consented. According to religious tradition [2] this city was from earliest times dedicated to Typhôn. Occupying this city and using the region as a base for revolt, they appointed as their leader one of the priests of Hêliopolis called Osarsêph,[3]

---

[1] The quarries of Tura were known to Herodotus (ii. 8, 124) as the source of building-stone for the Pyramids.
On forced labour in quarries in Ptolemaic times, Reinach refers to Bouché-Leclercq, *Histoire des Lagides*, iii. 241 ; iv. 193, 337 f.

[2] *Cf.* Fr. 42, § 78.

[3] Osarsêph, the leader of the movement, is later (§ 250) identified with Moses. The name Osarsêph is a possible Egyptian name: *cf.* Ranke, *Personennamen* I. p. 85, No. 3 *wsîr-sp'*. Wilcken (*Chrestomathie*, i. 1, p. 106) derives the name from a holy animal Sêph ; but the Jews would naturally see in it a form of the name Joseph.

FR. 54   MANETHO

τούτῳ πειθαρχήσοντες[1] ἐν πᾶσιν ὡρκωμότησαν.
239 ὁ δὲ πρῶτον μὲν αὐτοῖς νόμον ἔθετο μήτε προσκυνεῖν θεοὺς μήτε τῶν μάλιστα ἐν Αἰγύπτῳ
θεμιστευομένων ἱερῶν ζῴων ἀπέχεσθαι μηδενός,
πάντα δὲ θύειν καὶ ἀναλοῦν, συνάπτεσθαι δὲ
240 μηδενὶ πλὴν τῶν συνομωμοσμένων.[2] τοιαῦτα δὲ
νομοθετήσας καὶ πλεῖστα ἄλλα μάλιστα τοῖς
Αἰγυπτίοις ἐθισμοῖς ἐναντιούμενα ἐκέλευσεν πολυ-
χειρίᾳ τὰ τῆς πόλεως ἐπισκευάζειν τείχη καὶ πρὸς
πόλεμον ἑτοίμους γίνεσθαι τὸν πρὸς Ἀμένωφιν τὸν
241 βασιλέα. αὐτὸς δέ, προσλαβόμενος μεθ᾿ ἑαυτοῦ
καὶ τῶν ἄλλων ἱερέων καὶ συμμεμιαμμένων τινὰς[3]
ἔπεμψε πρέσβεις πρὸς τοὺς ὑπὸ Τεθμώσεως
ἀπελασθέντας Ποιμένας εἰς πόλιν τὴν καλουμένην
Ἱεροσόλυμα, καὶ τὰ καθ᾿ ἑαυτὸν καὶ τοὺς ἄλλους
τοὺς συνατιμασθέντας δηλώσας ἠξίου συνεπιστρα-
242 τεύειν ὁμοθυμαδὸν ἐπ᾿ Αἴγυπτον. ἐπάξειν[4] μὲν
οὖν αὐτοὺς ἐπηγγείλατο πρῶτον μὲν εἰς Αὔαριν τὴν
προγονικὴν αὐτῶν πατρίδα καὶ τὰ ἐπιτήδεια τοῖς
ὄχλοις παρέξειν ἀφθόνως, ὑπερμαχήσεσθαι δὲ ὅτε
δέοι καὶ ῥᾳδίως ὑποχείριον αὐτοῖς τὴν χώραν ποιή-
243 σειν. οἱ δὲ ὑπερχαρεῖς γενόμενοι πάντες προθύμως
εἰς κ΄ μυριάδας ἀνδρῶν συνεξώρμησαν καὶ μετ᾿

---

[1] *Ed. pr.*: -ήσαντες L.   [2] Niese: συνωμοσμένων L.
[3] τινὰς add. Reinach (*quosdam* Lat.).
[4] ἐπανάξειν conj. Cobet.

---

[1] "Does the author know that the Decalogue begins with an admonition to have no other god but Jehovah ? Or does he recall Greek lists of duties (Xen., *Mem.* iv. 4;

and took an oath of obedience to him in everything. First of all, he made it a law [1] that they should neither worship the gods nor refrain from any of the animals [2] prescribed as especially sacred in Egypt, but should sacrifice and consume all alike, and that they should have intercourse with none save those of their own confederacy. After framing a great number of laws like these, completely opposed to Egyptian custom, he ordered them with their multitude of hands, to repair the walls of the city and make ready for war against King Amenôphis. Then, acting in concert with certain other priests and polluted persons like himself, he sent an embassy to the Shepherds who had been expelled by Tethmôsis,[3] in the city called Jerusalem; and, setting forth the circumstances of himself and his companions in distress, he begged them to unite wholeheartedly in an attack upon Egypt. He offered to conduct them first to their ancestral home at Auaris, to provide their hosts with lavish supplies, to fight on their behalf whenever need arose, and to bring Egypt without difficulty under their sway. Overjoyed at the proposal, all the Shepherds, to the number of 200,000, eagerly set out,

---

19; *Carmen Aureum*, v. 1; *cf.* Dieterich, *Nekyia*, pp. 146 f.) which inculcate reverence for the gods as the first precept ?" (Reinach). Add Isocrates, *Ad Demonicum*, §§ 13, 16, and the *Precepts of Sansnôs* (ii./iii. A.D.), as inscribed in Nubia, *C.I.G.* iii. 5041 (Wilcken, *Chrestomathie*, I. ii. p. 147, No. 116)—the first precept is " Revere the divinity ".

[2] *Cf.* Tac., *Hist.* v. 4: the Jews under Moses sacrificed the ram as if to insult Ammôn, and the bull, because the Egyptians worship Apis. *Cf. O.T. Leviticus* xvi. 3.

[3] Tethmôsis for Amôsis, as in Fr. 50 (§ 94).

Fr. 54 MANETHO

οὐ πολὺ ἧκον εἰς Αὔαριν. Ἀμένωφις δ' ὁ τῶν Αἰγυπτίων βασιλεὺς ὡς ἐπύθετο τὰ κατὰ τὴν ἐνείνων ἔφοδον, οὐ μετρίως συνεχύθη, τῆς παρὰ Ἀμενώφεως τοῦ Παάπιος μνησθεὶς προδηλώσεως. 244 καὶ πρότερον συναγαγὼν πλῆθος Αἰγυπτίων καὶ βουλευσάμενος μετὰ τῶν ἐν τούτοις ἡγεμόνων, τά τε ἱερὰ ζῷα τὰ [πρῶτα]¹ μάλιστα ἐν τοῖς ἱεροῖς τιμώμενα ὡς ἑαυτὸν² μετεπέμψατο, καὶ τοῖς κατὰ μέρος ἱερεῦσι παρήγγελλεν ὡς ἀσφαλέστατα τῶν 245 θεῶν συγκρύψαι τὰ ξόανα. τὸν δὲ υἱὸν Σέθων, τὸν καὶ Ῥαμέσσην ἀπὸ Ῥαψηοῦς τοῦ πατρὸς ὠνομασμένον, πενταέτη ὄντα ἐξέθετο πρὸς τὸν ἑαυτοῦ φίλον. αὐτὸς δὲ διαβὰς ⟨σὺν⟩³ τοῖς ἄλλοις Αἰγυπτίοις, οὖσιν εἰς τριάκοντα μυριάδας ἀνδρῶν μαχιμωτάτων, καὶ τοῖς πολεμίοις ἀπ- 246 αντήσας⁴ οὐ συνέβαλεν, ἀλλὰ μὴ δεῖν⁵ θεομαχεῖν νομίσας παλινδρομήσας ἧκεν εἰς Μέμφιν, ἀναλαβών τε τόν τε Ἆπιν καὶ τὰ ἄλλα τὰ ἐκεῖσε μεταπεμφθέντα ἱερὰ ζῷα, εὐθὺς εἰς Αἰθιοπίαν σὺν ἅπαντι τῷ στόλῳ καὶ πλήθει τῶν Αἰγυπτίων ἀνήχθη· χάριτι γὰρ ἦν αὐτῷ ὑποχείριος ὁ τῶν Αἰθιόπων βασιλεύς. 247 ὃς⁶ ὑποδεξάμενος καὶ τοὺς ὄχλους πάντας ὑπολαβὼν οἷς ἔσχεν ἡ χώρα τῶν πρὸς ἀνθρωπίνην τροφὴν ἐπιτηδείων, καὶ πόλεις καὶ κώμας πρὸς τὴν τῶν

¹ Om. Lat.: bracketed by Bekker.
² Cobet: ὥς γε αὑτὸν L.
³ Conj. Niese (cum aliis Lat.).
⁴ Cobet (occurrens Lat.): ἀπαντήσασιν L.
⁵ Herwerden (cf. § 263): μέλλειν L.
⁶ Niese (after Lat.): ὅθεν L.

and before long arrived at Auaris. When Amenôphis, king of Egypt, learned of their invasion, he was sorely troubled, for he recalled the prediction of Amenôphis, son of Paapis. First, he gathered a multitude of Egyptians ; and having taken counsel with the leading men among them, he summoned to his presence the sacred animals which were held in greatest reverence in the temples, and gave instructions to each group of priests to conceal the images of the gods as securely as possible. As for his five-year-old son Sethôs, also called Ramessês after his grandfather Rapsês,[1] he sent him safely away to his friend.[2] He then crossed the Nile with as many as 300,000 of the bravest warriors of Egypt, and met the enemy. But, instead of joining battle, he decided that he must not fight against the gods, and made a hasty retreat to Memphis. There he took into his charge Apis and the other sacred animals which he had summoned to that place ; and forthwith he set off for Ethiopia[3] with his whole army and the host of Egyptians. The Ethiopian king, who, in gratitude for a service, had become his subject, welcomed him, maintained the whole multitude with such products of the country as were fit for human consumption,

[1] Rapsês : doubtless an error for Rampsês. There is confusion here : the grandfather is Ramessês II. See Meyer (*Aeg. Chron.* p. 91), who considers the words " Sethôs also called " an interpolation (*cf.* § 98), intended to identify a Sethôs son of Amenôphis and a Ramessês son of Amenôphis.
[2] A curious indefiniteness : the reference may be to the king of Ethiopia, mentioned in the next section.
[3] The truth is that Ethiopia (Nubia, Cush) was at that time a province of the kingdom of the Pharaohs.

Fr. 54 MANETHO

πεπρωμένων τρισκαίδεκα ἐτῶν ἀπὸ τῆς ἀρχῆς αὐτοῦ¹ ἔκπτωσιν αὐτάρκεις, οὐχ ἧττον δὲ καὶ στρατόπεδον Αἰθιοπικὸν πρὸς φυλακὴν ἐπέταξε τοῖς παρ' Ἀμενώφεως τοῦ βασιλέως ἐπὶ τῶν ὁρίων τῆς Αἰγύπτου. καὶ τὰ μὲν κατὰ τὴν Αἰθιοπίαν τοιαῦτα· οἱ δὲ Σολυμῖται κατελθόντες σὺν τοῖς μιαροῖς τῶν Αἰγυπτίων οὕτως ἀνοσίως καὶ ‹ὠμῶς›² τοῖς ἀνθρώποις προσηνέχθησαν, ὥστε τὴν τῶν προειρημένων ‹Ποιμένων›³ κράτησιν χρυσὸν φαίνεσθαι τοῖς τότε τὰ τούτων ἀσεβήματα θεωμένοις· καὶ γὰρ οὐ μόνον πόλεις καὶ κώμας ἐνέπρησαν, οὐδὲ ἱεροσυλοῦντες οὐδὲ λυμαινόμενοι ξόανα θεῶν ἠρκοῦντο, ἀλλὰ καὶ τοῖς ἀδύτοις⁴ ὀπτανίοις τῶν σεβαστευομένων ἱερῶν ζῴων χρώμενοι διετέλουν, καὶ θύτας καὶ σφαγεῖς τούτων ἱερεῖς καὶ προφήτας ἠνάγκαζον γίνεσθαι καὶ γυμνοὺς ἐξέβαλλον. λέγεται δὲ ὅτι ‹ὁ›⁵ τὴν πολιτείαν καὶ τοὺς νόμους αὐτοῖς καταβαλόμενος ἱερεύς, τὸ γένος Ἡλιοπολίτης, ὄνομα Ὀσαρσὴφ⁶ ἀπὸ τοῦ ἐν Ἡλιουπόλει θεοῦ Ὀσίρεως, ὡς μετέβη εἰς τοῦτο τὸ γένος, μετετέθη τοὔνομα καὶ προσηγορεύθη Μωυσῆς."

Ἃ μὲν οὖν Αἰγύπτιοι φέρουσι περὶ τῶν Ἰουδαίων ταῦτ' ἐστὶ καὶ ἕτερα πλείονα, ἃ παρίημι

---

¹ + εἰς τὴν L (repeating πρὸς τὴν above): a verb (e.g. παρέσχεν) seems to have dropped out.
² Add. Reinach.   ³ Add. Reinach.
⁴ Bekker: αὐτοῖς L.   ⁵ Cobet: om. L.
⁶ Cf. § 238: Ὀσαρσίφ edd.

---

[1] According to Meyer (*Aeg. Chron.* p. 77), this section with its identification of Osarsêph and Moses is due to an

assigned to them cities and villages sufficient for the destined period of 13 years' banishment from his realm, and especially stationed an Ethiopian army on the frontiers of Egypt to guard King Amenôphis and his followers. Such was the situation in Ethiopia. Meanwhile, the Solymites [or dwellers in Jerusalem] made a descent along with the polluted Egyptians, and treated the people so impiously and savagely that the domination of the Shepherds seemed like a golden age to those who witnessed the present enormities. For not only did they set towns and villages on fire, pillaging the temples and mutilating images of the gods without restraint, but they also made a practice of using the sanctuaries as kitchens to roast the sacred animals which the people worshipped; and they would compel the priests and prophets to sacrifice and butcher the beasts, afterwards casting the men forth naked. It is said that the priest who framed their constitution and their laws was a native of Hêliopolis, named Osarsêph after the god Osiris, worshipped at Hêliopolis; but when he joined this people, he changed his name and was called Moses." [1]

Such, then, are the Egyptian stories about the Jews,[2] together with many other tales which I pass

anti-Semitic commentator on Manetho. It is interesting that Osiris should be thus identified with the mysterious god of the Jews, whose name must not be uttered.

[2] *Cf.* Hecataeus of Abdera (in Diodorus Siculus, xl. 3): the Jews are foreigners expelled from Egypt because of a plague. See Meyer, *Geschichte* [2], ii. 1, p. 424. Hecataeus lived for some time at the court of Ptolemy I. (323-285 B.C.), and used Egyptian sources for his *Aegyptiaca*. *Cf.* Intro. pp. xxvi f.

Fr. 54 MANETHO

συντομίας ἕνεκα. λέγει δὲ ὁ Μανεθὼς πάλιν ὅτι μετὰ ταῦτα ἐπῆλθεν ὁ Ἀμένωφις ἀπὸ Αἰθιοπίας μετὰ μεγάλης δυνάμεως καὶ ὁ υἱὸς αὐτοῦ Ῥάμψης, καὶ αὐτὸς ἔχων δύναμιν, καὶ συμβαλόντες οἱ δύο τοῖς Ποιμέσι καὶ τοῖς μιαροῖς ἐνίκησαν αὐτοὺς καὶ πολλοὺς ἀποκτείναντες ἐδίωξαν αὐτοὺς ἄχρι τῶν 252 ὁρίων τῆς Συρίας. ταῦτα μὲν καὶ τὰ τοιαῦτα Μανεθὼς συνέγραψεν· ὅτι δὲ ληρεῖ καὶ ψεύδεται περιφανῶς ἐπιδείξω, προδιαστειλάμενος ἐκεῖνο, τῶν ὕστερον πρὸς ἄλλους[1] λεχθησομένων ἕνεκα. δέδωκε γὰρ οὗτος ἡμῖν καὶ ὡμολόγηκεν ἐξ ἀρχῆς τὸ[2] μὴ εἶναι τὸ γένος Αἰγυπτίους, ἀλλ' αὐτοὺς ἔξωθεν ἐπελθόντας κρατῆσαι τῆς Αἰγύπτου καὶ πάλιν ἐξ 253 αὐτῆς ἀπελθεῖν. ὅτι δ' οὐκ ἀνεμίχθησαν ἡμῖν ὕστερον τῶν Αἰγυπτίων οἱ τὰ σώματα λελωβημένοι, καὶ ὅτι ἐκ τούτων οὐκ ἦν Μωυσῆς ὁ τὸν λαὸν ἀγαγών, ἀλλὰ πολλαῖς ἐγεγόνει γενεαῖς πρότερον, ταῦτα πειράσομαι διὰ τῶν ὑπ' αὐτοῦ 82 λεγομένων ἐλέγχειν.
254 Πρώτην δὴ τὴν αἰτίαν τοῦ πλάσματος ὑποτίθεται καταγέλαστον. ὁ βασιλεὺς γάρ, φησίν, Ἀμένωφις ἐπεθύμησε τοὺς θεοὺς ἰδεῖν. ποίους; εἰ μὲν τοὺς παρ' αὐτοῖς νενομοθετημένους, τὸν βοῦν καὶ τράγον καὶ κροκοδείλους καὶ κυνοκεφά-
255 λους, ἑώρα. τοὺς οὐρανίους δὲ πῶς ἐδύνατο; καὶ διὰ τί ταύτην ἔσχε τὴν ἐπιθυμίαν; ὅτι νὴ Δία

---

[1] Niese: ἀλλήλους L (alterna gratia Lat.).
[2] Conj. Niese: τε L.

by for brevity's sake. Manetho adds, however, that, at a later date, Amenôphis advanced from Ethiopia with a large army, his son Rampsês also leading a force, and that the two together joined battle with the Shepherds and their polluted allies, and defeated them, killing many and pursuing the others to the frontiers of Syria. This then, with other tales of a like nature, is Manetho's account. Before I give proof that his words are manifest lies and nonsense, I shall mention one particular point, which bears upon my later refutation of other writers. Manetho has made one concession to us. He has admitted that our race was not Egyptian in origin, but came into Egypt from elsewhere, took possession of the land, and afterwards left it. But that we were not, at a later time, mixed up with disease-ravaged Egyptians, and that, so far from being one of these, Moses, the leader of our people, lived many generations earlier, I shall endeavour to prove from Manetho's own statements.

To begin with, the reason which he suggests for his fiction is ridiculous. "King Amenôphis," he says, "conceived a desire to see the gods." Gods indeed! If he means the gods established by their ordinances,—bull, goat, crocodiles, and dog-faced baboons,—he had them before his eyes; and as for the gods of heaven, how could he see them? And why did he conceive this eager desire? Because, by Zeus,[1] before his time another king

[1] A strange expression which seems to belong to an anti-Semitic polemic. In Josephus, c. *Apion.* ii. 263 (a passage about Socrates), νὴ Δία has been restored to the text by Niese's conjecture.

καὶ πρότερος αὐτοῦ βασιλεὺς ἄλλος ἑωράκει. παρ' ἐκείνου τοίνυν ἐπέπυστο ποταποί τινές εἰσι καὶ τίνα πρόπον αὐτοὺς εἶδεν, ὥστε καινῆς αὐτῷ τέχνης οὐκ ἔδει. ἀλλὰ σοφὸς ἦν ὁ μάντις, δι' οὗ τοῦτο κατορθώσειν ὁ βασιλεὺς ὑπελάμβανε. καὶ πῶς οὐ προέγνω τὸ ἀδύνατον αὐτοῦ τῆς ἐπιθυμίας; οὐ γὰρ ἀπέβη. τίνα δὲ καὶ λόγον εἶχε διὰ τοὺς ἠκρωτηριασμένους ἢ λεπρῶντας ἀφανεῖς εἶναι τοὺς θεούς; ὀργίζονται γὰρ ἐπὶ τοῖς ἀσεβήμασιν, οὐκ ἐπὶ τοῖς ἐλαττώμασι τῶν σωμάτων. ὀκτὼ δὲ μυριάδας τῶν λεπρῶν καὶ κακῶς διακειμένων πῶς οἷόν τε μιᾷ σχεδὸν ἡμέρᾳ συλλεγῆναι; πῶς δὲ παρήκουσεν τοῦ μάντεως ὁ βασιλεύς; ὁ μὲν γὰρ αὐτὸν ἐκέλευσεν ἐξορίσαι τῆς Αἰγύπτου τοὺς λελωβημένους, ὁ δ' αὐτοὺς εἰς τὰς λιθοτομίας ἐνέβαλεν, ὥσπερ τῶν ἐργασομένων δεόμενος, ἀλλ' οὐχὶ καθᾶραι τὴν χώραν προαιρούμενος. φησὶ δὲ τὸν μὲν μάντιν αὐτὸν ἀνελεῖν τὴν ὀργὴν τῶν θεῶν προορώμενον καὶ τὰ συμβησόμενα περὶ τὴν Αἴγυπτον, τῷ δὲ βασιλεῖ γεγραμμένην τὴν πρόρρησιν[1] καταλιπεῖν. εἶτα πῶς οὐκ ἐξ ἀρχῆς ὁ μάντις τὸν αὐτοῦ θάνατον προηπίστατο; πῶς δὲ οὐκ εὐθὺς ἀντεῖπεν τῷ βασιλεῖ βουλομένῳ τοὺς θεοὺς ἰδεῖν; πῶς δ' εὔλογος ὁ φόβος τῶν μὴ παρ' αὐτὸν συμβησομένων κακῶν; ἢ τί χεῖρον ἔδει παθεῖν οὗ δρᾶν[2] ἑαυτὸν ἔσπευδεν;

Τὸ δὲ δὴ πάντων εὐηθέστατον ἴδωμεν. πυθό-

---

[1] *Ed. pr.*: πρόσρησιν L.

[2] Herwerden (*quam quod se ipse perimere festinabat* Lat.): οὐδ' ἂν L.

had seen them! From this predecessor, then, he had learned their nature and the manner in which he had seen them, and in consequence he had no need of a new system. Moreover, the prophet by whose aid the king expected to succeed in his endeavour, was a sage. How, then, did he fail to foresee the impossibility of realizing this desire? It did, in fact, come to naught. And what reason had he for ascribing the invisibility of the gods to the presence of cripples or lepers? Divine wrath is due to impious deeds, not to physical deformities. Next, how could 80,000 lepers and invalids be gathered together in practically a single day? And why did the king turn a deaf ear to the prophet? The prophet had bidden him expel the cripples from Egypt, but the king cast them into stone-quarries, as if he needed labourers, not as if his purpose was to purge the land. Manetho says, moreover, that the prophet took his own life, because he foresaw the anger of the gods and the fate in store for Egypt, but left in writing his prediction to the king. Then how was it that the prophet had not from the first foreknowledge of his own death? Why did he not forthwith oppose the king's desire to see the gods? Was it reasonable to be afraid of misfortunes which were not to happen in his time? Or what worse fate could have been his than that which he hastened to inflict upon himself?

But let us now examine [1] the most ridiculous part

---

[1] The passage §§ 260-266 repeats unnecessarily the substance of §§ 237-250: possibly these are extracts from two treatises utilizing the same material.

μενος γὰρ ταῦτα καὶ περὶ τῶν μελλόντων φοβηθείς, τοὺς λελωβημένους ἐκείνους, ὧν αὐτῷ καθαρίσαι[1] προείρητο τὴν Αἴγυπτον, οὐδὲ τότε τῆς χώρας ἐξήλασεν, ἀλλὰ δεηθεῖσιν αὐτοῖς ἔδωκε πόλιν, ὥς φησι, τὴν πάλαι μὲν οἰκηθεῖσαν ὑπὸ τῶν Ποιμένων, 261 Αὔαριν δὲ καλουμένην. εἰς ἣν ἀθροισθέντας αὐτοὺς ἡγεμόνα φησὶν ἐξελέσθαι τῶν ἐξ Ἡλιουπόλεως πάλαι γεγονότων ἱερέων, καὶ τοῦτον αὐτοῖς εἰσηγήσασθαι μήτε θεοὺς προσκυνεῖν μήτε τῶν ἐν[2] Αἰγύπτῳ θρησκευομένων ζῴων ἀπέχεσθαι, πάντα δὲ θύειν καὶ κατεσθίειν, συνάπτεσθαι δὲ μηδενὶ πλὴν τῶν συνομωμοσμένων,[3] ὅρκοις τε τὸ πλῆθος ἐνδησάμενον, ἦ μὴν τούτοις ἐμμενεῖν τοῖς νόμοις, καὶ τειχίσαντα τὴν Αὔαριν πρὸς τὸν βασιλέα 262 πόλεμον ἐξενεγκεῖν. καὶ προστίθησιν ὅτι ἔπεμψεν εἰς Ἱεροσόλυμα παρακαλῶν ἐκείνους αὐτοῖς συμμαχεῖν καὶ δώσειν αὐτοῖς τὴν Αὔαριν ὑπισχνούμενος, εἶναι γὰρ αὐτὴν τοῖς ἐκ τῶν Ἱεροσολύμων ἀφιξομένοις προγονικήν, ἀφ' ἧς ὁρμωμένους αὐτοὺς 263 πᾶσαν τὴν Αἴγυπτον καθέξειν. εἶτα τοὺς μὲν ἐπελθεῖν εἴκοσι στρατοῦ μυριάσι λέγει, τὸν βασιλέα δὲ τῶν Αἰγυπτίων Ἀμένωφιν οὐκ οἰόμενον δεῖν θεομαχεῖν εἰς τὴν Αἰθιοπίαν εὐθὺς ἀποδρᾶναι, τὸν δὲ Ἆπιν καί τινα τῶν ἄλλων ἱερῶν ζῴων παρατεθεικέναι τοῖς ἱερεῦσι διαφυλάττεσθαι κελεύσαντα. 264 εἶτα τοὺς Ἱεροσολυμίτας ἐπελθόντας τάς τε πόλεις ἀνιστάναι καὶ τὰ ἱερὰ κατακαίειν καὶ τοὺς ἱερέας[4]

of the whole story. Although he had learned these facts, and had conceived a dread of the future, the king did not, even then, expel from his land those cripples of whose taint he had previously been bidden to purge Egypt, but instead, at their request, he gave them as their city (Manetho says) the former habitation of the Shepherds, Auaris, as it was called. Here, he adds, they assembled, and selected as their leader a man who had formerly been a priest in Heliopolis. This man (according to Manetho) instructed them not to worship the gods nor to refrain from the animals revered in Egypt, but to sacrifice and devour them all, and to have intercourse with none save those of their own confederacy. Then having bound his followers by oath to abide strictly by these laws, he fortified Auaris and waged war against the king. This leader, Manetho adds, sent to Jerusalem, inviting the people to join in alliance with him, and promising to give them Auaris, which, he reminded them, was the ancestral home of those who would come from Jerusalem, and would serve as a base for their conquest of the whole of Egypt. Then, continues Manetho, they advanced with an army of 200,000 men ; and Amenôphis, king of Egypt, thinking he ought not to fight against the gods, fled straightway into Ethiopia after enjoining that Apis and some of the other sacred animals should be entrusted to the custody of the priests. Thereafter, the men from Jerusalem came on, made desolate the cities, burned down the temples, massacred

---

[1] Cobet : καθαρεῦσαι L.
[3] Niese : συνωμοσμένων L.
[2] Conj. Niese : ἐπ' L.
[4] Bekker : ἱππέας L, Lat.

ἀποσφάττειν, ὅλως τε μηδεμιᾶς ἀπέχεσθαι παρα-
265 νομίας μηδὲ ὠμότητος. ὁ δὲ τὴν πολιτείαν καὶ
τοὺς νόμους αὐτοῖς καταβαλόμενος [1] ἱερεύς, φησίν,
ἦν τὸ γένος Ἡλιοπολίτης, ὄνομα δ᾽ Ὀσαρσὴφ [2]
ἀπὸ τοῦ ἐν Ἡλιουπόλει θεοῦ Ὀσίρεως, μεταθέμενος
266 δὲ Μωυσῆν αὐτὸν προσηγόρευσε. τρισκαιδεκάτῳ
δέ φησιν ἔτει τὸν Ἀμένωφιν,—τοσοῦτον γὰρ αὐτῷ
χρόνον εἶναι τῆς ἐκπτώσεως πεπρωμένον,—ἐξ
Αἰθιοπίας ἐπελθόντα μετὰ πολλῆς στρατιᾶς καὶ
συμβαλόντα τοῖς Ποιμέσι καὶ τοῖς μιαροῖς νικῆσαί
τε τῇ μάχῃ καὶ κτεῖναι πολλοὺς ἐπιδιώξαντα
29 μέχρι τῶν τῆς Συρίας ὅρων.
267 Ἐν τούτοις πάλιν οὐ συνίησιν ἀπιθάνως ψευ-
δόμενος. οἱ γὰρ λεπροὶ καὶ τὸ μετ᾽ αὐτῶν πλῆθος,
εἰ καὶ πρότερον ὠργίζοντο τῷ βασιλεῖ καὶ τοῖς
τὰ περὶ αὐτοὺς πεποιηκόσι κατὰ [τε] [3] τὴν τοῦ
μάντεως προαγόρευσιν, ἀλλ᾽ ὅτε τῶν λιθοτομιῶν
ἐξῆλθον καὶ πόλιν παρ᾽ αὐτοῦ καὶ χώραν ἔλαβον,
πάντως [4] ἂν γεγόνεισαν πρᾳότεροι πρὸς αὐτόν.
268 εἰ δὲ δὴ [5] κἀκεῖνον ἐμίσουν, ἰδίᾳ μὲν ἂν αὐτῷ [6]
ἐπεβούλευον, οὐκ ἂν δὲ πρὸς ἅπαντας ἤραντο
πόλεμον, δῆλον ὅτι πλείστας ἔχοντες συγγενείας
269 τοσοῦτοί γε τὸ πλῆθος ὄντες. ὅμως δὲ καὶ τοῖς
ἀνθρώποις πολεμεῖν διεγνωκότες, οὐκ ἂν εἰς τοὺς
αὐτῶν θεοὺς πολεμεῖν ἐτόλμησαν οὐδ᾽ ὑπεναν-
τιωτάτους ἔθεντο νόμους τοῖς πατρίοις αὐτῶν καὶ
270 οἷς ἐνετράφησαν. δεῖ δὲ ἡμᾶς τῷ Μανεθῷ [7] χάριν

[1] *Ed. pr.*: καταβαλλόμενος L.
[2] Ὀσαρσὶφ *ed. pr.*: Ἀρσὴφ L.
[3] Om. Lat., Bekker. [4] *Ed. pr.*: πάντες L, Lat.
[5] εἰ δ᾽ ἔτι conj. Niese (*porro si adhuc* Lat.).

the priests, and, in short, committed every possible kind of lawlessness and savagery. The priest who framed their constitution and their laws was, according to Manetho, a native of Hêliopolis, Osarsêph by name, after Osiris the god worshipped in Hêliopolis: but he changed his name and called himself Moses. Thirteen years later—this being the destined period of his exile—Amenôphis, according to Manetho, advanced from Ethiopia with a large army, and joining battle with the Shepherds and the polluted people, he defeated them, killing many, after pursuing them to the frontiers of Syria.

Here again Manetho fails to realize the improbability of his lying tale. Even if the lepers and their accompanying horde were previously angry with the king and the others who had treated them thus in obedience to the seer's prediction, certainly when they had left the stone-quarries and received from him a city and land, they would have grown more kindly disposed to him. If indeed they still hated him, they would have plotted against him personally, instead of declaring war against the whole people; for obviously so large a company must have had numerous relatives in Egypt. Notwithstanding, once they had resolved to make war on the Egyptians, they would never have ventured to direct their warfare against their gods, nor would they have framed laws completely opposed to the ancestral code under which they had been brought up. We must, however, be grateful to Manetho for stating that the

⁶ ἂν αὐτῷ ed. pr.: ἄνω (= ἀνθρώπῳ) L: ἂν (alone) conj. Niese: ἂν ἀνθρώπῳ Reinach.
⁷ Niese: Μανέθωνι L.

ἔχειν, ὅτι ταύτης τῆς παρανομίας οὐχὶ τοὺς ἐξ Ἱεροσολύμων ἐλθόντας ἀρχηγοὺς γενέσθαι φησίν, ἀλλ' αὐτοὺς ἐκείνους ὄντας Αἰγυπτίους καὶ τούτων μάλιστα τοὺς ἱερέας ἐπινοῆσαί τε ταῦτα καὶ ὁρκωμοτῆσαι τὸ πλῆθος.

271 Ἐκεῖνο μέντοι πῶς οὐκ ἄλογον, τῶν μὲν οἰκείων αὐτοῖς καὶ τῶν φίλων συναποστῆναι[1] οὐδένα μηδὲ τοῦ πολέμου τὸν κίνδυνον συνάρασθαι, πέμψαι δὲ τοὺς μιαροὺς εἰς Ἱεροσόλυμα καὶ τὴν παρ' ἐκείνων 272 ἐπάγεσθαι συμμαχίαν; ποίας αὐτοῖς φιλίας ἢ τίνος αὐτοῖς οἰκειότητος προϋπηργμένης; τοὐναντίον γὰρ ἦσαν πολέμιοι καὶ τοῖς ἔθεσι[2] πλεῖστον διέφερον. ὁ δέ φησιν εὐθὺς ὑπακοῦσαι τοῖς ὑπισχνουμένοις ὅτι τὴν Αἴγυπτον καθέξουσιν, ὥσπερ αὐτῶν οὐ σφόδρα τῆς χώρας ἐμπείρως ἐχόντων, 273 ἧς βιασθέντες ἐκπεπτώκασιν. εἰ μὲν οὖν ἀπόρως ἢ κακῶς ἔπραττον, ἴσως ἂν καὶ παρεβάλλοντο, πόλιν δὲ κατοικοῦντες εὐδαίμονα καὶ χώραν πολλὴν κρείττω τῆς Αἰγύπτου καρπούμενοι, διὰ τί ποτ' ἂν ἐχθροῖς μὲν πάλαι τὰ δὲ σώματα λελωβημένοις, οὓς μηδὲ τῶν οἰκείων οὐδεὶς ὑπέμενε, τούτοις ἔμελλον παρακινδυνεύσειν βοηθοῦντες; οὐ γὰρ δή γε τὸν γενησόμενον προῄδεσαν δρασμὸν 274 τοῦ βασιλέως· τοὐναντίον γὰρ αὐτὸς εἴρηκεν ὡς

---

[1] Bekker (*consensit* Lat.): συναποστῆσαι L.
[2] Hudson (*moribus* Lat.): ἤθεσι L.

---

[1] In § 245 we are told that Amenôphis himself led his host in this useless march, and that his son was only 5 years old. Only here is Pêlusium mentioned as the destination of the march.

[*Footnote continued on opposite page.*]

authors of this lawlessness were not the newcomers from Jerusalem, but that company of people who were themselves Egyptians, and that it was, above all, their priests who devised the scheme and bound the multitude by oath.

Moreover, how absurd it is to imagine that, while none of their relatives and friends joined in the revolt and shared in the perils of war, these polluted persons sent to Jerusalem and gained allies there! What alliance, what connexion had previously existed between them? Why, on the contrary, they were enemies, and differed widely in customs. Yet Manetho says that they lent a ready ear to the promise that they would occupy Egypt, just as if they were not thoroughly acquainted with the country from which they had been forcibly expelled! Now, if they had been in straitened or unhappy circumstances, they would perhaps have taken the risk; but dwelling, as they did, in a prosperous city and enjoying the fruits of an ample country, superior to Egypt, why ever should they be likely to hazard their lives by succouring their former foes, those maimed cripples, whom none even of their own kinsfolk could endure? For of course they did not foresee that the king would take flight. On the contrary, Manetho has himself stated that the son[1] of

---

Pêlusium, " the celebrated eastern seaport and key to Egypt " (Baedeker[8], pp. 197 f.), the famous frontier fortress, in Ancient Egyptian *Snw*. A scarab of the late Twelfth Dynasty or early Thirteenth, published by Newberry in J. *Eg. Arch.* xviii. (1932), p. 141, shows the place-name written within the fortress-sign. The name Pêlusium is from πηλός " mud ": *cf.* Strabo, 17. 1, 21, for the muddy pools or marshes around Pêlusium.

ὁ παῖς τοῦ Ἀμενώφιος τριάκοντα μυριάδας ἔχων εἰς τὸ Πηλούσιον ὑπηντίαζεν. καὶ τοῦτο μὲν ᾔδεισαν πάντως οἱ παραγινόμενοι, τὴν δὲ μετάνοιαν αὐτοῦ καὶ τὴν φυγὴν πόθεν εἰκάζειν ἔμελλον; 275 ἔπειτα[1] κρατήσαντάς φησι τῆς Αἰγύπτου πολλὰ καὶ δεινὰ δρᾶν τοὺς ἐκ τῶν Ἱεροσολύμων ἐπιστρατεύσαντας, καὶ περὶ τούτων ὀνειδίζει καθάπερ οὐ πολεμίους αὐτοὺς[2] ἐπαγαγὼν ἢ δέον τοῖς ἔξωθεν ἐπικληθεῖσιν ἐγκαλεῖν, ὁπότε ταῦτα πρὸ τῆς ἐκείνων ἀφίξεως ἔπραττον καὶ πράξειν ὠμωμό-276 κεσαν οἱ τὸ γένος Αἰγύπτιοι. ἀλλὰ καὶ χρόνοις ὕστερον Ἀμένωφις ἐπελθὼν ἐνίκησε μάχῃ καὶ κτείνων τοὺς πολεμίους μέχρι τῆς Συρίας ἤλασεν· οὕτω γὰρ παντάπασίν ἐστιν ἡ Αἴγυπτος τοῖς 277 ὁποθενδηποτοῦν ἐπιοῦσιν εὐάλωτος. καίτοι[3] οἱ τότε πολέμῳ κρατοῦντες αὐτήν, ζῆν πυνθανόμενοι τὸν Ἀμένωφιν, οὔτε τὰς ἐκ τῆς Αἰθιοπίας ἐμβολὰς ὠχύρωσαν, πολλὴν εἰς τοῦτο παρασκευὴν ἔχοντες, οὔτε τὴν ἄλλην ἡτοίμασαν δύναμιν. ὁ δὲ καὶ μέχρι τῆς Συρίας ἀναιρῶν, φησίν, αὐτοὺς ἠκολούθησε διὰ τῆς ψάμμου τῆς ἀνύδρου, δῆλον ὅτι οὐ ῥᾴδιον 30 οὐδὲ ἀμαχεὶ στρατοπέδῳ διελθεῖν.

278 Κατὰ μὲν οὖν τὸν Μανεθὼν οὔτε ἐκ τῆς Αἰγύπτου τὸ γένος ἡμῶν ἐστιν οὔτε τῶν ἐκεῖθέν τινες ἀνεμίχθησαν· τῶν γὰρ λεπρῶν καὶ νοσούντων πολλοὺς μὲν εἰκὸς ἐν ταῖς λιθοτομίαις ἀποθανεῖν πολὺν χρόνον ἐκεῖ γενομένους καὶ κακοπαθοῦντας, πολλοὺς δ᾽ ἐν ταῖς μετὰ ταῦτα μάχαις, πλείστους δ᾽ ἐν τῇ τελευταίᾳ καὶ τῇ φυγῇ.

[1] Hudson: εἶτα Niese: *deinde* Lat.: τὰ σιτία L.

Amenôphis marched with 300,000 men to confront them at Pêlusium. This was certainly known to those already present; but how could they possibly guess that he would change his mind and flee? Manetho next says that, after conquering Egypt, the invaders from Jerusalem committed many heinous crimes; and for these he reproaches them, just as if he had not brought them in as enemies, or as if he was bound to accuse allies from abroad of actions which before their arrival native Egyptians were performing and had sworn to perform. But, years later, Amenôphis returned to the attack, conquered the enemy in battle, and drove them, with slaughter, right to Syria. So perfectly easy a prey is Egypt to invaders, no matter whence they come! And yet those who at that time conquered the land, on learning that Amenôphis was alive, neither fortified the passes between it and Ethiopia, although their resources were amply sufficient, nor did they keep the rest of their forces in readiness! Amenôphis, according to Manetho, pursued them with carnage over the sandy desert right to Syria. But obviously it is no easy matter for an army to cross the desert even without fighting.

Thus, according to Manetho, our race is not of Egyptian origin, nor did it receive any admixture of Egyptians. For, naturally, many of the lepers and invalids died in the stone-quarries during their long term of hardship, many others in the subsequent battles, and most of all in the final engagement and the rout.

---

² Reinach : αὐτοῖς L.   ³ Conj. Thackeray : καὶ L.

31
279   Λοιπόν μοι πρὸς αὐτὸν εἰπεῖν περὶ Μωυσέως τοῦτον δὲ τὸν ἄνδρα θαυμαστὸν μὲν Αἰγύπτιοι καὶ θεῖον νομίζουσι, βούλονται δὲ προσποιεῖν αὐτοῖς μετὰ βλασφημίας ἀπιθάνου, λέγοντες Ἡλιοπολίτην εἶναι τῶν ἐκεῖθεν ἱερέων ἕνα διὰ τὴν
280 λέπραν συνεξεληλασμένον. δείκνυται δ' ἐν ταῖς ἀναγραφαῖς ὀκτωκαίδεκα σὺν τοῖς πεντακοσίοις πρότερον ἔτεσι γεγονὼς καὶ τοὺς ἡμετέρους ἐξαγαγὼν ἐκ τῆς Αἰγύπτου πατέρας εἰς τὴν
281 χώραν τὴν νῦν οἰκουμένην ὑφ' ἡμῶν. ὅτι δ' οὐδὲ συμφορᾷ τινι τοιαύτῃ περὶ τὸ σῶμα κεχρημένος ἦν, ἐκ τῶν λεγομένων ὑπ' αὐτοῦ δῆλός ἐστι· τοῖς γὰρ λεπρῶσιν ἀπείρηκε μήτε μένειν ἐν πόλει μήτ' ἐν κώμῃ κατοικεῖν, ἀλλὰ μόνους περιπατεῖν κατεσχισμένους τὰ ἱμάτια, καὶ τὸν ἁψάμενον αὐτῶν
282 ἢ ὁμωρόφιον γενόμενον οὐ καθαρὸν ἡγεῖται. καὶ μὴν κἂν θεραπευθῇ τὸ νόσημα καὶ τὴν αὐτοῦ φύσιν ἀπολάβῃ, προείρηκέν τινας ἁγνείας,[1] καθαρμοὺς πηγαίων ὑδάτων λουτροῖς καὶ ξυρήσεις πάσης τῆς τριχός, πολλάς τε κελεύει καὶ παντοίας ἐπιτελέσαντα θυσίας τότε παρελθεῖν εἰς τὴν
283 ἱερὰν πόλιν. καίτοι[2] τοὐναντίον εἰκὸς ἦν προνοίᾳ τινὶ καὶ φιλανθρωπίᾳ χρήσασθαι τὸν ἐν τῇ συμφορᾷ ταύτῃ γεγονότα πρὸς τοὺς ὁμοίως[3] αὐτῷ δυστυχήσαντας. οὐ μόνον δὲ περὶ τῶν λεπρῶν οὕτως ἐνομοθέτησεν, ἀλλ' οὐδὲ τοῖς καὶ τὸ βραχύτατόν τι τοῦ σώματος ἠκρωτηριασμένοις ἱερᾶσθαι
284 συγκεχώρηκεν, ἀλλ' εἰ καὶ μεταξύ τις ἱερώμενος

---

[1] + καὶ Lat., Reinach.   [2] *Ed. pr.*: καὶ L.
[3] *Ed. pr.*: ὁμοίους L, Lat.

It remains for me to reply to Manetho's statements about Moses. The Egyptians regard him as a wonderful, even a divine being, but wish to claim him as their own by an incredible calumny, alleging that he belonged to Hêliopolis and was dismissed from his priesthood there owing to leprosy. The records, however, show that he lived 518 years [1] earlier, and led our forefathers up out of Egypt to the land which we inhabit at the present time. And that he suffered from no such physical affliction is clear from his own words. He has, in fact, forbidden lepers [2] either to stay in a town or to make their abode in a village; they must go about in solitude, with their garments rent. Anyone who touches them or lives under the same roof with them he considers unclean. Moreover, even if the malady is cured and the leper resumes normal health, Moses has prescribed certain rites of purification—to cleanse himself in a bath of spring-water and to shave off all his hair,—and enjoins the performance of a number of different sacrifices before entrance into the holy city. Yet it would have been natural, on the contrary, for a victim of this scourge to show some consideration and kindly feeling for those who shared the same misfortune. It was not only about lepers that he framed such laws: those who had even the slightest mutilation of the body were disqualified for the priesthood; [3] and if a priest in the course of his ministry met with an

---

[1] 518 years. See n. on § 230.
[2] For the laws of leprosy, here summarized, see *O.T. Leviticus* xiii. (especially 45 f.) and xiv.
[3] *Cf. Leviticus* xxi. 17-23 (exclusion from the priesthood of anyone " that hath a blemish ").

Fr. 54 MANETHO

τοιαύτῃ χρήσαιτο συμφορᾷ, τὴν τιμὴν αὐτὸν
285 ἀφείλετο. πῶς οὖν εἰκὸς ἐκεῖνον¹ ταῦτα νομο-
θετεῖν ἀνοήτως ⟨ἢ τοὺς⟩² ἀπὸ τοιούτων συμ-
φορῶν συνειλεγμένους προσέσθαι³ καθ' ἑαυτῶν εἰς
286 ὄνειδός τε καὶ βλάβην νόμους συντιθεμένους; ἀλλὰ
μὴν καὶ τοὔνομα λίαν ἀπιθάνως μετατέθεικεν·
Ὀσαρσὴφ⁴ γάρ, φησίν, ἐκαλεῖτο. τοῦτο μὲν οὖν
εἰς τὴν μετάθεσιν οὐκ ἐναρμόζει, τὸ δ' ἀληθὲς
ὄνομα δηλοῖ τὸν ἐκ τοῦ ὕδατος σωθέντα [Μωσῆν]·⁵
τὸ γὰρ ὕδωρ οἱ Αἰγύπτιοι μῶϋ καλοῦσιν.
287 Ἱκανῶς οὖν γεγονέναι νομίζω κατάδηλον⁶ ὅτι
Μανεθώς, ἕως μὲν ἠκολούθει ταῖς ἀρχαίαις ἀναγραφαῖς, οὐ πολὺ τῆς ἀληθείας διημάρτανεν, ἐπὶ
δὲ τοὺς ἀδεσπότους μύθους τραπόμενος ἢ συνέθη-
κεν αὐτοὺς ἀπιθάνως ἤ τισι τῶν πρὸς ἀπέχθειαν
εἰρηκότων ἐπίστευσεν.

¹ ἢ 'κεῖνον Niese. ² Add. Niese.
³ Niese: προέσθαι L. ⁴ Ed. pr.: Ὀαρσὴφ L.
⁵ Bracketed as a gloss (Niese).
⁶ Bekker: καὶ δῆλον δ' L (δ' om. ed. pr.).

---

[1] The same etymology (with the necessary addition that ὑσῆς means " saved ") recurs in Josephus, *Antiq.* ii. 228: cf. Philo, *De Vita Moysis*, i. 4, § 17. There is a word in Ancient Egyptian, *mw*, meaning " water," but the connexion with the name Moses is hypothetical. Similar forms appear as personal names in Pharaonic times, *e.g.*

accident of this nature, he was deprived of his office. How improbable, then, that Moses should be so foolish as to frame these laws, or that men brought together by such misfortunes should approve of legislation against themselves, to their own shame and injury! But, further, the name, too, has been transformed in an extremely improbable way. According to Manetho, Moses was called Osarsêph. These names, however, are not interchangeable: the true name means "one saved out of the water," for water is called "mō-y" by the Egyptians.[1]

It is now, therefore, sufficiently obvious, I think, that, so long as Manetho followed the ancient records, he did not stray far from the truth; but when he turned to unauthorized legends, he either combined them in an improbable form or else gave credence to certain prejudiced informants.

Ms. from the Old Kingdom, *Ms* (very common) from the New Kingdom. In *Exodus* ii. 10 "Moses" is "drawn out" (Hebr. *mashah*) of the water—a derivation "hardly meant to be taken seriously" (T. H. Robinson, in Oesterley and Robinson, *History of Israel*, I. p. 81).
See further Alan H. Gardiner, ' The Egyptian Origin of some English Personal Names,' in *Journ. of Amer. Orient. Soc.* 56 (1936), pp. 192-4. Gardiner points out (p. 195, n. 28) that ὑσῆς (mentioned above) is clearly a perversion of ασιης [or ἐσιῆς, = Egyptian *ḥsy*, " praised," LS⁹], the Greek equivalent of the Coptic *hasie*, " favoured"; but an Egyptian became " favoured " by the fact of being drowned, not by being saved from drowning.

Fr. 55. Syncellus, p. 134. ΚΑΤΑ ΑΦΡΙΚΑΝΟΝ.

Ἐννεακαιδεκάτη δυναστεία βασιλέων ζ'[1] Διοσπολιτῶν.

α' Σέθως, ἔτη να'.
β' Ῥαψάκης, ἔτη ξα'.[2]
γ' Ἀμμενέφθης, ἔτη κ'.
δ' Ῥαμεσσῆς, ἔτη ξ'.
ε' Ἀμμενεμνῆς, ἔτη ε'.
ϛ' Θούωρις, ὁ παρ' Ὁμήρῳ[3] καλούμενος Πόλυβος, Ἀλκάνδρας ἀνήρ, ἐφ' οὗ[4] τὸ Ἴλιον ἑάλω, ἔτη ζ'.

Ὁμοῦ, ἔτη σθ'.

[1] MSS.: ϛ' Müller, who explains the error as due to someone who thought that Ἀλκάνδρας ἀνήρ denoted a seventh king.
[2] ξϛ' Müller.   [3] *Odyssey*, iv. 126.
[4] m.: ζ' Ἀλκάνδρος ἀνήρ, ἐφ' οὗ MSS.

---

[1] Dynasty XIX.: c. 1310-1200 B.C. The lists given by Africanus and Eusebius for Dynasty XIX. are in very bad confusion. Armaïs (Haremhab) should begin the line, which Meyer gives as follows :—
Haremhab : Ramessês I.: Sethôs I.: Ramessês II. (the Louis Quatorze of Egyptian history : 67 years, see Breasted, *Anc. Rec.* iv. § 471 ; *C.A.H.* ii. pp. 139 ff.) : Merneptah : Amenmesês : Merneptah II. Siptah : Sethôs II.: Ramessês Siptah : <Arsu the Syrian>.
W. Struve (*Die Ära ἀπὸ Μενόφρεως und die XIX. Dynastie Manethos*, in *Zeitschr. für äg. Sprache*, Bd. 63 (1928), pp. 45-50) gives a revised sequence with additional identifications : (1) Harmaïs (Haremhab), (2) Ramessês I., (3) Amenôphath (Seti I. Merneptah), (4) Sesôs (Struve's emendation for Sethôs), also called Ramessês Miamoun

AEGYPTIACA (EPITOME) Fr. 55

Dynasty XIX.

Fr. 55 (*from Syncellus*). According to Africanus.

The Nineteenth Dynasty [1] consisted of seven (six) kings of Diospolis.
1. Sethôs, for 51 years.
2. Rapsacês, for 61 (66) years.
3. Ammenephthês, for 20 years.
4. Ramessês, for 60 years.
5. Ammenemnês, for 5 years.
6. Thuôris, who in Homer is called Polybus, husband of Aleandra, and in whose time Troy was taken,[2] reigned for 7 years.

Total, 209 years.

(Ramessês II. Seso), (5) Amenephthês (Merneptah), (6) [Amenophthês or Menophthês, emended from the form Menophrês in Theon of Alexandria], (Seti II. Merneptah), (7) Ramessês III. Siptah, (8) Ammenemes (Amenmeses), (9) Thuôris or Thuôsris, also called Siphthas. *Cf.* Petrie, *History of Egypt*, iii. pp. 120 ff. Struve points also to a new Sôthis date, 1318 B.C., in the reign of Seti I. (according to Petrie's chronology, 1326-1300 B.C.).

² The Fall of Troy was traditionally dated 1183 B.C.: *cf.* p. 107 n. 3.

In Homer, *Odyssey*, iv. 126, a golden distaff and a silver work-basket with wheels beneath and golden rims,— treasures in the palace of Menelaus at Sparta,—are described as gifts to Helen from " Alcandrê, the wife of Polybus who dwelt in Egyptian Thebes where the amplest store of wealth is laid up in men's houses "; while to Menelaus himself Polybus had given two silver baths, two tripods, and ten talents of gold. See W. H. D. Rouse, *The Story of Odysseus*, 1937, p. 56: " Polybos was a great nobleman in the Egyptian Thebes, with a palace full of treasures ".

FR. 55, 56   MANETHO

Ἐπὶ τὸ αὐτὸ δευτέρου τόμου Μανεθῶ βασιλεῖς
μςʹ, ἔτη ͵βρκαʹ.

Fr. 56 (a).   Syncellus, p. 136.   ΚΑΤΑ ΕΥΣΕΒΙΟΝ

Ἐννεακαιδεκάτη δυναστεία βασιλέων εʹ Διοσπολιτῶν.

αʹ Σέθως, ἔτη νεʹ.
βʹ Ῥαμψής, ἔτη ξςʹ.
γʹ Ἀμμενεφθίς, ἔτη μʹ.
δʹ Ἀμμενέμης, ἔτη κςʹ.
εʹ Θούωρις, ὁ παρ' Ὁμήρῳ καλούμενος Πόλυβος, Ἀλκάνδρας ἀνήρ, ἐφ' οὗ τὸ Ἴλιον ἑάλω, ἔτη ζʹ.

Ὁμοῦ, ἔτη ρμδʹ.

Ἐπὶ τὸ αὐτὸ βʹ τόμου Μανεθῶ βασιλέων μβʹ
ἔτη ͵αρκαʹ.[1]

(b) EUSEBIUS, Chronica I. (Armenian Version),
p. 102.

Nona decima dynastia Diospolitarum regum V.
Sethos, annis LV.
Rampses, annis LXVI.
Amenephthis, annis VIII.
Ammenemes, annis XXVI.

[1] ͵βρκαʹ corr. Müller.

AEGYPTIACA (EPITOME) Fr. 55, 56

Sum total in the Second Book of Manetho, ninety-six kings, for 2121 years.[1]

Fr. 56 (a) (*from Syncellus*). ACCORDING TO EUSEBIUS.

The Nineteenth Dynasty consisted of five kings of Diospolis.
1. Sethôs, for 55 years.
2. Rampsês, for 66 years.
3. Ammenephthis, for 40 years.
4. Ammenemês, for 26 years.
5. Thuôris, who in Homer is called Polybus, husband of Aleandra, and in whose reign Troy was taken, reigned for 7 years.

Total, 194 years.
Sum total in the Second Book of Manetho, for ninety-two kings, 1121 (2121) years.

(b) ARMENIAN VERSION OF EUSEBIUS.

The Nineteenth Dynasty consisted of five kings of Diospolis.
1. Sethos, for 55 years.
2. Rampses, for 66 years.
3. Amenephthis, for 8 years.
4. Ammenemes, for 26 years.

---

[1] For the corrected total of Book II., see Fr. 4, n. 4 (246 or 289 kings for 2221 years). The wide difference between the number of kings (96 or 92 as compared with 246 or 289) is puzzling: Meyer conjectures that about 150 or 193 of the larger numbers were ephemeral or co-regents.

Fr. 56, 57   MANETHO

Thuoris, ab Homero dictus Polybus, vir strenuus et fortissimus,[1] cuius aetate Ilium captum est, annis VII.

Summa annorum CLXXXXIV.

Manethonis libro secundo conflatur summa LXXXXII regum, annorum MMCXXI.

ΤΟΜΟΣ ΤΡΙΤΟΣ

Fr. 57 (a).   *Syncellus*, p. 137.

ΚΑΤΑ ΑΦΡΙΚΑΝΟΝ.

Τρίτου τόμου Μανεθῶ.

Εἰκοστὴ δυναστεία βασιλέων Διοσπολιτῶν ιβ', οἳ ἐβασίλευσαν ἔτη ρλε'.

(b) *Syncellus*, p. 139.   ΚΑΤΑ ΕΥΣΕΒΙΟΝ.

Τρίτου τόμου Μανεθῶ.

Εἰκοστὴ δυναστεία βασιλέων Διοσπολιτῶν ιβ', οἳ ἐβασίλευσαν ἔτη ροη'.

[1] *I.e.* ἀνὴρ Ἀλκάνδρας Müller.

---

[1] Dynasty XX. c. 1200-1090 B.C.
Setnakht: Ramessês III. c. 1200-1168: Ramessês IV.-XI. c. 1168-1090. Manetho's 12 kings probably included

AEGYPTIACA (EPITOME) Fr. 56, 57

5. Thuoris, by Homer called the active and gallant Polybus, in whose time Troy was taken, reigned for 7 years.

Total, 194 years.

In the Second Book of Manetho there is a total of ninety-two kings, reigning for 2121 years.

BOOK III.

Dynasty XX.

Fr. 57 (a) (*from Syncellus*). According to Africanus.

From the Third Book of Manetho.
The Twentieth Dynasty [1] consisted of twelve kings of Diospolis, who reigned for 135 years.

(b) According to Eusebius.

From the Third Book of Manetho.
The Twentieth Dynasty consisted of twelve kings of Diospolis, who reigned for 178 years.

Ramessês XII. and Herihor. The Great Papyrus Harris (time of Ramessês III.) describes the anarchy between Dynasties XIX. and XX.: see Breasted, *Anc. Rec.* iv. § 398.

A revised list of Dynasty XX. is given by Newberry in Elliot Smith and Warren Dawson, *Egyptian Mummies*, 1924 : see also T. E. Peet in *J. of Eg. Arch.* xiv. (1928), pp. 52 f.

Fr. 57, 58   MANETHO

(c) Eusebius, *Chronica* I. (Armenian Version),
p. 103.

E Manethonis tertio libro.
Vicesima dynastia Diospolitanorum regum XII,
qui imperaverunt annis CLXXII.

Fr. 58.   Syncellus, p. 137.   ΚΑΤΑ ΑΦΡΙΚΑΝΟΝ.

Πρώτη καὶ εἰκοστὴ δυναστεία βασιλέων Τανιτῶν ζ'.

α' Σμενδῆς, ἔτη κϛ'.
β' Ψουσέννης,[1] ἔτη μϛ'.
γ' Νεφερχερής,[2] ἔτη δ'.
δ' Ἀμενωφθίς, ἔτη θ'.
ε' Ὀσοχώρ, ἔτη ϛ'.
ϛ' Ψιναχῆς, ἔτη θ'.
ζ' Ψουσέννης,[3] ἔτη ιδ'.
Ὁμοῦ, ἔτη ρλ'.

[1] Ψουσένης A.   [2] Νεφελχερής MSS.   [3] Σουσέννης A.

---

[1] Dynasty XXI., resident at Tanis, c. 1090-c. 950 B.C. (a dark period in Egyptian history). For identifications with monumental and other evidence see Meyer, *Geschichte*[2], ii. 2, p. 20 n. This Tanite Dynasty overlapped with the Theban Dynasty XX.: see the Report of Wenamon, Breasted, *Anc. Rec.* iv. §§ 557-591; *C.A.H.* ii. pp. 192 ff.

AEGYPTIACA (EPITOME) Fr. 57, 58

(c) ARMENIAN VERSION OF EUSEBIUS.

From the Third Book of Manetho.
The Twentieth Dynasty consisted of twelve kings of Diospolis, who reigned for 172 years.

DYNASTY XXI.

Fr. 58 (*from Syncellus*). ACCORDING TO AFRICANUS.

The Twenty-first Dynasty [1] consisted of seven kings of Tanis.

1. Smendês,[2] for 26 years.
2. Psusen(n)ês [I.],[3] for 46 years.
3. Nephercherês (Nephelcherês), for 4 years.
4. Amenôphthis, for 9 years.
5. Osochôr, for 6 years.
6. Psinachês, for 9 years.
7. Psusennês [II.] (Susennês), for 14 years.

Total, 130 years.[4]

[2] For Smendês or Nesbenebded, a local noble of Tanis, who seized the whole Delta and made himself king of Lower Egypt, see *C.A.H.* ii. p. 191; iii. pp. 253 f.

[3] In Egyptian, Psusennês is Psukhe'mnê, "the star appearing in Thebes". In 1939-40 tombs of certain kings of Dynasties XXI. and XXII. were excavated by P. Montet at Tanis, the most valuable being the intact tomb of Psusennês I., with its rich funerary equipment: in several chambers sarcophagi, vases of many kinds, and jewels were found, including the funerary outfit of Amenôphthis (Amon-em-apt, son of Psusennês I.) and the silver sarcophagus of a certain Sesonchôsis (not the first king of Dynasty XXII.), (*Ann. Serv. Antiq.*, tt. xxxix. f., 1939-40).

[4] Actual total of items, 114 years. Eusebius is probably correct with 41 years for 2nd king and 35 years for 7th (Meyer).

Fr. 59   MANETHO

Fr. 59 (a).   Syncellus, p. 139.   ΚΑΤΑ ΕΥΣΕΒΙΟΝ.

Εἰκοστὴ πρώτη δυναστεία βασιλέων Τανιτῶν ἑπτά.

α' Σμένδις, ἔτη κϛ'.
β' Ψουσέννης, ἔτη μα'.
γ' Νεφερχερής, ἔτη δ'.
δ' Ἀμενωφθίς, ἔτη θ'.
ε' Ὀσοχώρ, ἔτη ϛ'.
ϛ' Ψιναχῆς, ἔτη θ'.
ζ' Ψουσέννης, ἔτη λε'.

Ὁμοῦ, ἔτη ρλ'.

(b) EUSEBIUS, *Chronica* I. (Armenian Version),
p. 103.

Vicesima prima dynastia Tanitarum regum VII.

Smendis, annis XXVI.
Psusennes, annis XLI.
Nephercheres, annis IV.
Amenophthis, annis IX.
Osochor, annis VI.
Psinnaches, annis IX.
Psusennes, annis XXXV.

Summa annorum est CXXX.

AEGYPTIACA (EPITOME)   Fr. 59

Fr. 59 (a) (*from Syncellus*).   ACCORDING TO
EUSEBIUS.

The Twenty-first Dynasty consisted of seven kings of Tanis.

1. Smendis, for 26 years.
2. Psusennês, for 41 years.
3. Nephercherês, for 4 years.
4. Amenôphthis, for 9 years.
5. Osochôr, for 6 years.
6. Psinachês, for 9 years.
7. Psusennês, for 35 years.

Total, 130 years.

(b) ARMENIAN VERSION OF EUSEBIUS.

The Twenty-first Dynasty consisted of seven kings of Tanis.

1. Smendis, for 26 years.
2. Psusennês, for 41 years.
3. Nephercherês, for 4 years.
4. Amenôphthis, for 9 years.
5. Osochôr, for 6 years.
6. Psinnaches, for 9 years.
7. Psusennes, for 35 years.

Total, 130 years.

Fr. 60. Syncellus, p. 137. ΚΑΤΑ ΑΦΡΙΚΑΝΟΝ

Εἰκοστὴ δευτέρα δυναστεία Βουβαστιτῶν βασιλέων θ'.

α' Σέσωγχις,¹ ἔτη κα'.
β' Ὀσορθών,² ἔτη ιε'.
γ' δ' ε' Ἄλλοι τρεῖς, ἔτη κε'.³
ς' Τακέλωθις, ἔτη ιγ'.
ζ' η' θ' Ἄλλοι τρεῖς, ἔτη μβ'.
Ὁμοῦ, ἔτη ρκ'.

Fr. 61 (a). Syncellus, p. 139. ΚΑΤΑ ΕΥΣΕΒΙΟΝ.

Εἰκοστὴ δευτέρα δυναστεία Βουβαστιτῶν βασιλέων τριῶν.

α' Σεσώγχωσις,⁴ ἔτη κα'.
β' Ὀσορθών, ἔτη ιε'.
γ' Τακέλωθις, ἔτη ιγ'.
Ὁμοῦ ἔτη μθ'.

¹ B: Σέσογχις A. ² B: Ὀσωρθών A.
³ κθ' Boeckh.   ⁴ Σεσόγχωσις A.

---

[1] Dynasty XXII. c. 950–c. 730 B.C., kings of Libyan origin resident at Bubastis. For identifications with the monumental and other evidence see Meyer, *Geschichte*², ii. 2,

AEGYPTIACA (EPITOME) Fr. 60, 61

Dynasty XXII.

Fr. 60 (*from Syncellus*). According to Africanus.

The Twenty-second Dynasty [1] consisted of nine kings of Bubastus.
1. Sesônchis, for 21 years.
2. Osorthôn,[2] for 15 years.
3, 4, 5. Three other kings, for 25 [29] years.
6. Takelôthis, for 13 years.
7, 8, 9. Three other kings, for 42 years.
Total, 120 years.[3]

Fr. 61 (a) (*from Syncellus*). According to Eusebius.

The Twenty-second Dynasty consisted of three kings of Bubastus.
1. Sesônchôsis, for 21 years.
2. Osorthôn, for 15 years.
3. Takelôthis, for 13 years.
Total, 49 years.

p. 58. The first king, Sesonchôsis (Shishak, *O.T. 1 Kings* xiv. 25, *2 Chron.* xii.) overthrew the Tanites c. 940 B.C. About 930 B.C. he captured Jerusalem and plundered the Temple of Solomon: see Peet, *Egypt and the Old Testament*, 1922, pp. 158 ff. Albright (*The Archaeology of Palestine and the Bible*², 1932-3, p. 199), dates the conquest of Judah by Shishak between 924 and 917 B.C.

² The name Osorthôn is another form of Osorchô (Dynasty XXIII. No. 2—Africanus), the Egyptian Osorkon.

³ Actual total of items, 116 years.

Fr. 61, 62   MANETHO

(b) EUSEBIUS, *Chronica* I. (Armenian Version),
p. 103.

Vicesima secunda dynastia Bubastitarum regum III.

Sesonchosis, annis XXI.
Osorthon, annis XV.
Tacelothis, annis XIII.
Summa annorum XLIX.

Fr. 62. *Syncellus*, p. 138. ΚΑΤΑ ΑΦΡΙΚΑΝΟΝ.

Τρίτη καὶ εἰκοστὴ δυναστεία Τανιτῶν βασιλέων δ'.

α' Πετουβάτης, ἔτη μ', ἐφ' οὗ Ὀλυμπιὰς ἤχθη πρώτη.
β' Ὀσορχώ, ἔτη η', ὃν Ἡρακλέα Αἰγύπτιοι καλοῦσι.
γ' Ψαμμοῦς, ἔτη ι'.
δ' Ζήτ, ἔτη λα'.[1]
Ὁμοῦ, ἔτη πθ'.

[1] λδ' B.

---

[1] Osorthôs (Aueber, Karst).
[2] Dynasty XXIII., resident at Tanis: the records of these kings (dated by Breasted 745-718 B.C.) are much confused. The name Petubatês (see Fr. 63 for the usual Grecized form Petubastis) represents the Egyptian Pedibaste. For King Osorcho (Osorkon III.) see the *stele* of Piankhi, king of Ethiopia, whose vassal Osorkon became (Breasted, *Anc. Rec.* iv. §§ 807, 811, 872, 878). Psammûs has not been identified.

AEGYPTIACA (EPITOME) Fr. 61, 62

(b) Armenian Version of Eusebius.

The Twenty-second Dynasty consisted of three kings of Bubastus.
1. Sesônchôsis, for 21 years.
2. Osorthôn,[1] for 15 years.
3. Tacelôthis, for 13 years.

Total, 49 years.

Dynasty XXIII.

Fr. 62 (*from Syncellus*). According to Africanus.

The Twenty-third Dynasty[2] consisted of four kings of Tanis.
1. Petubatês, for 40 years: in his reign the Olympic festival[3] was first celebrated.
2. Osorchô, for 8 years: the Egyptians call him Hêraclês.*
3. Psammûs, for 10 years.
4. Zêt,[4] for 31 years (34).

Total, 89 years.

---

[3] The date of the first Olympic festival was conventionally fixed at 776-775 B.C.

* See G. A. Wainwright, *Sky-Religion*, pp. 35 f.

[4] The fact that the name Zêt, occurring in Africanus alone, is wrapped in obscurity, has led Flinders Petrie to suggest ("The Mysterious Zêt" in *Ancient Egypt*, 1914, p. 32) that the three Greek letters are a contraction for ζητεῖται or other word connected with ζητέω, meaning "A question (remains)," or "Query, about 31 years": for 31 years at this time no single ruler seemed to be predominant, and further search was needed to settle who should be entered as the king of Egypt. "Zêt." is found in wall-inscriptions at Pompeii: see Diehl, *Pompeianische Wandinschriften*, No. 682. The next inscription, No. 683, gives "Zêtêma" in full: a riddle follows.

Fr. 63 (a). *Syncellus*, p. 140. ΚΑΤΑ ΕΥΣΕΒΙΟΝ.

Εἰκοστὴ τρίτη δυναστεία Τανιτῶν βασιλέων τριῶν.

α´ Πετουβάστις, ἔτη κε´.
β´ Ὀσορθών, ἔτη θ´, ὃν Ἡρακλέα Αἰγύπτιοι ἐκάλεσαν.
γ´ Ψαμμοῦς, ἔτη ι´.
Ὁμοῦ, ἔτη μδ´.

(b) EUSEBIUS, *Chronica* I. (Armenian Version), p. 103.

Vicesima tertia dynastia Tanitarum regum III.

Petubastis, annis XXV.

Deinde Osorthon, quem Aegyptii Herculem nuncupaverunt, annis IX.[1]

Psammus,[2] annis X.

Summa annorum XLIV.

---

[1] annis IX. (Aucher).
[2] Phramus (Petermann): Psamus (Aucher, Karst).

AEGYPTIACA (EPITOME) Fr. 63

Fr. 63 (a) (*from Syncellus*). ACCORDING TO EUSEBIUS.

The Twenty-third Dynasty consisted of three kings of Tanis.
1. Petubastis,[1] for 25 years.
2. Osorthôn, for 9 years: the Egyptians called him Hêraclês.
3. Psammûs, for 10 years.

Total, 44 years.

(b) ARMENIAN VERSION OF EUSEBIUS.

The Twenty-third Dynasty consisted of three kings of Tanis.
1. Petubastis, for 25 years.
2. Osorthon, whom the Egyptians named Hercules: for 9 years.
3. Psammus, for 10 years.

Total, 44 years.

[1] For a demotic romance of the time of Petubastis in one of the Rainer Papyri, see Krall in *Vienna Oriental Journal*, xvii. (1903), 1: it is also found in papyri of Paris and Strassburg. Parallels may be drawn between this romance and Manetho; *cf.* Spiegelberg, *Der Sagenkreis des Königs Petubastis* (Leipzig, 1910), pp. 8 f.

Fr. 64. Syncellus, p. 138. ΚΑΤΑ ΑΦΡΙΚΑΝΟΝ.

Τετάρτη καὶ εἰκοστὴ δυναστεία.

Βόχχωρις Σαΐτης, ἔτη ϛ', ἐφ' οὗ ἀρνίον ἐφθέγξατο . . . ἔτη πμη'.

Fr. 65 (a). Syncellus, p. 140. ΚΑΤΑ ΕΥΣΕΒΙΟΝ.

Εἰκοστὴ τετάρτη δυναστεία.

Βόχχωρις Σαΐτης, ἔτη μδ', ἐφ' οὗ ἀρνίον ἐφθέγξατο. Ὁμοῦ, ἔτη μδ'.

---

[1] Dynasty XXIV., c. 720–c. 715 B.C. Before Bocchoris, his father Tefnachte of Saïs (Tnephachthus in Diodorus Siculus, i. 45, 2) became the most powerful among the chiefs of the Delta (c. 730–720 B.C.).

For King Bocchoris see Alexandre Moret, *De Bocchori Rege*, 1903. *Cf*. Diodorus Siculus, i. 65, 79, 1 (law of contract: Bocchoris legislated for commerce), and 94, 5. See Breasted, *Anc. Rec.* iv. § 884: the only extant monuments of King Bocchoris are a few Serapeum *stelae* and a wall inscription, which record the burial of an Apis in the sixth year of his reign.

[2] See especially the demotic story (8 B.C.) of the prophetic lamb, quoted by Krall in *Festgaben für Büdinger*, pp. 3-11 (Innsbruck, 1898): the lamb prophesied the conquest and enslavement of Egypt by Assyria, and the removal of her gods to Nineveh. *Cf*. Aelian, *De Nat. Anim.* xii. 3, and Manetho, Fr. 54, §§ 232 ff. A reference to Manetho's description of the oracular lamb is preserved in Pseudo-Plutarch, *De proverbiis Alexandrinorum* (Crusius, 1887), No. 21, τὸ ἀρνίον σοι λελάληκεν. Αἰγύπτιοι τοῦτο ἀνέγραψαν ὡς ἀνθρωπείᾳ φωνῇ λαλῆσαν (or, as in Suidas, ἐν Αἰγύπτῳ, ὥς φασιν, ἀνθρωπείᾳ φωνῇ ἐλάλησεν). εὑρέθη δὲ ἔχον

AEGYPTIACA (EPITOME) Fr. 64, 65

Dynasty XXIV.

Fr. 64 (*from Syncellus*). According to Africanus.

The Twenty-fourth Dynasty.[1]
Bochchôris of Saïs, for 6 years: in his reign a lamb[2] spoke[3] . . . 990 years.

Fr. 65 (a) (*from Syncellus*). According to Eusebius.

The Twenty-fourth Dynasty.

Bochchôris of Saïs, for 44 years: in his reign a lamb spoke. Total, 44 years.[4]

βασίλειον δράκοντα ἐπὶ τῆς κεφαλῆς αὐτοῦ πτερωτόν, (Suidas adds, ἔχοντα μῆκος πήχεων δ'), καὶ τῶν βασιλέων τινὶ λελάληκε τὰ μέλλοντα. ("The lamb has spoken to you. Egyptians have recorded a lamb speaking with a human voice [or, in Egypt, they say, a lamb spoke with a human voice]. It was found to have upon its head a royal winged serpent [4 cubits in length]; and it foretold the future to one of the kings.") See Meyer, *Ein neues Bruchstück Manethos über das Lamm des Bokchoris* in *Zeitschr. für Ägypt. Sprache*, xlvi. (1910), pp. 135 f.: he points out the Egyptian character of the description—the royal *uraeus*, four cubits long, with ostrich feathers on both sides. *Cf.* Weill, *La fin du moyen empire égyptien*, pp. 116, 622.

[3] Here some essential words have been omitted from the text.

[4] Contrast the " 6 years " assigned to Bocchoris by Africanus (Fr. 64): it is suspicious that Eusebius should give 44 years for each of Dynasties XXIII., XXIV., and XXV.

Fr. 65, 66, 67   MANETHO

(b) EUSEBIUS, *Chronica* I. (Armenian Version),
p. 104.

Vicesima quarta dynastia.

Bocchoris Saïtes, annis XLIV, sub quo agnus locutus est.

Fr. 66. *Syncellus*, p. 138. ΚΑΤΑ ΑΦΡΙΚΑΝΟΝ.

Πέμπτη καὶ εἰκοστὴ δυναστεία Αἰθιόπων βασιλέων τριῶν.

α′ Σαβάκων, ὃς αἰχμάλωτον Βόχχωριν ἑλὼν
   ἔκαυσε ζῶντα, καὶ ἐβασίλευσεν ἔτη η′.
β′ Σεβιχὼς υἱός, ἔτη ιδ′.
γ′ Τάρκος, ἔτη ιη′.
Ὁμοῦ, ἔτη μ′.

Fr. 67 (a). *Syncellus*, p. 140. ΚΑΤΑ ΕΥΣΕΒΙΟΝ.

Εἰκοστὴ πέμπτη δυναστεία Αἰθιόπων βασιλέων τριῶν.

α′ Σαβάκων, ὃς αἰχμάλωτον Βόχχωριν ἑλὼν
   ἔκαυσε ζῶντα, καὶ ἐβασίλευσεν ἔτη ιβ′.
β′ Σεβιχὼς υἱός, ἔτη ιβ′.
γ′ Ταρακός, ἔτη κ′.
Ὁμοῦ, ἔτη μδ′.

---

[1] Dynasty XXV. (Ethiopian), c. 715-663 B.C.: the three kings are Shabaka, Shabataka, and Taharka.

[2] *Cf.* Herodotus, ii. 137 (Sabacôs).

Shabaka had a great reputation for mildness and kind rule: Petrie (*Religious Life*, 1924, pp. 193 f.) explains that

AEGYPTIACA (EPITOME) FR. 65, 66, 67

(b) Armenian Version of Eusebius.

The Twenty-fourth Dynasty.
Bocchoris of Saïs, for 44 years: in his reign a lamb spoke.

Dynasty XXV.

Fr. 66 (*from Syncellus*). According to Africanus.

The Twenty-fifth Dynasty [1] consisted of three Ethiopian kings.
1. Sabacôn,[2] who, taking Bochchôris captive, burned him alive, and reigned for 8 years.
2. Sebichôs, his son, for 14 years.
3. Tarcus, for 18 years.

Total, 40 years.

Fr. 67 (a) (*from Syncellus*). According to Eusebius.

The Twenty-fifth Dynasty consisted of three Ethiopian kings.
1. Sabacôn, who, taking Bochchôris captive, burned him alive, and reigned for 12 years.
2. Sebichôs, his son, for 12 years.
3. Taracus, for 20 years.

Total, 44 years.

Bochchoris was treated like a mock king in the ancient festival, the burning ceremonially destroying his kingly character. See Wainwright, *Sky-Religion*, pp. 38 ff.

[2] Taharka: in *O.T. 2 Kings* xix. 9, Tirhakah, King of Ethiopia. See Peet, *Egypt and the Old Testament*, 1922, pp. 175 ff.

Fr. 67, 68   MANETHO

(b) Eusebius, *Chronica* I. (Armenian Version), p. 104.

Vicesima quinta dynastia Aethiopum regum III.
Sabacon, qui captum Bocchorim vivum combussit, regnavitque annis XII.
Sebichos eius filius, annis XII.
Saracus,[1] annis XX.

Summa annorum XLIV.

Fr. 68. *Syncellus*, p. 141. ΚΑΤΑ ΑΦΡΙΚΑΝΟΝ.

Ἕκτη καὶ εἰκοστὴ δυναστεία Σαϊτῶν βασιλέων ἐννέα.

α΄ Στεφινάτης, ἔτη ζ΄.
β΄ Νεχεψώς, ἔτη ϛ΄.
γ΄ Νεχαώ, ἔτη η΄.
δ΄ Ψαμμήτιχος, ἔτη νδ΄.
ε΄ Νεχαὼ δεύτερος, ἔτη ϛ΄. οὗτος εἷλε τὴν Ἱερουσαλήμ, καὶ Ἰωάχαζ τὸν βασιλέα αἰχμάλωτον εἰς Αἴγυπτον ἀπήγαγε.
ϛ΄ Ψάμμουθις ἕτερος, ἔτη ἕξ.

[1] Taracus, Aucher, m.: Tarakos, Karst.

---

[1] Dynasty XXVI., 663-525 B.C.
Saïs (see p. 91 n. 4), now grown in power, with foreign aid asserts independence, and rules over Egypt. Herodotus, ii. 151 ff., supports the version of Africanus but differs in (5) Necôs 16 years (Ch. 159), and (7) Apries 25 years (Ch. 161) (22 years in Diod. Sic. i. 68). Eusebius (Fr. 69) has preserved the Ethiopian Ammeris (*i.e.* Tanutamûn) at the beginning of Dynasty XXVI.: so in the *Book of Sothis* (App. IV.), No. 78, Amaês, 38 years.

AEGYPTIACA (EPITOME) Fr. 67, 68

(b) ARMENIAN VERSION OF EUSEBIUS.

The Twenty-fifth Dynasty consisted of three Ethiopian kings.
1. Sabacon, who, taking Bocchoris captive, burned him alive, and reigned for 12 years.
2. Sebichos, his son, for 12 years.
3. Saracus (Taracus), for 20 years.

Total, 44 years.

DYNASTY XXVI.

Fr. 68 (*from Syncellus*). ACCORDING TO AFRICANUS.

The Twenty-sixth Dynasty [1] consisted of nine kings of Saïs.
1. Stephinatês, for 7 years.
2. Nechepsôs, for 6 years.
3. Nechaô, for 8 years.
4. Psammêtichus,[2] for 54 years.
5. Nechaô [3] the Second, for 6 years: he took Jerusalem, and led King Iôachaz captive into Egypt.
6. Psammuthis the Second, for 6 years.

---

[2] Psammêtichus I. (Psametik) = Psammêtk, " man, or vendor, of mixed wine," *cf.* Herodotus, ii. 151 (Griffith in *Catalogue of Demotic Papyri in the Rylands Library*, iii. pp. 44, 201). See Diod. Sic. i. 66, 67.

[3] Nechaô is an old name, an Egyptian plural form, " belonging to the *kas* " or bulls (Apis and Mnevis), *O.T.* 2 *Chron.* xxxvi. 2-4. Battle of Megiddo, 609 B.C.: defeat and death of King Josiah by Necho (2 *Kings* xxiii. 29, xxiv. 1, xxv. 26). Johoahaz, son of Josiah, was led captive into Egypt. For these events, see Peet, *Egypt and the Old Testament*, 1922, p. 181 ff.

ζ΄ Οὔαφρις, ἔτη ιθ΄, ᾧ προσέφυγον ἁλούσης
  ὑπὸ Ἀσσυρίων Ἱερουσαλὴμ οἱ τῶν Ἰουδαίων
  ὑπόλοιποι.
η΄ Ἄμωσις, ἔτη μδ΄.
θ΄ Ψαμμεχερίτης, μῆνας ϛ΄.
Ὁμοῦ, ἔτη ρν΄ καὶ μῆνας ϛ΄.

Fr. 69 (a).   Syncellus, p. 143.   ΚΑΤΑ ΕΥΣΕΒΙΟΝ.

Ἕκτη καὶ εἰκοστὴ δυναστεία Σαϊτῶν βασιλέων θ΄.
α΄ Ἀμμέρις Αἰθίοψ, ἔτη ιβ΄.
β΄ Στεφινάθις, ἔτη ζ΄.
γ΄ Νεχεψώς, ἔτη ϛ΄.
δ΄ Νεχαώ, ἔτη η΄.
ε΄ Ψαμμήτιχος, ἔτη με΄.[1]
ϛ΄ Νεχαὼ δεύτερος, ἔτη ϛ΄. οὗτος εἷλε τὴν
  Ἱερουσαλήμ, καὶ Ἰωάχαζ τὸν βασιλέα
  αἰχμάλωτον εἰς Αἴγυπτον ἀπήγαγε.
ζ΄ Ψάμμουθις ἕτερος, ὁ καὶ Ψαμμήτιχος, ἔτη
  ιζ΄.

[1] μδ΄ Müller.

---

[1] Uaphris or Apries, in Egyptian Waḥibprē‘, the Hophra of the O.T. Capture of Jerusalem by Nebuchadnezzar, king of Babylon, 587 B.C. See Peet, op. cit. pp. 185 ff.

AEGYPTIACA (EPITOME) Fr. 68, 69

7. Uaphris,[1] for 19 years: the remnant of the Jews fled to him, when Jerusalem was captured by the Assyrians.
8. Amôsis,[2] for 44 years.
9. Psammecheritês,[3] for 6 months.

Total, 150 years 6 months.

Fr. 69 (a) (*from Syncellus*). ACCORDING TO EUSEBIUS.

The Twenty-sixth Dynasty consisted of nine kings of Saïs.
1. Ammeris the Ethiopian, for 12 years.
2. Stephinathis, for 7 years.
3. Nechepsôs, for 6 years.
4. Nechaô, for 8 years.
5. Psammêtichus, for 45 [44] years.
6. Nechaô the Second, for 6 years: he took Jerusalem, and led King Iôachaz captive into Egypt.
7. Psammuthis the Second, also called Psammêtichus, for 17 years.

[2] Amôsis should be Amasis (Ia'hmase), the general of Uaphris or Apries: Amasis was first made co-regent with Apries (569 B.C.), then two years later, after a battle, he became sole monarch.
On the character of Amasis, "the darling of the people and of popular legend," see the demotic papyrus translated by Spiegelberg, *The Credibility of Herodotus' Account of Egypt* (trans. Blackman), pp. 29 f.
[3] Psammêtichus III., defeated by Cambysês the Persian, 525 B.C. The three Psametiks are differentiated as Psammêtichus, Psammuthis, and Psammecheritês (*cf.* Fr. 20, n. 1).

Fr. 69 MANETHO

η΄ Οὔαφρις, ἔτη κε΄, ᾧ προσέφυγον ἁλούσης ὑπὸ Ἀσσυρίων τῆς Ἱερουσαλὴμ οἱ τῶν Ἰουδαίων ὑπόλοιποι.
θ΄ Ἄμωσις, ἔτη μβ΄.

Ὁμοῦ, ἔτη ρξγ΄.

(b) Eusebius, *Chronica* I. (Armenian Version), p. 104.

Vicesima sexta dynastia Saïtarum regum IX.

Ameres Aethiops, annis XVIII.
Stephinathes, annis VII.
Nechepsos, annis VI.
Nechao, annis VIII.
Psametichus, annis XLIV.
Nechao alter, annis VI. Ab hoc Hierosolyma capta sunt, Iochasusque rex in Aegyptum captivus abductus.
Psamuthes alter, qui et Psammetichus, annis XVII.
Uaphres, annis XXV, ad quem reliquiae Iudaeorum, Hierosolymis in Assyriorum potestatem redactis, confugerunt.
Amosis, annis XLII.

Summa annorum CLXVII.

8. Uaphris, for 25 years: the remnant of the Jews fled to him, when Jerusalem was captured by the Assyrians.
9. Amôsis, for 42 years.

Total, 163 years.[1]

(b) ARMENIAN VERSION OF EUSEBIUS.

The Twenty-sixth Dynasty consisted of nine kings of Saïs.
1. Ameres the Ethiopian, for 18 years.
2. Stephinathes, for 7 years.
3. Nechepsos, for 6 years.
4. Nechao, for 8 years.
5. Psametichus, for 44 years.
6. Nechao the Second, for 6 years: he took Jerusalem, and led King Ioachaz captive into Egypt.
7. Psamuthes the Second, also called Psammetichus, for 17 years.
8. Uaphres, for 25 years: the remnant of the Jews took refuge with him, when Jerusalem was subjugated by the Assyrians.
9. Amosis, for 42 years.

Total, 167 years.

[1] If 44 years are assigned to (5) Psammêtichus, the actual total is 167, as in the Armenian Version.

Fr. 70. *Syncellus*, p. 141. ΚΑΤΑ ΑΦΡΙΚΑΝΟΝ.

Ἑβδόμη καὶ εἰκοστὴ δυναστεία Περσῶν βασιλέων η'.

α' Καμβύσης ἔτει ε' τῆς ἑαυτοῦ βασιλείας Περσῶν ἐβασίλευσεν Αἰγύπτου ἔτη ϛ'.
β' Δαρεῖος Ὑστάσπου, ἔτη λϛ'.
γ' Ξέρξης ὁ μέγας, ἔτη κα'.
δ' Ἀρτάβανος, μῆνας ζ'.
ε' Ἀρταξέρξης, ἔτη μα'.
ϛ' Ξέρξης, μῆνας δύο.
ζ' Σογδιανός, μῆνας ζ'.
η' Δαρεῖος Ξέρξου, ἔτη ιθ'.

Ὁμοῦ, ἔτη ρκδ', μῆνες δ'.

---

[1] Persian Domination, 525-332 B.C.
Dynasty XXVII., 525-404 B.C. After conquering Egypt, Cambysês reigned three years, 525/4-523/2 B.C. See *Cambridge Ancient History*, vi. pp. 137 ff.

An interesting papyrus fragment (P. Baden 4 No. 59: V. / A.D.—see the facsimile in Plate III) contains this Dynasty in a form which differs in some respects from the versions given by Africanus and Eusebius. Like Eusebius the papyrus inserts the Magi, and calls Artaxerxês " the Long-handed " and his successor Xerxês " the Second ": as in Africanus, Darius is " son of Hysta[spês] " and Xerxês is " the Great ". To Cambysês the papyrus

AEGYPTIACA (EPITOME) FR. 70

Dynasty XXVII.

Fr. 70 (*from Syncellus*). According to Africanus.

The Twenty-seventh Dynasty[1] consisted of eight Persian kings.

1. Cambysês in the fifth year of his kingship over the Persians became king of Egypt, and ruled for 6 years.
2. Darius, son of Hystaspês, for 36 years.
3. Xerxês the Great, for 21 years.
4. Artabanus,[2] for 7 months.
5. Artaxerxês,[3] for 41 years.
6. Xerxês,[4] for 2 months.
7. Sogdianus, for 7 months.
8. Darius, son of Xerxês, for 19 years.

Total, 124 years 4 months.

---

gives $6\frac{1}{2}$ years: to the Magi, $7\frac{1}{2}$ months. The conquest of Egypt is assigned to the fourth year of Cambysês' reign, and it was in that year that the campaign began. Artaxerxês is described as "the son" (*i.e.* of Xerxês); while Darius II. is correctly named "the Illegitimate". See Bilabel's note on the papyrus (*l.c.*).

[2] Artabanus, vizier, and murderer of Xerxês I., 465 B.C.

[3] Artaxerxês I., "Long-hand" ("whether from a physical peculiarity or political capacity is uncertain," *C.A.H.* vi. p. 2), 465-424 B.C.

[4] Xerxês II. was murdered by his half-brother Sogdianus, who was in turn defeated and put to death in 423 B.C. by another half-brother Ochus (Darius II., nicknamed Nothos, "the Illegitimate,"), not "son of Xerxês". Darius II. died in 404 B.C.

Fr. 71 (a). Syncellus, p. 143. ΚΑΤΑ ΕΥΣΕΒΙΟΝ.

Εἰκοστὴ ἑβδόμη δυναστεία Περσῶν βασιλέων η'.

α' Καμβύσης ἔτει πέμπτῳ τῆς αὐτοῦ βασιλείας ἐβασίλευσεν Αἰγύπτου ἔτη γ'.
β' Μάγοι, μῆνας ζ'.
γ' Δαρεῖος. ἔτη λς'.
δ' Ξέρξης ὁ Δαρείου, ἔτη κα'.
ε' Ἀρταξέρξης ὁ μακρόχειρ, ἔτη μ'.
ς' Ξέρξης ὁ δεύτερος, μῆνας β'.
ζ' Σογδιανός, μῆνας ζ'.
η' Δαρεῖος ὁ Ξέρξου, ἔτη ιθ'.

Ὁμοῦ, ἔτη ρκ' καὶ μῆνες δ'.

(b) EUSEBIUS, *Chronica* I. (Armenian Version), p. 105.

Vicesima septima dynastia Persarum regum VIII.

Cambyses, qui regni sui quinto[1] anno Aegyptiorum potitus est, annis III.
Magi, mensibus septem.
Darius, annis XXXVI.
Xerxes Darii, annis XXI.
Artaxerxes, annis XL.
Xerxes alter, mensibus II.
Sogdianus, mensibus VII.
Darius Xerxis, annis XIX.
Summa annorum CXX, mensiumque IV.

[1] Aucher: XV. MSS.

AEGYPTIACA (EPITOME)   Fr. 71

Fr. 71 (a) (*from Syncellus*). ACCORDING TO EUSEBIUS.

The Twenty-seventh Dynasty consisted of eight Persian kings.
1. Cambysês in the fifth year of his kingship became king of Egypt, and ruled for 3 years.
2. Magi, for 7 months.
3. Darius, for 36 years.
4. Xerxês, son of Darius, for 21 years.
5. Artaxerxês of the long hand, for 40 years.
6. Xerxês the Second, for 2 months.
7. Sogdianus, for 7 months.
8. Darius, son of Xerxês, for 19 years.

Total, 120 years 4 months.

(b) ARMENIAN VERSION OF EUSEBIUS.

The Twenty-seventh Dynasty consisted of eight Persian kings.
1. Cambyses in the fifth [1] year of his kingship became king of Egypt, and ruled for 3 years.
2. Magi, for 7 months.
3. Darius, for 36 years.
4. Xerxes, son of Darius, for 21 years.
5. Artaxerxês, for 40 years.
6. Xerxês the Second, for 2 months.
7. Sogdianus, for 7 months.
8. Darius, son of Xerxes, for 19 years.

Total, 120 years 4 months.

[1] The Armenian text has "15th".

Fr. 72 (a). *Syncellus*, p. 142. ΚΑΤΑ ΑΦΡΙΚΑΝΟΝ.

Εἰκοστὴ ὀγδόη δυναστεία. Ἀμύρτεος Σαΐτης, ἔτη ϛ'.

(b) *Syncellus*, p. 144. ΚΑΤΑ ΕΥΣΕΒΙΟΝ.

Εἰκοστὴ ὀγδόη δυναστεία. Ἀμυρταῖος Σαΐτης, ἔτη ϛ'.

(c) EUSEBIUS, *Chronica* I. (Armenian Version), p. 105.

Vicesima octava dynastia. **Amyrtes Saïtes,** annis[1] VI.

Fr. 73 (a). *Syncellus*, p. 142. ΚΑΤΑ ΑΦΡΙΚΑΝΟΝ.

Ἐνάτη καὶ εἰκοστὴ δυναστεία. Μενδήσιοι βασιλεῖς δ'.

α' Νεφερίτης, ἔτη ϛ'.
β' Ἄχωρις, ἔτη ιγ'.
γ' Ψάμμουθις, ἔτος α'.
δ' Νεφερίτης, μῆνας δ'.
Ὁμοῦ, ἔτη κ', μῆνες δ'.

[1] Aucher, m.: mensibus MSS., according to Müller.

---

[1] Dynasty XXVIII.–XXX., Egyptian kings: 404-341 B.C.—a brief period of independence.

Dynasty XXVIII., Amyrtaeus of Saïs, 404-399 B.C.: no Egyptian king of this name is known on the monuments. See Werner Schur in *Klio*, xx. 1926, pp. 273 ff.

AEGYPTIACA (EPITOME) Fr. 72, 73

Dynasty XXVIII.

Fr. 72 (a) (*from Syncellus*). According to Africanus.

The Twenty-eighth Dynasty.[1] Amyrteos of Saïs, for 6 years.

(b) According to Eusebius.

The Twenty-eighth Dynasty. Amyrtaeus of Saïs, for 6 years.

(c) Armenian Version of Eusebius.

The Twenty-eighth Dynasty. Amyrtes of Saïs, for 6 years.[2]

Dynasty XXIX.

Fr. 73 (a) (*from Syncellus*). According to Africanus.

The Twenty-ninth Dynasty:[3] four kings of Mendês.
1. Nepherîtês, for 6 years.
2. Achôris, for 13 years.
3. Psammuthis, for 1 year.
4. Nepherîtês [II.], for 4 months.

Total, 20 years 4 months.

---

[2] 6 years (Aucher, Karst): 6 months (Müller). The Armenian words for "month" and "year" are so similar that corruption is likely (Margoliouth).

[3] Dynasty XXIX., resident at Mendês in E. Delta (Baedeker [8], p. 183), 398-381 B.C. On the sequence of these rulers see H. R. Hall in *C.A.H.* vi. p. 145 and n.

Fr. 73 MANETHO

(b) Syncellus. p. 144. ΚΑΤΑ ΕΥΣΕΒΙΟΝ.

Εἰκοστὴ ἐνάτη δυναστεία. Μενδήσιοι βασιλεῖς δ'.

α' Νεφερίτης, ἔτη ς'.
β' Ἄχωρις, ἔτη ιγ'.
γ' Ψάμμουθις, ἔτος α'.
δ' Νεφερίτης, μῆνας δ'.
ε' Μοῦθις, ἔτος α'.

'Ομοῦ' ἔτη κα' καὶ μῆνες δ'.

(c) EUSEBIUS, Chronica I. (Armenian Version), p. 106.

Vicesima nona dynastia Mendesiorum regum quattuor.

Nepherites, annis VI.
Achoris, annis XIII.
Psamuthes, anno I.
Muthes, anno I.
Nepherites mensibus IV.

Summa annorum XXI, mensiumque IV.

AEGYPTIACA (EPITOME) FR. 73

(b) ACCORDING TO EUSEBIUS.

The Twenty-ninth Dynasty: four kings [1] of Mendês.

1. Nepheritês, for 6 years.
2. Achôris, for 13 years.
3. Psammuthis, for 1 year.
4. Nepheritês [II.], for 4 months.
5. Muthis, for 1 year.

Total, 21 years 4 months.

(c) ARMENIAN VERSION OF EUSEBIUS.

The Twenty-ninth Dynasty consisted of four kings of Mendes.

1. Nepherites, for 6 years.
2. Achoris, for 13 years.
3. Psamuthes, for 1 year.
4. Muthes, for 1 year.
5. Nepherites [II.], for 4 months.

Total, 21 years and 4 months.

[1] Muthis or Muthês was a usurper, hence the number of kings is given as four. He is unknown to the Monuments. Aucher suggests that the name Muthis may be merely a repetition, curtailed, of the name Psammuthis.

Fr. 74   MANETHO

Fr. 74 (a). *Syncellus*, p. 144. ΚΑΤΑ ΑΦΡΙΚΑΝΟΝ.

Τριακοστὴ δυναστεία Σεβεννυτῶν βασιλέων τριῶν.

αʹ Νεκτανέβης, ἔτη ιηʹ.
βʹ Τεώς, ἔτη βʹ.
γʹ Νεκτανεβός, ἔτη ιηʹ.

Ὁμοῦ· ἔτη ληʹ.

(b) *Syncellus*, p. 145   ΚΑΤΑ ΕΥΣΕΒΙΟΝ.

Τριακοστὴ δυναστεία Σεβεννυτῶν βασιλέων τριῶν.

αʹ Νεκτανέβης, ἔτη ιʹ.
βʹ Τεώς, ἔτη βʹ.
γʹ Νεκτανεβός, ἔτη ηʹ.

Ὁμοῦ, ἔτη κʹ.

---

[1] Dynasty XXX., resident at Sebennytus (see Intro. p. xiii), 380-343 B.C.: Nectanebês I. (Nekhtenêbef), 380-363, Teôs or Tachôs (Zedḥôr), 362-361, Nectanebus II. (Nekhthorehbe), 360-343. See E. Meyer, *Zur Geschichte der 30. Dynastie* in *Zeitschrift für Ägyptische Sprache*, Bd. 67, pp. 68-70.

It is certain that Manetho knew only 30 dynasties and ended with the conquest of Egypt by Ochus: see Unger,

AEGYPTIACA (EPITOME)   Fr. 74

Dynasty XXX.

Fr. 74 (a) (*from Syncellus*).   According to Africanus.

The Thirtieth Dynasty [1] consisted of three kings of Sebennytus.

1. Nectanebês, for 18 years.
2. Teôs, for 2 years.
3. Nectanebus,[2] for 18 years.

Total, 38 years.

(b) According to Eusebius.

The Thirtieth Dynasty consisted of three kings of Sebennytus.

1. Nectanebês, for 10 years.
2. Teôs, for 2 years.
3. Nectanebus, for 8 years.

Total, 20 years.

---

[1] *Chronol. des Manetho*, pp. 334 f. Under Olymp. 107 (*i.e.* 352-348 B.C.) Jerome (*Chronicle*, p. 203 Fotheringham, p. 121 Helm) notes: Ochus Aegyptum tenuit, Nectanebo in Aethiopiam pulso, in quo Aegyptiorum regnum destructum est. Huc usque Manethos. ("Ochus possessed Egypt, when he had driven Nectanebô into Ethiopia: thereby the kingship of the Egyptians was destroyed. So far Manetho [or, Here ends the History of Manetho]").

[2] For the later renown of this king as magician in popular legend, see the *Dream of Nectonabôs*, in Wilcken, *Urkunden der Ptolemäerzeit*, i. pp. 369 ff.

Fr. 74, 75   MANETHO

(c) Eusebius, *Chronica* I. (Armenian Version), p. 106.

Tricesima dynastia Sebennytarum regum III.
Nectanebis, annis X.
Teos, annis II.
Nectanebus, annis VIII.
Summa annorum XX.

Fr. 75 (a). *Syncellus*, p. 145. ΚΑΤΑ ΑΦΡΙΚΑΝΟΝ.

Πρώτη καὶ τριακοστὴ δυναστεία Περσῶν βασιλέων τριῶν.

α΄ Ὦχος[1] εἰκοστῷ ἔτει τῆς ἑαυτοῦ βασιλείας Περσῶν ἐβασίλευσεν Αἰγύπτου ἔτη β΄.[2]
β΄ Ἀρσῆς, ἔτη γ΄.
γ΄ Δαρεῖος, ἔτη δ΄.
Ὁμοῦ, ἔτη τρίτου τόμου ‚αν΄.[3]
Μέχρι τῶνδε Μανεθῶ.

[1] Syncellus (p. 486) thus describes the scope of Manetho's *History*, wrongly putting λα΄ for λ΄: ἕως Ὤχου καὶ Νεκτανεβὼ ὁ Μανεθῶ τὰς λα΄ δυναστείας Αἰγύπτου περιέγραψε.
[2] This β΄ (instead of ϛ΄) is probably due to confusion with the β΄ at the beginning of the next line (Aucher).
[3] ων΄ Boeckh, Unger.

---

[1] Dynasty XXXI. is not due to Manetho, but was added later to preserve the continuity,—perhaps with the use of material furnished by Manetho himself. No total is given by Africanus and Eusebius,—a further proof that the whole Dynasty is additional. In another passage (p. 486) Syncellus states: "Manetho wrote an account of the 31

AEGYPTIACA (EPITOME) Fr. 74, 75

(c) ARMENIAN VERSION OF EUSEBIUS.

The Thirtieth Dynasty consisted of 3 kings of Sebennytus.
1. Nectanebis, for 10 years.
2. Teos, for 2 years.
3. Nectanebus, for 8 years.
Total, 20 years.

DYNASTY XXXI.

Fr. 75 (a) (*from Syncellus*). ACCORDING TO AFRICANUS.

The Thirty-first Dynasty[1] consisted of three Persian kings.
1. Ôchus in the twentieth year[2] of his kingship over the Persians became king of Egypt, and ruled for 2 years.
2. Arsês, for 3 years.
3. Darius, for 4 years.

Total of years in Book III., 1050 years[3] [850].

Here ends the *History* of Manetho.

(an error for 30) Dynasties of Egypt down to the time of Ôchus and Nectanebô ": although mistaken about the number of the Dynasties, Syncellus is in the main correct.

[2] The 20th year of the kingship of Ochus was 343 B.C.: the phrase is parallel to that used in Fr. 70, 1, and appears therefore to be Manetho's expression.

[3] The totals given by Africanus in Book III. are 135, 130, 120, 89, 6, 40, 150+, 124+, 6, 20+, 38, i.e. 858+ years. To reduce to 850, assign 116 years to Dynasty XXII. (as the items add), and 120 to Dynasty XXVII. (Meyer).

FR. 75 MANETHO

(b) Syncellus, p. 146. ΚΑΤΑ ΕΥΣΕΒΙΟΝ.

Τριακοστὴ πρώτη δυναστεία Περσῶν βασιλέων τριῶν.

α΄ Ὦχος εἰκοστῷ ἔτει τῆς αὐτοῦ Περσῶν βασιλείας κρατεῖ τῆς Αἰγύπτου ἔτη ς΄.
β΄ Μεθ᾽ ὃν Ἀρσῆς Ὤχου, ἔτη δ΄.
γ΄ Μεθ᾽ ὃν Δαρεῖος, ἔτη ἕξ· ὃν Ἀλέξανδρος ὁ Μακεδὼν καθεῖλε.

Ταῦτα τοῦ τρίτου ⟨τόμου⟩ Μανεθῶ.
Μέχρι τῶνδε Μανεθῶ.

(c) EUSEBIUS, *Chronica* I. (Armenian Version), p. 107.

Tricesima prima dynastia Persarum.

Ochus vicesimo iam anno Persis imperitans Aegyptum occupavit tenuitque annis VI.
Postea Arses Ochi, annis IV.
Tum Darius, annis VI, quem Macedo Alexander interfecit. Atque haec e Manethonis tertio[1] libro

[1] Aucher, m. : secundo MSS., according to Müller.

---

[1] Third Book (Aucher, Karst) : Second Book (Müller). The Armenian words for "second" and "third" have similar forms ; hence the corruption (Margoliouth).

AEGYPTIACA (EPITOME) FR. 75

(b) According to Eusebius.

The Thirty-first Dynasty consisted of three Persian kings.
1. Ôchus in the twentieth year of his kingship over the Persians conquered Egypt, and ruled for 6 years.
2. His successor was Arsês, son of Ochus, who reigned for 4 years.
3. Next, Darius reigned for 6 years: he was put to death by Alexander of Macedon.

These are the contents of the Third Book of Manetho.
Here ends the *History* of Manetho.

(c) Armenian Version of Eusebius.

The Thirty-first Dynasty consisted of Persian kings.
1. Ochus in the twentieth year of his kingship over the Persians seized Egypt and held it for 6 years.
2. His successor was Arsês, son of Ochus, who reigned for 4 years.
3. Next, Darius reigned for 6 years: he was put to death by Alexander of Macedon.

These are the contents of the Third Book[1] of Manetho.

Fr. 76, 77, 78   MANETHO

Η ΙΕΡΑ ΒΙΒΛΟΣ

Fr. 76. Eusebius, *Praeparatio Evangelica*, II Prooem., p. 44 C (Gifford).

Πᾶσαν μὲν οὖν τὴν Αἰγυπτιακὴν ἱστορίαν εἰς πλάτος τῇ Ἑλλήνων μετείληφε φωνῇ ἰδίως τε τὰ περὶ τῆς κατ' αὐτοὺς θεολογίας Μανεθὼς ὁ Αἰγύπτιος, ἔν τε ᾗ ἔγραψεν Ἱερᾷ βίβλῳ καὶ ἐν ἑτέροις αὐτοῦ συγγράμμασι.

Cf. Theodoretus, *Curatio*, II, p. 61 (Räder):

Μανεθὼς δὲ τὰ περὶ Ἴσιδος καὶ Ὀσίριδος καὶ Ἄπιδος καὶ Σαράπιδος καὶ τῶν ἄλλων θεῶν τῶν Αἰγυπτίων ἐμυθολόγησε.

Fr. 77. Plutarch, *De Is. et Osir.*, 9.

Ἔτι δὲ τῶν πολλῶν νομιζόντων ἴδιον παρ' Αἰγυπτίοις ὄνομα τοῦ Διὸς εἶναι τὸν Ἀμοῦν (ὃ παράγοντες ἡμεῖς Ἄμμωνα λέγομεν), Μανεθὼς μὲν ὁ Σεβεννύτης τὸ κεκρυμμένον οἴεται καὶ τὴν κρύψιν ὑπὸ ταύτης δηλοῦσθαι τῆς φωνῆς . . .

Fr. 78. Plutarch, *De Is. et Osir.*, 49.

Βέβωνα δὲ τινὲς μὲν ἕνα τῶν τοῦ Τυφῶνος ἑταίρων γεγονέναι λέγουσιν, Μανεθὼς δ' αὐτὸν

---

[1] Manetho's interpretation is from *imn*, "hidden, secret": see Sethe, *Abhandl. Berl. Akad.*, 1929, p. 78, § 153. Herodotus, ii. 42, 3, tells a story which is probably related to this meaning of Amûn.

THE SACRED BOOK.

Fr. 76 (*from* EUSEBIUS).

Now the whole history of Egypt and especially the details of Egyptian religion are expounded at length in Greek by Manetho the Egyptian, both in his *Sacred Book* and in other writings of his.

(*From* THEODORETUS.)

Manetho rehearsed the stories of Isis, Osiris, Apis, Serapis, and the other gods of Egypt.

Fr. 77 (*from* PLUTARCH, *Is. and Osir.*, ch. 9).

Further, the general belief is that the name Amûn,[1] which we transform into Ammôn, is an Egyptian proper noun, the title of Zeus[2]; but Manetho of Sebennytus is of opinion that this name has a meaning—" that which is concealed " and " concealment."

Fr. 78 (*from* PLUTARCH, *Is. and Osir.*, ch. 49).

Some say that Bebôn[3] was one of the comrades of Typhôn; but Manetho states that Typhôn himself

---

[2] The title Zeus Ammôn was already known to Pindar in the first half of the fifth century B.C. (*Pythians*, iv. 16, Fr. 36; see Pausanias, ix. 16, 1).

[3] The name " Bebôn," given to Typhôn, does not mean " prevention," but is the Egyptian *bᵓby*, an epithet of Sêth. In Greek, besides the form Βέβων, Βάβυς was used (Hellanicus in Athenaeus, xv. 25, p. 680a). Typhôn, an unpopular deity, came into favour in Dynasty XIX., two kings of which were Sethôs I. and II.

Fr. 78, 79 MANETHO

τὸν Τυφῶνα καὶ Βέβωνα καλεῖσθαι· σημαίνει δὲ τοὔνομα κάθεξιν ἢ κώλυσιν, ὡς τοῖς πράγμασιν ὁδῷ βαδίζουσι καὶ πρὸς ὃ χρὴ φερομένοις ἐνισταμένης τῆς τοῦ Τυφῶνος δυνάμεως.

Fr. 79. PLUTARCH, De Is. et Osir., 62.

Ἔοικε δὲ τούτοις καὶ τὰ Αἰγύπτια. τὴν μὲν γὰρ Ἶσιν πολλάκις τῷ τῆς Ἀθηνᾶς ὀνόματι καλοῦσι φράζοντι τοιοῦτον λόγον "ἦλθον ἀπ' ἐμαυτῆς," ὅπερ ἐστὶν αὐτοκινήτου φορᾶς δηλωτικόν· ὁ δὲ Τυφών, ὥσπερ εἴρηται, Σὴθ καὶ Βέβων καὶ Σμὺ ὀνομάζεται, βίαιόν τινα καὶ κωλυτικὴν ἐπίσχεσιν ⟨ἤ τιν'⟩[1] ὑπεναντίωσιν ἢ ἀναστροφὴν ἐμφαίνειν βουλομένων τῶν ὀνομάτων. ἔτι τὴν σιδηρῖτιν λίθον, ὀστέον Ὥρου, Τυφῶνος δὲ τὸν σίδηρον, ὡς ἱστορεῖ Μανεθώς, καλοῦσιν. ὥσπερ γὰρ ὁ σίδηρος πολλάκις μὲν ἑλκομένῳ καὶ ἑπομένῳ πρὸς τὴν λίθον ὅμοιός ἐστι, πολλάκις δ' ἀποστρέφεται καὶ ἀποκρούεται πρὸς τοὐναντίον, οὕτως ἡ σωτήριος

[1] ⟨ἤ τιν'⟩ Pohlenz.

---

[1] Explanation is difficult. The name of the goddess Neith with whom Athena is often identified has been interpreted " that which is, or exists " (Mallet, Le Culte de Neit à Saïs, p. 189). As a genuine etymology of the name, this is impossible ; but it may be that in the late period a connexion was imagined between Nt, " Neith," and nt(t), " that which is " (B.G.). It is suggestive that the Coptic word meaning " come " is na (A. Rusch, Pauly-Wissowa-Kroll, R.-E. xvi. 2 (1935), col. 2190).

THE SACRED BOOK Fr. 78, 79

was also called Bebôn. The name means "checking" or "prevention," and implies that, when actions are proceeding in due course and tending to their required end, the power of Typhôn obstructs them.

Fr. 79 (*from* PLUTARCH, *Is. and Osir.*, ch. 62).

The usage of the Egyptians is also similar. They often call Isis by the name of Athena, which expresses some such meaning as " I came from Myself,"[1] and is indicative of self-originated movement. But Typhôn, as I have already mentioned, is called Sêth, Bebôn, and Smy,[2] these names implying a certain violent and obstructive force, or a certain opposition or overthrow. Further, as Manetho records, they call the loadstone " the bone of Hôrus," but iron " the bone of Typhôn."[3] Just as iron is often like to be attracted and led after the stone, but often again turns away and is repelled in the opposite direction. so the

[2] Smy is not a name of Typhôn, but may mean " confederate " in Egyptian (from *sm*ꜣ, to unite). In religious texts the phrase Sêth and his *sm*ꜣ*yt*, i.e. " Sêth and his confederates," often occurs. See Kees on Sêth in Pauly-Wissowa-Kroll, *R.-E.* ii. A. 2 (1923), cols. 1896 ff.

[3] Interesting confirmation of the correctness of Plutarch and Manetho is given by G. A. Wainwright in his article " Iron in Egypt " (*J. Eg. Arch.* xviii. 1932, p. 14). He compares *Pyramid Texts*, § 14, " the *bi*ꜣ which came forth out of Seteꜣh," and refers to Petrie's discovery at Ḳâw (an important centre of Sêth worship) of great quantities of gigantic bones, collected in piles: they were chiefly of hippopotami,—mineralized, heavy, black bones, of metallic lustre and appearance. It is clear that they were considered sacred to Sêth, as they were wrapped in linen and were found here and there in tombs at Ḳâw.

Fr. 79, 80   MANETHO

καὶ ἀγαθὴ καὶ λόγον ἔχουσα τοῦ κόσμου κίνησις ἐπιστρέφεταί τε καὶ προσάγεται καὶ μαλακωτέραν ποιεῖ, πείθουσα τὴν σκληρὰν ἐκείνην καὶ τυφώνειον, εἶτ' αὖθις ἀνασχεθεῖσα εἰς ἑαυτὴν ἀνέστρεψε καὶ κατέδυσεν εἰς τὴν ἀπορίαν.

Fr. 80. PLUTARCH, *De Is. et Osir.*, 28.

Πτολεμαῖος δὲ ὁ Σωτὴρ ὄναρ εἶδε τὸν ἐν Σινώπῃ τοῦ Πλούτωνος κολοσσόν, οὐκ ἐπιστάμενος οὐδὲ ἑωρακὼς πρότερον οἷος ⟨ἦν⟩ τὴν μορφήν, κελεύοντα κομίσαι τὴν ταχίστην αὐτὸν εἰς Ἀλεξάνδρειαν. ἀγνοοῦντι δ' αὐτῷ καὶ ἀποροῦντι, ποῦ καθίδρυται,

---

[1] The story of the transport of the colossus of Serapis to Alexandria is told with variants by Tacitus, *Hist.* iv. 83, 84, Clement of Alexandria, *Protrep.* iv. p. 37, Stahlin, and Cyrillus *in Jul.* p. 13, Spanh.: *cf.* also Plutarch, *De sollert. anim.* 36, Eustathius on Dionys. Perieg. 254 (Müller, *Geogr. gr. min.* ii. p. 262). Both Tacitus and Plutarch agree in assigning the introduction of the statue to Ptolemy I.: Clement and Cyril attribute it to Ptolemy II. See Parthey, *Über Is. und Osir.* pp. 213 ff. Tacitus gives (from Lysimachus) the more circumstantial account, adding the name of the King of Pontus, Scydrothemis; but Plutarch mentions other names (*e.g.* Manetho) which Tacitus omits. The new cult of Serapis was intended to unite the Greek ruling class and their Egyptian subjects. (See Intro. p. xiv.) Georg Lippold (*Festschrift Paul Arndt*, 1925, p. 126) holds the sculptor of the statue to be the famous Bryaxis of Athens, c. 350 B.C.; and thus the image was worshipped at Sinôpe for about 70 years before it was taken to Alexandria. The most trustworthy copy of the statue is that in the Museum at Alexandria: see *Athen. Mitt.* xxxi. (1906), Plates VI, VII (A. W. Lawrence in

THE SACRED BOOK FR. 79, 80

salutary, good, and rational movement of the world at one time attracts, conciliates, and by persuasion mollifies that harsh Typhonian power; then again, when the latter has recovered itself, it overthrows the other and reduces it to helplessness.

Fr. 80 (from PLUTARCH, *Is. and Osir.*, ch. 28).

Ptolemy Sôtêr dreamed that he saw the colossal statue [1] of Pluto at Sinôpê,[2] although he did not know what manner of shape it had, having never previously seen it; and that it bade him convey it with all possible speed to Alexandria. The king was at a loss and did not know where the statue stood; but as he was describing the vision to his friends,

---

J. Eg. Arch. xi. (1925), p. 182). Only the Greek statue by Bryaxis was brought from Sinôpe: the cult was organized in Egypt itself, and Serapis became the paramount deity of Alexandria with a magnificent temple in Rhakôtis. If there were forty-two temples of Serapis in Egypt (Aristides, viii. 56, 1, p. 96 Dind.)—this number being one for each nome, the majority have left no trace: Parthey (*op. cit.* pp. 216 f.) identifies eleven.

See Wilamowitz, *Hell. Dichtung,* i. p. 154, Wilcken, *Urkunden der Ptolemäerzeit,* Intro. pp. 77 ff. (a full discussion of the origin of the cult of Serapis). *Cf.* also Rostovtzeff in *C.A.H.* vii. pp. 145 f.

For the dream as a vehicle of religious propaganda, *cf.* P. Cairo Zenon 34 (258-257 B.C.: see Deissmann, *Light from the Ancient East,* pp. 152 ff.), and *Inscr. Gr.* xi. 4, 1299 (c. 200 B.C.).

[2] In the districts by the Black Sea, a great god of the underworld was worshipped; and this deity, as Rostovtzeff holds, must be set in close connexion with the Alexandrine Serapis. See Julius Kaerst, *Geschichte des Hellenismus* [2], ii. (1926), pp. 246 f., and *cf.* the late Roman coins of Sinôpe with the Serapis-type (Plate IV, No. 3).

H

καὶ διηγουμένῳ τοῖς φίλοις τὴν ὄψιν, εὑρέθη πολυπλανὴς ἄνθρωπος, ὄνομα Σωσίβιος, ἐν Σινώπῃ φάμενος ἑωρακέναι τοιοῦτον κολοσσόν, οἷον ὁ βασιλεὺς ἰδεῖν ἔδοξεν. ἔπεμψεν οὖν Σωτέλη καὶ Διονύσιον, οἳ χρόνῳ πολλῷ καὶ μόλις, οὐκ ἄνευ μέντοι θείας προνοίας, ἤγαγον ἐκκλέψαντες. ἐπεὶ δὲ κομισθεὶς ὤφθη, συμβαλόντες οἱ περὶ Τιμόθεον τὸν ἐξηγητὴν καὶ Μανέθωνα τὸν Σεβεννύτην Πλούτωνος ὃν ἄγαλμα, τῷ Κερβέρῳ τεκμαιρόμενοι καὶ τῷ δράκοντι, πείθουσι τὸν Πτολεμαῖον, ὡς ἑτέρου θεῶν οὐδενὸς ἀλλὰ Σαράπιδός ἐστιν. οὐ γὰρ ἐκεῖθεν οὕτως ὀνομαζόμενος ἧκεν, ἀλλ' εἰς Ἀλεξάνδρειαν κομισθεὶς τὸ παρ' Αἰγυπτίοις ὄνομα τοῦ Πλούτωνος ἐκτήσατο τὸν Σάραπιν.

Fr. 81.   Aelian, *De Natura Animalium*, X, 16 (Hercher).

Ἀκούω δὲ καὶ Μανέθωνα τὸν Αἰγύπτιον, σοφίας ἐς ἄκρον ἐληλακότα ἄνδρα, εἰπεῖν ὅτι γάλακτος ὑείου ὁ γευσάμενος ἀλφῶν ὑποπίμπλαται καὶ λέπρας· μισοῦσι δὲ ἄρα οἱ Ἀσιανοὶ πάντες τάδε τὰ πάθη. πεπιστεύκασι δὲ Αἰγύπτιοι τὴν ὗν καὶ ἡλίῳ καὶ σελήνῃ ἐχθίστην εἶναι· ὅταν οὖν πανηγυρίζωσι τῇ σελήνῃ, θύουσιν αὐτῇ ἅπαξ τοῦ ἔτους ὗς, ἄλλοτε δὲ οὔτε ἐκείνῃ οὔτε ἄλλῳ τῳ τῶν θεῶν τόδε τὸ ζῷον ἐθέλουσι θύειν.

---

[1] Timotheus (of Eleusis), the Eumolpid, is believed to have introduced the Eleusinian Mysteries into Eleusis, the suburb of Alexandria.

there came forward a far-travelled man, by name Sôsibius, who declared that at Sinôpe he had seen just such a colossus as the king had dreamt he saw. He therefore despatched Sôtelês and Dionysius, who after a long time and with difficulty, though not unaided by divine providence, stole away the statue. When it was brought to Egypt and exhibited there, Timotheus [1] the *exégétés* (expounder or interpreter), Manetho [2] of Sebennytus, and their colleagues, judging by the Cerberus and the serpent, came to the conclusion that it was a statue of Pluto; and they convinced Ptolemy that it represented no other god than Serapis. For it had not come bearing this name from its distant home, but after being conveyed to Alexandria, it acquired the Egyptian name for Pluto, namely Serapis.

Fr. 81 (*from* AELIAN).

I am told also that Manetho the Egyptian, who attained the acme of wisdom, declared that one who tastes sow's milk is infected with leprosy or scall. All Asiatics, indeed, loathe these diseases. The Egyptians hold that the sow is abhorred by both Sun and Moon; so, when they celebrate the annual festival in honour of the Moon, they sacrifice swine [3] to the goddess, whereas at any other time they refuse to sacrifice this animal to the Moon or to any other deity.

[2] Manetho's connexion with the Serapis cult is vouched for by a bust in the Serapeum at Carthage, *Corpus Inscr. Lat.* viii. 1007: see Intro. p. xv.

[3] *Cf.* Herodotus, ii. 47, and see Newberry in *J. Eg. Arch.* xiv. p. 213.

ΕΠΙΤΟΜΗ ΤΩΝ ΦΥΣΙΚΩΝ

Fr. 82. Diogenes Laertius, Prooem, § 10 (Hicks, L.C.L.).

Θεοὺς δ' εἶναι ἥλιον καὶ σελήνην· τὸν μὲν Ὄσιριν, τὴν δ' Ἶσιν καλουμένην. αἰνίττεσθαί τε αὐτοὺς διά τε κανθάρου καὶ δράκοντος καὶ ἱέρακος καὶ ἄλλων, ὥς φησι Μανεθὼς ἐν τῇ τῶν Φυσικῶν Ἐπιτομῇ.

Fr. 83. Eusebius, Praepar. Evang., III, 2, p. 87 d (Gifford).

Τὴν Ἶσίν φασι καὶ τὸν Ὄσιριν τὸν ἥλιον καὶ τὴν σελήνην εἶναι, καὶ Δία μὲν τὸ διὰ πάντων χωροῦν πνεῦμα, Ἥφαιστον δὲ τὸ πῦρ, τὴν δὲ γῆν Δήμητραν ἐπονομάσαι· Ὠκεανόν τε τὸ ὑγρὸν ὀνομάζεσθαι παρ' Αἰγυπτίοις καὶ τὸν παρ' αὐτοῖς ποταμὸν Νεῖλον, ᾧ καὶ τὰς τῶν θεῶν ἀναθεῖναι γενέσεις· τὸν δὲ ἀέρα φασὶν αὐτοὺς προσαγορεύειν Ἀθηνᾶν. τούτους δὲ τοὺς πέντε θεούς, τὸν Ἀέρα λέγω καὶ τὸ Ὕδωρ τό τε Πῦρ καὶ τὴν Γῆν καὶ τὸ Πνεῦμα, τὴν πᾶσαν οἰκουμένην ἐπιπορεύεσθαι, ἄλλοτε ἄλλως εἰς μορφὰς καὶ ἰδέας ἀνθρώπων τε καὶ παντοίων ζῴων σχηματιζομένους· καὶ τούτων ὁμωνύμους παρ' αὐτοῖς Αἰγυπτίοις γεγονέναι θνητοὺς ἀνθρώπους, Ἥλιον

---

[1] The Ancient Egyptian name *Ha'pi* is applied both to the River Nile and to the god of the Nile. Cf. Diod. Sic. i. 12. 6 (the same phrase, with πρὸς ᾧ for ᾧ, and ὑπάρξαι for ἀναθεῖναι: τὰς γενέσεις—the same plural in Diod. Sic. i. 9, 6,

AN EPITOME OF PHYSICAL DOCTRINES

AN EPITOME OF PHYSICAL DOCTRINES.

Fr. 82 (*from* Diogenes Laertius).

The Egyptians hold the Sun and the Moon to be gods, the former being named Osiris, the latter Isis. They refer darkly to them under the symbols of beetle, serpent, hawk, and other creatures, as Manetho says in his *Epitome of Physical Doctrines*.

Fr. 83 (*from* Eusebius).

The Egyptians say that Isis and Osiris are the Moon and the Sun; that Zeus is the name which they gave to the all-pervading spirit, Hephaestus to fire, and Demeter to earth. Among the Egyptians the moist element is named Ocean and their own River Nile; and to him they ascribed the origin of the Gods.[1] To Air, again, they give, it is said, the name of Athena. Now these five deities,—I mean Air, Water, Fire, Earth, and Spirit,—traverse the whole world, transforming themselves at different times into different shapes and semblances of men and creatures of all kinds. In Egypt itself there have also been born mortal men of the same names as these deities:

θεῶν γενέσεις ὑπάρξαι). See also Plutarch, *Is. et Osir.* 66, p. 377 C. The name Νεῖλος appears first in Hesiod, *Theogony* 338, which may be dated to the eighth century B.C.

In a *Hymn to the Nile*, engraved upon the rocks at Gebel Silsileh in Upper Egypt by command of Ramessês II., the river is described as "the living and beautiful Nile, ... father of all the gods" (Wiedemann, *Religion of the Ancient Egyptians*, pp. 146 f.).

Fr. 83, 84, 85   MANETHO

καὶ Κρόνον καὶ ῾Ρέαν, ἔτι δὲ Δία καὶ ῞Ηραν καὶ ῞Ηφαιστον καὶ ῾Εστίαν ἐπονομασθέντας. γράφει δὲ καὶ τὰ περὶ τούτων πλατύτερον μὲν ὁ Μανεθώς, ἐπιτετμημένως δὲ ὁ Διόδωρος . . .

Cf. Theodoretus, *Curatio*, III, p. 80 (Räder).

ΠΕΡΙ ΕΟΡΤΩΝ

Fr. 84. Joannes Lydus, *De Mensibus*, IV, 87 (Wünsch).

᾿Ιστέον δέ, ὡς ὁ Μανέθων ἐν τῷ περὶ ἑορτῶν λέγει τὴν ἡλιακὴν ἔκλειψιν πονηρὰν ἐπίρροιαν ἀνθρώποις ἐπιφέρειν περί τε τὴν κεφαλὴν καὶ τὸν στόμαχον.

ΠΕΡΙ ΑΡΧΑΪΣΜΟΥ ΚΑΙ ΕΥΣΕΒΕΙΑΣ

Fr. 85. Porphyrius, *De Abstinentia*, II, 55 (Nauck).

Κατέλυσε δὲ καὶ ἐν ῾Ηλίου πόλει[1] τῆς Αἰγύπτου τὸν τῆς ἀνθρωποκτονίας νόμον ῎Αμωσις, ὡς μαρ-

---

[1] Εἰλειθυίας πόλει conj. Fruin.

---

[1] If the reference is not to a separate treatise, but to a passage in the *Sacred Book*, translate: "in his account of festivals".

[2] On human sacrifice in Egypt, see Meyer, *Geschichte*[5], I. ii. pp. 98 f. Herodotus, ii. 45, denies that men were sacrificed in Egypt in his time; but Seleucus, under

ON ANCIENT RITUAL AND RELIGION

they were called Hêlios, Cronos, Rhea, as well as Zeus, Hêra, Hêphaestus, and Hestia. Manetho writes on this subject at considerable length, while Diodorus gives a concise account. . . .

ON FESTIVALS.

Fr. 84 (*from* JOANNES LYDUS).

It must be understood that Manetho in his book *On Festivals*[1] states that a solar eclipse exerts a baneful influence upon men in their head and stomach.

ON ANCIENT RITUAL AND RELIGION.

Fr. 85 (*from* PORPHYRIUS).

The rite of human sacrifice[2] at Hêliopolis (Eileithyiaspolis)[3] in Egypt was suppressed by Amôsis,[4]

Tiberius, wrote an account of human sacrifice in Egypt (Athen. iv. p. 172*d*), and there is evidence for the sacrifice of captives in Dynasties XVIII. and XIX. See Diod. Sic. i. 88, 5, and *cf.* Frazer, *Golden Bough*, ii. pp. 254 ff.

Some writers have suggested that the contracted human figure (the *tekenu*), wrapped in a skin and drawn on a sledge, who is a regular feature of funeral processions in the New Kingdom, may have been a remnant of human sacrifice. This, however, is very doubtful: *cf.* N. de G. Davies, *Five Theban Tombs*, pp. 9, 14. See further G. A. Wainwright, *Sky-Religion*, pp. 33 f.

[3] See Fr. 86. The mention of Hêra (see *infra*) makes it very probable that "Eileithyiaspolis" is the correct reading here.

[4] Amôsis, c. 1570 B.C.

Fr. 85, 86 MANETHO

τυρεῖ Μανεθὼς ἐν τῷ περὶ ἀρχαϊσμοῦ καὶ εὐσεβείας. ἐθύοντο δὲ τῇ Ἥρᾳ, καὶ ἐδοκιμάζοντο καθάπερ οἱ ζητούμενοι καθαροὶ μόσχοι καὶ συσφραγιζόμενοι· ἐθύοντο δὲ τῆς ἡμέρας τρεῖς, ἀνθ' ὧν κηρίνους ἐκέλευσεν ὁ Ἄμωσις τοὺς ἴσους ἐπιτίθεσθαι.

See also Eusebius, *Praepar. Evang.*, IV, 16, p. 155d (Gifford): Theodoretus, *Curatio*, VII, p. 192 (Räder).

Fr. 86. PLUTARCH, *De Is. et Osir.*, 73.

Πολλῶν δὲ λεγόντων εἰς ταῦτα τὰ ζῷα τὴν Τυφῶνος αὐτοῦ διῃρῆσθαι[1] ψυχήν, αἰνίττεσθαι δόξειεν ἂν ὁ μῦθος, ὅτι πᾶσα φύσις ἄλογος καὶ θηριώδης τῆς τοῦ κακοῦ δαίμονος γέγονε μοίρας, κἀκεῖνον ἐκμειλισσόμενοι καὶ παρηγοροῦντες περιέπουσι ταῦτα καὶ θεραπεύουσιν· ἂν δὲ πολὺς ἐμπίπτῃ καὶ χαλεπὸς αὐχμὸς ἐπάγων ὑπερβαλλόντως ἢ νόσους ὀλεθρίους ἢ συμφορὰς ἄλλας παραλόγους καὶ ἀλλοκότους, ἔνια τῶν τιμωμένων οἱ ἱερεῖς ἀπάγοντες ὑπὸ σκότῳ μετὰ σιωπῆς καὶ ἡσυχίας

[1] Wyttenbach: διάρασθαι MSS.

---

[1] or ". . . . in discussing ancient ritual and religion.

[2] Drought is said to be a particular manifestation of Typhôn; see Plutarch, *Is. et Osir.*, 45, 51 *fin*. In reference to Egypt, drought naturally means, not absence of rain, but insufficient inundation.

[3] For this striking trait in Egyptian religion see Erman-Ranke, *Ägypten*, 1923, p. 184 n. 2, with the reference to Lacau, *Recueil de travaux*, 26 (1904), p. 72 (sarcophagi of Dynasty XII.); and *cf.* Alan H. Gardiner, *Hieratic Papyri in the British Museum*, iii. (1935), No. V. C (a spell of c. 1200 B.C. in which the reciter threatens the gods that he will cut off the head of a cow taken from the forecourt

ON ANCIENT RITUAL AND RELIGION

as Manetho testifies in his book *On Ancient Ritual and Religion*.[1] Men were sacrificed to Hêra : they were examined, like the pure calves which are sought out and marked with a seal. Three men used to be sacrificed each day; but in their stead Amôsis ordered that the same number of waxen images should be offered.

Fr. 86 (*from* PLUTARCH, *Is. and Osir.*, ch. 73).

Now many say that the soul of Typhôn himself is diffused among these animals ; and this fable would seem to hint that every irrational and bestial nature is partaker of the evil spirit, and that, while seeking to conciliate and appease him, men tend and worship these animals. Should a long and severe drought [2] occur, bringing with it an excess of deadly diseases or other strange and unaccountable calamities, the priests lead off some of the sacred animals quietly and in silence under cover of darkness, threatening them at first and trying to frighten [3] them ; but, should

of the temple of Hathor, and will cause the sky to split in the middle), No. VIII. B (the Book of Banishing an Enemy, also dated c. 1200 B.C., containing threats to tear out the soul and annihilate the corpse of Osiris, and set fire to every tomb of his), and *The Attitude of the Ancient Egyptians to Death and the Dead*, 1935, pp. 12, 16 f., 39, note 17.

Threats to the gods also appear later in the Greek papyri : see L.C.L., *Select Papyri*, i. (Hunt and Edgar), pp. 309, 345, Th. Hopfner, *Griechisch-Ägyptischer Offenbarungszauber* (= *Stud. zur Pal. und Pap.*, Wessely, xxiii. 1924), §§ 187, 210 *et al.*, and *cf.* Porphyrius, *Epistula ad Anebonem*, 27, who remarks that this is peculiarly Egyptian. See Wilcken, *Chrestomathie*, i. 1, pp. 124 f. ("perhaps a remnant of ancient fetishism").

ἀπειλοῦσι καὶ δεδίττονται τὸ πρῶτον, ἂν δ' ἐπιμένῃ,
καθιερεύουσι καὶ σφάττουσιν. ὡς δή τινα κολασμὸν
ὄντα τοῦ δαίμονος τοῦτον ἢ καθαρμὸν ἄλλως μέγαν
ἐπὶ μεγίστοις· καὶ γὰρ ἐν Εἰλειθυίας πόλει ζῶντας
ἀνθρώπους κατεπίμπρασαν, ὡς Μανεθὼς ἱστόρηκε,
Τυφωνείους καλοῦντες, καὶ τὴν τέφραν αὐτῶν λικ-
μῶντες ἠφάνιζον καὶ διέσπειρον. ἀλλὰ τοῦτο μὲν
ἐδρᾶτο φανερῶς καὶ καθ' ἕνα καιρὸν ἐν ταῖς κυνάσιν
ἡμέραις· αἱ δὲ τῶν τιμωμένων ζῴων καθιερεύσεις
ἀπόρρητοι καὶ χρόνοις ἀτάκτοις πρὸς τὰ συμπίπ-
τοντα γινόμεναι, τοὺς πολλοὺς λανθάνουσι, πλὴν
ὅταν ⟨Ἄπιδος¹⟩ ταφὰς ἔχωσι, καὶ τῶν ἄλλων ἀνα-
δεικνύντες ἔνια πάντων παρόντων συνεμβάλλωσιν,
οἰόμενοι τοῦ Τυφῶνος ἀντιλυπεῖν καὶ κολούειν τὸ
ἡδόμενον.

ΠΕΡΙ ΚΑΤΑΣΚΕΥΗΣ ΚΥΦΙΩΝ

Fr. 87. Plutarch, *De Is. et Osir.*, 80.

Τὸ δὲ κῦφι μῖγμα μὲν ἐκκαίδεκα μερῶν συν-
τιθεμένων ἐστί, μέλιτος καὶ οἴνου καὶ σταφίδος καὶ

¹ ⟨Ἄπιδος⟩ add. Xylander.

---

[1] El Kab on the right bank of the Nile, 53 miles S. of Luxor (Baedeker⁸, p. 365 ff.), the seat of Nekhebyt, the goddess of childbirth, and in prehistoric times the capital of the southern kingdom.

[2] Kyphi (Anc. Egyptian k³pt, from k³p, to burn) is mentioned in the Ebers Papyrus (Wreszinski, 98, 12 f.), where ten ingredients (without honey and wine) are given.

ON THE MAKING OF KYPHI Fr. 86, 87

the visitation continue, they consecrate the animals and slaughter them, intending thus to inflict a kind of chastisement upon the spirit, or at least to offer a great atonement for heinous offences. Moreover, in Eileithyiaspolis,[1] as Manetho has related, they used to burn men alive, calling them "Typhôn's followers"; and their ashes they would winnow and scatter broadcast until they were seen no more. But this was done openly and at a set time, namely in the dog-days; whereas the consecrations of sacred animals are secret ceremonies, taking place at irregular intervals as occasion demands, unknown to the common people except when the priests celebrate a funeral of Apis, and, displaying some of the animals, cast them together into the tomb in the presence of all, deeming that thus they are vexing Typhôn in return and curtailing his delight.

ON THE MAKING OF KYPHI.

Fr. 87 (from PLUTARCH, Is. and Osir., ch. 80).

Kyphi[2] is a mixture of sixteen ingredients—honey, wine, raisins, cyperus [? galingale], resin, myrrh,

Recipes of a similar nature have been found at Edfu (two) and at Philae (one): they were inscribed in hieroglyphs on temple-walls. Kyphi had a double use—as incense and as medicine. See further Ganszyniec in Pauly-Wissowa-Kroll, R.-E. (1924). Parthey (Isis und Osiris, pp. 277 ff.) describes the results of experiments with the recipes of Plutarch, of Galen (also sixteen ingredients), and of Dioscorides (ten ingredients): he gives first place to the kyphi prepared according to the prescription of Dioscorides.

κυπέρου, ῥητίνης τε καὶ σμύρνης καὶ ἀσπαλάθου καὶ σεσέλεως, ἔτι δὲ σχίνου τε καὶ ἀσφάλτου καὶ θρύου καὶ λαπάθου, πρὸς δὲ τούτοις ἀρκευθίδων ἀμφοῖν (ὧν τὴν μὲν μείζονα, τὴν δ' ἐλάττονα καλοῦσι) καὶ καρδαμώμου καὶ καλάμου.

[ΤΑ ΠΡΟΣ ΗΡΟΔΟΤΟΝ]

Fr. 88.[1]   *Etymologicum Magnum* (Gaisford), s.v. Λεοντοκόμος.

Τὸ δὲ λέων παρὰ τὸ λάω, τὸ θεωρῶ· ὀξυδερκέστατον γὰρ τὸ θηρίον, ὥς φησι Μανέθων ἐν τῷ πρὸς Ἡρόδοτον, ὅτι οὐδέποτε καθεύδει ὁ λέων, τοῦτο δὲ ἀπίθανον . . .

[1] *Cf.* also Fr. from Choeroboscus, *Orthogr.*, in Cramer, *Anecd. Graeca Ox.*, ii. 235, 32 (= *Etym. genuinum*): . . . ἀπὸ τούτου τοῦ λάω γέγονε λέων· ὀξυδερκέστατον γὰρ τὸ θηρίον· φασὶ γὰρ ὅτι οὐδέποτε καθεύδει ὁ λέων. τοῦτο δὲ ἀπίθανον . . . See Aelian, *De Nat. Anim.*, v. 39: Αἰγυπτίους ὑπὲρ αὐτοῦ κομπάζειν φασὶ λέγοντας ὅτι κρείττων ὕπνου λέων ἐστὶν ἀγρυπνῶν ἀεί.

---

[1] Aspalathus = Calycotome villosa.
[2] Cardamom = Elettaria cardamomum. See L.C.L., *Theophrastus*, ix. 7, 3 (Hort).
[3] Manetho's note may refer to such passages in Herodotus as ii. 65 ff. and iii. 108.

[*Footnote continued on opposite page.*]

[CRITICISMS OF HERODOTUS] Fr. 87, 88

aspalathus,[1] seselis [hartwort]; mastic, bitumen, thryon [a kind of reed or rush], dock [monk's rhubarb], as well as of both junipers (arceuthids—one called the greater, the other the less), cardamom,[2] and reed [orris-root, or root of sweet flag].

[CRITICISMS OF HERODOTUS]

Fr. 88 [3] (from the *Etymologicum Magnum*).

The word λέων ("lion") comes from λάω, "I see": the animal has indeed the keenest of sight, as Manetho says in his *Criticism of Herodotus* that the lion never sleeps.[4] But this is hard to believe.

Choeroboscus, in his work *On Orthography* (iv./v. A.D.), gives the derivation of λέων according to Orus or Hôrus in almost the same words as those quoted above from the *Etymologicum Magnum*; but he omits the clause "as Manetho says in his *Criticism of Herodotus*" (Cramer, *Anecdota Graeca e codd. manuscriptis bibliothecarum Oxoniensium*, ii. p. 235, ll. 32 ff. = *Etymologicum Genuinum*).

Cf. Aelian, *On the Nature of Animals*, v. 39: "the Egyptians, they say, boast about this, adding that the lion is superior to sleep, being always awake." Aelian quotes from Apion (see p. 19 n. 3), who may well have taken his statement from Manetho.

[4] By a curious coincidence, in Egyptian also the words for "lion" (*m'i*) and "to see" (*m'*) are very similar, and the word for "lion" is sometimes written as though it came from the verb "to see". Manetho possibly had this fact in mind when he stated that the lion never sleeps (Battiscombe Gunn).

FR. 88   MANETHO

Eustathius on Homer, *Iliad*, XI, 480:

(Τινὲς λέγουσιν) ὅτι ἐκ τοῦ λάω, τὸ βλέπω, γίνεται ὥσπερ ὁ λέων, οὕτω καὶ ὁ λίς, κατὰ τὸν γραμματικὸν Ὧρον, ὡς ὀξυδερκής, καὶ ὅτι, ὥς φησι Μανέθων ἐν τοῖς πρὸς Ἡρόδοτον, οὐ καθεύδει ὁ λέων ὅπερ ἀπίθανον . . .

[CRITICISMS OF HERODOTUS] Fr. 88

(*From* Eustathius.)

(Some say) that from λάω, " I see," comes not only λέων, but also λίς (a lion), according to Ôrus the grammarian,[1] because of its keen sight; and they add, as Manetho states in his *Criticisms of Herodotus*, that the lion never sleeps. This is hard to believe.

[1] Ôrus or Hôrus (v. A.D.) was, according to Suidas, an Alexandrian grammarian who taught at Constantinople: none of his numerous works is extant.

APPENDIX I

Pseudo-Manetho

Syncellus, p. 72.

Πρόκειται δὲ λοιπὸν καὶ περὶ τῆς τῶν Αἰγυπτίων δυναστείας μικρὰ διαλαβεῖν ἐκ τῶν Μανεθῶ τοῦ Σεβεννύτου, ὃς ἐπὶ Πτολεμαίου τοῦ Φιλαδέλφου 4 ἀρχιερεὺς τῶν ἐν Αἰγύπτῳ εἰδωλείων χρηματίσας ἐκ τῶν ἐν τῇ Σηριαδικῇ γῇ κειμένων στηλῶν ἱερᾷ, φησι, διαλέκτῳ καὶ ἱερογραφικοῖς γράμμασι κεχαρακτηρισμένων ὑπὸ Θὼθ τοῦ πρώτου Ἑρμοῦ, καὶ ἑρμηνευθεισῶν μετὰ τὸν κατακλυσμὸν [ἐκ τῆς ἱερᾶς διαλέκτου εἰς τὴν Ἑλληνίδα φωνήν][1] γράμμασιν ἱερογλυφικοῖς, καὶ ἀποτεθέντων[2] ἐν βίβλοις ὑπὸ τοῦ Ἀγαθοδαίμονος, υἱοῦ τοῦ δευτέρου Ἑρμοῦ, πατρὸς 12 δὲ τοῦ Τάτ, ἐν τοῖς ἀδύτοις τῶν ἱερῶν Αἰγύπτου, προσεφώνησε τῷ αὐτῷ Φιλαδέλφῳ βασιλεῖ δευτέρῳ Πτολεμαίῳ ἐν τῇ Βίβλῳ τῆς Σώθεος γράφων ἐπὶ λέξεως οὕτως·

[1] The words bracketed are probably a later interpolation.
[2] ἀποτεθεισῶν conj. Scaliger, Müller.

---

[1] Sêriadic land, *i.e.* Egypt, *cf.* Josephus, *Ant.* i. 71. In an inscription the home of Isis is Σειριὰς γῆ, and Isis herself is Νειλῶτις or Σειρίας, the Nile is Σείριος : see Reitzenstein, *Poimandres*, p. 183.

[2] For the god Thôth inscribing records, see p. xiv n. 1.

APPENDIX I.

PSEUDO-MANETHO.

(From SYNCELLUS).

It remains now to make brief extracts concerning the dynasties of Egypt from the works of Manetho of Sebennytus. In the time of Ptolemy Philadelphus he was styled high-priest of the pagan temples of Egypt, and wrote from inscriptions in the Sêriadic land,[1] traced, he says, in sacred language and holy characters by Thôth,[2] the first Hermês, and translated after the Flood ... in hieroglyphic characters. When the work had been arranged in books by Agathodaemôn, son of the second Hermês [3] and father of Tat, in the temple-shrines of Egypt, Manetho dedicated it to the above King Ptolemy II. Philadelphus in his *Book of Sôthis,* using the following words:

[3] The second Hermês is Hermês Trismegistus, the teacher.
For a discussion of the whole passage, see W. Scott, *Hermetica,* iii. pp. 492 f. He pointed out manifest breaches of continuity after χρηματίσας (end of l. 4) and after Αἰγύπτου (end of l. 12). If the intervening 8 lines are cut out (ἐκ τῶν ... Αἰγύπτου), the sentence runs smoothly; and Scott suggested that these 8 lines originally stood in Manetho's letter after ἃ ἔμαθον. Even with this insertion there still remains a gap before ἱερὰ βιβλία, but apart from that lacuna, the whole becomes intelligible.

App. I   PSEUDO-MANETHO

Ἐπιστολὴ Μανεθῶ τοῦ Σεβεννύτου πρὸς Πτολεμαῖον τὸν Φιλάδελφον.

"Βασιλεῖ μεγάλῳ Πτολεμαίῳ Φιλαδέλφῳ σεβαστῷ Μανεθῶ ἀρχιερεὺς καὶ γραμματεὺς τῶν κατ' Αἴγυπτον ἱερῶν ἀδύτων, γένει Σεβεννύτης ὑπάρχων Ἡλιουπολίτης, τῷ δεσπότῃ μου Πτολεμαίῳ χαίρειν.

Ἡμᾶς δεῖ λογίζεσθαι, μέγιστε βασιλεῦ, περὶ πάντων ὧν ἐὰν βούλῃ ἡμᾶς ἐξετάσαι πραγμάτων. ἐπιζητοῦντι οὖν[1] σοι περὶ τῶν μελλόντων τῷ κόσμῳ γίγνεσθαι, καθὼς ἐκέλευσάς μοι, παραφανήσεταί σοι ἃ ἔμαθον ἱερὰ βιβλία γραφέντα ὑπὸ τοῦ προπάτορος, τρισμεγίστου Ἑρμοῦ. ἔρρωσό μοι, δέσποτά μου βασιλεῦ."

Ταῦτα περὶ τῆς ἑρμηνείας τῶν ὑπὸ τοῦ δευτέρου Ἑρμοῦ γραφέντων βιβλίων λέγει. μετὰ δὲ ταῦτα καὶ περὶ ἐθνῶν Αἰγυπτιακῶν πέντε ἐν τριάκοντα δυναστείαις ἱστορεῖ[2] . . .

[1] οὖν add. Boeckh.
[2] For the continuation of this, see Fr. 2, p. 10.

[1] Augustus, a title of the Roman emperor, was not used in Ptolemaic times.
[2] For a curious juxtaposition of Manetho and Hermês Trismegistus, see Wellmann in *Hermes*, xxxv. p. 367.

PSEUDO-MANETHO   App. I

Letter of Manetho of Sebennytus to Ptolemy Philadelphus.

"To the great King Ptolemy Philadelphus Augustus.[1] Greeting to my lord Ptolemy from Manetho, high-priest and scribe of the sacred shrines of Egypt, born at Sebennytus and dwelling at Hêliopolis. It is my duty, almighty king, to reflect upon all such matters as you may desire me to investigate. So, as you are making researches concerning the future of the universe, in obedience to your command I shall place before you the Sacred Books which I have studied, written by your forefather, Hermês Trismegistus.[2] Farewell, I pray, my lord King."

Such is his account of the translation of the books written by the second Hermês. Thereafter Manetho tells also of five Egyptian tribes which formed thirty dynasties . . .

(Fr. 2, p. 11, follows directly after this.)

A MS. of Celsus gives a list of medical writers, Egyptian or Greek and Latin : they include (col. I, ll. 9-13) Hermês Trismegistus, Manetho (MS. emmanetos), Nechepsô, Cleopatra regina. Here Manetho is followed by Nechepsô, to whom, along with Petosiris (perhaps another name of Nechepsô), works on astrology were attributed in the Second Century B.C.: see W. Kroll and M. Pieper in *R.-E.* xvi. 2 (1935), *s.v.* Nechepsô.

211

APPENDIX II

Eratosthenes (?)

Fr. 7 (a). *Syncellus*, p. 171.

Θηβαίων βασιλεῖς.

Ἀπολλόδωρος χρονικὸς ἄλλην Αἰγυπτίων τῶν Θηβαίων λεγομένων βασιλείαν ἀνεγράψατο βασιλέων λη΄, ἐτῶν ‚αος΄. ἥτις ἤρξατο μὲν τῷ ‚βπ΄ ἔτει τοῦ κόσμου, ἔληξε δὲ εἰς τὸ ‚γμε΄ [1] ἔτος τοῦ κόσμου, ὧν τὴν γνῶσιν, φησὶν, ὁ Ἐρατοσθένης λαβὼν Αἰγυπτιακοῖς ὑπομνήμασι καὶ ὀνόμασι κατὰ πρόσταξιν βασιλικὴν τῇ Ἑλλάδι φωνῇ παρέφρασεν οὕτως·

Θηβαίων βασιλέων τῶν μετὰ ‚αρκδ΄ ἔτη τῆς διασπορᾶς λη΄ βασιλειῶν,

[1] ‚γπιος΄ m.

---

[1] This list of kings was said to have been taken by Apollodorus (ii. B.C.) from Eratosthenes of Cyrene (iii. B.C.) whom Apollodorus often followed as an authority; but according to Jacoby (*Apollodors Chronik*, pp. 399 ff., Fr. 117—Pseudo-Apollodorus) the list of "Theban" kings owes nothing either to Apollodorus or to Eratosthenes, but is the work of one who sought to recommend his compilation under two distinguished names. The list,

APPENDIX II.

ERATOSTHENES (?) (*From Syncellus*).

Fr. 7 (a).

Kings of Thebes.[1]

Apollodorus, the chronographer, recorded another dynasty of Egyptian kings,—the Thebans, as they are called,—thirty-eight kings ruling for 1076 years. This dynasty began in Anno Mundi 2900, and came to an end in Anno Mundi 3045 [3976]. The knowledge of these kings, he says, Eratosthenes took from Egyptian records and lists, and at the king's command he translated them into the Greek language, as follows:

Of the Theban kings in thirty-eight dynasties ruling 1124 years after the Dispersion,

---

containing thirty-eight kings, who ruled for 1076 years, is of Theban origin, derived from a Royal List such as that of Karnak: the explanations of the names are interesting, and the variations in Nos. 11 and 15 may be due to the priests themselves. Historically the list is of no great worth: several of the names are not proper names, but Throne-names, such as are found in the Royal Lists and the Turin Papyrus (Meyer, *Aeg. Chron.* pp. 99 ff.).

Kings 1-5 correspond to Dynasty I., 13-17 to Dynasty IV., 18-22 to Dynasty VI.

App. II   PSEUDO-MANETHO

α' ⟨πρῶτος⟩[1] ἐβασίλευσε Μήνης Θηβαῖος,[2] ὅ ἑρμηνεύεται αἰώνιος[3]· ἐβασίλευσεν ἔτη ξβ'. τοῦ δὲ κόσμου ἦν ἔτος ͵βπ'.

β' Θηβαίων δεύτερος ἐβασίλευσεν Ἀθώθης, υἱὸς Μήνεως, ἔτη νθ'. οὗτος ἑρμηνεύεται Ἑρμογένης.. ἔτος τοῦ κόσμου ͵βπξβ'.

γ' Θηβαίων Αἰγυπτίων τρίτος ἐβασίλευσεν Ἀθώθης ὁμώνυμος, ἔτη λβ'. τοῦ δὲ κόσμου ἦν ἔτος ͵γκα'.

Syncellus, p. 180.

δ' Θηβαίων ἐβασίλευσε δ' Μιαβαῆς,[4] υἱὸς Ἀθώθεως, ἔτη ιθ'. οὗτος ἑρμηνεύεται φιλόταυρος.[5] τοῦ δὲ κόσμου ἦν ἔτος ͵γνγ'.

ε' Θηβαίων ἐβασίλευσε ε' Πεμφῶς,[6] υἱὸς Ἀθώθους, ὅ ἐστιν Ἡρακλείδης, ἔτη ιη'. τοῦ δὲ κόσμου ἦν ἔτος ͵γοβ'.

Fr. 13.   Syncellus, p. 180.

ς' Θηβαίων Αἰγυπτίων ἐβασίλευσεν ς' Μομχειρὶ Μεμφίτης, ἔτη οθ'. οὗτος ἑρ-

[1] πρῶτος add. Goar.
[2] Θηβαῖος conj. Meyer: Θηνίτης B: Θηβινίτης Θηβαῖος Dindorf.
[3] αἰώνιος corr. Jablonski: διώνιος B, Διώνιος A.
[4] Διαβιῆς B.
[5] φιλόταυρος Bunsen: φιλέτεος codd.: φιλέταιρος Scaliger.
[6] Σεμψῶς Bunsen.

ERATOSTHENES (?) APP. II

1. The first was Mênês of Thebes, whose name, being interpreted, means "everlasting".[1] He reigned for 62 years. Anno mundi 2900.
2. The second king of Thebes was Athôthês, son of Mênês, for 59 years. His name, being interpreted, means "Born of Hermês".[2] Anno mundi 2962.
3. The third king of Thebes in Egypt was Athôthês II., for 32 years. Anno mundi 3021.
4. The fourth king of Thebes was Miabaês, son of Athôthis, for 19 years. His name, being interpreted, means "Bull-lover".[3] Anno mundi 3053.
5. The fifth king of Thebes was Pemphôs (? Sempsôs, Semempsês), son of Athôthis. His name is "descendant of Hêraclês," and he reigned for 18 years. Anno mundi 3072.

Fr. 13.

6. The sixth king of Thebes in Egypt was Momcheiri of Memphis, reigning for 79 years. His name, being interpreted, means

---

[1] The Egyptian form of the name Mênês may quite well be interpreted as "the abiding one," from *mn*, "to endure".

[2] This etymology obviously assumes the presence of the divine name Thôth in the name Athôthês.

[3] The first element of the name Miabaês is clearly some form of the verb *mr*, "to love".

App. II PSEUDO-MANETHO

μηνεύεται ἡγήσανδρος¹· περισσομελής, [τοιγὰρ ἄμαχος].² τοῦ δὲ κόσμου ἦν ‚γϞ´.

ζ´ Θηβαίων Αἰγυπτίων ἐβασίλευσεν ζ´ Στοῖχος, υἱὸς αὐτοῦ· ὅ ἐστιν Ἄρης ἀναίσθητος, ἔτη ϛ´. τοῦ δὲ κόσμου ἦν ἔτος ‚γρξθ´.

η´ Θηβαίων Αἰγυπτίων ἐβασίλευσεν ὄγδοος Γοσορμίης, ὅ ἐστιν αἰτησιπαντός,³ ἔτη λ´. τοῦ δὲ κόσμου ἦν ἔτος ‚γροε´.

θ´ Θηβαίων Αἰγυπτίων ἐβασίλευσεν θ´ Μάρης, υἱὸς αὐτοῦ, ὅ ἐστιν Ἡλιόδωρος, ἔτη κϛ´. τοῦ δὲ κόσμου ἦν ἔτος ‚γσε´.

Syncellus, p. 190.

ι´ Θηβαίων Αἰγυπτίων ι´ ἐβασίλευσεν Ἀνωΰφίς, ὅ ἐστιν ἐπίκωμος,⁴ ἔτη κ´. τοῦ δὲ κόσμου ἦν ἔτος ‚γσλα´.

ια´ Θηβαίων Αἰγυπτίων ια´ ἐβασίλευσε Σίριος, ὅ ἐστιν υἱὸς κόρης, ὡς δὲ ἕτεροι ἀβάσκαντος, ἔτη ιη´. τοῦ δὲ κόσμου ἦν ἔτος ‚γσνα´.

ιβ´ Θηβαίων Αἰγυπτίων ιβ´ ἐβασίλευσε Χνοῦβος ἢ Γνεῦρος, ὅ ἐστι Χρυσὸς ἢ Χρυσοῦς

¹ Conj. Bunsen: τῆς ἀνδρός codd.: ἔτης ἀνδρός Gutschmid.
² A gloss, which the codd. have before Μομχειρί.
³ ἐτησιπαντός A: ἔτης παντος Gutschmid.
⁴ B: ἐπίκομος A.

---

¹ With this interpretation of the name Marês (which may correctly explain the second element as Rê, " the Sun "), cf. ἥλιος εὐφεγγής, " a brilliant Sun," in *Hymn IV.*,

"leader of men". He had exceeding large limbs (and was therefore irresistible). Anno mundi 3090.

7. The seventh king of Thebes in Egypt was his son, Stoichos. The name means "unfeeling Arês". He reigned for 6 years. Anno mundi 3169.

8. The eighth king of Thebes in Egypt was Gosormiês, whose name means "all-demanding". He reigned for 30 years. Anno mundi 3175.

9. The ninth king of Thebes in Egypt was his son, Marês, whose name means "gift of the Sun".[1] He reigned for 26 years. Anno mundi 3205.

10. The tenth king of Thebes in Egypt was Anôÿphis, whose name means "revelling".[2] He reigned for 20 years. Anno mundi 3231.

11. The eleventh king of Thebes in Egypt was Sirius, whose name means "son of the iris of the eye,"[3] or, as others say, "unharmed by the evil eye". He reigned for 18 years. Anno mundi 3251.

12. The twelfth king of Thebes in Egypt was Chnubos or Gneuros, which means "gold"[4]

---

line 32, A. Vogliano, *Madinet Madi, Primo Rapporto* (1936): see note on No. 35 *infra*, p. 224.

[2] Possibly this explanation is based upon the Egyptian word *unóf*, "to rejoice" (B.G.).

[3] In Egyptian *si-iri* means "son of the eye".

[4] *Nûb* is Egyptian for "gold".

App. II   PSEUDO-MANETHO

υἱός,¹ ἔτη κβ'. τοῦ δὲ κόσμου ἦν ἔτος ,γσξθ'.

ιγ' Θηβαίων Αἰγυπτίων ιγ' ἐβασίλευσε 'Ραΰωσις, ὅ ἐστιν ἀρχικράτωρ, ἔτη ιγ'. τοῦ δὲ κόσμου ἦν ἔτος ,γσϟα'.

ιδ' Θηβαίων Αἰγυπτίων ιδ' ἐβασίλευσε Βιύρης, ἔτη ι'. τοῦ δὲ κόσμου ἦν ἔτος ,γτδ'.

Fr. 17.   Syncellus, p. 190.

ιε' Θηβαίων Αἰγυπτίων ιε' ἐβασίλευσε Σαῶφις, κωμαστής, κατὰ δὲ ἐνίους χρηματιστής, ἔτη κθ'. τοῦ δὲ κόσμου ἦν ἔτος ,γτιδ'.

Syncellus, p. 195.

ις' Θηβαίων ις' ἐβασίλευσε Σαῶφις β', ἔτη κζ'. τοῦ δὲ κόσμου ἦν ἔτος ,γτμγ'.

ιζ' Θηβαίων ιζ' ἐβασίλευσε Μοσχερῆς,² ἡλιόδοτος, ἔτη λα'. τοῦ δὲ κόσμου ἦν ἔτος ,γτο'.

ιη' Θηβαίων ιη' ἐβασίλευσε Μοσθῆς,³ ἔτη λγ'. τοῦ δὲ κόσμου ἦν ἔτος ,γυα'.

ιθ' Θηβαίων ιθ' ἐβασίλευσε Παμμῆς, ἀρχοειδής,⁴ ἔτη λε'. τοῦ δὲ κόσμου ἦν ἔτος ,γυλδ'.

¹ Corr. Bunsen : Χνοῦβος Γνευρός, ὅ ἐστι Χρύσης Χρύσου υἱός codd.
² Μεγχερῆς conj. Bunsen.
³ Μεγχερῆς β' conj. Bunsen.
⁴ Conj. Gutschmid: ἀρχονδής codd.

ERATOSTHENES (?)   App. II

or "golden son" (or his son). He reigned for 22 years. Anno mundi 3269.

13. The thirteenth king of Thebes in Egypt was Raÿôsis, which means "the arch-masterful".[1] He reigned for 13 years Anno mundi 3291.
14. The fourteenth king of Thebes in Egypt was Biÿrês, who reigned for 10 years. Anno mundi 3304.

Fr. 17.

15. The fifteenth king of Thebes in Egypt was Saôphis, "reveller," or, according to some, "money-getter, trafficker". He reigned for 29 years. Anno mundi 3314.
16. The sixteenth king of Thebes was Saôphis II, who reigned for 27 years. Anno mundi 3343.
17. The seventeenth king of Thebes was Moscherês (? Mencherês), "gift of the Sun," who reigned for 31 years. Anno mundi 3370.
18. The eighteenth king of Thebes was Mosthês (? Mencherês II.), who reigned for 33 years. Anno mundi 3401.
19. The nineteenth king of Thebes was Pammês, "leader-like," who reigned for 35 years. Anno mundi 3434.

---

[1] Possibly, according to this explanation, Ra- (or Rha-) is the Egyptian *ḥry*, "master," and the rest of the name *wôse(r), "powerful" (B.G.).

App. II   PSEUDO-MANETHO

Fr. 22.   Syncellus, p. 195.

κ' Θηβαίων κ' ἐβασίλευσεν Ἀπάππους, μέγιστος. οὗτος, ὥς φασι, παρὰ ὥραν μίαν ἐβασίλευσεν ἔτη ρ'. τοῦ δὲ κόσμου ἦν ἔτος ͵γυξθ'.
κα' Θηβαίων κα' ἐβασίλευσεν Ἐχεσκοσοκάρας,¹ ἔτος α'. τοῦ δὲ κόσμου ἦν ἔτος ͵γφξθ'.
κβ' Θηβαίων κβ' ἐβασίλευσε Νίτωκρις, γυνὴ ἀντὶ ἀνδρός, ὅ ἐστιν Ἀθηνᾶ νικηφόρος, ἔτη ϛ'. τοῦ δὲ κόσμου ἦν ἔτος ͵γφο'.

Fr. 33.   Syncellus, p. 196.

κγ' Θηβαίων κγ' ἐβασίλευσε Μυρταῖος² Ἀμμωνόδοτος, ἔτη κβ'. τοῦ δὲ κόσμου ἦν ἔτος ͵γφοϛ'.³

Syncellus, p. 204.

κδ' Θηβαίων κδ' ἐβασίλευσεν Οὐωσιμάρης,⁴ κραταιός ἐστιν⁵ ἥλιος, ἔτη ιβ'. τοῦ δὲ κόσμου ἦν ἔτος ͵γφϟη'.
κε' Θηβαίων κε' ἐβασίλευσε Σεθίνιλος,⁶ ὅ ἐστιν αὐξήσας τὸ πάτριον κράτος, ἔτη η'. τοῦ δὲ κόσμου ἦν ἔτος ͵γχι'.

¹ B : ἐχεσκὸς ὀκάρας A.   ² Conj. Ἀμυρταῖος.
³ m. : ͵γφϟη' codd.   ⁴ Jablonski : Θυωσιμάρης B.
⁵ Bunsen : ὅ ἐστιν codd.
⁶ B : Θίριλλος A : Θίνιλλος Dindorf.

ERATOSTHENES (?) APP. II

Fr. 22.

20. The twentieth king of Thebes was Apappûs (Pepi),[1] "the very great". He, they say, ruled for 100 years all but one hour. Anno mundi 3469.
21. The twenty-first king of Thebes was Echeskosokaras, for 1 year. Anno mundi 3569.
22. The twenty-second ruler of Thebes was Nitôcris,[2] a queen, not a king. Her name means "Athêna the victorious," and she reigned for 6 years. Anno mundi 3570.

Fr. 33.

23. The twenty-third king of Thebes was Myrtaeus (Amyrtaeus), "gift of Ammôn,"[3] for 22 years. Anno mundi 3576.
24. The twenty-fourth king of Thebes was Uôsimarês, "Mighty is the Sun,"[4] for 12 years. Anno mundi 3598.
25. The twenty-fifth king of Thebes was Sethinilus (Thirillus), which means "having increased his ancestral power," for 8 years. Anno mundi 3610.

[1] Apappûs is the Phiôps of Fr. 20. 4, with a curious misunderstanding of his reign of 94 years.

[2] See p. 54 n. 2, and Wainwright, *Sky-Religion*, pp. 41, 45.

[3] This interpretation is based upon the common Egyptian name Amenerdais, "Amûn has given him".

[4] The Egyptian *Wôse-mi-Rê* means "Mighty like the Sun": Uôsimarês may however be intended for the first half of the *praenomen* of Ramessês II., *Wese-mê-Rê*, but this means "Rê is mighty in justice" (B.G.).

App. II   PSEUDO-MANETHO

κϛ' Θηβαίων κϛ' ἐβασίλευσε Σεμφρουκράτης, ὅ ἐστιν Ἡρακλῆς Ἁρποκράτης, ἔτη ιη'. τοῦ δὲ κόσμου ἦν ἔτος ,γχιη'.

κζ' Θηβαίων κζ' ἐβασίλευσε Χουθήρ, ταῦρος τύραννος, ἔτη ζ'. τοῦ δὲ κόσμου ἦν ἔτος ,γχλϛ'.

κη' Θηβαίων κη' ἐβασίλευσε Μευρής,¹ φίλος κόρης,² ἔτη ιβ'. τοῦ δὲ κόσμου ἦν ἔτος ,γχμγ'.

κθ' Θηβαίων κθ' ἐβασίλευσε Χωμαεφθά,³ κόσμος φιλήφαιστος, ἔτη ια'. τοῦ δὲ κόσμου ἦν ἔτος ,γχνε'.

λ' Θηβαίων λ' ἐβασίλευσε Σοικούνιος⁴ ὀχοτύραννος,⁵ ἔτη ξ'. τοῦ δὲ κόσμου ἦν ἔτος ,γχξϛ'.

Syncellus, p. 233.

λα' Θηβαίων λα' ἐβασίλευσε Πετεαθυρῆς, ἔτη ιϛ'. τοῦ δὲ κόσμου ἦν ἔτος ,γψκϛ'.

Fr. 37.

λβ' Θηβαίων λβ' ἐβασίλευσε ⟨Σταμμενέμης α',⁶ ἔτη κϛ'. τοῦ δὲ κόσμου ἦν ἔτος ,γψμβ'.

---

¹ Conj. Μιειρής. ² Gutschmid: φιλόσκορος codd.
³ Τωμαεφθά Bunsen. ⁴ Σοικοῦνις Bunsen.
⁵ ὡς Ὦχος τύραννος Bunsen: Σοῦχος τύραννος Gutschmid.
⁶ Ἀμμενέμης Bunsen. A lacuna here in codd.

---

¹ The first syllable of the name Chuthêr may represent the Egyptian *kŏ*, "bull".
² In Egyptian, "loving the eye" is *mai-îri*.

ERATOSTHENES (?)   App. II

26. The twenty-sixth king of Thebes was Semphrucratês, which means "Heraclês Harpocratês," for 18 years. Anno mundi 3618.
27. The twenty-seventh king of Thebes was Chuthêr, "bull-lord,"[1] for 7 years. Anno mundi 3636.
28. The twenty-eighth king of Thebes was Meurês (Mieirês), "loving the iris of the eye,"[2] for 12 years. Anno mundi 3643.
29. The twenty-ninth king of Thebes was Chômaephtha (Tômaephtha), "world, loving Hêphaestus,"[3] for 11 years. Anno mundi 3655.
30. The thirtieth king of Thebes was Soicunius (or Soicunis), † hochotyrannos, †[4] (or Soicuniosochus the lord), for 60 years. Anno mundi 3666.
31. The thirty-first king of Thebes was Peteathyrês,[5] for 16 years. Anno mundi 3726.

Fr. 37.

32. The thirty-second king of Thebes was ⟨Stammenemês I. (Ammenemês I.), for 26 years. Anno mundi 3742.

[3] As to the latter part of the name, "loving Hêphaestus" is in Egyptian *mai-Ptah*: the emended Tô- represents the Egyptian *tŏ*, "world" (B.G.).
[4] Bunsen emends this *vox nihili* to mean "a tyrant like Ôchus": Gutschmid, to mean "Suchus the lord". The latter description may refer to one of the Sebekḥotpes.
[5] Peteathyrês, a well-formed name Pede-hathor, which does not occur as a king's name.

App. II PSEUDO-MANETHO

λγ' Θηβαίων λγ' ἐβασίλευσε⟩ Σταμμενέμης β',
ἔτη κγ'. τοῦ δὲ κόσμου ἦν ἔτος ͵γψξη'.

λδ' Θηβαίων λδ' ἐβασίλευσε Σιστοσιχερμῆς,
Ἡρακλῆς κραταιός,¹ ἔτη νε'. τοῦ δὲ κόσμου
ἦν ἔτος ͵γψϙα'.

λε' Θηβαίων λε' ἐβασίλευσε Μάρης, ἔτη μγ'.
τοῦ δὲ κόσμου ἦν ἔτος ͵γωμϛ'.

Fr. 40.

λϛ' Θηβαίων λϛ' ἐβασίλευσε Σιφθὰς² ὁ καὶ
Ἑρμῆς, υἱὸς Ἡφαίστου, ἔτη ε'. τοῦ δὲ
κόσμου ἦν ἔτος ͵γωπθ'.

Syncellus, p. 278.

λζ' Θηβαίων λζ' ἐβασίλευσε Φρουορῶ³ ἤτοι
Νεῖλος, ἔτη ε'.⁴ τοῦ δὲ κόσμου ἦν ἔτος
͵γωϞδ'.⁵

λη' Θηβαίων λη' ἐβασίλευσε Ἀμουθαρταῖος, ἔτη
ξγ'. τοῦ δὲ κόσμου ἦν ἔτος ͵γϡιγ'.

¹ Σεσόρτωσις, Ἑρμῆς ἢ Ἡρακλῆς κραταιός conj. Bunsen.
² Bunsen: Σιφόας codd.   ³ Φουορῶ Bunsen.
⁴ ιθ' corr. Müller.   ⁵ ͵γωπθ' codd.

---

[1] Besides Marês and derived forms (Marrês, Aelian, *De Nat. Anim.* vi. 7; Marros and Mendês, Diod. Sic. i. 61, 1; Imandês, Strabo, 17. 1. 37, 42), there are two types of variants on the name of Amenemhêt III.—(1) Lamarês (Fr. 34), Lamaris (Fr. 35), Labarês, Labaris; and (2) Pramarrês, Premanrês (Pr- = Pharaoh): *cf.* Poremanrês, P. Mich. Zen. 84, lines 18, 21, Porramanrês in A. Vogliano, *Madinet Madi, Primo Rapporto* (1936), *Hymn* IV., line 34, where the first two syllables must be eliminated if

ERATOSTHENES (?) APP. II

33. The thirty-third king of Thebes was⟩ Stammenemês II. (Ammenemês II.), for 23 years. Anno mundi 3768.
34. The thirty-fourth king of Thebes was Sistosichermês, " valiant Hêraclês " (Sistosis or Sesortôsis, " valiant Hermês or Hêraclês "), for 55 years. Anno mundi 3791.
35. The thirty-fifth king of Thebes was Marês,[1] for 43 years. Anno mundi 3846.

Fr. 40.

36. The thirty-sixth king of Thebes was Siphthas,[2] also called Hermês, " son of Hêphaestus," for 5 years. Anno mundi 3889.
37. The thirty-seventh king of Thebes was Phruorô[3] (Phuorô) or " the Nile," for 5 (? 19) years. Anno mundi 3894.
38. The thirty-eighth king of Thebes was Amuthartaeus, for 63 years. Anno mundi 3913.

[Syncellus then adds (p. 279) in much the same phrase as that quoted at the beginning of Appendix II.: " These names Eratosthenes took from the sacred scribes at Diospolis and translated from Egyptian into the Greek language."]

---

the pentameter is to scan. [See note on p. 50. The temple at the vestibule of which the Hymn was inscribed is dated 95 B.C.]

[2] Siphthas is King Siptah ("son of Ptah "), probably Thuôris (Thuôsris), of Dynasty XIX.

[3] The Egyptian name for the River Nile is *p-yeor-o*. For comparisons of the King of Egypt with the River Nile, see Grapow, *Die Bildlichen Ausdrückedes Aegyptischen*, p. 62.

APPENDIX III

Το Παλαιον Χρονικον.

Syncellus, p. 95.

Φέρεται γὰρ παρ' Αἰγυπτίοις παλαιόν τι χρονογραφεῖον, ἐξ οὗ καὶ τὸν Μανεθῶ πεπλανῆσθαι νομίζω, περιέχον λ' δυναστειῶν ἐν γενεαῖς πάλιν ριγ' χρόνον ἄπειρον [καὶ οὐ τὸν αὐτὸν τοῦ¹ Μανεθῶ] ἐν μυριάσι τρισὶ καὶ ͵ϛφκε΄, πρῶτον μὲν τῶν Ἀεριτῶν,² δεύτερον δὲ τῶν Μεστραίων, τρίτον δὲ Αἰγυπτίων, οὕτω πως ἐπὶ λέξεως ἔχον·

Θεῶν βασιλεία κατὰ τὸ Παλαιὸν Χρονικόν.

Ἡφαίστου χρόνος οὐκ ἔστι διὰ τὸ νυκτὸς καὶ ἡμέρας αὐτὸν φαίνειν.

¹ Hopfner: τὸν A: ὃν Boeckh, Bunsen.
² Αὐριτῶν codd.

---

[1] The Old Chronicle is dated by Gutschmid to the end of the second century after Christ. Gelzer would refer its statements to another source than Manetho, perhaps Ptolemy of Mendês; while Meyer regards it as the work of Panodôrus, c. A.D. 400 (cf. Fr. 2).

[2] By the name Manetho Syncellus refers, as always, to the *Book of Sôthis* (App. IV.).

[3] The actual total of years from the items given, if 6 years be assigned to Dynasty XXVIII., is 36,347, *i.e.* 178 years

APPENDIX III.

THE OLD CHRONICLE.

(From Syncellus).

Now, among the Egyptians there is current an old chronography,[1] by which indeed. I believe, Manetho[2] has been led into error.

In 30 dynasties with 113 generations, it comprises an immense period of time [not the same as Manetho gives] in 36,525 years,[3] dealing first with the Aeritae,[4] next with the Mestraei, and thirdly with the Egyptians. Its contents are somewhat as follows:—

Dynasties of the Gods according to the Old Chronicle.

Hêphaestus has no period assigned, because he shines night and day. Hêlios [the Sun], son of

less than the total given in the text. The number of generations, 113, is obtained by counting 1 for Dynasty XXVIII. and 7 for XXIX. This vast world-period of 36,525 years is 25 times the Sôthic period of 1461 calendar years (or 1460 Sôthic years): see *infra*, and for the Sôthic period, Intro. pp. xxix f.

[4] Aeritae and Mestraei are really the same as the third race, the Egyptians, the three names apparently referring to Egypt at three different dates. Aeria is an old name of Egypt (Euseb., *Chron.* in Syncellus, p. 293, Armenian Version (Schöne, p. 30), Aegyptus quae prius Aeria dicebatur . . .). Mestraei (Josephus, *Antiq.* 1. 6. 2)—from Mestraïm (p. 7 n. 2).

App. III PSEUDO-MANETHO

Ἥλιος Ἡφαίστου ἐβασίλευσεν ἐτῶν μυριάδας τρεῖς.

Ἔπειτα Κρόνος, φησί, καὶ οἱ λοιποὶ πάντες θεοὶ δώδεκα ἐβασίλευσαν ἔτη ͵γψπδ'.

Ἔπειτα ἡμίθεοι βασιλεῖς ὀκτὼ ἔτη σιζ'.

Καὶ μετ' αὐτοὺς γενεαὶ ιε' Κυνικοῦ κύκλου ἀνεγράφησαν ἐν ἔτεσιν υμγ'.

Εἶτα Τανιτῶν ις' δυναστεία, γενεῶν η', ἐτῶν ρϟ'.

Πρὸς οἷς ιζ' δυναστεία Μεμφιτῶν, γενεῶν δ', ἐτῶν ργ'.

Μεθ' οὓς ιη' δυναστεία Μεμφιτῶν, γενεῶν ιδ', ἐτῶν τμη'.

Ἔπειτα ιθ' δυναστεία Διοσπολιτῶν, γενεῶν ε', ἐτῶν ρϟδ'.

Εἶτα κ' δυναστεία Διοσπολιτῶν, γενεῶν η', ἐτῶν σκη'.

Ἔπειτα κα' δυναστεία Τανιτῶν, γενεῶν ς', ἐτῶν ρκα'.

Εἶτα κβ' δυναστεία Τανιτῶν, γενεῶν γ', ἐτῶν μη'.

Ἔπειτα κγ' δυναστεία Διοσπολιτῶν, γενεῶν β', ἐτῶν ιθ'.

Εἶτα κδ' δυναστεία Σαϊτῶν, γενεῶν γ', ἐτῶν μδ'.

Πρὸς οἷς κε' δυναστεία Αἰθιόπων, γενεῶν γ', ἐτῶν μδ'.

Μεθ' οὓς κς' δυναστεία Μεμφιτῶν, γενεῶν ζ', ἐτῶν ροζ'.

THE OLD CHRONICLE   App. III

Hêphaestus, ruled for 30,000 years. Then Cronos (it says) and the remaining gods, 12 in number, reigned altogether for 3984 years. Next, the eight demi-gods were kings for 217 years; and after them 15 generations of the Sôthic Cycle are recorded with 443 years.[1]

Then follow:

The Sixteenth Dynasty of Kings of Tanis, in 8 generations, for 190 years.

The Seventeenth Dynasty of Kings of Memphis, in 4 generations, for 103 years.

The Eighteenth Dynasty of Kings of Memphis, in 14 generations, for 348 years.

The Nineteenth Dynasty of Kings of Diospolis, in 5 generations, for 194 years.

The Twentieth Dynasty of Kings of Diospolis, in 8 generations, for 228 years.

The Twenty-first Dynasty of Kings of Tanis, in 6 generations, for 121 years.

The Twenty-second Dynasty of Kings of Tanis, in 3 generations, for 48 years.

The Twenty-third Dynasty of Kings of Diospolis, in 2 generations, for 19 years.

The Twenty-fourth Dynasty of Kings of Saïs, in 3 generations, for 44 years.

The Twenty-fifth Dynasty of Ethiopian Kings, in 3 generations, for 44 years.

The Twenty-sixth Dynasty of Kings of Memphis, in 7 generations, for 177 years.

---

[1] This total comes, not from the *Book of Sôthis* which gives 395 for the first 15, but from Eratosthenes (App. II.). A smaller total than Manetho's 3357 years was desired in order to shorten the duration of the historical age of Egypt.

App. III PSEUDO-MANETHO

Καὶ μετ' αὐτοὺς κζ' δυναστεία¹ Περσῶν, γενεῶν ε', ἐτῶν ρκδ'.

Ἔπειτα κθ' δυναστεία Τανιτῶν γενεῶν ⟨ζ'⟩, ἐτῶν λθ'.
Καὶ ἐπὶ πάσαις λ' δυναστεία Τανίτου ἑνός, ἔτη ιη'.
Τὰ πάντα ὁμοῦ τῶν λ' δυναστειῶν ἔτη Μγ' καὶ ͵ϛφκε'.

Ταῦτα ἀναλυόμενα, εἴτουν μεριζόμενα, παρὰ τὰ ͵αυξα' ἔτη εἴκοσι πεντάκις, τὴν παρ' Αἰγυπτίοις καὶ Ἕλλησιν ἀποκατάστασιν τοῦ ζωδιακοῦ μυθολογουμένην δηλοῖ, τοῦτ' ἔστι τὴν ἀπὸ τοῦ αὐτοῦ σημείου ἐπὶ τὸ αὐτὸ σημεῖον, ὅ ἐστι πρῶτον λεπτὸν τῆς πρώτης μοίρας τοῦ ἰσημερινοῦ ζῳδίου, κριοῦ λεγομένου παρ' αὐτοῖς, ὥσπερ καὶ ἐν τοῖς Γενικοῖς τοῦ Ἑρμοῦ καὶ ἐν Κυραννίσι βίβλοις εἴρηται.

Ἐντεῦθεν δὲ οἶμαι καὶ Πτολεμαῖον τὸν Κλαύδιον τοὺς προχείρους κανόνας τῆς ἀστρονομίας διὰ κε' ἐτηρίδων ψηφίζεσθαι θεσπίσαι . . .

Ἐντεῦθεν δέ ἐστι καὶ τὸ ἀσύμφωνον τῶν τοιούτων ἐκδόσεων πρός τε τὰς θείας ἡμῶν γραφὰς καὶ πρὸς ἄλληλα ἐπιγνῶναι, ὅτι αὕτη μὲν ἡ παλαιοτέρα νομιζομένη Αἰγυπτίων συγγραφὴ Ἡφαίστου μὲν ἄπειρον εἰσάγει χρόνον, τῶν δὲ λοιπῶν κθ' δυναστειῶν ἔτη τρισμύρια ͵ϛφκε', καίτοι τοῦ Ἡφαίστου πολλοῖς ἔτεσι μετὰ τὸν κατακλυσμὸν καὶ τὴν πυργοποιΐαν

¹ Scaliger: codd. μετὰ τὰς κζ' δυναστείας, omit. γενεῶν.

THE OLD CHRONICLE App. III

The Twenty-seventh Dynasty of Persian Kings, in 5 generations, for 124 years.

[The Twenty-eighth Dynasty is here omitted— one king of Saïs reigning for 6 years.]

Then comes the Twenty-ninth Dynasty of Kings of Tanis in ‹7› generations for 39 years; and finally the Thirtieth Dynasty consists of one King of Tanis for 18 years. The sum total of all the 30 Dynasties comprises 36,525 years.

If this total is broken up, or divided, 25 times into periods of 1461 years, it reveals the periodic return of the Zodiac which is commonly referred to in Egyptian and Greek books, that is, its revolution from one point back to that same point again, namely, the first minute of the first degree of the equinoctial sign of the Zodiac, the Ram as it is called by them, according to the account given in *The General Discourses of Hermês* and in the *Cyranides*.

Hence it was, I suppose, that Claudius Ptolemaeus [1] announced that the ready astronomical tables should be calculated in periods of 25 years . . .

Hence, too, the lack of harmony between such systems and our Holy Scriptures, as well as between one system and another, may be explained by the fact that this Egyptian record, which is held to be of great antiquity, assigns an immense period to Hêphaestus, and to the remaining 29 [2] Dynasties 36,525 years, although Hêphaestus ruled over Egypt

---

[1] Claudius Ptolemaeus, the famous mathematician, astronomer, and geographer, c. A.D. 100-178: for his *Ready Tables* see p. 5 in the other section of this volume.

[2] An obviously incorrect summary of the enumeration of Dynasties given above.

App. III PSEUDO-MANETHO

τῆς Αἰγύπτου βασιλεύσαντος, ὡς δειχθήσεται ἐν τῷ δέοντι τόπῳ.

Ὁ δὲ παρ' Αἰγυπτίοις ἐπισημότατος Μανεθῶ περὶ τῶν αὐτῶν λ' δυναστειῶν γράψας, ἐκ τούτων δηλαδὴ λαβὼν τὰς ἀφορμάς, κατὰ πολὺ διαφωνεῖ περὶ τοὺς χρόνους πρὸς ταῦτα, καθὼς ἔστι καὶ ἐκ τῶν προειρημένων ἡμῖν ἀνωτέρω μαθεῖν καὶ ἐκ τῶν ἑξῆς λεχθησομένων. τῶν γὰρ ἐν τοῖς τρισὶ τόμοις ριγ' γενεῶν ἐν δυναστείαις λ' ἀναγεγραμμένων, αὐτῷ[1] ὁ χρόνος τὰ πάντα συνῆξεν ἔτη ͵γφνε', ἀρξάμενα τῷ ͵αφπς' ἔτει τοῦ κόσμου καὶ λήξαντα εἰς τὸ ͵ερμζ'[2] κοσμικὸν ἔτος, ἤτοι πρὸ τῆς Ἀλεξάνδρου τοῦ Μακεδόνος κοσμοκρατορίας ἔτη που ιε'.

Ἐκ τούτων οὖν ἀφελών τις τὰ πρὸ τοῦ κατακλυσμοῦ χνς' πρὸς ἀναπλήρωσιν τῶν ͵βσμβ' ἐξ Ἀδὰμ ἕως τοῦ κατακλυσμοῦ, ὡς ψευδῆ καὶ ἀνύπαρκτα, καὶ τὰ ἀπὸ τοῦ κατακλυσμοῦ ἕως τῆς πυργοποιίας καὶ συγχύσεως τῶν γλωσσῶν καὶ διασπορᾶς τῶν ἐθνῶν φλδ', ἕξει σαφῶς τὴν ἀρχὴν τῆς Αἰγυπτιακῆς βασιλείας ἐκ τοῦ πρώτου βασιλεύσαντος τῆς Αἰγύπτου Μεστραίμ, τοῦ καὶ Μήνεος λεγομένου παρὰ τῷ Μανεθῶ, ἀπὸ τοῦ ͵βψος' ἔτους τοῦ ἐξ Ἀδὰμ ἕως Νεκταναβῶ τοῦ ἐσχάτου βασιλέως Αἰγύπτου, ὡς εἶναι τὰ πάντα ἀπὸ Μεστραὶμ ἕως τοῦ αὐτοῦ Νεκταναβῶ ἔτη ͵βτξε', ἃ καὶ ἔφθασεν, ὡς προείρηται, εἰς τὸ κοσμικὸν ͵ερμζ'[3] ἔτος πρὸ τῆς Ἀλεξάνδρου τοῦ κτίστου ἀρχῆς ἔτεσι ιε' ἐγγύς.

[1] Boeckh : αὐτῶν codd., probably corrupt.

many years after the Flood and the Building of the Tower, as will be shown in the appropriate place.

The illustrious Egyptian Manetho, writing of these same 30 Dynasties, and obviously taking this as his starting-point, is widely divergent thereafter in the dates he gives, as one may learn both from what I have already said above, and from the remarks that will follow immediately. For in his three books, 113 generations are recorded in 30 Dynasties, and the time which he assigns amounts in all to 3555 years, beginning with Anno mundi 1586 and ending with 5147 [5141], or some 15 years before the conquest of the world by Alexander of Macedon.

If therefore one subtracts from this total the 656 years before the Flood in order to make up [with 1586] the 2242 years from Adam to the Flood,— these 656 years being regarded as falsely assigned or non-existent,—and the 534 years from the Flood to the Building of the Tower, the Confusion of Tongues, and the Dispersion of the Peoples, one will clearly find the rise of the kingdom of Egypt under the first Egyptian king, Mestraïm, who is by Manetho called Mênês, which began in the year 2776, the year of Adam, and continued down to Nectanabô, the last king of Egypt. Thus the sum total from Mestraïm down to this Nectanabô is 2365 years, which takes us, as has already been stated, to Anno mundi 5147 [5141], approximately 15 years before the rule of Alexander the Founder.

---

²1. ͵ερμα΄.   ³ ͵ερμα΄, marginal note in Goar.

APPENDIX IV.

Ἡ Βιβλοσ Τησ Σωθεωσ Ἢ Ὁ Κυνικοσ Κυκλοσ.

Syncellus, p. 170.

Αἰγύπτου τῆς πάλαι Μεστραίας βασιλέων ἔτη.

α΄ Μεστραὶμ ὁ καὶ Μήνης, ἔτη λε΄.
β΄ Κουρώδης, ἔτη ξγ΄.
γ΄ Ἀρίσταρχος, ἔτη λδ΄.
δ΄ Σπάνιος, ἔτη λς΄.
ε΄ καὶ ς΄, βασιλέων δυοῖν ἀνεπιγράφων ἔτη οβ΄.
ζ΄ Ὠσιροπίς,¹ ἔτη κγ΄.
η΄ Σεσόγχωσις, ἔτη μθ΄.
θ΄ Ἀμενέμης, ἔτη κθ΄.

Syncellus, p. 179.

ι΄ Ἄμασις, ἔτη β΄.
ια΄ Ἀκεσέφθρης, ἔτη ιγ΄.
ιβ΄ Ἀγχορεύς, ἔτη θ΄.
ιγ΄ Ἀρμιϋσῆς, ἔτη δ΄.

¹ Cod. B: ὁ Σάραπις Goar, Dindorf.

---

[1] The *Book of Sôthis* which Syncellus believed to be the genuine Manetho, but which in its original form was based upon Eusebius and Josephus, is dated by Gutschmid to the

APPENDIX IV.

The Book of Sôthis[1] or The Sôthic Cycle.

(From Syncellus.)

The years of the kings of Egypt, called Mestraea of old.

1. **Mestraïm**, also called Mênês, 35 years.
2. Kourôdês, 63 years.
3. Aristarchus, 34 years.
4. Spanius, 36 years.
5 and 6. Two kings, unrecorded, 72 years.
7. Ôsiropis, 23 years.
8. Sesonchôsis, 49 years.
9. Amenemês, 29 years.
10. Amasis, 2 years.
11. Acesephthrês, 13.
12. Anchoreus, 9 years.
13. Armiÿsês, 4 years.

third century after Christ. It is not possible to divide the kings of this " Cycle " into dynasties, for their sequence is unchronological : *e.g.* 18-24 belong to Dynasties XIX. and XX., 26-29, 32 to the Hyksôs period, 33-48 to Dynasty XVIII., 49, 58 to Dynasty XIX., 50, 51 to Dynasty XXVI., 59-61 to Dynasty I., 63-67 to Dynasty XXI., 68-70 to Dynasty XXIII., 74 to Dynasty XXIV., 75-77 to Dynasty XXV., and 79-86 to Dynasty XXVI.

The *Book of Sôthis* includes names taken from another source than Manetho.

App. IV PSEUDO-MANETHO

ιδ' Χαμοῖς, ἔτη ιβ'·
ιε' Μιαμούς, ἔτη ιδ'.
ις' Ἀμεσῆσις, ἔτη ξε'.
ιζ' Οὔσης, ἔτη ν'.
ιη' Ῥαμεσής, ἔτη κθ'.

Syncellus, p. 189.

ιθ' Ῥαμεσομενής,[1] ἔτη ιε'.
κ' Οὐσιμάρη,[2] ἔτη λα'.
κα' Ῥαμεσσήσεως, ἔτη κγ'.
κβ' Ῥαμεσσαμένω, ἔτη ιθ'.
  Οὗτος πρῶτος Φαραὼ ἐν τῇ θείᾳ γραφῇ μνημονεύεται. ἐπὶ τούτου ὁ πατριάρχης Ἀβραὰμ κατῆλθεν εἰς Αἴγυπτον.
κγ' Ῥαμεσσῆ Ἰουβασσῆ, ἔτη λθ'.

Syncellus, p. 193.

κδ' Ῥαμεσσῆ Οὐάφρου, ἔτη κθ'.
κε' Κόγχαρις, ἔτη ε'.
  Τούτῳ τῷ ε' ἔτει τοῦ κε' βασιλεύσαντος Κογχάρεως τῆς Αἰγύπτου ἐπὶ τῆς

[1] B: Ῥαμεσσομενής A.   [2] B: Οὐσιμάρης A.

---

[1] The name Chamoïs is probably the Greek form of the name Khamuas: for Khamuas, the principal son of Ramessēs II., see Griffith, *Stories of the High Priests*, p. 2 n. 2.

THE BOOK OF SOTHIS   App. IV

14. Chamoïs,[1] 12 years.
15. Miamûs, 14 years.
16. Amesêsis, 65 years.
17. Usês, 50 years.
18. Ramesês, 29 years.
19. Rames(s)omenês, 15 years.
20. Usimarê(s),[2] 31 years.
21. Ramessêseôs,[3] 23 years.
22. Ramessamenô, 19 years.
   He is the first Pharaoh mentioned in the Holy Scriptures. In his reign the patriarch Abraham went down into Egypt.[4]
23. Ramessê Iubassê, 39 years.
24. Ramessê, son of Uaphrês,[5] 29 years.
25. Concharis, 5 years.
   In this 5th year of Concharis, the 25th king of Egypt, during the Sixteenth

[2] The name Usimarê(s) is the first part of the *praenomen* of Ramessês II.: see p. 221 n. 4.

[3] It is tempting to see in this name the Egyptian *Ramesese-o*, "Ramessês the Great," although this term, so commonly used in modern times, is not found in Egyptian records (B.G.).

[4] On Abraham's descent into Egypt, see Peet, *Egypt and the Old Testament*, 1922, pp. 47 ff. (Abraham went down into Egypt in the First Intermediate Period, during Dynasties VII.-X., and left Egypt before 2081 B.C.) Sir L. Woolley, on the other hand, is satisfied with the traditional date of the birth of Abraham at Ur, c. 2000 B.C.; but he believes that the patriarch was not a single man, but a composite character (Abram, Abraham)—see *Abraham: Recent Discoveries and Hebrew Origins*, 1936.

[5] This description "son of Uaphrês" is a remarkable anachronism: a king of Dynasty XIX. or XX. is said to be the son of a king of Dynasty XXVI.

App. IV PSEUDO-MANETHO

ις΄ δυναστείας τοῦ Κυνικοῦ λεγομένου κύκλου παρὰ τῷ Μανεθῷ, ἀπὸ τοῦ πρώτου βασιλέως καὶ οἰκιστοῦ Μεστραὶμ τῆς Αἰγύπτου, πληροῦνται ἔτη ψ΄, βασιλέων κε΄, τοῦτ' ἔστιν ἀπὸ τοῦ καθολικοῦ κοσμικοῦ ‚βψος΄ ἔτους, καθ' ὃν χρόνον ἡ διασπορὰ γέγονεν, ἐν τῷ λδ΄ ἔτει τῆς ἡγεμονίας Ἀρφαξάδ, ε΄ δὲ ἔτει τοῦ Φαλέκ. καὶ διεδέξαντο Τανῖται βασιλεῖς δ΄, οἳ καὶ ἐβασίλευσαν Αἰγύπτου ἐπὶ τῆς ιζ΄ δυναστείας ἔτη σνδ΄,[1] ὡς ἑξῆς ἐστοιχείωται.

Syncellus, p. 195.

κς΄ Σιλίτης, ἔτη ιθ΄, πρῶτος τῶν ς΄ τῆς ιζ΄ δυναστείας παρὰ Μανεθῷ.

Syncellus, p. 204.

κζ΄ Βαίων, ἔτη μδ΄.
κη΄ Ἀπαχνάς, ἔτη λς΄.
κθ΄ Ἄφωφις, ἔτη ξα΄.

Τοῦτον λέγουσί τινες πρῶτον κληθῆναι Φαραώ, καὶ τῷ τετάρτῳ ἔτει τῆς βασιλείας αὐτοῦ τὸν Ἰωσὴφ ἐλθεῖν εἰς Αἴγυπτον δοῦλον. οὗτος κατέστησε τὸν Ἰωσὴφ κύριον Αἰγύπτου καὶ πάσης τῆς βασιλείας αὐτοῦ τῷ ιζ΄ ἔτει τῆς ἀρχῆς αὐτοῦ, ἡνίκα καὶ τὴν τῶν ὀνείρων διασάφησιν ἔμαθε παρ' αὐτοῦ, καὶ τῆς θείας συνέσεως αὐτοῦ διὰ πείρας

[1] σνθ΄ corr. Müller.

THE BOOK OF SÔTHIS   App. IV

Dynasty of the Sôthic Cycle as it is called in Manetho, the total of years from the first king and founder of Egypt, Mestraïm, is 700 belonging to 25 kings, *i.e.* from the general cosmic year 2776, in which the Dispersion took place in the 34th year of the rule of Arphaxad [1] and the 5th year of Phalec.[2] Next in the succession were 4 kings of Tanis, who ruled Egypt in the Seventeenth Dynasty for 254 [259] years, according to the following computation.

26. Silitês (the first of the 6 kings of the Seventeenth Dynasty in Manetho), 19 years.
27. Baiôn, 44 years.
28. Apachnas, 36 years.
29. Aphôphis, 61 years.

Some say that this king was at first called Pharaoh, and that in the 4th year of his kingship Joseph came as a slave into Egypt.[3] He appointed Joseph lord of Egypt and all his kingdom in the 17th year of his rule, having learned from him the interpretation of the dreams and having thus proved his divine wisdom.

---

[1] Arphaxad, son of Shem: *O.T. Genesis* x. 22. See p. 26 n. 1.

[2] Phalec or Peleg (= division): " for in his days was the earth divided " (*Genesis* x. 25). *Cf.* the name of the town Phaliga on the Euphrates,—not that the patriarch Peleg is to be connected directly with this town (W. F. Albright, *The Archaeology of Palestine and the Bible* [2], 1932-3, p. 210).

[3] For the Sojourn in Egypt during the Hyksôs period, see Peet, *Egypt and the Old Testament*, pp. 73 ff.; Albright, *The Archaeology of Palestine and the Bible* [2], pp. 143 f.; Garstang, *The Heritage of Solomon*, 1934, p. 147.

App. IV   PSEUDO-MANETHO

γέγονεν. ἡ δὲ θεία γραφὴ καὶ τὸν ἐπὶ τοῦ Ἀβραὰμ βασιλέα Αἰγύπτου Φαραὼ καλεῖ.

Syncellus, p. 232.

λ' Σέθως, ἔτη ν'.
λα' Κήρτως, ἔτη κθ', κατὰ Ἰώσηππον, κατὰ δὲ τὸν Μανεθῶ, ἔτη μδ'.
λβ' Ἀσήθ, ἔτη κ'.
  Οὗτος προσέθηκε τῶν ἐνιαυτῶν τὰς ε' ἐπαγομένας, καὶ ἐπὶ αὐτοῦ, ὥς φασιν, ἐχρημάτισεν τξε' ἡμερῶν ὁ Αἰγυπτιακὸς ἐνιαυτός, τξ' μόνον ἡμερῶν πρὸ τούτου μετρούμενος. ἐπὶ αὐτοῦ ὁ μόσχος θεοποιηθεὶς Ἆπις ἐκλήθη.
λγ' Ἄμωσις ὁ καὶ Τέθμωσις, ἔτη κϛ'.

Syncellus, p. 278.

λδ' Χεβρών, ἔτη ιγ'.
λε' Ἀμεμφίς,[1] ἔτη ιε'.
λϛ' Ἀμενσῆς, ἔτη ια'.
λζ' Μισφραγμούθωσις, ἔτη ιϛ'.
λη' Μισφρής, ἔτη κγ'.
λθ' Τούθμωσις, ἔτη λθ'.

Syncellus, p. 286.

μ' Ἀμενῶφθις, ἔτη λδ'.
  Οὗτος ὁ Ἀμενῶφθίς ἐστιν ὁ Μέμνων εἶναι νομιζόμενος καὶ φθεγγόμενος λίθος·

THE BOOK OF SÔTHIS App. IV

The Holy Scriptures, however, give the name of Pharaoh also to the king of Egypt in the time of Abraham.

30. Sethôs, 50 years.
31. Cêrtôs, according to Josephus, 29 years; according to Manetho, 44 years.
32. Asêth, 20 years.

    This king added the 5 intercalary days to the year :[1] in his reign, they say, the Egyptian year became a year of 365 days, being previously reckoned as 360 days only. In his time the bull-calf was deified and called Apis.

33. Amôsis, also called Tethmôsis, 26 years.
34. Chebrôn, 13 years.
35. Amemphis, 15 years.
36. Amensês, 11 years
37. Misphragmuthôsis, 16 years.
38. Misphrês, 23 years.
39. Tuthmôsis, 39 years.
40. Amenôphthis, 34 years.

    This is the king who was reputed to be Memnôn and a speaking statue. Many

---

[1] See p. 99 n. 3.

[1] B : ’Αμεμφής A.

App. IV   PSEUDO-MANETHO

ὃν λίθον χρόνοις ὕστερον Καμβύσης ὁ
Περσῶν τέμνει, νομίζων εἶναι γοητείαν ἐν
αὐτῷ, ὡς Πολύαινος ὁ Ἀθηναῖος ἱστορεῖ.
    Αἰθίοπες ἀπὸ Ἰνδοῦ ποταμοῦ ἀναστάντες
πρὸς τῇ Αἰγύπτῳ ᾤκησαν.
μα΄ Ὧρος, ἔτη μη΄.
μβ΄ Ἀχενχερής, ἔτη κε΄.
μγ΄ Ἀθωρίς, ἔτη κθ΄.
μδ΄ Χενχερής, ἔτη κϛ΄.

Syncellus, p. 293.
με΄ Ἀχερρής, ἔτη η΄ ἢ καὶ λ΄.
μϛ΄ Ἁρμαῖος, ὁ καὶ Δαναός, ἔτη θ΄.
    Ἁρμαῖος, ὁ καὶ Δαναός, φεύγων τὸν
ἀδελφὸν Ῥαμεσσῆν τὸν καὶ Αἴγυπτον[1]
ἐκπίπτει τῆς κατ᾽ Αἴγυπτον βασιλείας
αὐτοῦ, εἰς Ἑλλάδα τε ἀφικνεῖται. Ῥαμεσσῆς δέ, ὁ ἀδελφὸς αὐτοῦ, ὁ καὶ Αἴγυπτος καλούμενος, ἐβασίλευσεν Αἰγύπτου ἔτη
ξη΄, μετονομάσας τὴν χώραν Αἴγυπτον τῷ
ἰδίῳ ὀνόματι, ἥτις πρότερον Μεστραία,
παρ᾽ Ἕλλησι δὲ Ἀερία ἐλέγετο. Δαναὸς
δέ, ὁ καὶ Ἁρμαῖος, κρατήσας τοῦ Ἄργους
καὶ ἐκβαλὼν Σθένελον τὸν Κροτωποῦ Ἀργείων ἐβασίλευσε· καὶ οἱ ἀπόγονοι αὐτοῦ
μετ᾽ αὐτὸν Δαναΐδαι καλούμενοι ἐπ᾽ Εὐ-
ρυσθέα τὸν Σθενέλου τοῦ Περσέως· μεθ᾽
οὓς οἱ Πελοπίδαι ἀπὸ Πέλοπος παρα-
λαβόντες τὴν ἀρχήν, ὧν πρῶτος Ἀτρεύς.

[1] Αἰγύπτιον codd.: Αἴγυπτον Scaliger: καὶ add. Müller.

years later Cambysês, the Persian king, cut this statue in two, deeming that there was sorcery in it, as Polyaenus of Athens [1] relates.

The Ethiopians, removing from the River Indus, settled near Egypt.

41. Ôrus, 48 years.
42. Achencherês, 25 years.
43. Athôris, 29 years.
44. Chencherês, 26 years.
45. Acherrês, 8 or 30 years.
46. Armaeus, also called Danaus, 9 years.

This king, fleeing from his brother Ramessês, also called Aegyptus, was driven from his kingdom of Egypt and came to Greece. Ramessês, his brother, whose other name was Aegyptus, ruled Egypt for 68 years, changing the name of his country to Egypt after his own name. Its previous name was Mestraea, and among the Greeks Aeria. Now Danaus or Armaeus took possession of Argos and, driving out Sthenelus the son of Crotôpus, ruled over the Argives. His descendants thereafter were called Danaïdae down to Eurystheus son of Sthenelus, the son of Perseus. Next to these, after Pelops the Pelopidae succeeded to the kingdom: the first of these was Atreus.

---

[1] Polyaenus of Athens (? of Sardis or of Macedonia), a writer of history, lived in the time of Gaius (Caligula).

App. IV   PSEUDO-MANETHO

Syncellus, p. 302.

μζ´ Ῥαμεσσῆς, ὁ καὶ Αἴγυπτος, ἔτη ξη´.
μη´ Ἀμένωφις, ἔτη η´.
μθ´ Θούωρις, ἔτη ιζ´.
ν´ Νεχεψώς, ἔτη ιθ´.
να´ Ψαμμουθίς, ἔτη ιγ´.
νβ´ —, ἔτη δ´.
νγ´ Κήρτως, ἔτη κ´.[1]
νδ´ Ῥάμψις, ἔτη με´.
νε´ Ἀμενσῆς, ὁ καὶ Ἀμμενέμης, ἔτη κϛ´.

Syncellus, p. 319.

νϛ´ Ὀχυράς, ἔτη ιδ´.
νζ´ Ἀμενδής, ἔτη κζ´.
νη´ Θούωρις, ἔτη ν´.
    Οὗτός ἐστιν ὁ παρ᾽ Ὁμήρῳ Πόλυβος, Ἀλκάνδρας ἀνήρ, ἐν Ὀδυσσείᾳ φερόμενος, παρ᾽ ᾧ φησι τὸν Μενέλαον σὺν τῇ Ἑλένῃ μετὰ τὴν ἅλωσιν Τροίας κατῆχθαι πλανώμενον.
νθ´ Ἄθωθις, ὁ καὶ Φουσανός, ἐφ᾽ οὗ σεισμοὶ κατὰ τὴν Αἴγυπτον ἐγένοντο, μηδέπω γεγονότες ἐν αὐτῇ πρὸ τούτου, ἔτη κη´.
ξ´ Κενκένης, ἔτη λθ´.
ξα´ Οὐέννεφις, ἔτη μβ´.[2]

[1] Corr. Goar: ιϛ´ codd.   [2] λβ´ cod. B.

THE BOOK OF SÔTHIS

47. Ramessês, also called Aegyptus, 68 years.
48. Amenôphis, 8 years.
49. Thuôris, 17 years.
50. Nechepsôs,[1] 19 years.
51. Psammuthis, 13 years.
52. —, 4 years.
53. Cêrtôs,[2] 20 years.
54. Rampsis, 45 years.
55. Amensês, also called Ammenemês, 26 years.
56. Ochyras, 14 years.
57. Amendês, 27 years.
58. Thuôris, 50 years.

>This is the Polybus of Homer, who appears in the *Odyssey* as husband of Alcandra: the poet tells how Menelaus and Helen dwelt with him in their wanderings after the capture of Troy.

59. Athôthis, also called Phusanus,[3] 28 years.

>In his reign earthquakes occurred in Egypt, although previously unknown there.

60. Cencenês, 39 years.
61. Uennephis, 42 years.

---

[1] See p. 211 n. 2. Nechepsôs appears again as Nechepsus, No. 80.

[2] 53-58 may be the 6 kings of Dynasty XIX., some of them repeated. 53 Cêrtôs may be Sethôs: 54 Rampsis = 47 Ramessês: 55 Amensês = Amenmesês: while Thuôris appears as 58 and 49.

[3] With Phusanus *cf.* Psusennês of Dynasty XXI.

App. IV   PSEUDO-MANETHO

Syncellus, p. 332.

ξβ' Σουσακείμ, ἔτη λδ'.
    Σουσακεὶμ Λίβυας καὶ Αἰθίοπας καὶ Τρωγλοδύτας παρέλαβε πρὸ τῆς Ἱερουσαλήμ.
ξγ' Ψούενος, ἔτη κε'.
ξδ' Ἀμμενῶφις, ἔτη θ'.
ξε' Νεφεχέρης, ἔτη ϛ'.
ξϛ' Σαΐτης, ἔτη ιε'.
ξζ' Ψινάχης, ἔτη θ'.
ξη' Πετουβάστης, ἔτη μδ'.
ξθ' Ὀσώρθων, ἔτη θ'.
ο' Ψάμμος, ἔτη ι'.
οα' Κόγχαρις, ἔτη κα'.

Syncellus, p. 347.

οβ' Ὀσόρθων, ἔτη ιε'.
ογ' Τακαλῶφις, ἔτη ιγ'.
οδ' Βόκχωρις, ἔτη μδ'.
    Βόκχωρις Αἰγυπτίοις ἐνομοθέτει, ἐφ' οὗ λόγος ἀρνίον φθέγξασθαι.
οε' Σαβάκων Αἰθίοψ, ἔτη ιβ'.
    Οὗτος, τὸν Βόκχωριν αἰχμάλωτον λαβών, ζῶντα ἔκαυσεν.
οϛ' Σεβήχων, ἔτη ιβ'.

THE BOOK OF SÔTHIS

62. Susakeim,[1] 34 years.
    This king brought up Libyans, Ethiopians, and Trôglodytes [2] before Jerusalem.
63. Psuenus, 25 years.
64. Ammenôphis, 9 years.
65. Nephecherês, 6 years.
66. Saïtês, 15 years.
67. Psinachês, 9 years.
68. Petubastês, 44 years.
69. Osôrthôn, 9 years.
70. Psammus, 10 years.
71. Concharis, 21 years.
72. Osŏrthôn, 15 years.
73. Tacalôphis, 13 years.
74. Bocchôris, 44 years.
    This king made laws for the Egyptians: in his time report has it that a lamb spoke.[3]
75. Sabacôn, an Ethiopian, 12 years.
    This king, taking Bocchôris captive, burned him alive.[4]
76. Sebêchôn, 12 years.

---

[1] Susakeim, apparently, is Shoshenḳ, or Sesonchôsis, the first king of Dynasty XXII. (Fr. 60, 1): Josephus, *Antiq.*, viii. § 210, has Susakos.

[2] In *O.T.* 2 *Chron.* xii. 3 it is said that Shishak brought up, along with the Ethiopians, the Lubims (Libyans) and the Sukkiims: in the LXX the last are the Trôglodytes, *i.e.* the "Cave-dwellers" along the west shore of the Red Sea (see Strabo, xvi. 4. 17). G. W. Murray, *Sons of Ishmael*, 1935, p. 18, suspects that the Ethiopians were negro troops or perhaps Beja nomads (*i.e.* Bedouin). "At any rate Shishak, like the great Mohammed Ali after him, realized the importance of Bedouin auxiliaries on a desert campaign."

[3] See p. 164 n. 2.   [4] See p. 166 n. 2.

App. IV   PSEUDO-MANETHO

Syncellus, p. 360.

οζ' Ταράκης, ἔτη κ'.
οη' Ἀμαῆς, ἔτη λη'.
οθ' Στεφινάθης, ἔτη κζ'.
π' Νεχεψός, ἔτη ιγ'.

Syncellus, p. 396.

πα' Νεχαώ, ἔτη η'.
πβ' Ψαμμήτιχος, ἔτη ιδ'.
πγ' Νεχαὼ β' Φαραώ, ἔτη θ'.
πδ' Ψαμουθὴς ἕτερος, ὁ καὶ Ψαμμήτιχος, ἔτη ιζ'.
πε' Οὔαφρις,[1] ἔτη λδ'.
πς' Ἄμωσις,[2] ἔτη ν'.

[1] Οὐαφρής codd.   [2] Ἄμασις codd.

THE BOOK OF SÔTHIS App. IV

77. Taraĉês, 20 years.
78. Amaês,[1] 38 years.
79. Stephinathês, 27 years.
80. Nechepsus, 13 years.
81. Nechaô, 8 years.
82. Psammêtichus, 14 years.
83. Nechaô II. (Pharaoh), 9 years.
84. Psamuthês the Second, also called Psammêtichus, 17 years.
85. Uaphris, 34 years.
86. Amôsis, 50 years.

[1] Amaês corresponds to Ammeris or Ameres the Ethiopian, Fr. 69, 1, *i.e.* Tanutamûn, Dynasty XXVI.

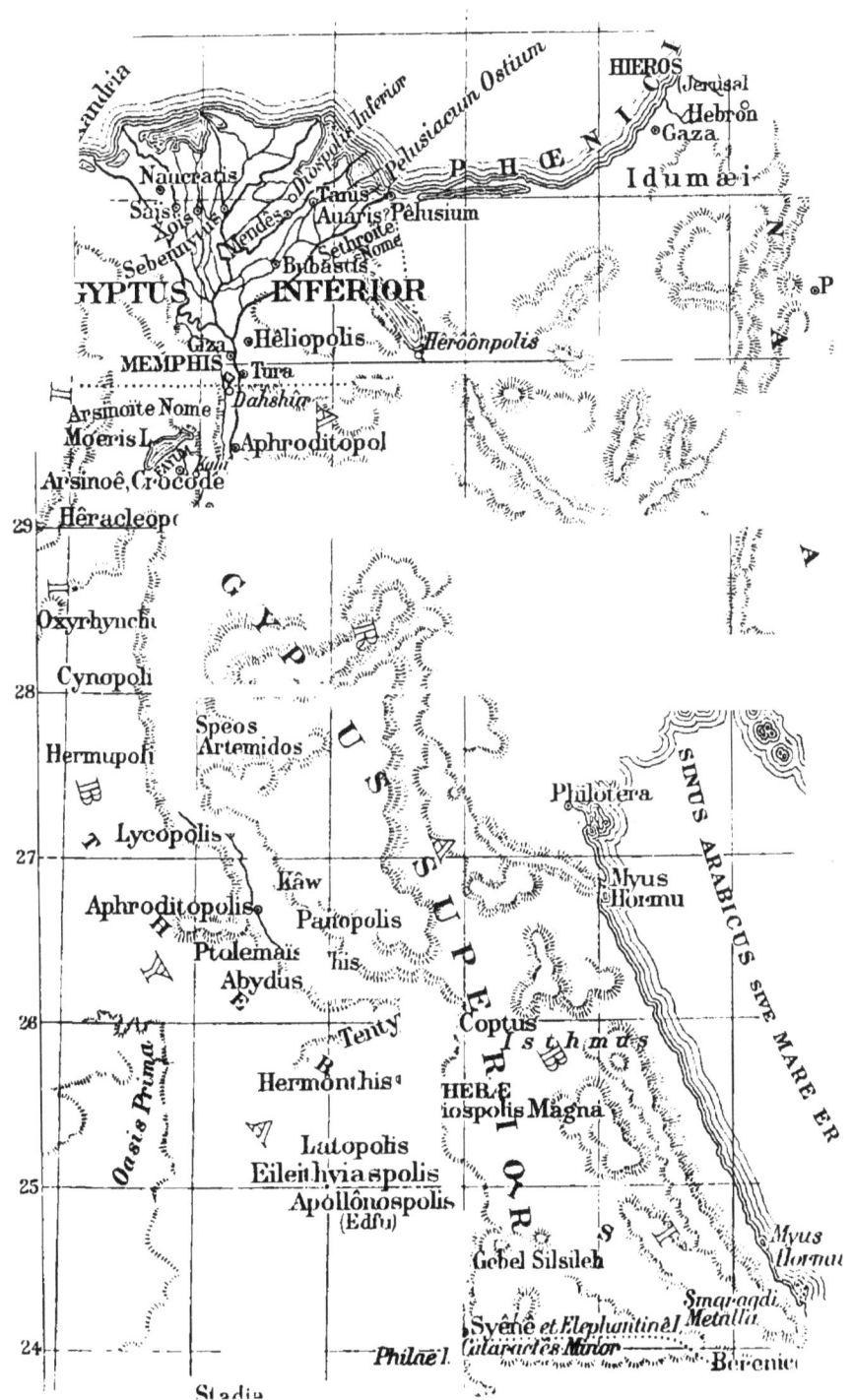

SCARABS

1. Apôphis.

2. Khian.

3. Amôsis.

THE PALERMO STONE.

Old Egyptian Annals of the Kings. Dimensions of fragment: c. 17½ inches high by 10 inches wide.

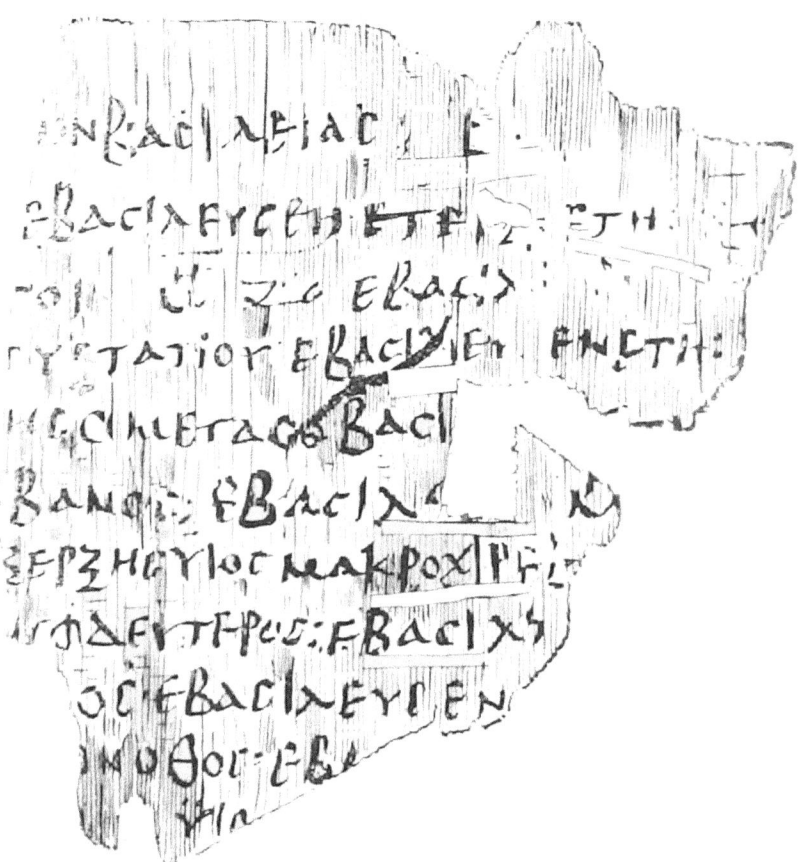

FACSIMILE OF P. BADEN 4. 59.
Papyrus of an Epitome of Manetho, v./A.D.

PLATE IV

(1)

(2)

(3)

INDEX TO MANETHO.

Abraham, 25, 27, 237, 241.
Acenchérès I. (King), 103, 109, 119; II. (King), 103, 109.
Acencherès II., 103, 109.
Acesephthrès, 235.
Achencherès, 243.
Achencherses, 243.
Acherrès, 113, 117, 119, 243.
Achês, 69.
Achôris, 179, 181.
Achthoês, 61.
Adam, 7, 11, 13, 25, 27, 233.
Aegyptiaca, i.
Aegyptus, 7, 105, 117, 119, 121, 243, 245.
Aeria, 243.
Aeritae, 227.
Aesculapius, 45.
Africanus, i, xxi, 27, 43, 47, 83, 111, 113, 115, 117.
Agathodaemon, 15, 209.
Air, 197.
Alcandra, 149, 151, 245.
Alexander the Great, 187, 233.
Alexandria, 193, 195.
Amaes, 249.
Amasis, 235.
Amemphis, 241.
Amendès, 245.
Amenemès, 235.
Amenôph, Amenôphath, 113.
Amenôphis I., 101, 109, 115, ? 245, ? 247; II., 101, 109; III., 103, 109, 113, 115, 117; IV., 103, 111, 113, 117, 119, 121, 123 n. 1, 127, 129, 131, 133, 137, 139, 143.
Amenôphis, son of Hapu, 123, 125, 129.
Amenôphthis, 111, 155, 157, 241.
Amenses (-is), 111, 115, 241, 245.
Amerês, 69, 173.
Amersis, 111.
Amesêsis, 237.
Amessê, 109.
Amessis, 101.

Ammanemès, 67, 71.
Ammenemès, 63, 65, 69, 71; (I.), 223; (II.), 225, 245.
Ammenemnes, 149, 151.
Ammenephthès (59), 149, 151.
Ammenôphis: see Amenôphis.
Ammôn, 17, 189, 239.
Amôphis, 117.
Amôsis (Amosès, Amusis), 19, 113, 115, 117, 171, 173, 199, 201, 241, 245.
Amôs, 189.
Amuthartaeus, 225.
Amyrtaeus (-taeos, -taes), 179, 221.
Anchoreus, 235.
Annianus, ii n. 2, 17 n. 2.
Anôÿphis, 217.
Anubis, 17.
Apachnan (-as), 83, 239.
Apappus, 221.
Aphrodite, 17.
Apiôn, 19.
Apis, 25, 27, 39, 105, 137, 189, 203, 241.
Apollo, 17.
Apollodorus, 213.
Apôphis (Aphobis, Aphôphis), 83, 91, 97, 99, 239.
Arabs, 85.
Archaês, 99.
Archlês, 91, 97.
Arês, 17, 23, 217.
Argives, 107, 117, 119, 243.
Argos, 19, 107, 117, 119, 243.
Aristarchus, 235.
Armaeus, 243.
Armais, 117, 119.
Armesis, 113.
Armiÿsês, 235.
Arphaxad, 27, 239.
Arsês, 185, 187.
Arsinoïte nome, 69, 71, 73.
Artabanus, 175.
Artaxerxès, 175, 177.

251

PLATE IV

(1)

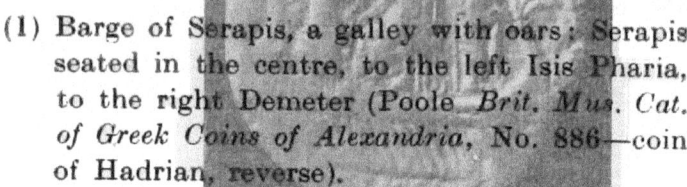

(1) Barge of Serapis, a galley with oars: Serapis seated in the centre, to the left Isis Pharia, to the right Demeter (Poole *Brit. Mus. Cat. of Greek Coins of Alexandria*, No. 886—coin of Hadrian, reverse).

(2) **Temple of Serapis, with a distyle portico**: Serapis seated, with Cerberus at his feet (*ibid.*, No. 872).

(3) Serapis reclining, an eagle in his right hand, a sceptre in his left (Babelon et Reinach, *Recueil général des monnaies grecques*, I., Plate XXVII, 23—bronze coin of Sinope, A.D. 159/160, reverse).

INDEX TO MANETHO

Abraham, 25, 27, 237, 241.
Acenchĕrēs I. (King), 103, 109, 119; II. (King), 103, 109.
Acenchĕrēs (Queen), 103, 109.
Acesephthrēs, 235.
Achencherēs, 243.
Achenchersēs, 115.
Acherrēs, 113, 117, 119, 243.
Achēs, 43.
Achōris, 179, 181.
Achthoēs, 61.
Adam, 7, 11, 13, 25, 27, 233.
Aegyptiaca, 99.
Aegyptus, 7, 105, 117, 119, 121, 243, 245.
Aeria, 243.
Aeritae, 227.
Aesculapius, 45.
Africanus, 25, 27, 29, 37, 43, 47, 57, 111, 113, 115, 117.
Agathodaemōn, 15, 209.
Air, 197.
Alcandra, 149, 151, 245.
Alexander the Great, 187, 233.
Alexandria, 193, 195.
Amaes, 249.
Amasis, 235.
Amemphis, 241.
Amendēs, 245.
Amenemēs, 235.
Amenōph, Amenōphath, 113.
Amenōphis I., 101, 109, 115, ? 245, ? 247; II., 101, 109; III., 103, 109, 113, 115, 117; IV., 103, 111, 113, 117, 119, 121, 123 n. 1, 127, 129, 131, 133, 137, 139, 143.
Amenōphis, son of Hapu, 123, 125, 129.
Amenōphthis, 111, 155, 157, 241.
Amensēs (-is), 111, 115, 241, 245.
Amerēs, 69, 173.
Amersis, 111.
Amesêsis, 237.
Amessē, 109.
Amessis, 101.
Ammanemēs, 67, 71.
Ammenemēs, 63, 65, 69, 71; (I.), 223; (II.), 225, 245.
Ammenem(n)ēs, 149, 151.
Am(m)enephthēs(-is), 149, 151.
Ammenōphis: see Amenōphis.
Ammeris, 171.
Ammōn, 17, 189, 221.
Amophis, 117.
Amōs, 111, 113.
Amōsis (Amosēs, Amusis), 19, 113, 115, 117, 171, 173, 199, 201, 241, 249.
Amûn, 189.
Amuthartaeus, 225.
Amyrtaeus (-teos, -tes), 179, 221.
Anchoreus, 235.
Annianus, 11 n. 2, 17 n. 3.
Anōÿphis, 217.
Anubis (-es), 17, 19.
Apachnan (-as), 83, 239.
Apappūs, 221.
Aphrodite, 23.
Apiōn, 19.
Apis, 35, 37, 39, 129, 137, 189, 203, 241.
Apollo, 17.
Apollodorus, 213.
Apōphis (Aphobis, Aphōphis), 83, 91, 97, 99, 239.
Arabs, 85.
Archaēs, 99.
Archlēs, 91, 97.
Arēs, 17, 23, 217.
Argives, 107, 117, 119, 243.
Argos, 19, 107, 117, 119, 243.
Aristarchus, 235.
Armaeus, 243.
Armais, 117, 119.
Armesis, 113.
Armlÿsēs, 235.
Arphaxad, 27, 239.
Arsēs, 185, 187.
Arsinoïte nome, 69, 71, 73.
Artabanus, 175.
Artaxerxēs, 175, 177.

251

INDEX

Asclepios, 41, 43.
Asêth, 241.
Asia, 67, 71, 73, 89.
Asiatics, 195.
Assis, 83.
Assyrians, 81, 89, 103, 171, 173.
Athena, 191, 197, 221.
Athens, 243.
Athôris, 115, 243.
Athôthês I., 215 ; II., 215.
Athôthis, 29, 31, 33, 215, 245.
Atreus, 243.
Auaris, 81, 87, 125, 127, 129, 137.

Babylon, 15.
Baiôn, 239.
Behôn, 189, 191.
Bêrôssos, 15.
Bicheris, 47.
Biènechès, 29.
Binôthris, 37.
Biophis, 39.
Bites, 5.
Biyrês, 219.
Bnôn, 83, 91, 97.
Bocchôris, Bochchôris, 165, 167, 169, 247.
Bôchos (-us), 21, 37, 39.
Boéthos, 35.
Bubastis (-us), 21, 35, 37, 39, 159, 161.
Bubastite branch, 81.
Bydis, 5.

Caïnan, 27.
Calendar, xxviii., 99 n. 3, 233, 241.
Cambysês, 175, 177, 243.
Cechous, 39 (see Kaiochôs).
Cencenês, 33 (see Kenkenês), 245.
Cencherês, 115.
Cerberus, 195.
Certôs, 241, 245.
Chairês, 37.
Chaldea, 15.
Cham (Ham), 7, 23.
Chamois, 237.
Chebrês, 113.
Chebrôn, 101, 109, 115, 117, 241.
Chebrôs, 111.
Chencherês, 243.
Chencrês, 37.
Cheops, 47, 49.
Cherês, 51.
Cherrês, 117, 119.

Chnubos, 217.
Cho, 33 (see Kôchômê).
Chomaephtha, 223.
Chôos, 37 (see Kaichôos).
Chuthêr, 223.
Concharis, 237, 247.
Cronos, 3, 17, 23, 199, 229.
Crotôpus, 243.
Cyprus, 103.

Danaïdae, 243.
Danaus, 105, 107, 117, 119, 121, 243.
Darius I., 175, 177 ; II., 175, 177.
Darius, 3, 185, 187.
Demeter, 197.
Deucalion, 113.
Diodorus, 199.
Dionysius, 195.
Diospolis (or Thebes), 21, 63, 65, 67, 69, 71, 73, 75, 93, 95, 111, 115, 117, 149, 151, 153, 155, 225, 229.
Dispersion, 213, 233, 239.

Earth, 197.
Earthquakes, 35 n. 3.
Echeskosokaras, 221.
Egregori, 11.
Egypt, 3, 5, 7, 15, 17, 19, 23, 25, 27, 29, 41, 43, 45, 47, 61, 63, 85, 87, 89, 91, 95, 97, 101, 103, 105, 107, 111, 115, 117, 119, 121, 123, 125, 127, 129, 133, 135, 137, 139, 141, 143, 145, 169, 171, 173, 175, 177, 185, 187, 189, 195, 197, 199, 209, 211, 215, 217, 219, 231, 233, 235, 237, 239, 241, 243, 245 ; Lower, 81 ; Upper, 81
Egyptians, 121, 125, 129, 133, 139, 141, 143, 145, 147, 161, 163, 191, 195, 197, 227, 247.
Eileithyiaspolis, 199, 203.
Elephantine, 51, 53.
Enoch, 11.
Eratosthenes, 213, 225.
Ethiopia, 9, 129, 131, 133, 137, 139, 143.
Ethiopian, 167, 169, 171, 173, 229, 243, 247.
Europe, 67, 71, 73.
Eurystheus, 243.
Eusebius, 11, 13, 25, 27, 29, 31, 39, 43, 49, 57, 115, 117.

252

INDEX

Exodus, 19 n. 3, 107, 110 n. 2, 115, 119.

Fire, 197.
Flood, 7, 13, 15, 25, 27, 31, 37, 47, 49, 113, 209, 233.

Gneuros, 217.
Gosormiês, 217.
Greece, 117, 119, 243.
Greeks, 243.

Ham, 7, 23.
Harmaïs, 103, 105, 109.
Harmessês Miamûn, 103
Harpocratês, 223.
Hebrews, 119.
Hecataeus of Abdera, xxiv., 131 n. 2.
Helen, 245.
Hêliopolis, 23, 35, 125, 131, 139, 145, 199, 211.
Hêlios, 3, 15, 17, 23, 199, 227.
Hêphaestus, 3, 15, 17, 23, 197, 199, 223, 227, 229, 231.
Hêra, 199, 201.
Hêracleopolis, 61, 63.
Hêraclês, Hercules, 17, 161, 163, 215, 223, 225.
Hermaeus, 121.
Hermês, 23, 209, 215, 225.
Hermês (Trismegistus), 209, 211.
Hermupolis, 23.
Herodotus, 31, 33, 47, 49, 79, 205, 207.
Hestia, 199.
Homer, 149, 151, 153, 245.
Hôrus, 23, 191.
Hyksôs, 85.
Hystaspês, 175.

Iannas, 83.
Imuthes, 41.
Inachus, 19.
Indus, River, 243.
Iôachaz, 169, 171, 173.
Isis, 5, 17, 189, 191, 197.
Israel, 115.

Jerusalem 88 n. 2, 89, 101, 119, 121, 127, 137, 141, 143, 169, 171, 173, 247.
Jews, 77, 107, 115, 121, 131, 171, 173.
Joseph 25, 89, 97, 239.

Josephus, 77, 241.
Judaea, 89, 119.
Jupiter, 23.

Kaiechôs, Kaichôos, 35, 37.
Kenkenês, 29, 31.
Kerpherês, 43.
Khian, 83 n. 2.
Kings, co-existing, 8 n. 1.
Kôchômê, 29, 31.
Kourôdês, 235.
Kyphi, 203.

Labyrinth, 69, 71, 73.
Lachares, Lamares (-is), Lampares, 69, 71, 73.
Lamb, prophetic, 164 n. 2.
Libyans, 41, 43, 45, 247.
Luke, 27.

Macedon, 187.
Magi, 177.
Malalas, 23.
Manetho, 3, 11, 15, 17, 21, 23, 25, 63, 65, 67, 69, 71, 77, 79, 85, 87, 89, 99, 101, 107, 109, 119, 125, 133, 135, 137, 139, 141, 143, 145, 147, 151, 153, 155, 185, 187, 189, 195, 197, 199, 201, 203, 205, 207, 209, 211, 227, 233, 239, 241.
Marês, 217, 225.
Mars, 23.
Medes, 105.
Memnôn, 113, 115, 117, 241.
Memphis, 5, 9, 23, 29, 31, 33, 35, 41, 43, 45, 49, 53, 57, 59, 81, 91, 95, 97, 129, 215, 229.
Memphrês, 117.
Mempses, 35.
Mencherês I., II., 47, 51, 219.
Mendês, Mendesian, 35, 37, 39, 179, 181.
Menelaus, 245.
Menes, Mên, Min, Mineus, 21, 29, 31, 33, 215, 233, 235.
Menthesuphis, 55.
Mêphram(m)uthôsis, 101, 109.
Mêphrês, 101, 109.
Mercury, 23.
Mesôchris, 43.
Mestraea, 235, 243.
Mestraei, 227.
Mestraïm, Mestrem, Mizraïm, 7, 9, 15, 25, 233, 235, 239.
Methusuphis, 53.

253

INDEX

Meurês, 223.
Miabaês, 215.
Miamûs, 237.
Miebis, 29.
Mieirês, 223.
Min, Mineus : see Menes.
Miphrês, 115.
Misaphris, 113.
Mispharmuthosis, 117.
Misphragmuthôsis, 87, 113, 115, 241.
Misphrês, 241.
Mnevis, 35, 37, 39.
Momcheiri, 215.
Moon, 195, 197.
Moscherês, 219.
Moses, 25, 107, 111, 115, 119, 131, 133, 139, 145, 147.
Mosthês, 219.
Muthes (-is), 181.
Myrtaeus, 221.

Narachô, 23, 25.
Nechao I., 169, 171, 173, 249; II., 169, 171, 173, 249.
Nechepsôs, 169, 171, 173, 245.
Nechepsus, 249.
Necherocheus, 21.
Necherôchis, 43, 45.
Necherôphês, 41.
Nectanabô, 25, 233.
Nectanebês (-is), 183, 185.
Nectanebus, 183, 185.
Nephecherês, 247.
Nephelcherês, Nephercherês, 37, 51, 155, 157.
Nepheritês I., 179, 181 : II., 179, 181.
Niebaïs, 31, 35.
Nile, 37, 39, 81, 125, 129, 197, 225.
Nitôcris, 55, 57, 221.
Noah, 7, 23.

Ocean, 197.
Ochthôis, 61.
Ôchus, 185, 187.
Ochyras, 245.
O*dyssey*, 245.
Olympic festival, 161.
Onnus, 51.
Ôr, Orus, 5, 17, 19, 103, 109, 113, 115, 117, 121, 243.
Ôrus the grammarian, 207.
Osarsêph, 125, 131, 139, 147.

Osiris, 5, 17, 19, 23, 69, 71, 73, 131, 139, 189, 197.
Ôsiropis, 235.
Osochôr, 155, 157.
Osorchô, 161.
Osôrthôn, 159, 161, 163, 247.
Osôrthôn, 247.
Othius, 53.
Othoês, 51, 53.
Othoi, 21.

Paapis, 123, 129.
Pachnan, 91.
Palaephatus, 23.
Pammês, 219.
Pamphilus, 11, 25.
Panodôrus, 11, 13.
Pelopidae, 243.
Pelops, 243.
Pelusium, 105, 140 n., 143.
Pemphôs, 215.
Pepi, 221.
Perseus, 243.
Persian Kings, 175, 177, 185, 187, 231, 243.
Persians, 3, 175, 185, 187.
Peteathyrês, 223.
Petubastês (-is), 163, 247.
Petubatês, 161.
Phaethôn, 23.
Phalec, 239.
Pharaôh, 23, 109, 237, 239, 241, 249.
Phiôps, 53, 55.
Phius, 53.
Phoenicia, 91, 95, 97, 99, 103.
Phruorô (Phuorô), 225.
Phusanus, 245.
Pluto, 193, 195.
Polyaenus, 243.
Polybus, 149, 151, 153, 245.
Potter's oracle, viii. n. 1, 123 n. 1.
Psammecheritês, 171.
Psam(m)êtichus I., 169, 171, 173, 249; II., 169, 171, 173, 249 : III., 171.
Psammus, 247.
Psammûs, 161, 163.
Psammuthis, Psamuthês, 169, 173, 179, 181, 245, 249.
Psin(n)achês, 155, 157, 247.
Psuenus, 247.
Psusennês I., 155, 157 ; II., 155, 157.
Ptolemaeus, Claudius, 231.

INDEX

Ptolemy of Mendes, viii., x., 19 n. 3, 226 n. 1.
Ptolemy Philadelphus, 15, 209, 211.
Ptolemy Sôtêr, 193, 195.
Pyramid, the Great, 47, 49.

Queens, 37 n. 1, 54 n. 2.

Ram, 231.
Ramessamenô, 237.
Ramessê, 237.
Ramessê Iubassê, 237.
Rames(s)ês, 103, 109, 113, 117, 119, 237, 243 (= Aegyptus), 245.
Ramessês II., 103, 149.
Ramessês Miammû(n), 109.
Ramessêseôs, 237.
Rames(s)omenês, 237.
Rampsês (-is), 121, 133, 151, 245.
Rapsacês, 149.
Rapsês, 129.
Rathôs, 113.
Rathôtis, 103, 109.
Rathurês, 51.
Ratoisês, 47.
Raÿôsis, 219.
Rhea, 199.

Sabacôn, 167, 169, 247.
Sacrifice, human, 198 n. 2.
Saïs, 9, 91 n. 4, 99, 165, 167, 168 n. 1, 169, 171, 173, 179, 229, 231.
Saïte nome, 81, 91, 95, 97, 99.
Saïtês, 91, 95, 97, 99, 247.
Saitic, 99.
Salitis, 81, 83.
Saôphis I., 219 ; II., 219.
Saracus, 160.
Saturn(us), 2, 23.
Scemiophris, 69.
Scripture, Holy Scriptures, 13, 25, 231, 237, 241.
Sebêchôn, 247.
Sebennytus, xi. n. 1, 15, 23, 183, 185, 189, 195, 209, 211.
Sebercherês, 47.
Sebichôs, 167, 169.
Semempsês, 29, 33, 215.
Semphrucratês, 223.
Sempsôs, 215.
Sephrês, 51.
Sêphuris, 43.
Serapis, 189, 195.
Sêriadic, 209.
Sesôchris, 87, 39, 41.

Sesônchis, 159.
Sesonchosis, 67, 69, 71, 159, 161, 235.
Sesorthos, Sosorthus, 43, 45.
Sesortôsis, 225.
Sesôstris, 67, 71.
Sêth, 191.
Sethenês, 37.
Sethinilus, 221.
Sethôs (Ramessês), 103, 105, 111, 121, 129, 149, 151, 241.
Sethôsis, 105.
Sethroïte nome, 80 n. 3, 81, 91, 95, 97, 99.
Shepherds, Shepherd Kings, 85, 87, 89, 91, 93, 95, 97, 99, 101, 107, 121, 125, 127, 131, 133, 137, 139.
Silitês, 239.
Sinôpê, 193, 195.
Siphthas, 225.
Sirius, 217.
Sisirês, 51.
Sistosichermês, 225.
Sistosis, 225.
Smendês (-is), 155, 157.
Smy, 191.
Sogdianus, 175, 177.
Soicuniosochus, 223.
Soicunis (-ius), 223.
Sol, 2, 17.
Solymites, 131.
Sôris, 47.
Sôsibius, 195.
Sosinosiris, 19.
Sôsis, 3, 19, 23.
Sôsus, 17.
Sôtatês (? Sôtadês), 23.
Sôtelês, 195.
Sothic Cycle, xxvii. f., 229, 235, 239.
Sôthis, xxvii n., 235.
Sôÿphis, 43.
Spanius, 235.
Spirit, 197.
Staan, 91.
Stammenemês I., 223 ; II., 225.
Stephinatês (-thês, -this), 169, 171, 173, 249.
Sthenelus, 243.
Stoichos, 217.
Sun, 3, 15, 17, 195, 197, 217, 221, 227.
Suphis I., 47, 49 ; II., 47.
Susakeim, 247.
Susennês, 155.
Syria, 89, 133, 139, 143.

INDEX

Tacalôphis, 247.
Tacelothis, Takelôthis, 159, 161.
Tancheres, 51.
Tanis, 23. 155 157. 161, 163, 229 231, 239.
Tanite nome, 80 n. 3.
Taracês, 249.
Taracus, Tarcus, 167, 169.
Tat, 209.
Temple (Solomon's), 118 n., 119, 159 n. 1.
Tethmôsis, 101, 109 121, 127, 241
Teôs, 183, 185.
Thamphthis, 47.
Thebaïd, 87.
Thebans, 213.
Thebes, 93, 95, 215, 217, 219, 221, 223, 225: see Diospolis.
Thirillus, 221.
This, 5, 9, 29, 31, 33, 35.
Thmôsis, 101.
Thôth, 209.
Thrace, 67, 71, 73.
Threats to the gods, 200 n. 3.
Thulis, 23.
Thummôsis, 87.
Thuôris, 149, 151, 153, 245.
Timotheus, 195.
Tithoês, 17.
Tlas, 37.
Tômaephtha, 223.
Tongues, Confusion of, 233.
Tosertasis, 43.
Tosorthros, 41.
Tower (of Babel), 233.

Trôglodytes, 247.
Trojan war, 107.
Troy, 149, 151, 153, 245.
Tuthmôses (-is). 109 113. 115 117. 241
Tutimaeus, 79.
Typhon, 5, 17, 19, 125, 189, 191, 201, 203.
Typhonian, 193.
Tyreis, Tyris, 43.

Uaphrês (-is), 171, 173, 237, 249.
Ubienthês, 33.
Uenephês, 29, 31.
Uennephis, 245.
Uôsimarês, 221.
Usaphaïs, 29, 31, 35.
Usercherês, 51.
Usês, 237.
Usimare(s), 237.

Vavenephis (see Uenephês), 33.
Venus, 23.
Vibenthis, 35.
Vulcanus, 2.

Water, 197.

Xerxes I. (the Great), 175, 177, II., 175, 177.
Xoïs, 75.

Zêt, 161.
Zeus, 17, 23, 133, 189, 197, 199.
Zodiac, 13, 231.

PTOLEMY
TETRABIBLOS

EDITED AND TRANSLATED INTO
ENGLISH BY

F. E. ROBBINS, Ph.D.
UNIVERSITY OF MICHIGAN

CAMBRIDGE, MASSACHUSETTS
HARVARD UNIVERSITY PRESS

LONDON
WILLIAM HEINEMANN LTD.
MCMLXIV

FIRST PRINTED . 1940
REPRINTED   . 1948, 1956, 1964

Printed in Great Britain at The University Press, Aberdeen

CONTENTS

	PAGE
INTRODUCTION	v
THE LUMINARIES AND PLANETS	xxiii
THE SIGNS OF THE ZODIAC	xxiii

BOOK I

1. INTRODUCTION 2
2. THAT KNOWLEDGE BY ASTRONOMICAL MEANS IS ATTAINABLE, AND HOW FAR . . . 4
3. THAT IT IS ALSO BENEFICIAL . . . 20
4. OF THE POWER OF THE PLANETS . . 34
5. OF BENEFICENT AND MALEFICENT PLANETS . 38
6. OF MASCULINE AND FEMININE PLANETS . . 40
7. OF DIURNAL AND NOCTURNAL PLANETS . . 42
8. OF THE POWER OF THE ASPECTS TO THE SUN . 44
9. OF THE POWER OF THE FIXED STARS . . 46
10. OF THE EFFECT OF THE SEASONS AND OF THE FOUR ANGLES 58
11. OF SOLSTITIAL, EQUINOCTIAL, SOLID, AND BICORPOREAL SIGNS 64
12. OF MASCULINE AND FEMININE SIGNS . . 68
13. OF THE ASPECTS OF THE SIGNS . . 72
14. OF COMMANDING AND OBEYING SIGNS . . 74
15. OF SIGNS WHICH BEHOLD EACH OTHER AND SIGNS OF EQUAL POWER . . . 76
16. OF DISJUNCT SIGNS 76
17. OF THE HOUSES OF THE SEVERAL PLANETS . 78
18. OF THE TRIANGLES 82
19. OF EXALTATIONS 88
20. OF THE DISPOSITION OF TERMS . . . 90
21. ACCORDING TO THE CHALDAEANS . . . 98
22. OF PLACES AND DEGREES . . . 108
23. OF FACES, CHARIOTS, AND THE LIKE . . 110
24. OF APPLICATIONS AND SEPARATIONS AND THE OTHER POWERS 112

BOOK II

1. INTRODUCTION 116
2. OF THE CHARACTERISTICS OF THE INHABITANTS OF THE GENERAL CLIMES . . . 120
3. OF THE FAMILIARITIES BETWEEN COUNTRIES AND THE TRIPLICITIES AND STARS . . . 128

CONTENTS

		PAGE
4.	Method of Making Particular Predictions	160
5.	Of the Examination of the Countries Affected	162
6.	Of the Time of the Predicted Events	164
7.	Of the Class of those Affected	168
8.	Of the Quality of the Predicted Event	176
9.	Of the Colours of Eclipses, Comets, and the Like	190
10.	Concerning the New Moon of the Year	194
11.	Of the Nature of the Signs, Part by Part, and their Effect upon the Weather	200
12.	Of the Investigation of Weather in Detail	206
13.	Of the Significance of Atmospheric Signs	212

BOOK III

1.	Introduction	220
2.	Of the Degree of the Horoscopic Point	228
3.	The Subdivision of the Science of Nativities	234
4.	Of Parents	240
5.	Of Brothers and Sisters	250
6.	Of Males and Females	254
7.	Of Twins	256
8.	Of Monsters	260
9.	Of Children that are not Reared	264
10.	Of Length of Life	270
11.	Of Bodily Form and Temperament	306
12.	Of Bodily Injuries and Diseases	316
13.	Of the Quality of the Soul	332
14.	Of Diseases of the Soul	362

BOOK IV

1.	Introduction	372
2.	Of Material Fortune	372
3.	Of the Fortune of Dignity	376
4.	Of the Quality of Action	380
5.	Of Marriage	392
6.	Of Children	408
7.	Of Friends and Enemies	412
8.	Of Foreign Travel	422
9.	Of the Quality of Death	426
10.	Of the Division of Times	436
	Index	461

INTRODUCTION

I.

From his own day well into the Renaissance Claudius Ptolemy's name was well-nigh pre-eminent in astronomy, geography, and astrology alike. "The divine Ptolemy," he is called by Hephaestion of Thebes,[1] and the expression shows that the reverence accorded him fell little short of idolatry. In such circumstances it is surprising that all we know of Ptolemy's personal history must be pieced together from passages in his own works, two scholia in ancient manuscripts, and brief notices to be found in later writers, some of them Arabian.[2] The result, when the reliable is summed up and the false or fanciful subtracted, is meagre indeed. We can probably rely upon the reports that he was born at Ptolemaïs in Egypt[3] and lived to the age of 78;[4] he tells us that his astronomical observations were made on the

[1] In *Catalogus Codicum Astrologicorum Graecorum* (hereafter cited as *CCAG*), viii. 2, p. 81, 2.

[2] The sources are collected and discussed by F. Boll, "Studien über Claudius Ptolemäus," *Jahrb. f. Cl. Ph.*, Supplementbd. xxi. 1894, pp. 53-66 (hereafter cited as Boll, *Studien*).

[3] Theodore of Melitê is the authority; Boll, *op. cit.*, pp. 54-55. An eleventh-century work of Abulwafa (*ibid.*, pp. 58-62) gave rise to the belief that he was born at Pelusium, so that, *e.g.*, he is called $Πηλουσιεύς$ in the title of the first edition of the *Tetrabiblos*.

[4] This comes from Abulwafa.

PTOLEMY

parallel of Alexandria, which convinces Boll that Alexandria was his home, although there is another tradition [1] that for 40 years he observed at Canopus, which was about 15 miles east of Alexandria, and it is known that he erected votive stelae in the temple at Canopus inscribed with the fundamental principles of his doctrines.[2] Combining the various traditions with the fact that the earliest of his observations recorded in the *Almagest* was made in 127 and the latest in 151, we may conclude, further, that his life fell approximately in the years 100-178,[3] covering the first three-quarters of the second century of our era and the reigns of Trajan, Hadrian, Antoninus Pius, and Marcus Aurelius.

A detailed and not too flattering description of Ptolemy's personal appearance and habits goes back, again, to the Arabic tradition, and has been repeated in some of the modern editions of Ptolemy's works,[4]

---

[1] Preserved by Olympiodorus (fourth century), *In Plat. Phaed.*, p. 47, 16 (Finckh).

[2] Boll, *Studien*, p. 66. Heiberg gives the text in his edition of the *Opera astronomica minora* of Ptolemy (Leipzig, 1907), pp. 149 ff.

[3] This is Boll's conclusion (*op. cit.*, p. 64), accepted by Christ, *Griechische Litteraturgeschichte*, 6th ed., 1924, ii. 2, p. 896. Boll, *ibid.*, pp. 63, 65, cites the passages of the *Almagest* which refer to the dated observations. He points out that a very slight change in the text of *Almagest*, x. 1, would make the date of the latest observation 141 instead of 151, but though this would, perhaps, agree better with some of the traditions, there is no real reason for altering the figure.

[4] *E.g.* in the preface of the Latin version of the *Almagest* published at Venice in 1515; and the preface of the translation of the *Tetrabiblos* by Whalley (see below, p. xiii).

INTRODUCTION

but on examination it proves to be nothing but the stock characterization of the philosopher given by the Greek physiognomists.[1] There is, in fact, no more to be learned about Ptolemy from external sources, and his own works contain little that is biographical. We learn from them, however, that he took, in general, an Aristotelian position philosophically, though his predilection for mathematics led him to regard that division of science with far greater reverence than the more biologically minded Aristotle.[2] One of his minor works and chapters in the longer ones are philosophical and testify to his knowledge of and interest in the subject. Though he was himself amply capable of original thought, he was acquainted with the work and writings of his predecessors, of Menelaüs in mathematics, of Hipparchus in astronomy, of Marinus of Tyre in geography, of Didymus in music, and of Posidonius in astrological ethnology and the arguments whereby astrology was defended. He drew freely and openly from them, and had the gift of systematizing the materials with which he dealt, a characteristic which is especially evident in the *Tetrabiblos*.

The works, genuine and false, ascribed to Ptolemy are: (1) the *Almagest* or *Syntaxis Mathematica*, in 13 books, the great treatise on astronomy; (2) Φάσεις ἀπλανῶν ἀστέρων καὶ συναγωγὴ ἐπισημασιῶν (" On the Apparitions of the Fixed Stars and a Collection of Prognostics "); (3) Ὑποθέσεις τῶν πλανωμένων (" On the Planetary Hypothesis "); (4) Κανὼν βασιλειῶν (" Table of Reigns "), a chrono-

---
[1] Boll, *Studien*, pp. 58-62.
[2] *Op. cit.*, pp. 66-111, 131-163.

PTOLEMY

logical table of reigns; (5) Ἁρμονικῶν βιβλία γ´ ("On Music," in three books); (6) the *Tetrabiblos*, of which later; (7) Περὶ ἀναλήμματος, *De Analemmate*, the description of a sphere on a plane (extant only in translation); (8) *Planisphaerium*, "The Planisphere"; (9) the *Optics*, in 5 books (its genuineness has been doubted); (10) the Καρπός or *Centiloquium*, a collection of astrological aphorisms (generally thought to be spurious); (11) the *Geography*; (12) the Πρόχειροι κανόνες or "Ready (astronomical) Tables"; (13) Προχείρων κανόνων διάταξις καὶ ψηφοφορία, "Scheme and Manipulation of the Ready Tables"; (14) Περὶ κριτηρίου καὶ ἡγεμονικοῦ, a short treatise dealing with the theory of knowledge and the soul. Of these, the *Almagest*, since it is mentioned in the *Geography*, the Ὑποθέσεις, and the *Tetrabiblos*, and since it contains no reference to observations after the year 151, was certainly not the latest. The three books mentioned, and possibly others, belong to the last third of the author's life.

II.

The treatise with which we are especially concerned is now, and usually has been, called the *Tetrabiblos* or *Quadripartitum*, but more accurately it should be Μαθηματικὴ τετράβιβλος σύνταξις, "Mathematical Treatise in Four Books," which is the title found in some of the MSS.[1] and is likely to have been that used by Ptolemy himself. Many of the MSS., however, use the title Τὰ πρὸς

[1] *E.g.* N (see below). Τετράβιβλος alone is used by P and E.

INTRODUCTION

Σύρον ἀποτελεσματικά,[1] "The Prognostics addressed to Syrus," in which certain of them substitute the similar but less common word συμπερασματικά for ἀποτελεσματικά.[2] The book is a systematic treatise on astrology, but it should be remembered that in Ptolemy's time the two words ἀστρολογία and ἀστρονομία meant much the same thing, " astronomy," and that he called what we mean by " astrology " τὸ δι' ἀστρονομίας προγνωστικόν,[3] "prognostication through astronomy," which indeed it was, in his estimation.

In antiquity and the middle ages no one thought it inconsistent with Ptolemy's reputation as a scientific astronomer that he should also have written upon astrology, and consequently the *Tetrabiblos* passed without question as genuine.[4] More lately, however, this wedding of astrology to astronomy has come to seem incongruous and for that reason the authenticity of the work has been challenged by certain scholars.[5] In this brief introduction the question, of course, cannot be argued fully. There are, however, two reasons for dismissing any doubts concerning the authorship of the book. The first is that by the second century of our era the triumph of astrology

[1] *E.g.* VMDE. Syrus is otherwise unknown. The Anonymous who comments on the *Tetrabiblos* says that some considered it a fictitious name, others that Syrus was a physician skilled in astrology. Several other works of Ptolemy—notably the *Almagest*—are dedicated to him.
[2] *E.g.* A. [3] *Tetrabiblos,* i. *ad init.*
[4] Boll, *Studien*, pp. 127-131.
[5] Chiefly Hultsch. *Cf.* Boll's remarks in his paper " Zur Ueberlieferungsgeschichte der griechischen Astrologie und Astronomie," *Sitzungsber. d. Münch. Ak., phil.-hist. Cl.,* 1899, pp. 77 ff.

PTOLEMY

was complete.¹ With few exceptions every one, from emperor to the lowliest slave, believed in it, and having weathered the criticism of the New Academy, astrology was defended by the powerful Stoic sect. Its position was strengthened by the prevalence of stellar and solar religion throughout the world, and it even captured the sciences, such as medicine, botany, mineralogy, chemistry, and ethnography. Furthermore, this continued to be the situation, in general, well into the Renaissance. Regiomontanus, Copernicus, Tycho Brahe, Galileo, Kepler, and Leibnitz all either practised astrology themselves or countenanced its practice. There is really no basis, therefore, for thinking it incongruous that Ptolemy should have believed in astrology or written upon it. The second reason for accepting him as the author of the *Tetrabiblos* is, as Boll ² has sufficiently demonstrated, that the book, in its general philosophic views, its language, and its astronomy, is entirely in accord with the Ptolemaic works whose genuineness has never been questioned. These arguments are too lengthy to be repeated here.

III.

Though the *Tetrabiblos* enjoyed almost the authority of a Bible among the astrological writers of a thousand years or more, its Greek text has been

---

¹ See, for example, Chapters II-III of Boll-Bezold, *Sternglaube und Sterndeutung* (ed. 3, revised by W. Gundel). Leipzig: B. G. Teubner, 1926. F. Cumont, *Astrology and Religion among the Greeks and Romans.* New York: Putnam, 1912.

² *Studien*, pp. 111-181.

INTRODUCTION

printed only three times, and not at all since the sixteenth century. The editions are as follows:

(1) The first edition, edited by Joachim Camerarius, was printed by Froben at Nürnberg in 1535 in quarto. Besides the text, it contains Camerarius' Latin translation of Bks. I-II and of parts of Bks. III-IV, and his notes on Bks. I-II, the Greek text of the Καρπός, and a Latin translation by J. Pontanus.

(2) The second edition, also by Camerarius, was printed by Joannes Oporinus in octavo at Basel in 1553.[1] This contains the Greek text of the *Tetrabiblos*, a Latin translation by Philip Melanchthon, and the Καρπός in both Greek and Latin. In the preparation of the first edition Camerarius had relied upon the Nürnberg codex (N in the list on p. xvii), in which his marks to guide the printer are still to be seen. He claims for his second edition to have corrected many mistakes in the text, and he has indeed managed to do away with many errors and misprints which are to be found in the first edition; but apparently, too, he made use of one or more additional MSS., probably of the general type of A in our list below, from which he introduced nearly a hundred readings at variance with N, and

[1] Κλαυδίου Πτολεμαίου Πηλουσιέως τετράβιβλος σύνταξις πρὸς Σύρον ἀδελφόν. Τοῦ αὐτοῦ Καρπός, πρὸς τὸν αὐτὸν Σύρον. *Claudii Ptolemaei Pelusiensis libri quatuor, compositi Syro fratri. Eiusdem Fructus librorum suorum, sive Centum dicta, ad eundem Syrum. Innumeris quibus hucusque scatebant mendis, purgati.* Basileae, per Ioannem Oporinum. This is the title page of the Greek text. The portion containing the translations has a separate title page.

PTOLEMY

in some seventy-five other instances he altered the text by outright emendation. In spite of the attempted improvement the second edition retains some forty misprints or mistakes, half of them newly introduced; its punctuation is most illogical, and it is far from reproducing what seems to be the best tradition of the manuscripts.

(3) Fr. Junctinus included the Greek text of the *Tetrabiblos* in his *Speculum astrologiae*, the second edition of which, in two folio volumes, was issued at Leyden in 1581. Junctinus made no attempt to improve the text as already published.

Professor Franz Boll, whose studies of Ptolemy have been cited many times already, had begun work upon a new edition of the *Tetrabiblos* prior to his lamented death, July 3, 1924. His pupil, Fräulein Emilie Boer, however, continued Boll's task, and the appearance of their completed text has been awaited since 1926.[1] I regret very much that my own work on the present text and translation could not have profited from the results of the textual studies of these two scholars.

Translations of the *Tetrabiblos* have been more numerous than texts. The oldest of them is the Arabian version, by Ishaq ben Hunein, made in the ninth century. Thence in turn Plato Tiburtinus, in 1138, and Aegidius de Thebaldis, in the middle of the thirteenth century, made Latin translations,

---

[1] I am told that the work was completed in this year. It has been announced as Vol. III, Fasc. 1, of *Ptolemaei opera omnia* in the well-known *Bibliotheca Classica*, published by B. G. Teubner, Leipzig. The year of publication is unknown to the writer as this is written.

INTRODUCTION

which were the chief means whereby Western Europe knew the *Tetrabiblos* up to the time of the first edition of the Greek text. Printed editions of these translations—the first dated 1484—appeared,[1] and they were also circulated in manuscript form. More important are the Latin translations made directly from the Greek, beginning with that of Camerarius himself, which was printed both with his text, as noted above, and by itself.[2] The translation by Antonius Gogava, first issued at Louvain in 1543, was several times reprinted at other places, for instance, at Padua in 1658, and was the version used by Cardanus to accompany his commentary. Philip Melanchthon's translation made its appearance in 1553, as we have seen; this, too, was issued separately later.[3] An English translation by John Whalley was published in 1701 and in a second edition in 1786,[4] which, as Ashmand says, " was not, in any one instance, purified from the blunders and obscurities which disgraced its predecessor." In

---

[1] On the early Latin versions see Thorndike, *History of Magic and Experimental Science* (New York, 1923), I, p. 110. MSS. of the Arabic version exist at the Escurial and in the Laurentian Library at Florence.

[2] Printed by Joannes Petreius, Nürnberg, 1535, with Camerarius' notes.

[3] *E.g.* a rudely printed duodecimo from the press of the heirs of Petrus Thomasius, Perusia, 1646, is in the writer's own library.

[4] *The Quadripartite; or, Four Books Concerning the Influences of the Stars . . . by Claudius Ptolemy. . . .* By John Whalley, Professor of Physic and Astrology, and Others. The Second Edition, Revised, Corrected, and Improved. London: Printed for the Editors, and sold by M. Sibley . . . and E. Sibley . . . 1786.

PTOLEMY

truth, Ptolemy is not easy to translate accurately, and though Whalley's version is worse than the others, all show a certain willingness to disguise the difficulties with smooth-sounding but non-committal phrases.[1]

The importance and popularity of the *Tetrabiblos* is shown by the number of commentaries upon it which have been made. In antiquity, as we deduce from expressions used in writings still extant, a considerable number existed;[2] the name of one commentator, Pancharios, survives, but none of his work except a few quotations.[3] Three such treatises which did survive, however, were edited by Hieronymus Wolf and published with Latin translations in folio at Basel in 1559. These are (1) an anonymous commentary on the *Tetrabiblos*, attributed by some, as Wolf says, to Proclus; (2) an introduction to the *Tetrabiblos*, to which the name of Porphyry is attached, though its authorship is by no means certain; (3) the scholia of Demophilus. These have not been republished, but are to be found in a number of manuscripts. Of greater importance for the study of the *Tetrabiblos* is the *Paraphrase* attributed to Proclus, but which, of course, may not have been his at all. Since it follows the *Tetrabiblos* very

---

[1] German translations also exist; *e.g.* by J. W. Pfaff in his *Astrologisches Taschenbuch*, 1822-23 (mentioned by Christ, *Gr. Litteraturgeschichte*), and one by M. E. Winkel, Linseverlag, 1923, which is based on the Latin of Melanchthon (*v.* W. Gundel in *Jahresb. ü. die Fortschritte d. Kl. Alt.* 241, 1934, p. 74).

[2] Boll, *Studien*, p. 127.

[3] *E.g.* ap. *CCAG*, viii. 2, p. 67, 18 ff.; *cf.* Kroll, *Philologus*, lvii (1897), p. 123.

INTRODUCTION

closely, and since, as it happens, one manuscript of the *Paraphrase* is older than any of those of the *Tetrabiblos*, this document must be taken into consideration by any editor of the latter work. The first and only edition of the *Paraphrase*, with a preface by Melanchthon, appeared at Basel in 1554,[1] and the standard Latin version, from which at least two English translations have been made,[2] is that of Leo Allatius (Elzevir, Leyden, 1635). Besides the *Paraphrase* and the ancient commentaries, the elaborate commentary by Hieronymus Cardanus, published in the sixteenth century, should also be mentioned.[3]

IV.

There are in European libraries at least thirty-five manuscripts containing all or a large part of the *Tetrabiblos*, besides a considerable number which contain partial texts or astrological miscellanies in which Ptolemy is cited along with other writers. Parts of the *Tetrabiblos*, too, are quoted by other

---

[1] Πρόκλου τοῦ διαδόχου τῶν ἀσαφῶς εἰρημένων Πτολεμαίῳ, καὶ δυσπαρακολουθήτως ἐν τῷ αὐτοῦ τετραβίβλῳ, ἐπὶ τὸ σαφέστερον καὶ δυσπαρακολούθητον [sic] μεταχείρησις. *Procli paraphrasis in quatuor Ptolemaei libros de Siderum effectionibus. Cum praefatione Philippi Melanthonis.* Basileae, apud Joannem Oporinum [1554].

[2] J. M. Ashmand, *Ptolemy's Tetrabiblos or Quadripartite*, etc. London: Davis and Dickson, 1822. James Wilson, *The Tetrabiblos or Quadripartite of Ptolemy*, etc. London: W. Hughes [1828]. Charpulier, *Les Discourses*, etc., 130, n. 2, cites a Ptolemy's *Tetrabiblos*, by J. M. Ashmand, London, 1917.

[3] Editions were published at Basel in 1554 and 1579, at Leyden in 1555, and in the fifth volume of Cardanus' works (Leyden: Huguetan and Revaud, 1663).

PTOLEMY

authors, like Hephaestion of Thebes. Finally, there are a few manuscripts with Latin or Arabic translations. In spite of this volume of material, however, the earliest text of the *Tetrabiblos* itself is only of the thirteenth century. There is but one full manuscript even of this degree of antiquity, and only two or three from the fourteenth century; most of them are from the fifteenth and sixteenth. In view of this fact it is fortunate that we have one (but only one) manuscript of the *Paraphrase* which antedates all of these, having been written in the tenth century.

In preparing the present text of the *Tetrabiblos* I have been obliged to work entirely with photographs and photostats. However, by a fortunate circumstance, I was able to secure a collection of these which had been brought together by a German scholar unknown to me and which apparently includes the most important manuscripts.[1] Those manuscripts, therefore, which have been collated and used, and the symbols which I have used to refer to them, are as follows:[2]

V : Vaticanus gr. 1038, S. XIII. Contains a number of the works of Euclid, Hypsicles, and Hero, and an almost complete collection of the writings of Ptolemy, with the *Tetrabiblos* on ff. 352-384v.; the ending, after p. 207, 19 (Cam.²), does not appear. Heiberg (*Deutsche Litteraturzeitung*, 1900, p. 417)

---

[1] The purchase of this collection was made possible by the Faculty Research Fund of the University of Michigan. It was accompanied by an anonymous description of the MSS. of the *Tetrabiblos*, to which I am indebted for information about many MSS. which I could not personally inspect.

[2] Of F and H only a few sample pages have been available.

INTRODUCTION

believes that it was largely copied from Vat. gr. 1594, S. IX, which contains other Ptolemaic texts in a relatively pure form but does not, now at least, include the *Tetrabiblos*. A distinctive feature of this manuscript is the large number of small lacunæ left by the scribe when he could not read his archetype or found it defective. In this Boll sees an indication of faithfulness and reliability. *Cf.* F. Boll, " Zur Ueberlieferungsgeschichte der griechischen Astrologie und Astronomie," S*itzungsberichte d. K. B. Akad. d. Wiss. zu München, phil.-hist. Cl.*, 1899, pp. 77 ff.; *CCAG*, v. 1, no. 9.

D: Parisinus gr. 2509, S. XV. Contains the *Tetrabiblos* on ff. 14-81v., followed by the Καρπός. *Cf.* Omont, *Inv.* ii. 274; *CCAG*, viii. 3, no. 82. A copy of V, but the lacunæ were filled in from another source.

P: Parisinus gr. 2425, S. XV. Contains the *Tetrabiblos* on ff. 8-63v. The most immediately striking feature of this manuscript is its constant mis-spelling of words due to the confusion of αι and ε, ει, η, and ι, ο and ω, for example: that is, the confusions typical of late Greek. They may indicate that the manuscript (or an ancestor) was copied from dictation. P also has an ending which differs from the final sentences of the Camerarius editions and most other manuscripts.

L: Oxon. Laud, gr. 50, S. XVI. A copy of P, of no independent value. Paris. Suppl. gr. 597 is another copy of P.

N: Norimbergensis Cent. V, app. 8, S. XVI. This is the basis of Camerarius' text. It contains the *Tetrabiblos* (to p. 187, 6 Cam. only) on ff. 1-59v. *Cf. CCAG*, vii. no. 42.

PTOLEMY

A: Vaticanus gr. 208, S. XIV *exeuntis*. This manuscript uses the term συμπερασματικά in the title instead of ἀποτελεσματικά. F and H below are related to A. Mercati and De' Cavalieri, *Codices Vaticani graeci*, i (Rome, 1923); *CCAG*, v. 1, no. 6.

E: Monacensis gr. 419, S. XIV. In this manuscript book and chapter headings are missing, and the ending is omitted (from p. 212, 7 Cam.). It is closely related to M (below), but in the latter the missing parts have been supplied in a second hand.

F: Venetus Marc. 323, S. XV. Contains the *Tetrabiblos* on ff. 403-461. Zanetti, *Bibliotheca*, p. 146; Morelli, *Bibliotheca*, p. 195; *CCAG*, ii. no. 4.

G: Vindobonensis philos. gr. 115, S. XIII. Contains a portion of Book II of the *Tetrabiblos* in ff. 7-16v. *Cf.* Boll, *Sitzungsb. Münch. Ak.* 1899, i. p. 84.

H: Venetus Marc. 324, S. XIV-XV. The *Tetrabiblos* is on ff. 156r.-189v. Zanetti, p. 149; Morelli, p. 207; *CCAG*, ii. no. 5.

M: Venetus Marc. 314, S. XIV *ineuntis*. Contains the *Tetrabiblos* on ff. 1-76v. See on E, above. Zanetti, p. 146; Morelli, p. 195; *CCAG*, ii. no. 3.

Besides the manuscripts of the *Tetrabiblos* itself the oldest manuscript of the *Paraphrase* has been utilized: Vaticanus gr. 1453, S. X, containing this text on ff. 1-219. This is cited as Proc. Camerarius' two editions of the *Tetrabiblos* are cited respectively as Cam.[1] and Cam.[2], or simply Cam., if they agree.

A puzzling problem connected with the manuscripts of the *Tetrabiblos* concerns their ending. In one group the conclusion is entirely missing, and has

INTRODUCTION

either been left so [1] or an ending supplied which is identical with that of Proclus' *Paraphrase*; [2] in the other an ending appears which is considerably longer than the former, but which is precisely the same in its general content, and is to be found in the Arabic version of the *Tetrabiblos*.[3] One thing is certain: the first of these endings is spurious. Of course it does not follow that the other is genuine; if it is not, however, the original ending of the book must have been lost so early that it is missing in all the manuscripts. This is a situation that not infrequently occurred in ancient times, especially when a book was from the first existent in the form of a codex, not a roll; yet I am not ready to concede it in this instance, for these reasons: (a) the ending shown in P could readily, from its language, have

---

[1] V breaks off at p. 207, 19 Cam.², E at p. 212, 7 (the beginning of the concluding passage). N also in its present state lacks the conclusion (from p. 187, 6 Cam.²), but this may have been lost at the time the first edition was made, and since Camerarius probably made some use of at least one other MS. we cannot be sure whether N originally had the conclusion or, if so, if it was of the type which Camerarius actually printed (*i.e.* the one taken from the *Paraphrase*). N in general resembles P and one would have expected it to have the same conclusion as P. On the other hand, if it did, one would have expected Camerarius to reproduce it, for it is unlikely that he would have departed from his preferred MS. in so important a particular.

[2] MAD. D, after the point at which V ends, is written in a different ink; the conclusion of M (p. 212, 7 ff. Cam.²) is in a different hand.

[3] P and its copies alone have this ending. My colleague, Professor William H. Worrell, has examined the conclusion of the Arabic version as it appears in Cod. Laur. Orient. 352, ff. 234v.-235r. It is close to, but perhaps not identical with, the ending of P.

PTOLEMY

been written by Ptolemy himself;[1] (*b*) the ending taken from the *Paraphrase* is obviously a summary of that found in P, and I cannot conceive how anyone (except perhaps Ptolemy) could have reversed the process and evolved the tortuous, crabbed Greek of the latter from the comparatively simple language of the former. Thus the ending found in P has the better claim to originality, and if it was not written by Ptolemy in the first place it is extremely difficult to explain how it came to be written at all in the form in which we find it. Since the question, however, is admittedly complicated, and not all the extant manuscripts could be studied in preparing this edition, both endings have been included in the text and translation.

In constructing the text which follows, my underlying purpose has been to abide by the best manuscript tradition; very few emendations have been

---

[1] It echoes many words and thoughts found in p. 106, 25-108, 10 Cam.², which need not be separately enumerated; not, however, in a manner which would indicate that it is a forgery based on the passage, for Ptolemy elsewhere repeats phrases in much the same way, especially when he wishes to point out that he is carrying out a predetermined scheme. Note, however, in addition, that ἁρμόζειν and ἐφαρμόζειν are favourite words of Ptolemy, and *cf.*, for example, pp. 17. 1-2, 117. 6, 120. 9 Cam.² and p. 1. 21 (with Boll, *Studien*, p. 171); *cf.* with διοδευομένου the similar forms of ἐφοδεύω and ἐφοδικῶς, pp. 103. 13, 18; 106. 26; 202. 16 Cam.²; and Boll, *op. cit.*, p. 179; and with διὰ τὴν . . . πρόθεσιν, *cf.* p. 202. 18, ὥσπερ ἐν ἀρχῇ προεθέμεθα. In fact practically every word of the passage except the doubtful χρηματείαις is to be paralleled in the *Tetrabiblos*, usually many times; to arrange them in so exact an approximation to Ptolemy's usual style would demand a forger of superhuman ingenuity.

INTRODUCTION

attempted, and I think no great amount of emendation is necessary. My collations have been made against Camerarius' second edition, because thus far this has been the standard text and it was most convenient; I have not, however, allowed Camerarius' choice of readings to influence me unduly, for his text, in the first place, was not based upon the oldest and best manuscripts and it is, besides, full of his emendations. It was quite evident that this edition of the *Tetrabiblos* should be built up anew, independently of Camerarius' work. Without making the exhaustive studies of the relationships of the manuscripts which should eventually be carried out, I have proceeded on the assumption that V and P best preserve the original text, representing somewhat different strains. With V and its copy D, the oldest text of Proclus' *Paraphrase* is evidently in close alliance, and among the *Tetrabiblos* manuscripts MAEFHG are inclined in general to follow the lead of V, ME and AFH being related between themselves, as has already been stated. N apparently belongs rather to the P family, if there is such, but it is far from presenting a pure text; its peculiarities are, in my opinion, the result of attempts to edit or improve. The later manuscripts, however, all show aberration to a greater or less extent, and VPLD Proc. are frequently to be found arrayed against MNAE (I leave FGH out of consideration because only a few pages of each of them have come into the reckoning). In such cases I have seldom hesitated to follow VPLD, and in general, too, I agree with Boll that V is the best single guide that we have.

I am conscious that in many passages this

PTOLEMY

translation falls short of the intended goal, a version which, in spite of the technical, unfamiliar subject, could readily be understood by itself or at least with the help of a few notes. Ptolemy, however, was a difficult author even for the ancients; the existence of the *Paraphrase* and the frequent flounderings of the anonymous commentator testify to this. He displays a certain enthusiasm for his subject, but beyond this it would be impossible to commend his literary style or even the clearness of his exposition. He is fond of long, involved sentences and has a number of mannerisms, among them a fondness for the infinitive with the article and an almost Teutonic habit of piling up long strings of modifiers between article and substantive, which often results in sequences of two or even three articles. It would, under the circumstances, be almost impossible to make him crystal clear, but I trust there are not too many Heraclitean passages.

Annotation of the *Tetrabiblos* could be carried to great lengths by collecting comparable passages from other astrological writers. The comments attached to this translation, however, are intended only to help the reader over difficulties and have been kept at minimum length.

Many friends have assisted, in one way or another, with this work. Some I cannot thank as I would like to do; but I must express appreciation to Professor W. Carl Rufus for criticizing the astronomy of my translation; to Dr. William Warner Bishop, Librarian of the University of Michigan, for procuring much-needed books and the photostatic reproductions of the manuscripts; and to Franz Cumont for ever helpful interest and suggestions.

THE LUMINARIES AND PLANETS

Symbols.

Sun ☉   Saturn ♄   Venus ♀
Moon ☽   Jupiter ♃   Mercury ☿
               Mars ♂

Classifications.

Effect (i. 5).   *Gender* (i. 6).   *Sect* (i. 7).
Beneficent ♃ ♀ ☽   Masculine ☉ ♄ ♃ ♂   Diurnal ☉ ♃ ♄
Maleficent ♄ ♂   Feminine ☽ ♀   Nocturnal ☽ ♀ ♂
Common ☿   Common ☿   Common ☿

THE SIGNS OF THE ZODIAC

Symbols and Order.

Aries ♈   Cancer ♋   Libra ♎   Capricornus ♑
Taurus ♉   Leo ♌   Scorpio ♏   Aquarius ♒
Gemini ♊   Virgo ♍   Sagittarius ♐   Pisces ♓

The order Aries to Pisces is that "of the following signs," or direct; from Pisces to Aries that "of the leading signs," or reverse.

THE SIGNS OF THE ZODIAC, CONTINUED

Classifications.

i. 11

Equinoctial ♈ ♎
Solstitial ♋ ♑
Solid ♉ ♌ ♏ ♒
Bicorporeal ♊ ♍ ♐ ♓

i. 12

Masculine and diurnal ♈ ♊ ♌ ♎ ♐ ♒
Feminine and nocturnal ♉ ♋ ♍ ♏ ♑ ♓
Commanding and obeying (i. 14) ♉ ♓; ♊ ♒; ♋ ♑; ♌ ♐; ♍ ♏
Beholding each other (i. 15) ♊ ♌; ♉ ♍; ♈ ♎; ♓ ♏; ♒ ♐

THE TRIANGLES (i. 18).

		Signs.	Governors.
I.	N.W.	♈ ♌ ♐	☉, ♃
II.	S.E.	♉ ♍ ♑	♀(d.), ☽(n.)
III.	N.E.	♊ ♎ ♒	♄(d.), ☿(n.)
IV.	S.W.	♋ ♏ ♓	♂, ♀(d.), ☽(n.)

d., day; n., night.

HOUSES, EXALTATIONS, DEPRESSIONS (i. 17, 19).

Planet.	Solar house.	Lunar house.	Exaltation.	Depression.
☉	♌	......	♈	♎
☽	......	♋	♉	♏
♄	♑	♒	♎	♈
♃	♐	♓	♋	♑
♂	♏	♈	♑	♋
♀	♎	♉	♓	♍
☿	♍	♊	♍	♓

PTOLEMY
TETRABIBLOS

Κλαυδίου Πτολεμαίου μαθηματικῆς
τετραβίβλου συντάξεως

ΒΙΒΛΙΟΝ Α'.

⟨ᾱ. Προοίμιον⟩

Τῶν τὸ δι' ἀστρονομίας προγνωστικὸν τέλος παρασκευαζόντων,[1] ὦ Σύρε, δύο τῶν μεγίστων καὶ κυριωτάτων ὑπαρχόντων, ἑνὸς μὲν τοῦ πρώτου καὶ τάξει καὶ δυνάμει, καθ' ὃ τοὺς γινομένους ἑκάστοτε σχηματισμοὺς τῶν κινήσεων ἡλίου καὶ σελήνης καὶ ἀστέρων[2] πρὸς ἀλλήλους τε καὶ τὴν γῆν καταλαμβανόμεθα· δευτέρου δὲ καθ' ὃ διὰ τῆς φυσικῆς τῶν σχηματισμῶν αὐτῶν ἰδιοτροπίας τὰς ἀποτελουμένας μεταβολὰς τῶν ἐμπεριεχομένων ἐπισκεπτόμεθα· τὸ μὲν πρῶτον ἰδίαν ἔχον καὶ δι' ἑαυτὴν αἱρετὴν θεωρίαν, κἂν μὴ τὸ ἐκ τῆς ἐπιζεύξεως τοῦ δευτέρου τέλος συμπεραίνηται, κατ' ἰδίαν σύνταξιν ὡς μάλιστα ἐνῆν ἀποδεικτικῶς σοι[3] περιώδευται. περὶ δὲ τοῦ δευτέρου καὶ μὴ ὡσαύτως αὐτοτελοῦς ἡμεῖς ἐν τῷ παρόντι ποιησόμεθα λόγον κατὰ τὸν ἁρμόζοντα φιλοσοφίᾳ τρόπον καὶ ὡς ἄν τις φιλαλήθει μάλιστα χρώμενος σκοπῷ μήτε τὴν κατάληψιν αὐτοῦ παραβάλλοι τῇ τοῦ πρώτου καὶ ἀεὶ ὡσαύτως ἔχοντος βεβαιότητι, τὸ ἐν πολλοῖς ἀσθενὲς

---

[1] κατασκευαζόντων P.
[2] τῶν ἀστέρων NCam.; τῶν om. VPMADE.
[3] σοι] ἐν τῇ συντάξει P.

THE QUADRIPARTITE MATHEMATICAL TREATISE, OR "TETRABIBLOS," OF CLAUDIUS PTOLEMY.

BOOK I.

1. *Introduction.*

OF the means of prediction through astronomy, O Syrus, two are the most important and valid. One, which is first [1] both in order and in effectiveness, is that whereby we apprehend the aspects of the movements of sun, moon, and stars in relation to each other and to the earth, as they occur from time to time; the second is that in which by means of the natural character of these aspects themselves we investigate the changes which they bring about in that which they surround. The first of these, which has its own science, desirable in itself even though it does not attain the result given by its combination with the second, has been expounded to you as best we could in its own treatise [2] by the method of demonstration. We shall now give an account of the second and less self-sufficient method in a properly philosophical way, so that one whose aim is the truth might never compare its perceptions with the sureness of the first, unvarying science, for he ascribes to it the weakness and unpredictability

---

[1] Astronomy proper.
[2] The *Almagest*.

PTOLEMY

2 καὶ δυσείκαστον τῆς ὑλικῆς ποιότητος προσποιούμενος, μήτε πρὸς τὴν κατὰ τὸ ἐνδεχόμενον ἐπίσκεψιν ἀποκνοίη, τῶν τε πλείστων καὶ ὁλοσχερῶν συμπτωμάτων ἐναργῶς οὕτω τὴν ἀπὸ τοῦ περιέχοντος αἰτίαν ἐμφανιζόντων. ἐπεὶ δὲ πᾶν μὲν τὸ δυσέφικτον παρὰ τοῖς πολλοῖς εὐδιάβλητον ἔχει φύσιν, ἐπὶ δὲ τῶν προκειμένων δύο καταλήψεων αἱ μὲν τῆς προτέρας[1] διαβολαὶ τυφλῶν ἂν εἶεν παντελῶς, αἱ δὲ τῆς δευτέρας εὐπροφασίστους ἔχουσι τὰς ἀφορμάς (ἢ γὰρ τὸ ἐπ' ἐνίων δυσθεώρητον ἀκαταληψίας τελείας δόξαν[2] παρέσχεν, ἢ τὸ τῶν γνωσθέντων δυσφύλακτον καὶ τὸ τέλος ὡς ἄχρηστον διέσυρε), πειρασόμεθα διὰ βραχέων πρὸ τῆς κατὰ μέρος ὑφηγήσεως τὸ μέτρον ἑκατέρου τοῦ τε δυνατοῦ καὶ τοῦ χρησίμου τῆς τοιαύτης προγνώσεως ἐπισκέψασθαι· καὶ πρῶτον τοῦ δυνατοῦ.

⟨β̄.⟩ Ὅτι καταληπτικὴ ἡ δι' ἀστρονομίας γνῶσις, καὶ μέχρι τίνος

Ὅτι μὲν τοίνυν διαδίδοται καὶ διικνεῖταί τις δύναμις ἀπὸ τῆς αἰθερώδους καὶ ἀιδίου φύσεως

---
[1] τάξει καὶ δυνάμει post προτέρας add. NCam.
[2] δόξαν om. NCam.

---

[1] Ptolemy is contrasting, after the manner of Aristotle, the unchangeability of the heavenly bodies and their regular motions, which can be known and predicted by astronomy, with the constant and unpredictable changes of material objects in the sublunary region.
[2] On the arguments against astrology, see Bouché-Leclercq, pp. 570 ff. The Academic school, led by

of material qualities found in individual things,¹ nor yet refrain from such investigation as is within the bounds of possibility, when it is so evident that most events of a general nature draw their causes from the enveloping heavens. But since everything that is hard to attain is easily assailed ² by the generality of men, and in the case of the two before-mentioned disciplines the allegations against the first could be made only by the blind, while there are specious grounds for those levelled at the second—for its difficulty in parts has made them think it completely incomprehensible, or the difficulty of escaping what is known ³ has disparaged even its object as useless— we shall try to examine briefly the measure of both the possibility and the usefulness of such prognostication before offering detailed instruction on the subject. First as to its possibility.

2. *That Knowledge by Astronomical Means is Attainable, and How Far.*

A very few considerations would make it apparent to all that a certain power emanating from the eternal ethereal substance ⁴ is dispersed through and

Carneades, initiated the most serious attack against it in antiquity. The answers given by Ptolemy in the two chapters following are, as Boll (*Studien*, pp. 131 ff.) shows, largely derived from the Stoic Posidonius, who defended divination.

³ Proclus paraphrases, " the difficulty of retaining in the memory what has been learned," but the reference is clearly to the subject discussed in i. 3.

⁴ The ether, or fifth element, contrasted with the usual four ; this is an Aristotelian (Peripatetic) doctrine.

PTOLEMY

ἐπὶ πᾶσαν τὴν περιγείαν καὶ δι' ὅλων μεταβλητήν, τῶν ὑπὸ τὴν σελήνην πρώτων στοιχείων πυρὸς καὶ ἀέρος περιεχομένων μὲν καὶ τρεπομένων ὑπὸ τῶν κατὰ τὸν αἰθέρα κινήσεων, περιεχόντων δὲ καὶ συντρεπόντων τὰ λοιπὰ πάντα, γῆν καὶ ὕδωρ καὶ τὰ ἐν αὐτοῖς φυτὰ καὶ ζῷα, πᾶσιν ἂν ἐναργέστατον[1]
3 καὶ δι' ὀλίγων φανείη. ὅ τε γὰρ ἥλιος διατίθησί πως ἀεὶ μετὰ τοῦ περιέχοντος πάντα τὰ περὶ τὴν γῆν, οὐ μόνον διὰ τῶν κατὰ τὰς ἐτησίους ὥρας μεταβολῶν πρὸς γονὰς ζῴων καὶ φυτῶν καρποφορίας καὶ ῥύσεις ὑδάτων καὶ σωμάτων μετατροπὰς ἀλλὰ καὶ διὰ τῶν καθ' ἑκάστην ἡμέραν περιόδων, θερμαίνων τε καὶ ὑγραίνων καὶ ξηραίνων καὶ ψύχων τεταγμένως τε καὶ ἀκολούθως τοῖς πρὸς τὸν κατὰ κορυφὴν ἡμῶν γινομένοις ὁμοιοτρόποις σχηματισμοῖς. ἥ τε σελήνη πλείστην,[2] ὡς περιγειοτάτη, διαδίδωσιν ἐπὶ τὴν γῆν[3] τὴν ἀπόρροιαν, συμπαθούντων αὐτῇ καὶ συντρεπομένων τῶν πλείστων καὶ ἀψύχων καὶ ἐμψύχων, καὶ ποταμῶν μὲν συναυξόντων καὶ συμμειούντων τοῖς φωσὶν αὐτῆς τὰ ῥεύματα, θαλαττῶν δὲ συντρεπουσῶν ταῖς ἀνατολαῖς καὶ ταῖς δύσεσι τὰς ἰδίας ὁρμάς, φυτῶν δὲ καὶ ζῴων ἢ ὅλων ἢ κατά τινα μέρη συμπληρουμένων τε αὐτῇ καὶ συμμειουμένων. αἵ τε τῶν ἀστέρων τῶν τε ἀπλανῶν καὶ τῶν πλανωμένων πάροδοι πλείστας ποιοῦσι ἐπισημασίας τοῦ περιέχοντος καυματώδεις καὶ πνευματώδεις[4] καὶ νιφετώδεις, ὑφ' ὧν καὶ τὰ ἐπὶ τῆς

---

[1] ἐνεργέστατον MAECam.　　　[2] πλείστην om. NCam.
[3] ἐπὶ τὴν γῆν VMADE, ὑπὸ τὴν γῆν P, πρὸς τῇ γῇ NCam.
[4] καὶ πνευματώδεις om. NCam.

permeates the whole region about the earth, which throughout is subject to change, since, of the primary sublunar elements, fire and air are encompassed and changed by the motions in the ether, and in turn encompass and change all else, earth and water and the plants and animals therein. For the sun,[1] together with the ambient, is always in some way affecting everything on the earth, not only by the changes that accompany the seasons of the year to bring about the generation of animals, the productiveness of plants, the flowing of waters, and the changes of bodies, but also by its daily revolutions furnishing heat, moisture, dryness, and cold in regular order and in correspondence with its positions relative to the zenith. The moon, too, as the heavenly body nearest the earth, bestows her effluence[2] most abundantly upon mundane things, for most of them, animate or inanimate, are sympathetic to her and change in company with her; the rivers increase and diminish their streams with her light, the seas turn their own tides with her rising and setting, and plants and animals in whole or in some part wax and wane with her. Moreover, the passages of the fixed stars and the planets through the sky often signify hot, windy, and snowy conditions of the air, and mundane

---

[1] Boll, *Studien*, pp. 133 ff., enumerates parallels to this passage concerning the sun and the moon in Cicero, Philo Judaeus, Cleomedes, and Manilius, and ascribes their likeness to the influence of Posidonius.

[2] This word, ἀπόρροια, has another meaning, "separation," as a technical term of astrology; see c. 24 below and my note on P. Mich. 149, col. iii, 33.

PTOLEMY

γῆς οἰκείως διατίθεται. ἤδη δὲ καὶ οἱ πρὸς ἀλλήλους αὐτῶν σχηματισμοί, συνερχομένων πως[1] καὶ συγκιρναμένων τῶν διαδόσεων, πλείστας καὶ ποικίλας μεταβολὰς ἀπεργάζονται, κατακρατούσης μὲν τῆς τοῦ ἡλίου δυνάμεως πρὸς τὸ καθ' ὅλου τῆς ποιότητος τεταγμένον, συνεργούντων δὲ ἢ ἀποσυνεργούντων 4 κατά τι τῶν λοιπῶν, καὶ τῆς μὲν σελήνης ἐκφανέστερον καὶ συνεχέστερον ὡς ἐν ταῖς συνόδοις καὶ διχοτόμοις καὶ πανσελήνοις, τῶν δὲ ἀστέρων περιοδικώτερον καὶ ἀσημότερον ὡς ἐν ταῖς φάσεσι καὶ κρύψεσι καὶ προσνεύσεσιν. ὅτι δὲ τούτων οὕτω θεωρουμένων οὐ μόνον τὰ ἤδη συγκραθέντα διατίθεσθαί πως ὑπὸ τῆς τούτων κινήσεως ἀναγκαῖον ἀλλὰ καὶ τῶν σπερμάτων τὰς ἀρχὰς καὶ τὰς πληροφορήσεις διαπλάττεσθαι καὶ διαμορφοῦσθαι πρὸς τὴν οἰκείαν τοῦ τότε περιέχοντος ποιότητα, πᾶσιν ἂν δόξειεν ἀκόλουθον εἶναι. οἱ γοῦν παρατηρητικώτεροι τῶν γεωργῶν καὶ τῶν νομέων ἀπὸ τῶν κατὰ τὰς ὀχείας καὶ τὰς τῶν σπερμάτων καταθέσεις συμβαινόντων πνευμάτων στοχάζονται τῆς ποιότητος τῶν ἀποβησομένων, καὶ ὅλως τὰ μὲν ὁλοσχερέστερα καὶ διὰ τῶν ἐπιφανεστέρων συσχηματισμῶν ἡλίου καὶ σελήνης καὶ ἀστέρων ἐπισημαινόμενα καὶ παρὰ τοῖς μὴ φυσικῶς, μόνον δὲ παρατηρητικῶς σκεπτομένοις, ὡς ἐπὶ πᾶν προγινωσκόμενα θεωροῦμεν, τὰ μὲν ἐκ μείζονός τε δυνάμεως καὶ ἁπλουστέρας

[1] πως] τε NCam.

---

[1] Positions relative to one another in the heavens. For the names of the aspects recognized by Ptolemy *cf.* the note on i. 13 (pp. 72-73).

things are affected accordingly. Then, too, their aspects[1] to one another, by the meeting and mingling of their dispensations, bring about many complicated changes. For though the sun's power prevails in the general ordering of quality, the other heavenly bodies aid or oppose it in particular details, the moon more obviously and continuously, as for example when it is new, at quarter, or full, and the stars at greater intervals and more obscurely, as in their appearances, occultations, and approaches.[2] If these matters be so regarded, all would judge it to follow that not only must things already compounded be affected in some way by the motion of these heavenly bodies, but likewise the germination and fruition of the seed must be moulded and conformed to the quality proper to the heavens at the time. The more observant farmers and herdsmen,[3] indeed, conjecture, from the winds prevailing at the time of impregnation and of the sowing of the seed, the quality of what will result; and in general we see that the more important consequences signified by the more obvious configurations of sun, moon, and stars are usually known beforehand, even by those who inquire, not by scientific means, but only by observation. Those which are consequent upon greater forces and simpler natural orders, such as

[2] By "stars" (ἀστέρων) in this passage Ptolemy means primarily the planets rather than the fixed stars. Their "appearances" and "occultations" are their heliacal risings and settings (cf. Bouché-Leclercq, p. 111, n. 3). πρόσνευσις is used to mean both "inclination" and, as here, the "approach" of one heavenly body to another.

[3] Cicero, de divinatione, i. 112: Multa medici, multa gubernatores, agricolae etiam multa praesentiunt.

PTOLEMY

τάξεως καὶ παρὰ τοῖς πάνυ ἰδιώταις, μᾶλλον δὲ καὶ παρ' ἐνίοις τῶν ἀλόγων ζῴων, ὡς τῶν ὡρῶν καὶ τῶν πνευμάτων τὰς ἐτησίους διαφοράς· τούτων γὰρ ὡς ἐπὶ πᾶν ὁ ἥλιος αἴτιος· τὰ δὲ ἧττον οὕτως ἔχοντα παρὰ τοῖς ἤδη κατὰ τὸ ἀναγκαῖον ταῖς παρατηρή-
5 σεσιν ἐνειθισμένοις, ὡς τοῖς ναυτιλλομένοις τὰς κατὰ μέρος τῶν χειμώνων καὶ τῶν πνευμάτων ἐπισημασίας, ὅσαι γίνονται κατὰ τὸ περιοδικώτερον ὑπὸ τῶν τῆς σελήνης ἢ καὶ τῶν ἀπλανῶν ἀστέρων πρὸς τὸν ἥλιον συσχηματισμῶν. παρὰ μέντοι τὸ μήτε αὐτῶν τούτων τοὺς χρόνους καὶ τοὺς τόπους ὑπὸ ἀπειρίας ἀκριβῶς δύνασθαι κατανοεῖν, μήτε τὰς τῶν πλανωμένων ἀστέρων περιόδους, πλεῖστον καὶ αὐτὰς συμβαλλομένας, τὸ πολλάκις αὐτοῖς[1] σφάλλεσθαι συμβαίνει. τί δὴ οὖν κωλύει τὸν ἠκριβωκότα μὲν τὰς πάντων τῶν ἀστέρων καὶ ἡλίου καὶ σελήνης κινήσεις, ὅπως αὐτὸν μηδενὸς τῶν σχηματισμῶν μήτε ὁ τόπος μήτε ὁ χρόνος λανθάνοι, διειληφότα δὲ ἐκ τῆς ἔτι ἄνωθεν συνεχοῦς ἱστορίας ὡς ἐπὶ πᾶν αὐτῶν τὰς φύσεις,[2] κἂν μὴ τὰς κατ' αὐτὸ τὸ ὑποκείμενον ἀλλὰ τάς γε δυνάμει ποιητικάς,[3] οἷον ὡς τὴν τοῦ ἡλίου ὅτι θερμαίνει καὶ τὴν τῆς σελήνης ὅτι ὑγραίνει καὶ ἐπὶ τῶν λοιπῶν ὁμοίως, ἱκανὸν δὲ πρὸς ταῦτα τοιαῦτα ὄντα φυσικῶς ἅμα καὶ εὐστόχως ἐκ τῆς συγκράσεως[4] πάντων τὸ ἴδιον τῆς ποιότητος διαλαβεῖν, ὡς δύνασθαι μὲν ἐφ' ἑκάστου τῶν διδομένων καιρῶν ἐκ

---

[1] αὐτοῖς VPMNDE ; αὐτοὺς ACam.
[2] ὥς . . . φύσεις post διειληφότα δὲ NCam. ; αὐτῶν PMAE, αὐτὰ VDNCam.; τὰς φύσεις MAEProc., φύσει VDNCam., φήσῃ P.

the annual variations of the seasons and the winds, are comprehended by very ignorant men, nay even by some dumb animals; for the sun is in general responsible for these phenomena. Things that are not of so general a nature, however, are comprehended by those who have by necessity become used to making observations, as, for instance, sailors know the special signs of storms and winds that arise periodically by reason of the aspects of the moon and fixed stars to the sun. Yet because they cannot in their ignorance accurately know the times and places of these phenomena, nor the periodic movements of the planets, which contribute importantly to the effect, it happens that they often err. If, then, a man knows accurately the movements of all the stars, the sun, and the moon, so that neither the place nor the time of any of their configurations escapes his notice, and if he has distinguished in general their natures as the result of previous continued study, even though he may discern, not their essential, but only their potentially effective qualities, such as the sun's heating and the moon's moistening, and so on with the rest; and if he is capable of determining in view of all these data, both scientifically and by successful conjecture, the distinctive mark of quality resulting from the combination of all the factors, what is to prevent him from being able to tell on each given occasion the characteristics of the air from the rela-

---

³ ποιητικάς VPMNDECam.¹ ; ποιότητας ACam.²
⁴ συγκρίσεως PCam.

PTOLEMY

τῆς τότε τῶν φαινομένων σχέσεως τὰς τοῦ περιέχοντος ἰδιοτροπίας εἰπεῖν, οἷον ὅτι θερμότερον ἢ ὑγρότερον ἔσται, δύνασθαι δὲ καὶ καθ' ἕνα ἕκαστον τῶν ἀνθρώπων τήν τε καθ' ὅλου ποιότητα τῆς ἰδιοσυγκρασίας ἀπὸ τοῦ κατὰ τὴν σύστασιν περιέχοντος συνιδεῖν, οἷον ὅτι τὸ μὲν σῶμα τοιόσδε, τὴν δὲ ψυχὴν τοιόσδε, καὶ τὰ κατὰ καιροὺς συμπτώματα διὰ τοῦ τὸ μὲν τοιόνδε περιέχον τῇ τοιᾷδε συγκράσει σύμμετρον ἢ καὶ πρόσφορον γίνεσθαι πρὸς εὐεξίαν, τὸ δὲ τοιόνδε ἀσύμμετρον καὶ πρόσφορον πρὸς κάκωσιν; ἀλλὰ γὰρ τὸ μὲν δυνατὸν τῆς τοιαύτης καταλήψεώς διὰ τούτων καὶ τῶν ὁμοίων ἔστι συνιδεῖν.

Ὅτι δὲ εὐπροφασίστως μέν, οὐ προσηκόντως δέ, τὴν πρὸς τὸ ἀδύνατον ἔσχε διαβολὴν οὕτως ἂν κατανοήσαιμεν. πρῶτον μὲν γὰρ τὰ πταίσματα τῶν μὴ ἀκριβούντων τὸ ἔργον, πολλὰ ὄντα, ὡς ἐν μεγάλῃ καὶ πολυμερεῖ θεωρίᾳ, καὶ τοῖς ἀληθευομένοις τὴν τούτου ἐκ τύχης παρέσχε δόξαν, οὐκ ὀρθῶς. τὸ γὰρ τοιοῦτον οὐ τῆς ἐπιστήμης, ἀλλὰ τῶν μεταχειριζομένων ἐστὶν ἀδυναμία· ἔπειτα καὶ οἱ πλεῖστοι τοῦ πορίζειν ἕνεκεν ἑτέραν τέχνην τῷ ταύτης ὀνόματι καταξιοπιστευόμενοι[1] τοὺς μὲν ἰδιώτας ἐξαπατῶσι, πολλὰ προλέγειν δοκοῦντες καὶ τῶν μηδεμίαν φύσιν ἐχόντων προγινώσκεσθαι, τοῖς

---

[1] καταξιοπιστευόμενοι VPMADE; διὰ τὴν ἀξιοπιστίαν Proc.; καὶ ἀξίᾳ προστησάμενοι καὶ πιστευόμενοι NCam.

---

[1] The first part of the pseudo-Lucianic Περὶ ἀστρολογίης closely parallels this passage, as Boll, *Studien*, pp. 151-153, shows.

tions of the phenomena at the time, for instance, that it will be warmer or wetter ? Why can he not, too, with respect to an individual man, perceive the general quality of his temperament from the ambient at the time of his birth, as for instance that he is such and such in body and such and such in soul, and predict occasional events, by use of the fact that such and such an ambient is attuned to such and such a temperament and is favourable to prosperity, while another is not so attuned and conduces to injury ? Enough, however ; for the possibility of such knowledge can be understood from these and similar arguments.

The following considerations might lead us to observe that criticism of the science on the score of impossibility has been specious but undeserved. In the first place, the mistakes [1] of those who are not accurately instructed in its practice, and they are many, as one would expect in an important and many-sided art, have brought about the belief that even its true predictions depend upon chance, which is incorrect. For a thing like this is an impotence, not of the science, but of those who practise it. Secondly, most, for the sake of gain, claim credence for another art in the name of this,[2] and deceive the vulgar, because they are reputed to foretell many things, even those that cannot naturally be known

[2] Cardanus (p. 104) gives a number of examples, among them the *geomantici*, those who make elaborate predictions from the mere fact that a man was born on a certain day of the week, of the moon, or of the month, those who predict by reckoning the numerical equivalents of the letters in a man's name (arithmologists), and so on. *Cf.* also Plato's remarks about unworthy pretenders to philosophy, *Republic*, 495C ff.

PTOLEMY

δὲ ζητητικωτέροις διὰ τούτου παρέσχον ἀφορμὴν ἐν ἴσῳ¹ καὶ τῶν φύσιν ἐχόντων προλέγεσθαι² καταγινώσκειν. οὐδὲ τοῦτο δεόντως· οὐδὲ γὰρ φιλοσοφίαν ἀναιρετέον, ἐπεί τινες τῶν προσποιουμένων αὐτὴν πονηροὶ καταφαίνονται. ἀλλ' ὅμως ἐναργές ἐστιν ὅτι κἂν διερευνητικῶς τις ὡς ἔνι μάλιστα καὶ γνησίως τοῖς μαθήμασι προσέρχηται, πολλάκις πταίειν αὐτὸν ἐνδέχεται, δι' οὐδὲν μὲν τῶν εἰρημένων, δι' αὐτὴν δὲ τὴν τοῦ πράγματος φύσιν καὶ τὴν πρὸς τὸ μέγεθος τῆς ἐπαγγελίας ἀσθένειαν. καθ' ὅλου γὰρ πρὸς τῷ τὴν περὶ τὸ ποιὸν τῆς ὕλης θεωρίαν πᾶσαν εἰκαστικὴν εἶναι καὶ οὐ διαβεβαιωτικήν, καὶ μάλιστα τὴν ἐκ πολλῶν ἀνομοίων συγκιρναμένην, ἔτι καὶ τοῖς παλαιοῖς τῶν πλανωμένων συσχηματισμοῖς, ἀφ' ὧν ἐφαρμόζομεν τοῖς ὡσαύτως ἔχουσι τῶν νῦν τὰς ὑπὸ τῶν προγενεστέρων ἐπ' ἐκείνων παρατετηρημένας προτελέσεις,³ παρόμοιοι μὲν⁴ δύνανται γίνεσθαι μᾶλλον ἢ ἧττον καὶ οὗτοι διὰ μακρῶν περιόδων, ἀπαράλλακτοι δὲ οὐδαμῶς, τῆς πάντων ἐν τῷ οὐρανῷ μετὰ τῆς γῆς κατὰ τὸ ἀκριβὲς συναποκαταστάσεως, εἰ μή τις κενο-

¹ ἴσῳ VPD; ἑκάστῳ MNAECam.
² προλέγεσθαι VMADEProc.; πως λέγεσθαι (post φύσιν) P; προγινώσκεσθαι NCam.
³ μὴ καθάπαξ τοὺς αὐτοὺς συμβεβηκέναι τοῖς νῦν add. NCam.; om. VPMADE Proc.
⁴ γὰρ add. codd.; om. Proc.

[1] On rascals in philosophy cf. Plato, *Republic* 487D, and the discussion which follows.
[2] By various ancient authors it was claimed that the Chaldaean observations extended over periods of from 470,000 to 720,000 years: Boll-Bezold-Gundel, pp. 25, 99.

TETRABIBLOS I. 2

beforehand, while to the more thoughtful they have thereby given occasion to pass equally unfavourable judgement upon the natural subjects of prophecy. Nor is this deservedly done; it is the same with philosophy—we need not abolish it because there are evident rascals among those that pretend to it.[1] Nevertheless it is clear that even though one approach astrology in the most inquiring and legitimate spirit possible, he may frequently err, not for any of the reasons stated, but because of the very nature of the thing and his own weakness in comparison with the magnitude of his profession. For in general, besides the fact that every science that deals with the quality of its subject-matter is conjectural and not to be absolutely affirmed, particularly one which is composed of many unlike elements, it is furthermore true that the ancient configurations of the planets,[2] upon the basis of which we attach to similar aspects of our own day the effects observed by the ancients in theirs, can be more or less similar to the modern aspects, and that, too, at long intervals, but not identical, since the exact return of all the heavenly bodies and the earth to the same positions,[3] unless one

[3] " The Stoics say that the planets, returning to the same point of longitude and latitude which each occupied when first the universe arose, at fixed periods of time bring about a conflagration and destruction of things, and that the universe again reverts anew to the same condition, and that as the stars again move in the same way everything that took place in the former period is exactly reproduced. Socrates, they say, and Plato will again exist, and every single man, with the same friends and countrymen; the same things will happen to them, they will meet with the same fortune, and deal with the same things," etc. (Nemesius, *De natura hominis*, 38, p. 309, Matthaei).

PTOLEMY

δοξοίη περὶ τὴν τῶν ἀκαταλήπτων κατάληψιν καὶ γνῶσιν.[1] ἢ μηδ' ὅλως ἢ[2] μὴ κατά γε τὸν αἰσθητὸν ἀνθρώπῳ χρόνον ἀπαρτιζομένης, ὡς διὰ τοῦτο τὰς προρρήσεις[3] ἀνομοίων ὄντων τῶν ὑποκειμένων παραδειγμάτων ἐνίοτε διαμαρτάνεσθαι. περὶ μὲν οὖν τὴν ἐπίσκεψιν τῶν κατὰ τὸ περιέχον γινομένων συμπτωμάτων, τοῦτ' ἂν εἴη μόνον τὸ δυσχερές, μηδεμιᾶς ἐνταῦθα συμπαραλαμβανομένης αἰτίας τῇ κινήσει τῶν οὐρανίων. περὶ δὲ τὰς γενεθλιο-
8 λογικάς,[4] καὶ ὅλως τὰς κατ' ἰδίαν τῆς ἑκάστου συγκρίσεως,[5] οὐ μικρὰ οὐδὲ τὰ τυχόντα ἔστιν ἰδεῖν συναίτια καὶ αὐτὰ γινόμενα τῆς τῶν συνισταμένων ἰδιοτροπίας. αἵ τε γὰρ τῶν σπερμάτων διαφοραὶ πλεῖστον δύνανται πρὸς τὸ τοῦ γένους ἴδιον, ἐπειδήπερ τοῦ περιέχοντος καὶ τοῦ ὁρίζοντος ὑποκειμένου τοῦ αὐτοῦ κατακρατεῖ τῶν σπερμάτων ἕκαστον εἰς τὴν καθ' ὅλου τοῦ οἰκείου μορφώματος διατύπωσιν, οἷον ἀνθρώπου καὶ ἵππου καὶ τῶν ἄλλων· οἵ τε τόποι τῆς γενέσεως οὐ μικρὰς ποιοῦνται τὰς περὶ τὰ συνιστάμενα παραλλαγάς. καὶ τῶν σπερμάτων γὰρ κατὰ γένος ὑποκειμένων τῶν αὐτῶν, οἷον ἀνθρωπίνων, καὶ τῆς τοῦ περιέχοντος καταστάσεως τῆς αὐτῆς, παρὰ τὸ τῶν χωρῶν διάφορον πολὺ καὶ τοῖς σώμασι καὶ ταῖς ψυχαῖς οἱ γενόμενοι διήνεγκαν. πρὸς δὲ τούτοις αἵ τε τροφαὶ καὶ τὰ ἔθη, πάντων τῶν προκειμένων ἀδιαφόρων ὑποτιθεμένων, συμβάλλονταί τι πρὸς τὰς κατὰ μέρος τῶν βίων διαγωγάς.

[1] καὶ γνῶσιν om. Cam.
[2] ἢ . . . ἢ VMADE; εἰ . . . εἰ NCam.; ἢ . . . ἡμῖν P.
[3] προρρήσεις libri (πρω- P) Proc.Cam.¹ (*notatum); παρατηρήσεις Cam.²

TETRABIBLOS I. 2

holds vain opinions of his ability to comprehend and know the incomprehensible, either takes place not at all or at least not in the period of time that falls within the experience of man; so that for this reason predictions sometimes fail, because of the disparity of the examples on which they are based. As to the investigation of atmospheric phenomena, this would be the only difficulty, since no other cause besides the movement of the heavenly bodies is taken into consideration. But in an inquiry concerning nativities and individual temperaments in general, one can see that there are circumstances of no small importance and of no trifling character, which join to cause the special qualities of those who are born. For differences of seed exert a very great influence on the special traits of the genus, since, if the ambient and the horizon are the same, each seed prevails to express in general its own form, for example, man, horse, and so forth; and the places of birth bring about no small variation in what is produced. For if the seed is generically the same, human for example, and the condition of the ambient the same, those who are born differ much, both in body and soul, with the difference of countries.[1] In addition to this, all the aforesaid conditions being equal, rearing and customs contribute to influence the particular way in which a

---

[1] The first three chapters of Book ii deal with astrological ethnology, and in iv. 10 Ptolemy points out that in all nativities such general considerations as nationality and age take precedence over more particular details.

---

⁴ γενεθλιολογικάς VD, cf. Proc.; γενεθλιολογίας cett. Cam.
⁵ συγκρίσεως VP (-κρη-) MDECam.¹; συγκράσεως Cam.²

ὧν ἕκαστον ἐὰν μὴ συνδιαλαμβάνηται ταῖς ἀπὸ τοῦ περιέχοντος αἰτίαις, εἰ καὶ ὅτι μάλιστα τὴν πλείστην ἔχει τοῦτο δύναμιν (τῷ τὸ μὲν περιέχον κἀκείνοις αὐτοῖς εἰς τὸ τοιοῖσδε εἶναι συναίτιον γίνεσθαι, τούτῳ δ' ἐκεῖνα μηδαμῶς), πολλὴν ἀπορίαν δύνανται παρέχειν τοῖς ἐπὶ τῶν τοιούτων οἰομένοις ἀπὸ μόνης 9 τῆς τῶν μετεώρων κινήσεως, πάντα, καὶ τὰ μὴ τέλεον ἐπ' αὐτῇ, δύνασθαι διαγινώσκειν.

Τούτων δὲ οὕτως ἐχόντων, προσῆκον ἂν εἴη μήτε, ἐπειδὴ διαμαρτάνεσθαί ποτε τὴν τοιαύτην πρόγνωσιν ἐνδέχεται, καὶ τὸ πᾶν αὐτῆς ἀναιρεῖν, ὥσπερ οὐδὲ τὴν κυβερνητικὴν[1] διὰ τὸ πολλάκις πταίειν ἀποδοκιμάζομεν· ἀλλ' ὡς ἐν μεγάλοις, οὕτω καὶ θείοις ἐπαγγέλμασιν, ἀσπάζεσθαι καὶ ἀγαπητὸν ἡγεῖσθαι τὸ δυνατόν, μήτ' αὖ πάλιν πάντα[2] ἡμῖν ἀνθρωπίνως καὶ ἐστοχασμένως αἰτεῖν παρ' αὐτῆς, ἀλλὰ συμφιλοκαλεῖν, καὶ ἐν οἷς οὐκ ἦν ἐπ' αὐτῇ τὸ πᾶν ἐφοδιάζειν· καὶ ὥσπερ τοῖς ἰατροῖς, ὅταν ἐπιζητῶσί τινα, καὶ περὶ αὐτῆς τῆς νόσου καὶ περὶ τῆς τοῦ κάμνοντος ἰδιοτροπίας οὐ μεμψόμεθα λέγουσιν,[3] οὕτω καὶ ἐνταῦθα τὰ γένη καὶ τὰς χώρας καὶ τὰς τροφάς, ἢ καί τινα τῶν ἤδη συμβεβηκότων, μὴ ἀγανακτεῖν ὑποτιθεμένοις.

[1] τὴν κυβερνητικὴν VPMDEProc.; κυβερνητικοὺς NACam.
[2] πάντα] μὴ πάντα VPD.
[3] λέγουσιν NCam., λέγοντες VPMADE.

life is lived. Unless each one of these things is examined together with the causes that are derived from the ambient, although this latter be conceded to exercise the greatest influence (for the ambient is one of the causes for these things being what they are, while they in turn have no influence upon it), they can cause much difficulty for those who believe that in such cases everything can be understood, even things not wholly within its jurisdiction, from the motion of the heavenly bodies alone.

Since this is the case, it would not be fitting to dismiss all prognostication of this character because it can sometimes be mistaken, for we do not discredit the art of the pilot for its many errors; but as when the claims are great, so also when they are divine, we should welcome what is possible and think it enough. Nor, further, should we gropingly and in human fashion demand everything of the art, but rather join in the appreciation of its beauty, even in instances wherein it could not provide the full answer; and as we do not find fault with the physicians, when they examine a person, for speaking both about the sickness itself and about the patient's idiosyncrasy, so too in this case we should not object to astrologers using as a basis for calculation nationality, country, and rearing, or any other already existing accidental qualities.

PTOLEMY

⟨γ.⟩ Ὅτι καὶ ὠφέλιμος

Τίνα μὲν οὖν τρόπον δυνατὸν γίνεται τὸ δι' ἀστρονομίας προγνωστικόν, καὶ ὅτι μέχρι μόνον ἂν φθάνοι τῶν τε κατ' αὐτὸ τὸ περιέχον συμπτωμάτων καὶ τῶν ἀπὸ τῆς τοιαύτης αἰτίας τοῖς ἀνθρώποις παρακολουθούντων, ταῦτα δ' ἂν εἴη περί τε τὰς ἐξ ἀρχῆς ἐπιτηδειότητας τῶν δυνάμεων καὶ πράξεων σώματος καὶ ψυχῆς καὶ τὰ κατὰ καιροὺς αὐτῶν πάθη, πολυχρονιότητάς τε καὶ ὀλιγοχρονιότητας, ἔτι δὲ καὶ ὅσα τῶν ἔξωθεν κυρίαν τε καὶ φυσικὴν ἔχει πρὸς τὰ πρῶτα συμπλοκήν, ὡς πρὸς τὸ σῶμα μὲν ἡ κτῆσις καὶ ἡ συμβίωσις, πρὸς δὲ τὴν ψυχὴν ἥ τε τιμὴ καὶ τὸ ἀξίωμα, καὶ τὰς τούτων κατὰ καιροὺς τύχας, σχεδὸν ὡς ἐν κεφαλαίοις[1] γέγονεν ἡμῖν δῆλον· λοιπὸν δ' ἂν εἴη τῶν προκειμένων τὴν κατὰ τὸ χρήσιμον ἐπίσκεψιν διὰ βραχέων ποιήσασθαι, πρότερον διαλαβοῦσι τίνα τρόπον, καὶ πρὸς τί τέλος ἀφορῶντες τὴν αὐτοῦ τοῦ χρησίμου δύναμιν ἐκδεξόμεθα. εἰ μὲν γὰρ πρὸς τὰ τῆς ψυχῆς ἀγαθά, τί ἂν εἴη συμφορώτερον[2] πρὸς εὐπραγίαν καὶ χαρὰν καὶ ὅλως εὐαρέστησιν τῆς τοιαύτης προγνώσεως, καθ' ἣν τῶν τε ἀνθρωπίνων καὶ τῶν θείων γινόμεθα συνορατικοί; εἰ δὲ πρὸς τὰ τοῦ σώματος, πάντων ἂν μᾶλλον ἡ τοιαύτη κατάληψις ἐπιγινώσκοι τὸ οἰκεῖόν τε καὶ πρόσφορον τῇ καθ' ἑκάστην σύγκρασιν ἐπιτηδειότητι· εἰ δὲ μὴ πρὸς πλοῦτον ἢ δόξαν ἢ

[1] κεφαλαίοις libri, -ῳ Cam.
[2] συμφορώτερον VD, συμφερότερον PL, σπουδαιότερον MAE Cam.; post προγνώσεως MAE.

TETRABIBLOS I. 3

3. *That it is also Beneficial.*

In somewhat summary fashion it has been shown how prognostication by astronomical means is possible, and that it can go no further than what happens in the ambient and the consequences to man from such causes—that is, it concerns the original endowments of faculties and activities of soul and body, their occasional diseases, their endurance for a long or a short time, and, besides, all external circumstances that have a directive and natural connection with the original gifts of nature, such as property and marriage in the case of the body and honour and dignities in that of the soul, and finally what befalls them from time to time.[1] The remaining part of our project would be to inquire briefly as to its usefulness,[2] first distinguishing how and with what end in view we shall take the meaning of the word usefulness. For if we look to the goods of the soul, what could be more conducive to well-being, pleasure, and in general satisfaction than this kind of forecast, by which we gain full view of things human and divine? And if we look to bodily goods, such knowledge, better than anything else, would perceive what is fitting and expedient for the capabilities of each temperament. But if it does not aid in the acquisition of riches, fame, and the like, we shall be able

---

[1] Note that in this sentence Ptolemy refers to several of the subjects of chapters in Books iii and iv.

[2] According to Cicero, *De divinatione*, ii. 105, Dicaearchus wrote a book to prove that divination was useless; Plutarch took the other side, in an essay of which only fragments are preserved.

PTOLEMY

τὰ τοιαῦτα συνεργεῖ, προχωρήσει καὶ περὶ πάσης φιλοσοφίας τὸ αὐτὸ τοῦτο φάσκειν· οὐδενὸς γὰρ τῶν τοιούτων ἐστίν, ὅσον ἐφ' ἑαυτῇ, περιποιητική. ἀλλ' οὔτ' ἐκείνης διὰ τοῦτ' ἂν οὔτε ταύτης καταγινώσκοιμεν δικαίως, ἀφέμενοι τοῦ πρὸς τὰ μείζω συμφέροντος.

11 Ὅλως δ' ἂν ἐξετάζουσι φανεῖεν ἂν οἱ τὸ ἄχρηστον τῆς καταλήψεως ἐπιμεμφόμενοι πρὸς οὐδὲν τῶν κυριωτάτων ἀφορῶντες, ἀλλὰ πρὸς αὐτὸ τοῦτο μόνον, ὅτι τῶν πάντη πάντως ἐσομένων ἡ πρόγνωσις περιττή, καὶ τοῦτο δὲ ἁπλῶς πάνυ, καὶ οὐκ εὖ διειλημμένως. πρῶτον μὲν γὰρ δεῖ σκοπεῖν, ὅτι καὶ ἐπὶ τῶν ἐξ ἀνάγκης ἀποβησομένων τὸ μὲν ἀπροσδόκητον τούς τε θορύβους ἐκστατικοὺς καὶ τὰς χαρὰς ἐξοιστικὰς μάλιστα πέφυκε ποιεῖν· τὸ δὲ προγινώσκειν ἐθίζει καὶ ῥυθμίζει τὴν ψυχὴν τῇ μελέτῃ τῶν ἀπόντων ὡς παρόντων, καὶ παρασκευάζει μετ' εἰρήνης καὶ εὐσταθείας ἕκαστα τῶν ἐπερχομένων ἀποδέχεσθαι. ἔπειθ' ὅτι μηδ' οὕτως ἕκαστα χρὴ νομίζειν τοῖς ἀνθρώποις ἀπὸ τῆς ἄνωθεν αἰτίας παρακολουθεῖν, ὥσπερ ἐξ ἀρχῆς ἀπό τινος ἀλύτου καὶ θείου προστάγματος καθ' ἕνα ἕκαστον νενομοθετημένα καὶ ἐξ ἀνάγκης ἀποβησόμενα, μηδεμιᾶς ἄλλης ἁπλῶς αἰτίας ἀντιπρᾶξαι δυναμένης, ἀλλ' ὡς μὲν τῆς τῶν οὐρανίων κινήσεως καθ' εἱμαρμένην θείαν καὶ ἀμετάπτωτον ἐξ αἰῶνος ἀποτελουμένης, τῆς δὲ τῶν ἐπιγείων[1] ἀλλοιώσεως καθ' εἱμαρμένην φυσικὴν καὶ μεταπτώτην τὰς πρώτας αἰτίας ἄνωθεν λαμβανούσης κατὰ συμβεβηκὸς καὶ κατ' ἐπακολούθησιν· καὶ ὡς τῶν μὲν διὰ καθολικωτέρας περιστά-

to say the same of all philosophy, for it does not provide any of these things as far as its own powers are concerned. We should not, however, for that reason be justified in condemning either philosophy or this art, disregarding its greater advantages.

To a general examination it would appear that those who find fault with the uselessness of prognostication have no regard for the most important matters, but only for this—that foreknowledge of events that will happen in any case is superfluous; this, too, quite unreservedly and without due discrimination. For, in the first place, we should consider that even with events that will necessarily take place their unexpectedness is very apt to cause excessive panic and delirious joy, while foreknowledge accustoms and calms the soul by experience of distant events as though they were present, and prepares it to greet with calm and steadiness whatever comes. A second reason is that we should not believe that separate events attend mankind as the result of the heavenly cause as if they had been originally ordained for each person by some irrevocable divine command and destined to take place by necessity without the possibility of any other cause whatever interfering. Rather is it true that the movement of the heavenly bodies, to be sure, is eternally performed in accordance with divine, unchangeable destiny, while the change of earthly things is subject to a natural and mutable fate, and in drawing its first causes from above it is governed by chance and natural sequence. Moreover, some things happen to mankind through more general

---

[1] περιγείων PMECam.

PTOLEMY

σεις τοῖς ἀνθρώποις συμβαινόντων, οὐχὶ δὲ ἐκ τῆς 12 ἰδίας ἑκάστου¹ φυσικῆς ἐπιτηδειότητος, ὡς ὅταν κατὰ μεγάλας καὶ δυσφυλάκτους τοῦ περιέχοντος τροπὰς ἐκ πυρώσεων ἢ λοιμῶν ἢ κατακλυσμῶν κατὰ πλήθη διαφθαρῶσιν, ὑποπιπτούσης ἀεὶ τῆς βραχυτέρας αἰτίας τῇ μείζονι καὶ ἰσχυροτέρᾳ, τῶν δὲ κατὰ τὴν ἑνὸς ἑκάστου φυσικὴν ἰδιοσυγκρασίαν διὰ μικρὰς καὶ τὰς τυχούσας τοῦ περιέχοντος ἀντιπαθείας. τούτων γὰρ οὕτω διαληφθέντων, φανερὸν ὅτι καὶ καθ᾽ ὅλου καὶ κατὰ μέρος, ὅσων μὲν συμπτωμάτων τὸ πρῶτον αἴτιον² ἄμαχόν τέ ἐστι καὶ μεῖζον παντὸς τοῦ ἀντιπράττοντος, ταῦτα καὶ πάντη πάντως ἀποβαίνειν ἀνάγκη· ὅσα δὲ μὴ οὕτως ἔχει, τούτων τὰ μὲν ἐπιτυγχάνοντα τῶν ἀντιπαθησόντων³ εὐανάτρεπτα γίνεται, τὰ δὲ μὴ εὐπορήσοντα⁴ καὶ αὐτὰ ταῖς πρώταις φύσεσιν ἀκολουθεῖ, δι᾽ ἄγνοιαν μέντοι καὶ οὐκέτι διὰ τὴν τῆς ἰσχύος ἀνάγκην. τὸ αὐτὸ δ᾽ ἄν τις ἴδοι συμβεβηκὸς καὶ ἐπὶ πάντων ἁπλῶς τῶν φυσικὰς ἐχόντων τὰς ἀρχάς. καὶ γὰρ καὶ λίθων καὶ φυτῶν καὶ ζῴων, ἔτι δὲ τραυμάτων καὶ παθῶν καὶ νοσημάτων, τὰ μὲν ἐξ ἀνάγκης τι ποιεῖν πέφυκε, τὰ δ᾽ εἰ μηδὲν τῶν ἐναντίων ἀντιπράξει. οὕτως οὖν χρὴ νομίζειν καὶ τὰ τοῖς ἀνθρώποις συμβησόμενα προλέγειν τοὺς φυσικοὺς τῇ

¹ ἐκ τῆς ἰδίας ἑκάστου VMADE; ἰδίας om. PL; ἀπὸ ἑκάστης φυσικῆς ἰδίας Cam.²
² ὃ post αἴτιον add. Cam., om. libri.
³ ἀντιπαθησόντων VADCam., -σάντων PME.
⁴ εὐπορήσοντα VADCam., -σαντα PME.

---

¹ *Cf.* ii. 1, "the particular always falls under the general." Ptolemy distinguishes carefully between uni-

TETRABIBLOS I. 3

circumstances and not as the result of an individual's own natural propensities—for example, when men perish in multitudes by conflagration or pestilence or cataclysms, through monstrous and inescapable changes in the ambient, for the lesser cause always yields to the greater [1] and stronger; other occurrences, however, accord with the individual's own natural temperament through minor and fortuitous antipathies of the ambient. For if these distinctions are thus made, it is clear that both in general and in particular whatever events depend upon a first cause, which is irresistible and more powerful than anything that opposes it, must by all means take place; on the contrary, of events that are not of this character, those which are provided with resistant forces are easily averted, while those that are not follow the primary natural causes, to be sure, but this is due to ignorance and not to the necessity of almighty power. One might observe this same thing happening in all events whatsoever that have natural causes. For even of stones, plants, and animals, and also of wounds, mishaps, and sicknesses, some are of such a nature as to act of necessity, others only if no opposing thing interferes. One should therefore believe that physical philosophers predict what is to befall men with foreknowledge of

versal (καθολική) and particular or genethlialogical (γενεθλιαλογική) astrology. The former deals with astrological influences which affect all mankind or whole countries and races of men, and is treated in Books i-ii; the latter concerns the nativities of individuals, and is the subject of Books iii-iv.

PTOLEMY

τοιαύτῃ προγνώσει, καὶ μὴ κατὰ κενὰς δόξας προσερχομένους, ὡς τῶν μὲν διὰ τὸ πολλὰ καὶ μεγάλα 13 τὰ ποιητικὰ τυγχάνειν, ἀφυλάκτων ὄντων, τῶν δὲ διὰ τοὐναντίον μετατροπὰς ἐπιδεχομένων. καθάπερ καὶ τῶν ἰατρῶν ὅσοι δυνατοὶ σημειοῦσθαι τὰ παθήματα προγινώσκουσι τά τε πάντως ἀνελόντα,[1] καὶ τὰ χωροῦντα [2] βοήθειαν. ἐπὶ δὲ τῶν μεταπεσεῖν δυναμένων, οὕτως ἀκουστέον τοῦ γενεθλιαλόγου, φέρ᾽ εἰπεῖν, ὅτι τῇ τοιᾷδε συγκράσει κατὰ τὴν τοιάνδε τοῦ περιέχοντος ἰδιοτροπίαν τραπεισῶν ἐπὶ τὸ πλέον ἢ ἔλαττον τῶν ὑποκειμένων συμμετριῶν, τὸ τοιόνδε [3] παρακολουθήσει πάθος· ὡς καὶ τοῦ μὲν ἰατροῦ, ὅτι τόδε τὸ ἕλκος νομὴν ἢ σῆψιν ἐμποιεῖ, τοῦ δὲ μεταλλικοῦ, λόγου ἕνεκεν, ὅτι τὸν σίδηρον ἡ λίθος ἡ μαγνῆτις ἕλκει. ὥσπερ γὰρ τούτων ἑκάτερον, ἐαθὲν μὲν δι᾽ ἀγνωσίαν τῶν ἀντιπαθησόντων, πάντῃ πάντως παρακολουθήσει τῇ τῆς πρώτης φύσεως δυνάμει, οὔτε δὲ τὸ ἕλκος τὴν νομὴν ἢ τὴν σῆψιν κατεργάσεται τῆς ἀντικειμένης θεραπείας τυχόν, οὔτε τὸν σίδηρον ἡ μαγνῆτις ἑλκύσει παρατριβέντος αὐτῇ σκορόδου. καὶ αὐτὰ δὲ ταῦτα τὰ κωλύοντα φυσικῶς καὶ καθ᾽ εἱμαρμένην ἀντεπάθησεν· οὕτω καὶ ἐπ᾽ ἐκείνων, ἀγνοούμενα μὲν τὰ συμβησόμενα τοῖς ἀνθρώποις, ἢ ἐγνωσμένα μέν, μὴ τυχόντα δὲ τῶν ἀντιπαθούντων, πάντῃ πάντως ἀκολουθήσει τῷ τῆς πρώτης φύσεως εἱρμῷ. προγνωσθέντα δὲ καὶ εὐπορήσαντα τῶν θεραπευόντων

---

[1] ἀναιροῦνται Cam.¹, ἀναιροῦντα Cam.²
[2] χωροῦντα VMADE; cf. τὰ θεραπείαν ἐπιδεχόμενα Proc.; χωρηγοῦντα Cam.¹, Cam.² (χορ-), P (χωρι-).
[3] ἄν post τοιόνδε add. PMECam.

this character and do not approach their task under false impressions; for certain things, because their effective causes are numerous and powerful, are inevitable, but others for the opposite reason may be averted. Similarly those physicians who can recognize ailments know beforehand those which are always fatal and those which admit of aid. In the case of events that may be modified we must give heed to the astrologer, when, for example, he says that to such and such a temperament, with such and such a character of the ambient, if the fundamental proportions increase or decrease, such and such an affection will result. Similarly we must believe the physician, when he says that this sore will spread or cause putrefaction, and the miner, for instance, that the lodestone attracts iron: just as each of these, if left to itself through ignorance of the opposing forces, will inevitably develop as its original nature compels, but neither will the sore cause spreading or putrefaction if it receives preventive treatment, nor will the lodestone attract the iron if it is rubbed with garlic;[1] and these very deterrent measures also have their resisting power naturally and by fate; so also in the other cases, if future happenings to men are not known, or if they are known and the remedies are not applied, they will by all means follow the course of primary nature; but if they are recognized ahead of time and remedies are provided, again quite in accord

[1] A current belief; cf. Thorndike, *History of Magic and Experimental Science*, I, p. 213, for an instance of its occurrence in Plutarch.

PTOLEMY

φυσικῶς πάλιν καθ' εἱμαρμένην, ἢ ἀγένητα[1] τέλεον,
ἢ μετριώτερα καθίσταται. ὅλως δὲ τῆς τοιαύτης
δυνάμεως τῆς αὐτῆς οὔσης ἐπί τε τῶν ὁλοσχερῶς
θεωρουμένων καὶ ἐπὶ τῶν κατὰ μέρος, θαυμάσειεν
ἄν τις διὰ τίνα δή ποτε αἰτίαν ἐπὶ μὲν τῶν[2] καθ'
ὅλου πιστεύουσι πάντες καὶ τῷ δυνατῷ τῆς προγνώσεως καὶ τῷ πρὸς τὸ φυλάττεσθαι χρησίμῳ (τάς τε
γὰρ ὥρας καὶ τὰς τῶν ἀπλανῶν ἐπισημασίας καὶ
τοὺς τῆς σελήνης σχηματισμοὺς οἱ πλεῖστοι προγινώσκειν ὁμολογοῦσι, καὶ πολλὴν πρόνοιαν ποιοῦνται
τῆς φυλακῆς αὐτῶν, πεφροντικότες ἀεὶ πρὸς μὲν τὸ
θέρος τῶν ψύχειν δυναμένων, πρὸς δὲ τὸν χειμῶνα
τῶν θερμαινόντων, καὶ ὅλως προπαρασκευάζοντες
αὐτῶν τὰς φύσεις ἐπὶ τὸ εὔκρατον· καὶ ἔτι πρὸς μὲν
τὸ ἀσφαλὲς τῶν τε ὡρῶν καὶ τῶν ἀναγωγῶν παρα-
φυλάττοντες τὰς τῶν ἀπλανῶν ἀστέρων ἐπισημασίας,
πρὸς δὲ τὰς ἀρχὰς τῶν ὀχειῶν καὶ φυτειῶν τοὺς
κατὰ πλήρωσιν τῶν φώτων τῆς σελήνης σχηματισμούς, καὶ οὐδεὶς οὐδαμῇ τῶν τοιούτων κατέγνωκεν
οὔθ' ὡς ἀδυνάτων, οὔθ' ὡς ἀχρήστων), ἐπὶ δὲ τῶν κατὰ
μέρος καὶ ἐκ τῆς τῶν λοιπῶν συγκράσεως ἰδιωμάτων, οἷον μᾶλλον καὶ ἧττον, χειμώνων ἢ καὶ
καυμάτων, καὶ τῆς καθ' ἕκαστον ἰδιοσυγκρασίας,
οὔτε τὸ προγινώσκειν ἔτι δυνατὸν ἡγοῦνταί τινες
οὔτε τὰ πολλὰ ἐγχωρεῖν φυλάξασθαι· καίτοι προ-
δήλου τυγχάνοντος, ὅτι πρὸς τὰ καθ' ὅλου καύματα

[1] ἀγένητα VADE, ἀγέννητα PMCam.
[2] τῶν libri, τοῖς Cam.

---

[1] Hesiod's *Works and Days*, 383 ff. (ed. Flach), well illustrates how such stars and constellations as the Pleiades,

with nature and fate, they either do not occur at all or are rendered less severe. And in general, since such power is the same whether applied to things regarded universally or particularly, one would wonder why all believe in the efficacy of prediction in universal matters, and in its usefulness for guarding one's interests (for most people admit that they have foreknowledge of the seasons, of the significance of the constellations, and of the phases of the moon, and take great forethought for safe-guarding themselves, always contriving cooling agents against summer and the means of warmth against winter, and in general preparing their own natures with moderation as a goal; furthermore, to ensure the safety of the seasons and of their sailings they watch the significance of the fixed stars, and, for the beginning of breeding and sowing, the aspects of the moon's light at its full,[1] and no one ever condemns such practices either as impossible or useless); but, on the other hand, as regards particular matters and those depending upon the mixture of the other qualities—such as predictions of more or less, of cold or of heat, and of the individual temperament—some people believe neither that foreknowledge is still possible nor that precautions can be taken in most instances. And yet, since it is obvious that, if we happen to have cooled ourselves against heat in general, we shall

Orion, Hyades, Sirius, and Arcturus, and the solstices were observed in ordinary rural life in such connections as those mentioned by Ptolemy; also in navigation (618 ff.). The favourable and unfavourable days of the month (*i.e.* of the moon) are enumerated in lines 769 ff.

PTOLEMY

εἰ τύχοιμεν προκαταψύξαντες ἑαυτοὺς ἧττον καυσούμεθα, δύναται τὸ ὅμοιον ἐνεργεῖν καὶ πρὸς τὰ ἰδίως τήνδε τὴν σύγκρασιν εἰς ἀμετρίαν αὔξαντα¹ τοῦ θερμοῦ. ἀλλὰ γὰρ αἴτιον τῆς τοιαύτης ἁμαρτίας τό τε δύσκολον καὶ ἄηθες τῆς τῶν κατὰ μέρος προγνώσεως, ὅπερ καὶ ἐπὶ τῶν ἄλλων σχεδὸν ἁπάντων ἀπιστίαν ἐμποιεῖ. καὶ τὸ μὴ συναπτομένης ὡς ἐπὶ πᾶν τῆς ἀντιπαθούσης δυνάμεως τῇ προγνωστικῇ, διὰ τὸ σπάνιον τῆς οὕτω τελείας διαθέσεως, καὶ περὶ τὰς πρώτας φύσεις ἀνεμποδίστως ἀποτελουμένης, δόξαν ὡς περὶ ἀτρέπτων καὶ ἀφυλάκτων παρέσχε καὶ πάντων ἁπλῶς τῶν ἀποβησομένων

Ὥσπερ δέ, οἶμαι, καὶ ἐπ' αὐτοῦ τοῦ προγνωστικοῦ, καὶ εἰ μὴ² διὰ παντὸς ἦν ἄπταιστον, τό γε δυνατὸν αὐτοῦ μεγίστης ἄξιον σπουδῆς κατεφαίνετο, τὸν αὐτὸν τρόπον καὶ ἐπὶ τοῦ φυλακτικοῦ, καὶ εἰ μὴ πάντων ἐστὶ θεραπευτικόν, ἀλλὰ τό γ' ἐπ' ἐνίων, κἂν ὀλίγα κἂν μικρὰ ᾖ, ἀγαπᾶν καὶ ἀσπάζεσθαι καὶ κέρδος οὐ τὸ τυχὸν ἡγεῖσθαι προσήκει.

Τούτοις δέ, ὡς ἔοικε, συνεγνωκότες οὕτως ἔχουσι, καὶ οἱ μάλιστα τὴν τοιαύτην δύναμιν τῆς τέχνης προαγαγόντες Αἰγύπτιοι συνῆψαν πανταχῇ τῷ δι' ἀστρονομίας προγνωστικῷ τὴν ἰατρικήν. οὐ γὰρ

---

¹ αὔξαντα PL, -οντα VMADECam.
² καὶ εἰ μὴ MAE, κἂν μὴ VDCam., καὶ ἢ μὴ P, καὶ εἰ μὲν L.

¹ Ptolemy's language is highly condensed and obscure; the translation gives the probable meaning. Proclus' *Paraphrase*, pp. 31-32, thus renders the passage: "But the reason for such an assumption is the difficulty of prognostication in particular cases, the accurate and truth-

suffer less from it, similar measures can prove effective against particular forces which increase this particular temperament to a disproportionate amount of heat. For the cause of this error is the difficulty and unfamiliarity of particular prognostication, a reason which in most other situations as well brings about disbelief. And since for the most part the resisting faculty is not coupled with the prognostic, because so perfect a disposition is rare, and since the force of nature takes its course without hindrance when the primary natures are concerned, an opinion has been produced that absolutely all future events are inevitable and unescapable.[1]

But, I think, just as with prognostication, even if it be not entirely infallible, at least its possibilities have appeared worthy of the highest regard, so too in the case of defensive practice, even though it does not furnish a remedy for everything, its authority in some instances at least, however few or unimportant, should be welcomed and prized. and regarded as profitable in no ordinary sense.

Recognizing, apparently, that these things are so, those who have most advanced this faculty of the art, the Egyptians, have entirely united medicine with astronomical prediction.[2] For they would

ful handling of these matters, and the fact that, because a person is rarely found who has so perfect a disposition that none of the remedies escapes him, the faculty which generally resists the force which, unhindered, is effective through the primary natures, is not coupled with the prognostication, and, not being so coupled, creates the opinion concerning all future events without exception that they are inevitable and that it is impossible to ward them off." [2] See Bouché-Leclercq, pp. 517-520.

PTOLEMY

ἄν ποτε ἀποτροπιασμούς τινας καὶ φυλακτήρια καὶ θεραπείας συνίσταντο πρὸς τὰς ἐκ τοῦ περιέχοντος ἐπιούσας ἢ παρούσας περιστάσεις καθολικάς τε καὶ μερικάς, εἴ τις αὐτοῖς ἀκινησίας καὶ ἀμετατρεψίας τῶν ἐσομένων ὑπῆρχε δόξα. νῦν δὲ καὶ τὸ κατὰ τὰς ἐφεξῆς φύσεις ἀντιπρᾶξαι δυνάμενον ἐν δευτέρᾳ χώρᾳ τοῦ καθ' εἱμαρμένην λόγου[1] τιθέμενοι, συνέζευξαν τῇ τῆς προγνώσεως δυνάμει τὴν κατὰ τὸ χρήσιμον καὶ ὠφέλιμον διὰ τῶν καλουμένων παρ' αὐτοῖς ἰατρομαθηματικῶν συντάξεων,[2] ὅπως διὰ μὲν ἀστρονομίας τάς τε τῶν ὑποκειμένων συγκράσεων ποιότητας[3] εἰδέναι συμβαίνῃ, καὶ τὰ διὰ τὸ περιέχον ἐσόμενα συμπτώματα, καὶ τὰς ἰδίας αὐτῶν αἰτίας (ὡς ἄνευ τῆς τούτων γνώσεως, καὶ τῶν βοηθημάτων κατὰ τὸ πλεῖστον διαπίπτειν ὀφειλόντων, ἅτε μὴ πᾶσι σώμασιν ἢ πάθεσι τῶν αὐτῶν συμμέτρων ὄντων), διὰ δὲ τῆς ἰατρικῆς ἀπὸ τῶν ἑκάστοις οἰκείως συμπαθούντων ἢ ἀντιπαθούντων, τάς τε τῶν μελλόντων παθῶν προφυλακὰς καὶ τὰς τῶν ἐνεστώτων θεραπείας ἀδιαπτώτους, ὡς ἔνι μάλιστα, ποιούμενοι διατελῶσιν.[4]

Ἀλλὰ ταῦτα μὲν μέχρι τοσούτων ἡμῖν κατὰ τὸ κεφαλαιῶδες προτετυπώσθω. ποιησόμεθα δὲ ἤδη τὸν λόγον κατὰ τὸν εἰσαγωγικὸν τρόπον, ἀρξάμενοι περὶ τῆς ἑκάστου τῶν οὐρανίων περὶ αὐτὸ τὸ ποιητικὸν ἰδιοτροπίας, ἀκολούθως ταῖς ὑπὸ τῶν

[1] λόγου VMADE, λόγον PL, om. Cam.
[2] Post συντάξεων add. μέθοδον Cam.; in libris deest.
[3] ποιότητας libri, ἰδιότητας Cam.
[4] διατελοῦσι Cam.

never have devised certain means of averting or warding off or remedying the universal and particular conditions that come or are present by reason of the ambient, if they had had any idea that the future cannot be moved and changed. But as it is, they place the faculty of resisting by orderly natural means in second rank to the decrees of fate, and have yoked to the possibility of prognostication its useful and beneficial faculty, through what they call their iatromathematical systems (medical astrology), in order that by means of astronomy they may succeed in learning the qualities of the underlying temperatures, the events that will occur in the future because of the ambient, and their special causes, on the ground that without this knowledge any measures of aid ought for the most part to fail, because the same ones are not fitted for all bodies or diseases;[1] and, on the other hand, by means of medicine, through their knowledge of what is properly sympathetic or antipathetic in each case, they proceed, as far as possible, to take precautionary measures against impending illness and to prescribe infallible treatment for existing disease.

Let this be, to this point, our summarily stated preliminary sketch. We shall now conduct our discussion after the manner of an introduction,[2] beginning with the character of each of the heavenly

[1] Perhaps "affections," the more general sense of the word πάθος.
[2] "Introductions" (εἰσαγωγαί), or systematic elementary treatises, are a common literary form in antiquity. Nicomachus' *Introduction to Arithmetic* (εἰσαγωγὴ ἀριθμητική) is a good example. The "art" (τέχνη) was a similar form of treatise, and might deal with any art or science.

παλαιῶν κατὰ τὸν φυσικὸν τρόπον ἐφηρμοσμέναις παρατηρήσεσι, καὶ πρώταις[1] ταῖς τῶν πλανωμένων ἀστέρων δυνάμεσι ἡλίου τε καὶ σελήνης.

⟨δ.⟩ Περὶ τῆς τῶν πλανωμένων ἀστέρων[2] δυνάμεως

Ὁ ἥλιος κατείληπται τὸ ποιητικὸν ἔχων τῆς οὐσίας ἐν τῷ θερμαίνειν, καὶ ἠρέμα ξηραίνειν. ταῦτα δὲ μάλιστα τῶν ἄλλων ἡμῖν εὐαισθητότερα γίνεται διά τε τὸ μέγεθος αὐτοῦ καὶ τὸ τῶν κατὰ τὰς ὥρας μεταβολῶν ἐναργές, ἐπειδήπερ ὅσῳ ἂν μᾶλλον ἐγγίζῃ τοῦ κατὰ κορυφὴν ἡμῶν τόπου,[3] μᾶλλον ἡμᾶς οὕτω διατίθησιν. ἡ δὲ σελήνη τὸ μὲν πλέον ἔχει τῆς δυνάμεως ἐν τῷ ὑγραίνειν, διὰ τὴν περιγειότητα δηλονότι καὶ τὴν τῶν ὑγρῶν ἀναθυμίασιν. καὶ διατίθησιν οὕτως ἄντικρυς τὰ σώματα πεπαίνουσα καὶ διασήπουσα τὰ πλεῖστα, κεκοινώνηκε δὲ ἠρέμα καὶ τοῦ θερμαίνειν διὰ τοὺς ἀπὸ τοῦ ἡλίου φωτισμούς.

Ὁ δὲ τοῦ Κρόνου ἀστὴρ τὸ πλέον ἔχει τῆς ποιότητος ἐν τῷ ψύχειν καὶ τῷ ἠρέμα ξηραίνειν, διὰ τὸ

[1] πρώταις VD, πρώτης MAE, πρὸ τῆς P, πρὸς τῆς L, πρῶτον Proc., πρώτως Cam.
[2] πλανωμένων ἀστέρων VADEProc., om. ἀστέρων M, πλανητῶν PLCam. [3] τῷ . . . τόπῳ MAECam.

---

[1] In this chapter and elsewhere Ptolemy makes use of the four Aristotelian principles, hot, cold, wet, dry (*e.g. De generatione et corruptione*, ii. 2, 3). *Cf.* Boll-Bezold-Gundel, p. 50.
[2] It was a doctrine as old as Thales that the moisture arising from the earth nourished the heavenly bodies ; *cf.*

TETRABIBLOS I. 3-4

bodies with respect to its active power, in agreement with the physical observations attached to them by the ancients, and in the first place the powers of the planets, sun, and moon.

4. *Of the Power of the Planets.*

The active power of the sun's essential nature is found to be heating and, to a certain degree, drying.[1] This is made more easily perceptible in the case of the sun than any other heavenly body by its size and by the obviousness of its seasonal changes, for the closer it approaches to the zenith the more it affects us in this way. Most of the moon's power consists of humidifying, clearly because it is close to the earth and because of the moist exhalations [2] therefrom. Its action therefore is precisely this, to soften and cause putrefaction in bodies for the most part, but it shares moderately also in heating power because of the light which it receives from the sun.

It is Saturn's [3] quality chiefly to cool and, moderately, to dry, probably because he is furthest

---

Diels, *Doxographi Graeci* (Berlin, 1879), p. 276 ; J. Burnet, *Early Greek Philosophy* (London, 1920), p. 49.

[3] Ptolemy ordinarily says " the (star) of Saturn," " the (star) of Jupiter," etc. (ὁ τοῦ Κρόνου, ὁ τοῦ Διός), and less often merely " Saturn," " Jupiter," and the like, a form of speech which tends to identify the planet and the divinity whose name it bears. On the other hand, he does not use the older Greek names such as Φωσφόρος, Φαίνων, etc. (though Πυροείς occurs for Ἄρης in one of the MSS.). See F. Cumont, " Antiochus d'Athènes et Porphyre," *Annuaire de l'Inst. de Philologie et d'Histoire Orientale*, ii. 139, and " Les noms de planètes et d'astrolatrie chez les grecs," *L'Antiquité Classique*, iv. 1, pp. 5-43 ; Boll-Bezold-Gundel, p. 48.

πλεῖστον, ὡς ἔοικεν, ἀπέχειν[1] ἅμα τῆς τε τοῦ ἡλίου θερμασίας καὶ τῆς τῶν περὶ τὴν γῆν ὑγρῶν ἀναθυμιάσεως. συνίστανται δὲ δυνάμεις ἐπί τε τούτου καὶ τῶν λοιπῶν, καὶ διὰ τῆς τῶν πρὸς τὸν ἥλιον καὶ τὴν σελήνην σχηματισμῶν παρατηρήσεως, ἐπειδήπερ οἱ μὲν οὕτως, οἱ δὲ οὕτω τὴν τοῦ περιέχοντος κατάστασιν ἐπὶ τὸ μᾶλλον ἢ ἧττον συντρέποντες φαίνονται.

Ὁ δὲ τοῦ Ἄρεως[2] ξηραίνειν μάλιστα καὶ καυσοῦν ἔχει φύσιν, τῷ τε πυρώδει τοῦ χρώματος οἰκείως καὶ τῇ πρὸς τὸν ἥλιον ἐγγύτητι, ὑποκειμένης αὐτῷ τῆς ἡλιακῆς σφαίρας.

Ὁ δὲ τοῦ Διὸς εὔκρατον ἔχει τὸ ποιητικὸν τῆς δυνάμεως, μεταξὺ γινομένης τῆς κινήσεως αὐτοῦ τοῦ τε κατὰ τὸν Κρόνον ψυκτικοῦ καὶ τοῦ κατὰ τὸν Ἄρην καυστικοῦ. θερμαίνει τε γὰρ ἅμα καὶ ὑγραίνει, καὶ διὰ τὸ μᾶλλον εἶναι θερμαντικός, ὑπὸ τῶν ὑποκειμένων σφαιρῶν, γονίμων πνευμάτων γίνεται ποιητικός.

Καὶ ὁ τῆς Ἀφροδίτης δὲ τῶν μὲν αὐτῶν ἐστι κατὰ τὸ εὔκρατον ποιητικός,[3] ἀλλὰ κατὰ τὸ ἐναντίον. θερμαίνει μὲν γὰρ ἠρέμα διὰ τὴν ἐγγύτητα τὴν πρὸς τὸν ἥλιον· μάλιστα δὲ ὑγραίνει καθάπερ ἡ σελήνη καὶ αὐτὸς διὰ τὸ μέγεθος τῶν ἰδίων φωτῶν, νοσφιζόμενος τὴν ἀπὸ τῶν περιεχόντων τὴν γῆν ὑγρῶν ἀναθυμίασιν.

[1] ἀπέχειν VMADE, om. PLCam.; ἀφεστάναι add. post ἀναθυμιάσεως Cam.
[2] Πυρόεντος ME. Ordinem restauravi quam praebent VPLADProc.; in MECam. ordo est ὁ δὲ τοῦ Διὸς ... ποιητικός. ὁ δὲ τοῦ Ἄρεως . . σφαίρας.

TETRABIBLOS I. 4

removed[1] both from the sun's heat and the moist exhalations about the earth. Both in Saturn's case and in that of the other planets there are powers, too, which arise through the observation of their aspects to the sun and the moon, for some of them appear to modify conditions in the ambient in one way, some in another, by increase or by decrease.

The nature of Mars is chiefly to dry and to burn, in conformity with his fiery colour and by reason of his nearness to the sun, for the sun's sphere lies just below him.

Jupiter has a temperate active force because his movement takes place between the cooling influence of Saturn and the burning power of Mars. He both heats and humidifies; and because his heating power is the greater by reason of the underlying spheres, he produces fertilizing winds.

Venus has the same powers and tempered nature as Jupiter, but acts in the opposite way; for she warms moderately because of her nearness to the sun, but chiefly humidifies, like the moon, because of the amount of her own light and because she appropriates the exhalations from the moist atmosphere surrounding the earth.

---

[1] The order of the heavenly bodies followed by Ptolemy is Saturn, Jupiter, Mars, Sun, Venus, Mercury, Moon; *cf.* Bouché-Leclercq, pp. 107-108.

---

² ποιητικός . . . ἐναντίον VPLMADE (καὶ κατὰ ME); *cf.* Proc.; τῷ Ζηνὶ κατὰ μέντοι τὸ ἀντικείμενον ποιητικός Cam. (om. τῷ Ζηνὶ ed. pr.).

PTOLEMY

Ὁ δὲ τοῦ Ἑρμοῦ ὡς ἐπὶ πᾶν ἐξ ἴσου ποτὲ μὲν ξηραντικὸς καταλαμβάνεται καὶ τῶν ὑγρῶν ἀναπωτικός,[1] διὰ τὸ μηδέποτε πολὺ τῆς τοῦ ἡλίου θερμασίας κατὰ μῆκος ἀφίστασθαι, ποτὲ δ' αὖ ὑγραντικός, διὰ τὸ τῇ περιγειοτάτῃ σφαίρᾳ τῆς σελήνης ἐπικεῖσθαι, ταχείας δὲ ποιεῖσθαι τὰς ἐν ἀμφοτέροις[2] μεταβολάς, πνευματούμενος ὥσπερ ὑπὸ τῆς περὶ αὐτὸν τὸν ἥλιον ὀξυκινησίας.

⟨ε.⟩ Περὶ ἀγαθοποιῶν καὶ κακοποιῶν[3]

Τούτων οὕτως ἐχόντων, ἐπειδὴ τῶν τεττάρων χυμάτων δύο μέν ἐστι τὰ γόνιμα καὶ ποιητικά, τό τε τοῦ θερμοῦ καὶ τὸ τοῦ ὑγροῦ · διὰ τούτων γὰρ πάντα συγκρίνεται καὶ αὔξεται · δύο δὲ τὰ φθαρτικὰ καὶ παθητικά, τό τε τοῦ ξηροῦ καὶ τὸ τοῦ ψυχροῦ, δι' ὧν πάντα πάλιν διακρίνεται καὶ φθίνει,[4] τοὺς μὲν δύο τῶν πλανητῶν, τόν τε τοῦ Διὸς καὶ τὸν τῆς Ἀφροδίτης, καὶ ἔτι τὴν σελήνην, ὡς ἀγαθοποιοὺς οἱ παλαιοὶ παρειλήφασι, διὰ τὸ εὔκρατον καὶ τὸ πλέον ἔχειν ἔν τε τῷ θερμῷ καὶ τῷ ὑγρῷ, τὸν δὲ τοῦ Κρόνου καὶ τὸν τοῦ Ἄρεως[5] τῆς ἐναντίας φύσεως ποιητικούς, τὸν μὲν τῆς ἄγαν ψύξεως ἕνεκεν, τὸν δὲ τῆς ἄγαν ξηρότητος · τὸν δὲ ἥλιον καὶ τὸν τοῦ Ἑρμοῦ διὰ τὸ κοινὸν τῶν φύσεων ὡς ἀμφότερα δυναμένους, καὶ μᾶλλον συντρεπομένους, οἷς ἂν τῶν ἄλλων προσγένωνται.[6]

---

[1] ἀναπαυτικός PL.
[2] ἐν ἀμφοτέροις VMADE, ἀμφοτερ P, ἀμφοτέρας L, ἐπ' ἀμφότερα Proc. Cam.
[3] Titulum capitis om. Cam., habent VPLMADE.

Mercury in general is found at certain times alike to be drying and absorptive of moisture, because he never is far removed in longitude from the heat of the sun; and again humidifying, because he is next above the sphere of the moon, which is closest to the earth; and to change quickly from one to the other, inspired as it were by the speed of his motion in the neighbourhood of the sun itself.

5. *Of Beneficent and Maleficent Planets.*

Since the foregoing is the case, because two of the four humours are fertile and active, the hot and the moist (for all things are brought together and increased by them), and two are destructive and passive, the dry and the cold, through which all things, again, are separated and destroyed, the ancients accepted two of the planets, Jupiter and Venus, together with the moon, as beneficent because of their tempered nature and because they abound in the hot and the moist, and Saturn and Mars as producing effects of the opposite nature, one because of his excessive cold and the other for his excessive dryness; the sun and Mercury, however, they thought to have both powers, because they have a common nature, and to join their influences with those of the other planets, with whichever of them they are associated.

---

⁴ φθίνει VMADE, διαφθείρεται LCam., διαφθείρῃ P, φθείρεται Proc.
⁵ Post Ἄρεως add. κακοποιούς, ὡς MAECam., om. VPLD.
⁶ προσγένωνται VMADE, παραγίγνωνται P, παραγίνονται L Cam.; add. ὡς μέσους Cam.², μέσους Cam.¹

PTOLEMY

⟨ς̄.⟩ Περὶ ἀρρενικῶν καὶ θηλυκῶν ἀστέρων

Πάλιν ἐπειδὴ τὰ πρῶτα γένη τῶν φύσεών ἐστι δύο, τό τε ἀρρενικὸν καὶ τὸ θῆλυ, τῶν δὲ προκειμένων δυνάμεων ἡ τῆς ὑγρᾶς οὐσίας μάλιστα θηλυκὴ τυγχάνει (πλέον γὰρ ἐγγίνεται καθ' ὅλου τοῦτο τὸ μέρος πᾶσι τοῖς θήλεσι, τὰ δ' ἄλλα μᾶλλον τοῖς ἄρρεσιν), εἰκότως τὴν μὲν σελήνην καὶ τὸν τῆς Ἀφροδίτης ἀστέρα θηλυκοὺς ἡμῖν παραδεδώκασι διὰ τὸ πλέον ἔχειν ἐν τῷ ὑγρῷ, τὸν δὲ ἥλιον καὶ τὸν τοῦ Κρόνου καὶ τὸν τοῦ Διὸς καὶ τὸν τοῦ Ἄρεως ἀρρενικούς, τὸν δὲ τοῦ Ἑρμοῦ κοινὸν ἀμφοτέρων τῶν γενῶν, καθ' ὃ ἐξ ἴσου τῆς τε ξηρᾶς καὶ τῆς ὑγρᾶς οὐσίας ἐστὶ ποιητικός. ἀρρενοῦσθαι δέ φασι τοὺς ἀστέρας καὶ θηλύνεσθαι παρά τε τοὺς πρὸς τὸν ἥλιον σχηματισμούς· ἑῴους μὲν γὰρ ὄντας καὶ προηγουμένους ἀρρενοῦσθαι, ἑσπερίους δὲ καὶ ἑπομένους θηλύνεσθαι. καὶ ἔτι παρὰ τοὺς πρὸς τὸν ὁρίζοντα· ἐν μὲν γὰρ τοῖς ἀπὸ ἀνατολῆς μέχρι μεσουρανήσεως, ἢ καὶ ἀπὸ δύσεως μέχρι τῆς ὑπὸ γῆν ἀντιμεσουρανήσεως[1] σχηματισμοῖς, ὡς ἀπηλιωτικοὺς ἀρρενοῦσθαι· ἐν δὲ τοῖς λοιποῖς δυσὶ τεταρτημορίοις ὡς λιβυκοὺς[2] θηλύνεσθαι.

[1] μέχρι πάλιν τοῦ ἀντικειμένου μεσουρανήματος Cam.; om. PL.
[2] δυτικοὺς Cam.

---

[1] Or matutine; that is, stars which are above the earth when the sun rises, as evening, or vespertine, stars set after the sun. Cardanus (p. 127) says that whatever planet is

TETRABIBLOS I. 6

6. *Of Masculine and Feminine Planets.*

Again, since there are two primary kinds of natures, male and female, and of the forces already mentioned that of the moist is especially feminine—for as a general thing this element is present to a greater degree in all females, and the others rather in males—with good reason the view has been handed down to us that the moon and Venus are feminine, because they share more largely in the moist, and that the sun, Saturn, Jupiter, and Mars are masculine, and Mercury common to both genders, inasmuch as he produces the dry and the moist alike. They say too that the stars become masculine or feminine according to their aspects to the sun, for when they are morning stars [1] and precede the sun they become masculine, and feminine when they are evening stars and follow the sun. Furthermore this happens also according to their positions with respect to the horizon; for when they are in positions from the orient to mid-heaven,[2] or again from the occident to lower mid-heaven, they become masculine because they are eastern, but in the other two quadrants, as western stars, they become feminine.

less than 6 signs removed from the sun in the order of the signs is feminine and occidental; any that is more than 6 signs distant, masculine and oriental.

[2] Cardanus (*l.c.*) remarks that some do not accept this statement but count all stars from the inferior to the superior mid-heaven (4th to the 10th house) masculine and from the superior to the inferior mid-heaven (10th to the 4th house) feminine. Planets may also become masculine or feminine in consequence of occupying a masculine or feminine sign; see Bouché-Leclercq, p. 103.

PTOLEMY

<ζ.> Περὶ ἡμερινῶν καὶ νυκτερινῶν

Ὁμοίως δὲ ἐπειδὴ τῶν ποιούντων τὸν χρόνον τὰ ἐκφανέστατα διαστήματα δύο ταῦτα τυγχάνει τό τε τῆς ἡμέρας ἠρρενωμένον μᾶλλον διὰ τὸ ἐν αὐτῇ θερμὸν καὶ δραστικὸν καὶ τὸ τῆς νυκτὸς τεθηλυσμένον μᾶλλον διὰ τὸ κατ' αὐτὴν δίϋγρον καὶ ἀναπαυστικόν, νυκτερινοὺς μὲν ἀκολούθως παραδεδώκασι τήν τε σελήνην καὶ τὸν τῆς Ἀφροδίτης, ἡμερινοὺς δὲ τόν τε ἥλιον καὶ τὸν τοῦ Διός, ἐπίκοινον δὲ κατὰ ταὐτὰ τὸν τοῦ Ἑρμοῦ καὶ ἐν μὲν τῷ ἑῴῳ σχήματι ἡμερινόν, ἐν δὲ τῷ ἑσπερίῳ νυκτερινόν. προσένειμαν δὲ ἑκατέρᾳ τῶν αἱρέσεων καὶ τοὺς δύο τοὺς τῆς φθαρτικῆς οὐσίας, οὐκ ἔτι μέντοι κατὰ τὰς αὐτὰς τῆς φύσεως αἰτίας, ἀλλὰ κατὰ τὰς ἐναντίας. τοῖς μὲν γὰρ τῆς ἀγαθῆς κράσεως οἰκειούμενα τὰ ὅμοια μεῖζον αὐτῶν τὸ ὠφέλιμον ποιεῖ, τοῖς δὲ φθαρτικοῖς τὰ ἀνοίκεια μιγνύμενα παραλύει τὸ πολύ[1] τῆς κακώσεως αὐτῶν. ἔνθεν τὸν μὲν τοῦ Κρόνου ψυκτικὸν ὄντα τῷ θερμῷ τῆς ἡμέρας ἀπένειμαν, τὸν δὲ τοῦ Ἄρεως ξηρὸν ὄντα τῷ ὑγρῷ τῆς νυκτός· οὕτω γὰρ ἑκάτερος ὑπὸ τῆς κράσεως[2] τῆς συμμετρίας τυχὼν οἰκεῖος γίνεται τῆς τὸ εὔκρατον παρασχούσης αἱρέσεως.

[1] πολύ VMADEFProc., κακόν PL, σφοδρόν Cam.
[2] ἐναντίας κράσεως Cam.; ἐναντίας om. libri.

TETRABIBLOS I. 7

7. *Of Diurnal and Nocturnal*[1] *Planets.*

Similarly, since of the two most obvious intervals of those which make up time, the day is more masculine because of its heat and active force, and night more feminine because of its moisture and its gift of rest, the tradition has consequently been handed down that the moon and Venus are nocturnal, the sun and Jupiter diurnal, and Mercury common as before, diurnal when it is a morning star and nocturnal as an evening star. They also assigned to each of the sects the two destructive stars, not however in this instance on the principle of similar natures,[2] but of just the opposite; for when stars of the same kind are joined with those of the good temperament their beneficial influence is increased, but if dissimilar stars are associated with the destructive ones the greatest part of their injurious power is broken. Thus they assigned Saturn, which is cold, to the warmth of day, and Mars, which is dry, to the moisture of night, for in this way each of them attains good proportion through admixture and becomes a proper member of its sect, which provides moderation.

---

[1] These are the sects (αἵρεσις, *conditio*, *secta*) of the sun and moon respectively; *cf.* Vettius Valens, ii. 1, iii. 5; Rhetorius, *ap. CCAG*, i. 146.

[2] *I.e.* that "birds of a feather flock together," in various forms a proverbial expression in Greek; *e.g.* Odyssey, 17. 218, ὡς αἰεὶ τὸν ὁμοῖον ἄγει θεὸς ὡς τὸν ὁμοῖον; Plato, *Republic*, 329 A, *Phaedrus*, 240 C, etc.

PTOLEMY

⟨η.⟩ Περὶ τῆς δυνάμεως τῶν πρὸς τὸν ἥλιον σχηματισμῶν

Ἤδη μέντοι καὶ παρὰ τοὺς πρὸς τὸν ἥλιον συσχηματισμοὺς ἥ τε σελήνη καὶ οἱ τρεῖς τῶν πλανωμένων[1] τὸ μᾶλλον καὶ ἧττον λαμβάνουσιν ἐν ταῖς οἰκείαις ἑαυτῶν δυνάμεσιν. ἥ τε γὰρ σελήνη κατὰ μὲν τὴν ἀπὸ ἀνατολῆς μέχρι τῆς πρώτης διχοτόμου αὔξησιν ὑγρότητός ἐστι μᾶλλον ποιητική· κατὰ δὲ τὴν ἀπὸ πρώτης διχοτόμου μέχρι πανσελήνου, θερμότητος· κατὰ δὲ τὴν ἀπὸ πανσελήνου μέχρι δευτέρας διχοτόμου ξηρότητος· κατὰ δὲ τὴν ἀπὸ δευτέρας διχοτόμου[2] μέχρι κρύψεως[3] ψυχρότητος. οἵ τε πλανώμενοι καὶ ἑῷοι μόνον ἀπὸ μὲν τῆς ἀνατολῆς μέχρι τοῦ πρώτου στηριγμοῦ μᾶλλόν εἰσιν ὑγραντικοί, ἀπὸ δὲ τοῦ πρώτου στηριγμοῦ μέχρι τῆς ἀκρονύκτου μᾶλλον θερμαντικοί, ἀπὸ δὲ τῆς ἀκρονύκτου μέχρι τοῦ δευτέρου στηριγμοῦ μᾶλλον ξηραντικοί, ἀπὸ δὲ τοῦ δευτέρου στηριγμοῦ μέχρι δύσεως μᾶλλον ψυκτικοί· δῆλον δὲ ὅτι καὶ ἀλλήλοις συγκιρνάμενοι παμπληθεῖς διαφορὰς ποιοτήτων εἰς τὸ περιέχον ἡμᾶς ἀπεργάζονται, κατακρατούσης μὲν ὡς ἐπὶ πᾶν τῆς ἰδίας ἑκάστου δυνάμεως, τρεπομένης δὲ κατὰ τὸ ποσὸν ὑπὸ τῆς τῶν σχηματιζομένων.[4]

[1] Post πλανωμένων add. ὅ τε τοῦ Κρόνου καὶ ὁ τοῦ Διὸς καὶ ὁ τοῦ Ἄρεως AFCam., om. VPLMDE.
[2] μειώσιν post διχοτόμου add. Cam.²
[3] κρύψεως VMDEProc.Cam.: τρήψεως P, τρέψεως L; συνόδου AFH et Cam.² in marg.
[4] ἐναντιώσεως post σχηματιζομένων add. Cam., om. libri.

TETRABIBLOS I. 8

8. *Of the Power of the Aspects to the Sun.*

Now, mark you, likewise, according to their aspects to the sun, the moon and three of the planets[1] experience increase and decrease in their own powers. For in its waxing from new moon to first quarter the moon is more productive of moisture; in its passage from first quarter to full, of heat; from full to last quarter, of dryness, and from last quarter to occultation,[2] of cold. The planets, in oriental aspects only, are more productive of moisture from rising to their first station,[3] of heat from first station to evening rising, of dryness from evening rising to the second station, of cold from second station to setting; and it is clear that when they are associated with one another they produce very many variations of quality in our ambient, the proper force of each one for the most part persisting, but being changed in quantity by the force of the stars that share the configuration.

[1] Saturn, Jupiter, and Mars; a gloss to this effect has been incorporated into the text of certain MSS. and of Camerarius' editions (see the critical note).
[2] *I.e.* new moon.
[3] By "rising" heliacal rising is meant. The stations are the points in the motion of the planets at which they appear to stand still before beginning retrograde movement. Ptolemy explained these irregularities of movement by the theory of epicycles. *Cf.* Bouché-Leclercq, pp. 111-123.

PTOLEMY

⟨θ̄.⟩ Περὶ τῆς τῶν ἀπλανῶν
ἀστέρων δυνάμεως

Ἑξῆς δὲ ὄντος καὶ τὰς τῶν ἀπλανῶν φύσεις κατὰ τὸ ἰδίως αὐτῶν ποιητικὸν ἐπιδραμεῖν, ἐκθησόμεθα καὶ τὰς ἐπ' αὐτῶν τετηρημένας ἰδιοτροπίας κατὰ τὸ ὅμοιον ταῖς τῶν πλανωμένων φύσεσι τὸν ἐμφανισμὸν ποιούμενοι· καὶ πρῶτον τῶν περὶ αὐτὸν τὸν διὰ μέσων κύκλον[1] ἐχόντων τὰς μορφώσεις.

Τοῦ Κριοῦ τοίνυν οἱ μὲν ἐν τῇ κεφαλῇ τὸ ποιητικὸν ὅμοιον ἔχουσι κεκραμένον τῇ τε τοῦ Ἄρεως καὶ τῇ τοῦ Κρόνου δυνάμει· οἱ δὲ ἐν τῷ στόματι τῇ τε τοῦ Ἑρμοῦ καὶ ἠρέμα τῇ τοῦ Κρόνου· οἱ δὲ ἐν τῷ ὀπισθίῳ ποδὶ τῇ τοῦ Ἄρεως, οἱ δὲ ἐπὶ τῆς οὐρᾶς τῇ τῆς Ἀφροδίτης.

Τῶν δὲ ἐν τῷ Ταύρῳ ἀστέρων[2] οἱ μὲν ἐπὶ τῆς ἀποτομῆς ὁμοίαν ἔχουσι κρᾶσιν τῷ τε τῆς Ἀφροδίτης, καὶ ἠρέμα τῷ τοῦ Κρόνου· οἱ δ' ἐν τῇ Πλειάδι τῇ τε τῆς σελήνης καὶ τῷ τοῦ Διός· τῶν δὲ ἐν τῇ κεφαλῇ ὁ μὲν λαμπρὸς ὁ τῆς Ὑάδος[3] καὶ ὑπόκιρρος,[4] καλούμενος δὲ Λαμπαδίας, τῷ τοῦ Ἄρεως· οἱ δὲ λοιποὶ[5] τῷ τοῦ Κρόνου καὶ ἠρέμα τῷ τοῦ Ἑρμοῦ· οἱ δ' ἐν ἄκροις τοῖς κέρασι τῇ τοῦ Ἄρεως.

[1] διὰ μέσων κύκλον] ζῳδιακὸν NCam.
[2] τῶν . . . ἀστέρων] τοῦ δὲ Ταύρου NCam.
[3] ὁ τῆς Ὑάδος VDProc., τῆς Ὑάδος PLMAEFH, τῶν Ὑάδων NCam.
[4] ἀπόκιρρος NCam.
[5] οἱ δὲ λοιποὶ . . . τῷ τοῦ Ἄρεως] haec post l. 21, Ἄρεως VPLMADEProc., om. NFHCam.¹; post l. 16, τοῦ Διός Cam.²; post λοιποὶ add. ἐκεῖ ὄντες Cam.², om. libri.

TETRABIBLOS I. 9

9. *Of the Power of the Fixed Stars.*

As it is next in order to recount the natures of the fixed stars with reference to their special powers, we shall set forth their observed characters in an exposition like that of the natures of the planets, and in the first place those of the ones that occupy the figures in the zodiac [1] itself.

The stars in the head of Aries, then, have an effect like the power of Mars and Saturn, mingled; those in the mouth like Mercury's power and moderately like Saturn's; those in the hind foot like that of Mars, and those in the tail like that of Venus.

Of those in Taurus,[2] the stars along the line where it is cut off have a temperature like that of Venus and in a measure like that of Saturn; those in the Pleiades, like those of the moon and Jupiter; of the stars in the head, the one of the Hyades that is bright and somewhat reddish, called the Torch,[3] has a temperature like that of Mars; the others, like that of Saturn and moderately like that of Mercury; those in the tips of the horns, like that of Mars.

---

[1] Strictly, "around the ecliptic itself." Properly, the zodiac is ὁ ζῳδιακὸς κύκλος, and the ecliptic, the path of the sun through its middle, is ὁ διὰ μέσων (*sc.* τῶν ζῳδίων) κύκλος or ὁ διὰ μέσου (*sc.* τοῦ ζῳδιακοῦ) κύκλος, "the circle through the midst of the signs" or "through the middle of the zodiac."

[2] Taurus was represented as the head and fore parts only of a charging bull.

[3] Aldebaran.

PTOLEMY

Τῶν δὲ ἐν τοῖς Διδύμοις ἀστέρων οἱ μὲν ἐπὶ τῶν ποδῶν τῆς ὁμοίας κεκοινωνήκασι ποιότητος τῷ τε τοῦ Ἑρμοῦ καὶ ἠρέμα τῷ τῆς Ἀφροδίτης· οἱ δὲ περὶ τοὺς μηροὺς λαμπροὶ τῷ τοῦ Κρόνου· τῶν δὲ ἐν ταῖς κεφαλαῖς δύο λαμπρῶν ὁ μὲν ἐν τῇ προηγουμένῃ τῷ τοῦ Ἑρμοῦ, καλεῖται δὲ καὶ Ἀπόλλωνος· ὁ δὲ ἐν τῇ ἑπομένῃ τῷ τοῦ Ἄρεως, καλεῖται δὲ καὶ Ἡρακλέους.

Τῶν δὲ ἐν τῷ Καρκίνῳ ἀστέρων οἱ μὲν ἐπὶ τῶν ὀφθαλμῶν δύο τῆς αὐτῆς ἐνεργείας εἰσὶ ποιητικοὶ τῷ τε τοῦ Ἑρμοῦ καὶ ἠρέμα τῷ τοῦ Ἄρεως· οἱ δὲ ἐν ταῖς χηλαῖς τῷ τε τοῦ Κρόνου καὶ τῷ τοῦ Ἑρμοῦ. ἡ δὲ ἐν τῷ στήθει νεφελοειδὴς συστροφή, καλουμένη δὲ Φάτνη, τῷ τε τοῦ Ἄρεως καὶ τῇ σελήνῃ· οἱ δὲ ἑκατέρωθεν αὐτῆς δύο, καλούμενοι δὲ Ὄνοι, τῷ τοῦ Ἄρεως καὶ τῷ ἡλίῳ.

Τῶν δὲ περὶ τὸν Λέοντα οἱ μὲν ἐπὶ τῆς κεφαλῆς δύο τὸ ὅμοιον ποιοῦσι τῷ τε τοῦ Κρόνου καὶ ἠρέμα τῷ τοῦ Ἄρεως, οἱ δὲ ἐν τῷ τραχήλῳ τρεῖς τῷ τοῦ Κρόνου καὶ ἠρέμα τῷ τοῦ Ἑρμοῦ· ὁ δὲ ἐπὶ τῆς καρδίας λαμπρός, καλούμενος δὲ Βασιλίσκος, τῷ τοῦ Ἄρεως καὶ τῷ τοῦ Διός· οἱ δὲ ἐν τῇ ὀσφύϊ καὶ ὁ ἐπὶ τῆς οὐρᾶς λαμπρὸς τῷ τοῦ Κρόνου καὶ τῷ τῆς Ἀφροδίτης· οἱ δὲ ἐν τοῖς μηροῖς τῷ τε τῆς Ἀφροδίτης καὶ ἠρέμα τῷ τοῦ Ἑρμοῦ.

Τῶν δὲ κατὰ τὴν Παρθένον οἱ μὲν ἐν τῇ κεφαλῇ καὶ ὁ ἐπ' ἄκρας τῆς νοτίου πτέρυγος ὅμοιον ἔχουσι τὸ ποιητικὸν τῷ τε τοῦ Ἑρμοῦ καὶ ἠρέμα τῷ τοῦ Ἄρεως· οἱ δὲ λοιποὶ τῆς πτέρυγος λαμπροὶ καὶ οἱ

TETRABIBLOS I. 9

Of the stars in Gemini, those in the feet share the same quality as Mercury and, to a less degree, as Venus; the bright stars in the thighs, the same as Saturn; of the two bright stars in the heads,[1] the one in the head in advance the same as Mercury; it is also called the star of Apollo; the one in the head that follows, the same as Mars; it is also called the star of Hercules.

Of the stars in Cancer, the two in the eyes produce the same effect as Mercury, and, to a less degree, as Mars; those in the claws, the same as Saturn and Mercury; the cloud-like cluster in the breast, called the Manger,[2] the same as Mars and the moon; and the two on either side of it, which are called Asses,[3] the same as Mars and the sun.

Of those in Leo, the two in the head act in the same way as Saturn and, to a less degree, as Mars; the three in the throat, the same as Saturn and, to a less degree, as Mercury; the bright star upon the heart, called Regulus, the same as Mars and Jupiter; those in the hip and the bright star in the tail,[4] the same as Saturn and Venus; and those in the thighs, the same as Venus and, to a less degree, Mercury.

Of the stars in Virgo,[5] those in the head and the one upon the tip of the southern wing have an effect like that of Mercury and, in less degree, of Mars; the other bright stars of the wing and those on the

---

[1] These are Castor ("in advance") and Pollux.
[2] Praesepe; more popularly, Beehive.
[3] Asinus Borealis and Asinus Australis.
[4] β Leonis.
[5] Virgo was represented as a winged woman bearing in her left hand a stem of wheat, the head of which was marked by the bright star Spica.

κατὰ τὰ περιζώματα τῷ τε τοῦ Ἑρμοῦ καὶ ἠρέμα τῷ τῆς Ἀφροδίτης· ὁ δὲ ἐν τῇ βορείᾳ πτέρυγι λαμπρός, καλούμενος δὲ Προτρυγητήρ, τῷ τοῦ Κρόνου καὶ τῷ τοῦ Ἑρμοῦ· ὁ δὲ καλούμενος Στάχυς τῷ τῆς Ἀφροδίτης καὶ ἠρέμα τῷ τοῦ Ἄρεως· οἱ δὲ ἐν ἄκροις τοῖς ποσὶ καὶ τῷ σύρματι[1] τῷ τοῦ Ἑρμοῦ[2] καὶ ἠρέμα τῷ τοῦ Ἄρεως.

Τῶν δὲ Χηλῶν τοῦ Σκορπίου[3] οἱ μὲν ἐν ἄκραις αὐταῖς ὡσαύτως διατιθέασι τῷ τε τοῦ Διὸς καὶ τῷ τοῦ Ἑρμοῦ· οἱ δὲ ἐν μέσαις τῷ τε τοῦ Κρόνου καὶ ἠρέμα τῷ τοῦ Ἄρεως.

Τῶν δὲ ἐν τῷ σώματι τοῦ Σκορπίου οἱ μὲν ἐν τῷ μετώπῳ λαμπροὶ τὸ αὐτὸ ποιοῦσι τῷ τε τοῦ Ἄρεως καὶ ἠρέμα τῷ τοῦ Κρόνου· οἱ δὲ ἐν τῷ σώματι τρεῖς, ὧν ὁ μέσος ὑπόκιρρος καὶ λαμπρότερος, καλεῖται δὲ Ἀντάρης, τῷ τοῦ Ἄρεως καὶ ἠρέμα τῷ τοῦ Διός· οἱ δὲ ἐν τοῖς σφονδύλοις τῷ τε τοῦ Κρόνου καὶ ἠρέμα τῷ τῆς Ἀφροδίτης· οἱ δὲ ἐπὶ τοῦ κέντρου τῷ τε τοῦ Ἑρμοῦ καὶ τῷ τοῦ Ἄρεως· ἡ δὲ λεγομένη νεφελοειδὴς συστροφὴ τῷ τοῦ Ἄρεως καὶ τῇ σελήνῃ.

Τῶν δὲ περὶ τὸν Τοξότην οἱ μὲν ἐπὶ τῆς ἀκίδος τοῦ βέλους ὅμοιον ἔχουσι τὸ ποιητικὸν τῷ τοῦ Ἄρεως καὶ τῇ σελήνῃ· οἱ δὲ περὶ τὸ τόξον καὶ τὴν λαβὴν τῆς χειρὸς τῷ τε τοῦ Διὸς καὶ τῷ τοῦ Ἄρεως· ἡ

---

[1] Post σύρματι add. τοῦ ματίου NProc.Cam.; om. VPMADEFH.
[2] τοῦ Ἑρμοῦ VPADEFHProc., τοῦ Ἀφροδίτης MNCam,
[3] Σκορπίου VPDProc., Ζυγοῦ NCam., om. LN (lac. 6 litt.) AEFH.

girdles like that of Mercury and, in a measure, of Venus; the bright star in the northern wing, called Vindemiator, like those of Saturn and Mercury; the so-called Spica, like that of Venus and, in a less degree, that of Mars; those in the tips of the feet and the train[1] like that of Mercury and, in a less degree, Mars.

Of those in the Claws of the Scorpion,[2] the ones at their very extremities exercise the same influence as do Jupiter and Mercury; those in the middle parts the same as do Saturn and, to a less degree, Mars.

Of the stars in the body of Scorpio, the bright stars on the forehead act in the same way as does Mars and in some degree as does Saturn; the three in the body, the middle one of which is tawny and rather bright and is called Antares, the same as Mars and, in some degree, Jupiter; those in the joints, the same as Saturn and, in some degree, Venus; those in the sting, the same as Mercury and Mars; and the so-called cloud-like cluster, the same as Mars and the moon.

Of the stars in Sagittarius,[3] those in the point of his arrow have an effect like that of Mars and the moon; those in the bow and the grip of his hand, like that of Jupiter and Mars; the cluster in his forehead,

---

[1] "Of the garment" is added in the Nuremberg MS., by Proclus, and in the printed editions; see the critical note.

[2] "Claws of the Scorpion" was the earlier name of Libra (Ζυγός); the latter came into general use in the first century before Christ. Ptolemy uses both names.

[3] Represented as a centaur preparing to shoot an arrow; a mantle flies above and behind his shoulders.

δὲ ἐν τῷ προσώπῳ συστροφὴ τῷ τε ἡλίῳ καὶ τῷ τοῦ Ἄρεως· οἱ δὲ ἐν ταῖς ἐφαπτίσι[1] καὶ τῷ νώτῳ τῷ τοῦ Διὸς καὶ ἠρέμα τῷ τοῦ Ἑρμοῦ· οἱ δὲ ἐν τοῖς ποσὶ τῷ τοῦ Διὸς καὶ τῷ τοῦ Κρόνου· τὸ δὲ ἐπὶ τῆς οὐρᾶς τετράπλευρον τῷ τῆς Ἀφροδίτης καὶ ἠρέμα τῷ τοῦ Κρόνου.

Τῶν δὲ κατὰ τὸν Αἰγόκερων ἀστέρων οἱ μὲν ἐπὶ τῶν κεράτων ὡσαύτως ἐνεργοῦσι τῷ τῆς Ἀφροδίτης καὶ ἠρέμα τῷ τοῦ Ἄρεως· οἱ δὲ ἐν τῷ στόματι τῷ τοῦ Κρόνου καὶ ἠρέμα τῷ τῆς Ἀφροδίτης· οἱ δὲ ἐν τοῖς ποσὶ καὶ τῇ κοιλίᾳ τῷ τοῦ Ἄρεως καὶ τῷ τοῦ Ἑρμοῦ· οἱ δὲ ἐπὶ τῆς οὐρᾶς τῷ τοῦ Κρόνου καὶ τῷ τοῦ Διός.

Τῶν δὲ περὶ τὸν Ὑδροχόον οἱ μὲν ἐν τοῖς ὤμοις ὁμοίως διατιθέασι τῷ τε τοῦ Κρόνου καὶ τῷ τοῦ Ἑρμοῦ, σὺν τοῖς ἐν τῇ ἀριστερᾷ χειρὶ καὶ τῷ ἱματίῳ· οἱ δὲ ἐπὶ τῶν μηρῶν μᾶλλον μὲν τῷ τοῦ Ἑρμοῦ, ἧττον δὲ τῷ τοῦ Κρόνου· οἱ δὲ ἐν τῇ ῥύσει τοῦ ὕδατος τῷ τε τοῦ Κρόνου καὶ ἠρέμα τῷ τοῦ Διός.

Τῶν δὲ περὶ τοὺς Ἰχθῦς οἱ μὲν ἐν τῇ κεφαλῇ τοῦ νοτιωτέρου ἰχθύος τὸ αὐτὸ ποιοῦσι τῷ τοῦ Ἑρμοῦ καὶ ἠρέμα τῷ τοῦ Κρόνου· οἱ δὲ ἐν τῷ σώματι τῷ τοῦ Διὸς καὶ τῷ τοῦ Ἑρμοῦ· οἱ δὲ ἐπὶ τῆς οὐρᾶς καὶ τοῦ νοτίου λίνου τῷ τοῦ Κρόνου καὶ ἠρέμα τῷ τοῦ Ἑρμοῦ· οἱ δὲ ἐν τῷ σώματι καὶ τῇ ἀκάνθῃ τοῦ βορείου ἰχθύος τῷ τοῦ Διὸς[2] καὶ ἠρέμα

---

[1] ἐφαπτίσι VMADEFHProc.; ἐφαπτρίσι Cam.²; πτέρηξιν P, πτέρυξι LNCam.¹

[2] Διὸς VMADFHProc., Ἄρεως PLNCam., Ἑρμοῦ E.

like that of the sun and Mars; those in the cloak and his back, like that of Jupiter and, to a less degree, of Mercury; those in his feet, like that of Jupiter and Saturn; the quadrangle upon the tail, like that of Venus and, to a less degree, of Saturn.

Of the stars in Capricorn,[1] those in the horns act in the same way as Venus and, in some degree, as Mars; those in the mouth, as Saturn and, in some degree, as Venus; those in the feet and the belly, as Mars and Mercury; and those in the tail, as Saturn and Jupiter.

Of the stars in Aquarius, those in the shoulders exert an influence like that of Saturn and Mercury, together with those in the left arm and the cloak; those in the thighs, like that of Mercury in a greater degree and like that of Saturn in a lesser degree; those in the stream of water, like that of Saturn and, in some degree, like that of Jupiter.

Of the stars in Pisces,[2] those in the head of the southern Fish act in the same way as Mercury and somewhat as does Saturn; those in the body, as do Jupiter and Mercury; those in the tail and the southern cord, as do Saturn and, in some degree, Mercury; those in the body and backbone of the northern Fish, as do Jupiter and, in some degree,

---

[1] Represented as a monster with a goat's head and fore feet and a fish's tail.

[2] The southern Fish (not to be confused with the extra-zodiacal constellation Piscis Australis, mentioned later) is toward Aquarius; the two fishes are represented as being joined by a cord from tail to tail.

τῷ τῆς Ἀφροδίτης· οἱ δὲ ἐν τῷ βορείῳ τοῦ λίνου τῷ τοῦ Κρόνου καὶ τῷ τοῦ Διός· ὁ δὲ ἐπὶ τοῦ συνδέσμου λαμπρὸς τῷ τοῦ Ἄρεως καὶ ἠρέμα τῷ τοῦ Ἑρμοῦ.

Τῶν δὲ ἐν ταῖς βορειοτέραις τοῦ ζῳδιακοῦ μορφώσεσιν οἱ μὲν περὶ τὴν μικρὰν Ἄρκτον λαμπροὶ τὴν ὁμοίαν ἔχουσι ποιότητα τῷ τε τοῦ Κρόνου καὶ ἠρέμα τῷ τῆς Ἀφροδίτης· οἱ δὲ περὶ τὴν μεγάλην Ἄρκτον τῷ τοῦ Ἄρεως· ἡ δὲ ὑπὸ τὴν οὐρὰν αὐτῆς τοῦ Πλοκάμου συστροφὴ τῇ σελήνῃ καὶ τῷ τῆς Ἀφροδίτης· οἱ δὲ ἐν τῷ Δράκοντι λαμπροὶ τῷ τοῦ Κρόνου καὶ τῷ τοῦ Ἄρεως καὶ τῷ τοῦ Διός· οἱ δὲ τοῦ Κηφέως τῷ τε τοῦ Κρόνου καὶ τῷ τοῦ Διός· οἱ δὲ περὶ τὸν Βοώτην τῷ τοῦ Ἑρμοῦ καὶ τῷ τοῦ Κρόνου· ὁ δὲ λαμπρὸς καὶ ὑπόκιρρος τῷ τοῦ Διὸς καὶ Ἄρεως, ὁ καὶ Ἀρκτοῦρος καλούμενος· οἱ δὲ ἐν τῷ βορείῳ Στεφάνῳ τῷ τε τῆς Ἀφροδίτης καὶ τῷ τοῦ Ἑρμοῦ· οἱ δὲ κατὰ τὸν ἐν γόνασι τῷ τοῦ Ἑρμοῦ· οἱ δὲ ἐν τῇ Λύρᾳ τῷ τῆς Ἀφροδίτης καὶ τῷ τοῦ Ἑρμοῦ· καὶ οἱ ἐν τῇ Ὄρνιθι δὲ ὡσαύτως· οἱ δὲ κατὰ τὴν Κασσιέπειαν τῷ τε τοῦ Κρόνου καὶ τῷ τῆς Ἀφροδίτης· οἱ δὲ κατὰ τὸν Περσέα τῷ τοῦ Διὸς καὶ τῷ τοῦ Κρόνου· ἡ δὲ ἐν τῇ λαβῇ τῆς μαχαίρας συστροφὴ τῷ τοῦ Ἄρεως καὶ τῷ τοῦ Ἑρμοῦ· οἱ δὲ ἐν τῷ Ἡνιόχῳ λαμπροὶ τῷ τοῦ Ἄρεως καὶ τῷ τοῦ Ἑρμοῦ· οἱ δὲ κατὰ τὸν Ὀφιοῦχον τῷ τοῦ Κρόνου καὶ ἠρέμα τῷ τῆς Ἀφροδίτης· οἱ δὲ περὶ τὸν ὄφιν αὐτοῦ τῷ τε τοῦ Κρόνου καὶ τῷ τοῦ Ἄρεως· οἱ δὲ κατὰ τὸν Ὀϊστὸν τῷ τε τοῦ Ἄρεως καὶ ἠρέμα τῷ τῆς

TETRABIBLOS I. 9

Venus; those in the northern part of the cord, as do Saturn and Jupiter; and the bright star on the bond, as do Mars and, in some degree, Mercury.

Of the stars in the configurations north of the zodiac, the bright stars in Ursa Minor have a similar quality to that of Saturn and, to a less degree, to that of Venus; those in Ursa Major, to that of Mars; and the cluster of the Coma Berenices beneath the Bear's tail, to that of the moon and Venus; the bright stars in Draco, to that of Saturn, Mars, and Jupiter; those of Cepheus, to that of Saturn and Jupiter; those in Boötes, to that of Mercury and Saturn; the bright, tawny star, to that of Jupiter and Mars, the star called Arcturus; the star in Corona Septentrionalis, to that of Venus and Mercury; those in Geniculator,[1] to that of Mercury; those in Lyra,[2] to that of Venus and Mercury; and likewise those in Cygnus. The stars in Cassiopeia have the effect of Saturn and Venus; those in Perseus, of Jupiter and Saturn; the cluster in the hilt of the sword, of Mars and Mercury; the bright stars in Auriga,[3] of Mars and Mercury; those in Ophiuchus, of Saturn and, to some degree, of Venus; those in his serpent, of Saturn and Mars; those in Sagitta, of Mars and, to some degree, of

---
[1] *I.e.* Hercules.
[2] The bright star Vega is in Lyra.
[3] Capella is the brightest in this constellation.

PTOLEMY

Ἀφροδίτης· οἱ δὲ περὶ τὸν Ἀετὸν τῷ τοῦ Ἄρεως καὶ τῷ τοῦ Διός· οἱ δὲ ἐν τῷ Δελφῖνι τῷ τοῦ Κρόνου καὶ τῷ τοῦ Ἄρεως· οἱ δὲ κατὰ τὸν Ἵππον λαμπροὶ τῷ τοῦ Ἄρεως καὶ τῷ τοῦ Ἑρμοῦ· οἱ δὲ ἐν τῇ Ἀνδρομέδῃ τῷ τῆς Ἀφροδίτης· οἱ δὲ τοῦ Τριγώνου[1] τῷ τοῦ Ἑρμοῦ.

Τῶν δὲ ἐν τοῖς νοτιωτέροις τοῦ ζῳδιακοῦ μορφώμασιν ὁ μὲν ἐν τῷ στόματι τοῦ νοτίου Ἰχθύος λαμπρὸς ὁμοίαν ἔχει τὴν ἐνέργειαν τῷ τε τῆς Ἀφροδίτης καὶ τῷ τοῦ Ἑρμοῦ· οἱ δὲ περὶ τὸ Κῆτος τῷ τοῦ Κρόνου· τῶν δὲ περὶ τὸν Ὠρίωνα οἱ μὲν ἐπὶ τῶν ὤμων τῷ τε τοῦ Ἄρεως καὶ τῷ τοῦ Ἑρμοῦ, οἱ δὲ λοιποὶ λαμπροὶ τῷ τε τοῦ Διὸς καὶ τῷ τοῦ Κρόνου· τῶν δὲ ἐν τῷ Ποταμῷ ὁ μὲν ἔσχατος καὶ ὁ λαμπρὸς τῷ τοῦ Διός, οἱ δὲ λοιποὶ τῷ τοῦ Κρόνου· οἱ δὲ ἐν τῷ Λαγῷ τῷ τε τοῦ Κρόνου καὶ[2] τῷ τοῦ Ἑρμοῦ· τῶν δὲ περὶ τὸν Κύνα, οἱ μὲν ἄλλοι τῷ τῆς Ἀφροδίτης, ὁ δὲ ἐπὶ τοῦ στόματος λαμπρὸς τῷ τοῦ Διὸς καὶ ἠρέμα τῷ τοῦ Ἄρεως· ὁ δὲ ἐν τῷ Προκυνὶ λαμπρὸς τῷ τε τοῦ Ἑρμοῦ καὶ ἠρέμα τῷ τοῦ Ἄρεως· οἱ δὲ κατὰ τὸν Ὕδρον λαμπροὶ τῷ τε τοῦ Κρόνου καὶ τῷ τῆς Ἀφροδίτης· οἱ δὲ ἐν τῷ Κρατῆρι τῷ τε τῆς Ἀφροδίτης καὶ ἠρέμα τῷ τοῦ Ἑρμοῦ· οἱ δὲ περὶ τὸν Κόρακα τῷ τοῦ Ἄρεως καὶ τῷ τοῦ Κρόνου· οἱ δὲ τῆς Ἀργοῦς λαμπροὶ τῷ τοῦ Κρόνου καὶ τῷ τοῦ Διός· τῶν δὲ περὶ τὸν Κένταυρον οἱ μὲν ἐν τῷ ἀνθρωπείῳ σώματι

---

[1] τοῦ Τριγώνου VMADEFHProc., τοῦ Δέλτῳ P, τοῦ^{δτ'} L, ἐν τῷ Δέλτα NCam.

[2] τῷ τε τοῦ Κρόνου καὶ om. Cam.

TETRABIBLOS I. 9

Venus; those in Aquila,[1] of Mars and Jupiter; those in Delphinus, of Saturn and Mars; the bright stars in the Horse,[2] of Mars and Mercury; those in Andromeda, of Venus; those in Triangulum, of Mercury.

Of the stars in the formations south of the zodiac the bright star in the mouth of Piscis Australis [3] has an influence similar to that of Venus and Mercury; those in Cetus, similar to that of Saturn; of those in Orion,[4] the stars on his shoulders similar to that of Mars and Mercury, and the other bright stars similar to that of Jupiter and Saturn; of the stars in Eridanus the last bright one [5] has an influence like that of Jupiter and the others like that of Saturn; the star in Lepus, like that of Saturn and Mercury; of those in Canis, the others like that of Venus, and the bright star in the mouth,[6] like that of Jupiter and, to a less degree, of Mars; the bright star Procyon, like that of Mercury and, in a less degree, that of Mars; the bright stars in Hydra,[7] like that of Saturn and Venus; those in Crater, like that of Venus and, in a less degree, of Mercury; those in Corvus, like that of Mars and Saturn; the bright stars of Argo,[8] like that of Saturn and Jupiter; of those in Centaurus, the ones

---

[1] Altair is in this group.
[2] Pegasus.
[3] The bright star is Fomalhaut.
[4] Rigel and Betelgeuse are the brightest stars here.
[5] The "last bright star" in Eridanus is Achernar.
[6] Sirius, which is in Canis.
[7] The brightest star is Alphard.
[8] These are Canopus and Var.

τῷ τε τῆς Ἀφροδίτης καὶ τῷ τοῦ Ἑρμοῦ, οἱ δὲ ἐν τῷ ἵππῳ λαμπροὶ τῷ τε τῆς Ἀφροδίτης καὶ τῷ τοῦ Διός· οἱ δὲ περὶ τὸ Θηρίον λαμπροὶ τῷ τε τοῦ Κρόνου καὶ ἠρέμα τῷ τοῦ Ἄρεως· οἱ δὲ ἐν τῷ Θυμιατηρίῳ τῷ τε τῆς Ἀφροδίτης καὶ ἠρέμα τῷ τοῦ Ἑρμοῦ·[1] οἱ δὲ ἐν τῷ νοτίῳ Στεφάνῳ λαμπροὶ τῷ τε τοῦ Κρόνου καὶ τῷ τοῦ Ἑρμοῦ.[2]

Αἱ μὲν οὖν τῶν ἀστέρων καθ' ἑαυτὰς δυνάμεις τοιαύτης ἔτυχον ὑπὸ τῶν παλαιοτέρων παρατηρήσεως.

⟨i.⟩ *Περὶ τῆς τῶν ὡρῶν καὶ δ' γωνιῶν δυνάμεως*

Καὶ τῶν ὡρῶν δὲ τῶν τοῦ ἔτους δ' οὐσῶν, ἔαρος τε καὶ θέρους καὶ μετοπώρου καὶ χειμῶνος, τὸ μὲν ἔαρ ἔχει τὸ μᾶλλον ἐν τῷ ὑγρῷ διὰ τὴν κατὰ τὸ παρῳχημένον ψῦχος, ἀρχομένης δὲ τῆς θερμασίας, διάχυσιν·[3] τὸ δὲ θέρος τὸ πλέον ἐν τῷ θερμῷ διὰ τὴν τοῦ ἡλίου πρὸς τὸν κατὰ κορυφὴν ἡμῶν τόπον[4] ἐγγύτητα· τὸ δὲ μετόπωρον τὸ μᾶλλον ἐν τῷ ξηρῷ, διὰ τὴν κατὰ τὸ παρῳχημένον καῦμα τῶν ὑγρῶν ἀνάποτιν· ὁ δὲ χειμὼν τὸ πλέον ἐν τῷ ψυχρῷ διὰ τὸ τὸν ἥλιον πλεῖστον ἀφίστασθαι τοῦ κατὰ κορυφὴν ἡμῶν τόπου. διόπερ, καὶ τοῦ ζῳδιακοῦ μηδεμιᾶς οὔσης φύσει ἀρχῆς ὡς κύκλου, τὸ ἀπὸ τῆς ἐαρινῆς ἰσημερίας ἀρχόμενον δωδεκατημόριον, τὸ τοῦ Κριοῦ,

---

[1] Ἑρμοῦ VPLMADEFHProc., Κρόνου NCam.
[2] Titulum capitis post Ἑρμοῦ posuerunt PLMNEFH.

in the human body, like that of Venus and Mercury, and the bright stars in the equine body like that of Venus and Jupiter; the bright stars in Lupus, like that of Saturn and, in less degree, of Mars; those in Ara, like that of Venus and, to a lesser degree, of Mercury; and the bright stars in Corona Australis, like that of Saturn and Mercury.

Such, then, are the observations of the effects of the stars themselves as made by our predecessors.

10. *Of the Effect of the Seasons and of the Four Angles.*

Of the four seasons of the year, spring, summer, autumn, and winter, spring exceeds in moisture on account of its diffusion after the cold has passed and warmth is setting in; the summer, in heat, because of the nearness of the sun to the zenith; autumn more in dryness, because of the sucking up of the moisture during the hot season just past; and winter exceeds in cold, because the sun is farthest away from the zenith. For this reason, although there is no natural beginning of the zodiac, since it is a circle, they assume that the sign which begins with

---

³ διὰ τὴν . . . . . διάχυσιν] τῆς κατὰ τὸ παρ. ψ. συστάσεως, ἀρχ. δὲ τῆς θ. διαχεῖσθαι NCam.
⁴ τόπον om. NCam.

καὶ τῶν ὅλων ἀρχὴν ὑποτίθενται, καθάπερ ἐμψύχου ζῴου τοῦ ζωδιακοῦ τὴν ὑγρὰν τοῦ ἔαρος ὑπερβολὴν προκαταρκτικὴν ποιούμενοι, καὶ ἐφεξῆς τὰς λοιπὰς ὥρας διὰ τὸ καὶ πάντων ζῴων τὰς μὲν πρώτας ἡλικίας τὸ πλέον ἔχειν τῆς ὑγρᾶς οὐσίας, παραπλησίως τῷ ἔαρι ἁπαλὰς οὔσας καὶ ἔτι τρυφεράς· τὰς δὲ δευτέρας τὰς μέχρι τῆς ἀκμαιότητος[1] τὸ πλέον ἔχειν ἐν τῷ θερμῷ[2] παραπλησίως τῷ θέρει· τὰς δὲ τρίτας καὶ ἤδη ἐν παρακμῇ καὶ ἀρχῇ φθίσεως τὸ πλέον ἤδη καὶ αὐτὰς ἔχειν ἐν τῷ ξηρῷ παραπλησίως τῷ μετοπώρῳ· τὰς δὲ ἐσχάτας καὶ πρὸς τῇ διαλύσει τὸ πλέον ἔχειν ἐν τῷ ψυχρῷ καθάπερ καὶ ὁ χειμών.[3]

Ὁμοίως δὲ καὶ τῶν δ' τοῦ ὁρίζοντος τόπων καὶ γωνιῶν, ἀφ' ὧν καὶ οἱ καθ' ὅλα μέρη πνέοντες ἄνεμοι τὰς ἀρχὰς ἔχουσι, ὁ μὲν πρὸς τὰς ἀνατολὰς αὐτός τε τὸ πλέον ἔχει ἐν τῷ ξηρῷ διὰ τὸ κατ' αὐτὸν γινομένου τοῦ ἡλίου τὰ ἀπὸ τῆς νυκτὸς ὑγρανθέντα τότε πρῶτον ἄρχεσθαι ξηραίνεσθαι· οἵ τε ἀπ' αὐτοῦ πνέοντες ἄνεμοι, οὓς κοινότερον

[1] ἀκμαιότητος VMADEF, ἀκμαιοτάτης PLNCam.
[2] θερμῷ VMADEF, θερμαίνειν PLNCam.
[3] Hic inser. titulum Περὶ τῆς τῶν τεττάρων γωνιῶν δυνάμεως VADFProc.

---

[1] *Cf. Almagest*, iii. 1 (p. 192, 19-22), where Ptolemy defines the year as the return of the sun to the points fixed by the equinoxes and solstices. The sign of Aries, defined as the 30° beginning with the vernal equinox, is, of course, very different from the sign considered as the actual constellation. This gave rise to an argument against astrology, first expressed by Origen. *Cf.* Boll-Bezold-Gundel,

TETRABIBLOS I. 10

the vernal equinox, that of Aries,[1] is the starting-point of them all, making the excessive moisture of the spring the first part of the zodiac as though it were a living creature, and taking next in order the remaining seasons, because in all creatures the earliest ages,[2] like the spring, have a larger share of moisture and are tender and still delicate. The second age, up to the prime of life, exceeds in heat, like summer; the third, which is now past the prime and on the verge of decline, has an excess of dryness, like autumn; and the last, which approaches dissolution, exceeds in its coldness, like winter.

Similarly, too, of the four regions and angles of the horizon, from which originate the winds from the cardinal points,[3] the eastern one likewise excels in dryness because, when the sun is in that region, whatever has been moistened by the night then first begins to be dried; and the winds which blow from

pp. 131-132; Bouché-Leclercq, p. 129, n. 1; Ashmand, Ptolemy's *Tetrabiblos*, p. 32, n.

[2] Ptolemy here enumerates four ages of man, as do also many Pythagorizing arithmologists, when they praise the number 4, as, for example, *Theologoumena Arithmetica*, p. 20 Ast, Diogenes Laertius, viii. 1. 10, Martianus Capella, vii. 734, etc. Ptolemy later (iv. 10) speaks of seven ages, assigning one to each planet; the arithmologists have also a series of seven ages which they cite in praise of the number 7; *e.g.* Philo, *De mundi opificio* 36. There are also lists in which the ages are merely made up of hebdomadic groups of years.

[3] Proclus' paraphrase for οἱ καθ' ὅλα μέρη πνέοντες ἄνεμοι is οἱ καθολικοὶ ἄνεμοι, which is closer than the Latin translations, *totas illas partes occupantes venti* (Gogava), and *venti, qui totas illas partes occupant* (Melanchthon). Ptolemy means the winds from the cardinal points and around them.

PTOLEMY

ἀπηλιώτας καλοῦμεν,[1] ἄνικμοί τέ εἰσι καὶ ξηραντικοί. ὁ δὲ πρὸς μεσημβρίαν τόπος αὐτός τέ ἐστι θερμότατος διά τε τὸ πυρῶδες τῶν τοῦ ἡλίου μεσουρανήσεων καὶ διὰ τὸ ταύτας κατὰ τὴν τῆς ἡμετέρας οἰκουμένης ἔγκλισιν πρὸς μεσημβρίαν μᾶλλον ἀποκλίνειν· οἵ τε ἀπ' αὐτοῦ πνέοντες ἄνεμοι, οὓς κοινῶς νότους καλοῦμεν, θερμοί τέ εἰσι καὶ μανωτικοί. ὁ δὲ πρὸς ταῖς δυσμαῖς τόπος αὐτός τέ ἐστιν ὑγρὸς διὰ τὸ κατ' αὐτὸν γινομένου τοῦ ἡλίου τὰ ἀπὸ τῆς ἡμέρας ἀναποθέντα τότε πρῶτον ἄρχεσθαι διυγραίνεσθαι· οἵ τε ἀπ' αὐτοῦ φερόμενοι ἄνεμοι, οὓς κοινότερον ζεφύρους καλοῦμεν, νεαροί τέ εἰσι καὶ ὑγραντικοί. ὁ δὲ πρὸς ταῖς ἄρκτοις τόπος αὐτός τέ ἐστι ψυχρότατος διὰ τὸ κατὰ τὴν τῆς ἡμετέρας οἰκουμένης ἔγκλισιν τὰς τῆς θερμότητος αἰτίας τῶν τοῦ ἡλίου μεσουρανήσεων πλέον αὐτοῦ διεστάναι, ὥσπερ[2] ἀντιμεσουρανοῦντος· οἵ τε ἀπ' αὐτοῦ πνέοντες ἄνεμοι, οἱ καλούμενοι κοινῶς βορέαι, ψυχροί τε ὑπάρχουσι καὶ πυκνωτικοί.

Χρησίμη δὲ καὶ ἡ τούτων διάληψις πρὸς τὸ τὰς συγκράσεις πάντα τρόπον ἑκάστοτε δύνασθαι[3] διακρίνειν. εὐκατανόητον γὰρ διότι καὶ παρὰ τὰς τοιαύτας καταστάσεις ἤτοι τῶν ὡρῶν ἢ τῶν ἡλικιῶν ἢ τῶν γωνιῶν τρέπεταί πως τὸ ποιητικὸν τῆς τῶν ἀστέρων δυνάμεως, καὶ ἐν μὲν ταῖς οἰκείαις καταστάσεσιν ἀκρατοτέραν τε ἔχουσι τὴν ποιότητα καὶ τὴν ἐνέργειαν ἰσχυροτέραν, οἷον ἐν ταῖς θερμαῖς οἱ

---
[1] καλοῦσιν NCam.
[2] Post ὥσπερ add. τοῦ ἡλίου NCam., om. alii.

it, which we call in general *Apeliotes*,[1] are without moisture and drying in effect. The region to the south is hottest because of the fiery heat of the sun's passages through mid-heaven and because these passages, on account of the inclination of our inhabited world, diverge more to the south; and the winds which blow thence and are called by the general name *Notus* are hot and rarefying. The region to the west is itself moist, because when the sun is therein the things dried out during the day then first begin to become moistened; likewise the winds which blow from this part, which we call by the general name *Zephyrus*, are fresh and moist. The region to the north is the coldest, because through our inhabited world's inclination it is too far removed from the causes of heat arising from the sun's culmination, as it is also when the sun is at its lower culmination; and the winds which blow thence, which are called by the general name *Boreas*, are cold and condensing in effect.

The knowledge of these facts is useful to enable one to form a complete judgement of temperatures in individual instances. For it is easily recognizable that, together with such conditions as these, of seasons, ages, or angles, there is a corresponding variation in the potency of the stars' faculties, and that in the conditions akin to them their quality is purer and their effectiveness stronger, those that are heating by nature, for instance, in heat, and those that

---

[1] This is the usual Attic form; the alternative, ἀφηλιώτης, shows more clearly its derivation from ἥλιος, "the wind that blows from the sun."

---

[3] δύνασθαι om. NCam.

θερμαντικοὶ τὴν φύσιν, καὶ ἐν ταῖς ὑγραῖς οἱ ὑγραντικοί, ἐν δὲ ταῖς ἐναντίαις κεκραμένην καὶ ἀσθενεστέραν· ὡς ἐν ταῖς ψυχραῖς οἱ θερμαντικοὶ καὶ ἐν ταῖς ξηραῖς οἱ ὑγραντικοὶ καὶ ἐν ταῖς ἄλλαις δὲ ὡσαύτως κατὰ τὸ ἀνάλογον τῇ διὰ τῆς μίξεως συγκιρναμένῃ ποιότητι.

31 ⟨ιαʹ.⟩ *Περὶ τροπικῶν καὶ ἰσημερινῶν καὶ στερεῶν*[1] *καὶ δισώμων ζῳδίων*

Τούτων δὲ οὕτω προεκτεθέντων ἀκόλουθον ἂν εἴη συνάψαι καὶ τὰς αὐτῶν τῶν τοῦ ζῳδιακοῦ δωδεκατημορίων παραδεδομένας φυσικὰς ἰδιοτροπίας. αἱ μὲν γὰρ ὁλοσχερέστεραι καθ' ἕκαστον αὐτῶν κράσεις ἀνάλογον ἔχουσι ταῖς κατ' αὐτὰ γινομέναις ὥραις, συνίστανται δέ τινες αὐτῶν ἰδιότητες ἀπό τε τῆς πρὸς τὸν ἥλιον καὶ τὴν σελήνην καὶ τοὺς ἀστέρας οἰκειώσεως, ὡς ἐν τοῖς ἐφεξῆς διελευσόμεθα, προτάξαντες τὰς κατὰ τὸ ἀμιγὲς αὐτῶν μόνων τῶν δωδεκατημορίων καθ' αὑτά τε καὶ πρὸς ἄλληλα θεωρουμένας δυνάμεις.

Πρῶται μὲν τοίνυν εἰσὶ διαφοραὶ τῶν καλουμένων τροπικῶν καὶ ἰσημερινῶν καὶ στερεῶν καὶ δισώμων.

[1] καὶ στερεῶν om. MNECam. Titulum post l. 19 δυνάμεις ponunt VDProc.

---

[1] κράσεις, " mixtures "; astrologically used to designate the resultant qualities derived from the mingling of various influences. *Cf. The Life and Opinions of Tristram Shandy*, Bk. I, Chapter 11, "who . . . seemed not to have had one single drop of Danish blood in his whole crasis."

are moistening in the moist, while under opposite conditions their power is adulterated and weaker. Thus the heating stars in the cold periods and the moistening stars in the dry periods are weaker, and similarly in the other cases, according to the quality produced by the mixture.

11. *Of Solstitial, Equinoctial, Solid, and Bicorporeal Signs.*

After the explanation of these matters the next subject to be added would be the natural characters of the zodiacal signs themselves, as they have been handed down by tradition. For although their more general temperaments [1] are each analogous to the seasons that take place in them,[2] certain peculiar qualities of theirs arise from their kinship [3] to the sun, moon, and planets, as we shall relate in what follows, putting first the unmingled powers of the signs themselves alone, regarded both absolutely and relatively to one another.

The first distinctions, then, are of the so-called solstitial, equinoctial, solid, and bicorporeal signs.[4]

[2] That is, when the sun is in these signs.
[3] οἰκείωσις, also translated "familiarity," is a common astrological term denoting the various relationships of affinity derived from the positions of signs or planets with reference to the universe or to each other, as, for example, through the aspects (c. 13).
[4] All but Virgo are represented as bicorporeal in fact. Ptolemy, as a learned writer, pays less attention to the fanciful and mythological classification of the signs into terrestrial, aquatic, four-footed, etc. (although he refers to them in i. 12), and gives greater prominence to the astronomical classification.

δύο μὲν γάρ ἐστι τροπικά, τό τε πρῶτον ἀπὸ τῆς θερινῆς τροπῆς λ' μοῖρον, τὸ τοῦ Καρκίνου · καὶ τὸ πρῶτον ἀπὸ τῆς χειμερινῆς τροπῆς, τὸ κατὰ τὸν Αἰγόκερων. ταῦτα δὲ ἀπὸ τοῦ συμβεβηκότος εἴληφε τὴν ὀνομασίαν. τρέπεται γὰρ ἐν ταῖς ἀρχαῖς αὐτῶν γινόμενος ὁ ἥλιος, ἐπιστρέφων εἰς τὰ ἐναντία τὴν κατὰ πλάτος πάροδον, καὶ κατὰ μὲν τὸν Καρκίνον θέρος ποιῶν, κατὰ δὲ τὸν Αἰγόκερων χειμῶνα. δύο δὲ καλεῖται ἰσημερινά, τό τε ἀπὸ τῆς ἐαρινῆς ἰσημερίας πρῶτον δωδεκατημόριον, τὸ τοῦ Κριοῦ, καὶ τὸ ἀπὸ τῆς μετοπωρινῆς τὸ τῶν Χηλῶν, 32 ὠνόμασται δὲ καὶ ταῦτα πάλιν ἀπὸ τοῦ συμβεβηκότος, ἐπειδὴ κατὰ τὰς ἀρχὰς αὐτῶν γινόμενος ὁ ἥλιος ἴσας ποιεῖ πανταχῆ τὰς νύκτας ταῖς ἡμέραις.

Τῶν δὲ λοιπῶν ὀκτὼ δωδεκατημορίων τέτταρα μὲν καλεῖται στερεά, τέτταρα δὲ δίσωμα. καὶ στερεὰ μέν ἐστι τὰ ἑπόμενα τοῖς τε τροπικοῖς καὶ τοῖς ἰσημερινοῖς, Ταῦρος, Λέων, Σκορπίος, Ὑδροχόος, ἐπειδὴ τῶν ἐν ἐκείνοις ἀρχομένων ὡρῶν αἵ τε ὑγρότητες καὶ θερμότητες καὶ ξηρότητες καὶ ψυχρότητες, ἐν τούτοις γινομένου τοῦ ἡλίου,[1] μᾶλλον καὶ στερεώτερον ἡμῶν καθικνοῦνται, οὐ τῶν καταστημάτων φύσει γινομένων τότε ἀκρατοτέρων, ἀλλ' ἡμῶν ἐγκεχρονικότων αὐτοῖς ἤδη καὶ διὰ τοῦτο τῆς ἰσχύος[2] εὐαισθητότερον ἀντιλαμβανομένων.

Δίσωμα δέ ἐστι τὰ τοῖς στερεοῖς ἑπόμενα, Δίδυμοι, Παρθένος, Τοξότης, Ἰχθῦς, διὰ τὸ μεταξύ τε

---

[1] Post ἡλίου add. καὶ ἐπιτεταγμέναι Cam., ἐπιτεταγμέναι N; om. alii.
[2] Post ἰσχύος add. αὐτῶν NADECam.

TETRABIBLOS I. 11

For there are two solstitial signs, the first interval of 30° from the summer solstice, the sign of Cancer, and the first from the winter solstice, Capricorn; and they have received their name [1] from what takes place in them. For the sun turns when he is at the beginning of these signs and reverses his latitudinal progress, causing summer in Cancer and winter in Capricorn. Two signs are called equinoctial, the one which is first from the spring equinox, Aries, and the one which begins with the autumnal equinox, Libra; and they too again are named from what happens there, because when the sun is at the beginning of these signs he makes the nights exactly equal to the days.

Of the remaining eight signs four are called solid and four bicorporeal. The solid signs, Taurus, Leo, Scorpio, and Aquarius, are those which follow the solstitial and equinoctial signs; and they are so called because when the sun is in them the moisture, heat, dryness, and cold of the seasons that begin in the preceding signs touch us more firmly, not that the weather is naturally any more intemperate at that time, but that we are by then inured to them and for that reason are more sensible of their power.

The bicorporeal signs, Gemini, Virgo, Sagittarius, and Pisces, are those which follow the solid signs,

---

[1] *I.e.* τροπικόν, "having to do with turning (τροπή)." Astronomers to-day usually call them "solstitial" instead of "tropical," since "tropic" generally refers to the terrestrial circles, the Tropic of Cancer and the Tropic of Capricorn.

PTOLEMY

εἶναι τῶν στερεῶν καὶ τῶν τροπικῶν καὶ ἰσημερινῶν, καὶ ὥσπερ κεκοινωνηκέναι κατὰ τὰ τέλη καὶ τὰς ἀρχὰς τῆς τῶν δύο καταστημάτων φυσικῆς ἰδιοτροπίας.

⟨ιβ.⟩ Περὶ ἀρρενικῶν καὶ θηλυκῶν ζῳδίων

Πάλιν δὲ ὡσαύτως ἐξ μὲν τῶν δωδεκατημορίων ἀπένειμαν τῇ φύσει τῇ ἀρρενικῇ καὶ ἡμερινῇ, τὰ δὲ ἴσα τῇ θηλυκῇ καὶ νυκτερινῇ. καὶ ἡ μὲν τάξις
33 αὐτοῖς ἐδόθη παρ' ἕν διὰ τὸ συνεζεῦχθαι καὶ ἐγγὺς ἀεὶ τυγχάνειν τήν τε ἡμέραν τῇ νυκτὶ καὶ τὸ θῆλυ τῷ ἄρρενι. τῆς δὲ ἀρχῆς ἀπὸ τοῦ Κριοῦ δι' ἃς εἴπομεν αἰτίας λαμβανομένης, ὡσαύτως δὲ καὶ τοῦ ἄρρενος ἄρχοντος καὶ πρωτεύοντος, ἐπειδὴ καὶ τὸ ποιητικὸν ἀεὶ τοῦ παθητικοῦ πρῶτόν ἐστι τῇ δυνάμει, τὸ μὲν τοῦ Κριοῦ δωδεκατημόριον καὶ ἔτι τὸ τῶν Χηλῶν ἀρρενικὰ ἔδοξε καὶ ἡμερινά, καὶ ἅμα ἐπειδήπερ ὁ ἰσημερινὸς κύκλος δι' αὐτῶν γραφόμενος τὴν πρώτην καὶ ἰσχυροτάτην τῶν ὅλων φορὰν ἀποτελεῖ· τὰ δὲ ἐφεξῆς αὐτῶν ἀκολούθως[1] τῇ παρ' ἕν, ὡς ἔφαμεν, τάξει.

Χρῶνται δέ τινες τῇ τάξει τῶν ἀρρενικῶν καὶ θηλυκῶν[2] καὶ ἀπὸ τοῦ ἀνατέλλοντος δωδεκατημορίου, ὃ δὴ καλοῦσιν ὡρόσκοπον, τὴν ἀρχὴν τοῦ ἄρρενος[3] ποιούμενοι. ὥσπερ γὰρ καὶ τὴν τῶν

[1] ἀκολούθως VMDEProc., ἀκόλουθα PLNACam.
[2] καὶ θηλυκῶν om. NCam.
[3] τοῦ ἄρρενος om. NCam.

and are so called because they are between the solid and the solstitial and equinoctial signs and share, as it were, at end and beginning, the natural properties of the two states of weather.

12. *Of Masculine and Feminine Signs.*

Again, in the same way they assigned six of the signs to the masculine and diurnal nature [1] and an equal number to the feminine and nocturnal. An alternating order was assigned to them because day is always yoked to night and close to it, and female to male. Now as Aries is taken as the starting-point for the reasons we have mentioned, and as the male likewise rules and holds first place, since also the active is always superior to the passive in power, the signs of Aries and Libra were thought to be masculine and diurnal, an additional reason being that the equinoctial circle which is drawn through them completes the primary and most powerful movement of the whole universe.[2] The signs in succession after them correspond, as we said, in alternating order.

Some, however, employ an order of masculine and feminine signs whereby the masculine begins with the sign that is rising, called the horoscope.[3] For just as some begin the solstitial signs with the moon's

[1] The signs of the zodiac, as well as the planets, are divided between the two sects (*cf.* i. 7).

[2] *I.e.* the general revolution of the heavens, carrying the fixed stars and the other heavenly bodies (according to the Ptolemaic and other ancient systems).

[3] Obviously, in a system like this, a given sign would not always belong to the same sect.

PTOLEMY

τροπικῶν ἀρχὴν ἀπὸ τοῦ σεληνιακοῦ ζῳδίου¹ λαμβάνουσιν ἔνιοι διὰ τὸ ταύτην τάχιον τῶν ἄλλων τρέπεσθαι, οὕτω καὶ τὴν τῶν ἀρρενικῶν ἀπὸ τοῦ ὡροσκοποῦντος διὰ τὸ ἀπηλιωτικώτερον,² καὶ οἱ μὲν ὁμοίως παρ' ἓν πάλιν τῇ τάξει χρώμενοι, οἱ δὲ καθ' ὅλα τεταρτημόρια διαιροῦντες καὶ ἑῷα μὲν ἡγούμενοι³ καὶ ἀρρενικὰ τό τε ἀπὸ τοῦ ὡροσκόπου μέχρι τοῦ μεσουρανοῦντος καὶ τὸ κατ' ἀντίθεσιν ἀπὸ τοῦ δύνοντος μέχρι τοῦ ὑπὸ γῆν μεσουρανοῦν-
34 τος,⁴ ἑσπέρια δὲ καὶ θηλυκὰ τὰ λοιπὰ δύο τεταρτημόρια. καὶ ἄλλας δέ τινας τοῖς δωδεκατημορίοις προσηγορίας ἐφήρμοσαν ἀπὸ τῶν περὶ αὐτὰ μορφώσεων· λέγω δὲ οἷον τετράποδα καὶ χερσαῖα καὶ ἡγεμονικὰ καὶ πολύσπορα καὶ τὰ τοιαῦτα· ἃς⁵ αὐτόθεν τό τε αἴτιον⁶ καὶ τὸ ἐμφανιστικὸν ἐχούσας περιττὸν ἡγούμεθα καταριθμεῖν, τῆς ἐκ τῶν τοιούτων διατυπώσεων ποιότητος ἐν αἷς ἂν τῶν προτελέσεων χρησίμη φαίνηται δυναμένης⁷ προεκτίθεσθαι.

¹ ζῳδίου VPLADE, κύκλου MNCam.
² τὸ ἀπηλιωτικώτερον VD (ἀφηλ-) Proc.; τὴν ἀπηλιώτην alii Cam.
³ ἡγούμενοι VMADE, om. PLNCam.
⁴ ὑπὸ γῆν μεσουρανοῦντος VMADEProc., ἀντιμεσουρανοῦντος PLNCam.
⁵ ἃς VDME, om. PL, ὡς NACam.; καλέσαντες post τοιαῦτα inser. PLMNCam., om. VDAE.
⁶ τό τε αἴτιον om. Cam.².
⁷ δυναμένης VD, δυναμης P, δύναμις LMNAECam. προεκτίθεσθαι VMDEAProc., πρωεκτεθηō P, προεκτίθης L, προεκτεθείσης NCam.

sign because the moon changes direction more swiftly than the rest, so they begin the masculine signs with the horoscope because it is further to the east, some as before making use of the alternate order of signs, and others dividing by entire quadrants, and designating as matutinal and masculine signs those of the quadrant from the horoscope to mid-heaven and those of the opposite quadrant from the occident to the lower mid-heaven, and as evening and feminine the other two quadrants. They have also attached other descriptions [1] to the signs, derived from their shapes; I refer, for example, to "four-footed," " terrestrial," " commanding," " fecund," and similar appellations. These, since their reason and their significance are directly derived, we think it superfluous to enumerate, since the quality resulting from such conformations can be explained in connection with those predictions wherein it is obviously useful.

[1] For this type of classification, *cf.* Bouché-Leclercq, pp. 149-152. Vettins Valens, pp. 5 ff. (Kroll), attaches many epithets to the signs; *cf.* also Antiochus, *ap. CCAG*, viii. 112; Rhetorius, *ap. CCAG*, i. 164 ff. Some of them figure in ii. 7, below.

PTOLEMY

⟨ιγ.⟩ Περὶ τῶν συσχηματιζομένων δωδεκατημορίων

Οἰκειοῦται δὲ ἀλλήλοις τῶν μερῶν τοῦ ζωδιακοῦ πρῶτον τὰ συσχηματιζόμενα. ταῦτα δ' ἐστὶν ὅσα διάμετρον ἔχει στάσιν, περιέχοντα δύο ὀρθὰς γωνίας καὶ ἐξ τῶν δωδεκατημορίων καὶ μοίρας ρπ΄· καὶ ὅσα τρίγωνον ἔχει στάσιν, περιέχοντα μίαν ὀρθὴν γωνίαν καὶ τρίτον καὶ δ΄ δωδεκατημόρια καὶ μοίρας ρκ΄· καὶ ὅσα τετραγωνίζειν λέγεται, περιέχοντα μίαν ὀρθὴν καὶ γ΄ δωδεκατημόρια καὶ μοίρας ϙ΄· καὶ ἔτι ὅσα ἑξάγωνον ποιεῖται στάσιν, περιέχοντα δίμοιρον μιᾶς ὀρθῆς καὶ β΄ δωδεκατημόρια καὶ μοίρας ξ΄.

Δι' ἣν δὲ αἰτίαν αὗται μόναι τῶν διαστάσεων παρελήφθησαν ἐκ τούτων ἂν μάθοιμεν. τῆς μὲν γὰρ κατὰ τὸ διάμετρον αὐτόθεν ἐστὶν ὁ λόγος φανερὸς ἐπειδήπερ ἐπὶ μιᾶς εὐθείας ποιεῖται τὰς συναντήσεις. λαμβανομένων δὲ τῶν δύο μεγίστων καὶ διὰ συμφωνίας μορίων τε καὶ ἐπιμορίων, μορίων μὲν πρὸς τὴν τῶν β΄ ὀρθῶν διάμετρον τοῦ τε ἡμίσους καὶ τοῦ τρίτου, τὸ μὲν εἰς δύο τὴν τοῦ

---

[1] *Cf.* the note on οἰκείωσις (i. 11). οἰκειοῦσθαι is the corresponding verb.

[2] The aspects are geometrical relationships between the heavenly bodies. Ptolemy recognizes here only four—opposition, trine, quartile, and sextile—as having significance, and does not class "conjunction" as an aspect, although it is treated as such throughout the *Tetrabiblos*.

TETRABIBLOS I. 13

13. *Of the Aspects of the Signs.*

Of the parts of the zodiac those first are familiar[1] one to another which are in aspect.[2] These are the ones which are in opposition, enclosing two right angles, six signs, and 180 degrees; those which are in trine, enclosing one and one-third right angles, four signs, and 120 degrees; those which are said to be in quartile, enclosing one right angle, three signs, and 90 degrees, and finally those that occupy the sextile position, enclosing two-thirds of a right angle, two signs, and 60 degrees.

We may learn from the following why only these intervals have been taken into consideration. The explanation of opposition is immediately obvious, because it causes the signs to meet on one straight line. But if we take the two fractions and the two superparticulars[3] most important in music, and if the fractions one-half and one-third be applied to

---

Kepler is said to have invented several others, based on other aliquot parts of 360°, the semiquadrate, quintile, sesquiquadrate, biquintile, etc. (*cf.* Ashmand, pp. 40-41, nn.); these have been employed by modern astrologers, but the Ptolemaic doctrines of this and the 16th chapter are inconsistent with their use. The intervals between bodies in aspect in the four ways here mentioned can be measured in whole signs.

[3] Nicomachus of Gerasa, *Introduction to Arithmetic,* i. 19, defines the superparticular as "a number that contains within itself the whole of the number compared with it, and some one factor of it besides." The "two superparticulars most important to music" are the first two in the series, the sesquialter $\left(\frac{3}{2}\right)$ and the sesquitertian $\left(\frac{4}{3}\right)$, which correspond to the diapente and diatessaron respectively (*cf.* Nicomachus, *op. cit.,* ii. 26).

τετραγώνου πεποίηκε, τὸ δὲ εἰς τρία τὴν τοῦ ἑξαγώνου καὶ τὴν τοῦ τριγώνου·[1] ἐπιμορίων δὲ πρὸς τὸ τῆς μιᾶς ὀρθῆς τετράγωνον μεταξὺ λαμβανομένου τοῦ τε ἡμιολίου καὶ τοῦ ἐπιτρίτου, τὸ μὲν ἡμιόλιον ἐποίησε τὴν τοῦ τετραγώνου πρὸς τὴν τοῦ ἑξαγώνου, τὸ δὲ ἐπίτριτον τὴν τοῦ τριγώνου πρὸς τὴν τοῦ τετραγώνου. τούτων μέντοι τῶν σχηματισμῶν οἱ μὲν τρίγωνοι καὶ ἑξάγωνοι σύμφωνοι καλοῦνται διὰ τὸ ἐξ ὁμογενῶν συγκεῖσθαι δωδεκατημορίων ἢ ἐκ πάντων θηλυκῶν ἢ ἀρρενικῶν· ἀσύμφωνοι δὲ οἱ τετράγωνοι καὶ οἱ κατὰ διάμετρον διότι κατὰ ἀντίθεσιν τῶν ὁμογενῶν τὴν σύστασιν λαμβάνουσιν.

⟨ιδ.⟩ Περὶ προσταττόντων καὶ ἀκουόντων

Ὡσαύτως δὲ προστάττοντα καὶ ἀκούοντα λέγεται τμήματα τὰ κατ' ἴσην διάστασιν ἀπὸ τοῦ αὐτοῦ, ἢ καὶ ὁποτέρου, τῶν ἰσημερινῶν σημείων ἐσχηματισμένα διὰ τὸ ἐν τοῖς ἴσοις χρόνοις ἀναφέρεσθαι καὶ ἐπὶ τῶν ἴσων εἶναι παραλλήλων.

[1] καὶ τὴν τοῦ τριγώνου libri omnes Proc.; καὶ τ. τ. τετραγώνου Cam.[1]; om. Cam.[2]

---

[1] That is, $\frac{1}{2}$ of 180° = 90° (quartile) and $\frac{1}{3}$ of 180° = 60° (sextile). All the MSS. and Proclus add here "and trine," which perhaps we should, with Camerarius (ed. 2), discard. The trine, however, could be regarded as $\frac{1}{3}$ of 360° or as twice the sextile.

[2] That is, the sesquialter = $\frac{3}{2} = \frac{90°}{60°}$ and the sesquitertian = $\frac{4}{3} = \frac{120°}{90°}$.

opposition, composed of two right angles, the half makes the quartile and the third the sextile and trine.[1] Of the superparticulars, if the sesquialter and sesquitertian be applied to the quartile interval of one right angle, which lies between them, the sesquialter makes the ratio of the quartile to the sextile and the sesquitertian that of trine to quartile.[2] Of these aspects trine and sextile are called harmonious because they are composed of signs of the same kind, either entirely of feminine or entirely of masculine signs; while quartile and opposition are disharmonious because they are composed of signs of opposite kinds.

14. *Of Commanding and Obeying Signs.*

Similarly the names "commanding" and "obeying"[3] are applied to the divisions of the zodiac which are disposed at an equal distance from the same equinoctial sign, whichever it may be, because they ascend[4] in equal periods of time and are on equal parallels. Of these the ones in the summer

---

[3] *Cf.* Bouché-Leclercq, pp. 159-164, on this and the following chapter. The pairs which "command" and "obey" (the "commanding" sign first) are: Taurus-Pisces, Gemini-Aquarius, Cancer-Capricorn, Leo-Sagittarius, Virgo-Scorpio. Aries and Libra are left out of the scheme, being the equinoctial signs from which the start is made; so Manilius, ii. 485, 501. The original notion seems to have been that these signs "heard" (ἀκούειν) each other, and the idea of "obeying" (ὑπακούειν) was a pseudo-scientific elaboration.

[4] *Cf.* the note on iii. 10 (pp. 286 ff.) for the ascension of the signs.

τούτων δὲ τὰ μὲν ἐν τῷ θερινῷ ἡμικυκλίῳ προστάττοντα καλεῖται, τὰ δ' ἐν τῷ χειμερινῷ ὑπακούοντα, διὰ τὸ κατ' ἐκεῖνο μὲν γινόμενον τὸν ἥλιον μείζονα ποιεῖν τῆς νυκτὸς τὴν ἡμέραν, κατὰ τοῦτο δὲ ἐλάττω.

36 ⟨ιε.⟩ Περὶ βλεπόντων καὶ ἰσοδυναμούντων

Πάλιν δὲ ἰσοδυναμεῖν φασιν ἀλλήλοις μέρη τὰ τοῦ αὐτοῦ καὶ ὁποτέρου τῶν τροπικῶν σημείων τὸ ἴσον ἀφεστῶτα, διὰ τὸ καθ' ἑκάτερον αὐτῶν τοῦ ἡλίου γινομένου τάς τε ἡμέρας ταῖς ἡμέραις καὶ τὰς νύκτας ταῖς νυξὶ καὶ τὰ διαστήματα τῶν οἰκείων ὡρῶν ἰσοχρόνως[1] ἀποτελεῖσθαι. ταῦτα δὲ καὶ βλέπειν ἄλληλα λέγεται διά τε τὰ προειρημένα καὶ ἐπειδήπερ ἑκάτερον αὐτῶν ἔκ τε τῶν αὐτῶν μερῶν τοῦ ὁρίζοντος ἀνατέλλει καὶ εἰς τὰ αὐτὰ καταδύνει.

⟨ι϶.⟩ Περὶ ἀσυνδέτων

Ἀσύνδετα δὲ καὶ ἀπηλλοτριωμένα καλεῖται τμήματα ὅσα μηδένα λόγον ἁπλῶς ἔχει πρὸς ἄλληλα τῶν προκατειλεγμένων οἰκειώσεων. ταῦτα δέ ἐστιν ἃ μήτε τῶν προσταττόντων ἢ ἀκουόντων τυγχάνει μήτε τῶν βλεπόντων ἢ ἰσοδυναμούντων, ἔτι καὶ τῶν ἐκκειμένων τεττάρων σχηματισμῶν,

[1] ἰσοχρόνως VMAE, -ων P, -ος D, -α Proc., -ια NLCam.

---

[1] In the summer hemisphere are the signs Aries, Taurus, Gemini, Cancer, Leo, and Virgo; Libra, Scorpio, Sagittarius,

hemisphere [1] are called " commanding " and those in the winter hemisphere " obedient," because the sun makes the day longer than the night when he is in the summer hemisphere, and shorter in the winter.

15. *Of Signs which Behold each other and Signs of Equal Power.*

Again they say that the parts which are equally removed from the same tropical sign, whichever it may be, are of equal power,[2] because when the sun comes into either of them the days are equal to the days, the nights to the nights, and the lengths of their own hours [3] are the same. These also are said to "behold" one another both for the reasons stated and because each of the pair rises from the same part of the horizon and sets in the same part.

16. *Of Disjunct Signs.*

" Disjunct " and " alien " are the names applied to those divisions of the zodiac which have none whatever of the aforesaid familiarities with one another. These are the ones which belong neither to the class of commanding or obeying, beholding or of equal power, and furthermore they are found

---

Capricorn, Aquarius, and Pisces are in the winter hemisphere; see the diagram in Bouché-Leclercq, p. 161.

[2] These pairs are Gemini-Leo, Taurus-Virgo, Aries-Libra, Pisces-Scorpio, and Aquarius-Sagittarius; Cancer and Capricorn are left without mates (ἄζυγα).

[3] " Their own hours " are " ordinary " or " civil " hours (καιρικαὶ ὧραι; cf. p. 286, n. 3), which are always one-twelfth of the day (sunrise to sunset) or night (sunset to sunrise). Of course, they are equal if the days and nights are equal.

τοῦ τε διαμέτρου καὶ τοῦ τριγώνου καὶ τοῦ τετραγώνου καὶ τοῦ ἑξαγώνου κατὰ τὸ παντελὲς ἀμέτοχα καταλαμβανόμενα, καὶ ἤτοι δι' ἑνὸς ἢ διὰ πέντε γινόμενα δωδεκατημορίων, ἐπειδήπερ τὰ μὲν δι' ἑνὸς ἀπέστραπται ὥσπερ ἀλλήλων καὶ δύο αὐτὰ ὄντα ἑνὸς περιέχει γωνίαν, τὰ δὲ διὰ πέντε εἰς ἄνισα διαιρεῖ τὸν ὅλον κύκλον, τῶν ἄλλων σχηματισμῶν εἰς ἴσα τὴν τῆς περιμέτρου διαίρεσιν ποιουμένων.

⟨ιζ.⟩ Περὶ οἴκων ἑκάστου ἀστέρος[1]

Συνοικειοῦνται δὲ καὶ οἱ πλάνητες τοῖς τοῦ ζωδιακοῦ μέρεσι κατά τε τοὺς καλουμένους οἴκους καὶ τρίγωνα καὶ ὑψώματα καὶ ὅρια καὶ τὰ τοιαῦτα. καὶ τὸ μὲν τῶν οἴκων τοιαύτην ἔχει φύσιν. ἐπειδὴ γὰρ τῶν ιβ' ζῳδίων τὰ βορειότατα καὶ συνεγγίζοντα μᾶλλον τῶν ἄλλων τοῦ κατὰ κορυφὴν ἡμῶν τόπου, θερμασίας τε καὶ ἀλέας διὰ τοῦτο περιποιητικὰ τυγχάνοντα, τό τε τοῦ Καρκίνου ἐστὶ καὶ τὸ τοῦ Λέοντος, τὰ δύο ταῦτα τοῖς μεγίστοις καὶ κυριωτάτοις, τουτέστι τοῖς φωσίν, ἀπένειμαν οἴκους, τὸ μὲν τοῦ Λέοντος ἀρρενικὸν ὂν τῷ ἡλίῳ, τὸ δὲ τοῦ Καρκίνου θηλυκὸν τῇ σελήνῃ. καὶ ἀκολούθως τὸ μὲν ἀπὸ τοῦ Λέοντος μέχρις Αἰγόκερω ἡμικύκλιον ἡλιακὸν ὑπέθεντο, τὸ δὲ ἀπὸ Ὑδροχόου μέχρι Καρκίνου σεληνιακόν, ὅπως ἐν ἑκατέρῳ τῶν ἡμικυκλίων ἓν ζῴδιον καθ' ἕκαστον τῶν πέντε[2] ἀστέρων οἰκείως ἀπονεμηθῇ, τὸ μὲν πρὸς ἥλιον, τὸ δὲ πρὸς

---

[1] Titulum sic habent VADEProc.; om. ἑκάστου ἀστέρος alii Cam.
[2] πέντε om. PLNCam.

to be entirely without share in the four aforesaid aspects, opposition, trine, quartile, and sextile, and are either one or five signs apart; for those which are one sign apart are as it were averted from one another and, though they are two, bound the angle of one, and those that are five signs apart divide the whole circle into unequal parts, while the other aspects make an equal division of the perimeter.

17. *Of the Houses of the Several Planets.*

The planets also have familiarity with the parts of the zodiac, through what are called their houses, triangles, exaltations, terms,[1] and the like. The system of houses is of the following nature. Since of the twelve signs the most northern, which are closer than the others to our zenith and therefore most productive of heat and of warmth are Cancer and Leo, they assigned these to the greatest and most powerful heavenly bodies, that is, to the luminaries, as houses, Leo, which is masculine, to the sun and Cancer, feminine, to the moon. In keeping with this they assumed the semicircle from Leo to Capricorn to be solar and that from Aquarius to Cancer to be lunar, so that in each of the semicircles one sign might be assigned to each of the five planets as its own, one bearing aspect to the

[1] ὅρια, *termini*, literally "boundaries"; see c. 20. The triangles or triplicities are treated in c. 18 and the exaltations in c. 19.

σελήνην ἐσχηματισμένον, ἀκολούθως ταῖς τῶν κινήσεων αὐτῶν σφαίραις καὶ ταῖς τῶν φύσεων ἰδιοτροπίαις. τῷ μὲν γὰρ τοῦ Κρόνου ψυκτικῷ μᾶλλον ὄντι τὴν φύσιν κατ' ἐναντιότητα τοῦ θερμοῦ καὶ τὴν ἀνωτάτω καὶ μακρὰν τῶν φωτῶν ἔχοντι ζώνην ἐδόθη τὰ διάμετρα ζῴδια τοῦ τε Καρκίνου καὶ τοῦ Λέοντος, ὅ τε Αἰγόκερως καὶ Ὑδροχόος, μετὰ τοῦ καὶ ταῦτα τὰ δωδεκατημόρια ψυχρὰ καὶ χειμερινὰ τυγχάνειν, καὶ ἔτι τὸν κατὰ διάμετρον συσχηματισμὸν ἀσύμφωνον πρὸς ἀγαθοποιΐαν εἶναι. τῷ δὲ τοῦ Διὸς ὄντι εὐκράτῳ καὶ ὑπὸ τὴν τοῦ Κρόνου σφαῖραν ἐδόθη τὰ ἐχόμενα δύο τῶν προκειμένων πνευματικὰ ὄντα καὶ γόνιμα, ὅ τε Τοξότης καὶ οἱ Ἰχθῦς, κατὰ τριγωνικὴν πρὸς τὰ φῶτα διάστασιν, ἥτις ἐστὶ συμφώνου καὶ ἀγαθοποιοῦ σχηματισμοῦ. ἐφεξῆς δὲ τῷ τοῦ Ἄρεως ξηραντικῷ μᾶλλον ὄντι τὴν φύσιν καὶ ὑπὸ τὴν τοῦ Διὸς ἔχοντι τὴν σφαῖραν τὰ ἐχόμενα πάλιν ἐκείνων ἐδόθη δωδεκατημόρια τὴν ὁμοίαν ἔχοντα φύσιν, ὅ τε Σκορπίος καὶ ὁ Κριός, ἀκολούθως τῇ φθαρτικῇ καὶ ἀσυμφώνῳ[1] ποιότητι, τὴν τετράγωνον πρὸς τὰ φῶτα ποιοῦντα διάστασιν. τῷ δὲ τῆς Ἀφροδίτης εὐκράτῳ τε ὄντι καὶ ὑπὸ τὸν τοῦ Ἄρεως τὰ ἐχόμενα ἐδόθη δύο ζῴδια γονιμώτατα ὄντα, αἵ τε Χηλαὶ καὶ ὁ Ταῦρος, τηροῦντα τὴν συμφωνίαν τῆς ἑξαγώνου

[1] ἀσυμφώνῳ VPLMADE, ἀκολούθως N, om. Cam. (locum * notaus).

sun and the other to the moon, consistently with the spheres of their motion [1] and the peculiarities of their natures.[2] For to Saturn, in whose nature cold prevails, as opposed to heat, and which occupies the orbit highest and farthest from the luminaries, were assigned the signs opposite Cancer and Leo, namely Capricorn and Aquarius,[3] with the additional reason that these signs are cold and wintry, and further that their diametrical aspect is not consistent with beneficence. To Jupiter, which is moderate and below Saturn's sphere, were assigned the two signs next to the foregoing, windy and fecund, Sagittarius and Pisces, in triangular aspect [4] to the luminaries, which is a harmonious and beneficent configuration. Next, to Mars, which is dry in nature and occupies a sphere under that of Jupiter, there were assigned again the two signs, contiguous to the former, Scorpio and Aries, having a similar nature, and, agreeably to Mars' destructive and inharmonious quality, in quartile aspect [5] to the luminaries. To Venus, which is temperate and beneath Mars, were given the next two signs, which are extremely fertile, Libra and Taurus. These

---

[1] That is, they are in the order of their distance from the centre of the universe, the earth.

[2] *Cf.* c. 4.

[3] Capricorn opposes Cancer and Aquarius Leo.

[4] Sagittarius is triangular to Leo, the sun's house, and Pisces to Cancer. *Cf.* c. 13 on the " harmonious " nature of the trine and sextile, in contrast with quartile and opposition.

[5] Aries is quartile to the moon's house, Cancer, and Scorpio to the sun's house, Leo. They are, however, also triangular to these houses, Aries to Leo and Scorpio to Cancer.

διαστάσεως, καὶ ἐπειδήπερ οὐ πλέον δύο δωδεκατημορίων ὁ ἀστὴρ οὗτος ἐφ' ἑκάτερον τὸ πλεῖστον ἀφίσταται τοῦ ἡλίου· ἐπὶ τέλει δὲ τῷ τοῦ Ἑρμοῦ μηδέποτε πλέον ἑνὸς δωδεκατημορίου τὴν ἀπὸ τοῦ ἡλίου ἐφ' ἑκάτερα διάστασιν ποιουμένῳ καὶ ὑπὸ μὲν τοὺς ἄλλους ὄντι, σύνεγγυς δὲ μᾶλλόν πως ἀμφοτέρων τῶν φώτων, τὰ λοιπὰ καὶ συνεχῆ τοῖς ἐκείνων οἴκοις ἐδόθη δύο δωδεκατημόρια τό τε τῶν Διδύμων καὶ τὸ τῆς Παρθένου.

39 ⟨ιη.⟩ Περὶ τριγώνων

Ἡ δὲ πρὸς τὰ τρίγωνα συνοικείωσις τοιαύτη τις οὖσα τυγχάνει. ἐπειδὴ γὰρ τὸ τρίγωνον καὶ ἰσόπλευρον σχῆμα συμφωνότατόν ἐστιν ἑαυτῷ καὶ ὁ ζῳδιακὸς ὑπὸ τριῶν κύκλων ὁρίζεται, τοῦ τε ἰσημερινοῦ καὶ τῶν δύο τροπικῶν, διαιρεῖται δὲ τὰ ιβ' αὐτοῦ μέρη εἰς τρίγωνα ἰσόπλευρα δ,[1] τὸ μὲν πρῶτον, ὅ[2] ἐστι διά τε τοῦ Κριοῦ καὶ τοῦ Λέοντος καὶ τοῦ Τοξότου, ἐκ τριῶν ἀρρενικῶν ζῳδίων συγκείμενον, καὶ οἴκους ἔχον ἡλίου τε καὶ Ἄρεως καὶ Διός, ἐδόθη τῷ ἡλίῳ καὶ Διὶ παρὰ τὴν αἵρεσιν τὴν ἡλιακὴν ὄντος[3] τοῦ Ἄρεως. λαμβάνει δὲ αὐτοῦ τὴν πρώτην οἰκοδεσποτίαν ἡμέρας μὲν ὁ ἥλιος, νυκτὸς δὲ ὁ τοῦ Διός, καί ἐστιν ὁ μὲν Κριὸς μᾶλλον πρὸς τῷ ἰσημερινῷ, ὁ δὲ Λέων μᾶλλον

[1] ὧν post δ' add NCam.
[2] ὅ VAD; om. cett. Cam.
[3] ὄντος libri Cam.¹; ὑπάρχοντος Proc.; ἐξωσθέντος Cam.²

TETRABIBLOS I. 17-18

preserve the harmony of the sextile aspect;[1] another reason is that this planet at most is never more than two signs removed from the sun in either direction. Finally, there were given to Mercury, which never is farther removed from the sun than one sign in either direction and is beneath the others and closer in a way to both of the luminaries, the remaining signs, Gemini and Virgo, which are next to the houses of the luminaries.

18. *Of the Triangles.*

The familiarity by triangles is as follows. Inasmuch as the triangular and equilateral form is most harmonious with itself,[2] the zodiac also is bounded by three circles, the equinoctial and the two tropics, and its twelve parts are divided into four equilateral triangles. The first of these, which passes through Aries, Leo, and Sagittarius, is composed of three masculine signs and includes the houses of the sun, of Mars, and of Jupiter. This triangle was assigned to the sun and Jupiter, since Mars is not of the solar sect.[3] The sun assumes first governance of it by day and Jupiter by night. Also, Aries is close to the equinoctial circle, Leo to the summer solstice and

---

[1] Taurus is sextile to Cancer and Libra to Leo.

[2] This statement savours of Neo-Pythagoreanism; *cf.*, for example, the demonstration by Nicomachus (*Introduction to Arithmetic*, ii. 7. 4) of the proposition that the triangle is the most elementary plane figure, which is also Platonic doctrine (*Timaeus* 53C ff.); note likewise the much repeated statement that the number 3 is the first plane surface; Theon of Smyrna, p. 46, 14 (ed. Hiller), Macrobius, *Somnium Scipionis*, i. 6. 22, etc.

[3] See c. 7.

πρὸς τῷ θερινῷ, ὁ δὲ Τοξότης πρὸς τῷ χειμερινῷ. γίνεται δὲ καὶ προηγουμένως μὲν τοῦτο τὸ τρίγωνον βόρειον, διὰ τὴν τοῦ Διὸς συνοικοδεσποτίαν, ἐπειδήπερ οὗτος γόνιμός τέ ἐστι καὶ πνευματώδης οἰκείως τοῖς ἀπὸ τῶν ἄρκτων ἀνέμοις. διὰ δὲ τὸν τοῦ Ἄρεως οἶκον λαμβάνει μῖξιν τοῦ λιβὸς καὶ συνίσταται[1] βορρολιβυκόν, ἐπειδήπερ ὁ τοῦ Ἄρεως τοιούτων ἐστὶ πνευμάτων ποιητικός, διά τε τὴν τῆς σελήνης αἵρεσιν καὶ τὸ τῶν δυσμῶν τεθηλυσμένον.

Τό τε δεύτερον τρίγωνον, ὅ ἐστι διά τε τοῦ Ταύρου καὶ Παρθένου καὶ Αἰγόκερω, συγκείμενον ἐκ τριῶν θηλυκῶν, ἀκολούθως ἐδόθη σελήνῃ τε καὶ Ἀφροδίτῃ, οἰκοδεσποτούσης αὐτοῦ[2] νυκτὸς μὲν τῆς σελήνης, ἡμέρας δὲ τοῦ τῆς Ἀφροδίτης. καὶ ἔστιν ὁ μὲν Ταῦρος πρὸς τῷ θερινῷ κύκλῳ μᾶλλον, ἡ δὲ Παρθένος πρὸς τῷ ἰσημερινῷ, ὁ δὲ Αἰγόκερως πρὸς τῷ χειμερινῷ. γίνεται δὲ καὶ τοῦτο τὸ τρίγωνον προηγουμένως μὲν νότιον διὰ τὴν τῆς Ἀφροδίτης οἰκοδεσποτίαν, ἐπειδήπερ ὁ ἀστὴρ οὗτος τῶν ὁμοίων ἐστὶ πνευμάτων διὰ τὸ θερμὸν καὶ ἔνικμον τῆς δυνάμεως ποιητικός. προσλαβὼν δὲ μῖξιν ἀπηλιώτου διὰ τὸ τὸν τοῦ Κρόνου οἶκον ἐν αὐτῷ τυγχάνειν τὸν Αἰγόκερων συνίσταται καὶ αὐτὸ νοταπηλιωτικὸν κατ' ἀντίθεσιν τοῦ πρώτου, ἐπειδήπερ καὶ ὁ τοῦ Κρόνου τοιούτων ἐστὶ πνευμάτων ποιητικὸς οἰκειούμενος καὶ αὐτὸς ταῖς ἀνατολαῖς διὰ τὴν πρὸς τὸν ἥλιον αἵρεσιν.

[1] συνίσταται] γίνεται VDProc.
[2] αὐτοῦ PLMA, αὐτῶν VDNECam.

Sagittarius to the winter solstice. This triangle is preëminently northern because of Jupiter's share in its government, since Jupiter is fecund and windy,[1] similarly to the winds from the north. However, because of the house of Mars it suffers an admixture of the south-west wind [2] and is constituted *Borrolibycon*, because Mars causes such winds and also because of the sect of the moon and the feminine quality of the occident.[3]

The second triangle, which is the one drawn through Taurus, Virgo, and Capricorn, is composed of three feminine signs, and consequently was assigned to the moon and Venus; the moon governs it by night and Venus by day. Taurus lies toward the summer tropic, Virgo toward the equinox, and Capricorn toward the winter tropic. This triangle is made preëminently southern because of the dominance of Venus, since this star through the heat and moisture of its power produces similar winds; but as it receives an admixture of Apeliotes because the house of Saturn, Capricornus, is included within it, it is constituted *Notapeliotes* [4] in contrast to the first triangle, since Saturn produces winds of this kind and is related to the east through sharing in the sect of the sun.

[1] *Cf.* c. 4.   [2] *Africus, Lips.*
[3] In c. 10 the west is characterized as moist, which is regarded as a feminine quality (*cf.* c. 6).
[4] *I.e.* south-east.

PTOLEMY

Τὸ δὲ τρίτον τρίγωνον ὅ ἐστι[1] τὸ διά τε Διδύμων καὶ Χηλῶν καὶ Ὑδροχόου, ἐκ τριῶν ἀρρενικῶν ζωδίων συγκείμενον, καὶ πρὸς μὲν τὸν τοῦ Ἄρεως μηδένα λόγον ἔχον, πρὸς δὲ τὸν τοῦ Κρόνου καὶ τὸν τοῦ Ἑρμοῦ διὰ τοὺς οἴκους, τούτοις ἀπενεμήθη,[2] πάλιν οἰκοδεσποτοῦντος ἡμέρας μὲν τοῦ Κρόνου διὰ τὴν αἵρεσιν, νυκτὸς δὲ τοῦ Ἑρμοῦ. καὶ ἔστι τὸ μὲν τῶν Διδύμων δωδεκατημόριον πρὸς τῷ θερινῷ, τὸ δὲ τῶν Χηλῶν πρὸς τῷ ἰσημερινῷ, τὸ δὲ τοῦ Ὑδροχόου πρὸς τῷ χειμερινῷ. συνίσταται δὲ καὶ τοῦτο τὸ τρίγωνον προηγουμένως μὲν ἀπηλιωτικὸν διὰ τὸν τοῦ Κρόνου· κατὰ δὲ τὴν μῖξιν βορραπηλιωτικὸν διὰ τὴν τοῦ Διὸς αἵρεσιν τῷ τοῦ Κρόνου πρὸς τὸ τὸν ἡμερινὸν λόγον συνοικειοῦσθαι.

41 Τὸ δὲ τέταρτον τρίγωνον, ὅ ἐστι διά τε Καρκίνου καὶ Σκορπίου καὶ Ἰχθύων, κατελείφθη μὲν[3] λοιπῷ ὄντι τῷ τοῦ Ἄρεως καὶ λόγον ἔχοντι πρὸς αὐτὸ διὰ τὸν οἶκον τὸν Σκορπίον· συνοικοδεσποτοῦσι δὲ αὐτῷ διά τε τὴν αἵρεσιν καὶ τὸ θηλυκὸν τῶν ζωδίων νυκτὸς μὲν ἡ σελήνη, ἡμέρας δὲ ὁ τῆς Ἀφροδίτης, καὶ ἔστιν ὁ μὲν Καρκίνος πρὸς τῷ θερινῷ κύκλῳ, ὁ δὲ Σκορπίος πρὸς τῷ χειμερινῷ μᾶλλον, οἱ δὲ Ἰχθῦς πρὸς τῷ ἰσημερινῷ. καὶ τοῦτο δὲ τὸ τρίγωνον συνίσταται προηγουμένως μὲν λιβυκὸν διὰ τὴν τοῦ Ἄρεως καὶ τῆς σελήνης οἰκοδεσποτίαν, κατὰ μῖξιν δὲ νοτολιβυκὸν διὰ τὴν τῆς Ἀφροδίτης οἰκοδεσποτίαν.

[1] τρίτον δὲ τρίγωνόν ἐστι PLNCam.
[2] ἀπενεμήθη VPMADE, om. L, ἀπονεμηθέν NCam.

TETRABIBLOS I. 18

The third triangle is the one drawn through Gemini, Libra, and Aquarius, composed of three masculine signs, and having no relation to Mars but rather to Saturn and Mercury because of their houses. It was assigned in turn to these, with Saturn governing during the day on account of his sect and Mercury by night. The sign of Gemini lies toward the summer tropic, Libra toward the equinox, and Aquarius toward the winter tropic. This triangle also is primarily of eastern constitution, because of Saturn, but by admixture north-eastern, because the sect of Jupiter has familiarity with Saturn, inasmuch as it is diurnal.

The fourth triangle, which is the one drawn through Cancer, Scorpio, and Pisces, was left to the only remaining planet, Mars, which is related to it through his house, Scorpio; and along with him, on account of the sect and the femininity of the signs, the moon by night and Venus by day are co-rulers. Cancer is near the summer circle, Scorpio lies close to the winter one, and Pisces to the equinox. This triangle is constituted preëminently western, because it is dominated by Mars and the moon; but by admixture it becomes south-western through the domination of Venus.

---

[3] μέν VD, om. PL, μόνῳ MNAECam.

PTOLEMY

⟨ιθ.⟩ Περὶ ὑψωμάτων

Τὰ δὲ καλούμενα τῶν πλανωμένων ὑψώματα λόγον ἔχει τοιόνδε. ἐπειδὴ γὰρ ὁ ἥλιος ἐν μὲν τῷ Κριῷ γενόμενος τὴν εἰς τὸ ὑψηλὸν καὶ βόρειον ἡμικύκλιον μετάβασιν ποιεῖται, ἐν δὲ ταῖς Χηλαῖς τὴν εἰς τὸ ταπεινὸν καὶ νότιον, εἰκότως[1] τὸν μὲν Κριὸν ὡς ὕψωμα ἀνατεθήκασιν αὐτῷ καθ' ὃν ἄρχεται καὶ τὸ τῆς ἡμέρας μέγεθος καὶ τὸ τῆς φύσεως αὐτοῦ θερμαντικὸν αὔξεσθαι, τὰς δὲ Χηλὰς ὡς ταπείνωμα διὰ τὰ ἐναντία.

Ὁ δὲ τοῦ Κρόνου πάλιν ἵνα πρὸς τὸν ἥλιον διάμετρον στάσιν ἔχῃ, ὥσπερ καὶ ἐπὶ τῶν οἴκων, τὸν μὲν Ζυγὸν ἀντικειμένως ὡς ὕψωμα ἔλαβε, τὸν δὲ Κριὸν ὡς ταπείνωμα. ὅπου γὰρ τὸ θερμὸν αὔξεται, μειοῦται ἐκεῖ τὸ ψυχρόν, καὶ ὅπου ἐκεῖνο μειοῦται, τὸ ψυχρὸν αὔξεται.[2] πάλιν ἐπειδὴ[3] ἐν τῷ ὑψώματι τοῦ ἡλίου ἐν τῷ Κριῷ συνοδεύουσα ἡ σελήνη πρώτην ποιεῖται φάσιν καὶ ἀρχὴν τῆς τοῦ φωτὸς αὐξήσεως καὶ ὡσπερεὶ ὑψώσεως ἐν τῷ τοῦ ἰδίου τριγώνου πρώτῳ ζῳδίῳ τῷ Ταύρῳ, τοῦτο μὲν αὐτῆς ὕψωμα ἐκλήθη, τὸ δὲ διάμετρον τὸ τοῦ Σκορπίου ταπείνωμα.

Μετὰ ταῦτα δὲ ὁ μὲν τοῦ Διὸς τῶν βορείων καὶ τῶν γονίμων πνευμάτων ἀποτελεστικὸς ὢν ἐν Καρκίνῳ μάλιστα βορειότατος γινόμενος αὔξεται

---

[1] εἰκότως VMADE, οἰκείως (οἰκίως) PLNCam.
[2] καὶ ὅπου . . αὔξεται NMAECam. (αὐξάνει NECam.); κ. ὅπου τὸ ψυχρὸν αὔξεται, ἐκεῖ ἐκμειοῦται τὸ θερμόν VD; κ. ὅπου ἐκείνῳ μειοῦτε, τὸ θερμὸν αὔξεται P.

TETRABIBLOS I. 19

19. *Of Exaltations.*

The so-called exaltations [1] of the planets have the following explanation. Since the sun, when he is in Aries, is making his transition to the northern and higher semicircle, and in Libra is passing into the southern and lower one, they have fittingly assigned Aries to him as his exaltation, since there the length of the day and the heating power of his nature begin to increase, and Libra as his depression for the opposite reasons.

Saturn again, in order to have a position opposite to the sun, as also in the matter of their houses,[2] took, contrariwise, Libra as his exaltation and Aries as his depression. For where heat increases there cold diminishes, and where the former diminishes cold on the contrary increases. And since the moon, coming to conjunction in the exaltation of the sun, in Aries, shows her first phase and begins to increase her light and, as it were, her height, in the first sign of her own triangle, Taurus, this was called her exaltation, and the diametrically opposite sign, Scorpio, her depression.

Then Jupiter, which produces the fecund north winds, reaches farthest north in Cancer and brings

---

[1] These have nothing to do with aphelion or perihelion; the planets are exalted or depressed in power in these positions: Boll-Bezold-Gundel, p. 59; Bouché-Leclercq pp. 192-199.
[2] *Cf.* c. 17; the houses of Saturn are the signs in opposition to the houses of the sun and moon.

---

[3] πάλιν ἐπειδὴ VADE; πάλιν ἐπὶ δεῖ P; πάλιν. ἐπεὶ δὲ libri alii Cam.

PTOLEMY

πάλιν καὶ πληροῖ τὴν ἰδίαν δύναμιν· ὅθεν τοῦτο μὲν τὸ δωδεκατημόριον ὕψωμα πεποιήκασιν αὐτοῦ, τὸν δὲ Αἰγόκερων ταπείνωμα.

Ὁ δὲ τοῦ Ἄρεως φύσει καυσώδης ὢν καὶ μᾶλλον ἐν Αἰγόκερῳ διὰ τὸ νοτιώτατον γίνεσθαι καυστικώτερος γινόμενος, καὶ αὐτὸς μὲν εἰκότως ἔλαβεν ὕψωμα κατ' ἀντίθεσιν τῷ τοῦ Διὸς τὸν Αἰγόκερων, ταπείνωμα δὲ τὸν Καρκίνον.

Πάλιν ὁ μὲν [1] τῆς Ἀφροδίτης ὑγραντικὸς ὢν φύσει καὶ μᾶλλον ἐν τοῖς Ἰχθύσι, ἐν οἷς ἡ τοῦ ὑγροῦ ἔαρος ἀρχὴ προσημαίνεται, καὶ αὐτὸς αὐξάνων τὴν οἰκείαν δύναμιν, τὸ μὲν ὕψωμα ἔσχεν ἐν τοῖς Ἰχθύσι, τὸ δὲ ταπείνωμα ἐν τῇ Παρθένῳ.

Ὁ δὲ τοῦ Ἑρμοῦ τὸ ἐναντίον μᾶλλον [2] ὑπόξηρος ὢν εἰκότως καὶ κατὰ τὸ ἀντικείμενον ἐν μὲν τῇ Παρθένῳ, καθ' ἣν τὸ ξηρὸν μετόπωρον προσημαίνεται,[3] καὶ αὐτὸς ὥσπερ ὑψοῦται, κατὰ δὲ τοὺς Ἰχθῦς ταπεινοῦται.

43 ⟨κ.⟩ Περὶ ὁρίων διαθέσεως[4]

Περὶ δὲ τῶν ὁρίων δισσοὶ μάλιστα φέρονται τρόποι, καὶ ὁ μέν ἐστιν Αἰγυπτιακός, ὁ πρὸς τὰς τῶν οἴκων ὡς ἐπὶ πᾶν κυρίας· ὁ δὲ Χαλδαϊκός, ὁ πρὸς τὰς τῶν τριγώνων οἰκοδεσποτίας. ὁ μὲν οὖν Αἰγυπτιακὸς ὁ τῶν κοινῶς φερομένων ὁρίων οὐ πάνυ τοι σῴζει τὴν ἀκολουθίαν οὔτε τῆς τάξεως οὔτε τῆς καθ' ἕκαστον ποσότητος. πρῶτον μὲν γὰρ ἐπὶ τῆς

---

[1] πάλιν ὁ μὲν PLME ; πάλιν ὁ VAD ; πάλιν. ὁ μέντοι NCam.
[2] μᾶλλον VP (μᾶλον) AD, πάλιν MNECam., πάλιν ἢ μᾶλλον L.

his own power to fullness; they therefore made this sign his exaltation and Capricorn his depression.

Mars, which by nature is fiery and becomes all the more so in Capricorn because in it he is farthest south, naturally received Capricorn as his exaltation, in contrast to Jupiter, and Cancer as his depression.

Venus, however, as she is moist by nature and increases her own proper power all the more in Pisces, where the beginning of the moist spring is indicated, has her exaltation in Pisces and her depression in Virgo.

Mercury, on the contrary, since he is drier, by contrast naturally is exalted, as it were, in Virgo, in which the dry autumn is signified, and is depressed in Pisces.

20. *Of the Disposition of Terms.*

With regard to the terms two systems are most in circulation; the first is the Egyptian,[1] which is chiefly based on the government of the houses, and the second the Chaldaean, resting upon the government of the triplicities. Now the Egyptian system of the commonly accepted terms does not at all preserve the consistency either of order or of individual quantity. For in the first place, in the

---

[1] Probably the system of the mythical Nechepso and Petosiris; it is the system of Dorotheus of Sidon, Firmicus Maternus, and Paulus Alexandrinus. *Cf.* Bouché-Leclercq, pp. 206-210, who discusses Ptolemy's criticism of the Egyptian *termini*.

[3] προσημαίνεται NCam.; προσημαίνει VLMADE; προσημένη P.
[4] *Sic* VADEProc.; Π. τῶν ὁρίων NCam.; Π. ὁρίων PLM.

τάξεως πῆ μὲν τοῖς τῶν οἴκων κυρίοις τὰ πρωτεῖα δεδώκασιν, πῆ δὲ τοῖς τῶν τριγώνων· ἐνίοτε δὲ καὶ τοῖς τῶν ὑψωμάτων. ἐπεὶ παραδείγματος ἕνεκεν,[1] εἴ γε[2] τοῖς οἴκοις ἠκολουθήκασι, διὰ τί τῷ τοῦ Κρόνου εἰ τύχοι πρώτῳ δεδώκασιν ἐν Ζυγῷ καὶ οὐ τῷ τῆς Ἀφροδίτης, καὶ διὰ τί ἐν Κριῷ τῷ τοῦ Διὶ καὶ οὐ τῷ τοῦ Ἄρεως; εἴτε τοῖς τριγώνοις, διὰ τί τῷ τοῦ Ἑρμοῦ δεδώκασιν ἐν Αἰγόκερῳ καὶ οὐ τῷ τῆς Ἀφροδίτης; εἴτε καὶ τοῖς ὑψώμασι, διὰ τί τῷ τοῦ Ἄρεως ἐν Καρκίνῳ καὶ οὐ τῷ τοῦ Διός; εἴτε τοῖς τὰ πλεῖστα τούτων ἔχουσι, διὰ τί ἐν Ὑδροχόῳ τῷ τοῦ Ἑρμοῦ δεδώκασι, τρίγωνον ἔχοντι μόνον, καὶ οὐχὶ τῷ τοῦ Κρόνου· τούτου γὰρ καὶ οἶκός ἐστι καὶ τρίγωνον. ἢ διὰ τί ὅλως[3] ἐν Αἰγόκερῳ τῷ τοῦ Ἑρμοῦ πρώτῳ[4] δεδώκασι μηδένα λόγον ἔχοντι πρὸς τὸ ζῴδιον οἰκοδεσποτίας; καὶ ἐπὶ τῆς λοιπῆς διατάξεως[5] τὴν αὐτὴν ἀναλογίαν[6] ἄν τις εὕροι.

Δεύτερον δὲ καὶ ἡ ποσότης τῶν ὁρίων οὐδεμίαν ἀκολουθίαν ἔχουσα φαίνεται. ὁ γὰρ καθ' ἕνα ἕκαστον ἀστέρα ἐπισυναγόμενος ἐκ πάντων ἀριθμός, πρὸς ὃν φασιν αὐτῶν τὰ χρονικὰ ἐπιμερίζεσθαι, οὐδένα οἰκεῖον οὐδὲ εὐαπόδεκτον ἔχει λόγον.

---

[1] ἐπεὶ παραδείγματος ἕνεκεν VD; ἐπὶ παρ. δὲ ἕν. PL, ἐπὶ παρ. τοῦ (τό E) γε ἕν. ME, παραδείγματος δὲ ἕνεκεν NCam.
[2] εἴ γε ME, εἴτε VD, εἴπερ γάρ A, ὅτε PLNCam.
[3] ὅλως VMNDE, ὅλο P, ὅλου L, ὅλος ACam.
[4] πρώτῳ VMADE, -ον PLNCam.
[5] διατάξεως P (-ξαι-) L, δὲ τάξεως alii Cam.
[6] ἀναλογίαν libri, ἀνακολουθίαν Cam.

TETRABIBLOS I. 20

matter of order, they have sometimes assigned the first place to the lords of the houses and again to those of the triplicities, and sometimes also to the lords of the exaltations. For example, if it is true that they have followed the houses, why have they assigned precedence to Saturn, say, in Libra,[1] and not to Venus, and why to Jupiter in Aries and not to Mars? And if they follow the triplicities, why have they given Mercury, and not Venus,[2] first place in Capricorn? Or if it be exaltations, why give Mars, and not Jupiter, precedence in Cancer[3]; and if they have regard for the planets that have the greatest number of these qualifications, why have they given first place in Aquarius to Mercury, who has only his triplicity there, and not to Saturn, for it is both the house and the triplicity of Saturn? Or why have they given Mercury first place in Capricorn at all, since he has no relation of government to the sign? One would find the same kind of thing in the rest of the system.

Secondly, the number of the terms manifestly has no consistency; for the number derived for each planet from the addition of its terms in all the signs, in accordance with which they say the planets assign years of life,[4] furnishes no suitable or acceptable argument. But even if we rely upon the

[1] Libra is the solar house of Venus; Saturn's houses are Capricorn and Aquarius. Similarly Mars is at home in Aries, Jupiter's houses being Pisces and Sagittarius.

[2] *Cf.* c. 18; Venus and the moon govern the second triangle.   [3] *Cf.* c. 19; Mars' exaltation is in Capricorn.

[4] For the doctrine that the sum of the terms of each planet determines the life-time of those born under its influence, *cf.* Bouché-Leclercq, p. 408.

PTOLEMY

ἐὰν δὲ καὶ τούτῳ τῷ κατὰ τὴν ἐπισυναγωγὴν ἀριθμῷ πιστεύσωμεν, ὡς ἄντικρυς ὑπ' Αἰγυπτίων ὁμολογουμένῳ, πολλαχῶς μὲν καὶ ἄλλως τῆς κατὰ τὸ ζῴδιον ποσότητος ἐναλλασσομένης, ὁ αὐτὸς ἀριθμὸς ἂν συναγόμενος εὑρεθείη. καὶ ὃ πιθανολογεῖν δὲ καὶ σοφίζεσθαί τινες ἐπιχειροῦσι περὶ αὐτῶν, ὅτι κατὰ παντὸς κλίματος ἀναφορικὸν λόγον οἱ καθ' ἕκαστον ἀστέρα συσχηματιζόμενοί πως χρόνοι τὴν αὐτὴν ἐπισυνάγουσι ποσότητα, ψεῦδός[1] ἐστι. πρῶτον μὲν γὰρ ἀκολουθοῦσι[2] τῇ κοινῇ πραγματείᾳ καὶ τῇ πρὸς ὁμαλὰς ὑπεροχὰς τῶν ἀναφορῶν συνισταμένῃ, μὴ κατὰ μικρὸν ἐγγὺς οὔσῃ τῆς ἀληθείας· καθ' ἣν ἐπὶ τοῦ διὰ τῆς κάτω χώρας τῆς Αἰγύπτου παραλλήλου τὸ μὲν τῆς Παρθένου καὶ τῶν Χηλῶν δωδεκατημόριον ἐν λη' χρόνοις ἑκάτερον καὶ ἔτι τρίτῳ θέλουσιν ἀναφέρεσθαι, τὸ δὲ τοῦ Λέοντος καὶ τοῦ Σκορπίου ἑκάτερον ἐν λε', δεικνυμένου διὰ τῶν γραμμῶν ὅτι ταῦτα μὲν ἐν πλείοσι τῶν λε' χρόνων ἀναφέρεται, τὸ δὲ τῆς Παρθένου καὶ τὸ τῶν Χηλῶν ἐν ἐλάττοσιν· ἔπειτα καὶ οἱ τοῦτο ἐπιχειρήσαντες κατασκευάζειν οὐκέτι φαίνονται κατηκολουθηκότες οὐδ' οὕτω τῇ παρὰ τοῖς πλείστοις φερομένῃ ποσότητι τῶν ὁρίων, κατὰ[3] πολλὰ διηναγκασμένοι καταψεύσασθαι· καί που καὶ μορίοις μορίων ἐχρήσαντο, τοῦ σῶσαι τὸ προκείμενον αὐτοῖς ἕνεκεν, οὐδ' αὐτοῖς,[4] ὡς ἔφαμεν, ἀληθοῦς ἐχομένοις[5] σκοποῦ.

[1] ψεῦδος VMADEProc., ψευδές PLNCam.
[2] ἠκολουθήκασι NCam.
[3] κατὰ PL, καὶ τὰ VMDE, καίτοι NACam.

number derived from this summation, in accordance with the downright claim of the Egyptians, the sum would be found the same, even though the amounts, sign by sign, be frequently changed in various ways. And as for the specious and sophistic assertion [1] about them that some attempt to make, namely that the times assigned to each single planet by the schedule of ascensions in all the climes add up to this same sum, it is false. For, in the first place, they follow the common method, based upon evenly progressing increases in the ascensions, which is not even close to the truth. By this scheme they would have each of the signs Virgo and Libra, on the parallel which passes through lower Egypt, ascend in $38\frac{1}{3}$ times,[2] and Leo and Scorpio each in 35, although it is shown by the tables [3] that these latter ascend in more than 35 times and Virgo and Libra in less. Furthermore, those who have endeavoured to establish this theory even so do not seem to follow the usually accepted number of terms, and are compelled to make many false statements, and they have even made use of fractional parts of fractions in the effort to save their hypothesis, which, as we said, is itself not a true one.

[1] This perhaps means that the sum of the times of ascension of the two signs assigned as houses to each planet gave, according to the theory of these unnamed astrologers, the number of years of life which they assigned to those born under them; cf. Bouché-Leclercq, p. 209.

[2] A "time" is the period taken by one degree of the equator to rise above the horizon.

[3] In *Almagest*, ii. 8.

[4] αὐτοῖς VMDE, αὐτῆς APL, αὐτό NCam.

[5] ἐχομένοις VDE, -ης M, -ον NACam., ἔχομεν L, ἔχωμεν P.

PTOLEMY

Τὰ μέντοι φερόμενα παρὰ τοῖς πολλοῖς διὰ τὴν τῆς ἐπάνωθεν παραδόσεως ἀξιοπιστίαν τοῦτον ὑπόκειται τὸν τρόπον.[1]

ὅρια κατ' Αἰγυπτίους[2]

Κριοῦ			Ταύρου			Διδύμων		
♃	ς'	ς'	♀	η'	η'	☿	ς'	ς'
♀	ς'	ιβ'	☿	ς'	ιδ'	♃	ς'	ιβ'
☿	η'	κ'	♃	η'	κβ'	♀	ε'	ιζ'
♂	ε'	κε'	♄	ε'	κζ'	♂	ζ'	κδ'
♄	ε'	λ'	♂	γ'	λ	♄	ς'	λ'

Καρκίνου			Λέοντος			Παρθένου		
♂	ζ'	ζ'	♃	ς'	ς'	☿	ζ'	ζ'
♀	ς'	ιγ'	♀	ε'	ια'	♀	ι'	ιζ'
☿	ς'	ιθ'	♄	ζ'	ιη'	♃	δ'	κα'
♃	ζ'	κς'	☿	ς'	κδ'	♂	ζ'	κη'
♄	δ'	λ'	♂	ς'	λ	♄	β'	λ'

Ζυγοῦ			Σκορπίου			Τοξότου		
♄	ς'	ς'	♂	ζ'	ζ'	♃	ιβ'	ιβ'
☿	η'	ιδ'	♀	δ'	ια'	♀	ε'	ιζ'
♃	ζ'	κα'	☿	η'	ιθ'	☿	δ'	κα'
♀	ζ'	κη'	♃	ε'	κδ'	♄	ε'	κς'
♂	β'	λ'	♄	ς'	λ'	♂	δ'	λ'

Αἰγόκερω			Ὑδροχόου			Ἰχθύων		
☿	ζ'	ζ'	☿	ζ'	ζ'	♀	ιβ'	ιβ'
♃	ζ'	ιδ'	♀	ς'	ιγ'	♃	δ'	ις'
♀	η'	κβ'	♃	ζ'	κ'	☿	γ'	ιθ'
♄	δ'	κς'	♂	ε'	κε'	♂	θ'	κη'
♂	δ'	λ'	♄	ε'	λ	♄	β'	λ'

[1] Post hanc lineam add. VMPLADProc. haec aut similia: συνάγεται δὲ ἑκάστου αὐτῶν ὁ ἀριθμὸς οὕτως· Κρόνου μὲν μοῖραι νζ', Διὸς οθ', Ἄρεως ξς', Ἀφροδίτης πβ', Ἑρμοῦ ος'· γίνονται τξ'.

TETRABIBLOS I. 20

However, the terms most generally accepted on the authority of ancient tradition are given in the following fashion :—

Terms according to the Egyptians.[1]

Aries	♃ 6	♀ 6	☿ 8	♂ 5	♄ 5
Taurus	♀ 8	☿ 6	♃ 8	♄ 5	♂ 3
Gemini	☿ 6	♃ 6	♀ 5	♂ 7	♄ 6
Cancer	♂ 7	♀ 6	☿ 6	♃ 7	♄ 4
Leo	♃ 6	♀ 5	♄ 7	☿ 6	♂ 6
Virgo	☿ 7	♀ 10	♃ 4	♂ 7	♄ 2
Libra	♄ 6	☿ 8	♃ 7	♀ 7	♂ 2
Scorpio	♂ 7	♀ 4	☿ 8	♃ 5	♄ 6
Sagittarius	♃ 12	♀ 5	☿ 4	♄ 5	♂ 4
Capricornus	☿ 7	♃ 7	♀ 8	♄ 4	♂ 4
Aquarius	☿ 7	♀ 6	♃ 7	♂ 5	♄ 5
Pisces	♀ 12	♃ 4	☿ 3	♂ 9	♄ 2

[1] The Greek tables on p. 96 show also, within each sign, the cumulative totals up to 30°; these have been omitted in the translation. *Cf.* p. 107, n. 1, and for the symbols p. xxv.

---

[2] Tabulas codicis Vat. gr. 1453 (Procli Paraphrasin continentis) secutus sum, cum illis quae ab Camerario impressae sunt congruentes solis lineis 26 et 28 (sub Αἰγόκερῳ) exceptis ubi Cam. ♀ ζ' et ♂ ε' offert. Tabulae in PLMNAD inventae sunt; om. VE.

PTOLEMY

⟨κα.⟩ Κατὰ Χαλδαίους

Ὁ δὲ Χαλδαϊκὸς τρόπος ἁπλῆν μέν τινα ἔχει καὶ μᾶλλον πιθανήν, οὐχ οὕτω δὲ αὐταρκῆ[1] πρός τε[2] τὰς τῶν τριγώνων δεσποτίας ἀκολουθίαν[3] καὶ τὴν τῆς ποσότητος τάξιν, ὥστε μέντοι καὶ χωρὶς ἀναγραφῆς δύνασθαι ῥᾳδίως τινὰ[4] ἐπιβαλεῖν αὐταῖς. ἐν μὲν γὰρ τῷ πρώτῳ τριγώνῳ Κριῷ καὶ Λέοντι καὶ Τοξότῃ τὴν αὐτὴν ἔχοντι παρ' αὐτοῖς κατὰ ζῴδιον διαίρεσιν, πρῶτος μὲν λαμβάνει ὁ τοῦ τριγώνου κύριος, ὁ τοῦ Διός, εἶθ' ἑξῆς ὁ τοῦ ἐφεξῆς τριγώνου, λέγω δὴ τὸν τῆς Ἀφροδίτης, ἐφεξῆς δὲ ὁ τῶν Διδύμων,[5] ὅ τε τοῦ Κρόνου καὶ ὁ τοῦ Ἑρμοῦ· τελευταῖος δὲ ὁ τοῦ λοιποῦ τριγώνου κύριος, ὁ τοῦ Ἄρεως. ἐν δὲ τῷ δευτέρῳ τριγώνῳ Ταύρῳ καὶ Παρθένῳ καὶ Αἰγόκερῳ πάλιν τὴν αὐτὴν κατὰ ζῴδιον ἔχοντι διαίρεσιν ὁ μὲν τῆς Ἀφροδίτης πρῶτος, εἶθ' ὁ τοῦ Κρόνου, πάλιν καὶ ὁ τοῦ Ἑρμοῦ, μετὰ ταῦτα δὲ ὁ τοῦ Ἄρεως,

---

[1] τήν τε post αὐταρκῆ add. PNCam., τῆς τε L, om. VMDE, τὴν ἀκολουθίαν A.
[2] πρός τε VMADE, τε om. PLNCam.
[3] τὴν ἀκολουθίαν VMDE.
[4] τινὰ VMADE (post δύνασθαι ME): om. PLNCam.
[5] ὁ τῶν Διδύμων VPLDProc., οἱ τ. Δ. ME, ὁ τοῦ τρίτου NCam.

---

[1] This method, as Bouché-Leclercq remarks (p. 210), is less "optimistic" than the Egyptian or the Ptolemaic method, because it assigned to the maleficent planets a larger number of terms and more first places in the various signs.

[2] The *Paraphrase* of Proclus, by connecting the ὥστε

TETRABIBLOS I. 21

21. *According to the Chaldaeans.*

The Chaldaean method [1] involves a sequence, simple, to be sure, and more plausible, though not so self-sufficient with respect to the government of the triangles and the disposition of quantity, so that, nevertheless, one could easily understand them even without a diagram.[2] For in the first triplicity, Aries, Leo, and Sagittarius, which has with them the same division by signs as with the Egyptians, the lord of the triplicity, Jupiter,[3] is the first to receive terms, then the lord of the next triangle, Venus, next the lord of the triangle of Gemini, Saturn, and Mercury, and finally the lord of the remaining triplicity, Mars. In the second triplicity, Taurus, Virgo, and Capricorn, which again has the same division by signs, Venus is first, then Saturn, and again Mercury, after these Mars, and finally

clause solely with the expression οὐχ οὕτω δὲ αὐταρκῆ κ.τ.λ., interprets this sentence to mean that because of the lack of self-sufficiency mentioned one cannot readily understand the Chaldaean system without a diagram. Against this view two considerations are to be urged: (1) the Chaldaean system actually is simplicity itself compared with those of the Egyptians and of Ptolemy; (2) the adversative μέντοι ("nevertheless," "in spite of all this") and the intrusive καί have no meaning in Proclus' interpretation of the passage. The ὥστε clause is really dependent upon all that precedes, not merely a portion of it. The anonymous commentator (p. 41, ed. Wolf) agrees with the present interpretation. What Ptolemy misses in the Chaldaean system is the elaborate accompaniment of justifying reasons, dear to his heart even in a pseudo-science.

[3] The sun is the diurnal ruler of this triplicity (see c. 18), but no terms are assigned to the luminaries. Similarly the moon is disregarded in the second and fourth triangles.

τελευταῖος δὲ ὁ τοῦ Διός σχεδὸν δὲ καὶ ἐπὶ τῶν λοιπῶν δύο τριγώνων ἡ τάξις ἥδε συνορᾶται. τῶν μέντοι τοῦ αὐτοῦ τριγώνου δύο κυρίων, λέγω δὲ τοῦ τοῦ Κρόνου καὶ τοῦ τοῦ Ἑρμοῦ, τὸ πρωτεῖον τῆς κατὰ τὸ οἰκεῖον τάξεως ἡμέρας μὲν ὁ τοῦ Κρόνου λαμβάνει, νυκτὸς δὲ ὁ τοῦ Ἑρμοῦ. καὶ ἡ καθ' ἕκαστον δὲ ποσότης ἁπλῆ τις οὖσα τυγχάνει. ἵνα γὰρ καθ' ὑπόβασιν τῆς τῶν πρωτείων τάξεως καὶ ἡ ποσότης τῶν ἑκάστου ὁρίων μιᾷ μοίρᾳ λείπηται τῆς προτεταγμένης, τῷ μὲν πρώτῳ πάντοτε διδόασι μοίρας η', τῷ δὲ δευτέρῳ ζ', τῷ δὲ τρίτῳ ϛ', τῷ δὲ τετάρτῳ ε', τῷ δὲ τελευταίῳ δ', συμπληρουμένων οὕτω τῶν κατὰ τὸ ζῴδιον λ' μοιρῶν. συνάγονται δὲ καὶ ἐκ τούτων τοῦ μὲν Κρόνου μοῖραι ἡμέρας μὲν οη', νυκτὸς δὲ ξϛ'· τοῦ δὲ Διὸς οβ'· τοῦ δὲ Ἄρεως ξθ'· τῆς δὲ Ἀφροδίτης οε'· τοῦ δὲ Ἑρμοῦ ἡμέρας μὲν ξϛ', νυκτὸς δὲ οη'. γίνονται μοῖραι τξ'.

Τούτων μὲν οὖν τῶν ὁρίων ἀξιοπιστότερα, ὡς ἔφαμεν, τυγχάνει[1] τὰ κατὰ τὸν Αἰγυπτιακὸν τρόπον καὶ διὰ τὸ τὴν συναγωγὴν αὐτῶν παρὰ τοῖς Αἰγυπτίοις συγγραφεῦσιν ὡς χρησίμην ἀναγραφῆς ἠξιῶσθαι καὶ διὰ τὸ συμφωνεῖν αὐτοῖς ὡς ἐπὶ πᾶν τὰς μοίρας τῶν ὁρίων ταῖς κατατεταγμέναις ὑπ' αὐτῶν παραδειγματικαῖς γενέσεσιν. αὐτῶν μέντοι τούτων τῶν συγγραφέων μηδαμῇ τὴν σύνταξιν αὐτῶν μηδὲ τὸν ἀριθμὸν ἐμφανισάντων, ὕποπτον ἂν

---

[1] ὡς ἔφαμεν τυγχάνει VPLNAD, φαμεν τυγχάνειν ME, om. Cam.

TETRABIBLOS I. 21

Jupiter. This arrangement in general is observed also in the remaining two triplicities.[1] Of the two lords of the same triplicity, however, Saturn and Mercury, by day [2] Saturn takes the first place in the order of ownership, by night Mercury. The number assigned to each is also a simple matter. For in order that the number of terms of each planet may be less by one degree than the preceding, to correspond with the descending order in which first place is assigned, they always assign 8° to the first, 7° to the second, 6° to the third, 5° to the fourth, and 4° to the last; thus the 30° of a sign is made up. The sum of the number of degrees thus assigned to Saturn is 78 by day and 66 by night, to Jupiter 72, to Mars 69, to Venus 75, to Mercury 66 by day and 78 by night; the total is 360 degrees.

Now of these terms those which are constituted by the Egyptian method are, as we said, more worthy of credence, both because in the form in which they have been collected by the Egyptian writers they have for their utility been deemed worthy of record, and because for the most part the degrees of these terms are consistent with the nativities which have been recorded by them as examples. As these very writers, however, nowhere explain their arrangement or their number, their failure to agree in an account

---

[1] *I.e.* the order of the planets is always the same, but the leader (or pair of leaders, in the case of Saturn and Mercury) in one triangle is shifted to the last position when one comes to the next triangle. Hence, since the number of terms in each sign are also always 8, 7, 6, 5, 4, the Chaldaean system makes the assignment of terms exactly the same in the corresponding signs of each triangle.

[2] *I.e.* in a diurnal nativity.

εἰκότως καὶ εὐδιάβλητον αὐτῶν γένοιτο τὸ περὶ τὴν τάξιν ἀνομόλογον.[1] ἤδη μέντοι περιτετυχήκαμεν ἡμεῖς ἀντιγράφῳ παλαιῷ καὶ τὰ πολλὰ[2] διεφθαρμένῳ, περιέχοντι φυσικὸν καὶ σύμφωνον λόγον τῆς τάξεως καὶ τῆς ποσότητος αὐτῶν μετὰ τοῦ τάς τε τῶν προειρημένων[3] γενέσεων μοιρογραφίας καὶ τὸν τῶν συναγωγῶν ἀριθμὸν σύμφωνον εὑρίσκεσθαι τῇ τῶν παλαιῶν ἀναγραφῇ. τὸ δὲ κατὰ λέξιν τοῦ βιβλίου πάνυ μακρὸν ἦν καὶ μετὰ περιττῆς ἀποδείξεως, ἀδιάγνωστον[4] δὲ διὰ τὸ διεφθάρθαι,[5] καὶ μόλις αὐτὴν τὴν τοῦ καθ' ὅλου προαίρεσιν δυνάμενον ἡμῖν ὑποτυπῶσαι· καὶ ταῦτα συνεφοδιαζούσης καὶ τῆς αὐτῶν τῶν ὁρίων ἀναγραφῆς μᾶλλόν πως διὰ τὸ πρὸς τῷ τέλει τοῦ βιβλίου κατατετάχθαι διασεσωσμένης. ἔχει γοῦν ὁ τύπος τῆς ὅλης αὐτῶν 48 ἐπιβολῆς τὸν τρόπον τοῦτον· ἐπὶ μὲν γὰρ τῆς τάξεως τῆς καθ' ἕκαστον δωδεκατημόριον παραλαμβάνεται τά τε ὑψώματα καὶ τὰ τρίγωνα καὶ οἱ οἶκοι. καθ' ὅλου μὲν γὰρ ὁ μὲν β΄ τούτων ἔχων ἀστὴρ οἰκοδεσποτίας[6] ἐν τῷ αὐτῷ ζῳδίῳ προτάττεται, κἂν κακοποιὸς ᾖ· ὅπου δὲ τοῦτο οὐ συμβαίνει οἱ μὲν κακοποιοὶ πάντοτε ἔσχατοι τάττονται, πρῶτοι δὲ οἱ τοῦ ὑψώματος κύριοι, εἶτα οἱ τοῦ τριγώνου, εἶτα οἱ τοῦ οἴκου ἀκολούθως

---

[1] ἀνομόλογον VPLD, ἀνομολόγητον MAE, ἀνωμολόγητον N Cam.
[2] καὶ τὰ πολλὰ VMLAD, κατὰ πολλὰ PNECam.
[3] προειρημένων ME; προγενομένων PLNCam. (προ- P, -γιν- L); om. A; τῶν γενέσεων προειρημένας μοιρ. VD. Ll. 6-14 om. Proc.
[4] ἀδιάγνωστον MAE, ἀδιάσωστον alii Cam.

TETRABIBLOS I. 21

of the system might well become an object of suspicion and a subject for criticism. Recently, however, we have come upon an ancient manuscript, much damaged, which contains a natural and consistent explanation of their order and number, and at the same time the degrees reported in the aforesaid nativities and the numbers given in the summations were found to agree with the tabulation of the ancients. The book was very lengthy in expression and excessive in demonstration, and its damaged state made it hard to read, so that I could barely gain an idea of its general purport; that too, in spite of the help offered by the tabulations of the terms, better preserved because they were placed at the end of the book.[1] At any rate the general scheme of assignment of the terms is as follows. For their arrangement within each sign, the exaltations, triplicities, and houses are taken into consideration. For, generally speaking, the star that has two rulerships of this sort in the same sign is placed first, even though it may be maleficent. But wherever this condition does not exist, the maleficent planets are always put last, and the lords of the exaltation first, the lords of the triplicity next, and then those of the

[1] Ptolemy's ancient manuscript, therefore, if it really existed, was probably in the form of a roll, for there the last pages would be protected. The first and last pages of a codex would be liable to damage, since they would be outermost.

---

[5] διὰ τὸ διεφθάρθαι VMADE, καὶ διεφθάρθαι PL, καὶ διεφθαρμένον NCam.
[6] οἰκοδεσποτ(ε)ίας VMADEProc.; om. alii.

τῇ ἐφεξῆς τάξει τῶν ζῳδίων, πάλιν δὲ ἐφεξῆς οἱ ἀνὰ δύο ἔχοντες οἰκοδεσποτίας προταττόμενοι τοῦ μίαν ἔχοντος ἐν τῷ αὐτῷ ζῳδίῳ. ὁ μέντοι Καρκίνος καὶ ὁ Λέων οἶκοι ὄντες ἡλίου καὶ σελήνης, ἐπεὶ οὐ δίδοται τοῖς φωσὶ ὅρια, ἀπονέμονται τοῖς κακοποιοῖς διὰ τὸ ἐν τῇ τάξει πλεονεκτεῖσθαι, ὁ μὲν Καρκίνος τῷ τοῦ Ἄρεως, ὁ δὲ Λέων τῷ τοῦ Κρόνου, ἐν οἷς καὶ ἡ τάξις αὐτοῖς ἡ οἰκεία φυλάττεται. ἐπὶ δὲ τῆς ποσότητος τῶν ὁρίων, ὡς μὲν μηδενὸς εὑρισκομένου κατὰ δύο τρόπους κυρίου ἤτοι ἐν αὐτῷ τῷ ζῳδίῳ ἢ καὶ ἐν τοῖς ἐφεξῆς μέχρι τεταρτημορίου, τοῖς μὲν ἀγαθοποιοῖς, τουτέστι τῷ τε τοῦ Διὸς καὶ τῷ τῆς Ἀφροδίτης ἑκάστῳ, δίδονται μοῖραι ζ', τοῖς δὲ κακοποιοῖς, τουτέστι τῷ τοῦ Κρόνου καὶ τῷ τοῦ Ἄρεως ἑκάστῳ μοῖραι ε', τῷ δὲ τοῦ Ἑρμοῦ ἐπικοίνῳ ὄντι μοῖραι ϛ', εἰς συμπλήρωσιν τῶν λ'.[1] ἐπεὶ δὲ ἔχουσί τινες ἀεὶ δύο λόγους, ὁ γὰρ τῆς Ἀφροδίτης μόνος γίνεται οἰκοδεσπότης τοῦ κατὰ τὸν Ταῦρον τριγώνου τῆς σελήνης εἰς τὰ ὅρια μὴ παραλαμβανομένης, προσδίδοται μὲν ἑκάστῳ τῶν οὕτως ἐχόντων ἄν τε ἐν αὐτῷ τῷ ζῳδίῳ ἄν τε ἐν τοῖς ἐφεξῆς μέχρι τεταρτημορίου μοῖρα μία, οἷς καὶ παρέκειντο στιγμαί. ἀφαιροῦνται δὲ αἱ προστιθέμεναι τῆς διπλῆς ἀπὸ τῶν λοιπῶν καὶ μοναχῶν, ὡς ἐπὶ τὸ πολὺ δὲ ἀπὸ τοῦ τοῦ Κρόνου, εἶτα καὶ τοῦ τοῦ Διός, διὰ τὸ

---

[1] Post λ add. glossa in marg. codicis N et Cam.[2] εἴ γε μὴ ἔχουσί τινες δύο λόγους; om. libri omnes et Proclus.

house, following the order of the signs.[1] And again in order, those that have two lordships each are preferred to the one which has but one in the same sign. Since terms are not allotted to the luminaries, however, Cancer and Leo, the houses of the sun and moon, are assigned to the maleficent planets because they were deprived of their share in the order, Cancer to Mars and Leo to Saturn;[2] in these the order appropriate to them is preserved. As for the number of the terms, when no star is found with two prerogatives, either in the sign itself or in those which follow it within the quadrant, there are assigned to each of the beneficent planets, that is, to Jupiter and Venus, 7°; to the maleficent, Saturn and Mars, 5° each; and to Mercury, which is common, 6°; so that the total is 30°. But since some always have two prerogatives—for Venus alone becomes the ruler of the triplicity of Taurus, since the moon does not participate in the terms—there is given to each one of those in such condition, whether it be in the same sign or in the following signs within the quadrant, one extra degree; these were marked with dots.[3] But the degrees added for double prerogatives are taken away from the others, which have but one, and, generally speaking, from Saturn and Jupiter

---

[1] *I.e.* in the order Aries, Taurus, Gemini, etc., which the Greeks called "the order of the following signs" and regarded as proceeding to the left.

[2] According to the anonymous commentator (p. 42, ed. Wolf), this is because Mars belongs to the nocturnal sect and Saturn to the diurnal, the leaders of which are, respectively, the moon and the sun.

[3] In Ptolemy's ancient manuscript; so says the anonymous commentator (p. 44, ed. Wolf).

PTOLEMY

βραδύτερον αὐτῶν τῆς κινήσεως. ἔστι δὲ καὶ ἡ
τούτων τῶν ὁρίων ἔκθεσις τοιαύτη.

[1] Κριοῦ

♃	ϛ′	ϛ′
♀	η′	ιδ′
☿	ζ′	κα′
♂	ε′	κϛ′
♄	δ′	λ′

Ταύρου

♀	η′	η′
☿	ζ′	ιε′
♃	ζ′	κβ′
♄	β′	κδ′
♂	ϛ′	λ′

Διδύμων

☿	ζ′	ζ′
♃	ϛ′	ιγ′
♀	ζ′	κ′
♂	ϛ′	κϛ′
♄	δ′	λ′

Καρκίνου

♂	ϛ′	ϛ′
♃	ζ′	ιγ′
☿	ζ′	κ′
♀	ζ′	κζ′
♄	γ′	λ′

Λέοντος

♃	ϛ′	ϛ′
☿	ζ′	ιγ′
♄	ϛ′	ιθ′
♀	ϛ′	κε′
♂	ε′	λ

Παρθένου

☿	ζ′	ζ′
♀	ϛ′	ιγ′
♃	ε′	ιη′
♄	ϛ′	κδ′
♂	ϛ′	λ′

Ζυγοῦ

♄	ϛ′	ϛ′
♀	ε′	ια′
☿	ε′	ιϛ′
♃	η′	κδ′
♂	ϛ′	λ′

Σκορπίου

♂	ϛ′	ϛ′
♀	ζ′	ιγ′
♃	η′	κα′
☿	ϛ′	κζ′
♄	γ′	λ′

Τοξότου

♃	η′	η′
♀	ϛ′	ιδ′
☿	ε′	ιθ′
♄	ϛ′	κε′
♂	ε′	λ′

Αἰγόκερω

♀	ϛ′	ϛ′
☿	ϛ′	ιβ′
♃	ζ′	ιθ′
♄	ϛ′	κε′
♂	ε′	λ

Ὑδροχόου

♄	ϛ′	ϛ′
☿	ϛ′	ιβ′
♀	η′	κ′
♃	ε′	κε′
♂	ε′	λ

Ἰχθύων

♀	η′	η′
♃	ϛ′	ιδ′
☿	ϛ′	κ′
♂	ε′	κε′
♄	ε′	λ

[1] Tabulas quae in cod. Vat. gr. 1453 (Procli Paraphrasin continentis) inventae sunt sequor. Hae cum illis quae ab Camerario impressae sunt congruunt solis ll. 4-5 sub Αἰγόκερω exceptis ubi ordo Camerarii est: ♂ ε′, ♄ ϛ′. Proclus autem non nullas notitias duplices habet, viz.: l. 4 sub Ταύρου, ♄ β′ aut δ′; l. 2 sub Καρκίνου ☿ aut ♃,

TETRABIBLOS I. 21

because of their slower motion. The tabulation [1] of these terms is as follows:—

Terms according to Ptolemy.

Aries	♃ 6	♀ 8	☿ 7	♂ 5	♄ 4
Taurus	♀ 8	☿ 7	♃ 7	♄ 2	♂ 6
Gemini	☿ 7	♃ 6	♀ 7	♂ 6	♄ 4
Cancer	♂ 6	♃ 7	☿ 7	♀ 7	♄ 3
Leo	♃ 6	☿ 7	♄ 6	♀ 6	♂ 5
Virgo	☿ 7	♀ 6	♃ 5	♄ 6	♂ 6
Libra	♄ 6	♀ 5	☿ 5	♃ 8	♂ 6
Scorpio	♂ 6	♀ 7	♃ 8	☿ 6	♄ 3
Sagittarius	♃ 8	♀ 6	☿ 5	♄ 6	♂ 5
Capricornus	♀ 6	☿ 6	♃ 7	♄ 6	♂ 5
Aquarius	♄ 6	☿ 6	♀ 8	♃ 5	♂ 5
Pisces	♀ 8	♃ 6	☿ 6	♂ 5	♄ 5

[1] The Greek tables contain, under each sign, (1) the name of the planet, (2) the number of its terms in this sign, and (3) the cumulative totals of terms, up to the 30° of the sign. The third detail has been omitted in the English tables. The anonymous commentator (pp. 44–47, ed. Wolf) demonstrates in detail how the assignment of terms is made.

---

l. 3 ♃ aut ☿; l. 3 sub Λέοντος ♄ aut ♀; l. 3 sub Ζυγοῦ ☿ aut ♃, ε′ aut η′, l. 4 ♃ aut ☿, η′ aut ε′; l. 2 sub Σκορπίου ♀ aut ♃, ζ′ aut η′, l. 3 ♃ aut ♀, η′ aut ζ′; l. 4 sub Αἰγόκερῳ ♄ aut ♂, l. 5 ♂ aut ♄; l. 4 sub Ἰχθύων ♂ ε′ aut ϛ′, l. 5, ♄ ε′ aut δ′.

PTOLEMY

⟨κβ.⟩ Περὶ τόπων καὶ μοιρῶν[1]

Διεῖλον δέ τινες καὶ εἰς ἔτι τούτων λεπτομερέστερα τμήματα[2] τῆς οἰκοδεσποτίας, τόπους καὶ μοίρας ὀνομάσαντες, καὶ τόπον μὲν ὑποτιθέμενοι τὸ τοῦ δωδεκατημορίου δωδεκατημόριον, τουτέστι 50 μοίρας β′ ἥμισυ,[3] καὶ διδόντες αὐτῶν τὴν κυρίαν τοῖς ἐφεξῆς ζῳδίοις. ἄλλοι δὲ καὶ κατ' ἄλλας τινὰς ἀλόγους τάξεις, μοῖραν δὲ ἑκάστην[4] πάλιν ἀπ' ἀρχῆς ἑκάστῳ[5] διδόντες τῶν ἀστέρων ἀκολούθως τῇ τάξει τῶν Χαλδαϊκῶν ὁρίων. ταῦτα μὲν οὖν πιθανὸν καὶ οὐ φυσικὸν ἀλλὰ κενόδοξον ἔχοντα λόγον παρήσομεν. ἐκεῖνο δὲ ἐπιστάσεως ἄξιον τυγχάνον οὐ παραλείψομεν, ὅτι καὶ τὰς τῶν δωδεκατημορίων ἀρχὰς ἀπὸ τῶν ἰσημερινῶν καὶ τῶν τροπικῶν σημείων εὔλογόν ἐστι ποιεῖσθαι, καὶ τῶν συγγραφέων τοῦτό πως ἐμφανισάντων, καὶ μάλιστα διότι τὰς φύσεις καὶ τὰς δυνάμεις καὶ τὰς συνοικειώσεις αὐτῶν ὁρῶμεν ἐκ τῶν προαποδεδειγμένων ἀπὸ τῶν τροπικῶν καὶ ἰσημερινῶν ἀρχῶν

---

[1] Post tabulas add. VMDProc. haec aut similia: γίνεται δὲ καὶ τούτων ἐκ τῆς ἐπισυνθέσεως Κρόνου μοῖραι νζ′, Διὸς οθ′, Ἄρεως ξϛ′, Ἀφροδίτης πβ′, Ἑρμοῦ οϛ′ · γίνονται τξ′. Titulum habent VPLMADEProc.; om. NCam.
[2] τὰ τμήματα PLNCam.
[3] ἀρχόμενοι ἀπὸ τοῦ δωδεκατημορίου καθ' ὅ ἐστιν ὁ ἀστὴρ add. NCam.; om. VPLMDEProc.; ἀρχόμενοι ἀπὸ τοῦ //// καὶ διδόντες A.   [4] ἑκάστην VMADE, -ῳ PLNCam.
[5] ἑκάστῳ VPLMADE, -ου NCam.

---

[1] After the tables and before this chapter-heading some of the MSS. have: "There result from the addition of

TETRABIBLOS I. 22

22. *Of Places and Degrees.*[1]

Some have made even finer divisions of rulership than these, using the terms "places" and "degrees." Defining "place" as the twelfth part of a sign, or 2½°, they[2] assign the domination over them to the signs in order. Others follow other illogical orders; and again they assign each "degree" from the beginning to each of the planets of each sign in accordance with the Chaldaean order of terms. These matters, as they have only plausible and not natural, but, rather, unfounded, arguments in their favour, we shall omit. The following, however, upon which it is worth while to dwell, we shall not pass by, namely, that it is reasonable to reckon the beginnings of the signs also from the equinoxes and solstices,[3] partly because the writers make this quite clear, and particularly because from our previous demonstrations we observe that their natures, powers, and familiarities take their cause from the solstitial

---

these, of Saturn, 57°; of Jupiter, 79°; of Mars, 66°; of Venus, 82°; of Mercury, 76°; the total is 360°."

[2] One MS. and the printed editions insert here, "begin with the sign in which the star is and"; *cf.* the critical note.

[3] That is, Ptolemy's zodiac, made up of 12 divisions of 30° each, measured on the ecliptic from one of the solstices or equinoxes, is entirely different from the zodiac made up of signs determined by the actual constellations. Because of the precession of the equinoxes the two by no means coincide; and because the powers of the signs are derived from their relations to the solstitial and equinoctial points, says Ptolemy, the former definition of the zodiac is preferable. *Cf.* cc. 10-11, and the distinction between solstitial, equinoctial, solid, and bicorporeal signs, as an example of what he means.

PTOLEMY

καὶ οὐκ ἀπ' ἄλλου τινὸς ἐχούσας¹ τὴν αἰτίαν. ἄλλων μὲν γὰρ ἀρχῶν ὑποτιθεμένων ἢ μηκέτι συγχρῆσθαι ταῖς φύσεσιν αὐτῶν εἰς τὰς προτελέσεις ἀναγκασθησόμεθα ἢ συγχρώμενοι διαπίπτειν, παραβάντων καὶ ἀπαλλοτριωθέντων² τῶν τὰς δυνάμεις αὐτοῖς ἐμπεριποιησάντων τοῦ ζωδιακοῦ διαστημάτων.

⟨κγ.⟩ Περὶ προσώπων καὶ λαμπηνῶν καὶ τῶν τοιούτων

Αἱ μὲν οὖν συνοικειώσεις τῶν ἀστέρων καὶ τῶν δωδεκατημορίων σχεδὸν ἂν εἶεν τοσαῦται. λέγονται δὲ καὶ ἰδιοπρόσωποι μὲν ὅταν ἕκαστος αὐτῶν τὸν αὐτὸν διασώζῃ πρὸς ἥλιον ἢ καὶ σελήνην σχηματισμὸν ὅνπερ καὶ ὁ οἶκος αὐτοῦ πρὸς τοὺς ἐκείνων οἴκους· οἷον ὅταν ὁ τῆς Ἀφροδίτης λόγου ἕνεκεν ἑξάγωνον ποιῇ πρὸς τὰ φῶτα διάστασιν, ἀλλὰ πρὸς ἥλιον μὲν ἑσπέριος ὤν, πρὸς σελήνην δὲ ἑῷος, ἀκολούθως τοῖς ἐξ ἀρχῆς οἴκοις· λαμπήναις δὲ ἐν ἰδίαις εἶναι καὶ θρόνοις καὶ τοῖς τοιούτοις ὅταν κατὰ δύο ᾖ καὶ πλείους τῶν προεκτεθειμένων

¹ ἔχοντας NCam.
² ἀπαλλοτριωθέντων VPLD, ἀλλοτριωθέντων MNAECam. (ἄλλω- Cam.).

---

[1] Just as, with the precession of the equinoxes, the fictive sign Aries is now almost entirely in Pisces.

[2] The scholiast on Ptolemy says that, in addition to the conditions laid down by Ptolemy, a planet, to be in proper face, must also be in its own house and must be in the necessary aspect with *both* the luminaries (not with one of them, as Ptolemy says).

and equinoctial starting-places, and from no other source. For if other starting-places are assumed, we shall either be compelled no longer to use the natures of the signs for prognostications or, if we use them, to be in error, since the spaces of the zodiac which implant their powers in the planets would then pass over to others [1] and become alienated.

23. *Of Faces, Chariots, and the Like.*

Such, then, are the natural affinities of the stars and the signs of the zodiac. The planets are said to be in their " proper face " [2] when an individual planet keeps to the sun or moon the same aspect which its house has to their houses ; as, for example, when Venus is in sextile to the luminaries, provided that she is occidental to the sun and oriental to the moon, in accordance with the original arrangement of their houses.[3] They are said to be in their own " chariots " and " thrones " [4] and the like when they

---

[3] Venus' solar house, Libra, is sextile dexter (*i.e.* toward the west) to Leo, the sun's house, and her lunar house, Taurus, is sextile sinister (*i.e.* toward the east) to the moon's house, Cancer.

[4] Ptolemy pays little attention to the thrones and chariots, which were apparently, as Bouché-Leclercq (p. 244) asserts, not to his taste as a scientific astrologer. In the Michigan astrological roll (P. Mich. 149, col. 3A, 22-34) the " thrones " are identified with the (astrological) exaltations and the depressions of the planets are called their " prisons " (φυλακαί) ; upon the thrones the planets have " royal power," in their prisons they " are abased and oppose their own powers." Sarapion (*CCAG.* viii. 4, p. 228, 25, and p. 231, 13) and Balbillus (*ibid.*, p. 237, 8) use the word ἰδιοθρονεῖν.

PTOLEMY

τρόπων συνοικειούμενοι τυγχάνωσι τοῖς τόποις ἐν οἷς καταλαμβάνονται, τότε¹ μάλιστα τῆς δυνάμεως αὐτῶν αὐξανομένης πρὸς ἐνέργειαν διὰ τὸ ὅμοιον καὶ συμπρακτικὸν τῆς τῶν περιεχόντων δωδεκατημορίων ὁμοφυοῦς οἰκειότητος.² χαίρειν δέ φασιν αὐτοὺς ὅταν κἂν μὴ πρὸς αὐτοὺς ᾖ ἡ συνοικείωσις τῶν περιεχόντων ζῳδίων ἀλλὰ μέντοι πρὸς τοὺς τῶν αὐτῶν αἱρέσεων, ἐκ μακροῦ μᾶλλον οὕτω γινομένης τῆς συμπαθείας. κοινωνοῦσι δὲ ὅμως καὶ κατὰ τὸν αὐτὸν τρόπον τῆς ὁμοιότητος· ὥσπερ ὅταν ἐν τοῖς ἠλλοτριωμένοις καὶ τῆς ἐναντίας αἱρέσεως τόποις καταλαμβάνωνται, πολὺ παραλύεται τὸ τῆς οἰκείας αὐτῶν δυνάμεως, ἄλλην τινὰ φύσιν μικτὴν ἀποτελούσης τῆς κατὰ τὸ ἀνόμοιον τῶν περιεχόντων ζῳδίων κράσεως.

52 ⟨κδ̄.⟩ *Περὶ συναφειῶν καὶ ἀπορροιῶν καὶ τῶν ἄλλων δυνάμεων*

Καὶ καθ' ὅλου δὲ συνάπτειν μὲν λέγονται τοῖς ἑπομένοις οἱ προηγούμενοι, ἀπερρυηκέναι δὲ οἱ ἑπόμενοι τῶν προηγουμένων, ἐφ' ὅσον ἂν μὴ μακρὸν ᾖ τὸ μεταξὺ αὐτῶν διάστημα. παραλαμβάνεται δὲ

¹ τότε γὰρ MNAECam.; γὰρ om. VPLD.
² ἰδιοθρονεῖν καὶ λάμπειν λέγονται add. MNAECam.; om. VPLD.

---

[1] Vettius Valens uses this word several times in a broader sense than that of this definition.
[2] *I.e.* are more occidental.
[3] συνάπτειν, *applicare* (noun συναφή, *applicatio*) is used of planets which are on or are closely approaching the same meridian. κόλλησις is a similar term. "Separation,"

happen to have familiarity in two or more of the aforesaid ways with the places in which they are found; for then their power is most increased in effectiveness by the similarity and co-operation of the kindred property of the signs which contain them. They say they " rejoice "[1] when, even though the containing signs have no familiarity with the stars themselves, nevertheless they have it with the stars of the same sect; in this case the sympathy arises less directly. They share, however, in the similarity in the same way; just as, on the contrary, when they are found in alien regions belonging to the opposite sect, a great part of their proper power is paralysed, because the temperament which arises from the dissimilarity of the signs produces a different and adulterated nature.

24. *Of Applications and Separations and the Other Powers.*

In general those which precede [2] are said to " apply "[3] to those which follow, and those that follow to " be separated " from those that precede, when the interval between them is not great.[4] Such

ἀπόρροια, *defluxio*, on the contrary, refers to the movement apart of two bodies after " application." ἀπόρροια is also used by astrologers to designate the " emanations " of the heavenly bodies which affect the earth and its inhabitants, as for example in Vettius Valens, p. 160, 6-7; 249, 3; 270, 24 fl.; 330, 19 fl.

[4] Ashmand says this is generally understood to mean, when the heavenly bodies are within each other's orbs (Saturn 10°, Jupiter 12°, Mars 7° 30', sun 17°, Venus 8°, Mercury 7° 30', moon 12° 30'). The anonymous commentator mentions 15° as the maximum distance (p. 51, ed. Wolf).

PTOLEMY

τὸ τοιοῦτον ἐάν τε σωματικῶς ἐάν τε καὶ κατά τινα τῶν παραδεδομένων σχηματισμῶν συμβαίνῃ, πλὴν ὅτι γε πρὸς μὲν τὰς δι' αὐτῶν τῶν σωμάτων συναφὰς καὶ ἀπορροίας καὶ τὰ πλάτη παρατηρεῖν αὐτῶν χρήσιμον εἰς τὸ μόνας τὰς ἐπὶ τὰ αὐτὰ μέρη τοῦ διὰ μέσων εὑρισκομένας παρόδους παραδέχεσθαι. πρὸς δὲ τὰς διὰ τῶν συσχηματισμῶν¹ περιττόν ἐστι τὸ τοιοῦτον, πασῶν ἀεὶ τῶν ἀκτίνων ἐπὶ ταὐτά, τουτέστιν ἐπὶ τὸ κέντρον τῆς γῆς, φερομένων καὶ ὁμοίως πανταχόθεν συμβαλλουσῶν.

Ἐκ δὴ τούτων ἁπάντων εὐσύνοπτον ὅτι τὸ μὲν ποιὸν ἑκάστου τῶν ἀστέρων ἐπισκεπτέον ἔκ τε τῆς ἰδίας αὐτῶν φυσικῆς ἰδιοτροπίας καὶ ἔτι τῆς τῶν περιεχόντων δωδεκατημορίων, ἢ καὶ τῆς τῶν πρός τε τὸν ἥλιον καὶ τὰς γωνίας σχηματισμῶν κατὰ τὸν ἐκτεθειμένον ἡμῖν περὶ πάντων τούτων τρόπον· τὴν δὲ δύναμιν πρῶτον μὲν ἐκ τοῦ ἤτοι ἀνατολικοὺς αὐτοὺς εἶναι καὶ προσθετικοὺς ταῖς ἰδίαις κινήσεσι,

¹ τὰς διὰ τῶν συσχηματισμῶν] τὸν γινόμενον σχηματισμὸν NCam.

---

[1] That is, when the planets themselves come to the same meridian, as opposed to the conjunction of one planet with the ray projected by another from the sextile, quartile, or trine aspect.

[2] The ecliptic bisects the zodiac longitudinally. Planets, to "apply" in the "bodily" sense, must both be to the north, or the south, of it; that is, in the same latitude. *Cf.* the anonymous commentator (pp. 50-51, ed. Wolf).

[3] See the note on iii. 10 concerning the projection of rays (ἀκτινοβολία). To judge from the remarks of the anonymous

TETRABIBLOS I. 24

a relation is taken to exist whether it happens by bodily conjunction [1] or through one of the traditional aspects, except that with respect to the bodily applications and separations of the heavenly bodies it is of use also to observe their latitudes, in order that only those passages may be accepted which are found to be on the same side of the ecliptic.[2] In the case of applications and separations by aspect, however, such a practice is superfluous, because all rays always fall and similarly converge from every direction upon the same point, that is, the centre of the earth.[3]

From all this, then, it is easy to see that the quality of each of the stars must be examined with reference both to its own natural character and that also of the signs that include it, or likewise from the character of its aspects to the sun and the angles, in the manner which we have explained. Their power must be determined, in the first place, from the fact that they are either oriental and adding to their proper motion [4]

commentator, the thought is that, while the rays of planets closely approaching each other but in different latitudes would miss each other, the rays of those in aspect in any case mingle at their common meeting-place, the centre of the earth.

[4] The theory of epicycles assigns to each planet at least one epicycle, on which it moves from west to east, while the centre of the epicycle likewise moves from west to east on the orbit, or deferent. Thus when the planet is in the outer semicircle of its epicycle (away from the earth) both motions will be in the same direction and the planet will be " adding to its motion "; conversely on the inner semicircle (toward the earth) the motion on the epicycle is in the opposite direction to that on the deferent and the apparent speed of the planet is diminished.

τότε γὰρ μάλιστά εἰσιν ἰσχυροί· ἢ δυτικοὺς καὶ ἀφαιρετικούς, τότε γὰρ ἀσθενεστέραν ἔχουσι τὴν ἐνέργειαν· ἔπειτα καὶ ἐκ τοῦ πως ἔχειν πρὸς τὸν ὁρίζοντα, μεσουρανοῦντες μὲν γὰρ ἢ ἐπιφερόμενοι τῷ μεσουρανήματι μάλιστά εἰσι δυναμικοί· δεύτερον δὲ ὅταν ἐπ' αὐτοῦ τοῦ ὁρίζοντος ὦσιν ἢ ἐπαναφέρωνται, καὶ μᾶλλον ὅταν ἐπὶ τοῦ ἀνατολικοῦ, ἧττον δὲ ὅταν ὑπὸ γῆν μεσουρανῶσιν ἢ ἄλλως συσχηματίζωνται τῷ ἀνατέλλοντι τόπῳ· μὴ οὕτω δὲ ἔχοντες ἀδύναμοι παντελῶς τυγχάνουσιν.

ΒΙΒΛΙΟΝ Β'

⟨ᾱ.⟩ Προοίμιον

Τὰ μὲν δὴ κυριώτερα τῶν πινακικῶς προεκτεθειμένων νῦν εἰς τὴν τῶν κατὰ μέρος προρρήσεων ἐπίσκεψιν ὡς ἐν κεφαλαίοις μέχρι τοσούτων ἡμῖν ἐφοδευέσθω, συνάψωμεν δὲ ἤδη κατὰ τὸ ἑξῆς τῆς ἀκολουθίας τὰς καθ' ἕκαστα τῶν εἰς τὸ δυνατὸν τῆς τοιαύτης προρρήσεως ἐμπιπτόντων πραγματείας, ἐχόμενοι πανταχῇ τῆς κατὰ τὸν φυσικὸν τρόπον ὑφηγήσεως.

Εἰς δύο τοίνυν τὰ μέγιστα καὶ κυριώτατα μέρη διαιρουμένου τοῦ δι' ἀστρονομίας προγνωστικοῦ, καὶ πρώτου μὲν ὄντος καὶ γενικωτέρου τοῦ καθ'

—for then they are most powerful—or occidental and diminishing in speed, for then their energy is weaker. Second, it is to be determined from their position relative to the horizon; for they are most powerful when they are in mid-heaven or approaching it, and second when they are exactly on the horizon or in the succedent place;[1] their power is greater when they are in the orient, and less when they culminate beneath the earth or are in some other aspect to the orient; if they bear no aspect[2] at all to the orient they are entirely powerless.

BOOK II.

1. *Introduction.*

LET it be considered that thus far we have furnished in brief the most important details of the tabular exposition needful for the inquiry into particular prognostications. Let us now add in proper sequence the procedures for dealing in detail with those matters which lie within the limits of possibility of this kind of prognostication, holding everywhere to the natural method of exposition.

Since, then, prognostication by astronomical means is divided into two great and principal parts, and since the first and more universal is that which

---

[1] That is, the space of 30° ("place," or "house") immediately following, or rising next after, the horoscopic sign (*cf.* iii. 10, p. 273). This place is called the ἐπαναφορά of the horoscope.

[2] That is, if they are disjunct (*cf.* c. 16).

54 ὅλα ἔθνη καὶ χώρας καὶ πόλεις λαμβανομένου, ὃ καλεῖται καθολικόν, δευτέρου δὲ καὶ εἰδικωτέρου τοῦ καθ' ἕνα ἕκαστον τῶν ἀνθρώπων, ὃ καὶ αὐτὸ καλεῖται γενεθλιαλογικόν, προσήκειν ἡγούμεθα περὶ τοῦ καθολικοῦ πρῶτον ποιήσασθαι τὸν λόγον, ἐπειδήπερ ταῦτα μὲν κατὰ μείζους καὶ ἰσχυροτέρας αἰτίας τρέπεσθαι πέφυκε μᾶλλον τῶν μερικῶς ἀποτελουμένων. ὑποπιπτουσῶν δὲ ἀεὶ τῶν ἀσθενεστέρων φύσεων ταῖς δυνατωτέραις καὶ τῶν κατὰ μέρος ταῖς καθ' ὅλου, παντάπασιν ἀναγκαῖον ἂν εἴη τοῖς προαιρουμένοις περὶ ἑνὸς ἑκάστου σκοπεῖν πολὺ πρότερον περὶ τῶν ὁλοσχερεστέρων περιειληφέναι.

Καὶ αὐτῆς δὲ τῆς καθολικῆς ἐπισκέψεως τὸ μὲν πάλιν κατὰ χώρας ὅλας λαμβάνεται, τὸ δὲ κατὰ πόλεις.[1] καὶ ἔτι τὸ μὲν κατὰ μείζους καὶ περιοδικωτέρας περιστάσεις, οἷον πολέμων ἢ λιμῶν ἢ λοιμῶν[2] ἢ σεισμῶν ἢ κατακλυσμῶν καὶ τῶν τοιούτων· τὸ δὲ κατὰ ἐλάττους καὶ καιρικωτέρας,[3] οἷαί εἰσιν αἱ τῶν ἐτησίων ὡρῶν καὶ κατὰ τὸ μᾶλλον καὶ ἧττον ἀλλοιώσεις, περί τε ἀνέσεις ἢ ἐπιτάσεις χειμώνων καὶ καυμάτων καὶ πνευμάτων εὐφορίας[4] τε καὶ ἀφορίας καὶ τὰ τοιαῦτα. προηγεῖται δὲ καὶ τούτων εἰκότως ἑκατέρου τό τε[5] κατὰ χώρας ὅλας καὶ τὸ κατὰ μείζους περι-
55 στάσεις διὰ τὴν αὐτὴν αἰτίαν τῇ προειρημένῃ·

[1] τὸ δὲ κατὰ χώρας καὶ κατὰ πόλεις NCam.Proc.; κατὰ χώρας καὶ om. libri alii.
[2] ἢ λιμῶν ἢ λοιμῶν VMD; καὶ λοιμ. καὶ λιμ. Proc.; ἢ λοιμ. ἢ λιμ. A; ἢ λοιμ. ἢ λοιμ. E, ἢ λοιμῶν PLNCam.
[3] καιρικωτέρας VAD, καιριωτέρας ME, cf. Proc.; μικροτέρας PLNCam.

relates to whole races, countries, and cities, which is called general, and the second and more specific is that which relates to individual men, which is called genethlialogical, we believe it fitting to treat first of the general division, because such matters are naturally swayed by greater and more powerful causes than are particular events. And since weaker natures always yield to the stronger, and the particular always falls under the general,[1] it would by all means be necessary for those who purpose an inquiry about a single individual long before to have comprehended the more general considerations.

Of the general inquiry itself, a part, again, is found to concern whole countries, and a part to concern cities;[2] and further, a part deals with the greater and more periodic conditions, such as wars, famines, pestilences, earthquakes, deluges, and the like; and another with the lesser and more occasional, as for example the changes in temperature[3] in the seasons of the year, and the variations of the intensity of storms, heat, and winds, or of good and bad crops, and so on. But in each of these cases, as is reasonable, procedure by entire countries and by more important conditions is preferred, for the same reason as before. And since in the examination

---

[1] *Cf.* i. 3.
[2] Or, as the variant reading has it, "to concern both countries and cities." See the *cr. n.*
[3] Literally, "variations of more and less."

---

[4] ἢ εὐφορίας PLMNAECam, ἢ om. VD.
[5] σκοπεῖν ἢ τὸ λαμβάνεσθαι add. post τό τε Cam.², om. libri Cam.¹

PTOLEMY

πρὸς δὲ τὴν τούτων ἐπίσκεψιν μάλιστα παραλαμβανομένων δύο τούτων, τῆς τε τῶν δωδεκατημορίων τοῦ ζῳδιακοῦ καὶ ἔτι τῆς τῶν ἀστέρων πρὸς ἕκαστα τῶν κλιμάτων συνοικειώσεως καὶ τῶν ἐν τοῖς οἰκείοις μέρεσι κατὰ καιροὺς γινομένων ἐπισημασιῶν, κατὰ μὲν τὰς συζυγίας ἡλίου καὶ σελήνης τῶν ἐκλειπτικῶν, κατὰ δὲ τὰς τῶν πλανωμένων παρόδους τῶν περὶ τὰς ἀνατολὰς καὶ τοὺς στηριγμούς, προεκθησόμεθα τὸν τῶν εἰρημένων συμπαθειῶν φυσικὸν λόγον, ἅμα παριστάντες ἐξ ἐπιδρομῆς[1] καὶ τὰς καθ' ὅλα ἔθνη θεωρουμένας ὡς ἐπὶ πᾶν σωματικάς τε καὶ ἠθικὰς ἰδιοτροπίας, οὐκ ἀλλοτρίας τυγχανούσας τῆς τῶν συνοικειουμένων ἀστέρων τε καὶ δωδεκατημορίων φυσικῆς περιστάσεως.

⟨β̄.⟩ Περὶ τῶν καθ' ὅλα κλίματα[2] ἰδιωμάτων

Τῶν τοίνυν ἐθνικῶν ἰδιωμάτων τὰ μὲν καθ' ὅλους παραλλήλους καὶ γωνίας ὅλας διαιρεῖσθαι συμβέβηκε ὑπὸ τῆς πρὸς τὸν διὰ μέσων τῶν ζῳδίων κύκλον καὶ τὸν ἥλιον αὐτῶν σχέσεως. τῆς γὰρ καθ' ἡμᾶς οἰκουμένης ἐν ἑνὶ τῶν βορείων τεταρτημορίων οὔσης, οἱ μὲν ὑπὸ τοὺς νοτιωτέρους παραλλήλους, λέγω δὲ τοὺς ἀπὸ τοῦ ἰσημερινοῦ

---

[1] ἐπιδρομῆς VPLNDE, ὑποδρομῆς MA, περιδρομῆς Cam.
[2] κλίματα VPLMADProc., ἔθνη NCam.; tit. om. E.

of these questions these two things particularly are taken into consideration, the familiarity of the signs of the zodiac and also of the stars with the several climes,[1] and the significances of heavenly bodies in their own proper regions [2] at a given time, manifested through the ecliptical conjunctions of the sun and moon and the transits [3] of the planets at rising and at their stationary periods, we shall first explain the natural reason for the aforesaid sympathies, and at the same time briefly survey the bodily and ethical peculiarities generally observed to belong to whole nations, which are not alien to the natural character of the stars and signs that are familiar to them.

2. *Of the Characteristics of the Inhabitants of the General Climes.*

The demarcation of national characteristics [4] is established in part by entire parallels and angles,[5] through their position relative to the ecliptic and the sun. For while the region which we inhabit is in one of the northern quarters, the people who live under the more southern parallels, that is, those

[1] Latitudes, or general regions determined by latitude.
[2] Such as houses (i. 17) or terms (i. 20-21).
[3] πάροδοι; the passage of a heavenly body through the zodiac.
[4] In the astrological ethnography which follows Ptolemy probably depends upon the Stoic Posidonius. Boll, *Studien*, pp. 181-238, enumerates many details in which, for this reason, Ptolemy here diverges from views expressed in the *Geography*.
[5] "Parallels" relate to latitude, *i.e.* position north or south; "angles" to position east or west.

PTOLEMY

μέχρι τοῦ θερινοῦ τροπικοῦ, κατὰ κορυφὴν λαμ-
56 βάνοντες τὸν ἥλιον καὶ διακαιόμενοι, μέλανες τὰ
σώματα καὶ τὰς τρίχας οὖλοί τε καὶ δασεῖς καὶ
τὰς μορφὰς συνεσπασμένοι καὶ τὰ μεγέθη συν-
τετηγμένοι καὶ τὰς φύσεις θερμοὶ καὶ τοῖς ἤθεσιν
ὡς ἐπὶ πᾶν ἄγριοι τυγχάνουσι διὰ τὴν ὑπὸ καύματος
συνέχειαν τῶν οἰκήσεων, οὓς δὴ καλοῦμεν κοινῶς[1]
Αἰθίοπας. καὶ οὐ μόνον αὐτοὺς ὁρῶμεν οὕτως
ἔχοντας ἀλλὰ καὶ τὸ περιέχον αὐτοὺς τοῦ ἀέρος
κατάστημα καὶ τὰ ἄλλα ζῷα καὶ τὰ φυτὰ παρ'
αὐτοῖς ἐμφανίζοντα τὴν διαπύρωσιν.[2]

Οἱ δὲ ὑπὸ τοὺς βορειοτέρους παραλλήλους, λέγω
δὲ τοὺς ὑπὸ τὰς ἄρκτους τὸν κατὰ κορυφὴν ἔχοντες
τόπον, πολὺ τοῦ ζῳδιακοῦ καὶ τῆς τοῦ ἡλίου θερμότητος ἀφεστῶτες,[3] κατεψυγμένοι μέν εἰσι διὰ
τοῦτο, δαψιλεστέρας[4] δὲ μεταλαμβάνοντες τῆς
ὑγρᾶς οὐσίας, θρεπτικωτάτης οὔσης καὶ ὑπὸ μηδενὸς
ἀναπινομένης θερμοῦ, λευκοί τε τὰ χρώματά εἰσι
καὶ τετανοὶ τὰς τρίχας τά τε σώματα μεγάλοι καὶ
εὐτραφεῖς τοῖς μεγέθεσι καὶ ὑπόψυχροι τὰς φύσεις,
ἄγριοι δὲ καὶ αὐτοὶ τοῖς ἤθεσι διὰ τὴν ὑπὸ τοῦ
κρύους συνέχειαν τῶν οἰκήσεων. ἀκολουθεῖ δὲ
τούτοις καὶ ὁ τοῦ περιέχοντος αὐτοὺς ἀέρος χειμὼν
καὶ τῶν φυτῶν τὰ μεγέθη καὶ τὸ δυσήμερον τῶν
ζῴων. καλοῦμεν δὲ καὶ τούτους ὡς ἐπὶ πᾶν Σκύθας.

Οἱ δὲ μεταξὺ τοῦ θερινοῦ τροπικοῦ καὶ τῶν
ἄρκτων, μήτε κατὰ κορυφὴν γινομένου παρ' αὐτοῖς

---

[1] κοινῶς VMADEProc., om. alii Cam.
[2] διαπύρωσιν VDP(-πιρ-)L(-πιον-), τὸ διάπυρον Proc., διάθεσιν MNAECam.

from the equator to the summer tropic, since they have the sun over their heads and are burned by it, have black skins and thick, woolly hair, are contracted in form and shrunken in stature, are sanguine of nature, and in habits are for the most part savage because their homes are continually oppressed by heat; we call them by the general name Ethiopians. Not only do we see them in this condition, but we likewise observe that their climate and the animals and plants of their region plainly give evidence of this baking by the sun.

Those who live under the more northern parallels, those, I mean, who have the Bears over their heads, since they are far removed from the zodiac and the heat of the sun, are therefore cooled; but because they have a richer share of moisture, which is most nourishing and is not there exhausted by heat, they are white in complexion, straight-haired, tall and well-nourished, and somewhat cold by nature; these too are savage in their habits because their dwelling-places are continually cold. The wintry character of their climate, the size of their plants, and the wildness of their animals are in accord with these qualities. We call these men, too, by a general name, Scythians.

The inhabitants of the region between the summer tropic and the Bears, however, since the sun is

---

³ ἀφεστῶτες VD, -τα A, διεστηκότες NLCam., διεστηκῶτες P, -κότα ME; cf. ἀπέχει Proc.
⁴ δαψιλεστέρας VMDE, -ρως LNACam., δαψηλέσταιρος -

PTOLEMY

57 τοῦ ἡλίου μήτε πολὺ κατὰ τὰς μεσημβρινὰς παρόδους ἀφισταμένου, τῆς τε τῶν ἀέρων εὐκρασίας μετειλήφασι, καὶ αὐτῆς μὲν διαφερούσης ἀλλ' οὐ σφόδρα μεγάλην τὴν παραλλαγὴν τῶν καυμάτων πρὸς τὰ ψύχη λαμβανούσης. ἔνθεν τοῖς χρώμασι μέσοι καὶ τοῖς μεγέθεσι μέτριοι καὶ ταῖς φύσεσιν εὔκρατοι καὶ ταῖς οἰκήσεσι συνεχεῖς καὶ τοῖς ἤθεσιν ἥμεροι τυγχάνουσι. τούτων δὲ οἱ πρὸς νότον ὡς ἐπὶ πᾶν ἀγχινούστεροι καὶ εὐμήχανοι μᾶλλον καὶ περὶ τὴν τῶν θείων ἱστορίαν ἱκανώτεροι διὰ τὸ συνεγγίζειν αὐτῶν τὸν κατὰ κορυφὴν τόπον τοῦ ζωδιακοῦ καὶ τῶν περὶ αὐτὸν πλανωμένων ἀστέρων,[1] οἷς οἰκείως καὶ αὐτοὶ τὰς ψυχικὰς κινήσεις εὐεπηβόλους[2] τε ἔχουσι καὶ διερευνητικὰς καὶ τῶν ἰδίως καλουμένων μαθημάτων περιοδευτικάς. καὶ τούτων δὲ πάλιν οἱ μὲν πρὸς ἕω μᾶλλόν εἰσιν ἠρρενωμένοι καὶ εὔτονοι τὰς ψυχὰς[3] καὶ πάντα ἐκφαίνοντες, ἐπειδὴ τὰς ἀνατολὰς ἄν τις εἰκότως τῆς ἡλιακῆς φύσεως ὑπολάβοι[4] καὶ τὸ μέρος ἐκεῖνο ἡμερινόν τε καὶ ἀρρενικὸν καὶ δεξιόν, καθ' ὃ κἂν τοῖς ζώοις ὁρῶμεν τὰ δεξιὰ μέρη μᾶλλον ἐπιτηδειότητα ἔχοντα πρὸς ἰσχὺν καὶ εὐτονίαν. οἱ δὲ πρὸς ἑσπέραν τεθηλυσμένοι μᾶλλόν εἰσι καὶ τὰς ψυχὰς ἁπαλώτεροι καὶ τὰ πολλὰ κρύπτοντες, ἐπειδὴ πάλιν τοῦτο τὸ μέρος
58 σεληνιακὸν τυγχάνει, πάντοτε τῆς σελήνης τὰς

---

[1] τῷ ζωδιακῷ καὶ τοῖς πλανωμένοις περὶ αὐτὸν ἀστράσιν NCam.
[2] εὐεπιβούλους VPLD.
[3] ταῖς ψυχαῖς PLNCam.
[4] διὰ τοῦτο post ὑπολάβοι add. NACam.

neither directly over their heads nor far distant at its noon-day transits, share in the equable temperature of the air, which varies, to be sure, but has no violent changes from heat to cold. They are therefore medium in colouring, of moderate stature, in nature equable, live close together, and are civilized in their habits. The southernmost of them [1] are in general more shrewd and inventive, and better versed in the knowledge of things divine because their zenith is close to the zodiac and to the planets revolving about it. Through this affinity the men themselves are characterized by an activity of the soul which is sagacious, investigative, and fitted for pursuing the sciences specifically called mathematical. Of them, again, the eastern group are more masculine, vigorous of soul, and frank in all things,[2] because one would reasonably assume that the orient partakes of the nature of the sun.[3] This region therefore is diurnal, masculine, and right-handed, even as we observe that among the animals too their right-hand parts are better fitted for strength and vigour. Those to the west are more feminine, softer of soul, and secretive, because this region, again, is lunar, for it is always in the west that the

---

[1] The anonymous commentator (p. 56, ed. Wolf) says that he means the Egyptians and the Chaldaeans, and is referring to the fact that they discovered astrology.

[2] This phrase (πάντα ἐκφαίνοντες) is contrasted with τὰ πολλὰ κρύπτοντες, below. The anonymous commentator says that some understood it to refer to the freedom of speech of the eastern group; others, to their gift of felicitous expression.

[3] *Cf.* i. 6; not only the sun, but also the oriental quadrant, is masculine.

PTOLEMY

πρώτας ἐπιτολὰς καὶ[1] ἀπὸ συνόδου φαντασίας ἀπὸ λιβὸς ποιουμένης. διὰ δὴ τοῦτο νυκτερινὸν δοκεῖ κλίμα θηλυκὸν[2] καὶ εὐώνυμον ἀντικειμένως τῷ ἀνατολικῷ.

Ἤδη δέ τινες καὶ ἐν ἑκάστοις τούτοις τῶν ὅλων μερῶν[3] ἰδιότροποι περιστάσεις ἠθῶν καὶ νομίμων φυσικῶς ἐξηκολούθησαν. ὥσπερ γὰρ ἐπὶ τῶν τοῦ περιέχοντος καταστημάτων καὶ ἐν τοῖς[4] ὡς ἐπὶ πᾶν κατειλεγμένοις θερμοῖς ἢ ψυχροῖς ἢ εὐκράτοις καὶ κατὰ μέρος ἰδιάζουσι τόποι καὶ χῶραί τινες ἐν τῷ μᾶλλον ἢ ἧττον ἤτοι διὰ θέσεως τάξιν ἢ ὕψος ἢ ταπεινότητα ἢ διὰ παράθεσιν· ἔτι δὲ ὡς ἱππικοί τινες μᾶλλον διὰ τὸ τῆς χώρας πεδινόν, καὶ ναυτικοὶ διὰ τὴν τῆς θαλάττης ἐγγύτητα, καὶ ἥμεροι διὰ τὴν τῆς χώρας εὐθηνίαν, οὕτω καὶ ἐκ τῆς πρὸς τοὺς ἀστέρας κατὰ τὰ δωδεκατημόρια φυσικῆς τῶν κατὰ μέρος κλιμάτων[5] συνοικειώσεως ἰδιοτρόπους ἄν τις εὕροι φύσεις παρ' ἑκάστοις, καὶ αὐτὰς δὲ ὡς ἐπὶ πᾶν οὐχ ὡς καὶ καθ' ἕνα ἕκαστον πάντως ἐνυπαρχούσας. ἀναγκαῖον οὖν ἐφ' ὧν ἂν εἴη χρήσιμον πρὸς τὰς κατὰ μέρος ἐπισκέψεις κεφαλαιωδῶς ἐπελθεῖν.[6]

[1] καὶ om. NAECam.
[2] κλίμα θηλυκὸν om. Cam.
[3] ὅλων μερῶν VMADE, δώδεκα μερῶν PL, δωδεκατημορίων NCam.
[4] τοῖς VD, αὐτοῖς PMNAECam., om. L.
[5] κλιμάτων VLMADE, λημμάτων PNCam.
[6] Post ἐπελθεῖν capitis titulum habent VMADProc.

moon emerges and makes its appearance after conjunction. For this reason it appears to be a nocturnal clime, feminine, and, in contrast with the orient, left-handed.

And now in each of these general regions certain special conditions of character and customs [1] naturally ensue. For as likewise, in the case of the climate, even within the regions that in general are reckoned as hot, cold, or temperate, certain localities and countries have special peculiarities of excess or deficiency by reason of their situation, height, lowness, or adjacency; and again, as some peoples are more inclined to horsemanship because theirs is a plain country, or to seamanship because they live close to the sea, or to civilization because of the richness of their soil, so also would one discover special traits in each arising from the natural familiarity of their particular climes with the stars in the signs of the zodiac. These traits, too, would be found generally present, but not in every individual. We must, then, deal with the subject summarily, in so far as it might be of use for the purpose of particular investigations.

[1] *I.e.* variations from the normal or general characteristics of the whole region.

PTOLEMY

⟨γ.⟩ Περὶ τῆς τῶν χωρῶν πρὸς τὰ τρίγωνα καὶ τοὺς ἀστέρας συνοικειώσεως

Τεττάρων δὴ τριγωνικῶν σχημάτων ἐν τῷ ζωδιακῷ θεωρουμένων, ὡς δέδεικται διὰ τῶν ἔμπροσθεν ἡμῖν, ὅτι τὸ μὲν κατὰ Κριὸν καὶ Λέοντα καὶ Τοξότην βορρολυβικόν τέ ἐστι καὶ οἰκοδεσποτεῖται μὲν προηγουμένως ὑπὸ τοῦ τοῦ Διὸς διὰ τὸ βόρειον, συνοικοδεσποτεῖται δὲ καὶ ὑπὸ τοῦ Ἄρεως διὰ τὸ λιβυκόν· τὸ δὲ κατὰ τὸν Ταῦρον καὶ τὴν Παρθένον καὶ τὸν Αἰγόκερων νοταπηλιωτικόν τέ ἐστι καὶ οἰκοδεσποτεῖται πάλιν προηγουμένως μὲν ὑπὸ τοῦ τῆς Ἀφροδίτης διὰ τὸ νότιον, συνοικοδεσποτεῖται δὲ ὑπὸ τοῦ Κρόνου διὰ τὸ ἀπηλιωτικόν· τὸ δὲ κατὰ τοὺς Διδύμους καὶ τὰς Χηλὰς καὶ τὸν Ὑδροχόον βορραπηλιωτικόν τέ ἐστι καὶ οἰκοδεσποτεῖται προηγουμένως μὲν ὑπὸ τοῦ Κρόνου διὰ τὸ ἀπηλιωτικόν, συνοικοδεσποτεῖται δὲ ὑπὸ τοῦ Διὸς διὰ τὸ βόρειον· τὸ δὲ κατὰ τὸν Καρκίνον καὶ τὸν Σκορπίον καὶ τοὺς Ἰχθῦς νοτολιβυκόν τέ ἐστι καὶ οἰκοδεσποτεῖται προηγουμένως μὲν ὑπὸ τοῦ τοῦ Ἄρεως διὰ τὸ λιβυκόν, συνοικοδεσποτεῖται δὲ ὑπὸ τοῦ τῆς Ἀφροδίτης διὰ τὸ νότιον—

Τούτων δὲ οὕτως ἐχόντων διαιρουμένης τε τῆς καθ' ἡμᾶς οἰκουμένης εἰς τέτταρα τεταρτημόρια, τοῖς τριγώνοις ἰσάριθμα, κατὰ μὲν πλάτος ὑπό τε τῆς καθ' ἡμᾶς θαλάττης ἀπὸ τοῦ Ἡρακλείου πορθμοῦ μέχρι τοῦ Ἰσσικοῦ κόλπου καὶ τῆς ἐφεξῆς

TETRABIBLOS II. 3

3. *Of the Familiarities between Countries and the Triplicities and Stars.*

Now of the four triangular formations recognized in the zodiac, as we have shown above,[1] the one which consists of Aries, Leo, and Sagittarius is northwestern, and is chiefly dominated by Jupiter on account of the north wind, but Mars joins in its government because of the south-west wind. That which is made up of Taurus, Virgo, and Capricornus is south-eastern, and again is governed primarily by Venus on account of the south wind, but conjointly by Saturn because of the east wind. The one consisting of Gemini, Libra, and Aquarius is north-eastern and is governed primarily by Saturn because of the east wind, and conjointly by Jupiter because of the north wind. The triangle of Cancer, Scorpio, and Pisces is south-western and is governed primarily, because of the west wind, by Mars, who is joined by Venus as co-ruler on account of the south wind.

As this is so, and since our inhabited world is divided into four quarters,[2] equal in number to the triangles, and is divided latitudinally by our sea from the Straits of Hercules[3] to the Gulf of Issus and the mountainous ridge adjacent on the east,[4]

---

[1] *Cf.* i. 18.
[2] Cardanus, p. 181, diagrammatically figures the "inhabited world" as a trapezium, narrower at the top (north) than the bottom, and bounded by arcs; this is divided into quadrants by north-south and east-west lines. The "parts closer to the centre" are then marked off by lines joining the ends of the two latter, dividing each quadrant and producing 4 right-angled triangles at the centre.
[3] Straits of Gibraltar.   [4] Probably the Taurus range.

PTOLEMY

πρὸς ἀνατολὰς ὀρεινῆς ῥάχεως,[1] ὑφ' ὧν χωρίζεται τό τε νότιον καὶ τὸ βόρειον αὐτῆς μέρος, κατὰ δὲ μῆκος ὑπὸ τοῦ Ἀραβικοῦ κόλπου, διὰ καὶ τοῦ Αἰγαίου πελάγους καὶ Πόντου καὶ τῆς Μαιώτιδος λίμνης, ὑφ' ὧν χωρίζεται τό τε ἀπηλιωτικὸν καὶ τὸ λιβυκὸν μέρος, γίνεται τεταρτημόρια τέτταρα, σύμφωνα τῇ θέσει τῶν τριγώνων· ἓν μὲν πρὸς βορρολίβα[2] τῆς ὅλης οἰκουμένης κείμενον, τὸ κατὰ τὴν Κελτογαλατίαν, ὃ δὴ κοινῶς Εὐρώπην καλοῦμεν· τούτῳ δὲ ἀντικείμενον καὶ πρὸς τὸν νοταπηλιώτην τὸ κατὰ τὴν ἑῴαν Αἰθιοπίαν, ὃ δὴ τῆς μεγάλης Ἀσίας νότιον μέρος ἂν καλοῖτο· καὶ πάλιν τὸ μὲν πρὸς βορραπηλιώτην τῆς ὅλης οἰκουμένης τὸ κατὰ τὴν Σκυθίαν, ὃ δὴ καὶ αὐτὸ βόρειον μέρος τῆς μεγάλης Ἀσίας γίνεται· τὸ δὲ ἀντικείμενον τούτῳ καὶ πρὸς λιβόνοτον ἄνεμον τὸ κατὰ τὴν ἑσπερίαν Αἰθιοπίαν, ὃ δὴ κοινῶς Λιβύην καλοῦμεν.

Πάλιν δὲ καὶ ἑκάστου τῶν προκειμένων τεταρτημορίων τὰ μὲν πρὸς τὸ μέσον μᾶλλον ἐσχηματισμένα τῆς ὅλης οἰκουμένης τὴν ἐναντίαν λαμβάνει θέσιν[3] πρὸς αὐτὸ τὸ περιέχον τεταρτημορίον, ὥσπερ[4] ἐκεῖνο πρὸς ὅλην τὴν οἰκουμένην, τοῦ τε κατὰ τὴν Εὐρώπην πρὸς βορρολίβα κειμένου τῆς ὅλης οἰκουμένης τὰ περὶ τὸ μέσον αὐτοῦ καὶ ἀντιγώνια πρὸς νοταπηλιώτην τοῦ αὐτοῦ τεταρτημορίου τὴν θέσιν ἔχοντα φαίνεται. καὶ ἐπὶ τῶν ἄλλων ὁμοίως, ὡς

---

[1] ῥάχεως VMADE, ῥαχείας NCam., ῥαχαίας PL.
[2] βορρᾶν καὶ λίβα NMECam.
[3] θέσιν VMADE, φύσιν PNCam., om. L.
[4] ὥσπερ VD, ἤπερ NCam., ἤνπερ PLMAE. Cf. Proc.: ἐναντίως κεῖται πρὸς . . . . καθ' ὥσπερ ἐκεῖνο . . . κεῖται κτλ.

TETRABIBLOS II. 3

and by these its southern and northern portions are separated, and in longitude by the Arabian Gulf, the Aegean Sea, the Pontus,[1] and the Lake Maeotis, whereby the eastern and western portions are separated, there arise four quarters, and these agree in position with the triangles. The first quarter lies in the north-west of the whole inhabited world; it embraces Celtic Gaul [2] and we give it the general name Europe. Opposite this is the south-eastern quarter; this includes eastern Ethiopia,[3] which would be called the southern part of Greater Asia. Again, the north-eastern quarter of the whole inhabited world is that which contains Scythia, which likewise is the northern part of Greater Asia; and the quarter opposite this and toward the south-west wind, the quarter of western Ethiopia, is that which we call by the general term Libya.

Again, of each of the aforesaid quarters the parts which are placed closer to the centre of the inhabited world are placed in a contrary fashion with respect to the surrounding quarters, just as are the latter in comparison with the whole world; and since the European quarter lies in the north-west of the whole world, the parts about the centre, which are allied to the opposite angle, obviously are situated in the south-east part of the quarter. The

---

[1] The Pontus Euxinus, or Black Sea. The Lake Maeotis is the Sea of Azov.

[2] As opposed to Galatia in Asia Minor.

[3] The designation of India as "Eastern Ethopia" is at variance with Ptolemy's *Geography*, and a mark of the influence of Posidonius (Boll, *Studien*, pp. 211-212). The distinction of two Ethiopias rests on the well-known Homeric passage, *Odyssey*, i. 22-24.

PTOLEMY

ἐκ τούτων ἕκαστον τῶν τεταρτημορίων δυσὶ τοῖς ἀντικειμένοις τριγώνοις συνοικειοῦσθαι· τῶν μὲν ἄλλων μερῶν πρὸς· τὴν καθ᾿ ὅλου πρόσνευσιν ἐφαρμοζομένων, τῶν δὲ περὶ τὸ μέσον πρὸς τὴν κατ᾿ αὐτὸ τὸ μέρος ἀντικειμένην συμπαραλαμβανομένων πρὸς τὴν οἰκείωσιν, καὶ τῶν ἐν τοῖς οἰκείοις τριγώνοις τὴν οἰκοδεσποτίαν ἐχόντων ἀστέρων, ἐπὶ μὲν τῶν ἄλλων οἰκήσεων πάλιν αὐτῶν μόνων,[1] ἐπὶ δὲ τῶν περὶ τὸ μέσον τῆς οἰκουμένης κἀκείνων καὶ ἔτι τοῦ τοῦ Ἑρμοῦ διὰ τὸ μέσον καὶ κοινὸν αὐτὸν ὑπάρχειν τῶν αἱρέσεων.

Ἐκ δὴ τῆς[2] τοιαύτης διατάξεως τὰ μὲν ἄλλα μέρη τοῦ πρώτου τῶν τεταρτημορίων, λέγω δὲ τοῦ κατὰ τὴν Εὐρώπην, πρὸς βορρολίβα κείμενα τῆς ὅλης[3] οἰκουμένης, συνοικειοῦται μὲν τῷ βορρολιβυκῷ τριγώνῳ τῷ κατὰ τὸν Κριὸν καὶ Λέοντα καὶ Τοξότην, οἰκοδεσποτεῖται δὲ εἰκότως ὑπὸ τῶν κυρίων τοῦ τριγώνου Διὸς καὶ Ἄρεως ἑσπερίων. ἔστι δὲ ταῦτα καθ᾿ ὅλα ἔθνη λαμβανόμενα Βρεττανία, Γαλατία, Γερμανία, Βασταρνία, Ἰταλία, Γαλλία, Ἀπουλία,

[1] μόνων VPLNE, -ον MADCam.
[2] ἐκ δὴ τῆς κτλ. VPLMADE ; cf. Proc. ; ἐν δὲ τῇ κτλ. NCam.
[3] ὅλης VMADEProc. ; om. PLNCam.

---

[1] Cardanus (p. 182) gives four reasons why Mercury governs these central portions ; that he may have some dominion in the world ; because the inhabitants of the central regions are more given to the arts and sciences, of which Mercury is the patron ; because they are addicted to commerce, likewise in Mercury's field ; and because Mercury's nature lies midway between those of the other four planets.

[2] That Jupiter and Mars must be in the occidental

same holds of the other quarters, so that each of them is related to two oppositely situated triangles; for while the other parts are in harmony with the general inclination of the quarter, the portions at the centre [of the world] share in familiarity with the opposite inclination, and, again, of the stars that govern in their own triangles, in all the other domiciles they alone govern, but in the parts about the centre of the world likewise the other group, and Mercury besides,[1] because he is mid-way between and common to the two sects.

Under this arrangement, the remainder of the first quarter, by which I mean the European quarter, situated in the north-west of the inhabited world, is in familiarity with the north-western triangle, Aries, Leo, and Sagittarius, and is governed, as one would expect, by the lords of the triangle, Jupiter and Mars, occidental.[2] In terms of whole nations these parts consist of Britain, (Transalpine) Gaul, Germany, Bastarnia,[3] Italy, (Cisalpine) Gaul, Apulia,

position is an additional requirement which does not appear in the original statement of the government of the triangles. Cardanus, p. 182, points out that in Ptolemy's scheme Jupiter governs the whole north, Venus the south, Saturn the east, and Mars the west, but in the first quadrant Mars and Jupiter dominate *non simpliciter, sed occidentales*, in the second, Saturn and Venus, not absolutely, but in oriental aspects, and so on. This, he says, is to display the variety of the customs of the nations, for a planet in oriental aspect is so different from the same planet occidental that practically it is two planets instead of one.

[3] The south-western part of Russia and southern Poland. Boll, *op. cit.*, p. 197, n. 2, points out that Hephaestion, who follows Ptolemy closely, and Proclus do not mention Bastarnia, and that the name may not have been in Ptolemy's original text.

PTOLEMY

Σικελία, Τυρρηνία, Κελτική, Ἱσπανία. εἰκότως δὲ τοῖς προκειμένοις ἔθνεσιν ὡς ἐπὶ πᾶν συνέπεσε,[1] διά τε τὸ ἀρχικὸν τοῦ τριγώνου καὶ τοὺς συνοικοδεσποτήσαντας ἀστέρας, ἀνυποτάκτοις[2] τε εἶναι καὶ φιλελευθέροις καὶ φιλόπλοις καὶ φιλοπόνοις καὶ πολεμικωτάτοις καὶ ἡγεμονικοῖς καὶ καθαροῖς καὶ μεγαλοψύχοις· διὰ μέντοι τὸν ἑσπέριον σχηματισμὸν Διὸς καὶ Ἄρεως, καὶ ἔτι διὰ τὸ τοῦ προκειμένου 82 τριγώνου τὰ μὲν ἐμπρόσθια ἠρρενῶσθαι, τὰ δὲ ὀπίσθια τεθηλύσθαι, πρὸς μὲν τὰς γυναῖκας ἀζήλοις αὐτοῖς εἶναι συνέπεσε[3] καὶ καταφρονητικοῖς τῶν ἀφροδισίων, πρὸς δὲ τὴν τῶν ἀρρένων συνουσίαν κατακορεστέροις τε καὶ μᾶλλον ζηλοτύποις· αὐτοῖς δὲ τοῖς διατιθεμένοις μήτε αἰσχρὸν ἡγεῖσθαι τὸ γινόμενον μήτε ὡς ἀληθῶς ἀνάνδροις διὰ τοῦτο καὶ μαλακοῖς ἀποβαίνειν, ἕνεκεν τοῦ μὴ παθητικῶς διατίθεσθαι, συντηρεῖν δὲ τὰς ψυχὰς ἐπάνδρους καὶ κοινωνικὰς καὶ πιστὰς καὶ φιλοικείους καὶ εὐεργετικάς. καὶ τούτων δὲ αὐτῶν τῶν χωρῶν Βρεττανία μὲν καὶ Γαλατία καὶ Γερμανία καὶ Βασταρνία μᾶλλον τῷ Κριῷ συνοικειοῦνται καὶ τῷ τοῦ Ἄρεως· ὅθεν ὡς ἐπὶ πᾶν οἱ ἐν αὐταῖς ἀγριώτεροι καὶ αὐθαδέστεροι καὶ θηριώδεις τυγχάνουσιν. Ἰταλία δὲ καὶ Ἀπουλία, Γαλλία καὶ Σικελία τῷ Λέοντι καὶ τῷ ἡλίῳ· διόπερ ἡγεμονικοὶ μᾶλλον

---

[1] συνέπεσε VADE, συνέπεται alii Cam.
[2] ἀνυποτάκτοις κτλ. VMADE, -ους PLN Cam.
[3] συνέπεσε(ν) VADE, συνέπεται PLN, om. MCam.

---

[1] Tuscany.
[2] Probably western Spain (Boll, *op. cit.*, p. 205).

TETRABIBLOS II. 3

Sicily, Tyrrhenia,¹ Celtica,² and Spain. As one might expect, it is the general characteristic of these nations, by reason of the predominance of the triangle and the stars which join in its government, to be independent, liberty-loving, fond of arms, industrious, very warlike, with qualities of leadership, cleanly, and magnanimous. However, because of the occidental aspect of Jupiter and Mars, and furthermore because the first parts of the aforesaid triangle are masculine and the latter parts feminine,³ they are without passion for women⁴ and look down upon the pleasures of love, but are better satisfied with and more desirous of association with men. And they do not regard the act as a disgrace to the paramour, nor indeed do they actually become effeminate and soft thereby, because their disposition is not perverted, but they retain in their souls manliness, helpfulness, good faith, love of kinsmen, and benevolence. Of these same countries Britain, (Transalpine) Gaul, Germany, and Bastarnia are in closer familiarity with Aries and Mars. Therefore for the most part their inhabitants are fiercer, more headstrong, and bestial. But Italy, Apulia, (Cisalpine) Gaul, and Sicily have their familiarity with Leo and the

Γαλατία is used to designate Gaul proper, between the Rhine and the Pyrenees, and Γαλλία for northern Italy.

³ All the signs of this triangle are masculine; cf. i. 17. Perhaps Ptolemy merely means that when Aries is rising Sagittarius will be occidental and therefore feminine; so Ashmand.

⁴ This preference of the northern barbarians is charged against them by Aristotle and following him by Posidonius, Diodorus, Strabo, Athenaeus, Sextus Empiricus and others; cf. the instances collected by Bouché-Leclercq, p. 340, n. 2, and the discussion in Boll, *Studien*, pp. 207-208.

οὗτοι καὶ εὐεργετικοὶ καὶ κοινώνικοι. Τυρρηνία δὲ καὶ Κελτικὴ καὶ Ἱσπανία τῷ Τοξότῃ καὶ τῷ τοῦ Διός· ὅθεν τὸ φιλελεύθερον[1] αὐτοῖς[2] καὶ τὸ ἁπλοῦν καὶ τὸ φιλοκάθαρον. τὰ δὲ ἐν τούτῳ μὲν ὄντα τῷ τεταρτημορίῳ, περὶ δὲ τὸ μέσον ἐσχηματισμένα τῆς οἰκουμένης, Θράκη τε καὶ Μακεδονία καὶ Ἰλλυρία καὶ Ἑλλὰς καὶ Ἀχαία καὶ Κρήτη, ἔτι δὲ αἵ τε Κυκλάδες καὶ τὰ παράλια τῆς μικρᾶς Ἀσίας καὶ Κύπρου[3] πρὸς νοταπηλιώτην κείμενα τοῦ ὅλου τεταρτημορίου, προσλαμβάνει τὴν συνοικείωσιν τοῦ νοταπηλιωτικοῦ τριγώνου, τοῦ κατὰ τὸν Ταῦρον καὶ τὴν Παρθένον καὶ τὸν Αἰγόκερων, ἔτι δὲ συνοικοδεσπότας τόν τε τῆς Ἀφροδίτης καὶ τὸν τοῦ Κρόνου καὶ τὸν τοῦ Ἑρμοῦ· ὅθεν οἱ κατοικοῦντες τὰς χώρας[4] συγκατεσχηματισμένοι μᾶλλον ἀπέβησαν καὶ κεκραμένοι τοῖς τε σώμασι καὶ ταῖς ψυχαῖς· ἡγεμονικοὶ μὲν καὶ αὐτοὶ τυγχάνοντες καὶ γενναῖοι καὶ ἀνυπότακτοι διὰ τὸν τοῦ Ἄρεως, φιλελεύθεροι δὲ καὶ αὐτόνομοι καὶ δημοκρατικοὶ καὶ νομοθετικοὶ διὰ τὸν τοῦ Διός, φιλόμουσοι[5] δὲ καὶ φιλομαθεῖς καὶ φιλαγωνισταὶ καὶ καθάριοι ταῖς διαίταις[6] διὰ τὸν τῆς Ἀφροδίτης, κοινωνικοὶ δὲ καὶ φιλόξενοι καὶ φιλοδίκαιοι καὶ φιλογράμματοι καὶ ἐν λόγοις πρακτικώτατοι διὰ τὸν τοῦ Ἑρμοῦ, μυστηρίων δὲ μάλιστα συντελεστικοὶ διὰ τὸν τῆς Ἀφροδίτης ἑσπέριον σχηματισμόν. πάλιν δὲ κατὰ μέρος καὶ τούτων οἱ μὲν περὶ τὰς Κυκλάδας καὶ τὰ

[1] τὸ φιλελεύθερον . . . ἁπλοῦν καὶ om. Cam.
[2] αὐτοῖς VD, -ῶν PLMNAE.
[3] Κύπρου VDProc.; Κύπρον al. Cam.

sun; wherefore these peoples are more masterful, benevolent, and co-operative. Tyrrhenia, Celtica, and Spain are subject to Sagittarius and Jupiter, whence their independence, simplicity, and love of cleanliness. The parts of this quarter which are situated about the centre of the inhabited world, Thrace, Macedonia, Illyria, Hellas, Achaia,[1] Crete, and likewise the Cyclades, and the coastal regions of Asia Minor and Cyprus, which are in the south-east portion of the whole quarter, have in addition familiarity with the south-east triangle, Taurus, Virgo, and Capricornus, and its co-rulers Venus, Saturn, and Mercury. As a result the inhabitants of those countries are brought into conformity with these planets and both in body and soul are of a more mingled constitution. They too have qualities of leadership and are noble and independent, because of Mars; they are liberty-loving and self-governing, democratic and framers of law, through Jupiter; lovers of music and of learning, fond of contests and clean livers, through Venus; social, friendly to strangers, justice-loving, fond of letters, and very effective in eloquence, through Mercury; and they are particularly addicted to the performance of mysteries, because of Venus's occidental aspect. And again, part by part, those of this group who live in the

[1] Hellas is northern Greece and Achaia the Peloponnesus.

---

[4] ἐκείνας post χώρας add. MNAECam.
[5] φιλόμουσοι . . . φιλομαθεῖς post Ἄρεως ins. NCam.
[6] καθάριοι ταῖς διαίταις VMADE, καθ. τὰς διαγωγὰς Proc.; φιλοκάθαροι ταῖς καρδίαις PLNCam.

PTOLEMY

παράλια τῆς μικρᾶς Ἀσίας καὶ Κυπρου[1] τῷ τε Ταύρῳ καὶ τῷ τῆς Ἀφροδίτης μᾶλλον συνοικειοῦνται· ὅθεν ὡς ἐπὶ τὸ πολὺ τρυφηταί τέ εἰσι καὶ καθάριοι καὶ τοῦ σώματος ἐπιμέλειαν ποιούμενοι. οἱ δὲ περὶ τὴν Ἑλλάδα καὶ τὴν Ἀχαίαν καὶ τὴν Κρήτην τῇ τε Παρθένῳ καὶ τῷ τοῦ Ἑρμοῦ, διὸ μᾶλλον λογικοὶ τυγχάνουσι καὶ φιλομαθεῖς καὶ τὰ τῆς ψυχῆς ἀσκοῦντες πρὸ τοῦ σώματος. οἱ δὲ περὶ τὴν Μακεδονίαν καὶ Θρᾴκην καὶ Ἰλλυρίδα τῷ τε Αἰγόκερῳ καὶ τῷ τοῦ Κρόνου· διὸ φιλοκτήματοι μέν, οὐχ ἥμεροι δὲ οὕτως, οὐδὲ κοινωνικοὶ τοῖς νόμοις.

Τοῦ δὲ δευτέρου τεταρτημορίου τοῦ κατὰ τὸ νότιον μέρος τῆς μεγάλης Ἀσίας τὰ μὲν ἄλλα μέρη τὰ περιέχοντα Ἰνδικήν, Ἀριανήν, Γεδρωσίαν, Παρθίαν, Μηδίαν, Περσίδα, Βαβυλωνίαν, Μεσοποταμίαν, Ἀσσυρίαν, καὶ τὴν θέσιν ἔχοντα πρὸς νοταπηλιώτην τῆς ὅλης οἰκουμένης, εἰκότως καὶ αὐτὰ συνοικειοῦται μὲν τῷ νοταπηλιωτικῷ τριγώνῳ τοῦ Ταύρου καὶ Παρθένου καὶ Αἰγόκερῳ, οἰκοδεσποτοῦνται δὲ ὑπὸ[2] τοῦ τῆς Ἀφροδιτης καὶ τοῦ Κρόνου ἐπὶ ἑῴων σχηματισμῶν· διόπερ καὶ τὰς φύσεις τῶν ἐν αὐτοῖς ἀκολούθως ἄν τις εὕροι τοῖς ὑπὸ τῶν οὕτως οἰκοδεσποτησάντων ἀποτελουμένας· σέβουσί τε γὰρ τὸν μὲν τῆς Ἀφροδίτης Ἶσιν ὀνομάζοντες, τὸν δὲ τοῦ Κρόνου Μίθραν ἥλιον.[3] καὶ προθεσπίζουσιν οἱ πολλοὶ τὰ μέλλοντα· καθιεροῦνταί τε παρ'

---

[1] Κύπρου VPLDProc.; Κύπρον al. Cam.
[2] οἰκοδεσποτοῦνται δὲ ὑπὸ κτλ. PLMNAECam. (οἰκοδεσποτεῖται MAE, -οῦντα L); συνοικειοῦται δὲ τῷ τῆς Ἀφρ. VD, cf. Proc.

TETRABIBLOS II. 3

Cyclades and on the shores of Asia Minor and Cyprus are more closely familiar to Taurus and Venus. For this reason they are, on the whole, luxurious, clean, and attentive to their bodies. The inhabitants of Hellas, Achaia, and Crete, however, have a familiarity with Virgo and Mercury, and are therefore better at reasoning, and fond of learning, and they exercise the soul in preference to the body. The Macedonians, Thracians, and Illyrians have familiarity with Capricorn and Saturn, so that, though they are acquisitive, they are not so mild of nature, nor social in their institutions.

Of the second quarter, which embraces the southern part of Greater Asia, the other parts, including India, Ariana, Gedrosia,[1] Parthia, Media, Persia, Babylonia, Mesopotamia, and Assyria, which are situated in the south-east of the whole inhabited world, are, as we might presume, familiar to the south-eastern triangle, Taurus, Virgo, and Capricorn, and are governed by Venus and Saturn in oriental aspects. Therefore one would find that the natures of their inhabitants conform with the temperaments governed by such rulers; for they revere the star of Venus under the name of Isis,[2] and that of Saturn as Mithras Helios. Most of them, too, divine future events; and among

---

[1] Gedrosia is modern Baluchistan, and Ariana lay north of it, between Parthia and the Indus.
[2] For this region it would have been more accurate to identify Venus with Astarte or Istar. It was, of course, the original home of the worship of Mithras.

---

[3] Μίθραν ἥλιον VPLMDE, Μιθρανήλιον Proc., om. ἥλιον A, Μίθραν δὲ τὸν ἥλιον NCam.

αὐτοῖς τὰ γεννητικὰ μόρια διὰ τὸν τῶν προκειμένων ἀστέρων συσχηματισμὸν σπερματικὸν ὄντα φύσει. ἔτι δὲ θερμοὶ καὶ ὀχευτικοὶ καὶ καταφερεῖς πρὸς τὰ ἀφροδίσια τυγχάνουσιν· ὀρχηστικοί τε καὶ πηδηταὶ καὶ φιλόκοσμοι μὲν διὰ τὸν τῆς Ἀφροδίτης, ἁβροδίαιτοι[1] δὲ διὰ τὸν τοῦ Κρόνου. ἀναφανδὸν δὲ ποιοῦνται καὶ οὐ κρύβδην τὰς πρὸς τὰς γυναῖκας συνουσίας διὰ τὸ ἑῷον τοῦ σχηματισμοῦ, τὰς δὲ πρὸς τοὺς ἄρρενας ὑπερεχθραίνουσι. διὰ ταῦτα δὲ καὶ τοῖς πλείστοις αὐτῶν συνέπεσεν ἐκ τῶν μητέρων τεκνοῦν,[2] καὶ τὰς προσκυνήσεις τῷ στήθει ποιεῖσθαι διὰ τὰς ἑῴας ἀνατολὰς καὶ τὸ τῆς καρδίας ἡγεμονικὸν οἰκείως ἔχον πρὸς τὴν ἡλιακὴν δύναμιν. εἰσὶ δὲ ὡς ἐπὶ πᾶν καὶ τἄλλα μὲν[3] τὰ περὶ τὰς στολὰς καὶ κόσμους[4] καὶ ὅλως τὰς σωματικὰς σχέσεις τρυφεροὶ καὶ τεθηλυσμένοι διὰ τὸν τῆς Ἀφροδίτης, τὰς δὲ ψυχὰς καὶ τὰς προαιρέσεις μεγαλόφρονες καὶ γενναῖοι καὶ πολεμικοὶ διὰ τὸ οἰκείως ἔχειν τὸν τοῦ Κρόνου πρὸς τὸ τῶν ἀνατολῶν σχῆμα. κατὰ μέρος δὲ πάλιν τῷ μὲν Ταύρῳ καὶ τῷ τῆς Ἀφροδίτης μᾶλλον συνοικειοῦνται ἥ τε Παρθία καὶ ἡ Μηδία καὶ ἡ Περσίς·[5] ὅθεν οἱ ἐνταῦθα στολαῖς τε ἀνθίναις[6] χρῶνται κατακαλυπτόντες ἑαυτοὺς ὅλους πλὴν τοῦ στήθους, καὶ ὅλως εἰσὶν ἁβροδίαιτοι καὶ καθάριοι. τῇ δὲ Παρθένῳ καὶ τῷ τοῦ Ἑρμοῦ τὰ περὶ τὴν Βαβυλῶνα καὶ Μεσοποταμίαν καὶ Ἀσσυρίαν· διὸ καὶ παρὰ τοῖς ἐνταῦθα

---

[1] ἁβροδίαιτοι MNAECam. Anon. (ed. Wolf, p. 61); ἁπλοδίαιτοι VLPD; ἁπλῶς...διάγοντες Proc.
[2] τεκνοῦν VMADE, τέκνα PLNCam., τεκνοποιοῦσι Proc.

them there exists the practice of consecrating the genital organs because of the aspect of the aforesaid stars, which is by nature generative. Further, they are ardent, concupiscent, and inclined to the pleasures of love; through the influence of Venus they are dancers and leapers and fond of adornment, and through that of Saturn luxurious livers. They carry out their relations with women [1] openly and not in secret, because of the planets' oriental aspect, but hold in detestation such relations with males. For these reasons most of them beget children by their own mothers, and they do obeisance to the breast, by reason of the morning rising of the planets and on account of the primacy of the heart, which is akin to the sun's power. As for the rest, they are generally luxurious and effeminate in dress, in adornment, and in all habits relating to the body, because of Venus. In their souls and by their predilection they are magnanimous, noble, and warlike, because of the familiarity of Saturn oriental. Part by part, again, Parthia, Media, and Persia are more closely familiar to Taurus and Venus; hence their inhabitants use embroidered clothing, which covers their entire body except the breast, and they are as a general thing luxurious and clean. Babylonia, Mesopotamia, and Assyria are familiar to Virgo and

---

[1] Here again see the citations collected by Bouché-Leclercq, p. 341, n. 2, of the charges of sexual immorality and incest made in antiquity against these peoples.

---

[3] τἆλλα μὲν VD, τὰ μὲν ἄλλα PLMAE, om. NCom.
[4] καὶ κόσμους VMAD (κόσμος) E, κατά τε τοὺς κόσμους NCam., ἀνατολλὰς καὶ κόσμους P, ἀνατολικὰς καὶ κόσκου L.
[5] Περσική NCam.   [6] ἀνθηραῖς NCam.

PTOLEMY

τὸ μαθηματικὸν καὶ παρατηρητικὸν τῶν πέντε[1] ἀστέρων ἐξαίρετον συνέπεσε.[2] τῷ δὲ Αἰγόκερῳ καὶ τῷ τοῦ Κρόνου τὰ περὶ τὴν Ἰνδικὴν καὶ Ἀριανὴν καὶ Γεδρωσίαν, ὅθεν καὶ τὸ τῶν νεμομένων[3] τὰς χώρας ἄμορφον καὶ ἀκάθαρτον καὶ θηριῶδες. τὰ δὲ λοιπὰ τοῦ τεταρτημορίου μέρη περὶ τὸ μέσον ἐσχηματισμένα τῆς ὅλης οἰκουμένης Ἰδουμαία, Κοίλη Συρία, Ἰουδαία, Φοινίκη, Χαλδαϊκή, Ὀρχηνία, Ἀραβία Εὐδαίμων, τὴν θέσιν ἔχοντα πρὸς βορρολίβα τοῦ ὅλου τεταρτημορίου προσλαμβάνει πάλιν τὴν συνοικείωσιν τοῦ βορρολιβυκοῦ τριγώνου, Κριοῦ, Λέοντος, Τοξότου, ἔτι δὲ συνοικοδεσπότας τόν τε τοῦ Διὸς καὶ τὸν τοῦ Ἄρεως καὶ ἔτι τὸν τοῦ Ἑρμοῦ· διὸ μᾶλλον οὗτοι τῶν ἄλλων ἐμπορικώτεροι καὶ συναλλακτικώτεροι, πανουργότεροι δὲ καὶ δειλοκαταφρόνητοι καὶ ἐπιβουλευτικοὶ καὶ δουλόψυχοι καὶ ὅλως ἀλλοπρόσαλλοι διὰ τὸν τῶν προκειμένων ἀστέρων συσχηματισμόν. καὶ τούτων δὲ πάλιν οἱ μὲν περὶ τὴν Κοίλην Συρίαν καὶ Ἰδουμαίαν καὶ Ἰουδαίαν τῷ τε Κριῷ καὶ τῷ τοῦ Ἄρεως μᾶλλον συνοικειοῦνται· διόπερ ὡς ἐπὶ πᾶν θρασεῖς τέ εἰσι καὶ ἄθεοι καὶ ἐπιβουλευτικοί. Φοίνικες δὲ καὶ Χαλδαῖοι καὶ Ὀρχήνιοι τῷ Λέοντι

[1] πέντε VProc., om. alii Cam.
[2] συνέπεσε VMADE, συνέπεται NCam., συνέπεστι P, συνετίεται L.
[3] τὸ τῶν νεμομένων κτλ.] οἱ νεμόμενοι .... ἄμορφοι κτλ. NCam.

---

[1] Idumaea is the region around the south end of the Dead Sea; Coelê Syria, north of Palestine and between Lebanon and Anti-Libanus; Judaea, between the Dead Sea and the

Mercury, and so the study of mathematics and the observation of the five planets are special traits of these peoples. India, Ariana, and Gedrosia have familiarity with Capricorn and Saturn; therefore the inhabitants of these countries are ugly, unclean, and bestial. The remaining parts of the quarter, situated about the centre of the inhabited world, Idumaea, Coelê Syria, Judaea, Phoenicia, Chaldaea, Orchinia, and Arabia Felix,[1] which are situated toward the north-west of the whole quarter, have additional familiarity with the north-western triangle, Aries, Leo, and Sagittarius, and, furthermore, have as co-rulers Jupiter, Mars, and Mercury. Therefore these peoples are, in comparison with the others, more gifted in trade and exchange; they are more unscrupulous, despicable cowards, treacherous, servile, and in general fickle, on account of the aspect of the stars mentioned. Of these, again, the inhabitants of Coelê Syria, Idumaea, and Judaea are more closely familiar to Aries and Mars, and therefore these peoples are in general bold, godless,[2] and scheming. The Phoenicians, Chaldaeans, and Orchinians have familiarity with Leo and the sun, so that

coast; Phoenicia the coastal strip north of Judaea and Samaria; Chaldaea, south-west of the Euphrates and north of the Arabian peninsula; what is meant by Orchinia is somewhat doubtful; and Arabia Felix is the south-western coastal region of the Arabian peninsula. In the *Geography*, v. 20, Chaldaea is treated merely as a part of Babylonia, not an entirely separate country, as here (*cf.* Boll, *Studien*, p. 205).

[2] The Jews, because of their monotheism and disregard of all pagan gods, were generally branded as atheists by their neighbours.

καὶ τῷ ἡλίῳ, διόπερ ἁπλούστεροι καὶ φιλάνθρωποι καὶ φιλαστρόλογοι καὶ μάλιστα πάντων σέβοντες τὸν ἥλιον. οἱ δὲ κατὰ τὴν Ἀραβίαν τὴν Εὐδαίμονα τῷ Τοξότῃ καὶ τῷ τοῦ Διός· ὅθεν ἀκολούθως τῇ προσηγορίᾳ τό τε τῆς χώρας εὔφορον συνέπεσε καὶ τὸ τῶν ἀρωμάτων πλῆθος καὶ τὸ τῶν ἀνθρώπων εὐάρμοστον πρός τε διαγωγὰς ἐλεύθερον καὶ συναλλαγὰς καὶ πραγματείας.

Τοῦ δὲ τρίτου τεταρτημορίου τοῦ κατὰ τὸ βόρειον μέρος τῆς μεγάλης Ἀσίας τὰ μὲν ἄλλα μέρη τὰ περιέχοντα τὴν Ὑρκανίαν, Ἀρμενίαν, Ματιανήν, 67 Βακτριανήν, Κασπηρίαν,¹ Σηρικήν, Σαυροματικήν, Ὀξειανήν, Σουγδιανήν, καὶ τὰ πρὸς βορραπηλιώτην κείμενα τῆς ὅλης οἰκουμένης συνοικειοῦνται μὲν τῷ βορραπηλιωτικῷ τριγώνῳ, Διδύμων καὶ Ζυγοῦ καὶ Ὑδροχόου, οἰκοδεσποτεῖται δὲ εἰκότως ὑπό τε τοῦ Κρόνου καὶ τοῦ Διὸς ἐπὶ σχημάτων ἀνατολικῶν· διόπερ οἱ ταύτας ἔχοντες τὰς χώρας σέβουσι μὲν Δία καὶ Κρόνον,² πλουσιώτατοι δέ εἰσι καὶ πολύχρυσοι, περί τε τὰς διαίτας καθάριοι καὶ εὐδιάγωγοι, σοφοί τε ἐπὶ τὰ θεῖα καὶ μάγοι καὶ τὰ ἤθη δίκαιοι καὶ ἐλεύθεροι καὶ τὰς ψυχὰς μεγάλοι καὶ γενναῖοι, μισοπόνηροί τε καὶ φιλόστοργοι καὶ ὑπεραποθνήσκοντες ἑτοίμως τῶν οἰκειοτάτων ἕνεκεν τοῦ καλοῦ καὶ ὁσίου, πρός τε τὰς ἀφροδισίους χρήσεις σεμνοὶ

---

¹ Κασπειρίαν VD, -ηρίαν NMAE, -ιρίαν Proc., -ίαν Cam., om. PL.
² ἥλιον VMADEProc., Κρόνον PLNCam.

---

[1] Astrology indeed began in the ancient Babylonian and Assyrian kingdoms.

they are simpler, kindly, addicted to astrology,[1] and beyond all men worshippers of the sun. The inhabitants of Arabia Felix are familiar to Sagittarius and Jupiter; this accounts for the fertility of the country, in accordance with its name, and its multitudes of spices, and the grace of its inhabitants and their free spirit in daily life, in exchange, and in business.

Of the third quarter, which includes the northern part of Greater Asia, the other parts, embracing Hyrcania, Armenia, Matiana, Bactriana, Casperia, Serica, Sauromatica, Oxiana, Sogdiana, and the regions in the north-east of the inhabited world,[2] are in familiarity with the north-eastern triangle, Gemini, Libra, and Aquarius, and are, as might be expected, governed by Saturn and Jupiter in oriental aspect. Therefore the inhabitants of these lands worship Jupiter and Saturn, have much riches and gold, and are cleanly and seemly in their living, learned and adepts in matters of religion, just and liberal in manners, lofty and noble in soul, haters of evil, and affectionate, and ready to die for their friends in a fair and holy cause. They are dignified and

[2] Of these Armenia lies south of the Caucasus between the Black Sea and the Caspian; Matiana and Hyrcania are around the south end of the Caspian, the former to the east and the latter to the west; Bactriana, Oxiana, and Sogdiana are still further east, around the upper courses of the Oxus; by Casperia is probably meant the region around the northern part of the Caspian Sea; Serica is China, or its western portion, and Sauromatica (called Sarmatia by the Romans) is the general name for Russia, here used of its Asiatic part. In the *Geography*, vi. 12, Ptolemy treats Oxiana as but one part of Sogdiana (Boll, *Studien*, p. 205).

PTOLEMY

καὶ καθάριοι καὶ περὶ τὰς ἐσθῆτας πολυτελεῖς, χαριστικοί τε καὶ μεγαλόφρονες, ἅπερ ὡς ἐπὶ πᾶν ὁ τοῦ Κρόνου καὶ ὁ τοῦ Διὸς ἀνατολικῶν συσχηματισμὸς ἀπεργάζεται.[1] καὶ τούτων δὲ πάλιν τῶν ἐθνῶν τὰ μὲν περὶ τὴν Ὑρκανίαν καὶ Ἀρμενίαν καὶ Ματιανὴν μᾶλλον συνοικειοῦται τοῖς τε Διδύμοις καὶ τῷ τοῦ Ἑρμοῦ· διόπερ εὐκινητότερα μᾶλλον καὶ ὑποπόνηρα. τὰ δὲ περὶ τὴν Βακτριανὴν καὶ Κασπηρίαν καὶ Σηρικὴν τῷ τε Ζυγῷ καὶ τῷ τῆς Ἀφροδίτης· ὅθεν οἱ κατέχοντες τὰς χώρας πλουσιώτατοι καὶ φιλόμουσοι καὶ μᾶλλον ἁβροδίαιτοι. τὰ δὲ περὶ τὴν Σαυροματικὴν καὶ τὴν Ὀξειανὴν καὶ Σουγδιανὴν τῷ τε Ὑδροχόῳ καὶ τῷ τοῦ Κρόνου· διὸ καὶ ταῦτα τὰ ἔθνη μᾶλλον ἀνήμερα καὶ αὐστηρὰ καὶ θηριώδη. τὰ δὲ λοιπὰ τούτου τοῦ τεταρτημορίου καὶ περὶ τὸ μέσον κείμενα τῆς ὅλης οἰκουμένης, Βιθυνία, Φρυγία, Κολχική, Συρία, Κομμαγηνή, Καππαδοκία, Λυδία, Λυκία,[2] Κιλικία, Παμφυλία, τὴν θέσιν ἔχοντα πρὸς λιβόνοτον αὐτοῦ τοῦ τεταρτημορίου, προσλαμβάνει τὴν συνοικείωσιν τοῦ νοτολιβυκοῦ τεταρτημορίου Καρκίνου καὶ Σκορπίου καὶ Ἰχθύων, καὶ συνοικοδεσπότας τόν τε τοῦ Ἄρεως καὶ ἔτι τὸν τῆς Ἀφροδίτης καὶ τὸν τοῦ Ἑρμοῦ· διόπερ οἱ περὶ τὰς χώρας ταύτας σέβουσι μὲν ὡς ἐπὶ πᾶν τὴν Ἀφροδίτην ὡς μητέρα θεῶν, ποικίλοις καὶ ἐγχωρίοις ὀνόμασι προσαγορεύοντες, καὶ τὸν τοῦ Ἄρεως ὡς Ἄδωνιν ἢ ἄλλως πως πάλιν ὀνομάζοντες· καὶ μυστήριά τινα μετὰ θρηνῶν ἀπο-

---

[1] ἀνατολικῶν συσχηματισμὸς ἀπεργάζεται VD, -ὸς -ὸς -εται MAE, -ὸν -ὸν -εται PL, κατὰ -ὸν -ὸν -ονται NCam.

pure in their sexual relations, lavish in dress, gracious and magnanimous; these things in general are brought about by Saturn and Jupiter in eastern aspects. Of these nations, again, Hyrcania, Armenia, and Matiana are more closely familiar to Gemini and Mercury; they are accordingly more easily stirred and inclined to rascality. Bactriana, Casperia, and Serica are akin to Libra and Venus, so that their peoples are rich and followers of the Muses, and more luxurious. The regions of Sauromatica, Oxiana, and Sogdiana are in familiarity with Aquarius and Saturn; these nations therefore are more ungentle, stern, and bestial. The remaining parts of this quarter, which lie close to the centre of the inhabited world, Bithynia, Phrygia, Colchica, Syria, Commagenê, Cappadocia, Lydia, Lycia, Cilicia, and Pamphylia,[1] since they are situated in the south-west of the quarter, have in addition familiarity with the south-western quarter, Cancer, Scorpio, and Pisces, and their co-rulers are Mars, Venus, and Mercury; therefore those who live in these countries generally worship Venus as the mother of the gods, calling her by various local names, and Mars as Adonis,[2] to whom again they give other names, and they celebrate in their honour certain mysteries accompanied

---

[1] These are all parts of Asia Minor.
[2] Ptolemy identifies Venus and Mars, who are coupled in Greek mythology, with the female and male divinities of this region worshipped under various names as the Mother of the Gods, Magna Mater, etc., and Attis, Adonis, etc.

---

[2] Λυκία VDProc., om. alii Cam.

PTOLEMY

διδόντες αὐτοῖς. περίκακοι δέ εἰσι καὶ δουλόψυχοι καὶ πονικοὶ καὶ πονηροὶ καὶ ἐν μισθοφόροις στρατείαις καὶ ἁρπαγαῖς καὶ αἰχμαλωσίαις γινόμενοι, καταδουλούμενοί τε αὐτοὺς καὶ πολεμικαῖς ἀπωλείαις περιπίπτοντες. διά τε τὸν τοῦ Ἄρεως καὶ τὸν τῆς Ἀφροδίτης κατὰ ἀνατολικὴν συναρμογήν, ὅτι ἐν μὲν τῷ τῆς Ἀφροδίτης τριγωνικῷ ζῳδίῳ τῷ Αἰγόκερῳ ὁ τοῦ Ἄρεως, ἐν δὲ τῷ τοῦ Ἄρεως τριγωνικῷ ζῳδίῳ τοῖς Ἰχθύσι ὁ τῆς Ἀφροδίτης ὑψοῦται, διὰ τοῦτο τὰς γυναῖκας συνέβη πᾶσαν εὔνοιαν πρὸς τοὺς ἄνδρας ἐνδείκνυσθαι, φιλοστόργους τε οὔσας καὶ οἰκουροὺς καὶ ἐργατικὰς καὶ 69 ὑπηρετικὰς καὶ ὅλως πονικὰς καὶ ὑποτεταγμένας. τούτων δὲ πάλιν οἱ μὲν περὶ τὴν Βιθυνίαν καὶ Φρυγίαν καὶ Κολχικὴν συνοικειοῦνται μᾶλλον τῷ τε Καρκίνῳ καὶ τῇ σελήνῃ· διόπερ οἱ μὲν ἄνδρες ὡς ἐπὶ πᾶν εἰσιν εὐλαβεῖς καὶ ὑποτακτικοί, τῶν δὲ γυναικῶν αἱ πλεῖσται διὰ τὸ τῆς σελήνης ἀνατολικὸν καὶ ἠρρενωμένον[1] σχῆμα ἔπανδροι καὶ ἀρχικαὶ καὶ πολεμικαὶ καθάπερ αἱ Ἀμαζόνες, φεύγουσαι[2] μὲν τὰς τῶν ἀνδρῶν συνουσίας, φίλοπλοι δὲ οὖσαι καὶ ἀρρενοποιοῦσαι τὰ θηλυκὰ πάντα[3] ἀπὸ βρέφους, ἀποκοπῇ τῶν δεξιῶν μαστῶν χάριν τῶν στρατιωτικῶν χρειῶν[4] καὶ ἀπογυμνοῦσαι ταῦτα τὰ μέρη κατὰ[5] τὰς παρατάξεις[6] πρὸς ἐπίδειξιν[7] τοῦ ἀθηλύντου τῆς φύσεως. οἱ δὲ περὶ τὴν Συρίαν καὶ Κομμαγηνὴν καὶ Καππαδοκίαν τῷ τε Σκορπίῳ

---

[1] ἠρ(ρ)ενωμένον PLME, -ων N, ἠρρωμένον alii Cam., ἀρσενικὸν Proc.   [2] φεύγουσι(ν) PLMA.
[3] τὰ θηλυκὰ πάντα VD, τὸ θῆλυ (aut θύλη) PLNCam., τὸ

TETRABIBLOS II. 3

by lamentations. They are exceedingly depraved. servile, laborious, rascally, are to be found in mercenary expeditions, looting and taking captives, enslaving their own peoples, and engaging in destructive wars. And because of the junction of Mars and Venus in the Orient, since Mars is exalted in Capricorn, a sign of Venus's triangle, and Venus in Pisces, a sign of Mars's triangle, it comes about that their women display entire goodwill to their husbands; they are affectionate, home-keepers, diligent, helpful, and in every respect laborious and obedient. Of these peoples, again, those who live in Bithynia, Phrygia, and Colchica are more closely familiar to Cancer and the moon; therefore the men are in general cautious and obedient, and most of the women, through the influence of the moon's oriental and masculine aspect, are virile,[1] commanding, and warlike, like the Amazons, who shun commerce with men, love arms, and from infancy make masculine all their female characteristics, by cutting off their right breasts for the sake of military needs and baring these parts in the line of battle, in order to display the absence of femininity in their natures. The people of Syria, Commagenê, and Cappadocia are

---

[1] *Cf.* the myth of Medea, the Colchian princess.

θῆλυ πᾶν ME, τοῦ θήλεος παντός A ; cf. τῶν θηλυκῶν βρεφῶν Proc.
  [4] χρειῶν VP (χρη-) LMAEProc., χρήσεων NDCam.
  [5] κατὰ VMADE, διὰ PLNCam.
  [6] παρατάξεις VMADE, -ης P, -εως L, πράξεις NCam. ; ἐν ταῖς παρατάξεσιν Proc.
  [7] πρὸς ἐπίδειξιν VD, εἰς ἐ. MAE, ὡς ἐπιδείξην P, ὡς ἐπίδειξιν L, ὡς ἐπιδείκνυσθαι NCam.

καὶ τῷ τοῦ Ἄρεως· διόπερ πολὺ παρ' αὐτοῖς συνέπεσε τὸ θρασὺ καὶ πονηρὸν καὶ ἐπιβουλευτικὸν καὶ ἐπίπονον. οἱ δὲ περὶ τὴν Λυδίαν καὶ Κιλικίαν καὶ Παμφυλίαν τοῖς τε Ἰχθύσι καὶ τῷ τοῦ Διός· ὅθεν οὗτοι μᾶλλον πολυκτήμονές τε καὶ ἐμπορικοὶ καὶ κοινωνικοὶ καὶ ἐλεύθεροι καὶ πιστοὶ περὶ τὰς συναλλαγάς.

Τοῦ δὲ λοιποῦ τεταρτημορίου τοῦ κατὰ τὴν κοινῶς καλουμένην[1] Διβύην, τὰ μὲν ἄλλα τὰ περιέχοντα Νουμηδίαν,[2] Καρχηδονίαν, Ἀφρικήν, Φαζανίαν,[3] Νασαμονῖτιν, Γαραμαντικήν, Μαυριτανίαν, Γαιτουλίαν, Μεταγωνῖτιν, καὶ τὰ τὴν θέσιν ἔχοντα πρὸς λιβόνοτον τῆς ὅλης οἰκουμένης, συνοικειοῦται μὲν τῷ νοτολιβυκῷ τριγώνῳ Καρκίνου καὶ Σκορπίου καὶ Ἰχθύων, οἰκοδεσποτεῖται δὲ εἰκότως ὑπό τε τοῦ Ἄρεως καὶ τοῦ τῆς Ἀφροδίτης ἐπὶ σχήματος ἑσπερίου· διόπερ συνέπεσε τοῖς πλείστοις αὐτῶν ἕνεκεν τῆς εἰρημένης τῶν ἀστέρων συναρμογῆς ὑπὸ ἀνδρὸς καὶ γυναικός,[4] δυοῖν ὁμομητρίων ἀδελφῶν, βασιλεύεσθαι, τοῦ μὲν ἀνδρὸς τῶν ἀνδρῶν ἄρχοντος, τῆς δὲ γυναικὸς τῶν γυναικῶν, συντηρουμένης τῆς τοιαύτης διαδοχῆς. θερμοὶ δέ εἰσι σφόδρα καὶ καταφερεῖς πρὸς τὰς τῶν γυναικῶν συνουσίας, ὡς

---

[1] καλουμένην om. NCam.   [2] Νουμιδίαν ACam.
[3] Φυζανίαν NCam.
[4] Post γυναικός add. ἢ PLNCam., om. VMADEProc.

---

[1] Here used of the continent in general; Africa is the Roman province.

familiar to Scorpio and Mars; therefore much boldness, knavery, treachery, and laboriousness are found among them. The people of Lydia, Cilicia, and Pamphylia have familiarity with Pisces and Jupiter; these accordingly are more wealthy, commercial, social, free, and trustworthy in their compacts.

Of the remaining quarter, which includes what is called by the common name Libya,[1] the other parts, including Numidia, Carthage, Africa, Phazania, Nasamonitis, Garamantica, Mauritania, Gaetulia, Metagonitis,[2] and the regions situated in the south-west of the inhabited world, are related by familiarity to the south-western triangle, Cancer, Scorpio, and Pisces, and are accordingly ruled by Mars and Venus in occidental aspect. For this reason it befalls most of the inhabitants, because of the aforesaid junction of these planets, to be governed by a man and wife who are own brother and sister,[3] the man ruling the men and the woman the women; and a succession of this sort is maintained. They are extremely ardent and disposed to commerce with women, so that even

[2] Along the Mediterranean coast, eastward from the Straits of Gibraltar, the regions are, first, Mauritania (of which Metagonitis is the portion east from the Straits), then Numidia, Africa (the Roman province, which includes Carthage), Tripolitana, Cyrenaica, Marmarica, and Egypt. The other nations mentioned are further inland and south of these, Gaetulia in the west, Garamantica and Phazania south of Tripoli, and Nasamonitis near Cyrenaica and Marmarica.

[3] Marriage between those of the same blood was a common practice in Hellenistic Egypt, including the royal family of the Ptolemies. *Cf.* Cumont, *L'Égypte des Astrologues* (Brussels, 1937), pp. 177-179.

καὶ τοὺς γάμους δι' ἁρπαγῶν ποιεῖσθαι[1] καὶ πολλαχῇ ταῖς γαμουμέναις τοὺς βασιλέας πρώτους[2] συνέρχεσθαι, παρ' ἐνίοις δὲ καὶ κοινὰς εἶναι τὰς γυναῖκας πάντων. φιλοκαλλωπισταὶ δὲ τυγχάνουσι[3] καὶ κόσμους γυναικείους περιζώννυνται διὰ τὸν τῆς Ἀφροδίτης, ἔπανδροι μέντοι ταῖς ψυχαῖς καὶ ὑποπόνηροι καὶ μαγευτικοί, νοθευταὶ δὲ καὶ παράβολοι καὶ ῥιψοκίνδυνοι διὰ τὸν τοῦ Ἄρεως. τούτων δὲ πάλιν οἱ μὲν περὶ τὴν Νουμηδίαν καὶ Καρχηδόνα[4] καὶ Ἀφρικὴν συνοικειοῦνται μᾶλλον τῷ τε Καρκίνῳ καὶ τῇ σελήνῃ· διόπερ οὗτοι κοινωνικοί τε καὶ ἐμπορικοὶ τυγχάνουσι καὶ ἐν εὐθηνίᾳ πάσῃ διατελοῦντες, οἱ δὲ περὶ τὴν Μεταγωνῖτιν 71 καὶ Μαυριτανίαν καὶ Γαιτουλίαν τῷ τε Σκορπίῳ καὶ τῷ τοῦ Ἄρεως· ὅθεν οὗτοι θηριωδέστεροί τέ εἰσι καὶ μαχιμώτατοι καὶ κρεοφάγοι καὶ σφόδρα[5] ῥιψοκίνδυνοι καὶ καταφρονητικοὶ τοῦ ζῆν, ὡς μηδὲ ἀλλήλων ἀπέχεσθαι. οἱ δὲ περὶ τὴν Φαζανίαν καὶ Νασαμωνῖτιν καὶ Γαραμαντικὴν τοῖς τε Ἰχθύσι καὶ τῷ τοῦ Διός· διόπερ ἐλεύθεροί τε καὶ ἁπλοῖ τοῖς ἤθεσι καὶ φίλεργοὶ καὶ εὐγνώμονες καθάριοί τε καὶ ἀνυπότακτοί εἰσιν ὡς ἐπὶ πᾶν καὶ[6] τὸν τοῦ Διὸς ὡς Ἄμμωνα[7] θρησκεύοντες. τὰ δὲ λοιπὰ τοῦ τεταρτημορίου μέρη καὶ πρὸς τὸ μέσον ἐσχηματισμένα τῆς ὅλης οἰκουμένης, Κυρηναϊκή, Μαρμαρική,

---

[1] ποιεῖσθαι] γίνεσθαι VAD.
[2] πρώτους VMDE, cf. Proc.; πρῶτα PLNACam.
[3] τυγχάνουσι(ν) VMADE, ὑπάρχουσι(ν) PLNCam.
[4] Καρχηδόνα VDProc., Καρχηδονίαν P (-δω-) LMNAECam.
[5] σφόδρα VMADEProc., om. PLNCam.
[6] καί (post ἐπὶ πᾶν) VMADE, διά NCam., om. PL.

TETRABIBLOS II. 3

their marriages are brought about by violent abduction, and frequently their kings enjoy the *jus primae noctis* with the brides, and among some of them the women are common to all the men. They are fond of beautifying themselves and gird themselves with feminine adornments, through the influence of Venus; through that of Mars, however, they are virile of spirit, rascally, magicians, impostors, deceivers, and reckless. Of these people, again, the inhabitants of Numidia, Carthage, and Africa are more closely familiar to Cancer and the moon. They therefore are social, commercial, and live in great abundance. Those who inhabit Metagonitis, Mauritania, and Gaetulia are familiar to Scorpio and Mars; they are accordingly fiercer and very warlike, meat-eaters, very reckless, and contemptuous of life to such an extent as not even to spare one another. Those who live in Phazania, Nasamonitis, and Garamantica are familiar to Pisces and Jupiter; hence they are free and simple in their characters, willing to work, intelligent, cleanly, and independent, as a general rule, and they are worshippers of Jupiter as Ammon. The remaining parts of the quarter, which are situated near the centre of the inhabited world, Cyrenaica, Marmarica, Egypt, Thebais,[1] the Oasis,

[1] Upper Egypt. By "Egypt" he doubtless means Lower Egypt. Cyrenaica and Marmarica are to the west. Troglodytica lies along the west coast of the Red Sea and Azania about where is now French Somaliland. By Arabia he may mean Arabia Petraea, the Sinai Peninsula and vicinity. Parts of Troglodytica, too, were sometimes called Arabia. The Greater and Lesser Oases lie west of the Thebais.

[7] ὡς Ἄμμωνα VMADE; *cf.* Proc.; τῷ Ἄμμονι PNCam.; τῷ σάμωνα L.

PTOLEMY

Αἴγυπτος, Θηβαΐς, Ὄασις, Τρωγλοδυτική, Ἀραβία, Ἀζανία, μέση Αἰθιοπία, πρὸς βορραπηλιώτην τετραμμένα τοῦ ὅλου τεταρτημορίου, προσλαμβάνει τὴν συνοικείωσιν τοῦ βορραπηλιωτικοῦ τριγώνου Διδύμων, Ζυγοῦ, καὶ Ὑδροχόου, καὶ συνοικοδεσπότας διὰ τοῦτο τόν τε τοῦ Κρόνου καὶ τὸν τοῦ Διὸς καὶ ἔτι τὸν τοῦ Ἑρμοῦ· ὅθεν οἱ κατὰ ταύτας τὰς χώρας κεκοινωνηκότες σχεδὸν τῆς τῶν πέντε[1] πλανήτων οἰκοδεσποτίας ἑσπερίου φιλόθεοι μὲν γεγόνασι καὶ δεισιδαίμονες καὶ θεοπρόσπλοκοι[2] καὶ φιλόθρηνοι καὶ τοὺς ἀποθνήσκοντας τῇ γῇ κρύπτοντες καὶ ἀφανίζοντες διὰ τὸ ἑσπέριον σχῆμα, παντοίοις δὲ νομίμοις καὶ ἔθεσι καὶ θεῶν παντοίων θρησκείαις χρώμενοι, καὶ ἐν μὲν ταῖς ὑποταγαῖς ταπεινοὶ καὶ δειλοὶ[3] καὶ μικρολόγοι καὶ ὑπομονητικοί, ἐν δὲ ταῖς ἡγεμονίαις εὔψυχοι καὶ μεγαλόφρονες, πολυγύναιοι δὲ καὶ πολύανδροι καὶ καταφερεῖς καὶ ταῖς ἀδελφαῖς συναρμοζόμενοι, καὶ πολύσποροι μὲν οἱ ἄνδρες, εὐσύλληπτοι δὲ αἱ γυναῖκες ἀκολούθως τῷ τῆς χώρας γονίμῳ.[4] πολλοὶ δὲ καὶ τῶν ἀρρένων σαθροὶ καὶ τεθηλυσμένοι ταῖς ψυχαῖς, ἔνιοι δὲ καὶ τῶν γεννητικῶν μορίων καταφρονοῦντες διὰ τὸν τῶν κακοποιῶν μετὰ τοῦ τῆς Ἀφροδίτης ἑσπερίου[5] σχηματισμόν. καὶ τούτων δὲ οἱ μὲν περὶ Κυρηναϊκὴν καὶ Μαρμαρικὴν καὶ μάλιστα οἱ περὶ τὴν κάτω χώραν τῆς Αἰγύπτου μᾶλλον συνοικειοῦνται τοῖς τε Διδύμοις καὶ τῷ τοῦ Ἑρμοῦ·

[1] πέντε libri Proc., μὲν Cam.
[2] θεοπρόσπλοκοι VPLD; προσπλεκόμενοι πρὸς θεούς Proc.; θεοπρόσπολοι MNAECam.

TETRABIBLOS II. 3

Troglodytica, Arabia, Azania, and Middle Ethiopia, which face the north-east of the whole quarter, have an additional familiarity with the north-eastern triangle Gemini, Libra, and Aquarius, and therefore have as co-rulers Saturn and Jupiter and, furthermore, Mercury. Accordingly those who live in these countries, because they all in common, as it were, are subject to the occidental rulership of the five planets, are worshippers of the gods, superstitious, given to religious ceremony and fond of lamentation; they bury their dead in the earth, putting them out of sight, on account of the occidental aspect of the planets; and they practice all kinds of usages, customs, and rites in the service of all manner of gods. Under command they are humble, timid, penurious, and long-suffering, in leadership courageous and magnanimous; but they are polygamous and polyandrous and lecherous, marrying even their own sisters, and the men are potent in begetting, the women in conceiving, even as their land is fertile. Furthermore, many of the males are unsound and effeminate of soul, and some even hold in contempt the organs of generation, through the influence of the aspect of the maleficent planets in combination with Venus occidental. Of these peoples the inhabitants of Cyrenaica and Marmarica, and particularly of Lower Egypt, are more closely familiar to Gemini and Mercury; on this account they are thoughtful and

---

³ δειλοὶ VMADEProc.; δεινοὶ LNCam., δηνοὶ P.
⁴ γονίμῳ VDMAEN (mg., γεννήματι) Cam.¹; γωνῇ P, γωνίσματι L; *γεννήματι Cam.²
⁵ ἑσπερίου VD; cf. Proc. γινόμενον ἐκ τῶν κακοποιῶν μετὰ τοῦ δυτικοῦ τῆς ('Αφ.); ἑσπέριον libri alii Cam.

διόπερ οὗτοι διανοητικοί τε καὶ συνετοὶ καὶ εὐεπήβολοι τυγχάνουσι περὶ πάντα καὶ μάλιστα περὶ τὴν τῶν σοφῶν τε καὶ θείων εὕρεσιν· μαγευτικοί[1] τε καὶ κρυφίων μυστηρίων ἐπιτελεστικοὶ καὶ ὅλως ἱκανοὶ περὶ τὰ μαθήματα. οἱ δὲ περὶ τὴν Θηβαΐδα καὶ Ὄασιν καὶ Τρωγλοδυτικὴν τῷ τε Ζυγῷ καὶ τῷ τῆς Ἀφροδίτης, ὅθεν καὶ αὐτοὶ θερμότεροί τέ εἰσι τὰς φύσεις καὶ κεκινημένοι καὶ ἐν εὐφορίαις ἔχοντες τὰς διαγωγάς· οἱ δὲ περὶ τὴν Ἀραβίαν καὶ Ἀζανίαν καὶ μέσην Αἰθιοπίαν τῷ Ὑδροχόῳ καὶ τῷ τοῦ Κρόνου,[2] διὸ καὶ οὗτοι κρεοφάγοι τε καὶ ἰχθυοφάγοι καὶ νομάδες εἰσίν, ἄγριον καὶ θηριώδη βίον ζῶντες.

Αἱ μὲν οὖν συνοικειώσεις τῶν τε ἀστέρων καὶ τῶν δωδεκατημορίων πρὸς τὰ κατὰ μέρος ἔθνη καὶ τὰ ὡς ἐπὶ πᾶν αὐτῶν ἰδιώματα κατὰ τὸ κεφαλαιῶδες τοῦτον ἡμῖν ὑποτετυπώσθωσαν τὸν τρόπον. ἐκθησόμεθα δὲ καὶ διὰ τὸ τῆς χρήσεως εὐεπήβολον ἐφ' ἑκάστου τῶν δωδεκατημορίων κατὰ ψιλὴν παράθεσιν ἕκαστα τῶν συνοικειουμένων ἐθνῶν ἀκολούθως τοῖς προκατειλεγμένοις περὶ αὐτῶν τὸν τρόπον τοῦτον.

Κριός[3]· Βρεττανία, Γαλατία, Γερμανία, Βασταρνία· περὶ τὸ μέσον Κοίλη Συρία Παλαιστίνη, Ἰδουμαία, Ἰουδαία.

Ταῦρος· Παρθία, Μηδία, Περσίς· περὶ τὸ μέσον Κυκλάδες νῆσοι, Κύπρος, παράλια τῆς μικρᾶς Ἀσίας.

[1] μαγευτικοί VPLMADEProc., μαγικοί NCam.
[2] Κρόνου VPLNDProc.Cam.¹, Διός AECam.²

TETRABIBLOS II. 3

intelligent and facile in all things, especially in the search for wisdom and religion; they are magicians and performers of secret mysteries and in general skilled in mathematics.¹ Those who live in Thebais, the Oasis, and Troglodytica are familiar to Libra and Venus; hence they are more ardent and lively of nature and live in plenty. The people of Arabia, Azania, and Middle Ethiopia are familiar to Aquarius and Saturn,² for which reason they are flesh-eaters, fish-eaters, and nomads, living a rough, bestial life.

Let this be our brief exposition of the familiarities of the planets and the signs of the zodiac with the various nations, and of the general characteristics of the latter. We shall also set forth, for ready use, a list of the several nations which are in familiarity, merely noted against each of the signs, in accordance with what has just been said about them, thus:—

Aries: Britain, Gaul, Germania, Bastarnia; in the centre, Coelê Syria, Palestine, Idumaea, Judaea.

Taurus: Parthia, Media, Persia; in the centre, the Cyclades, Cyprus, the coastal region of Asia Minor.

---

¹ "Mathematics" (literally, "the studies") here means astrology; *cf.* the title of Sextus Empiricus' book Πρὸς μαθηματικούς, "Against the Astrologers."

² Some MSS. and Camerarius' second edition have "Jupiter" in place of "Saturn."

---

³ Haec omiserunt omnino usque ad ἐκκειμένων δὲ τούτων PLNCam.¹; VMADEProc. res in columnis disponunt signorum nominibus in capite additis, verbis etiam περὶ τὸ μέσον (quae om. Cam.²) in propriis locis insertis.

PTOLEMY

Δίδυμοι· Ὑρκανία, Ἀρμενία, Ματιανή· περὶ τὸ μέσον Κυρηναϊκή,[1] Μαρμαρική, ἡ κάτω χώρα τῆς Αἰγύπτου.

Καρκίνος· Νουμηδία, Καρχηδονία, Ἀφρική· περὶ τὸ μέσον Βιθυνία, Φρυγία, Κολχική.

Λέων· Ἰταλία, Γαλλία, Σικελία, Ἀπουλία· περὶ τὸ μέσον Φοινίκη, Χαλδαία, Ὀρχηνία.

Παρθένος· Μεσοποταμία, Βαβυλωνία, Ἀσσυρία· περὶ τὸ μέσον Ἑλλάς, Ἀχαία, Κρήτη.

Ζυγός· Βακτριανή, Κασπηρία, Σηρική· περὶ τὸ μέσον Θηβαΐς, Ὄασις, Τρωγλοδυτική.

Σκορπίος· Μεταγωνῖτις, Μαυριτανία, Γαιτουλία· περὶ τὸ μέσον Συρία, Κομμαγηνή, Καππαδοκία.

Τοξότης· Τυρρηνία, Κελτική, Ἱσπανία· περὶ τὸ μέσον Ἀραβία ἡ εὐδαίμων.

74 Αἰγόκερως· Ἰνδική, Ἀριανή, Γεδρωσία· περὶ τὸ μέσον Θρᾴκη, Μακεδονία, Ἰλλυρίς.

Ὑδροχόος· Σαυροματική, Ὀξειανή, Σουγδιανή· περὶ τὸ μέσον Ἀραβία, Ἀζανία, μέση Αἰθιοπία.

Ἰχθῦς· Φαζανία, Νασαμωνῖτις, Γαραμαντική· περὶ τὸ μέσον Λυδία, Κιλικία, Παμφυλία.[2]

Ἐκκειμένων δὲ τούτων εὔλογον κἀκεῖνα τούτῳ τῷ μέρει προσθεῖναι, διότι καὶ τῶν ἀπλανῶν ἀστέρων ἕκαστος συνοικειοῦται ταῖς χώραις ὅσαις καὶ τὰ τοῦ ζῳδιακοῦ μέρη, μεθ' ὧν ἔχουσιν οἱ ἀπλανεῖς τὰς προσνεύσεις ἐπὶ τοῦ διὰ τῶν πόλων

---

[1] Κυρηναϊκή libri, om. Cam.
[2] γίνονται χῶραι οβ' post haec add. VMProc.

TETRABIBLOS II. 3

Gemini: Hyrcania, Armenia, Matiana; in the centre, Cyrenaica, Marmarica, Lower Egypt.

Cancer: Numidia, Carthage, Africa; in the centre, Bithynia, Phrygia, Colchica.

Leo: Italy, Cisalpine Gaul, Sicily, Apulia; in the centre, Phoenicia, Chaldaea, Orchenia.

Virgo: Mesopotamia, Babylonia, Assyria; in the centre, Hellas, Achaia, Crete.

Libra: Bactriana, Casperia, Serica; in the centre, Thebais, Oasis, Troglodytica.

Scorpio: Metagonitis, Mauritania, Gaetulia; in the centre, Syria, Commagenê, Cappadocia.

Sagittarius: Tyrrhenia, Celtica, Spain; in the centre, Arabia Felix.

Capricorn: India, Ariana, Gedrosia; in the centre, Thrace, Macedonia, Illyria.

Aquarius: Sauromatica, Oxiana, Sogdiana; in the centre, Arabia, Azania, Middle Ethiopia.

Pisces: Phazania, Nasamonitis, Garamantica; in the centre, Lydia, Cilicia, Pamphylia.[1]

Now that the subject at hand has been set forth, it is reasonable to attach to this section this further consideration—that each of the fixed stars has familiarity with the countries with which the parts of the zodiac, which have the same inclinations as the fixed stars[2] upon the circle drawn through its

[1] "Total, 72 countries," is found in some MSS. and Proclus. There are actually 73 in the list as given here, but there is a certain amount of confusion in the MSS.

[2] These are the so-called παρανατέλλοντα, stars which rise and set at the same time as the degrees or sections of the ecliptic, but to the north or south of them. See Boll-Bezold-Gundel, pp. 55, 141 ff.

αὐτοῦ[1] γραφομένου κύκλου, φαίνεται ποιούμενα τὴν συμπάθειαν, καὶ ὅτι ἐπὶ τῶν μητροπόλεων ἐκεῖνοι μάλιστα συμπαθοῦσιν οἱ τόποι τοῦ ζωδιακοῦ καθ' ὧν[2] ἐν ταῖς καταρχαῖς τῶν κτίσεων αὐτῶν ὡς ἐπὶ γενέσεως[3] ὅ τε ἥλιος καὶ ἡ σελήνη παροδεύοντες ἐτύγχανον καὶ τῶν κέντρων μάλιστα τὸ ὡροσκοποῦν· ἐφ' ὧν δ' οἱ χρόνοι τῶν κτίσεων οὐχ εὑρίσκονται, καθ' ὧν[4] ἐν ταῖς[5] τῶν κατὰ καιρὸν ἀρχόντων ἢ βασιλευόντων γενέσεσιν ἐκπίπτει τὸ μεσουράνημα.

⟨δ̄.⟩ **Ἔφοδος εἰς τὰς κατὰ μέρος προτελέσεις**

Τούτων οὕτως προεπεσκεμμένων[6] ἀκόλουθον ἂν εἴη λοιπὸν τὰς τῶν προτελέσεων ἐφόδους κεφαλαιωδῶς ἐπελθεῖν, καὶ πρῶτον τῶν καθ' ὅλας περιστάσεις χωρῶν ἢ πόλεων λαμβανομένων.[7] ἔσται δ' ὁ τρόπος τῆς ἐπισκέψεως τοιοῦτος· ἡ μὲν οὖν πρώτη καὶ ἰσχυροτάτη τῶν τοιούτων συμπτωμάτων αἰτία γίνεται παρὰ τὰς ἐκλειπτικὰς ἡλίου καὶ σελήνης συζυγίας καὶ τὰς ἐν αὐταῖς παρόδους τῶν ἀστέρων. τῆς δὲ προτελέσεως αὐτῆς τὸ μέν τί ἐστι τοπικόν, καθ' ὃ δεῖ προγινώσκειν ποίαις

---

[1] αὐτῶν NACam.   [2] ὧν PMAE, ὃν VLNDCam.
[3] γενέσεως VD, -εων (-αιων) PNMAECam., ἐπιγενέσεων L.
[4] καθ' ὧν MAE, καθ' ἣν VD, om. PLNCam.
[5] ἐν ταῖς VPLMADE, εἰς τὴν ... γένεσιν NCam.
[6] προεπεσκεμμένων VD, προεσκημένων P, προεσκευασμένων L, προκειμένων A, προεκκειμένων (-εγκ-) MNECam., προειρημένων Proc.
[7] λαμβανομένων VME, -ον D, -ας NACam., λαμβάνομεν PL.

poles, appear to exert sympathy; furthermore, that, in the case of metropolitan cities, those regions of the zodiac are most sympathetic through which the sun and moon, and of the centres especially the horoscope, were passing at the first founding of the city, as in a nativity. But in cases in which the exact times of the foundations are not discovered, the regions are sympathetic in which falls the mid-heaven of the nativities of those who held office or were kings at the time.[1]

4. *Method of Making Particular Predictions.*

After this introductory examination it would be the next task to deal briefly with the procedure of the predictions, and first with those concerned with general conditions of countries or cities. The method of the inquiry will be as follows: The first and most potent cause of such events lies in the conjunctions of the sun and moon at eclipse and the movements of the stars at the time. Of the prediction itself, one portion is regional;[2] therein we must foresee

---

[1] The procedure, therefore, is to treat a city like a person and cast its nativity, using instead of the time of birth the time of founding. If the latter is not accurately known, the astrologer should take the nativity of the founder, or other individual prominent in the enterprise, and observe where its mid-heaven falls.

[2] Ptolemy divides inquiries about cities and countries into four heads; what place is affected, the time and duration of the event, the generic classification of the event (*i.e.* what classes, *genera*, it will affect), and the quality, or nature, of the event itself. His terminology is Aristotelian. The next four chapters deal with the four phases of the inquiry.

χώραις ἢ πόλεσιν αἱ κατὰ μέρος ἐκλείψεις ἢ καὶ τῶν πλανωμένων αἱ κατὰ καιροὺς ἔμμονοι [1] στάσεις· αὗται δέ εἰσι Κρόνου τε καὶ Διὸς καὶ Ἄρεως, ὅταν στηρίζωσι· [2] ποιοῦνται γὰρ τότε τὰς [3] ἐπισημασίας· τὸ δέ τι χρονικόν, καθ' ὃ τὸν καιρὸν τῶν ἐπισημασιῶν καὶ τῆς παρατάσεως τὴν ποσότητα δεήσει προγινώσκειν· τὸ δέ τι γενικόν, καθ' ὃ προσήκει λαμβάνειν περὶ ποῖα τῶν γενῶν ἀποβήσεται τὸ σύμπτωμα· τελευταῖον δὲ τὸ εἰδικόν, καθ' ὃ τὴν αὐτοῦ τοῦ ἀποτελεσθησομένου ποιότητα θεωρήσομεν.

⟨ε.⟩ Περὶ τῆς τῶν διατιθεμένων χωρῶν ἐπισκέψεως

Περὶ μὲν οὖν τοῦ πρώτου καὶ τοπικοῦ τὴν διάληψιν ποιησόμεθα τοιαύτην· κατὰ γὰρ τὰς γινομένας ἐκλειπτικὰς συζυγίας ἡλίου καὶ σελήνης, καὶ μάλιστα τὰς εὐαισθητοτέρας, ἐπισκεψόμεθα τόν τε ἐκλειπτικὸν τοῦ ζῳδιακοῦ τόπον καὶ τὰς τῶν κατ' αὐτὸν [4] τριγώνων [5] συνοικειουμένας [6] χώρας· καὶ ὁμοίως τίνες τῶν πόλεων ἤτοι ἐκ τῆς κατὰ τὴν κτίσιν ὡροσκοπίας καὶ φωσφορίας ἢ ἐκ τῆς τῶν

---

[1] ἔμμονοι VMAD, ἔμμηνοι PNECam., ἔμμηνα L; cf. αἱ τῶν πλανωμένων ἐπιμένουσαι κατὰ καιροὺς στάσεις Proc.

[2] στηρίζωσι VADProc., -ονται L, -οντες PNMECam.

[3] ποιοῦνται... τὰς κτλ. VDProc.; ποιῶσι(ν) (aut ποιήσωσι) τὰς κτλ. alii libri Cam.

[4] κατ' αὐτόν VMADE, κατ' αὐτῶν L, κατὰ τῶν P, κατὰ τὰ NCam.

[5] τριγώνων VPLMDE, -ῳ A, -α NCam.

[6] συνοικειουμένας VADE, -ων MNCam., -ειωμένας P, -ειωμένων L.

for what countries or cities there is significance in the various eclipses or in the occasional regular stations of the planets, that is, of Saturn, Jupiter, and Mars, whenever they halt, for then they are significant. Another division of the prediction is chronological; therein the need will be to foretell the time of the portents and their duration. A part, too, is generic; through this we ought to understand with what classes the event will be concerned. And finally there is the specific aspect, by which we shall discern the quality of the event itself.

5. *Of the Examination of the Countries Affected.*

We are to judge of the first portion of the inquiry, which is regional, in the following manner: In the eclipses of sun and moon [1] as they occur, particularly those more easily observed,[2] we shall examine the region of the zodiac in which they take place, and the countries in familiarity with its triangles, and in similar fashion ascertain which of the cities, either from their horoscope [3] at the time of their founding and the position of the luminaries at the time, or

[1] Johannes Laurentius Lydus (*De ostentis*, 9) deals with a system of prediction whereby eclipses of the sun refer to Asia and those of the moon to Europe. Ptolemy makes no such sweeping distinction.

[2] Ptolemy takes no account of eclipses not visible at the place concerned.

[3] That is, the sign in the ascendant, or horoscopic position, at that time.

PTOLEMY

τότε ἡγεμονευόντων μεσουρανήσεως συμπάθειαν ἔχουσι πρὸς τὸ τῆς ἐκλείψεως δωδεκατημόριον. ἐφ' ὅσων δ' ἂν χωρῶν ἢ πόλεων εὑρίσκωμεν τὴν προκειμένην συνοικείωσιν, περὶ πάσας[1] μὲν ὡς ἐπὶ πᾶν ὑπονοητέον ἔσεσθαί τι σύμπτωμα, μάλιστα δὲ περὶ τὰς πρὸς αὐτὸ τὸ τῆς ἐκλείψεως δωδεκατημόριον λόγον ἐχούσας καὶ ἐν ὅσαις αὐτῶν ὑπὲρ γῆν οὖσα ἡ ἔκλειψις ἐφαίνετο.[2]

⟨ϛ.⟩ Περὶ τοῦ χρόνου τῶν ἀποτελουμένων

Τὸ δὲ δεύτερον καὶ χρονικὸν κεφάλαιον, καθ' ὃ τοὺς καιροὺς τῶν ἐπισημασιῶν καὶ τῆς παρατάσεως τὴν ποσότητα προσήκει διαγινώσκειν, ἐπισκεψόμεθα τρόπῳ τοιῷδε. τῶν γὰρ κατὰ τὸν αὐτὸν χρόνον γινομένων ἐκλείψεων μὴ κατὰ πᾶσαν οἴκησιν ἐν ταῖς αὐταῖς καιρικαῖς ὥραις ἀποτελουμένων, τῶν τε ἡλιακῶν τῶν αὐτῶν[3] μηδὲ τὰ μεγέθη τῶν ἐπισκοτήσεων ἢ τὸν χρόνον τῶν παρατάσεων κατὰ τὸ ἴσον πανταχῇ λαμβανουσῶν, πρῶτον μὲν κατὰ τὴν ἐν ἑκάστῃ τῶν λόγον ἐχουσῶν οἰκήσεων ἐκλειπτικὴν ὥραν καὶ τὸ τοῦ πόλου ἔξαρμα κέντρα[4] ὡς ἐπὶ

[1] πάσας] cf. Proc. πᾶσαι; ταύτας NCam.
[2] ἐφαίνετο VADEProc., φαίνεται P (φεν-) LMNCam.
[3] τῶν αὐτῶν VPLDProc.; δηλαδὴ καὶ τῶν σεληνιακῶν NACam.; καὶ τῶν σεληνιακῶν τῶν αὐτῶν ME.
[4] κέντρα VADProc., τά τε κέντρα PLNCam., καὶ τὰ κέντρα ME.

from the mid-heaven of the nativity [1] of their then rulers, are sympathetic [2] to the zodiacal sign of the eclipse. And in whatsoever countries or cities we discover a familiarity of this kind, we must suppose that some event will occur which applies, generally speaking, to all of them, particularly to those which bear a relation to the actual zodiacal sign of the eclipse and to those of them in which the eclipse, since it took place above the earth, was visible.

6. *Of the Time of the Predicted Events.*

The second and chronological heading, whereby we should learn the times of the events signified and the length of their duration, we shall consider as follows. Inasmuch as the eclipses which take place at the same time are not completed in the same number of ordinary hours [3] in every locality, and since the same solar eclipses do not everywhere have the same degree of obscuration or the same time of duration, we shall first set down for the hour of the eclipse, in each of the related localities, and for the altitude of the pole,[4] centres, as in a nativity;

[1] The mid-heaven was regarded by many, including Ptolemy, as the most important of the centres, or angles, even surpassing the horoscope itself in its significance in certain ways. *Cf.* Bouché-Leclercq, p. 271 (with n. 2).
[2] That is, bear an aspect to.
[3] Civil hours, twelfth parts of the day-time or the night-time. They vary in length according to the latitude and the time of the year. *Cf.* the note on horary periods, iii. 10 (p. 292, n. 2).
[4] That is, the latitude; from this the centres or angles can be determined.

PTOLEMY

γενεσεως διαθήσομεν· ἔπειτα καὶ ἐπὶ πόσας[1] ἰσημερινὰς ὥρας ἐν ἑκάστῃ[2] παρατείνει τὸ ἐπισκίασμα τῆς ἐκλείψεως· τούτων γὰρ ἐξετασθέντων ὅσας ἂν ἰσημερινὰς ὥρας εὕρωμεν, ἐφ' ἡλιακῆς μὲν ἐκλείψεως ἐπὶ τοσούτους ἐνιαυτοὺς παραμένειν ὑπονοήσομεν τὸ ἀποτελούμενον, ἐπὶ δὲ σεληνιακῆς ἐπὶ τοσούτους μῆνας, τῶν μέντοι καταρχῶν καὶ τῶν ὁλοσχερεστέρων ἐπιτάσεων[3] θεωρουμένων[4] ἐκ τῆς τοῦ ἐκλειπτικοῦ τόπου πρὸς τὰ κέντρα σχέσεως. πρὸς μὲν γὰρ τῷ ἀπηλιωτικῷ ὁρίζοντι ὁ τόπος ἐκπεσὼν τήν τε καταρχὴν τοῦ συμπτώματος κατὰ τὴν πρώτην τετράμηνον ἀπὸ τοῦ χρόνου τῆς ἐκλείψεως σημαίνει καὶ τὰς ὁλοσχερεῖς[5] ἐπιτάσεις περὶ τὸ πρῶτον τριτημόριον τοῦ καθ' ὅλην[6] τὴν παράτασιν[7] χρόνου· πρὸς[8] δὲ τῷ μεσουρανήματι, κατά τε τὴν δευτέραν τετράμηνον καὶ τὸ μέσον τριτημόριον· πρὸς δὲ τῷ λιβυκῷ ὁρίζοντι, κατὰ τὴν τρίτην τετράμηνον καὶ τὸ ἔσχατον τριτημόριον. τῶν δὲ κατὰ μέρος ἀνέσεων καὶ ἐπιτάσεων ἀπό τε τῶν ἀνὰ μέσον συζυγιῶν, ὅταν κατὰ τῶν τὸ αἴτιον ἐμποιούντων τόπων ἢ τῶν συσχηματιζομένων τόπων αὐτοῖς συμπίπτωσι, καὶ

---

[1] ὡς ἐπὶ πόσας PLMNECam., om. ὡς VADProc.
[2] Post ἑκάστῃ add. τῶν λόγον ἐχουσῶν οἰκήσεων PLNCam.; om. VMADE.
[3] τρόπους post ἐπιτάσεων add. Cam., om. libri.
[4] θεωρουμένων VMDE, θεωροῦμεν (θεορ-) PLNACam.
[5] τὰς ὅλας ὁλοσχερεῖς PLNACam.; ὅλας om. VMDEProc.
[6] καθ' ὅλην VMDE, καθ' ὅλου PLNACam.
[7] τὴν παράτασιν VPLMADE, τῆς παρατάσεως NCam.
[8] πρὸς libri et Cam.[1], ἐν Cam.[2]

TETRABIBLOS II. 6

secondly, how many equinoctial hours[1] the obscuration of the eclipse lasts in each. For when these data are examined, if it is a solar eclipse, we shall understand that the predicted event lasts as many years[2] as the equinoctial hours which we discover, and if a lunar eclipse, as many months. The nature of the beginnings[3] and of the more important intensifications[4] of the events, however, are deduced from the position of the place of the eclipse relative to the centres. For if the place of the eclipse falls on the eastern horizon, this signifies that the beginning of the predicted event is in the first period of four months from the time of the eclipse and that its important intensifications lie in the first third of the entire period of its duration; if on the mid-heaven, in the second four months and the middle third; if upon the western horizon, in the third four months and the final third. The beginnings of the particular abatements and intensifications of the event we deduce from the conjunctions which take place in the meantime,[5] if they occur in the significant regions or

---

[1] An equinoctial hour is the time measured by the passage of 15° of the equator ($\frac{1}{24}$ of 360°) past the horizon or other fixed point.

[2] A distinction is made because solar and lunar eclipses are of very different lengths; a total lunar eclipse may last nearly two hours, compared with eight minutes in the case of the sun.

[3] καταρχαί, that is, when the predicted event is due.

[4] ἐπιτάσεις, "intensifications," as opposed to "relaxations"; a metaphor drawn from the tightening and loosening of the strings of a musical instrument.

[5] During the period of the predicted effect (Bouché-Leclercq, p. 351).

PTOLEMY

ἀπὸ τῶν ἄλλων παρόδων,[1] ὅταν οἱ ποιητικοὶ τοῦ προτελέσματος ἀστέρες ἀνατολὰς ἢ δύσεις ἢ στηριγμοὺς ἢ ἀκρονύκτους φάσεις ποιῶνται, συσχηματιζόμενοι τοῖς τὸ αἴτιον ἔχουσι δωδεκατημορίοις· 78 ἐπειδήπερ ἀνατέλλοντες μὲν ἢ στηρίζοντες ἐπιτάσεις ποιοῦνται τῶν συμπτωμάτων, δύνοντες δὲ καὶ ὑπὸ τὰς αὐγὰς ὄντες ἢ ἀκρονύκτους ποιούμενοι προηγήσεις ἄνεσιν τῶν ἀποτελουμένων ποιοῦσιν.

⟨ζ⟩ Περὶ τοῦ γένους τῶν διατιθεμένων

Τρίτου δ' ὄντος κεφαλαίου τοῦ γενικοῦ, καθ' ὃ δεῖ διαλαβεῖν περὶ ποῖα τῶν γενῶν ἀποβήσεται τὸ σύμπτωμα, λαμβάνεται καὶ τοῦτο διὰ τῆς τῶν ζῳδίων ἰδιοτροπίας καὶ μορφώσεως καθ' ὧν ἂν τύχωσιν ὄντες οἵ τε τῶν ἐκλείψεων τόποι καὶ οἱ τὴν οἰκοδεσποτίαν λαβόντες τῶν ἀστέρων, τῶν τε πλανωμένων καὶ τῶν ἀπλανῶν, τοῦ τε τῆς ἐκλείψεως δωδεκατημορίου καὶ τοῦ κατὰ τὸ κέντρον τὸ πρὸ[2] τῆς ἐκλείψεως. λαμβάνεται δὲ ἡ τούτων οἰκοδεσποτία ἐπὶ μὲν τῶν πλανωμένων ἀστέρων οὕτως. ὁ γὰρ τοὺς πλείστους λόγους ἔχων πρὸς ἀμφοτέρους τοὺς ἐκκειμένους τόπους, τόν τε τῆς ἐκλείψεως καὶ τὸν τοῦ ἑπομένου αὐτῷ κέντρου, κατά τε τὰς ἔγγιστα καὶ φαινομένας συναφὰς ἢ ἀπορροίας καὶ τοὺς λόγους ἔχοντας τῶν συσχηματισμῶν, καὶ ἔτι κατὰ τὴν κυρίαν τῶν τε οἴκων καὶ τριγώνων καὶ ὑψωμάτων ἢ καὶ ὁρίων, ἐκεῖνος λήψεται μόνος τὴν

[1] παρόδων VP (παρρ-) LDProc.; παρανατελλόντων MNAE Cam.

the regions in some aspect to them, and also from the other movements of the planets, if those that effect the predicted event are either rising or setting or stationary or at evening rising, and are at the same time in some aspect to the zodiacal signs that hold the cause; for planets when they are rising or stationary produce intensifications in the events, but when setting, and under the rays of the sun,[1] or advancing at evening, they bring about an abatement.

7. *Of the Class of those Affected.*

The third heading is that of generic classification, whereby one must determine what classes the event will affect. This is ascertained from the special nature and form of the zodiacal signs in which happen to be the places of the eclipses and in which are the heavenly bodies, planets and fixed stars alike, that govern both the sign of the eclipse and that of the angle preceding the eclipse. In the case of the planets we discover the rulership of these regions thus: The one which has the greatest number of relationships to both the regions aforesaid, that of the eclipse and that of the angle which follows it, both by virtue of the nearest visible applications or recessions, and by those of the aspects which bear a relation, and furthermore by rulership of the houses, triangles, exaltations, and terms, that planet

---

[1] Too near the sun to be visible; *combustus;* cf. Bouché-Leclercq, p. 111, n. 3. "Advancing" is the same as "adding to its motion"; cf. above, p. 115, n. 4.

[2] τὸ κ. τὸ πρὸ P (πρώ) L ; τοῦ κέντρου τοῦ πρὸ MAE ; κατὰ τοῦ κέντρου πρὸ τῆς κτλ. Proc. ; τὸ πρὸ om. VDNCam.

PTOLEMY

οἰκοδεσποτίαν· εἰ δὲ μὴ ὁ αὐτὸς εὑρίσκοιτο τῆς τε ἐκλείψεως καὶ τοῦ κέντρου κύριος, δύο[1] τοὺς πρὸς ἑκάτερον τῶν τόπων τὰς πλείους ἔχοντας, ὡς πρόκειται, συνοικειώσεις συμπαραληπτέον, προκρινομένου τοῦ τῆς ἐκλείψεως κυρίου· εἰ δὲ πλείους εὑρίσκοιντο καθ' ἑκάτερον ἐφάμιλλοι, τὸν ἐπικεντρότερον ἢ χρηματιστικώτερον ἢ τῆς αἱρέσεως μᾶλλον ὄντα προκρινοῦμεν εἰς τὴν οἰκοδεσποτίαν. ἐπὶ δὲ τῶν ἀπλανῶν συμπαραληψόμεθα τόν τε αὐτῷ τῷ ἐκλειπτικῷ χρόνῳ[2] συγκεχρηματικότα πρῶτον τῶν λαμπρῶν[3] ἐπὶ τῆς παρῳχημένης κεντρώσεως κατὰ τοὺς διωρισμένους ἡμῖν ἐν τῇ πρώτῃ συντάξει τῶν ἐννέα τρόπων φαινομένους σχηματισμούς, καὶ τὸν ἐν τῇ φαινομένῃ κατὰ τὴν ἐκλειπτικὴν ὥραν διαθέσει, ἤτοι συνανατείλαντα ἢ συμμεσουρανήσαντα τῷ κατὰ τὰ ἑπόμενα κέντρῳ[4] τοῦ τόπου τῆς ἐκλείψεως.

Θεωρηθέντων δὲ οὕτως τῶν εἰς τὴν αἰτίαν τοῦ συμπτώματος παραλαμβανομένων ἀστέρων, συνεπισκεψώμεθα καὶ τὰς τῶν ζῳδίων μορφώσεις ἐν οἷς ἥ τε ἔκλειψις καὶ οἱ τὴν κυρίαν λαβόντες ἀστέρες ἔτυχον ὄντες, ὡς ἀπὸ τῆς τούτων ἰδιοτροπίας καὶ τοῦ ποιοῦ τῶν διατιθεμένων γενῶν ὡς ἐπὶ πᾶν λαμβανομένου. τὰ μὲν γὰρ ἀνθρωπόμορφα τῶν ζῳδίων τῶν τε περὶ τὸν διὰ μέσων τῶν ζῳδίων

---

[1] δύο δὲ PLNCam., ἀλλὰ δύο MAE, δὲ om. VDProc.
[2] χρόνῳ VDProc., τόπῳ alii Cam.
[3] τῶν λαμπρῶν VMADEProc., τὸν λαμπρὸν PL, τῷ λαμπρῷ NCam.   [4] κέντρῳ VMADEProc., -α PLNCam.

---

[1] The anonymous commentator on Ptolemy gives as examples of reasons for preferring one to another that it is

TETRABIBLOS II. 7

alone will hold the dominance. However, if the same planet is not found to be both lord of the eclipse and of the angle, we must take together the two which have the greatest number of familiarities, as aforesaid, to either one of the regions, giving preference to the lord of the eclipse. And if several rivals be found on either count, we shall prefer for the domination the one which is closest to an angle, or is more significant, or is more closely allied by sect.[1] In the case of the fixed stars, we shall take the first one of the brilliant stars which signifies upon the preceding angle at the actual time of the eclipse, according to the nine kinds of visible aspects defined in our first compilation,[2] and the star which of the group visible at the time of the eclipse has either risen or reached meridian with the angle following the place of the eclipse.

When we have thus reckoned the stars that share in causing the event, let us also consider the forms of the signs of the zodiac in which the eclipse and the dominating stars as well happened to be, since from their character the quality of the classes affected is generally discerned. Constellations of human form, both in the zodiac and among the

---

in the superior hemisphere, or is " adding to its motion," or rising, or if these characteristics appear in all the rivals, that it is of the proper sect.

[2] The reference is to the *Almagest*, viii. 4. They are πρωινὸς ἀπηλιώτης (matutine subsolar), πρωινὸν μεσουράνημα (matutine culmination), πρωινὸς λίψ (matutine setting), μεσημβρινὸς ἀπηλιώτης (meridianal subsolar), μεσημβρινὸν μεσουράνημα (meridianal culmination), μεσημβρινὸς λίψ (meridianal setting), ὀψινὸς ἀπηλιώτης (vespertine subsolar), ὀψινὸν μεσουράνημα (vespertine culmination), and ὀψινὸς λίψ (vespertine setting).

PTOLEMY

κύκλον καὶ τῶν κατὰ τοὺς ἀπλανεῖς ἀστέρας, περὶ τὸ τῶν ἀνθρώπων γένος ποιεῖ τὸ ἀποτελούμενον. 80 τῶν δὲ ἄλλων χερσαίων τὰ μὲν τετράποδα περὶ τὰ ὅμοια τῶν ἀλόγων ζώων, τὰ δὲ ἑρπυστικὰ περὶ τοὺς ὄφεις καὶ τὰ τοιαῦτα. καὶ πάλιν τὰ μὲν θηριώδη περὶ τὰ ἀνήμερα τῶν ζώων καὶ βλαπτικὰ τοῦ τῶν ἀνθρώπων γένους, τὰ δὲ ἥμερα περὶ τὰ χρηστικὰ καὶ χειροήθη[1] καὶ συνεργητικὰ πρὸς τὰς εὐετηρίας ἀναλόγως τοῖς καθ᾽ ἕκαστα μορφώμασιν, οἷον ἵππων ἢ βοῶν ἢ προβάτων καὶ τῶν τοιούτων. ἔτι δὲ τῶν χερσαίων τὰ μὲν πρὸς ταῖς ἄρκτοις μᾶλλον περὶ τὰς τῆς γῆς αἰφνιδίους κινήσεις, τὰ δὲ πρὸς μεσημβρίαν περὶ τὰς ἀπροσδοκήτους ἐκ τοῦ ἀέρος ῥύσεις. πάλιν δὲ ἐν μὲν τοῖς τῶν πτερωτῶν μορφώμασιν ὄντες οἱ κύριοι τόποι οἷον Παρθένῳ, Τοξότῃ, Ὄρνιθι,[2] Ἀετῷ[3] καὶ τοῖς τοιούτοις, περὶ τὰ πτηνὰ καὶ μάλιστα τὰ εἰς τροφὴν ἀνθρώπων τὸ σύμπτωμα ποιοῦσιν, ἐν δὲ τοῖς νηκτοῖς[4] περὶ τὰ ἔνυδρα καὶ τοὺς ἰχθῦς. καὶ τούτων ἐν μὲν τοῖς θαλαττίοις, οἷον Καρκίνῳ, Αἰγόκερῳ, Δελφῖνι,[5] περὶ τὰ θαλάττια, καὶ ἔτι τὰς τῶν στόλων

[1] καὶ καταχρηστικὰ post χειροήθη add. PLNCam.; om. VMADE.
[2] Ὄρνιθι VMADE, -ος PNCam., Ὀρνέων L.
[3] Ἀετῷ VMADE, cf. Proc.; τοῖς Ὀρνέοις PLNCam.
[4] νηκτοῖς NAECam.[1]; cf. νηχόμενα Proc.; νυκτοῖς alii Cam.[2]
[5] Δελφῖνι VMADE, -νῳ PL, -να NCam.

---

[1] Cf. i. 12 for classifications of the signs. Rhetorius, ap. CCAG, i. 164 ff., names as signs of human form Gemini, Virgo, Libra, Aquarius, and (in part) Sagittarius.

TETRABIBLOS II. 7

fixed stars, cause the event to concern the human race.[1] Of the other terrestrial signs,[2] the four-footed[3] are concerned with the four-footed dumb animals, and the signs formed like creeping things[4] with serpents and the like. Again, the animal[5] signs have significance for the wild animals and those which injure the human race; the tame signs concern the useful and domesticated animals, and those which help to gain prosperity, in consistency with their several forms; for example, horses, oxen, sheep, and the like. Again, of the terrestrial signs, the northern tend to signify sudden earthquakes and the southern unexpected rains from the sky. Yet again, those dominant regions that are in the form of winged creatures,[6] such as Virgo, Sagittarius, Cygnus, Aquila, and the like, exercise an effect upon winged creatures, particularly those which are used for human food, and if they are in the form of swimming things, upon water animals and fish. And of these, in the constellations pertaining to the sea,[7] such as Cancer, Capricorn, and the Dolphin, they influence the

---

Among the extra-zodiacal constellations might be cited Orion, Perseus, Andromeda, etc.

[2] Rhetorius, *loc. cit.*, names Aries, Taurus, Gemini, Leo, Virgo, Libra, Scorpio.

[3] Aries, Taurus, Leo, Sagittarius (Rhetorius, *loc. cit.*).

[4] To be sought among extra-zodiacal constellations, such as Draco, rather than the zodiac.

[5] θηριώδη; Taurus, Leo, and Scorpio, according to Rhetorius, *loc. cit.*

[6] Rhetorius, *loc. cit.*, names Virgo, Sagittarius, Pisces.

[7] Rhetorius, *loc. cit.*, designates as watery (ἔνυδρα) Pisces, Cancer, Capricorn, Aquarius, and Sagittarius, of the zodiac.

ἀναγωγάς· ἐν δὲ τοῖς ποταμίοις οἷον Ὑδροχόῳ καὶ Ἰχθύσι, περὶ τὰ ποτάμια καὶ τὰ πηγαῖα· κατὰ δὲ τὴν Ἀργὼ περὶ ἀμφότερα τὰ γένη. ὡσαύτως δ'[1] ἐν τοῖς τροπικοῖς ἢ ἰσημερινοῖς ὄντες κοινῶς μὲν περὶ τὰ τοῦ ἀέρος καταστήματα καὶ τὰς οἰκείας ἑκάστοις αὐτῶν ὥρας ἀποτελοῦσι τὰς ἐπισημασίας, 81 ἰδίως δὲ καὶ περὶ τὸ ἔαρ καὶ περὶ[2] τὰ ἐκ τῆς γῆς φυόμενα. κατὰ μὲν γὰρ τὴν ἐαρινὴν ἰσημερίαν ὄντες περὶ τοὺς βλαστοὺς τῶν δενδρικῶν καρπῶν, οἷον ἀμπέλου, συκῆς, καὶ τῶν συνακμαζόντων· κατὰ δὲ τὴν θερινὴν τροπὴν περὶ τὰς τῶν καρποφορηθέντων συγκομιδὰς καὶ ἀποθέσεις· ἐν Αἰγύπτῳ δὲ ἰδικῶς καὶ περὶ τὴν τοῦ Νείλου ἀνάβασιν· κατὰ δὲ τὴν μετοπωρινὴν ἰσημερίαν περὶ τὸν σπόρον καὶ τὰ χορτικὰ καὶ τὰ τοιαῦτα· κατὰ δὲ τὴν χειμερινὴν τροπὴν περὶ τὰς λαχανείας καὶ τὰ κατὰ τοῦτον τὸν καιρὸν ἐπιπολάζοντα ὀρνέων ἢ ἰχθύων γένη ἔτι δὲ καὶ τὰ μὲν ἰσημερινὰ τοῖς ἱεροῖς καὶ ταῖς περὶ τοὺς θεοὺς θρησκείαις ἐπισημαίνει· τὰ δὲ τροπικὰ ταῖς τῶν ἀέρων καὶ ταῖς τῶν πολιτικῶν εἰθισμένων[3] μεταβολαῖς· τὰ δὲ στερεὰ τοῖς θεμελίοις καὶ τοῖς οἰκοδομήμασι· τὰ δὲ δίσωμα καὶ τοῖς ἀνθρώποις καὶ τοῖς βασιλεῦσιν. ὁμοίως δὲ καὶ τὰ μὲν πρὸς ταῖς ἀνατολαῖς μᾶλλον ἔχοντα τὴν θέσιν ἐν τῷ χρόνῳ τῆς ἐκλείψεως περὶ τοὺς καρποὺς καὶ τὴν νέαν ἡλικίαν καὶ τοὺς θεμελίους τὸ ἐσόμενον σημαίνει· τὰ δὲ πρὸς τῷ ὑπὲρ γῆν μεσουρανήματι περὶ τὰ ἱερὰ καὶ τοὺς βασιλέας καὶ τὴν μέσην ἡλικίαν· τὰ δὲ πρὸς ταῖς δυσμαῖς περὶ τὰς τῶν

[1] ὡσαύτως. οἱ δ(ὲ) MNCam.

TETRABIBLOS II. 7

creatures of the sea and the sailing of fleets. In the constellations pertaining to rivers, such as Aquarius and Pisces, they concern the creatures of rivers and springs, and in Argo they affect both classes alike. Likewise stars in the solstitial [1] or equinoctial signs have significance in general for the conditions of the air and the seasons related to each of these signs, and in particular they concern the spring and things which grow from the earth. For when they are at the spring equinox they affect the new shoots of the arboreal crops, such as grapes and figs, and whatever matures with them; at the summer solstice, the gathering and storing of the crops, and in Egypt, peculiarly, the rising of the Nile; at the autumn solstice they concern the sowing, the hay crops, and such; and at the winter equinox the vegetables and the kinds of birds and fish most common at this season. Further, the equinoctial signs have significance for sacred rites and the worship of the gods; the solstitial signs, for changes in the air and in political customs; the solid signs,[2] for foundations and the construction of houses; the bicorporeal, for men and kings. Similarly, those which are closer to the orient at the time of the eclipse signify what is to be concerning the crops, youth, and foundations; those near the mid-heaven above the earth, concerning sacred rites, kings, and middle age; and

[1] *Cf.* i. 11.   [2] *Ibid.*

---

[2] τὸ ἔαρ καὶ περὶ PLNCam.Proc., om. VMADE; καὶ (post ἔαρ) om. PLN.
[3] ἐθισμένων VD, ἐθισμῶν MAE, ἐθίμων NCam., ἐθήμων P, εὐθύμων L.

PTOLEMY

νομίμων μετατροπὰς καὶ τὴν παλαιὰν ἡλικίαν καὶ τοὺς κατοιχομένους.

Καὶ περὶ τὸ πόστον δὲ μέρος τοῦ ὑποκειμένου γένους ἡ διάθεσις ἐπελεύσεται, τό τε τῆς ἐπισκοτήσεως τῶν ἐκλείψεων μέγεθος ὑποβάλλει καὶ αἱ τῶν τὸ αἴτιον ἐμποιούντων ἀστέρων πρὸς τὸν ἐκλειπτικὸν τόπου σχέσεις. ἑσπέριοι μὲν γὰρ σχηματιζόμενοι πρὸς τὰς ἡλιακὰς ἐκλείψεις,[1] ἑῷοι δὲ πρὸς τὰς σεληνιακάς, ἐπὶ τὸ ἔλαττον ὡς ἐπὶ πᾶν διατιθέασι· διαμετροῦντες δὲ ἐπὶ τὸ ἥμισυ· ἑῷοι δὲ σχηματιζόμενοι πρὸς τὰς ἡλιακὰς ἢ ἑσπέριοι πρὸς τὰς σεληνιακὰς ἐπὶ τὸ πλεῖον.

⟨η.⟩ *Περὶ τῆς αὐτοῦ τοῦ ἀποτελέσματος ποιότητος*

Τέταρτον δ' ἐστὶ κεφάλαιον τὸ περὶ αὐτῆς τῆς τοῦ ἀποτελέσματος ποιότητος, τουτέστι, πότερον ἀγαθῶν ἢ τῶν ἐναντίων ἐστὶ ποιητικὸν καὶ ποδαπὸν ἐφ' ἑκάτερον κατὰ τὸ τοῦ εἴδους ἰδιότροπον. τοῦτο δὲ ἀπὸ τῆς τῶν οἰκοδεσποτησάντων ἀστέρων τοὺς κυρίους τόπους ποιητικῆς φύσεως καταλαμβάνεται καὶ τῆς συγκράσεως τῆς τε πρὸς ἀλλήλους καὶ τοὺς τόπους καθ' ὧν ἂν ὦσι τετυχηκότες. ὁ μὲν γὰρ ἥλιος καὶ ἡ σελήνη διατάκται καὶ[2] ὥσπερ ἡγεμόνες

---

[1] ἐκλείψεις VMADEProc., om. PLNCam.
[2] διατάκται καὶ VD, διατέτακται καὶ MAE, διατακτικοί (om: κα') P (-τοικ-) LNCam.

---

[1] Planets become feminized by the occidental position (*cf.* i. 6) and hence oppose the sun; in oriental position

TETRABIBLOS II. 7-8

those near the occident, concerning change of customs, old age, and those who have passed away.

To the question, how large a portion of the class involved will the event affect, the answer is supplied by the extent of the obscuration of the eclipses, and by the positions relative to the place of the eclipse held by the stars which furnish the cause. For when they are occidental to solar eclipses,[1] or oriental to lunar, they usually affect a minority; in opposition, a half; and the majority, if they are oriental to solar eclipses or occidental to lunar.

8. *Of the Quality of the Predicted Event.*

The fourth heading concerns the quality of the predicted event, that is, whether it is productive of good or the opposite,[2] and of what sort is its effect in either direction, in accordance with the peculiar character of the species. This is apprehended from the nature of the activity of the planets which rule the dominant places and from their combination both with one another and with the places in which they happen to be. For the sun and the moon are the marshals and, as it were,

---

they are masculinized and oppose the moon. Hence the effect is minimized. When, however, they work with the sun (in oriental position and masculine) or with the moon, the eclipse has a greater effect. *Cf.* Bouché-Leclercq, p. 353, n. 3.

[2] As Bouché-Leclercq (p. 355) points out, the natural tendency in antiquity would be to assume that any eclipse portends evil. Ptolemy's predilection for classification causes him to examine the question in the light of the nature and characters of the planets (*cf.* i. 5).

εἰσὶ τῶν ἄλλων, αὐτοὶ αἴτιοι γενόμενοι τοῦ τε κατὰ τὴν ἐνέργειαν ὅλου καὶ τῆς τῶν ἀστέρων οἰκοδεσποτίας καὶ ἔτι τῆς τῶν οἰκοδεσποτησάντων ἰσχύος ἢ ἀδρανείας. ἡ δὲ τῶν τὴν κυρίαν λαβόντων συγκρατικὴ θεωρία τὴν τῶν ἀποτελεσμάτων δείκνυσι ποιότητα.

83 Ἀρξόμεθα δὲ τῆς καθ᾽ ἕκαστον τῶν πλανωμένων ποιητικῆς[1] ἰδιοτροπίας, ἐκεῖνο κοινῶς προεκθέμενοι ἔτι τῆς κεφαλαιώδους ὑπομνήσεως ἕνεκεν ὡς ὅταν καθ᾽ ὅλου τινὰ λέγωμεν τῶν πέντε ἀστέρων τὴν κρᾶσιν καὶ τὸ ποιητικὸν τῆς ὁμοίας φύσεως ὑποληπτέον, ἐάν τε αὐτὸς ἐν τῇ ἰδίᾳ ᾖ καταστάσει, ἐάν τε καὶ τῶν ἀπλανῶν τις ἢ τῶν τοῦ ζῳδιακοῦ τόπων κατὰ τὴν οἰκείαν αὐτοῦ κρᾶσιν θεωρῆται· καθάπερ ἂν εἰ τῶν φύσεων καὶ τῶν ποιοτήτων αὐτῶν καὶ μὴ τῶν ἀστέρων ἐτύγχανον αἱ προσηγορίαι. καὶ ὅτι ἐν ταῖς συγκράσεσι πάλιν οὐ μόνον τὴν πρὸς ἀλλήλους τῶν πλανωμένων μῖξιν δεῖ σκοπεῖν, ἀλλὰ καὶ τὴν πρὸς τοὺς τῆς αὐτῆς φύσεως κεκοινωνηκότας ἤτοι ἀπλανεῖς ἀστέρας ἢ τόπους τοῦ ζῳδιακοῦ κατὰ τὰς ἀποδεδειγμένας αὐτῶν πρὸς τοὺς πλάνητας συνοικειώσεις.

Ὁ μὲν οὖν τοῦ Κρόνου ἀστὴρ μόνος τὴν οἰκοδεσποτίαν λαβὼν καθ᾽ ὅλου μὲν φθορᾶς τῆς κατὰ

[1] ποιητικῆς VMADEProc., φυσικῆς PLNCam.

---

[1] According to the anonymous commentator (p. 71, ed. Wolf), the reason why the luminaries exert such power is that they are the ones which submit to eclipse and thereby determine the places of eclipses and the rulers of these places.

[2] Cardanus, p. 201: ". . . when he says, for example,

TETRABIBLOS II. 8

leaders of the others; for they are themselves responsible for the entirety of the power, and are the causes of the rulership of the planets, and, moreover, the causes of the strength or weakness of the ruling planets.[1] The comprehensive observation of the ruling stars shows the quality of the predicted events.

We shall begin with the characteristic active powers of the planets, one by one, first, however, making this general observation, as a summary reminder, that in general whenever we speak of any temperament of the five planets one must understand that whatever produces the like nature is also meant,[2] whether it be the planet itself in its own proper condition, or one of the fixed stars, or one of the signs of the zodiac, considered with reference to the temperament proper to it, just as though the characterizations were applied to the natures or the qualities themselves and not to the planets; and let us remember that in the combinations, again, we must consider not only the mixture of the planets one with another, but also their combination with the others that share in the same nature, whether they be fixed stars or signs of the zodiac, by virtue of their affinities with the planets, already set forth.[3]

Saturn,[4] when he gains sole dominance, is in general the cause of destruction by cold, and in

that Saturn does this or that, he understands this to refer not only to Saturn but to any star, even a fixed star, that may be of Saturn's nature; as those in Cetus and some in Orion " (*cf.* i. 9). Similarly signs of the zodiac, or terms, could thus substitute for the planets.

[3] *I.e.* in i. 9.

[4] *Cf.* i. 5. Saturn is one of the maleficent planets (*ibid.*).

PTOLEMY

ψύξιν ἐστὶν αἴτιος· ἰδίως δὲ περὶ μὲν ἀνθρώπους γινομένου τοῦ συμπτώματος νόσους μακρὰς καὶ φθίσεις καὶ συντήξεις καὶ ὑγρῶν ὀχλήσεις καὶ ῥευματισμοὺς καὶ τεταρταϊκὰς ἐπισημασίας, φυγαδείας τε καὶ ἀπορίας καὶ συνοχὰς καὶ πένθη καὶ φόβους[1] καὶ θανάτους μάλιστα τῶν τῇ ἡλικίᾳ προβεβηκότων ἐμποιεῖ. τῶν δὲ ἀλόγων ζῴων περὶ τὰ εὔχρηστα ὡς ἐπὶ πᾶν, σπάνιν τε καὶ τῶν ὄντων φθορὰς σωματικὰς καὶ νοσοποιούς, ὑφ᾽ ὧν καὶ οἱ χρησάμενοι τῶν ἀνθρώπων συνδιατιθέμενοι διαφθείρονται. περὶ δὲ τὴν τοῦ ἀέρος κατάστασιν ψύχη φοβερὰ παγώδη καὶ ὀμιχλώδη καὶ λοιμικά, δυσαερίας τε καὶ συννεφίας καὶ ζόφους· ἔτι δὲ νιφετῶν πλῆθος οὐκ ἀγαθῶν ἀλλὰ φθοροποιῶν, ἀφ᾽ ὧν καὶ τὰ κακοῦντα τὴν ἀνθρωπίνην φύσιν τῶν ἑρπετῶν συγκρίνεται. περὶ δὲ ποταμοὺς ἢ θαλάττας κοινῶς μὲν χειμῶνας καὶ στόλων ναυάγια καὶ δυσπλοίας καὶ τῶν ἰχθύων ἔνδειαν καὶ φθοράν, ἰδίως δὲ ἐν μὲν θαλάτταις ἀμπώτεις καὶ παλιρροίας, ἐπὶ δὲ ποταμῶν ὑπερμετρίαν καὶ κάκωσιν τῶν ποταμίων ὑδάτων. πρὸς δὲ τοὺς τῆς γῆς καρποὺς ἔνδειαν καὶ σπάνιν καὶ ἀπώλειαν μάλιστα τῶν εἰς τὰς ἀναγκαίας χρείας γινομένων ἤτοι ὑπὸ κάμπης ἢ ἀκρίδος ἢ κατακλυσμῶν ὑδάτων ἢ ὄμβρων ἐπιφορᾶς ἢ χαλάζης ἢ τῶν τοιούτων, ὡς καὶ μέχρι λιμοῦ[2] φθάνειν καὶ τῆς τοιαύτης τῶν ἀνθρώπων ἀπωλείας.

[1] φόβους VMADΞN (mg.) Proc. Cam.[2] (asterisco notatum); φόνους NCam.[1] (asterisco notatum), φων´ P, φόνοι L.
[2] λιμοῦ VMDEProc., λοιμοῦ PLNACam.

particular, when the event concerns men, causes long illnesses, consumptions, withering, disturbances caused by fluids, rheumatisms, and quartan fevers, exile, poverty, imprisonment, mourning, fears, and deaths, especially among those advanced in age.[1] He is usually significant with regard to those dumb animals that are of use to man, and brings about scarcity of them, and the bodily destruction by disease of such as exist, so that the men who use them are similarly affected and perish. With regard to weather, he causes fearful cold, freezing, misty, and pestilential; corruption of the air, clouds, and gloom; furthermore, multitudes of snowstorms, not beneficial but destructive, from which are produced the reptiles [2] harmful to man. As for the rivers and seas, in general he causes storms, the wreck of fleets, disastrous voyages, and the scarcity and death of fish, and in particular the high and ebb tides of the seas and in rivers excessive floods and pollution of their waters. As for the crops of the earth, he brings about want, scarcity, and loss, especially of those grown for necessary uses, either through worms or locusts or floods or cloud-burst or hail or the like, so that famine and the destruction of men thereby result.

[1] Saturn (Kronos) is pictured as an old man.

[2] For rains of fish, frogs, and other things *cf.* E. S. McCartney, *Trans. Am. Phil. Assn.*, 51, 112 ff., and *Classical Weekly*, 24, 27; also A. S. Pease, ed. of Cicero, *De divinatione*, p. 274. Mice, frogs, insects, and the like were thought to be spontaneously generated from earth, mud, or rain; *cf.* Thorndike, *History of Magic and Experimental Science*, i. 325, 491.

PTOLEMY

Ὁ δὲ τοῦ Διὸς μόνος τὴν κυρίαν λαχὼν καθ' ὅλου μὲν αὐξήσεώς ἐστι ποιητικός, ἰδίως δὲ περὶ μὲν ἀνθρώπους γενομένου τοῦ ἀποτελέσματος δόξας ἀποτελεῖ καὶ εὐετηρίας[1] καὶ εὐθηνίας καὶ καταστάσεις εἰρηνικὰς[2] καὶ τῶν ἐπιτηδείων αὐξήσεις, εὐεξίας τε σωματικὰς καὶ ψυχικάς· ἔτι δὲ εὐεργεσίας τε καὶ δωρεὰς ἀπὸ τῶν βασιλευόντων, αὐτῶν τε ἐκείνων αὐξήσεις καὶ μεγαλειότητας καὶ μεγαλοψυχίας. καθ' ὅλου τε εὐδαιμονίας ἐστὶν αἴτιος. περὶ δὲ τὰ ἄλογα ζῷα τῶν μὲν εἰς χρῆσιν ἀνθρωπίνην δαψίλειαν καὶ πολυπληθίαν ποιεῖ, τῶν δὲ εἰς τὸ ἐναντίον φθοράν τε καὶ ἀπώλειαν. εὔκρατον δὲ τὴν τῶν ἀέρων κατάστασιν καὶ ὑγιεινὴν καὶ πνευματώδη καὶ ὑγρὰν καὶ θρεπτικὴν τῶν ἐπιγείων ἀπεργάζεται, στόλων τε εὐπλοίας καὶ ποταμῶν συμμέτρους ἀναβάσεις καὶ τῶν καρπῶν δαψίλειαν καὶ ὅσα τούτοις παραπλήσια.

Ὁ δὲ τοῦ Ἄρεως μόνος τὴν οἰκοδεσποτίαν λαβὼν καθ' ὅλου μὲν τῆς κατὰ ξηρασίαν φθορᾶς ἐστιν αἴτιος, ἰδίως δὲ περὶ μὲν ἀνθρώπους γινομένου τοῦ συμπτώματος πολέμους ἐμποιεῖ καὶ στάσεις ἐμφυλίους καὶ αἰχμαλωσίας καὶ ἀνδραποδισμοὺς καὶ ἐπαναστάσεις[3] καὶ χόλους ἡγεμόνων τούς τε διὰ τῶν τοιούτων θανάτους αἰφνιδίους, ἔτι δὲ νόσους πυρεκτικὰς καὶ τριταϊκὰς ἐπισημασίας καὶ αἱμάτων ἀναγωγὰς καὶ ὀξείας βιαιοθανασίας[4] μάλιστα τῶν ἀκμαίων· ὁμοίως δὲ βίας τε καὶ

[1] ἑταιρείας Cam.²
[2] Post εἰρηνικὰς add. καὶ εὐετηρίας Cam.², om. libri Proc.

TETRABIBLOS II. 8

When Jupiter [1] rules alone he produces increase in general, and, in particular, when the prediction is concerned with men, he makes fame and prosperity, abundance, peaceful existence, the increase of the necessities of life, bodily and spiritual health, and, furthermore, benefits and gifts from rulers, and the increase, greatness, and magnanimity of these latter; and in general he is the cause of happiness. With reference to dumb animals he causes a multitude and abundance of those that are useful to men and the diminution and destruction of the opposite kind. He makes the condition of the air temperate and healthful, windy, moist, and favourable to the growth of what the earth bears; he brings about the fortunate sailing of fleets, the moderate rise of rivers, abundance of crops, and everything similar.

Mars, when he assumes the rulership alone, is in general the cause of destruction through dryness and in particular, when the event concerns men, brings about wars, civil faction, capture, enslavement, uprisings, the wrath of leaders, and sudden deaths arising from such causes; moreover, fevers, tertian agues, raising of blood, swift and violent deaths, especially in the prime of life; similarly, violence,

[1] A beneficent planet.

---

[3] ὄχλων ἐπαναστάσεις PLNCam., λαῶν ἐπαναστάσεις Proc.; ὄχλων om. VMADE.

[4] ὀρείας βιαιοθανασίας VD, ὀξεῖς καὶ βίαιοι θάνατοι Proc., ὀξείας βιοθανασίας MAE, ὀξείας καὶ βιοθανασίας P (βιω-) L, ὀξείας νόσους καὶ βιοθανασίας NCam.

ὕβρεις καὶ παρανομίας ἐμπρήσεις τε καὶ ἀνδροφονίας καὶ ἁρπαγὰς καὶ λῃστείας· περὶ δὲ τὴν τοῦ ἀέρος κατάστασιν καύσωνας καὶ πνεύματα θερμὰ λοιμικὰ καὶ συντηκτικὰ κεραυνῶν τε ἀφέσεις καὶ πρηστήρων καὶ ἀνομβρίας· περὶ δὲ θάλατταν¹ στόλων μὲν αἰφνίδια ναυάγια διὰ πνευμάτων ἀτάκτων ἢ κεραυνῶν ἢ τῶν τοιούτων, ποταμῶν δὲ λειψυδρίας καὶ ἀναξηράνσεις πηγῶν καὶ φθορὰν τῶν ποτίμων² ὑδάτων· περὶ δὲ τὰ ἐπὶ τῆς γῆς³ ἐπιτήδεια πρὸς χρῆσιν ἀνθρωπίνην τῶν τε ἀλόγων ζῴων καὶ τῶν ἐκ τῆς γῆς φυομένων σπάνιν καὶ φθορὰν καρπῶν τὴν γινομένην ἤτοι ἐκ τῶν τοῦ καύματος καταφλέξεων ἢ βρούχου ἢ τῆς τῶν πνευμάτων ἐκτινάξεως⁴ ἢ ἐκ τῆς ἐν ταῖς ἀποθέσεσι συγκαύσεως.

Ὁ δὲ τῆς Ἀφροδίτης μόνος κύριος γενόμενος τοῦ συμβαίνοντος καθ' ὅλου μὲν τὰ παραπλήσια τῷ τοῦ Διὸς μετά τινος ἐπαφροδισίας ἀποτελεῖ, ἰδίως δὲ περὶ μὲν ἀνθρώπους δόξας καὶ τιμὰς καὶ εὐφροσύνας καὶ εὐετηρίας εὐγαμίας τε καὶ πολυτεκνίας καὶ εὐαρεστήσεις πρὸς πᾶσαν συναρμογὴν καὶ τῶν κτήσεων συναυξήσεις καὶ διαίτας καθαρίους καὶ εὐαγωγοὺς καὶ πρὸς τὰ σεβάσμια τιμητικάς· ἔτι δὲ σωματικὰς εὐεξίας καὶ πρὸς τοὺς ἡγεμονεύοντας συνοικειώσεις καὶ τῶν ἀρχόντων ἐπαφροδισίας·⁵ περὶ δὲ τὰ τοῦ ἀέρος πνεύματα⁶ εὐκρασίας⁷ καὶ διύγρων καὶ θρεπτικωτάτων καταστάσεις εὐαερίας

---

¹ περὶ δὲ θάλασσαν AG; cf. Proc.; π. θαλ. δὲ ME; π. δὲ θαλάσσας VD; πάλιν δὲ ἐν θαλάσσαις PLNCam.
² ποτίμων VDGProc.; ποταμίων alii Cam.

TETRABIBLOS II. 8

assaults, lawlessness, arson and murder, robbery and piracy. With regard to the condition of the air he causes hot weather, warm, pestilential, and withering winds, the loosing of lightning and hurricanes, and drought. Again, at sea he causes sudden shipwreck of fleets through changeable winds or lightning or the like; the failure of the water of rivers, the drying up of springs, and the tainting of potable waters. With reference to the necessities produced upon the earth for human use, he causes a scarcity and loss of dumb animals and of things which grow from the earth, and the loss of crops by drying as the result of hot weather, or by locusts, or by the beating of the winds, or by burning in places of storage.

Venus, when she becomes sole ruler of the event, in general brings about results similar to those of Jupiter, but with the addition of a certain agreeable quality; in particular, where men are concerned, she causes fame, honour, happiness, abundance, happy marriage, many children, satisfaction in every mutual relationship, the increase of property, a neat and well conducted manner of life, paying honour to those things which are to be revered; further, she is the cause of bodily health, alliances with the leaders, and elegance of rulers; as to the winds of the air, of temperateness and settled conditions of moist and

---

³ ἐπὶ τῆς γῆς VG, ἐπη γῆς D, ἐκ τῆς γῆς Proc.; om. PLMNAECam.
⁴ ἢ βρούχου . . . ἐκτινάξεως om. NCam.
⁵ ἐπαφροδισίας codd. Cam.¹, εὐνοίας Cam.²
⁶ πνεύματα VAD, -ων alii Cam.
⁷ εὐκρασίας VMADEG, εὐκράτων PLNCam.

PTOLEMY

τε καὶ αἰθρίας καὶ ὑδάτων γονίμων δαψιλεῖς ἐπομ-
βρίας, στόλων τε εὐπλοίας καὶ ἐπιτυχίας καὶ ἐπικερ-
δίας[1] καὶ ποταμῶν πλήρεις ἀναβάσεις· ἔτι[2] δὲ
τῶν εὐχρήστων ζῴων[3] καὶ τῶν τῆς γῆς καρπῶν
μάλιστα δαψίλειαν καὶ εὐφορίαν καὶ ὄνησιν ἐμποιεῖ.

Ὁ δὲ τοῦ Ἑρμοῦ τὴν οἰκοδεσποτίαν λαβὼν καθ᾽
ὅλου μέν, ὡς ἂν ᾖ συγκιρνάμενος ἑκάστῳ τῶν ἄλλων,
συνοικειοῦται ταῖς ἐκείνων φύσεσιν· ἰδίως δέ ἐστι
πάντων μᾶλλον συγκινητικὸς καὶ ἐν μὲν ἀνθρωπίνοις
ἀποτελέσμασιν ὀξὺς καὶ πρακτικώτατος καὶ πρὸς
τὸ ὑποκείμενον εὐμήχανος, λῃστηρίων δὲ καὶ κλο-
πῶν καὶ πειρατικῶν ἐφόδων καὶ ἐπιθέσεων,[4] ἔτι δὲ
δυσπλοίας[5] ποιητικὸς ἐν τοῖς πρὸς τοὺς κακοποιοὺς
σχηματισμοῖς, νόσων τε αἴτιος ξηρῶν καὶ ἀμφη-
μερινῶν ἐπισημασιῶν καὶ βηχικῶν καὶ ἀναφορικῶν[6]
καὶ φθίσεων· ἀποτελεστικός τε καὶ τῶν περὶ τὸν
ἱερατικὸν λόγον καὶ τὰς τῶν θεῶν θρησκείας καὶ
τὰς βασιλικὰς προσόδους ἐπισυμβαινόντων καὶ τῆς
τῶν ἐθίμων ἢ νομίμων κατὰ καιροὺς ἐναλλοιώσεως
οἰκείως τῇ πρὸς αὐτοὺς ἑκάστοτε τῶν ἀστέρων
συγκράσει. πρὸς δὲ τὸ περιέχον μᾶλλον ξηρὸς ὢν
καὶ εὐκίνητος διὰ τὴν πρὸς τὸν ἥλιον ἐγγύτητα καὶ
τὸ τάχος τῆς ἀνακυκλήσεως πνευμάτων ἀτάκτων
καὶ ὀξέων καὶ εὐμεταβόλων μάλιστα κινητικὸς
ὑπάρχει, βροντῶν τε εἰκότως καὶ πρηστήρων καὶ
χασμάτων καὶ σεισμῶν καὶ ἀστραπῶν ἀποτελεσ-
τικός· τῆς τε διὰ τούτων ἐνίοτε περὶ τὰ τῶν ζῴων

---

[1] ἐπικερδ(ε)ίας VMADEG, ἐπικερδεῖς NLCam., ἐπεικερδεῖς P.
[2] ἔτι VMADEG, ἐν PLNCam.

very nourishing winds, of good air, clear weather, and generous showers of fertilizing waters; she brings about the fortunate sailing of fleets, successes, profits, and the full rising of rivers; of useful animals and the fruits of the earth she is the preëminent cause of abundance, good yields, and profit.

Mercury, if he gains the rulership, is, generally speaking, in nature like whatever of the other planets may be associated with him. In particular, he is above all stimulating, and in predictions concerning men is keen and very practical, ingenious in any situation; but he causes robbery, theft, piracy, and assault, and furthermore, brings about unsuccessful voyaging when he is in aspect with the maleficent planets, and occasions diseases of dryness, quotidian agues, coughs, raising, and consumption. He is the cause of events taking place which concern the priestly code, the worship of the gods, the royal revenues, and of change in customs and laws, from time to time, in consistency with his association with the other planets on each occasion. With reference to the air, since he is very dry and swift on account of his nearness to the sun, and the speed of his revolution, he is particularly apt to arouse irregular, fierce, and changeable winds, and, as might be expected, thunder, hurricanes, chasms in the earth, earthquakes, and lightning; sometimes by these

---

[3] τῶν εὐχρήστων ζώων κτλ (gen.) VMADEG, τοῖς εὐχρήστοις ζώοις κτλ. (dat.) PLNCam.

[4] καὶ ἐπιθέσεων VMADE; καὶ om. GPLCam.; ἐπιθἕ N, ἐπιθεικός Cam.¹, ἐπιθετικός PLCam.²

[5] δυσπλοίας VMADEG Proc., δυσπν(ο)ίας PLNCam.

[6] ἀναφορικῶν libri (ἀφορικῶν D) Cam.¹ Proc.; ἀναπνοικῶν Cam.²

καὶ τῶν φυτῶν εὔχρηστα φθορᾶς ποιητικός, ὑδάτων τε καὶ ποταμῶν ἐν μὲν ταῖς δύσεσι στερητικός, ἐν δὲ ταῖς ἀνατολαῖς πληρωτικός.

Ἰδίως μὲν οὖν τῆς οἰκείας φύσεως ἐπιτυχὼν ἕκαστος τὰ τοιαῦτα ἀποτελεῖ, συγκιρνάμενος δὲ ἄλλος ἄλλῳ κατὰ τοὺς συσχηματισμοὺς καὶ τὰς τῶν ζῳδίων ἐναλλοιώσεις[1] καὶ τὰς πρὸς ἥλιον φάσεις, ἀναλόγως τε καὶ τὴν ἐν τοῖς ἐνεργήμασι σύγκρασιν λαμβάνων, καὶ μεμιγμένην ἐκ τῶν κεκοινωνηκυιῶν φύσεων τὴν περὶ τὸ ἀποτελούμενον ἰδιοτροπίαν ποικίλην οὖσαν ἀπεργάζεται· ἀπείρου[2] δὲ ὄντος καὶ ἀδυνάτου τοῦ καθ' ἑκάστην σύγκρασιν τὸ ἴδιον ὑπομνηματίζειν ἀποτέλεσμα καὶ πάντας ἁπλῶς τοὺς καθ' ὁποιονουνδήποτε τρόπον συσχηματισμοὺς διεξελθεῖν οὕτω γε πολυμερῶς νοουμένους, εἰκότως ἂν καταλειφθείη τὸ τοιοῦτον εἶδος ἐπὶ τῇ τοῦ μαθηματικοῦ πρὸς τὰς κατὰ μέρος διακρίσεις ἐπιβολῇ καὶ ἐπινοίᾳ.

Παρατηρεῖν δὲ δεῖ[3] καὶ πῶς ἔχουσι οἰκειώσεως οἱ τοῦ προτελέσματος τὴν κυρίαν λαβόντες ἀστέρες πρὸς αὐτὰς τὰς χώρας ἢ τὰς πόλεις αἷς τὸ σύμπτωμα διασημαίνεται· ἀγαθοποιοὶ μὲν γὰρ ὄντες ἀστέρες καὶ συνοικειούμενοι τοῖς διατιθεμένοις καὶ μὴ καθυπερτερούμενοι ὑπὸ τῶν τῆς ἐναντίας αἱρέσεως ἔτι μᾶλλον ἀπεργάζονται τὸ κατὰ τὴν οἰκείαν φύσιν

---

[1] ἐναλλοιώσεις] ἐναλλαγὰς NCam.
[2] ἀπείρου] ἀπόρου NCam.
[3] δεῖ] δέον NCam.

---

[1] That is, exchange of houses.
[2] Cf. i. 8.

means he causes the destruction of useful animals and plants. At setting he diminishes waters and rivers, at rising fills them.

Such are the effects produced by the several planets, each by itself and in command of its own nature. Associated, however, now with one and now with another, in the different aspects, by the exchange of signs,[1] and by their phases with reference to the sun,[2] and experiencing a corresponding tempering of their powers, each produces a character, in its effect, which is the result of the mixture of the natures that have participated, and is complicated. It is of course a hopeless and impossible task to mention the proper outcome of every combination and to enumerate absolutely all the aspects of whatever kind, since we can conceive of such a variety of them. Consequently questions of this kind would reasonably be left to the enterprise and ingenuity of the mathematician,[3] in order to make the particular distinctions.

It is needful to observe what affinity exists between the planets which govern the prediction and the countries or the cities for which the event is signified. For if the ruling planets are beneficent, and have familiarity with the subjects affected, and are not overcome [4] by planets of the opposite sect, they more powerfully produce the benefits natural to them;

[3] $μαθηματικός$ is here used to mean " astrologer," as for example at the very end of the *Tetrabiblos* (p. 458, l. 21).

[4] $καθυπερτέρησις$, *supereminentia*, exists when one planet is superior to another, or is to the right of another in the astrological sense (*i.e.* preceding it in the direction of the diurnal movement of the heavens). *Cf.* Bouché-Leclercq, p. 250.

PTOLEMY

ὠφέλιμον, ὥσπερ μὴ συνοικειούμενοι ἢ καθυπερτερούμενοι ὑπὸ τῶν ἀντικειμένων ἧττον ὠφελοῦσι. τῆς δὲ βλαπτικῆς κράσεως ὄντες καὶ τὴν κυρίαν λαβόντες τοῦ προτελέσματος, ἐὰν μὲν συνοικειούμενοι τοῖς διατιθεμένοις τύχωσιν ἢ καθυπερτερηθῶσιν ὑπὸ τῶν τῆς ἐναντίας αἱρέσεως, ἧττον βλάπτουσιν· ἐὰν δὲ μήτε τὴν οἰκοδεσποτίαν ἔχωσι τῶν χωρῶν μήτε καθυπερτερῶνται ὑπὸ τῶν οἰκείως πρὸς αὐτὰς ἐχόντων, σφοδρότερον τὸ ἐκ τῆς κράσεως φθοροποιὸν ἐπισκήπτουσιν. ὡς ἐπὶ πᾶν μέντοι συνεμπίπτουσι τοῖς καθολικοῖς πάθεσιν ἐκεῖνοι τῶν ἀνθρώπων ὅσοι ποτ' ἄν[1] κατὰ τὰς ἰδίας γενέσεις τοὺς ἀναγκαιοτάτους τόπους, λέγω δὴ τοὺς φωσφοροῦντας ἢ τοὺς τῶν κέντρων, τοὺς αὐτοὺς τύχωσιν ἔχοντες τοῖς τὸ αἴτιον ἐμποιήσασι τῶν καθολικῶν συμπτωμάτων, τουτέστι τοῖς ἐκλειπτικοῖς ἢ καὶ τοῖς τούτων διαμέτροις. τούτων δὲ ἐπισφαλέσταται μάλιστα καὶ δυσφύλακτοι τυγχάνουσιν αἱ μοιρικαὶ καθέξεις ἢ διαμετρήσεις τῶν ἐκλειπτικῶν τόπων πρὸς ὁπότερον τῶν φώτων.

⟨θ.⟩ Περὶ χρωμάτων τῶν ἐκλείψεων καὶ κομητῶν καὶ τῶν τοιούτων

Τηρητέον δὲ πρὸς τὰς καθ' ὅλου περιστάσεις καὶ τὰ περὶ τὰς ἐκλείψεις χρώματα ἤτοι τῶν φώτων

[1] ποτ' ἂν om. PLNCam.

---

[1] A geniture (horoscope, nativity) of any individual or event has as its point of departure the horoscope in the proper sense, i.e. the degree of the ecliptic which is rising

even as, when they bear no familiarity, or are overcome by their opposites, they are less helpful. But when they are of the injurious temperament and govern the prediction, if they have familiarity with the subjects affected or are overcome by the opposite sect, they do less harm; but if they are neither lords of the countries nor are overcome by the planets that have familiarity with those countries, they exert all the more intensely the destructiveness of their temperament. Usually, however, those men are affected by the more universal ills who in their own genitures happen to have the most essential places,[1] by which I mean those of the luminaries or of the angles,[2] the same as those that furnish the cause of the general misfortunes, that is, the places of the eclipses or the places directly opposite. Of these the positions most dangerous and hardest to avoid are those in which either of their luminaries is in possession of the very degree of the place of the eclipse, or the degree opposite.

9. *Of the Colours of Eclipses, Comets, and the Like.*

For the prediction of general conditions we must also observe the colours at the time of the eclipses,

---

above the horizon (in the ascendant) at the moment. This point determines a series of divisions of the ecliptic of 30° each, a duodecimal system superimposed upon that of the zodiacal signs and differing therefrom. These divisions are the "places" (also called "houses," somewhat ambiguously) of the geniture.

[2] The angles, or centres, of a geniture are the horoscope or orient, the superior mid-heaven (upper culmination), the occident, and the inferior mid-heaven (lower culmination). See Bouché-Leclercq, pp. 257-259.

αὐτῶν ἢ τῶν περὶ αὐτὰ γινομένων συστημάτων, οἷον ῥάβδων ἢ ἅλων ἢ τῶν τοιούτων. μέλανα μὲν γὰρ ἢ ὑπόχλωρα φανέντα σημαντικὰ γίνεται τῶν ἐπὶ τῆς τοῦ Κρόνου φύσεως εἰρημένων· λευκὰ δὲ τῶν ἐπὶ τῆς τοῦ Διός· ὑπόκιρρα δὲ τῶν ἐπὶ τῆς τοῦ Ἄρεως· ξανθὰ δὲ τῶν ἐπὶ τοῦ τῆς Ἀφροδίτης· ποικίλα δὲ τῶν ἐπὶ τῆς τοῦ Ἑρμοῦ. κἂν μὲν ἐν ὅλοις τοῖς σώμασι τῶν φωτῶν ἢ ἐν ὅλοις τοῖς περὶ αὐτὰ τόποις τὸ γινόμενον ἰδίωμα τῆς χροιᾶς φαίνηται, περὶ τὰ πλεῖστα μέρη τῶν χωρῶν ἔσται τὸ ἀποτελεσθησόμενον. ἐὰν δὲ ἀπὸ μέρους οἱουδήποτε, περὶ ἐκεῖνο μόνον[1] τὸ μέρος, καθ' οὗ ἂν καὶ ἡ πρόσνευσις τοῦ ἰδιώματος γίνηται.

Τηρητέον δὲ ἔτι καὶ τὰς συνισταμένας ἤτοι κατὰ τοὺς ἐκλειπτικοὺς καιροὺς ἢ καὶ ὁτεδήποτε κομητῶν ἐπιφανείας πρὸς τὰς καθ' ὅλου περιστάσεις, οἷον τῶν καλουμένων δοκίδων ἢ σαλπίγγων ἢ πίθων καὶ τῶν τοιούτων, ὡς ἀποτελεσματικὰς μὲν φύσει. τῶν ἐπὶ τοῦ Ἄρεως καὶ τῶν τοῦ Ἑρμοῦ ἰδιωμάτων καὶ πολέμων δὲ καὶ καυσώδων[2] ἢ κινητικῶν καταστημάτων καὶ τῶν τούτοις ἐπισυμβαινόντων, δηλούσας δὲ διὰ μὲν τῶν τοῦ ζῳδιακοῦ μερῶν, καθ' ὧν ἂν οἱ συστάσεις αὐτῶν φαίνωνται, καὶ τῶν κατὰ τὰ

[1] μόνον VMADGProc., μὲν ὂν PL, om. NECam.
[2] καυσώδων VMADE; cf. Proc.; καυσώνων alii Cam.

---

[1] "Luminous sheaves," according to Bouché-Leclercq, p. 355. The expression must refer to rays of light.

either those of the luminaries themselves, or those of the formations that occur near them, such as rods,¹ halos, and the like. For if they appear black or livid they signify the effects which were mentioned in connection with Saturn's nature;² if white, those of Jupiter; if reddish, those of Mars; if yellow, those of Venus; and if variegated, those of Mercury. If the characteristic colour appears to cover the whole body of the luminary or the whole region surrounding it, the predicted event will affect most of the parts of the countries; but if it is in any one part, it will affect only that part against which the phenomenon is inclined.

We must observe, further, for the prediction of general conditions, the comets³ which appear either at the time of the eclipse or at any time whatever; for instance, the so-called "beams," "trumpets," "jars," and the like,⁴ for these naturally produce the effects peculiar to Mars and to Mercury—wars, hot weather, disturbed conditions, and the accompaniments of these; and they show, through the parts of the zodiac in which their heads appear and through the directions in which the shapes of their tails point,

² *Cf.* i. 4, for the powers of Saturn and the other planets.
³ *Cf.* Boll-Bezold-Gundel, pp. 51, 129; who quote *Julius Caesar*, ii. 2, "When beggars die, then are no comets seen; the heavens themselves blaze forth the death of princes."
⁴ Other astrologers and non-astrological writers classified the comets much more elaborately by their shapes and their associations with the planets, of which they were supposed to be the fiery missiles; Ptolemy is much more conservative in what he says. See Bouché-Leclercq, pp. 358-359, and for a more detailed ancient account Hephaestion of Thebes, pp. 97, 31—99, 22 (ed. Engelbrecht).

σχήματα τῆς κόμης προσνεύσεων τοὺς τόπους οἷς ἐπισκήπτουσι τὰ συμπτώματα· διὰ δὲ τῶν αὐτῆς τῆς συστάσεως ὥσπερ μορφώσεων τὸ εἶδος τοῦ ἀποτελέσματος καὶ τὸ γένος περὶ ὃ τὸ πάθος ἀποβήσεται·
91 διὰ δὲ τοῦ χρόνου τῆς ἐπιμονῆς τὴν παράτασιν τῶν συμπτωμάτων· διὰ δὲ τῆς πρὸς τὸν ἥλιον σχέσεως καὶ[1] τὴν καταρχήν, ἐπειδήπερ ἑῷοι μὲν ἐπὶ πολὺ φαινόμεναι τάχιον ἐπισημαίνουσιν, ἑσπέριοι δὲ βράδιον.

⟨i.⟩ *Περὶ τῆς τοῦ ἔτους νουμηνίας*[2]

Δεδειγμένης δὲ τῆς ἐφόδου τῆς περὶ τὰς καθ' ὅλου περιστάσεις χωρῶν τε καὶ πόλεων, λοιπὸν ἂν εἴη καὶ περὶ τῶν λεπτομερεστέρων ὑπομνηματίσασθαι· λέγω δὲ τῶν ἐνιαυσίως περὶ τὰς ὥρας ἀποτελουμένων, πρὸς ἣν ἐπίσκεψιν καὶ περὶ τῆς καλουμένης τοῦ ἔτους νουμηνίας ἁρμόζον ἂν εἴη προδιαλαβεῖν. ὅτι μὲν οὖν ἀρχὴν ταύτην εἶναι προσήκει τῆς τοῦ ἡλίου καθ' ἑκάστην περιστροφὴν ἀποκαταστάσεως, δῆλόν ἐστιν αὐτόθεν καὶ ἀπὸ τῆς δυνάμεως καὶ ἀπὸ τῆς ὀνομασίας. τίνα δ' ἄν τις ἀρχὴν ὑποστήσαιτο ἐν κύκλῳ μὲν αὐτὸ μόνον ἁπλῶς οὐδ' ἂν ἐπινοήσειεν, ἐν δὲ τῷ διὰ μέσον τῶν ζῳδίων μόνας ἂν εἰκότως ἀρχὰς λάβοι τὰ ὑπὸ τοῦ ἰσημερινοῦ καὶ τῶν τροπικῶν ἀφοριζόμενα σημεῖα, τουτέστι τά τε δύο ἰσημερινὰ καὶ τὰ δύο τροπικά. ἐνταῦθα μέντοι τις ἀπορήσειεν ἂν ἤδη, τίνι τῶν

[1] καὶ VPLDG; om. alii Cam.
[2] Titulum post προδιαλαβεῖν inser. GMProc.

the regions upon which the misfortunes impend. Through the formations, as it were, of their heads they indicate the kind of the event and the class upon which the misfortune will take effect; through the time which they last, the duration of the events; and through their position relative to the sun likewise their beginning; for in general their appearance in the orient betokens rapidly approaching events and in the occident those that approach more slowly.

10. *Concerning the New Moon of the Year.*

Now that we have described the procedure of prediction about the general states of countries and cities, it would remain to mention matters of greater detail; I refer to events that happen yearly in connection with the seasons. In the investigation of this subject it would be appropriate first to define the so-called new moon of the year.[1] That this should properly be the beginning of the sun's circular course in each of his revolutions is plain from the thing itself, both from its power and from its name. To be sure, one could not conceive what starting-point to assume in a circle, as a general proposition; but in the circle through the middle of the zodiac one would properly take as the only beginnings the points determined by the equator and the tropics, that is, the two equinoxes and the two solstices. Even then, however, one would still

[1] The new moon closest to the first of the year, as explained later.

τεττάρων ὡς προηγουμένῳ χρήσαιτο. κατὰ μὲν οὖν τὴν ἁπλῆν καὶ κυκλικὴν φύσιν οὐδὲν αὐτῶν ἐστιν ὡς ἐπὶ μιᾶς ἀρχῆς προηγούμενον· κέχρηνται δὲ οἱ περὶ τούτων γράψαντες, ἕν τι[1] ὑποτιθέμενοι διαφόρως, ἑκάστῳ τῶν τεττάρων ὡς ἀρχὴν κατά τινας οἰκείους λόγους καὶ φυσικὰς συμπαθείας[2] ἐνεχθέντες. καὶ γὰρ ἔχει τι τῶν μερῶν τούτων ἕκαστον ἐξαίρετον ἀφ' οὗ ἂν ἀρχὴ καὶ νέον ἔτος εἰκότως νομίζοιτο· τὸ μὲν ἐαρινὸν ἰσημερινὸν διά τε τὸ πρώτως τότε μείζονα τὴν ἡμέραν τῆς νυκτὸς ἄρχεσθαι γίνεσθαι καὶ διὰ τὸ τῆς ὑγρᾶς ὥρας εἶναι, ταύτην δὲ τὴν φύσιν, ὡς καὶ πρότερον ἔφαμεν, ἀρχομέναις ταῖς γενέσεσι πλείστην ἐνυπάρχειν· τὸ δὲ θερινὸν τροπικὸν διὰ τὸ κατ' αὐτὸ τὴν μεγίστην ἡμέραν ἀποτελεῖσθαι, παρὰ δὲ Αἰγυπτίοις καὶ τὴν τοῦ Νείλου ἀνάβασιν καὶ κυνὸς ἄστρου ἐπιτολὴν ἐπισημαίνειν· τὸ δὲ μετοπωρινὸν ἰσημερινὸν[3] διὰ τὸ γεγονέναι πάντων ἤδη τῶν καρπῶν συγκομιδήν, τότε δὲ ἀπ' ἄλλης ἀρχῆς τὸν τῶν ἐσομένων σπόρον καταβάλλεσθαι· τὸ δὲ χειμερινὸν τροπικὸν διὰ τὸ πρῶτον[4] ἄρχεσθαι τότε τὸ μέγεθος τῆς ἡμέρας ἀπὸ μειώσεως αὔξησιν λαμβάνειν. οἰκειότερον δέ μοι δοκεῖ καὶ φυσικώτερον πρὸς τὰς ἐνιαυσίους ἐπισκέψεις ταῖς τέτταρσιν ἀρχαῖς χρῆσθαι, παρατηροῦντας

[1] ἕν τι VPLMADE, ἐπί τινι NCam., ἐν τῇ G.
[2] συμπαθείας VPLMADEG, ἐμπαθείας NCam.
[3] ἰσημερινὸὶ om. NCam.
[4] πρῶτον VPLG, πρώτως alii Cam.

be at a loss which of the four to prefer. Indeed, in a circle, absolutely considered, no one of them takes the lead, as would be the case if there were one starting-point, but those who have written on these matters have made use of each of the four,[1] in various ways assuming some one as the starting-point, as they were led by their own arguments and by the natural characteristics of the four points. This is not strange, for each of these parts has some special claim to being reasonably considered the starting-point and the new year. The spring equinox might be preferred because first at that time the day begins to be longer than the night and because it belongs to the moist season, and this element, as we said before,[2] is chiefly present at the beginning of nativities; the summer solstice because the longest day occurs at that time and because to the Egyptians it signifies the flooding of the Nile and the rising of the dog star; the fall equinox because all the crops have by then been harvested, and a fresh start is then made with the sowing of the seed of future crops; and the winter solstice because then, after diminishing, the day first begins to lengthen. It seems more proper and natural to me, however, to employ the four starting-points for investigations which deal with the year, observing the syzygies

---

[1] Bouché-Leclercq, p. 129, with n. 1, points out that the Egyptian year began with the rising of Sirius, which is close to Cancer; that Cancer was the horoscope in the so-called Egyptian "theme of the world" (the horoscope of the universe, in which the planets, etc., were in the positions which they occupied at the very beginning); but that after Posidonius Aries was definitely recognized as the starting-point of the zodiac.   [2] i. 10.

τὰς ἔγγιστα αὐτῶν προγινομένας ἡλίου καὶ σελήνης συζυγίας συνοδικὰς ἢ πανσεληνιακάς, καὶ μάλιστα πάλιν τούτων τὰς ἐκλειπτικάς, ἵνα ἀπὸ μὲν τῆς ἐν τῇ[1] περὶ Κριὸν ἀρχῆς τὸ ἔαρ ὁποῖον ἔσται διασκεπτώμεθα, ἀπὸ δὲ τῆς περὶ τὸν Καρκίνον τὸ θέρος, ἀπὸ δὲ τῆς περὶ τὰς Χηλὰς τὸ μετόπωρον, ἀπὸ δὲ τῆς περὶ τὸν Αἰγόκερων τὸν χειμῶνα. τὰς μὲν γὰρ καθ' ὅλου τῶν ὡρῶν ποιότητας καὶ καταστάσεις ὁ ἥλιος ποιεῖ, καθ' ἃς καὶ οἱ παντελῶς ἄπειροι μαθημάτων πρόγνωσιν ἔχουσι τοῦ μέλλοντος.

Ἔτι δὲ καὶ τὰς τῶν ζῳδίων ἰδιοτροπίας εἴς τε τὰς παρασημασίας ἀνέμων τε καὶ τῶν ὁλοσχερεστέρων φύσεων παραληπτέον. τὰς δ' ἐν τῷ μᾶλλον ἢ ἧττον κατὰ καιροὺς ἐναλλοιώσεις καθ' ὅλου μὲν πάλιν αἱ περὶ τὰ προειρημένα σημεῖα γινόμεναι συζυγίαι καὶ οἱ τῶν πλανήτων πρὸς αὐτὰς σχηματισμοὶ δεικνύουσι, κατὰ μέρος δὲ καὶ αἱ καθ' ἕκαστον δωδεκατημόριον σύνοδοι καὶ πανσέληνοι καὶ τῶν ἀστέρων ἐπιπορεύσεις, ἣν δὴ μηνιαίαν[2] ἐπίσκεψιν ἄν τις προσαγορεύοι.[3]

Προεκτεθῆναι[4] δ' ὀφειλόντων εἰς τοῦτο καὶ τῶν ἐν μέρει κατὰ ζῴδιον πρὸς τὰ ἐνιαύσια καταστήματα τῶν φυσικῶν ἰδιωμάτων καὶ ἔτι τῶν καθ' ἕκαστον

[1] ἐν τῇ VDG, ἐν τῷ ME, om. PLNCam.; ἀπὸ μὲν τῆς περὶ τὸν Κρ. ἀρχῆς A; περὶ τὴν τοῦ Κριοῦ ἀρχὴν Cam.
[2] ἣν δὴ μην. VMDE, ἣν δ μην. G, ἣν διμηνέαν PL, ἣν διμηνιαίαν NCam.¹, ἥν' μηνιαίαν Cam.², ἣν δὴ νουμηνιαίαν A.
[3] προσαγορεύοι VPLND, -ῃ G, -οῇ A, -οοι MECam.
[4] προεκτεθῆναι P(-πεθη-)LMGE, -θεῖναι VNADCam.

of the sun and moon at new and full moon which most nearly precede them, and among these in particular the conjunctions at which eclipses take place, so that from the starting-point in Aries we may conjecture what the spring will be like, from that in Cancer the summer, from that in Libra the autumn, and from that in Capricorn the winter. For the sun creates the general qualities and conditions of the seasons, by means of which even those who are totally ignorant of astrology can foretell the future.[1]

Furthermore, we must take into consideration the special qualities of the signs of the zodiac to obtain prognostications of the winds and of the more general natures;[2] and the variations of degree from time to time are in general again shown by the conjunctions which take place at the aforesaid points and by the aspects of the planets to them, and in particular also by the conjunctions and full moons in the several signs and by the course of the planets. This might be called monthly investigation.

As it is proper that for this purpose there be enumerated the peculiar natural powers of the several signs to influence annual conditions, as well as those

[1] *Cf.* i. 2.
[2] The Latin versions interpret this sentence in substantially the way here shown. The Paraphrase of Proclus, however, understands it to mean that the sun governs the qualities of the signs, the winds, and "certain other general matters"; and the anonymous commentator also (p. 79, ed. Wolf) says, προϋπακουστέον ὁ ἥλιος ποιεῖ. By "the more general natures" doubtless are meant temperature and other things, besides the winds, that go to make up the weather.

PTOLEMY

ἀστέρων, τὴν μὲν τῶν πλανήτων καὶ τῶν τῆς ὁμοίας κράσεως ἀπλανῶν πρὸς τοὺς ἀέρας τε καὶ τοὺς ἀνέμους συνοικειώσιν καὶ ἔτι τὴν τῶν ὅλων δωδεκατημορίων πρός τε τοὺς ἀνέμους καὶ τὰς ὥρας, ἕκαστα[1] δεδηλώκαμεν ἐν τοῖς ἔμπροσθεν. ὑπόλοιπον δ' ἂν εἴη καὶ περὶ τῆς ἐπὶ μέρους τῶν ζῳδίων φύσεως εἰπεῖν.

⟨ιαʹ.⟩ Περὶ τῆς μερικῆς πρὸς τὰ καταστήματα φύσεως τῶν ζῳδίων

Τὸ μὲν οὖν τοῦ Κριοῦ δωδεκατημόριον καθ' ὅλου μέν ἐστι διὰ τὴν ἰσημερινὴν ἐπισημασίαν βροντῶδες ἢ χαλαζῶδες· κατὰ μέρος δὲ ἐν τῷ μᾶλλον καὶ ἧττον ἀπὸ τῆς τῶν κατὰ τῶν ἀπλανῶν ἀστέρων ἰδιότητος τὰ μὲν προηγούμενα αὐτοῦ ὀμβρώδη καὶ ἀνεμώδη, τὰ δὲ μέσα εὔκρατα, τὰ δ' ἑπόμενα καυσώδη καὶ λοιμικά, τὰ δὲ βόρεια καυματώδη καὶ φθαρτικά, τὰ δὲ νότια κρυσταλλώδη καὶ ὑπόψυχρα.

Τὸ δὲ τοῦ Ταύρου δωδεκατημόριον καθ' ὅλου μέν ἐστιν ἐπισημαντικὸν ἀμφοτέρων τῶν κράσεων καὶ ὑπόθερμον, κατὰ μέρος δὲ τὰ μὲν προηγούμενα αὐτοῦ, καὶ μάλιστα τὰ κατὰ τὴν Πλειάδα,[2] σεισμώδη καὶ πνευματώδη καὶ ὁμιχλώδη, τὰ δὲ μέσα ὑγραντικὰ καὶ ψυχρά, τὰ δὲ ἑπόμενα κατὰ τὴν

[1] ἕκαστα VMADE, om. alii Cam.
[2] τὴν Πλειάδα VMADEGProc., τὰς Πλειάδας P (Πλοι-) LNCam.

of the several planets, we have already, in what precedes, explained the familiarity of the planets,[1] and of the fixed stars of like temperament,[2] with the air and the winds, as well as that of the signs, as wholes,[3] with the winds and seasons. It would remain to speak of the nature of the signs, part by part.

11. *Of the Nature of the Signs, Part by Part, and their Effect upon the Weather.*

Now the sign of Aries as a whole, because it marks the equinox, is characterized by thunder or hail, but, taken part by part, through the variation in degree that is due to the special quality of the fixed stars, its leading[4] portion is rainy and windy, its middle temperate, and the following part hot and pestilential. Its northern parts are hot and destructive, its southern frosty and chilly.

The sign of Taurus as a whole is indicative of both temperatures and is somewhat hot; but taken part by part, its leading portion, particularly near the Pleiades, is marked by earthquakes, winds, and mists; its middle moist and cold, and its following

---

[1] i. 4 and 18.   [2] i. 9.
[3] *Cf.* the chapter on the triangles, i. 18.
[4] Ptolemy characterizes three parts of each sign, leading, middle, and following, besides the portions north and south of the ecliptic. The "leading" portion is so-called because it is the part which first rises above the horizon in the apparent diurnal movement of the heavens; the "following" portion is the last of the sign to appear. "Leading" degrees, or signs, are regarded as being to the right of the "middle" and the "following."

PTOLEMY

Ὑάδα πυρώδη καὶ κεραυνώδη καὶ ἀστραπῶν ποιητικά· τὰ δὲ βόρεια εὔκρατα, τὰ δὲ νότια κινητικὰ καὶ ἄτακτα.

Τὸ δὲ τῶν Διδύμων δωδεκατημόριον καθ' ὅλου μέν ἐστιν εὐκρασίας ποιητικόν, κατὰ μέρος δὲ τὰ μὲν προηγούμενα αὐτοῦ δίυγρα καὶ φθαρτικά, τὰ δὲ μέσα εὔκρατα, τὰ δὲ ἑπόμενα μεμιγμένα καὶ ἄτακτα· τὰ δὲ βόρεια πνευματώδη καὶ σεισμοποιά, τὰ δὲ νότια ξηρὰ καὶ καυσώδη.

Τὸ δὲ τοῦ Καρκίνου δωδεκατημόριον καθ' ὅλου μέν ἐστιν εὔδιον καὶ θερμόν, κατὰ μέρος δὲ τὰ μὲν προηγούμενα αὐτοῦ καὶ κατὰ τὴν Φάτνην πνιγώδη καὶ σεισμοποιὰ καὶ ἀχλυώδη, τὰ δὲ μέσα εὔκρατα, τὰ δὲ ἑπόμενα πνευματώδη· τὰ δὲ βόρεια καὶ τὰ νότια ἔκπυρα [1] καὶ καυσώδη.

Τὸ δὲ τοῦ Λέοντος δωδεκατημόριον καθ' ὅλου μέν ἐστι καυματῶδες καὶ πνιγῶδες, κατὰ μέρος δὲ τὰ μὲν προηγούμενα αὐτοῦ πνιγώδη καὶ λοιμικά, τὰ δὲ μέσα εὔκρατα, τὰ δὲ ἑπόμενα ἔνικμα [2] καὶ φθοροποιά· τὰ δὲ βόρεια κινητικὰ καὶ πυρώδη, τὰ δὲ νότια δίυγρα.

Τὸ δὲ τῆς Παρθένου δωδεκατημόριον καθ' ὅλου μέν ἐστι δίυγρον καὶ βροντῶδες, κατὰ μέρος δὲ τὰ μὲν προηγούμενα αὐτοῦ θερμότερα καὶ φθαρτικά, τὰ δὲ μέσα εὔκρατα, τὰ δὲ ἑπόμενα ὑδατώδη· τὰ δὲ βόρεια πνευματώδη, τὰ δὲ νότια εὔκρατα.

[1] Post ἔκπυρα add. καὶ φθαρτικὰ PLNCam.; om. VMADEG Proc.
[2] ἔνικμα VP(ἔνηκμα)LMADE; ἔνιγρα Proc.; ἄνικμα NCam.; αἴνιγμα G.

TETRABIBLOS II. 11

portion, near the Hyades, fiery and productive of thunder and lightning. Its northern parts are temperate, its southern unstable and irregular.

The sign of Gemini as a whole is productive of an equable temperature, but taken part by part its leading portion is wet and destructive, its middle temperate, and its following portion mixed and irregular. Its northern parts are windy and cause earthquakes; its southern parts dry and parching.

The sign of Cancer as a whole is one of fair, warm weather; but, part by part, its leading portion and the region of Praesepe is stifling, productive of earthquakes, and misty; its middle temperate, and its following parts windy. Its northern and southern parts are fiery and parching.[1]

The sign of Leo as a whole is hot and stifling; but, part by part, its leading portion is stifling and pestilential, its middle part temperate, and its following portion wet and destructive. Its northern parts are unstable and fiery, its southern parts moist.

The sign of Virgo as a whole is moist and marked by thunder-storms; but, taken part by part, its leading portion is rather warm and destructive, its middle temperate, and its following part watery. Its northern parts are windy and its southern parts temperate.

[1] "Fiery, destructive, and parching," according to certain MSS. See the critical note.

Τὸ δὲ τῶν Χηλῶν δωδεκατημόριον καθ' ὅλου μέν ἐστι τρεπτικὸν καὶ μεταβολικόν,[1] κατὰ μέρος δὲ τὰ μὲν προηγούμενα αὐτοῦ καὶ τὰ μέσα ἐστὶν εὔκρατα, τὰ δὲ ἑπόμενα ὑδατώδη· τὰ δὲ βόρεια πνευματώδη, τὰ δὲ νότια ἔνικμα καὶ λοιμικά.

Τὸ δὲ τοῦ Σκορπίου δωδεκατημόριον καθ' ὅλου μέν ἐστι βροντῶδες καὶ πυρῶδες, κατὰ μέρος δὲ τὰ μὲν προηγούμενα αὐτοῦ νιφετώδη, τὰ δὲ μέσα εὔκρατα, τὰ δὲ ἑπόμενα σεισμώδη· τὰ δὲ βόρεια καυσώδη, τὰ δὲ νότια ἔνικμα.

Τὸ δὲ τοῦ Τοξότου δωδεκατημόριον καθ' ὅλου μέν ἐστι πνευματῶδες, κατὰ μέρος δὲ τὰ μὲν προηγούμενα αὐτοῦ δίυγρα, τὰ δὲ μέσα εὔκρατα, τὰ δὲ ἑπόμενα πυρώδη· τὰ δὲ βόρεια πνευματώδη, τὰ δὲ νότια κάθυγρα καὶ μεταβολικά.

Τὸ δὲ τοῦ Αἰγόκερω δωδεκατημόριον καθ' ὅλου μέν ἐστι κάθυγρον, κατὰ μέρος δὲ τὰ μὲν προηγούμενα αὐτοῦ καυσώδη καὶ φθαρτικά, τὰ δὲ μέσα εὔκρατα, τὰ δὲ ἑπόμενα ὄμβρων κινητικά· τὰ δὲ βόρεια καὶ τὰ νότια κάθυγρα καὶ φθαρτικά.

Τὸ δὲ τοῦ Ὑδροχόου δωδεκατημόριον καθ' ὅλου μέν ἐστι ψυχρὸν καὶ ὑδατῶδες, κατὰ μέρος δὲ τὰ μὲν προηγούμενα αὐτοῦ κάθυγρα, τὰ δὲ μέσα εὔκρατα, τὰ δὲ ἑπόμενα πνευματώδη· τὰ δὲ βόρεια καυσώδη, τὰ δὲ νότια νιφετώδη.

Τὸ δὲ τῶν Ἰχθύων δωδεκατημόριον καθ' ὅλου μέν ἐστι ψυχρὸν καὶ πνευματῶδες, κατὰ μέρος δὲ τὰ μὲν προηγούμενα αὐτοῦ εὔκρατα, τὰ δὲ μέσα κάθυγρα, τὰ δὲ ἑπόμενα καυσώδη· τὰ δὲ βόρεια πνευματώδη, τὰ δὲ νότια ὑδατώδη.

TETRABIBLOS II. 11

The sign of Libra as a whole is changeable and variable; but, taken part by part, its leading and middle portions are temperate and its following portion watery. Its northern parts are windy and its southern moist and pestilential.

The sign of Scorpio as a whole is marked by thunder and fire, but, taken part by part, its leading portion is snowy, its middle temperate, and its following portion causes earthquakes. Its northern parts are hot and its southern moist.

The sign of Sagittarius as a whole is windy; but, taken part by part, its leading portion is wet, its middle temperate, and its following part fiery. Its northern parts are windy, its southern moist and changeable.

The sign of Capricorn as a whole is moist; but, taken part by part, its leading portion is marked by hot weather and is destructive, its middle temperate, and its following part raises rain-storms. Its northern and southern portions are wet and destructive.

The sign of Aquarius as a whole is cold and watery; but, taken part by part, its leading portion is moist, its middle temperate, its following part windy. Its northern portion brings hot weather and its southern clouds.

The sign of Pisces as a whole is cold and windy; but, taken part by part, its leading portion is temperate, its middle moist, and its following portion hot. Its northern parts are windy and its southern watery.

---

[1] μεταβολικόν VLADE, μεταβωλητικόν P, μεταβλητικόν MNGCam.

PTOLEMY

⟨ιβ.⟩ Περὶ τῆς ἐπὶ μέρους τῶν καταστημάτων ἐπισκέψεως

Τούτων δὲ οὕτως προεκτεθειμένων αἱ κατὰ μέρος ἔφοδοι τῶν ἐπισημασιῶν περιέχουσι τὸν τρόπον τοῦτον. μία μὲν γάρ ἐστιν ἡ ὁλοσχερέστερον πρὸς τὰ τεταρτημόρια νοουμένη, καθ' ἣν τηρεῖν, ὡς ἔφαμεν, δεήσει τὰς γινομένας ἔγγιστα πρὸ¹ τῶν τροπικῶν καὶ ἰσημερινῶν σημείων² συνόδους ἢ καὶ πανσελήνους, καὶ κατὰ τὴν μοῖραν³ ἤτοι συνοδικὴν ἢ πανσεληνιακὴν τὴν ἐν ἑκάστῳ τῶν ἐπιζητουμένων κλιμάτων⁴ τὰ κέντρα ὡς ἐπὶ γενέσεως διατιθέναι· ἔπειτα τοὺς οἰκοδεσπότας λαμβάνειν τοῦ τε συνοδικοῦ ἢ πανσεληνιακοῦ τόπου καὶ τοῦ ἑπομένου αὐτῷ κέντρου κατὰ τὸν ὑποδεδειγμένον ἡμῖν τρόπον ἐν τοῖς ἔμπροσθεν περὶ τῶν ἐκλείψεων, καὶ οὕτως τὸ μὲν καθ' ὅλου θεωρεῖν ἐκ τῆς τῶν τεταρτημορίων

¹ πρό PLMNEProc.Cam.¹, πρός Cam.², περὶ τὰ τροπικὰ κτλ. A, om. VD.
² σημείων VDMEProc., σημεῖα A, σημασιῶν alii Cam.
³ μοῖραν GMEProc., om. in lacuna fere 3 litt. VD, συζυγίαν A, om. alii Cam.
⁴ συζυγίαν post κλιμάτων add. NCam.

---

¹ In the latter part of ii. 10. Cardanus, pp. 228-229, commenting on this chapter, says, after admiring the genius of Ptolemy, " For in this chapter he does five things. In the first place, he has declared the proper nature of each part of the year in general, which is predicted from the new moon or full moon preceding the ingress of the sun to the cardinal point. In the second . . . , the quality of each month from the new or full moon, following the ingress of the sun to the cardinal point. In the third

TETRABIBLOS II. 12

12. *Of the Investigation of Weather in Detail.*

Now that these facts have been stated in introduction, the method of dealing with the significations in detail involves the following procedure. For one method is that which is more generally conceived, with relation to the quarters, which will demand, as we have said,[1] that we observe the new moons[2] or full moons which most nearly precede the solstitial and equinoctial signs, and that, as the degree of the new moon or of the full moon may fall in each latitude investigated, we dispose the angles as in a nativity.[3] It will then be necessary to determine the rulers of the place of the new moon or full moon and of the angle that follows it, after the fashion explained by us in the preceding sections dealing with eclipses,[4] and thus to judge of the general situation from the special nature of the

---

place, he tells us how to know the nature of the weather of the fourth part of each month . . . and this is discovered not only from new moons and full moons but also from the quarters. . . . In the fourth place, he shows us how to recognize each day the quality of the air . . . from the rising or setting of the bright stars. In the fifth he teaches us to learn that same thing hour by hour from the passage of the luminaries through the angles at the time." The "quarters" mentioned by Ptolemy are the quarters of the year, or of the zodiac.

[2] Literally "conjunctions" (συνόδους), but with special reference to those of the sun and moon; hence, "new moons."

[3] That is, determine the horoscopic point, mid-heaven, occident, etc., at the time of the conjunction and construct the horoscope for the event as though it were a birth.

[4] The reference is to ii. 4-8, especially c. 5, where the method of procedure is explained.

PTOLEMY

ἰδιότητος, τὸ δὲ μᾶλλον¹ ἢ ἧττον ἐπιτάσεων καὶ ἀνέσεων ἐκ τῆς τῶν οἰκοδεσποτησάντων φύσεως διαλαμβάνοντας ποίας τε ποιότητός εἰσι καὶ ποίων καταστημάτων κινητικοί.

Δευτέρα δ' ἐστὶν ἔφοδος ἡ μηνιαία, καθ' ἣν δεήσει τὰς καθ' ἕκαστον δωδεκατημόριον προσγινομένας συνόδους ἢ πανσελήνους κατὰ τὸν αὐτὸν τρόπον ἐπισκοπεῖν, ἐκεῖνο μόνον τηροῦντας, ἵνα συνόδου μὲν ἐμπεσούσης² τῆς ἔγγιστα τοῦ παρῳχημένου τροπικοῦ ἢ ἰσημερινοῦ σημείου καὶ ταῖς μέχρι τοῦ ἐφεξῆς τεταρτημορίου συνόδοις χρησώμεθα, πανσελήνου δὲ πανσελήνοις· ἐπισκοπεῖν δὲ ὁμοίως τὰ κέντρα καὶ τοὺς οἰκοδεσπότας ἀμφοτέρων τῶν τόπων καὶ μάλιστα τὰς ἔγγιστα φάσεις συναφάς τε καὶ ἀπορροίας τῶν πλανωμένων ἀστέρων, τάς τε ἰδιότητας αὐτῶν καὶ τῶν τόπων, καὶ ποίων ἀνέμων εἰσὶ κινητικοὶ αὐτοί τε καὶ τὰ μέρη τῶν ζῳδίων καθ' ὧν ἂν τύχωσιν· ἔτι δὲ καὶ ᾧ τὸ πλάτος τῆς σελήνης ἀνέμῳ προσνένευκε κατὰ τὴν λόξωσιν τοῦ διὰ μέσων, ὅπως ἐξ ἁπάντων τούτων κατὰ τὴν ἐπικράτησιν τὰ ὡς ἐπὶ πᾶν τῶν μηνῶν καταστήματα καὶ πνεύματα προγινώσκωμεν.

Τρίτη δ' ἐστὶ τὸ τὰς ἔτι λεπτομερεστέρας ἐπιση-

---

¹ τῶν μᾶλλον NAECam., τῶν om. VPLMDG.
² ἐμπεσούσης VDG ; ἐμπέσῃ Proc. ; ἐκπεσούσης alii Cam.

---

[1] The signs are taken as marking the months, and the new or full moons first occurring while the sun is in the several signs (hence *following* the entrance of the sun into

quarters, and determine the question of degree of intensification and relaxation from the nature of the ruling planets, their qualities, and the kinds of weather which they produce.

The second mode of procedure is based on the month. In this it will be necessary for us to examine in the same way the new moons or full moons that take place, in the several signs,[1] observing only this, that, if a new moon occurs nearest to the solstitial or equinoctial sign just past, we should use the new moons which take place as far as the next quadrant, and in the case of a full moon the full moons. It will be needful similarly that we observe the angles and the rulers of both the places, and especially the nearest appearances [2] of the planets, and their applications[3] and recessions, the peculiar properties of the planets and of their places, and the winds which are aroused both by the planets themselves and by the parts of the signs in which they chance to be; still further, to what wind the latitude of the moon is inclined through the obliquity of the ecliptic. From all these facts, by means of the principle of prevalence, we may predict the general conditions of weather and the winds of the months.

The third step is to observe the even more minutely

---

the sign, as Cardanus says) are to be observed. However, if, for example, in predicting the weather for the first quarter (spring), a new moon had preceded the first of Aries and had been used in determining the prediction in the way just described, we are to use the new moons in Aries, Taurus, and Gemini for the monthly predictions of this quadrant; if a full moon, the full moons.

[2] Or apparitions.   [3] See i. 24.

PTOLEMY

μασίας ἀνέσεων καὶ ἐπιτάσεων παρατηρεῖν. θεωρεῖται δὲ καὶ τοῦτο διά τε τῶν κατὰ μέρος τοῦ ἡλίου καὶ τῆς σελήνης συσχηματισμῶν, οὐ μόνον τῶν συνοδικῶν ἢ πανσεληνιακῶν ἀλλὰ καὶ τῶν κατὰ τὰς διχοτόμους, καταρχομένης ὡς ἐπὶ πᾶν τῆς κατὰ τὴν ἐπισημασίαν ἐναλλοιώσεως πρὸ τριῶν ἡμερῶν, ἐνίοτε δὲ καὶ μετὰ τρεῖς τῆς ἰσοστάθμου πρὸς τὸν ἥλιον ἐπιπορεύσεως, καὶ διὰ τοῦ καθ' ἑκάστην[1] τῶν τοιούτων[2] στάσεων ἢ καὶ τῶν ἄλλων, οἷον τριγώνων καὶ ἑξαγώνων, καὶ πρὸς τοὺς πλάνητας συσχηματισμοῦ. τούτων γὰρ ἀκολούθως τῇ φύσει καὶ ἡ τῆς ἐναλλοιώσεως ἰδιοτροπία καταλαμβάνεται συμφώνως ταῖς τε τῶν ἐπιθεωρούντων ἀστέρων καὶ ταῖς τῶν ζῳδίων πρός τε τὸ περιέχον καὶ τοὺς ἀνέμους φυσικαῖς συνοικειώσεσιν.

Αὐτῶν δὲ τούτων τῶν κατὰ μέρος ποιοτήτων αἱ καθ' ἡμέραν ἐπιτάσεις[3] ἀποτελοῦνται, μάλιστα μὲν ὅταν τῶν ἀπλανῶν οἱ λαμπρότεροι καὶ δραστικώτεροι φάσεις ἑῴας ἢ ἑσπερίας ἀνατολικὰς ἢ δυτικὰς ποιῶνται πρὸς τὸν ἥλιον· τρέπουσι γὰρ ὡς ἐπὶ πολὺ τὰς κατὰ μέρος καταστάσεις πρὸς τὰς ἑαυτῶν φύσεις, οὐδὲν δὲ ἔλαττον καὶ ὅταν τινὶ τῶν κέντρων τὰ φῶτα ἐπιπορεύηται.

Πρὸς γὰρ τὰς τοιαύτας αὐτῶν σχέσεις αἱ καθ' ὥραν ἀνέσεις καὶ ἐπιτάσεις τῶν καταστημάτων μεταβάλλουσι, καθάπερ πρὸς τὰς τῆς σελήνης αἵ τε

---

[1] ἑκάστην VMADGProc., -ον P, -ου NLECam.
[2] τῶν τοιούτων VMADEG, τούτων τῶν PL, τούτων NCam.¹, αὐτῶν Cam.²
[3] ἐπιτάσεις ἢ ἀνέσεις NACam.

TETRABIBLOS II. 12

detailed indications of relaxation and intensification.[1] This observation is based upon the configurations of the sun and the moon successively, not merely the new moons and full moons, but also the half moons, in which case the change signified generally has its beginning three days before, and sometimes three days after, the moon's progress matches that of the sun.[2] It is based also upon their aspects to the planets, when they are at each of the positions of this kind, or likewise others, such as trine and sextile. For it is in accordance with the nature of these that the special quality of the change is apprehended, in harmony with the natural affinities of the attending planets and of the signs of the zodiac for the ambient and the winds.

The day by day intensifications of these particular qualities are brought about chiefly when the more brilliant and powerful of the fixed stars make appearances, matutine or vespertine, at rising or setting, with respect to the sun.[3] For ordinarily they modulate the particular conditions to accord with their own natures, and none the less too when the luminaries are passing over one of the angles.

For the hour by hour intensifications and relaxations of the weather vary in response to such positions of the stars as these, in the same way that the ebb

---

[1] That is, in the predicted event. Ptolemy also uses the expression "the more or less" (τὸ μᾶλλον ἢ ἧττον) to refer to intensification and relaxation.

[2] *I.e.* conjunction.

[3] Heliacal risings and settings may be meant; but see also the list of configurations given in the note on ii. 7, p. 171.

ἀμπώτεις καὶ αἱ παλίρροιαι, καὶ αἱ τῶν πνευμάτων δὲ τροπαὶ μάλιστα περὶ τὰς τοιαύτας τῶν φωτῶν[1] κεντρώσεις ἀποτελοῦνται πρὸς οὓς ἂν τῶν ἀνέμων ἐπὶ τὰ αὐτὰ τὸ πλάτος τῆς σελήνης τὰς προσνεύσεις ποιούμενον καταλαμβάνηται. πανταχοῦ[2] μέντοι προσήκει διαλαμβάνειν ὡς προηγουμένης μὲν τῆς καθ' ὅλου καὶ πρώτης ὑποκειμένης αἰτίας, ἑπομένης δὲ τῆς τῶν κατὰ μέρος ἐπισυμβαινόντων, βεβαιουμένης δὲ μάλιστα καὶ ἰσχυροποιουμένης τῆς ἐνεργείας, ὅταν οἱ τῶν καθ' ὅλου φύσεων οἰκοδεσποτήσαντες ἀστέρες καὶ ταῖς ἐπὶ μέρους τύχωσι συσχηματιζόμενοι.

⟨ιγ.⟩ Περὶ τῆς τῶν μετεώρων σημειώσεως

Χρήσιμοι δ' ἂν εἶεν πρὸς τὰς τῶν κατὰ μέρος ἐπισημασιῶν προγνώσεις καὶ αἱ τῶν γινομένων σημείων περί τε τὸν ἥλιον καὶ τὴν σελήνην καὶ τοὺς ἀστέρας παρατηρήσεις.

Τὸν μὲν οὖν ἥλιον παρατηρητέον πρὸς μὲν τὰς ἡμερησίους καταστάσεις ἀνατέλλοντα, πρὸς δὲ τὰς νυκτερινὰς δύνοντα, πρὸς δὲ τὰς παρατεινούσας κατὰ τοὺς πρὸς τὴν σελήνην σχηματισμούς, ὡς ἑκάστου σχήματος τὴν μέχρι τοῦ ἑξῆς κατάστασιν ὡς ἐπὶ πᾶν προσημαίνοντος. καθαρὸς μὲν γὰρ καὶ ἀνεπισκότητος καὶ εὐσταθὴς καὶ ἀνέφελος ἀνατέλλων ἢ δύνων εὐδιεινῆς καταστάσεώς ἐστι δηλωτικός, ποικίλον δὲ τὸν κύκλον ἔχων ἢ ὑπόπυρρον ἢ ἀκτῖνας ἐρυθρὰς ἀποπέμπων ἤτοι εἰς τὰ ἔξω ἢ

and flow of the tide respond to the phases of the moon, and the changes in the air-currents are brought about especially at such appearances of the luminaries at the angles, in the direction of those winds towards which the latitude of the moon is found to be inclining. In every case, however, one should draw his conclusions on the principle that the universal and primary underlying cause takes precedence and that the cause of particular events is secondary to it, and that the force is most ensured and strengthened when the stars which are the lords of the universal natures are configurated with the particular causes.

13. *Of the Significance of Atmospheric Signs.*

Observations of the signs that are to be seen around the sun, moon, and planets would also be useful for a foreknowledge of the particular events signified.

We must, then, observe the sun at rising to determine the weather by day and at setting for the weather at night, and its aspects to the moon for weather conditions of longer extent, on the assumption that each aspect, in general, foretells the condition up to the next. For when the sun rises or sets clear, unobscured, steady, and unclouded, it signifies fair weather; but if its disk is variegated or reddish or sends out ruddy rays, either directly outward or turned back upon itself, or if it has the

---

¹ φωτῶν VPLDEG, φάσεων NACam., φύσεων M.
² πανταχοῦ PLNEProc.Cam., πανταχῇ VMADG.

PTOLEMY

ὡς ἐφ'[1] ἑαυτὸν κυκλουμένας[2] ἢ τὰ καλούμενα[3] παρήλια νέφη ἐξ ἑνὸς μέρους ἔχων ἢ σχήματα νεφῶν ὑπόκιρρα καὶ ὡσεὶ μακρὰς ἀκτῖνας ἀπομηκύνων, ἀνέμων σφοδρῶν ἐστι σημαντικὸς καὶ τοιούτων πρὸς ἃς ἂν γωνίας τὰ προειρημένα σημεῖα γίνηται. μέλας δὲ ἢ ὑπόχλωρος ἀνατέλλων ἢ δύνων μετὰ συννεφίας ἢ ἅλως ἔχων περὶ αὐτὸν καθ' ἓν μέρος ἢ ἐξ ἀμφοτέρων τῶν μερῶν παρήλια νέφη καὶ ἀκτῖνας ἢ ὑποχλώρους[4] ἢ μέλανας, χειμώνων καὶ ὑετῶν ἐστι δηλωτικός.

Τὴν δὲ σελήνην τηρητέον ἐν ταῖς πρὸ τριῶν ἡμερῶν ἢ μετὰ τρεῖς παρόδοις τῶν τε συνόδων καὶ πανσελήνων καὶ διχοτόμων. λεπτὴ μὲν γὰρ καὶ καθαρὰ φαινομένη καὶ μηδὲν ἔχουσα περὶ αὐτήν, εὐδιεινῆς καταστάσεώς ἐστι δηλωτική· λεπτὴ δὲ καὶ ἐρυθρὰ καὶ ὅλον τὸν τοῦ ἀφωτίστου κύκλον ἔχουσα διαφανῆ καὶ ὑποκεκινημένον, ἀνέμων ἐστὶν ἐπισημαντική, καθ' ὧν ἂν[5] μάλιστα ποιῆται τὴν πρόσνευσιν· μέλαινα δὲ ἢ χλωρὰ[6] καὶ παχεῖα θεωρουμένη χειμώνων καὶ ὄμβρων ἐστὶ δηλωτική.

Παρατηρητέον δὲ καὶ τὰς περὶ αὐτὴν γινομένας ἅλως. εἰ μὲν γὰρ μία εἴη καὶ αὐτὴ καθαρὰ καὶ ἠρέμα ὑπομαραινομένη, εὐδίαν· εἰ δὲ δύο ἢ καὶ τρεῖς εἶεν, χειμῶνας δηλοῦσιν· ὑπόκιρροι μὲν οὖσαι καὶ ὥσπερ[7] ῥηγνύμεναι, τοὺς διὰ σφοδρῶν ἀνέμων· ἀχλυώδεις δὲ καὶ παχεῖαι, τοὺς διὰ νιφετῶν· ὑπόχλωροι δὲ ἢ μέλαιναι καὶ ῥηγνύμεναι, τοὺς δι' ἀμφοτέρων· καὶ ὅσῳ[8] ἂν πλείους ὦσι, τοσούτῳ[9]

[1] ἐφ' om. AECam.

TETRABIBLOS II. 13

so-called parheliac clouds on one side, or yellowish formations of clouds, and as it were emits long rays, it indicates heavy winds and such as come from the angles to which the aforesaid signs point. If at rising or setting it is dark or livid, being accompanied by clouds, or if it has halos about it on one side, or the parheliac clouds on both sides, and gives forth either livid or dusky rays, it signifies storms and rain.

We must observe the moon in its course three days before or three days after new moon, full moon, and the quarters. For when it appears thin and clear and has nothing around it, it signifies clear weather. If it is thin and red, and the whole disk of the unlighted portion is visible and somewhat disturbed, it indicates winds, in that direction in which it is particularly inclined. If it is observed to be dark, or pale, and thick, it signifies storms and rains.

We must also observe the halos around the moon. For if there is one, and this is clear, and gradually fading, it signifies fair weather; if there are two or three, storms; if they are yellowish, and broken, as it were, storms accompanied by heavy winds; if they are thick and misty, snowstorms; pale, or dusky, and broken, storms with both winds and snow;

---

² κυκλουμένας G; κοιλούμενον VMDE, -ος A; καλλούμενον P, καλούμενον L; κλωμένας NCam.
³ καλούμενα VADEGProc.; λεγόμενα PLMNCam.
⁴ ὑποχλώρους VMADEGProc.; ὑπώχρους PLNCam.
⁵ καθ' ὧν ἂν VAD, καθ' ὃ ἂν ME, καθ' ὃ NPLCam.
⁶ χλωρά] cf. Proc.; χλορά VD; ὠχρά PLNACam.; ὠχρά ἢ χλωρά M, ἢ χλωρά ἢ ὠχρά E.
⁷ ὥσπερ VMADE; ὡσεί PNCam.; ὡς L.
⁸ ὅσῳ VMADE, -ον PLNCam.Proc.
⁹ τοσούτῳ VADE, -ους M, -ον PLNCam.Proc.

μείζονας. καὶ αἱ περὶ τοὺς ἀστέρας δὲ[1] τούς τε πλανωμένους καὶ τοὺς λαμπροὺς τῶν ἀπλανῶν ἅλως συνιστάμεναι ἐπισημαίνουσι τὰ οἰκεῖα τοῖς τε χρώμασιν ἑαυτῶν[2] καὶ ταῖς τῶν ἐναπειλημμένων φύσεσι.

Καὶ τῶν ἀπλανῶν δὲ τῶν κατά τι πλῆθος συνεγγὺς ὄντων παρατηρητέον τὰ χρώματα καὶ τὰ μεγέθη. λαμπρότεροι γὰρ καὶ μείζονες ὁρώμενοι παρὰ τὰς συνήθεις φαντασίας εἰς ὁποιονδήποτε μέρος ὄντες ἀνέμους τοὺς ἀπὸ τοῦ οἰκείου τόπου διασημαίνουσιν. οὐ μὴν ἀλλὰ καὶ τῶν ἰδίως νεφελοειδῶν συστροφῶν οἷον τῆς Φάτνης καὶ τῶν ὁμοίων, ἐπὰν αἰθρίας οὔσης αἱ συστάσεις ἀμαυραὶ καὶ ὥσπερ[3] ἀφανεῖς ἢ πεπαχυμέναι θεωρῶνται, φορᾶς ὑδάτων εἰσὶ δηλωτικαί· καθαραὶ δὲ καὶ παλλόμεναι συνεχῶς σφοδρῶν πνευμάτων· ἐπὰν δὲ τῶν ἀστέρων τῶν παρ' ἑκάτερα τῆς Φάτνης τῶν καλουμένων Ὄνων ὁ μὲν βόρειος ἀφανὴς γένηται, βορέαν πνεύσειν σημαίνει, ὁ δὲ νότιος νότον.[4]

Καὶ τῶν ἐπιγινομένων δὲ κατὰ καιροὺς ἐν τοῖς μετεώροις αἱ μὲν τῶν κομητῶν συστροφαὶ ὡς ἐπὶ πᾶν αὐχμοὺς καὶ ἀνέμους προσημαίνουσι καὶ τοσούτῳ μείζονας ὅσῳ ἂν ἐκ πλειόνων μερῶν καὶ ἐπὶ πολὺ ἡ σύστασις γένηται.

Αἱ δὲ διάδρομοι[5] καὶ οἱ ἀκοντισμοὶ[6] τῶν ἀστέρων,

---

[1] τοὺς ἀστέρας δὲ VMADE; om. alii Cam.
[2] ἑαυτῶν VMAD, αὐτῶν alii Cam.
[3] ὥσπερ VMADEProc., πᾶσαι PLNCam.
[4] ἐπὰν . . . νότον soli habent VDN(mg.)Cam.; om. PLNMAEProc.

and the more of them there are the more severe the storms. And the halos that gather about the stars, both the planets and the brilliant fixed stars, signify what is appropriate to their colours and to the natures of the luminaries which they surround.

As for the fixed stars which are close together in some number, we must observe their colours and magnitudes. For if they appear brighter and larger than usual, in whatever part of the sky they may be, they indicate the winds that blow from their own region. As for the clusters in the proper sense, however, such as Praesepe and the like, whenever in a clear sky their clusters appear to be dim, and, as it were, invisible, or thickened, they signify a downpour of water, but if they are clear and constantly twinkle, heavy winds. Whenever, of the stars called the Asses on each side of Praesepe, the one to the north becomes invisible, it means that the north wind will blow, and the one to the south, the south wind.[1]

Of occasional phenomena in the upper atmosphere, comets generally foretell droughts or winds, and the larger the number of parts that are found in their heads and the greater their size, the more severe the winds.

Rushing and shooting stars, if they come from one

---

[1] This sentence is perhaps an addition to the text, since it does not occur in all the MSS. nor in Proclus; it is to be found, however, in Hephaestion, p. 100, 31-33 (ed. Engelbrecht). Hephaestion's compilation dates, according to Engelbrecht, from the year 381.

---

⁵ διάδρομοι VD, -αὶ ME, διαδρομικαί A, δρόμοι Proc., διεκδρομαὶ PNCam., ἐκδρομαὶ L. ⁶ ἀκοντισταὶ NCam.

εἰ μὲν ἀπὸ μιᾶς γίνοιντο γωνίας, τὸν ἀπ' ἐκείνης ἄνεμον δηλοῦσιν· εἰ δ' ἀπὸ τῶν ἐναντίων, ἀκαταστασίαν πνευμάτων· εἰ δὲ ἀπὸ τῶν τεττάρων, παντοίους χειμῶνας μέχρι βροντῶν καὶ ἀστραπῶν καὶ τῶν τοιούτων. ὡσαύτως δὲ καὶ τὰ νέφη [1] πόκοις ἐρίων ὄντα παραπλήσια προδηλωτικὰ ἐνίοτε γίνεται χειμώνων. αἵ τε συνιστάμεναι κατὰ καιροὺς ἴριδες χειμῶνας μὲν ἐξ εὐδίας, εὐδίας δὲ ἐκ χειμώνων προσημαίνουσι· καὶ ὡς ἐπὶ πᾶν συνελόντι εἰπεῖν, αἱ καθ' ὅλου τοῦ ἀέρος ἐπιγινόμεναι ἰδιόχροοι [2] φαντασίαι τὰ ὅμοια δηλοῦσι τοῖς ὑπὸ τῶν οἰκείων συμπτωμάτων κατὰ τὰ προδεδηλωμένα διὰ τῶν ἔμπροσθεν ἀποτελουμένοις.

Ἡ μὲν δὴ τῶν καθολικῶν ἐπίσκεψις, τῶν τε ὁλοσχερεστέρων θεωρουμένων καὶ τῶν ἐπὶ μέρους, μέχρι τοσούτων ἡμῖν κατὰ τὸ κεφαλαιῶδες ὑπομνηματίσθω. τῆς δὲ κατὰ τὸ γενεθλιαλογικὸν εἶδος προγνώσεως τὰς πραγματείας ἐν τοῖς ἑξῆς κατὰ τὴν προσήκουσαν ἀκολουθίαν ἐφοδεύσομεν.

[1] Post νέφη add. ἐν ὁποίοις ἂν ὦσιν ὁρίοις NCam.; om. alii Proc.
[2] ἰδιόχροοι MA, ἰδιόχρωοι VPLD, ἰδιόχρονοι NECam. (*notatum); cf. τὰ ... χρώματα Proc.

angle, denote the wind from that direction, but if from opposite angles, a confusion of winds, and if from all four angles, storms of all kinds, including thunder, lightning, and the like. Similarly clouds resembling flocks of wool are sometimes significant of storms. And the rainbows that appear from time to time signify storms after clear weather and clear weather after storms. To sum up the whole matter, the visible phenomena, which appear with peculiar colours of their own in the atmosphere in general, indicate results similar to those brought about by their own proper occurrences, in the manner already explained in the foregoing.[1]

Let us, then, consider that thus far, in outline, there has been given an account of the investigation of general questions, both in their more universal aspects and in particular detail. In the following we shall supply in due order the procedure for the prediction which follows the genethlialogical form.

---

[1] The purpose of this clumsy sentence seems to be merely to refer the reader to the account already given in ii. 9.

PTOLEMY

ΒΙΒΛΙΟΝ Γʹ

⟨α.⟩ *Προοίμιον*[1]

Ἐφωδευμένης ἡμῖν ἐν τοῖς ἔμπροσθεν τῆς περὶ τὰ καθ' ὅλου συμπτώματα[2] θεωρίας, ὡς προηγουμένης καὶ τὰ πολλὰ κατακρατεῖν δυναμένης τῶν περὶ ἕνα ἕκαστον τῶν ἀνθρώπων κατὰ τὸ ἴδιον τῆς φύσεως ἀποτελουμένων, ὧν τὸ προγνωστικὸν μέρος 104 γενεθλιαλογικὸν καλοῦμεν, δύναμιν μὲν[3] μίαν καὶ τὴν αὐτὴν ἀμφοτέρων τῶν εἰδῶν ἡγεῖσθαι προσήκει καὶ περὶ τὸ ποιητικὸν καὶ περὶ τὸ θεωρητικόν, ἐπειδήπερ καὶ τῶν καθ' ὅλου καὶ τῶν καθ' ἕνα ἕκαστον συμπτωμάτων αἰτία μὲν ἡ τῶν πλανωμένων ἀστέρων ἡλίου τε καὶ σελήνης κίνησις, προγνωστικὴ δὲ ἡ τῆς τῶν ὑποκειμένων αὐτῆς φύσεων τροπῆς[4] κατὰ τὰς ὁμοιοσχήμονας τῶν οὐρανίων παρόδους διὰ τοῦ περιέχοντος ἐπιστημονικὴ παρατήρησις, πλὴν ἐφ' ὅσον ἡ μὲν καθολικὴ περίστασις μείζων τε καὶ αὐτοτελής, ἡ δ' ἐπὶ μέρους οὐχ ὁμοίως. ἀρχὰς δ' οὐκέτι τὰς αὐτὰς ἀμφοτέρων νομιστέον εἶναι, ἀφ' ὧν τὴν τῶν οὐρανίων διάθεσιν ὑποτιθέμενοι τὰ διὰ τῶν τότε σχηματισμῶν σημαινόμενα πειρώμεθα προγινώσκειν, ἀλλὰ τῶν μὲν καθολικῶν πολλάς, ἐπειδὴ μίαν τοῦ παντὸς οὐκ ἔχομεν· καὶ ταύτας οὐκ ἀπ'

---

[1] *Προοίμιον* VDProc.; *Περὶ σπορᾶς καὶ ἐκτροπῆς* PL (σπωρᾶς) NCam.

[2] τῶν συμπτωμάτων NCam., συμπτωμάτων PL.

[3] μὲν om. PLNCam.

BOOK III.

I. *Introduction.*

As in what precedes we have presented the theory of universal events, because this comes first and for the most part has power to control the predictions which concern the special nature of any individual, the prognostic part of which we call the genethlialogical art, we must believe that the two divisions have one and the same power both practically and theoretically. For the cause both of universal and of particular events is the motion of the planets, sun, and moon; and the prognostic art is the scientific observation of precisely the change in the subjcet natures which corresponds to parallel movements of the heavenly bodies through the surrounding heavens, except that universal conditions are greater and independent, and particular ones not similarly so. We must not, however, consider that both divisions[1] employ the same starting-points, from which, by reckoning the disposition of the heavenly bodies, we attempt to foretell the events signified by their aspects at that time. On the contrary, in the case of the universals we have to take many starting-points, since we have no single one for the universe;

---

[1] *I.e.* general astrology and genethlialogical astrology.

---

⁴ αὐτῆς φύσεων τροπῆς PL, αὐτῆς φύσεως τρ. VD, αὐτῶν φύσεων τρ. A, αὐτῶν φύσεως τρ. ME; αὐτῆς τροπῆς NCam.

αὐτῶν τῶν ὑποκειμένων πάντοτε λαμβανομένας, ἀλλὰ καὶ ἀπὸ τῶν περιεχόντων καὶ τὰς αἰτίας ἐπιφερόντων· σχεδὸν γὰρ πάσας[1] ἀπό τε τῶν τελειοτέρων ἐκλείψεων καὶ τῶν ἐπισήμως παροδευόντων ἀστέρων ἐπισκεπτόμεθα·[2] τῶν δὲ καθ' ἕνα ἕκαστον τῶν ἀνθρώπων καὶ μίαν καὶ πολλάς· μίαν μὲν τὴν αὐτοῦ τοῦ συγκρίματος ἀρχήν· καὶ ταύτην[3] γὰρ ἔχομεν· πολλὰς δὲ τὰς κατὰ τὸ ἑξῆς τῶν περιεχόντων πρὸς τὴν πρώτην ἀρχὴν ἐπισημασίας συμβαινούσας,[4] προηγουμένης μέντοι τῆς μιᾶς ἐνθάδε εἰκότως, ἐπειδήπερ αὐτὴ καὶ τὰς ἄλλας[5] ἀποτελεῖ. τούτων δ' οὕτως ἐχόντων ἀπὸ μὲν τῆς πρώτης ἀρχῆς θεωρεῖται τὰ καθ' ὅλου τῆς συγκρίσεως ἰδιώματα· διὰ δὲ τῶν ἄλλων τὰ κατὰ καιροὺς παρὰ τὸ μᾶλλον καὶ ἧττον συμβησόμενα κατὰ τὰς λεγομένας τῶν ἐφεξῆς χρόνων διαιρέσεις.[6]

Ἀρχῆς δὲ χρονικῆς ὑπαρχούσης τῶν ἀνθρωπίνων τέξεων[7] φύσει μὲν τῆς κατ' αὐτὴν τὴν σποράν, δυνάμει δὲ καὶ κατὰ τὸ συμβεβηκὸς τῆς κατὰ τὴν ἀποκύησιν ἐκτροπῆς, ἐπὶ μὲν τῶν ἐγνωκότων τὸν τῆς σπορᾶς καιρὸν ἤτοι συμπτωματικῶς ἢ καὶ παρατηρητικῶς ἐκείνῳ[8] μᾶλλον προσήκει πρός τε

---

[1] πάσας VPLAD; πάσαις MNECam.[2] (sed in mg. ἢ πάσας ἐπισκεπτόμεθα).

[2] ἐπισκεπτόμεθα VADECam.[1], Cam.[2] mg.; -ώμεθα PL; ἐπισκηπτόμεθα MNCam.[2]

[3] καὶ ταύτην VPLD; καὶ om. alii Cam.

[4] συμβαίνειν VPLMDE, -ουσας NACam.

[5] Post ἄλλας add. ὡς τὸ ὑποκείμενον εἰδικῶς (ἰδικῶς NCam.[1], ἠδικῇ P, ἐστικῇ L)PLNCam.; om. VMADEProc.

[6] Post διαιρέσεις titulum Περὶ σπορᾶς καὶ ἐκτροπῆς add. VMADProc.; om. E (spatio relicto) PLNCam.

TETRABIBLOS III. 1

and these too are not always taken from the subjects themselves, but also from the elements that attend them and carry with them the causes; for we investigate practically all the starting-points presented by the more complete eclipses and the significant passages of the planets. In predictions affecting individual men, however, we have both one and many starting-points. The one is the beginning of the temperament itself,[1] for this we have; and the many are the successive significances of the ambients which are relative to this first beginning, though to be sure the single starting-point is naturally in this case of greatest importance because it produces the others. As this is so, the general characteristics of the temperament are determined from the first starting-point, while by means of the others we predict events that will come about at specific times and vary in degree, following the so-called ages of life.[2]

Since the chronological starting-point of human nativities is naturally the very time of conception, but potentially and accidentally the moment of birth, in cases in which the very time of conception is known either by chance or by observation, it is more fitting that we should follow it in determining the special

---

[1] "Temperament" here is used in its astrological sense, of the mingling of physical and other traits which make up the individual. *Cf.* the similar use of κρᾶσις in i. 11, p. 64.

[2] The "divisions of the successive times," *i.e.* the ages of man, are discussed in iv. 10.

---

[7] τέξεων VD; γενέσεων (mg.: . . εξων) N; ἕξεων A; γενέσεων alii Proc.Cam.
[8] ἐκείνῳ MAEProc.; ἐκεῖνο alii Cam.

PTOLEMY

τὰ τοῦ σώματος καὶ τὰ τῆς ψυχῆς ἰδιώματα κατακολουθεῖν, τὸ ποιητικὸν τοῦ κατ' αὐτὸν τῶν ἀστέρων σχηματισμοῦ διασκεπτομένους. ἅπαξ γὰρ ἐν ἀρχῇ τὸ σπέρμα ποιόν πως γενόμενον ἐκ τῆς τοῦ περιέχοντος διαδόσεως, κἂν διάφορον τοῦτο γίνηται κατὰ τοὺς ἐφεξῆς τῆς σωματοποιήσεως χρόνους, αὐτὸ τὴν οἰκείαν μόνην ὕλην φυσικῶς προσεπισυγκρίνον ἑαυτῷ κατὰ τὴν αὔξησιν ἔτι μᾶλλον ἐξομοιοῦται τῇ τῆς πρώτης ποιότητος[1] ἰδιοτροπίᾳ.

Ἐπὶ δὲ τῶν μὴ γινωσκόντων, ὅπερ ὡς ἐπὶ πᾶν συμβαίνει, τῇ κατὰ τὴν ἐκτροπὴν ἀρχῇ καὶ ταύτῃ[2] προσανέχειν ἀναγκαῖον, ὡς μεγίστῃ καὶ αὐτῇ[3] καὶ μόνῳ τούτῳ τῆς πρώτης λειπομένῃ, τῷ δι' ἐκείνης καὶ τὰ πρὸ τῆς ἐκτέξεως δύνασθαι προγινώσκεσθαι· καὶ γὰρ εἰ τὴν μὲν ἀρχὴν ἄν τις εἴποι, τὴν δ' ὥσπερ καταρχήν, τὸ μέγεθος αὐτῆς τῷ μὲν χρόνῳ γίνεται δεύτερον, ἴσον δὲ καὶ μᾶλλον τελειότερον τῇ δυνάμει, σχεδόν τε δικαίως ἐκείνη μὲν ἂν ὀνομάζοιτο σπέρματος ἀνθρωπίνου γένεσις, αὕτη δὲ ἀνθρώπου. πλεῖστά τε γὰρ τότε προσλαμβάνει τὸ βρέφος ἃ μὴ πρότερον, ὅτε κατὰ γαστρὸς ἦν, προσῆν αὐτῷ, καὶ αὐτὰ τὰ ἴδια μόνης τῆς ἀνθρωπίνης φύσεως, ὅ τε σωματώδης σχηματισμός· κἂν μηδὲν αὐτῷ δοκῇ τὸ κατὰ τὴν ἔκτεξιν περιέχον εἰς τὸ τοιῷδε εἶναι συμβάλλεσθαι, αὐτὸ γοῦν τὸ κατὰ τὸν οἰκεῖον τοῦ

---

[1] ποιότητος VMADEProc. ; ἰδιότητος P (ἰδιω-) LNCam.
[2] ταύτῃ VAD, εἰς ταῦτα PNCam., εἰς ταύτην L, εἰς τὴν μετὰ ταύτῃ M, εἰς τὴν μετὰ ταῦτα E.
[3] αὐτῇ VPLMDE, ταύτῃ NACam.

nature of body and soul, examining the effective power of the configuration of the stars at that time. For to the seed is given once and for all at the beginning such and such qualities by the endowment of the ambient; and even though it may change as the body subsequently grows, since by natural process it mingles with itself in the process of growth only matter which is akin to itself, thus it resembles even more closely the type of its initial quality.

But if they do not know the time of conception, which is usually the case, we must follow the starting-point furnished by the moment of birth and give to this our attention, for it too is of great importance and falls short of the former only in this respect—that by the former it is possible to have foreknowledge also of events preceding birth. For if one should call the one "source" and the other, as it were, "beginning," its importance in time, indeed, is secondary, but it is equal or rather even more perfect in potentiality, and with reasonable propriety would the former be called the genesis of human seed and the latter the genesis of a man. For the child at birth and his bodily form take on many additional attributes which he did not have before, when he was in the womb, those very ones indeed which belong to human nature alone; and even if it seems that the ambient at the time of birth contributes nothing toward his quality, at least his very coming forth into the light under the appropriate conformation of the heavens contributes,

περιέχοντος σχηματισμὸν εἰς φῶς ἐλθεῖν συμβάλλεται, τῆς φύσεως μετὰ τὴν τελείωσιν πρὸς τὸ ὁμοιότυπον κατάστημα τῷ κατ' ἀρχὰς διαμορφώσαντι μερικῶς τὴν ὁρμὴν τῆς ἐξόδου ποιουμένης· ὥστ' εὐλόγως καὶ τῶν τοιούτων ἡγεῖσθαι δηλωτικὸν εἶναι τὸν κατὰ τὴν ἐκτροπὴν[1] τῶν ἀστέρων σχηματισμόν, οὐχ ὡς ποιητικὸν μέντοι πάντως, ἀλλ' ὡς ἐξ ἀνάγκης ἔχοντα καὶ κατὰ φύσιν ὁμοιότατον τῇ δυνάμει τὸ ποιητικόν.

Προθέσεως δὲ κατὰ τὸ παρὸν ἡμῖν οὔσης καὶ τοῦτο τὸ μέρος ἐφοδικῶς ἀναπληρῶσαι κατὰ τὸν ἐν ἀρχῇ τῆσδε τῆς συντάξεως ὑφηγημένον ἐπιλογισμὸν περὶ τοῦ δυνατοῦ τῆς τοιαύτης προγνώσεως, τὸν μὲν ἀρχαῖον τῶν προρρήσεων τρόπον τὸν κατὰ τὸ συγκρατικὸν[2] εἶδος τῶν ἀστέρων πάντων ἢ τῶν πλείστων, πολύχουν τε ὄντα καὶ σχεδὸν ἄπειρον, εἴ τις αὐτὸν ἀκριβοῦν ἐθέλοι κατὰ τὴν διέξοδον, καὶ μᾶλλον ἐν ταῖς κατὰ μέρος ἐπιβολαῖς τῶν φυσικῶς ἐπισκεπτομένων ἢ ἐν ταῖς παραδόσεσι ἀναθεωρεῖσθαι δυναμένων, παραιτησόμεθα διά τε τὸ δύσχρηστον καὶ τὸ δυσδιέξοδον. τὰς δὲ πραγματείας αὐτὰς δι' ὧν ἕκαστα τῶν εἰδῶν κατὰ τὸν ἐπιβληματικὸν τρόπον συνορᾶται καὶ τὰς κατὰ τὸ ἰδιότροπον καὶ ὁλοσχερέστερον τῶν ἀστέρων πρὸς ἕκαστα ποιητικὰς δυνάμεις ὡς ἔνι μάλιστα παρακολουθητικῶς τε ἅμα καὶ ἐπι-

---

[1] ἐκτροπὴν VADEProc., τροπὴν PLMNCam.
[2] συγκρατικὸν VAE; cf. κατὰ τὴν σύγκρασιν τῶν ἀστέρων Proc.; συγκριτικὸν MNDCam., -κροτικὸν PL.

TETRABIBLOS III. 1

since nature, after the child is perfectly formed, gives the impulse to its birth under a configuration of similar type to that which governed the child's formation in detail in the first place.[1] Accordingly one may with good reason believe that the position of the stars at the time of birth is significant of things of this sort, not, however, for the reason that it is causative in the full sense, but that of necessity and by nature it has potentially very similar causative power.

Since it is our present purpose to treat of this division likewise systematically on the basis of the discussion, introduced at the beginning of this compendium, of the possibility of prediction of this kind, we shall decline to present the ancient method of prediction, which brings into combination all or most of the stars, because it is manifold and well-nigh infinite, if one wishes to recount it with accuracy. Besides, it depends much more upon the particular attempts of those who make their inquiries directly from nature than of those who can theorize on the basis of the traditions; and furthermore we shall omit it on account of the difficulty in using it and following it. Those very procedures through which each kind of thing is apprehended by the practical method, and the active influences of the stars, both special and general, we shall, as far as possible, consistently and briefly, in accordance

[1] An assumption which Ptolemy does not think it necessary to demonstrate. The statement that the sign in which the moon was found at the conception would be in the ascendant at the nativity is attributed to " Nechepso and Petosiris "; Boll-Bezold-Gundel, p. 154; *cf.* Bouché-Leclercq, pp. 376, 379.

τετμημένως κατὰ τὸν φυσικὸν στοχασμὸν ἐκθησόμεθα· τοὺς μὲν τοῦ περιέχοντος τόπους πρὸς οὓς ἕκαστα θεωρεῖται τῶν ἀνθρωπίνων συμπτωμάτων, καθάπερ σκοπὸν οὗ δεῖ καταστοχάζεσθαι,[1] προυποτιθέμενοι, τὰς δὲ τῶν τοῖς τόποις κατ' ἐπικράτησιν τῶν συνοικειουμένων σωμάτων ποιητικὰς δυνάμεις, ὥσπερ ἀφέσεις βελῶν, κατὰ τὸ ὁλοσχερέστερον ἐφαρμόζοντες, τὸ δὲ ἐκ τῆς συγκράσεως τῆς ἐκ πλειόνων φύσεων περὶ τὸ ὑποκείμενον εἶδος συναγόμενον ἀποτέλεσμα καταλιπόντες, ὥσπερ 108 εὐστόχῳ τοξότῃ, τῷ τοῦ διασκεπτομένου λογισμῷ. πρῶτον δὲ περὶ τῶν καθ' ὅλου διὰ τῆς κατὰ τὴν ἐκτροπὴν ἀρχῆς θεωρουμένων ποιησόμεθα τὸν λόγον κατὰ τὴν προσήκουσαν τῆς τάξεως ἀκολουθίαν· πάντων μέν, ὡς ἔφαμεν, τῶν φύσιν ἐχόντων διὰ ταύτης λαμβάνεσθαι δυναμένων, συνεργησόντων δὲ εἴ τις ἔτι περιεργάζεσθαι θέλοι πρὸς μόνα τὰ κατ' αὐτὴν τὴν σύγκρισιν[2] ἰδιώματα καὶ τῶν κατὰ τὸν τῆς σπορᾶς[3] χρόνον[4] διὰ τῆς αὐτῆς θεωρίας ὑποπιπτόντων ἰδιωμάτων.

⟨β.⟩ Περὶ μοίρας ὡροσκοπούσης

Ἐπειδὴ περὶ τοῦ πρώτου καὶ κυριωτάτου, τουτέστι τοῦ μορίου τῆς κατὰ τὴν ἐκτροπὴν ὥρας, ἀπορία γίνεται πολλάκις, μόνης μὲν ὡς ἐπὶ πᾶν τῆς δι' ἀστρολάβων ὡροσκοπίων κατ' αὐτὴν τὴν ἔκτεξιν

[1] καταστοχάζεσθαι VMADE, προκαταστοχάζεσθαι PLNCam.
[2] κατ' αὐτὴν τὴν σύγκρισιν VDProc.; κατὰ τὴν σύγκ. PLA; κατὰ σύγκ. NCam., τὴν σύγκ. (om. κατὰ) ME.
[3] τὸν τῆς σπορᾶς VADE, τῆς σπορᾶς PLM, τὰς σπορὰς NCam.
[4] χρόνον libri; -ων Cam.

TETRABIBLOS III. 1-2

with natural conjecture, set forth. Our preface shall be an account of the places in the heavens to which reference is made when particular human events are theoretically considered, a kind of mark at which one must aim before proceeding further; to this we shall add a general discussion of the active powers of the heavenly bodies that gain kinship with these places by dominating them—the loosing of the arrow, as it were; but the predicted result, summed up by the combination of many elements applied to the underlying form, we shall leave, as to a skilful archer, to the calculation of him who conducts the investigation. First, then, we shall discuss in proper sequence the general matters the consideration of which is accomplished through the time of birth taken as the starting-point, for, as we have said, this furnishes an explanation of all natural events, but, if one is willing to take the additional trouble, by the same reasoning the properties that fall at the time of conception will also be of aid toward ascertaining the peculiar qualities that apply directly to the combination.

2. *Of the Degree of the Horoscopic Point.*

Difficulty often arises with regard to the first and most important fact, that is, the fraction of the hour of the birth; for in general only observation by means of horoscopic astrolabes [1] at the time of birth

---

[1] An instrument consisting of a graduated circle with a movable arm by which angles above the horizon could be taken.

PTOLEMY

διοπτεύσεως τοῖς ἐπιστημονικῶς παρατηροῦσι τὸ λεπτὸν¹ τῆς ὥρας ὑποβάλλειν δυναμένης, τῶν δ' ἄλλων σχεδὸν ἁπάντων ὡροσκοπίων, οἷς οἱ πλεῖστοι τῶν ἐπιμελεστέρων προσέχουσι, πολλαχῇ² διαψεύδεσθαι τῆς ἀληθείας δυναμένων, τῶν μὲν ἡλιακῶν παρὰ τὰς τῶν θέσεων καὶ τῶν γνωμόνων ἐπισυμπιπτούσας διαστροφάς, τῶν δὲ δι' ὑδρολογίων παρὰ τὰς τῆς ῥύσεως³ τοῦ ὕδατος ὑπὸ διαφόρων αἰτιῶν καὶ διὰ τὸ τυχὸν ἐποχάς τε καὶ ἀνωμαλίας, ἀναγκαῖον ἂν εἴη προπαραδοθῆναι τίνα ἄν τις τρόπον εὑρίσκοι τὴν ὀφείλουσαν ἀνατέλλειν μοῖραν τοῦ ζῳδιακοῦ κατὰ τὸν φυσικὸν καὶ ἀκόλουθον λόγον, προυποτεθείσης τῆς κατὰ τὴν διδομένην σύνεγγυς ὥραν διὰ τῆς τῶν ἀναφορῶν πραγματείας εὑρισκομένης. δεῖ δὴ λαμβάνειν τὴν τῆς ἐκτροπῆς προγενομένην ἔγγιστα συζυγίαν, ἐάν τε σύνοδος ᾖ ἐάν τε πανσέληνος, καὶ τὴν μοῖραν ἀκριβῶς διασκεψαμένους,⁴ συνόδου μὲν οὔσης τὴν ἀμφοτέρων τῶν φώτων, πανσελήνου δὲ τὴν τοῦ ὑπὲρ γῆν αὐτῶν

---

[1] τὸ λεπτὸν VMADE, τῶ λεπτὸν P, τῷ λεπτῷ NLCam.
[2] πολλαχῇ libri, πολλαχοῦ Proc., πολλάκι Cam.
[3] τῆς ῥύσεως PLME, ῥύσεως VAD. ῥύσεις N, τὴν ῥύσιν Proc., φύσεις Cam.
[4] διασκεψαμένους VAD, -ωμένους P, -ομένους LMNECam.

---

[1] The " solar instruments " are sun-dials, the gnomons of which cast shadows, the position and length of which

can for scientific observers give the minute of the hour, while practically all other horoscopic instruments on which the majority of the more careful practitioners rely are frequently capable of error, the solar instruments by the occasional shifting of their positions or of their gnomons,[1] and the water clocks by stoppages and irregularities in the flow of the water from different causes and by mere chance. It would therefore be necessary that an account first be given how one might, by natural and consistent reasoning, discover the degree of the zodiac which should be rising, given the degree of the known hour nearest the event, which is discovered by the method of ascensions.[2] We must, then, take the syzygy[3] most recently preceding the birth, whether it be a new moon or a full moon; and, likewise having ascertained the degree accurately, of both the luminaries if it is a new moon, and if it is a full moon that of the one of them that is above the earth, we must see what stars rule it at the

---

are significant. Clepsydrae, or water-clocks, operated on the principle of the hour-glass, except that water was used instead of sand. In addition to these instruments the practitioner would undoubtedly have tables of various sorts, including ephemerides, which gave the position of the sun, moon, and planets from day to day, tables of ascensions, etc. Examples of them are preserved among the papyri.

[2] The " ascensions " are the times, measured in arcs of the equator, in which the signs of the zodiac (which do not lie on the equator, but along the ecliptic, which is oblique to the equator) rise above the horizon. They will vary for the individual signs, and for the latitudes (Greek, " climes," κλίματα) at which observations are made.

[3] A conjunction or an opposition.

ὄντος, κατά τε¹ τὸν χρόνον τῆς ἐκτροπῆς ἰδεῖν τοὺς πρὸς αὐτὴν οἰκοδεσποτικὸν ἔχοντας λόγον τῶν ἀστέρων, τοῦ τρόπου καθ' ὅλου τοῦ κατὰ τὴν οἰκοδεσποτίαν ἐν πέντε τούτοις θεωρουμένου, τριγώνῳ τε καὶ οἴκῳ καὶ ὑψώματι καὶ ὁρίῳ καὶ φάσει ἢ συσχηματισμῷ, τουτέστιν ὅταν ἕν τι ᾖ πλείονα τούτων ἢ καὶ πάντα ὁ ζητούμενος ἔχει τόπος πρὸς τὸν μέλλοντα οἰκοδεσποτήσειν. ἐὰν μὲν οὖν ἕνα πρὸς ταῦτα πάντα ἢ τὰ πλεῖστα οἰκείως διακείμενον εὑρίσκωμεν, ἣν ἂν ἐπέχῃ μοῖραν οὗτος ἀκριβῶς καθ' ὃ παροδεύει δωδεκατημόριον, ἐν τῷ τῆς ἐκτροπῆς χρόνῳ τὴν ἰσάριθμον αὐτῇ κρινοῦμεν ἀνατέλλειν ἐν τῷ διὰ τῆς τῶν ἀναφορῶν πραγματείας εὑρημένῳ ἐγγυτέρῳ δωδεκατημορίῳ. ἐὰν δὲ δύο ᾖ καὶ πλείους συνοικοδεσποτοῦντας, οὗ ἂν αὐτῶν ἡ κατὰ τὴν ἐκτροπὴν
110 μοιρικὴ πάροδος ἐγγύτερον ἔχῃ τὸν ἀριθμὸν τῇ κατὰ τὰς ἀναφορὰς ἀνατελλούσῃ, τούτου τῇ ποσότητι τῶν μοιρῶν καταχρησόμεθα. εἰ δὲ δύο ἢ καὶ πλείους ἐγγὺς εἶεν² τῷ ἀριθμῷ,³ τῷ μᾶλλον ἔχοντι λόγον πρός τε τὰ κέντρα καὶ τὴν αἵρεσιν κατακολουθήσομεν· ἐὰν μέντοι πλείων ᾖ ἡ διάστασις τῶν τῆς οἰκοδεσποτίας μοιρῶν πρὸς τὴν κατὰ τὸ ὁλοσχερὲς ὡροσκόπιον ἤπερ πρὸς τὴν κατὰ τὸ

¹ τε VPD; cf. Anon. p. 91, Wolf; om. libri ceteri Proc. Cam. (sed * notat Cam.² et in mg. add. *videtur redundare*).
² ἐγγὺς εἶεν VPAD, ἐγγὺς ἐν L, ἐγγὺς ἔχοιεν E, ἔχοιεν MNCam., ἐγγύς εἰσιν Proc.
³ τῷ ἀριθμῷ VPLAD, τὸν ἀριθμόν MNECam.

TETRABIBLOS III. 2

time of the birth.[1] In general the mode of domination is considered as falling under these five forms: when it is trine, house, exaltation, term, and phase or aspect; that is, whenever the place in question is related in one or several or all of these ways to the star that is to be the ruler. If, then, we discover that one star is familiar with the degree in all or most of these respects, whatever degree this star by accurate reckoning occupies in the sign through which it is passing, we shall judge that the corresponding degree is rising at the time of the nativity in the sign which is found to be closest by the method of ascensions.[2] But if we discover two or more co-rulers, we shall use the number of degrees shown by whichever of them is, at the time of birth, passing through the degree that is closer to that which is rising according to the ascensions. But if two or more are close in the number of degrees, we shall follow the one which is most nearly related to the centres and the sect. If, however, the distance of the degree occupied by the ruler from that of the general horoscope is greater than its distance

---

[1] The text adopted is that of the two most important MSS. and is supported by the anonymous commentator. Bouché-Leclercq (p. 388, n. 1) would discard the words κατὰ τὸν χρόνον τῆς ἐκτροπῆς, but he had made no examination of the MSS. and presumably did not know that the best of them support κατά τε κτλ., the reading mentioned by the commentator. To observe the position of the luminary above the earth at the time of conjunction, rather than that of the one that is above the earth at the time of the nativity, seems much simpler and more natural.

[2] On Ptolemy's rule for determining the ascendant degree, cf. Bouché-Leclercq, pp. 387-388.

PTOLEMY

ὅμοιον μεσουράνημα,¹ τῷ αὐτῷ ἀριθμῷ πρὸς τὴν μεσουρανοῦσαν μοῖραν καταχρησάμενοι, διὰ ταύτης καὶ τὰ λοιπὰ τῶν κέντρων² διαστησόμεθα.

⟨γ̄.⟩ Διαίρεσις γενεθλιαλογίας

Τούτων δὴ προεκτεθειμένων, εἴ τις αὐτῆς τῆς τάξεως ἕνεκα διαιροίη τὸ καθ' ὅλου τῆς γενεθλιαλογικῆς θεωρίας, εὕροι ἂν τῶν κατὰ φύσιν καὶ δυνατῶν καταλήψεων τὴν μὲν τῶν πρὸ τῆς γενέσεως οὖσαν συμπτωμάτων μόνον, ὡς τὴν τοῦ περὶ γονέων λόγου, τὴν δὲ τῶν καὶ πρὸ τῆς γενέσεως καὶ μετὰ τὴν γένεσιν, ὡς τὴν τοῦ περὶ ἀδελφῶν λόγου, τὴν δὲ τῶν κατ' αὐτὴν τὴν γένεσιν, οὐκέθ' οὕτω μίαν οὖσαν καὶ ἁπλῆν· τελευταίαν δὲ τὴν τῶν μετὰ τὴν γένεσιν, πολυμερεστέραν καὶ ταύτην θεωρουμένην. ἔστι δὲ τῶν μὲν κατ' αὐτὴν τὴν γένεσιν ἐπιζητουμένων ὅ τε περὶ ἀρρενικῶν καὶ θηλυκῶν λόγος καὶ ὁ περὶ διδυμογόνων ἢ πλειστογόνων καὶ ὁ περὶ τεράτων καὶ ὁ περὶ ἀτρόφων· τῶν δὲ μετὰ τὴν γένεσιν ὅ τε περὶ χρόνων³ ζωῆς, ἐπειδήπερ οὐ συνῆπται τῷ περὶ ἀτρόφων, ἔπειτα ὁ περὶ μορφῆς σώματος καὶ ὁ περὶ παθῶν⁴ ἢ σινῶν σωματικῶν· ἑξῆς δὲ ὁ περὶ ψυχῆς ποιότητος καὶ ὁ περὶ παθῶν

---

¹ μεσουράνημα VMDEProc., -ισμα PL, -ηματι NACam.
² τῶν κέντρων VPLADEProc., τοῦ κέντρου MNCam.
³ χρόνων VPLMDEProc., -ου NACam.
⁴ ὁ περὶ παθῶν VPLD, om. ὁ E, om. ὁ περὶ MNACam.

---

[1] Ordinarily the horoscope, or ascendant, would be the point of reference by which the other centres (mid-heaven, occident, inferior mid-heaven) of the nativity would be

from that of the corresponding mid-heaven, we shall use this same number to constitute the mid-heaven and thereby establish the other angles.[1]

3. *The Subdivision of the Science of Nativities.*

After this preface, should any one simply for the sake of order attempt to subdivide the whole field of genethlialogical science, he would find that, of all the natural and possible predictions, one division concerns solely events preceding the birth, such as the account of the parents; another deals with events both before and after the birth, such as the account of brothers and sisters; another, with events at the very time of the birth, a subject which is no longer so unitary and simple; and finally that which treats of post-natal matters, which is likewise more complex in its theoretical development.[2] Among the subjects contemporary with the birth into which inquiry is made are those of sex, of twins or multiple births, of monsters, and of children that cannot be reared. To those dealing with post-natal events belong the account of the length of life, for this is not attached to the account of children that cannot be reared; second, that of the form of the body and that of bodily

---

established. In this case the mid-heaven is made the point of reference. The "general" (ὁλοσχερές; Proclus paraphrases with κατὰ τὸ καθ' ὅλου) horoscope seems to be the "presumable" one.

[2] What follows is practically a list of chapters in Books iii and iv. Since the subject of the last chapter of Book iv (the divisions of time and the ages of man) is not included, its genuineness has been questioned, but not seriously doubted.

ψυχικῶν· ἔπειθ' ὁ περὶ τύχης κτητικῆς καὶ ὁ περὶ τύχης ἀξιωματικῆς, μετὰ δὲ ταῦτα ὁ περὶ πράξεως ποιότητος· εἶτα ὁ περὶ συμβιώσεως γαμικῆς καὶ ὁ περὶ τεκνοποιίας καὶ ὁ περὶ συνεπιπλοκῶν καὶ συναρμογῶν καὶ φίλων·[1] ἑξῆς δ' ὁ περὶ ξενιτείας καὶ τελευταῖος ὁ περὶ τῆς τοῦ θανάτου ποιότητος, τῇ μὲν δυνάμει συνοικειούμενος τῷ περὶ χρόνων ζωῆς, τῇ τάξει δ' εἰκότως ἐπὶ πᾶσι τούτοις τιθέμενος· ὑπὲρ ὧν ἑκάστου κατὰ τὸ κεφαλαιῶδες ποιησόμεθα τὴν ὑφήγησιν, αὐτὰς τὰς τῆς ἐπισκέψεως πραγματείας μετὰ ψιλῶν τῶν ποιητικῶν δυνάμεων, ὡς ἔφαμεν, ἐκτιθέμενοι, καὶ τὰ μὲν περιέργως ὑπὸ τῶν πολλῶν φλυαρούμενα καὶ μὴ πιθανὸν ἔχοντα λόγον πρὸς τὰς ἀπὸ τῆς πρώτης[2] φύσεως αἰτίας ἀποπεμπόμενοι· τὰ δὲ ἐνδεχομένην ἔχοντα τὴν κατάληψιν, οὐ διὰ κλήρων καὶ ἀριθμῶν ἀναιτιολογήτων, ἀλλὰ δι' αὐτῆς τῆς τῶν σχηματισμῶν πρὸς τοὺς οἰκείους τόπους θεωρίας ἐπισκεπτόμενοι· καθ' ὅλου μέντοι καὶ ἐπὶ πάντων ἁπλῶς, ἵνα μὴ καθ' ἕκαστον εἶδος ταυτολογῶμεν.

112 Πρῶτον μὲν χρὴ σκοπεῖν[3] τὸν οἰκειούμενον τόπον τοῦ ζωδιακοῦ τῷ ζητουμένῳ τῆς γενέσεως κατ' εἶδος κεφαλαίῳ, καθάπερ λόγου ἕνεκεν τῷ περὶ πράξεων τὸν τοῦ μεσουρανήματος, ἢ τῷ περὶ πατρὸς τὸν ἡλιακόν· ἔπειτα θεωρεῖν τοὺς λόγον ἔχοντας πρὸς τὸν ὑποκείμενον τόπον τῶν ἀστέρων οἰκοδεσποτίας καθ' οὓς ἐπάνω[4] προείπομεν πέντε

[1] καὶ φίλων VPLD, καὶ om. MNAECam.
[2] πρώτης VPMADE, om. NL (in lacuna) Cam.
[3] σκοπεῖν om. MNCam. [4] ἐπάνω om. NCam.

TETRABIBLOS III. 3

illnesses and injuries; next, that of the quality of the mind and illnesses of the mind; then that which concerns fortune, both in the matter of possessions and in that of dignities; and after this the account of the quality of action; then that of marriage and of the begetting of children, and that of associations, agreements, and friends; following comes the account of journeys, and finally that of the quality of death, which is potentially akin to the inquiry about the length of life, but in order is reasonably placed at the end of all these subjects. We shall sketch each of these subjects briefly, explaining, as we said before, together with the effective powers by themselves, the actual procedure of investigation; as for the nonsense on which many waste their labour and of which not even a plausible account can be given, this we shall dismiss in favour of the primary natural causes. What, however, admits of prediction we shall investigate, not by means of lots and numbers of which no reasonable explanation can be given, but merely through the science of the aspects of the stars to the places with which they have familiarity, in general terms, however, which are applicable to absolutely all cases, that we may avoid the repetition involved in the discussion of particular cases.

In the first place, we should examine that place of the zodiac which is pertinent to the specific heading of the geniture which is subject to query; for example, the mid-heaven, for the query about action, or the place of the sun for the question about the father; then we must observe those planets which have the relation of rulership to the place in question

PTOLEMY

τρόπους. κἂν μὲν εἷς ᾖ ὁ κατὰ πάντας [1] κύριος, τούτῳ [2] διδόναι τὴν ἐκείνης τῆς προτελέσεως οἰκοδεσποτίαν· ἐὰν δὲ δύο ἢ τρεῖς, τοῖς τὰς πλείους ἔχουσι ψήφους· μετὰ δὲ ταῦτα πρὸς μὲν τὸ ποιὸν τοῦ ἀποτελέσματος σκοπεῖν τάς τε αὐτῶν τῶν οἰκοδεσποτησάντων ἀστέρων φύσεις καὶ τὰς τῶν δωδεκατημορίων ἐν οἷς εἰσιν αὐτοί τε καὶ οἱ συνοικειούμενοι[3] τόποι· πρὸς δὲ τὸ μέγεθος αὐτῶν σκοπεῖν καὶ τὴν δύναμιν[4] πότερον ἐνεργῶς τυγχάνουσι διακείμενοι κατά τε αὐτὸ τὸ κοσμικὸν καὶ τὸ κατὰ τὴν γένεσιν ἢ τὸ ἐναντίον· δραστικώτατοι μὲν γάρ εἰσιν ὅταν κοσμικῶς μὲν ἐν ἰδίοις ἢ ἐν οἰκείοις ὦσι τόποις· καὶ πάλιν ὅταν ἀνατολικοὶ τυγχάνωσι καὶ προσθετικοὶ τοῖς ἀριθμοῖς· κατὰ γένεσιν δὲ ὅταν ἐπὶ τῶν κέντρων ἢ τῶν ἐπαναφορῶν παροδεύωσι καὶ μάλιστα τῶν πρώτων, λέγω δὴ τῶν τε κατὰ τὰς ἀναφορὰς καὶ τὰς μεσουρανήσεις· ἀδρανέστατοι δὲ ὅταν κοσμικῶς μὲν[5] ἐν τοῖς ἀλλοτρίοις ἢ ἀνοικείοις ὦσι τόποις καὶ δυτικοὶ ἢ ἀναποδιστικοὶ[6] τοῖς δρόμοις ὦσι· κατὰ γένεσιν δὲ ὅταν ἀποκλίνωσι τῶν κέντρων· πρὸς δὲ τὸν καθ'

[1] πάντας VPMDEProc., πάντα LNACam.
[2] τούτῳ VAD ; cf. οὗτος λήψεται Proc. ; αὐτῷ PLMNECam.
[3] συνοικειούμενοι VP (-οικι-) LADProc. ; κυριευόμενοι MNE Cam.
[4] κα' τὴν δύναμιν VMNA (post αὐτῶν) DE ; om. Cam. ; πόθεν κρίνωμεν (-ομεν L) ἢ μέγα καὶ ἰσχυρὸν τὸ ἀποτέλεσμα ἡμῖν καὶ τὴν δύναμιν πότερον κτλ. PL.
[5] κοσμικῶς μὲν ὅταν NCam.
[6] ἀναποδιστικοὶ VMADEP (-τηκ-) L (-δεσ-); ἢ ἀφαιρετικοὶ in mg. A ; ἀναποδιτικοὶ N ; *ἀναποδυτικοὶ Cam. (in mg. ἀφαιρετικοί).

TETRABIBLOS III. 3

by the five ways aforesaid;[1] and if one planet is lord in all these ways, we must assign to him the rulership of that prediction; if two or three, we must assign it to those which have the more claims. After this, to determine the quality of the prediction, we must consider the natures of the ruling planets themselves and of the signs in which are the planets themselves, and the places familiar to them. For the magnitude of the event we must examine their power[2] and observe whether they are actively situated both in the cosmos itself and in the nativity,[3] or the reverse; for they are most effective when, with respect to the cosmos, they are in their own or in familiar regions, and again when they are rising and are increasing in their numbers;[4] and, with respect to the nativity, whenever they are passing through the angles or signs that rise after them,[5] and especially the principal of these, by which I mean the signs ascendant and culminating. They are weakest, with respect to the universe, when they are in places belonging to others or those unrelated to them, and when they are occidental or retreating in their course; and, with respect to the nativity, when they are declining from the angles. For the time of

[1] See c. 2, p. 233.
[2] The power of the ruling planets.
[3] The horoscopic point and other angles change for each nativity; the signs of the zodiac, houses of the planets, terms, etc., are cosmic, as being related to the universe itself and therefore fixed.
[4] *I.e.* when their movement in the zodiac is direct, not retrograde. The theory of epicycles was used to explain the stations and changes of direction in the movement of the planets.
[5] Or, the signs succedent (ἐπαναφοραί) to the angles.

PTOLEMY

ὅλου χρόνον τοῦ ἀποτελέσματος πότερον ἑῷοί εἰσιν ἢ ἑσπέριοι πρός τε τὸν ἥλιον καὶ τὸν ὡροσκόπον, ἐπειδήπερ τὰ μὲν προηγούμενα ἑκατέρου αὐτῶν τεταρτημόρια καὶ τὰ διάμετρα τούτοις ἑῷα γίνεται, τὰ δὲ λοιπὰ καὶ ἑπόμενα ἑσπέρια· καὶ πότερον ἐπὶ τῶν κέντρων τυγχάνουσιν ἢ τῶν ἐπαναφορῶν· ἑῷοι μὲν γὰρ ὄντες ἢ ἐπίκεντροι κατ' ἀρχὰς γίνονται δραστικώτεροι, ἑσπέριοι δὲ ἢ ἐπὶ τῶν ἐπαναφορῶν βραδύτεροι.

⟨δ.⟩ Περὶ γονέων

Ὁ μὲν οὖν προηγούμενος τύπος[1] τῆς κατ' εἶδος ἐπισκέψεως, οὗ διὰ παντὸς ἔχεσθαι προσήκει, τοῦτον ἔχει τὸν τρόπον. ἀρξόμεθα δὲ ἤδη κατὰ τὴν ἐκκειμένην τάξιν ἀπὸ πρώτου τοῦ περὶ γονέων λόγου. ὁ μὲν τοίνυν ἥλιος καὶ ὁ τοῦ Κρόνου ἀστὴρ τῷ πατρικῷ προσώπῳ συνοικειοῦνται κατὰ φύσιν, ἡ δὲ σελήνη καὶ ὁ τῆς Ἀφροδίτης τῷ μητρικῷ· καὶ ὅπως ἂν οὗτοι διακείμενοι τυγχάνωσι πρός τε ἀλλήλους καὶ πρὸς τοὺς ἄλλους, τοιαῦτα δεῖ καὶ τὰ περὶ τοὺς γονέας ὑπονοεῖν. τὰ μὲν γὰρ περὶ τῆς τύχης καὶ τῆς κτήσεως αὐτῶν ἐπισκεπτέον ἐκ τῆς δορυφορίας τῶν φώτων, ἐπειδήπερ περιεχόμενοι μὲν ὑπὸ τῶν ἀγαθοποιεῖν δυναμένων καὶ τῶν τῆς αὐτῆς αἱρέσεως, ἤτοι ἐν τοῖς αὐτοῖς ζῳδίοις ἢ καὶ ἐν τοῖς ἑξῆς, ἐπιφανῆ καὶ λαμπρὰ τὰ περὶ τοὺς γονέας διασημαίνουσι, καὶ μάλισθ' ὅταν τὸν μὲν ἥλιον ἑῷοι δορυφορῶσιν

---

[1] τύπος VPLD, τόπος MNAECam.

the predicted event in general we must observe whether they are oriental or occidental to the sun and to the horoscope; for the quadrants which precede each of them and those which are diametrically opposite are oriental, and the others, which follow, are occidental. Also we must observe whether they are at the angles or in the succedent signs; for if they are oriental or at the angles they are more effective at the beginning; if they are occidental or in the succeeding signs they are slower to take action.

4. *Of Parents.*

The guiding style of the specific inquiry, to which we should adhere throughout, runs after this fashion. We shall now, therefore, begin, following the order just stated, with the account of parents, which comes first. Now the sun and Saturn are by nature associated with the person of the father and the moon and Venus with that of the mother, and as these may be disposed with respect to each other and the other stars, such must we suppose to be the affairs of the parents. Now the question of their fortune and wealth must be investigated by means of the attendance[1] upon the luminaries; for when they are surrounded by planets that can be of benefit and by planets of their own sect, either in the same signs or in the next following, they signify that the circumstances of the parents will be conspicuously brilliant, particularly if morning stars attend the

---

[1] δορυφορία, " attendance," and δορυφόρος, " spear-bearer," " attendant," outside of astrology refer to the hired military guards of princes and tyrants.

ἀστέρες, τὴν δὲ σελήνην ἑσπέριοι, καλῶς καὶ αὐτοὶ διακείμενοι καθ' ὃν εἰρήκαμεν τρόπον.[1] ἐὰν δὲ καὶ ὁ τοῦ Κρόνου καὶ ὁ τῆς Ἀφροδίτης καὶ αὐτοὶ τυγχάνωσιν ἀνατολικοί τε καὶ ἰδιοπροσωποῦντες ἢ καὶ ἐπίκεντροι, εὐδαιμονίαν πρόδηλον ὑπονοητέον κατὰ τὸ οἰκεῖον ἑκατέρου τῶν γονέων· τὸ δὲ ἐναντίον, ἐὰν κενοδρομοῦντα ᾖ τὰ φῶτα καὶ ἀδορυφόρητα τυγχάνοντα, ταπεινότητος καὶ ἀδοξίας τῶν γονέων ἐστὶ δηλωτικὰ καὶ μάλισθ' ὅταν ὁ τῆς Ἀφροδίτης ἢ καὶ ὁ τοῦ Κρόνου μὴ καλῶς[2] φαίνωνται διακείμενοι. ἐὰν δὲ δορυφόρηται μέν, μὴ μέντοι ὑπὸ τῶν τῆς αὐτῆς αἱρέσεως, ὡς ὅταν Ἄρης μὲν ἐπαναφέρηται τῷ ἡλίῳ, Κρόνος δὲ τῇ σελήνῃ, ἢ μὴ ὑπὸ καλῶς κειμένων τῶν ἀγαθοποιῶν καὶ κατὰ τὴν αὐτὴν αἵρεσιν, μετριότητα καὶ ἀνωμαλίαν περὶ τὸν βίον αὐτῶν ὑπονοητέον. κἂν μὲν σύμφωνος ᾖ ὁ διασημανθησόμενος τῆς τύχης κλῆρος ἐν τῇ γενέσει τοῖς τὸν ἥλιον ἢ τὴν σελήνην[3] ἐπὶ καλῷ δορυφορήσασι, παραλήψονται σῶα τὰ τῶν γονέων· ἐὰν δὲ ἀσύμφωνος ᾖ ἢ ἐναντίος, μηδενὸς ἢ τῶν κακοποιῶν εἰληφότων τὴν δορυφορίαν, ἄχρηστος αὐτοῖς καὶ ἐπιβλαβὴς ἡ τῶν γονέων ἔσται κτῆσις.

Περὶ δὲ πολυχρονιότητος ἢ ὀλιγοχρονιότητος[4] αὐτῶν σκεπτέον ἀπὸ τῶν ἄλλων συσχηματισμῶν. ἐπὶ μὲν γὰρ τοῦ πατρός, ἐὰν ὁ τοῦ Διὸς ᾖ ὁ τῆς Ἀφροδίτης συσχηματισθῶσιν ὁπωσδήποτε

---

[1] καθ' ὃν ... τρόπον om. NCam.
[2] μὴ καλῶς MNAECam.Proc., κακῶς VD, om. μὴ PL.
[3] σελήνην VPLADProc., Ἀφροδίτην MNECam.
[4] ἢ ὀλιγοχρονιότητος om. NLCam.

sun and evening stars the moon, while the luminaries themselves are favourably placed in the way already described.[1] But if both Saturn and Venus, likewise, happen to be in the orient and in their proper faces,[2] or at the angles, we must understand it to be a prediction of conspicuous happiness, in accordance with what is proper and fitting for each parent. But, on the other hand, if the luminaries are proceeding alone and without attendants, they are indicative of low station and obscurity for the parents, particularly whenever Venus or Saturn do not appear in a favourable position. If, however, they are attended, but not by planets of the same sect, as when Mars rises close after the sun or Saturn after the moon, or if they are attended by beneficent planets which are in an unfavourable position and not of the same sect, we must understand that a moderate station and changing fortunes in life are predicted for them. And if the Lot of Fortune,[3] of which we shall make an explanation, is in agreement in the nativity with the planets which in favourable position attend the sun or the moon, the children will receive the patrimony intact; if, however, it is in disagreement or opposition, and if no planet attends, or the maleficent planets are in attendance, the estate of the parents will be useless to the children and even harmful.

With regard to the length or the shortness of their life one must inquire from the other configurations. For in the father's case, if Jupiter or Venus is in any

---

[1] *I.e.* in the preceding chapter.
[2] *Cf.* i. 23.   [3] See iii. 12.

PTOLEMY

τῷ τε ἡλίῳ καὶ τῷ τοῦ Κρόνου, ἢ καὶ αὐτὸς ὁ τοῦ Κρόνου σύμφωνον ἔχῃ σχηματισμὸν πρὸς τὸν ἥλιον ἤτοι συνὼν ἢ ἑξαγωνίζων ἢ τριγωνίζων, ἐν δυνάμει μὲν ὄντων αὐτῶν, πολυχρονιότητα τοῦ πατρὸς καταστοχαστέον· ἀδυναμούντων δὲ οὐχ ὁμοίως, οὐ μέντοιγε οὐδὲ ὀλιγοχρονιότητα· ἐὰν[1] δὲ τοῦτο μὲν μὴ ὑπάρχῃ, ὁ δὲ τοῦ Ἄρεως καθυπερτερήσῃ τὸν ἥλιον ἢ τὸν τοῦ Κρόνου, ἢ καὶ ἐπανενεχθῇ αὐτοῖς, ἢ καὶ αὐτὸς πάλιν ὁ τοῦ Κρόνου μὴ σύμφωνος ᾖ πρὸς τὸν ἥλιον ἀλλ' ἤτοι τετράγωνος ἢ διάμετρος, ἀποκεκλικότες μὲν τῶν κέντρων ἀσθενικοὺς μόνον[2] τοὺς πατέρας ποιοῦσιν, ἐπίκεντροι δὲ ἢ ἐπαναφερόμενοι τοῖς κέντροις ὀλιγοχρονίους ἢ ἐπισινεῖς· ὀλιχοχρονίους μὲν ὅταν ἐν τοῖς πρώτοις ὦσι δυσὶ κέντροις, τῷ τε ἀνατέλλοντι καὶ τῷ μεσουρανοῦντι, καὶ ταῖς τούτων ἐπαναφοραῖς· ἐπισινεῖς δὲ ἢ ἐπινόσους ὅταν ἐν τοῖς λοιποῖς δυσὶ κέντροις ὦσι, τῷ τε δύνοντι καὶ τῷ ὑπογείῳ, ἢ ταῖς τούτων ἐπαναφοραῖς.[3] ὁ μὲν γὰρ τοῦ Ἄρεως τὸν ἥλιον βλέψας καθ' ὃν εἰρήκαμεν τρόπον αἰφνιδίως ἀναιρεῖ τὸν πατέρα[4] ἢ σίνη περὶ τὰς ὄψεις ποιεῖ, τὸν δὲ τοῦ Κρόνου βλέψας ἢ θανάτοις ἢ ῥιγοπυρέτοις ἢ σίνεσι διὰ τομῶν καὶ καύσεων περικυλίει. ὁ δὲ τοῦ Κρόνου καὶ αὐτὸς κακῶς σχηματισθεὶς πρὸς τὸν ἥλιον καὶ τοὺς θανάτους τοὺς πατρικοὺς ἐπινόσους κατασκευάζει καὶ πάθη τὰ διὰ τῆς τῶν ὑγρῶν ὀχλήσεως.

[1] ἐὰν VPLDProc., ὅταν MNAECam.
[2] μόνους MNACam.
[3] ἐπισινεῖς ... ἐπαναφοραῖς libri Proc.; om. Cam.
[4] τοὺς πατέρας MNACam.

TETRABIBLOS III. 4

aspect whatever to the sun and to Saturn, or if Saturn himself is in an harmonious aspect to the sun, either conjunction, sextile, or trine, both being in power, we must conjecture long life for the father; if they are weak, however, the significance is not the same, though it does not indicate a short life. If, however, this condition is not present, but Mars overcomes [1] the sun or Saturn, or rises in succession to them, or when again Saturn is not in accord with the sun but is either in quartile or in opposition, if they are declining from the angles, they merely make the fathers weak, but if they are at the angles or rising after them, they make them short-lived or liable to injury: short-lived when they are upon the first two angles, the orient and the mid-heaven, and the succedent signs, and liable to injury or disease when they are in the other two angles, the occident and lower mid-heaven, or their succedent signs. For Mars, regarding the sun in the way described,[2] destroys the father suddenly or causes injuries to his sight; if he thus regards Saturn he puts him in peril of death or of chills and fever or of injury by cutting and cauterizing. Saturn himself in an unfavourable aspect to the sun brings about the father's death by disease and illnesses caused by gatherings of humours.

[1] The anonymous commentator on Ptolemy says that "stars are said to overcome (καθυπερτερεῖν) when they are of a smaller number of degrees," *i.e.* of the zodiac. The right takes precedent over the left, as a general rule. *Cf.* Bouché-Leclercq, p. 250, n. 1.

[2] In quartile or opposition.

PTOLEMY

Ἐπὶ δὲ τῆς μητρός, ἐὰν μὲν ὁ τοῦ Διὸς συσχηματισθῇ τῇ τε σελήνῃ καὶ τῷ τῆς Ἀφροδίτης ὁπωσδήποτε ᾖ καὶ αὐτὸς ὁ τῆς Ἀφροδίτης συμφώνως ἔχῃ πρὸς τὴν σελήνην, ἑξάγωνος ὢν ἢ τρίγωνος ἢ συνὼν αὐτῇ ἐν δυνάμει ὄντες, πολυχρόνιον δεικνύουσι τὴν μητέρα. ἐὰν δὲ ὁ τοῦ Ἄρεως βλέψῃ τὴν σελήνην ἢ τὸν τῆς Ἀφροδίτης ἐπανενεχθεὶς ἢ τετραγωνίσας ἢ διαμετρήσας, ἢ ὁ τοῦ Κρόνου τὴν σελήνην μόνην ὡσαύτως, ἀφαιρετικοὶ μὲν ὄντες ἢ ἀποκεκλικότες, πάλιν ἀντιπτώμασι μόνον ἢ ἀσθενείαις περικυλίουσι· προσθετικοὶ δὲ ἢ ἐπίκεντροι, ὀλιγοχρονίους ἢ ἐπισινεῖς ποιοῦσι τὰς μητέρας, ὀλιγοχρονίους μὲν ὁμοίως ἐπὶ τῶν ἀπηλιωτικῶν ὄντες κέντρων ἢ ἐπαναφορῶν, ἐπισινεῖς δὲ ἐπὶ τῶν δυτικῶν. Ἄρης μὲν γὰρ βλέψας τὴν σελήνην τοῦτον τὸν τρόπον, ἀνατολικὴν μὲν οὖσαν, τούς τε θανάτους τοὺς μητρικοὺς αἰφνιδίους καὶ σίνη περὶ τὰς ὄψεις ποιεῖ, ἀποκρουστικὴν δὲ τοὺς θανάτους ἀπὸ ἐκτρωσμῶν ἢ τῶν τοιούτων καὶ τὰ σίνη διὰ τομῶν καὶ καύσεων· τὴν δὲ Ἀφροδίτην βλέψας τούς τε θανάτους πυρεκτικοὺς ἀπεργάζεται καὶ πάθη τὰ δι' ἀποκρύφων καὶ σκοτισμῶν καὶ προσδρομῶν αἰφνιδίων. ὁ δὲ τοῦ Κρόνου τὴν σελήνην βλέψας θανάτους καὶ πάθη ποιεῖ, ἀνατολικῆς μὲν οὔσης αὐτῆς διὰ ῥιγοπυρέτων, ἀποκρουστικῆς δὲ διὰ νομῶν[1] ὑστερικῶν καὶ ἀναβρώσεων.

Προσπαραληπτέον δὲ εἰς τὰ κατὰ μέρος εἴδη τῶν σινῶν ἢ καὶ παθῶν ἢ καὶ θανάτων καὶ τὰς τῶν δωδεκατημορίων ἐν οἷς εἰσιν οἱ τὸ αἴτιον ἐμποιοῦντες ἰδιοτροπίας, ὑπὲρ ὧν εὐκαιρότερον ἐν τοῖς περὶ αὐτῆς

TETRABIBLOS III. 4

In the case of the mother, if Jupiter is in any aspect whatever to the moon and to Venus, or if Venus herself is concordant with the moon, in sextile, trine, or conjunction, when they are in power, they signify long life for the mother. If, however, Mars regards the moon or Venus, rising after her or in quartile or in opposition, or if Saturn similarly regards the moon by herself, when they are diminishing or declining, again they merely threaten with misfortune or sickness; but if they are increasing or angular, they make the mothers short-lived or subject to injury. They make them short-lived similarly when they are at the eastern angles or the signs that rise after them, and liable to injury when they are at the western angles. For when Mars in this way regards the waxing moon, it brings about sudden death and injury of the eyesight for the mothers; but if the moon is waning, death from abortions or the like, and injury from cutting and cauterizing. If he regards Venus, he causes death by fever, mysterious and obscure illnesses, and sudden attacks of disease. Saturn regarding the moon causes death and illnesses, when the moon is in the orient, by chills and fever; when she is in the occident, by uterine ulcers and cancers.

We must take into consideration, also, with reference to the particular kinds of injuries, diseases, or deaths, the special characters of the signs in which are the planets which produce the cause, with which

---

¹ νομῶν VPLD; νόσων MNAECam.

τῆς γενέσεως ἐπεξεργασόμεθα.¹ καὶ ἔτι παρατηρητέον ἡμέρας μὲν μάλιστα τόν τε ἥλιον καὶ τὴν Ἀφροδίτην, νυκτὸς δὲ τὸν τοῦ Κρόνου καὶ τὴν σελήνην.

Λοιπὸν δὲ ἐπὶ τῶν κατ' εἶδος ἐξεργασιῶν² ἁρμόζον καὶ ἀκόλουθον ἂν εἴη τὸν τῆς αἱρέσεως πατρικὸν ἢ μητρικὸν τόπον ὥσπερ ὡροσκόπον ὑποστησαμένους³ τὰ λοιπὰ ὡς ἐπὶ γενέσεως αὐτῶν τῶν γονέων ἐπισκοπεῖν⁴ κατὰ τὰς ἐφεξῆς ὑποδειχθησομένας τῶν ὁλοσχερεστέρων εἰδῶν πρακτικῶν τε καὶ συμβατικῶν⁵ ἐφόδους· τοῦ μέντοι συγκρατικοῦ τρόπου⁶ καὶ ἐνταῦθα καὶ ἐπὶ πάντων μεμνῆσθαι προσήκει, καταστοχαζομένους, ἐὰν μὴ μονοειδεῖς ἀλλὰ διάφοροι ἢ τῶν ἐναντίων ποιητικοὶ τυγχάνωσιν οἱ τὰς κυρίας τῶν ἐπιζητουμένων τόπων εἰληφότες ἀστέρες, τίνες ἐκ τῶν περὶ ἕκαστον⁷ συμβεβηκότων⁸ πρὸς δύναμιν πλεονεκτημάτων πλείους ἔχοντες εὑρίσκονται ψήφους πρὸς τὴν ἐπικράτησιν τῶν ἀποτελεσθησομένων, ἵνα ἢ ταῖς τούτων φύσεσιν ἀκόλουθον ποιώμεθα τὴν ἐπίσκεψιν, ἢ τῶν ψήφων ἰσορρόπων οὐσῶν, ὅταν μὲν ἅμα ὦσιν οἱ ἐπικρατοῦντες, τὸ ἐκ τῆς κράσεως τῶν διαφόρων

---

¹ ἐπεξεργασόμεθα VAD, -ώμεθα PL, ἐπεργαζόμεθα MNE Cam.; sententiam om. Proc.

² ἐξεργασιῶν VPLD, ἐπεξεργασιῶν MNAECam.

³ ὑποστησαμένους VPLDE, ἐπιστησαμένους MA, ἐπισταμένους NCam.; ὑποστήσασθαι Proc.

⁴ σκοπεῖν NCam.

⁵ πρακτικῶν τε καὶ συμβατικῶν VD, παρεκτικῶν τ. κ. σημαντικῶν PL (σημαντοτικῶν L), εἰδῶν τῶν τε κατὰ πρᾶξιν καὶ κατὰ σύμβασιν θεωρουμένων Proc.; πραγματικάς τε καὶ συμβατικάς MNAECam.

we shall find more appropriate occasion to deal in the discussion of the nativity itself,[1] and furthermore we must observe by day particularly the sun and Venus, and by night Saturn and the moon.

For the rest, in carrying out these particular inquiries, it would be fitting and consistent to set up the paternal or maternal place of the sect as a horoscope[2] and investigate the remaining topics as though it were a nativity of the parents themselves, following the procedure for the investigation of the general classifications, both practical and casual, the headings of which will be set forth in the following. However, both here and everywhere it is well to recall the mode of mixture of the planets, and, if it happens that the planets which rule the places under inquiry are not of one kind but different, or bring about opposite effects, we should aim to discover which ones have most claims, from the ways in which they happen to exceed in power in a particular case, to the rulership of the predicted events. This is in order that we may either guide our inquiry by the natures of these planets, or, if the claims of more than one are of equal weight, when the rulers are together, we may successfully calculate the combined result of the

[1] *Cf.* iii. 12, iv. 9.
[2] The anonymous commentator, on this passage, says that the significant planet is to be taken as the horoscope. *Cf.* a similar statement at the end of c. 5 and Bouché-Leclercq, p. 394.

---

[6] τρόπου VAD, -ον P, -ους L, τόπου MNECam.; τοῦ τρόπου τῆς συγκράσεως Proc.
[7] ἕκαστον VMADE, -α PLNCam.
[8] συμβεβηκότα NCam.

φύσεων συναγόμενον εὐστόχως ἐπιλογιζώμεθα· ὅταν δὲ διεστηκότες ἀνὰ μέρος ἑκάστοις¹ κατὰ τοὺς ἰδίους καιροὺς τὰ οἰκεῖα τῶν συμπτωμάτων ἀπομερίζωμεν,² προτέροις μὲν τοῖς ἑῴοις μᾶλλον, ὑστέροις δὲ τοῖς ἑσπερίοις. ἀπ' ἀρχῆς μὲν γὰρ ἀνάγκη συνοικειωθῆναι τῷ ζητουμένῳ τόπῳ τὸν μέλλοντά τι περὶ αὐτὸν ἀπεργάζεσθαι τῶν ἀστέρων, καὶ τούτου μὴ³ συμβεβηκότος οὐδὲν οἷόν τε καθ' ὅλου διαθεῖναι μέγα⁴ τὸν μηδ' ὅλως τῆς ἀρχῆς κοινωνήσαντα, τοῦ μέντοι χρόνου τῆς κατὰ⁵ τὸ ἀποτελούμενον ἐκβάσεως οὐκέτι τὸ τῆς πρώτης δεσποτίας αἴτιον, ἀλλ' ἡ τοῦ κυριεύσαντός πως πρός τε τὸν ἥλιον καὶ τὰς τοῦ κόσμου γωνίας διάστασις.

⟨ε.⟩ Περὶ ἀδελφῶν

Ὁ μὲν οὖν περὶ γονέων τόπος σχεδὸν καὶ ἀπὸ τούτων ἂν ἡμῖν γένοιτο καταφανής· ὁ δὲ περὶ ἀδελφῶν, εἴ τις κἀνταῦθα τὸ καθ' ὅλου μόνον ἐξετάζοι καὶ μὴ πέρα⁶ τοῦ δυνατοῦ τόν τε ἀριθμὸν ἀκριβῶς καὶ κατὰ μέρος ἐπιζητοίη, λαμβάνοιτ' ἂν φυσικώτερον ὅ τε περὶ ὁμομητρίων μόνον καὶ ἀπὸ τοῦ μεσουρανοῦντος δωδεκατημορίου τοῦ μητρικοῦ τόπου, τουτέστι τοῦ περιέχοντος ἡμέρας μὲν τὸν τῆς Ἀφροδίτης, νυκτὸς δὲ τὴν σελήνην, ἐπειδήπερ

---

¹ ἕκαστος codd. Cam.
² ἀπομερίζωμεν MNAECam., -όμεθα PL, -ομεν VDProc.
³ τούτου μὴ VPLAD ; τούτου γὰρ μὴ συμβάντος Proc. ; τούτου MNECam.¹, τοῦ Cam.²
⁴ μέγα VD ; οὐδὲν δύναται γίνεσθαι μέγα Proc. ; om. alii Cam.
⁵ κατὰ VPLD ; περὶ MNAE.   ⁶ πέρας Cam.²

mixture of their different natures; but when they are separated, that we may assign to each in turn at their proper times the events which belong to them, first to the more oriental among them and then to the occidental. For a planet must from the beginning have familiarity with the place about which the inquiry is made, if it is going to exercise any effect upon it, and in general, if this is not the case, a planet which had no share whatsoever in the beginning can exert no great influence; of the time of the occurrence of the event, however, the original dominance is no longer the cause, but the distance of the planet which dominates in any way from the sun and from the angles of the universe.

5. *Of Brothers and Sisters.*

The preceding may perhaps have made clear the topic of the parents. As for that of brethren, if here too one examines only the general subject and does not carry beyond the bounds of possibility his inquiry as to the exact number and other particulars, it is more naturally to be taken, when it is a question of blood-brethren alone, from the culminating sign, the place of the mother,[1] that is, that which contains by day Venus and by night the

---

[1] This is the reading of all the MSS. and Proclus. Camerarius, inserting a καί before τοῦ μητρικοῦ τόπου, would make it "the culminating sign *and* the place of the mother." While the best-attested reading has been left in the present text, the passage is extremely difficult to understand, whichever reading is preferred.

τοῦτο τὸ ζῴδιον καὶ τὸ ἐπαναφερόμενον αὐτῷ γίνεται τῆς μητρὸς ὁ περὶ τέκνων τόπος, ὁ αὐτὸς ὀφείλων εἶναι τῷ τοῦ γεννωμένου περὶ ἀδελφῶν. ἐὰν μὲν οὖν ἀγαθοποιοὶ τῷ τόπῳ συσχηματίζωνται, δαψίλειαν ἀδελφῶν ἐροῦμεν, πρός τε τὸ πλῆθος αὐτῶν τῶν ἀστέρων τὸν στοχασμὸν ποιούμενοι, καὶ πότερον ἐν μονοειδέσι τυγχάνουσι ζῳδίοις ἢ ἐν δισώμοις· ἐὰν δ' οἱ κακοποιοὶ καθυπερτερῶσιν αὐτῶν ἢ καὶ ἐναντιωθῶσι κατὰ διάμετρον, σπαναδελφίας εἰσὶ δηλωτικοί, μάλιστα δὲ κἂν τὸν ἥλιον συμπαραλαμβάνωσιν· εἰ δὲ καὶ ἐπὶ τῶν κέντρων ἡ ἐναντίωσις γένοιτο καὶ μάλιστα τοῦ ὡροσκοποῦντος, ἐπὶ μὲν Κρόνου καὶ πρωτότοκοι ἢ πρωτότροφοι γίνονται, ἐπὶ δὲ Ἄρεως θανάτῳ τῶν λοιπῶν[1] σπαναδελφοῦσιν. ἔτι[2] μέντοι τῶν διδόντων ἀστέρων ἐὰν μὲν καλῶς κατὰ τὸ κοσμικὸν τυγχάνωσι διακείμενοι, εὐσχήμονας καὶ ἐνδόξους ἡγητέον τοὺς διδομένους ἀδελφούς· ἐὰν δὲ ἐναντίως, ταπεινοὺς καὶ ἀνεπιφάντους· ἐὰν δὲ καθυπερτερήσωσι τοὺς διδόντας ἢ ἐπενεχθῶσιν αὐτοῖς οἱ κακοποιοί, καὶ ὀλιγοχρονίους· δώσουσι δὲ τοὺς μὲν ἄρρενας οἱ κοσμικῶς ἠρρενωμένοι, τὰς δὲ θηλείας οἱ τεθηλυσμένοι, καὶ πάλιν τοὺς μὲν πρώτους οἱ ἀπηλιωτικώτεροι, τοὺς δὲ ὑστέρους οἱ λιβυκώτεροι. πρὸς δὲ τούτοις ἐὰν οἱ διδόντες τοὺς ἀδελφοὺς

---

[1] λοιπῶν VPLD, ὄντων MNAECam.
[2] ἔτι VPLDProc., ἐπὶ MNAECam.

moon; for in this sign and that which succeeds it is the place of the children of the mother, which should be the same as the place of the brethren of the offspring. If, then, beneficent planets bear an aspect to this place, we shall predict an abundance of brethren, basing our conjecture upon the number of the planets and whether they are in signs of a simple or of a bicorporeal form. But if the malevolent planets overcome them or oppose them in opposition, they signify a dearth of brethren, especially if they have the sun among them. If the opposition is at the angles, and especially at the horoscope,[1] in case Saturn is in the ascendant, they are the first-born or the first to be reared; in case it is Mars, there is a small number of brethren by reason of the death of the others. If the planets which give brethren are in a favourable mundane[2] position, we must believe that the brethren thereby given will be elegant and distinguished; if the reverse is the case, humble and inconspicuous. But if the maleficent planets overcome those that give brethren, or rise after them, the brethren will also be short-lived; and the male planets in the mundane sense[3] will give males, the female females; again, those farther to the east the first and those farther to the west the later-born. Besides this, if the planets that give brethren are in harmonious aspect with the

---

[1] "Horoscope" is used here in its more original sense of the point rising above the horizon at the time the observation is made.

[2] See the note on iii. 3, p. 239.

[3] *I.e.* in the quadrant from the orient to mid-heaven or that from the occident to lower mid-heaven; *cf.* i. 6.

συμφώνως ἐσχηματισμένοι τυγχάνωσι τῷ κυριεύοντι τοῦ περὶ τῶν ἀδελφῶν δωδεκατημορίου, προσφιλεῖς ποιήσουσι τοὺς¹ διδομένους ἀδελφούς· ἐὰν δὲ καὶ τῷ κλήρῳ τῆς τύχης, καὶ κοινοβίους· ἐὰν δὲ ἐν τοῖς ἀσυνδέτοις τύχωσιν ἢ κατὰ τὴν ἐναντίαν στάσιν, φιλέχθρους καὶ φθονερούς, καὶ ὡς ἐπὶ πᾶν ἐπιβουλευτικούς. λοιπὸν δὲ καὶ τὰ καθ' ἕκαστον αὐτῶν εἴ τις ἐπιπολυπραγμονοίη,² συνεικάζοιτ' ἂν καὶ ἐνταῦθα πάλιν, τοῦ διδόντος ἀστέρος ὑποτιθεμένου κατὰ τὸν ὡροσκοπικὸν λόγον καὶ τῶν λοιπῶν ὡς ἐπὶ γενέσεως συνθεωρουμένων.³

⟨ϛ.⟩ Περὶ ἀρρενικῶν καὶ θηλυκῶν

Ὑπ'⁴ ὄψιν ἤδη καὶ τοῦ περὶ ἀδελφῶν λόγου κατὰ τὸν ἁρμόζοντα καὶ φυσικὸν τρόπον ἡμῖν γεγονότος,⁵ ἑξῆς ἂν εἴη τῶν κατ' αὐτὴν τὴν γένεσιν ἄρξασθαι, καὶ πρῶτον ἐπιδραμεῖν τὸν περὶ ἀρρενικῶν τε καὶ θηλυκῶν ἐπιλογισμόν. θεωρεῖται δ' οὗτος οὐ μονοειδῶς οὐδ' ἀφ' ἑνός τινος ἀλλ' ἀπό τε τῶν φώτων ἀμφοτέρων καὶ τοῦ ὡροσκόπου τῶν τε λόγον ἐχόντων πρὸς αὐτοὺς ἀστέρων, μάλιστα μὲν κατὰ τὴν τῆς σπορᾶς διάθεσιν, ὁλοσχερέστερον δὲ καὶ κατὰ τὴν τῆς ἐκτροπῆς. τὸ δ' ὅλον παρατηρητέον, πότερον οἱ προειρημένοι τρεῖς τόποι καὶ οἱ τούτων οἰκοδεσποτοῦντες ἀστέρες ἢ πάντες ἢ οἱ πλεῖστοι τυγχάνουσιν ἠρρενωμένοι πρὸς ἀρρενο-

---
¹ τοὺς VPLADE, μὲν MNCam.
² ἐπιπολυπραγμονοίη VPLAD, ἔτι πολ. MNECam.
³ συνθεωρουμένων om. NCam.

planet that rules the place of brethren,[1] they will make the given brethren friendly, and will also make them live together, if they are in harmonious aspect with the Lot of Fortune;[2] but if they are in disjunct signs or in opposition, they will produce quarrelsome, jealous, and for the most part, scheming brethren. Finally, if one would busy himself with further inquiries about details concerning individuals, he might in this case again make his conjecture by taking the planet which gives brethren as the horoscope and dealing with the rest as in a nativity.

6. *Of Males and Females.*

Now that the topic of brethren has been brought before our eyes in suitable and natural fashion, the next step would be to begin the discussion of matters directly concerned with the birth, and first to treat of the reckoning of males and females. This is determined by no simple theory based upon some one thing, but it depends upon the two luminaries, the horoscope, and the stars which bear some relation to them, particularly by their disposition at the time of conception, but more generally also by that at the time of the birth. The whole situation must be observed, whether the aforesaid three places and the planets which rule them are either all or the most of them masculine, to produce males, or feminine,

---

[1] *I.e.* the place (literally, "twelfth part" of the zodiac) which governs the inquiry about brethren; see the beginning of this chapter.
[2] For the Lot of Fortune see iii. 10.

---

[a] ὑπ' VPDE, ἐπ' MNLACam.
[b] ἐπιγεγονότος MNECam.

γονίαν ἢ τεθηλυσμένοι πρὸς θηλυγονίαν, καὶ οὕτως ἀποφαντέον. διακριτέον μέντοι τούς τε ἠρρενωμένους καὶ τοὺς τεθηλυσμένους καθ' ὃν ὑπεθέμεθα τρόπον ἐν ταῖς πινακικαῖς ἐκθέσεσι ἐν ἀρχῇ τῆς συντάξεως ἀπό τε τῆς τῶν δωδεκατημορίων ἐν οἷς εἰσι φύσεως, καὶ ἀπὸ τῆς αὐτῶν τῶν ἀστέρων, καὶ ἔτι ἀπὸ τῆς πρὸς τὸν κόσμον σχέσεως, ἐπειδήπερ ἀπηλιωτικοὶ μὲν ὄντες ἀρρενοῦνται, λιβυκοὶ δὲ θηλύνονται· πρὸς δὲ τούτοις ἀπὸ τῆς πρὸς τὸν ἥλιον, ἑῷοι μὲν γὰρ πάλιν ὄντες ἀρρενοῦνται, θηλύνονται δὲ ἑσπέριοι· δι' ὧν πάντων τὴν κατὰ τὸ πλεῖστον ἐπικράτησιν τοῦ γένους προσήκει καταστοχάζεσθαι.

⟨ζ.⟩ Περὶ διδυμογόνων

Καὶ περὶ τῶν γεννωμένων δὲ ὁμοίως ἀνὰ δύο ἢ καὶ πλειόνων τοὺς αὐτοὺς δύο τόπους παρατηρεῖν προσήκει, τουτέστι τά τε δύο φῶτα καὶ τὸν ὡροσκόπον. παρακολουθεῖν δὲ εἴωθε τοῦτο τὸ σύμπτωμα[1] παρὰ[2] τὰς συγκράσεις, ὅταν οἱ δύο ἢ καὶ οἱ τρεῖς τόποι δίσωμα περιέχωσι ζῴδια, καὶ μάλιστα ὅταν καὶ οἱ οἰκοδεσπόζοντες αὐτῶν ἀστέρες τὸ αὐτὸ πάθωσιν[3] ἢ τινες μὲν ἐν δισώμοις, τινὲς δὲ ἀνὰ δύο κείμενοι τυγχάνωσιν ἢ καὶ πλείους. ἐπὰν δὲ καὶ ἐν δισώμοις ὦσιν οἱ κύριοι τόποι καὶ κατὰ τὸ αὐτὸ

---

[1] τοῦτο τὸ σύμπτωμα VD; cf. συμβαίνει δὲ οὕτω γενέσθαι Proc.; τὸ τοιοῦτον σύμπτωμα libri alii Cam.
[2] παρὰ VD. περὶ libri alii Cam.
[3] πάθωσιν VPD; εἰς τοὺς οἰκοδεσποτοῦντας ... τὸ αὐτὸ συμβῇ Proc.; καθορῶσιν MNAECam., τιθῶσιν L.

to produce females, and on this basis the decision must be made. We must however distinguish the male and the female planets in the way set forth by us in the tabular series in the beginning of this compilation,[1] from the nature of the signs in which they are, and from the nature of the planets themselves, and furthermore from their position with reference to the universe, since they become masculine when they are in the east and feminine in the west; and besides, from their relation to the sun, for again when they rise in the morning they are made masculine, and feminine when they rise in the evening. By means of all these criteria one must conjecture what planet exercises preponderating control over the sex.

7. *Of Twins.*

Likewise with regard to the births of two or even more, it is fitting to observe the same two places, that is, the two luminaries and the horoscope. For such an event is apt to attend the intermixture [2] when either two or the three places [3] cover bicorporeal signs, and particularly when the same is true of the planets that rule them, or when some are in bicorporeal signs, and some are disposed in pairs or in larger groups. But when both the dominant places are in bicorporeal signs and most of the planets are similarly

[1] See i. 6.
[2] That is, of the influences of luminaries, signs, etc.
[3] The places or houses in which the luminaries and the horoscope are found.

PTOLEMY

πλείονες[1] τῶν ἀστέρων συνεσχηματισμένοι, τότε καὶ πλείονα τῶν δύο κυΐσκεσθαι[2] συμπίπτει, τοῦ μὲν πλήθους ἀπὸ τοῦ τὸ ἰδίωμα ποιοῦντος ἀστέρος τοῦ ἀριθμοῦ συνεικαζομένου, τοῦ δὲ γένους ἀπὸ τῶν συνεσχηματισμένων ἀστέρων τῷ τε ἡλίῳ καὶ τῇ σελήνῃ καὶ τῷ ὡροσκόπῳ πρὸς ἀρρενογονίαν ἢ θηλυγονίαν κατὰ τοὺς ἐν τοῖς ἔμπροσθεν εἰρημένους τρόπους. ὅταν δὲ ἡ τοιαύτη διάθεσις μὴ συμπερι-
122 λαμβάνῃ τοῖς φωσὶ τὸ τοῦ ὡροσκόπου κέντρον, ἀλλὰ τὸ[3] τοῦ μεσουρανήματος, αἱ τοιαῦται τῶν μητέρων δίδυμα ὡς ἐπὶ πᾶν ἢ καὶ πλείονα κυΐσκουσιν. ἰδίως δὲ τρεῖς μὲν ἄρρενας πληροφοροῦσιν ὑπὸ τὴν τῶν Ἀνακτόρων γένεσιν ἅμα τοῖς προκειμένοις τόποις ἐν δισώμοις συσχηματισθέντες Κρόνος, Ζεύς, Ἄρης· τρεῖς δὲ θηλείας ὑπὸ τὴν τῶν Χαρίτων Ἀφροδίτη, σελήνη μεθ' Ἑρμοῦ τεθηλυσμένου· δύο δ' ἄρρενας καὶ μίαν θήλειαν ὑπὸ τὴν τῶν Διοσκούρων Κρόνος, Ζεύς, Ἀφροδίτη· δύο δὲ θηλείας καὶ ἄρρενα ἕνα ὑπὸ τὴν Δήμητρος καὶ Κόρης[4] Ἀφροδίτη, σελήνη, Ἄρης· ἐφ' ὧν ὡς ἐπὶ τὸ πολὺ συμβαίνειν εἴωθε τό τε μὴ τελεσφορεῖσθαι τὰ γινόμενα καὶ τὸ μετὰ παρασήμων

---

[1] πλείονες VP (-οναις) LDProc., πλείοσι MNAECam.
[2] κυΐσκεσθαι VAD, κύεσθαι PL, τίκτεσθαι MNEProc.Cam.
[3] ἀλλὰ τὸ VADEProc., ἀλλὰ τῷ PL, ἀλλ' ἀπὸ MNCam.
[4] καὶ Διονύσου post Κόρης add. NCam., om. libri alii Proc.

---

[1] That is, from the planet that governs the dominant place.
[2] In the preceding chapter.

configurated, then it befalls that even more than two are conceived, for the number is conjectured from the star that causes the peculiar property of the number,[1] and the sex from the aspects which the planets have with respect to the sun and the moon and the horoscope for the production of males or of females, in accordance with the ways stated above.[2] But whenever such an arrangement of the planets does not include the horoscopic angle with the luminaries, but rather that of the mid-heaven, mothers with such genitures generally conceive twins or even more; and in particular, they give multiple birth, to three males, by the geniture of the Kings,[3] when Saturn, Jupiter, and Mars are in bicorporeal signs and bear some aspect to the aforesaid places; and to three females, by the geniture of the Graces, when Venus and the moon, with Mercury made feminine, are so arranged; to two males and one female, by the geniture of the Dioscuri, when Saturn, Jupiter, and Venus are so ordered, and to two females and a male, by the geniture of Demeter and Korê,[4] when Venus, the moon, and Mars are thus ordered. In these cases it generally happens that the children are not completely developed and are born with certain bodily

[3] Bouché-Leclercq, p. 398, n. 3, after remarking upon the various interpretations given this passage, says: " The title 'Ἀνάκτορες ("Ἄνακτες, "Ἄνακες) having been borne by the Dioscuri, the Cabiri, and the Curetes, I do not know to which group he alludes, and possibly he did not know very well himself." Cardanus remarks that Ptolemy regards three children as the largest number that can be born at one birth and survive.

[4] MS. N and Camerarius add here " and Dionysus," but the other MSS. agree in omitting the expression.

PTOLEMY

τινῶν σωματικῶν ἀποκυΐσκεσθαι καὶ ἔτι τὸ γίνεσθαί τινα τοῖς τόποις ἐξαίρετα καὶ ἀπροσδόκητα διὰ τῆς τῶν τοιούτων συμπτωμάτων ὥσπερ ἐπιφανείας.

⟨η̄.⟩ Περὶ τεράτων

Οὐκ ἀλλότριος δὲ τῆς προκειμένης σκέψεως οὐδ' ὁ περὶ τῶν τεράτων[1] λόγος. πρῶτον μὲν γὰρ ἐπὶ τῶν τοιούτων τὰ μὲν φῶτα ἀποκεκλικότα ἢ[2] ἀσύνδετα τῷ ὡροσκόπῳ κατὰ τὸ πλεῖστον εὑρίσκεται, τὰ δὲ κέντρα διειλημμένα ὑπὸ τῶν κακοποιῶν. ὅταν οὖν τοιαύτη τις ὑπ' ὄψιν πέσῃ διάθεσις, ἐπειδὴ γίνεται πολλάκις καὶ περὶ τὰς ταπεινὰς καὶ κακοδαίμονας γενέσεις, κἂν μὴ τερατώδεις ὦσιν, εὐθὺς ἐπισκοπεῖν προσήκει τὴν προγενομένην[3] συζυγίαν συνοδικὴν ἢ πανσεληνιακὴν καὶ τὸν οἰκοδεσποτήσαντα ταύτης τε καὶ τῶν τῆς ἐκτροπῆς φωτῶν.[4] ἐὰν γὰρ οἱ τῆς ἐκτροπῆς αὐτῶν τόποι καὶ ὁ τῆς σελήνης[5] καὶ ὁ τοῦ ὡροσκόπου πάντες ἢ οἱ πλείονες ἀσύνδετοι τυγχάνωσιν ὄντες τῷ τῆς προγενομένης συζυγίας τόπῳ, τὸ γεννώμενον αἰνιγματῶδες ὑπονοητέον. ἐὰν μὲν οὖν τούτων οὕτως ἐχόντων τά τε φῶτα ἐν τετράποσιν ἢ θηριώδεσιν εὑρίσκηται ζῳδίοις καὶ οἱ δύο κεκεντρωμένοι τῶν κακοποιῶν, οὐδ' ἐξ ἀνθρώπων ἔσται τὸ γεννώμενον, ἀλλὰ μηδενὸς μὲν μαρτυροῦντος

[1] τερατώδων VD.
[2] ἢ VPLMNDProc.; καὶ AECam.
[3] προγενομένην EProc., προγιν- A, προγεγωνυῖαν P, προτεγονίαν L, γενομένην MNCam., om. VD.

marks, and again the governing places may bear certain unusual and surprising marks by reason of the divine manifestation, as it were, of such portents.

8. *Of Monsters.*

The subject of monsters is not foreign to the present inquiry; for, in the first place, in such cases the luminaries are found to be as far as possible removed from the horoscope or in no way related to it, and the angles [1] are separated by the maleficent planets. Whenever, then, such a disposition is observed, for it frequently occurs in humble and unlucky nativities, even though they are not the genitures of monsters, one should at once look for the last preceding new or full moon, and the lord of this and of the luminaries of the birth. For if the places of the birth, of the moon, and of the horoscope, all or the majority of them, happen to be unrelated to the place of the preceding syzygy, it must be supposed that the child will be nondescript. Now if, under such conditions, the luminaries are found in four-footed or animal-shaped signs,[2] and the two maleficent planets are centred, the child will not even belong to the human race, but if no beneficent planet witnesses to

---

[1] Cardanus and Whalley say the ascendant and the midheaven are meant.

[2] *Cf.* i. 12. The only human signs are Virgo, Gemini, Sagittarius, and Aquarius.

---

[4] φωτῶν VPLMDEProc., τόπων NACam.
[5] ὁ τῆς σελήνης MNAECam.¹, ἡ τῆς σελ. P, οἱ τῆς σελ. VDLCam.

PTOLEMY

τοῖς φωσὶ ἀγαθοποιοῦ,[1] τῶν δὲ κακοποιῶν,[2] τέλεον ἀνήμερον καὶ τῶν ἀγρίαν καὶ κακωτικὴν ἐχόντων φύσιν· μαρτυρούντων δὲ Διὸς ἢ Ἀφροδίτης, τῶν ἐκθειαζομένων, οἷον κυνῶν ἢ αἰλούρων[3] ἢ τῶν τοιούτων· Ἑρμοῦ δέ, τῶν εἰς χρείαν ἀνθρωπίνην, οἷον ὀρνίθων ἢ συῶν ἢ βοῶν ἢ αἰγῶν καὶ τῶν τοιούτων. ἐὰν δὲ ἐν ἀνθρωποείδεσι τὰ φῶτα καταλαμβάνηται, τῶν ἄλλων ὡσαύτως ἐχόντων, ὑπ᾽ ἀνθρώπων μὲν ἢ παρ᾽ ἀνθρώποις ἔσται τὰ γεγενημένα, τέρατα δὲ[4] καὶ αἰνιγματώδη τῆς κατὰ τὸ ποιὸν ἰδιότητος, καὶ ἐνταῦθα συνορω-
124 μένης ἐκ τῆς τῶν ζῳδίων μορφώσεως, ἐν οἷς οἱ διειληφότες τὰ φῶτα ἢ τὰ κέντρα κακοποιοὶ τυγχάνουσιν. ἐὰν μὲν οὖν κἀνταῦθα μηδὲ εἷς τῶν ἀγαθοποιῶν ἀστέρων προσμαρτυρῇ[5] μηδενὶ τῶν προειρημένων τόπων, ἄλογα καὶ ὡς ἀληθῶς αἰνιγματώδη γίνεται τέλεον· ἐὰν δὲ ὁ τοῦ Διὸς ἢ ὁ τῆς Ἀφροδίτης μαρτυρήσῃ, τιμώμενον καὶ εὔσχημον ἔσται τὸ τοῦ τέρατος ἴδιον·[6] ὁποῖον περὶ τοὺς ἑρμαφροδίτους ἢ τοὺς καλουμένους ἁρποκρατιακοὺς καὶ τοὺς τοιούτους εἴωθε συμβαίνειν. εἰ δὲ καὶ ὁ τοῦ Ἑρμοῦ μαρτυρήσειε μετὰ τούτων μὲν καὶ ἀποφθεγγομένους καὶ διὰ[7] τῶν τοιούτων ποριστικούς· μόνος[8] δὲ ὁ τοῦ Ἑρμοῦ[9] νωδοὺς καὶ

---

[1] ἀγαθοποιοῦ PLMNEProc.Cam., ἀγαθοποιῶν VD, τῶν ἀγαθοποιῶν A; pos. post μὲν MNECam.
[2] τῶν δὲ κακοποιόν P, ἀποιούντων δὲ κακοποιῶν L, τῶν κακοποιῶν MNECam.¹, τῶν κακοποιῶν μαρτυρούντων Cam.², ἀλλὰ τῶν κακοποιῶν Proc.
[3] Post αἰλούρων add. ἢ πιθήκων MNAECam., om. VPLD.
[4] δὲ om. MNECam.

the luminaries, but the maleficent planets do so, it will be completely savage, an animal with wild and harmful nature; but if Jupiter or Venus witness, it will be one of the kinds regarded as sacred, as for example dogs, cats,[1] and the like; if Mercury witnesses, one of those that are of use to man, such as birds, swine, oxen, goats, and the like. If the luminaries are found in signs of human form, but the other planets are disposed in the same way, what is born will be, indeed, of the human race or to be classed with humans, but monsters and nondescript in qualitative character, and their qualities in this case too are to be observed from the form of the signs in which the maleficent planets which separate the luminaries or the angles happen to be. Now if even in this case not one of the beneficent planets bears witness to any of the places mentioned, the offspring are entirely irrational and in the true sense of the word nondescript; but if Jupiter or Venus bears witness, the type of monster will be honoured and seemly, such as is usually the case with hermaphrodites or the so-called harpocratiacs,[2] and the like. If Mercury should bear witness, along with the foregoing, this disposition produces prophets who also make money thereby; but when alone, Mercury

---

[1] The later MSS. here add "or apes."
[2] Deaf mutes.

---

[5] προσμαρτυρῇ PLProc., προσμαρτυρούμενα VD, συμμαρτυρῇ MNAECam.
[6] ἴδιον VPLAD; cf. Proc. τὴν ἰδιότητα ἕξει; om. MNECam.
[7] διὰ VPLAD, ἀπὸ MNECam.
[8] μόνος VPLMNADProc., -ον ECam.
[9] ὁ τοῦ Ἑρμοῦ VADProc.; om. PLMNECam.

κωφούς, εὐφυεῖς μέντοι καὶ πανούργους ἄλλως ἀπεργάζεται.[1]

⟨θ.⟩ Περὶ ἀτρόφων

Λοιποῦ δ' ὄντος εἰς τὰ κατ' αὐτὴν τὴν γένεσιν τοῦ περὶ ἀτρόφων λόγου, προσήκει διαλαβεῖν ὅτι πῇ μὲν ὁ τρόπος οὗτος ἔχεται τοῦ περὶ χρόνων ζωῆς λόγου,[2] ἐπειδὴ τὸ ζητούμενον εἶδος οὐκ ἀλλότριον ἑκατέρου, πῇ δὲ κεχώρισται παρὰ τὸ κατ' αὐτὴν τὴν τῆς ἐπισκέψεως δύναμιν διαφέρειν πως. ὁ μὲν γὰρ περὶ χρόνων ζωῆς ἐπὶ τῶν ὅλως ἐχόντων χρόνους αἰσθητοὺς θεωρεῖται, τουτέστι μὴ ἐλάττονας ἡλιακῆς περιόδου μιᾶς· χρόνος γὰρ ἰδίως ὁ τοιοῦτος ἐνιαυτὸς καταλαμβάνεται· δυνάμει δὲ καὶ ὁ ἐλάττων τούτου, μῆνές εἰσι καὶ ἡμέραι καὶ ὧραι. ὁ δὲ περὶ ἀτρόφων ἐπὶ τῶν μηδ' ὅλως φθανόντων ἐπὶ τὸν προκείμενον χρόνον, ἀλλ' ἐν τοῖς ἐλάττοσιν ἀριθμοῖς δι' ὑπερβολὴν τῆς κακώσεως φθειρομένων. ἔνθεν κἀκεῖνος μὲν πολυμερεστέραν ἔχει τὴν ἐπίσκεψιν, οὗτος δὲ τὴν ὁλοσχερεστέραν. ἁπλῶς γὰρ ἐάν τε κεκεντρωμένον ᾖ τὸ ἕτερον τῶν φώτων καὶ τῶν κακοποιῶν ὁ ἕτερος συνῇ ἢ καὶ

[1] ἀπεργάζεται VMDE, ἐργάζεται PL, ἀπεργάζηται NACam.
[2] λόγου om. MNECam.

---

[1] Either because they do not survive or because they are exposed; Ptolemy treats both classes in the same

TETRABIBLOS III. 8-9

makes them toothless and deaf and dumb, though otherwise clever and cunning.

9. *Of Children that are not Reared.*

As the account of children that are not reared [1] is still lacking in the discussion of matters related to the birth itself, it is fitting to see that in one way this procedure is connected with the inquiry concerning length of life, for the question in each case is of the same kind; but in another way they are distinct, because there is a certain difference in the actual meaning of the inquiry. For the question of length of life considers those who in general endure for perceptible lengths of time, that is, not less than one circuit of the sun, and such a space is properly understood to be a year; but potentially also lesser periods than this, months and days and hours, are perceptible lengths of time. But the inquiry concerning children that are not reared refers to those who do not attain at all to "time" thus defined, but perish in something less than "time" through excess of the evil influence. For this reason the investigation of the former question is more complex; but this is simpler. For it is merely the case that if one of the luminaries is angular [2] and one of the maleficent planets is in conjunction with it, or in

---

chapter, as does Firmicus Maternus, vii. 2 (*De expositis et non nutritis*). Cumont, *L'Égypte des astrologues*, p. 186, remarks that whereas the ancient Egyptian custom had been to bring up all children born, the Greeks introduced the practice of exposing unwanted babes.

[2] *I.e.* at one of the angles—rising, setting, or culminating.

διαμηκίζῃ, ταῦτα δὲ μοιρικῶς καὶ κατ' ἰσοσκελείαν, μηδενὸς μὲν ἀγαθοποιοῦ συσχηματιζομένου, τοῦ δ'[1] οἰκοδεσπότου τῶν φώτων ἐν τοῖς τῶν κακοποιῶν τόποις κατειλημμένου, τὸ γεννώμενον οὐ τραφήσεται, παρ' αὐτὰ δὲ ἕξει τὸ τέλος τῆς ζωῆς.[2] ἐὰν δὲ μὴ κατ' ἰσοσκελείαν μὲν τοῦτο συμβαίνῃ ἀλλ' ἐγγὺς ἐπαναφέρωνται τοῖς τῶν φώτων τόποις αἱ τῶν κακοποιῶν βολαί, δύο δ' ὦσιν οἱ κακοποιοί, καὶ ἤτοι τὸ ἕτερον τῶν φώτων ἢ καὶ ἀμφότερα βλάπτοντες ἢ κατ' ἐπαναφορὰν ἢ κατὰ διάμετρον ἢ ἐν μέρει τὸ ἕτερον ὁ ἕτερος ἢ ὁ μὲν ἕτερος διαμετρῶν ὁ δὲ ἕτερος ἐπαναφερόμενος, καὶ οὕτως ἄχρονα γίνεται, τοῦ πλήθους τῶν κακώσεων ἀφανίζοντος τὸ ἐκ τοῦ διαστήματος τῆς ἐπαναφορᾶς εἰς ἐπιμονὴν τῆς ζωῆς φιλάνθρωπον. βλάπτει δὲ ἐξαιρέτως κατὰ μὲν τὰς ἐπαναφορὰς ἥλιον μὲν ὁ τοῦ Ἄρεως, σελήνην δὲ ὁ τοῦ Κρόνου, κατὰ δὲ τὰς διαμετρήσεις ἢ καθυπερτερήσεις ἀνάπαλιν ἥλιον μὲν ὁ τοῦ Κρόνου, σελήνην δὲ ὁ τοῦ Ἄρεως, καὶ μάλιστα ἐὰν κατάσχωσι τοπικῶς ἤτοι[3] τὰ φῶτα

---

[1] δ' om. NCam. [2] τῆς ζωῆς om. NCam.
[3] ἤτοι VD, cf. Proc.; τῶν MNAECam.; ϛ' L.

---

[1] κατ' ἰσοσκελείαν, literally, "by equality of leg." The anonymous commentator does not explain this expression. Cardanus (pp. 264-265) understands it to mean that the two are exactly in opposition not only in longitude ("in degrees"), but also in latitude (as when the moon is in 10° of Aries, 3° north latitude, and Saturn or Mars in 10° of Libra, 3° south latitude).

[2] The planet which governs the sign in which the luminaries are found.

opposition, both in degrees and with equality of distance,[1] while no beneficent planet bears any aspect, and if the lord of the luminaries [2] is found in the places of the maleficent planets, the child that is born will not be reared, but will at once come to its end. But if this comes about without the equality of distance, but the shafts of the maleficent planets succeed closely upon the places of the luminaries, and there are two maleficent planets, and if they afflict [3] either one or both of the luminaries either by succeeding them or by opposition, or if one afflicts one luminary and the other the other in turn, or if one afflicts by opposition and the other by succeeding the luminary, in this way too children are born that do not live; for the number of afflictions dispels all that is favourable to length of life because of the distance of the maleficent planet through its succession. Mars especially afflicts the sun by succeeding it, and Saturn the moon; but conversely in opposition or in superior position Saturn afflicts the sun and Mars the moon, most of all if they occupy as rulers the

---

[3] Affliction, which in general is damage done by a maleficent planet to a beneficent one, is defined by the astrologer Antiochus (*CCAG*, viii. 3, p. 106, 34-38) as existing " when (*sc.* a beneficent planet) is smitten by the rays of maleficent planets, or is surrounded, or is in application with one of them, or in *glutinatio* (κόλλησις), or is governed by one of them, when the maleficent planet is in the inactive (non-signifying, ἀχρημάτιστοι) places. These are the sixth, third, second, eighth, and twelfth from the horoscope." Ptolemy says little about the " places " (less correctly " houses ") of a geniture; they are twelfth parts of the zodiacal circle marked off from the horoscope, each with some special significance; *cf.* Boll-Bezold-Gundel, pp. 62-63.

PTOLEMY

ἢ[1] τὸν ὡροσκόπον οἰκοδεσποτήσαντες.[2] ἐὰν δὲ δύο τυγχάνωσι διαμετρήσεις ἐπὶ κέντρων ὄντων τῶν φώτων καὶ τῶν κακοποιῶν κατ' ἰσοσκελείαν, τότε καὶ νεκρὰ ἢ ἡμιθανῆ τίκτεται τὰ βρέφη. τούτων δὲ οὕτως ἐχόντων, ἐὰν μὲν ἀπόρροιαν ἀπό τινος τῶν ἀγαθοποιῶν ἔχοντα τὰ φῶτα τυγχάνῃ[3] ἢ καὶ ἄλλως αὐτοῖς ᾖ συνεσχηματισμένα, ἐν τοῖς προηγουμένοις αὐτῶν[4] μέρεσι μέντοιγε τὰς ἀκτῖνας αὐτῶν ἐπιφερόντων, ἐπιζήσεται τὸ τεχθὲν ἄχρι τοῦ μεταξὺ τῆς τε ἀφέσεως καὶ τῶν ἐγγυτέρων[5] τῶν κακοποιῶν ἀκτίνων ἀριθμοῦ, τῶν μοιρῶν τοὺς ἴσους μῆνας ἢ ἡμέρας ἢ καὶ ὥρας πρὸς τὸ μέγεθος τῆς κακώσεως καὶ τὴν δύναμιν τῶν τὸ αἴτιον ποιούντων. ἐὰν δὲ αἱ τῶν κακοποιῶν ἀκτῖνες εἰς τὰ προηγούμενα φέρωνται τῶν φώτων, αἱ δὲ τῶν ἀγαθοποιῶν εἰς τὰ ἑπόμενα, τὸ γεννώμενον ἐκτεθὲν ἀναληφθήσεται καὶ ζήσεται. καὶ πάλιν ἐὰν μὲν οἱ συσχηματισθέντες ἀγαθοποιοὶ καθυπερτερηθῶσιν ὑπὸ τῶν κακοποιῶν εἰς κάκωσιν καὶ ὑποταγήν, ἐὰν δὲ καὶ καθυπερτερήσωσιν εἰς ὑποβολὴν ἄλλων γονέων. εἰ δὲ καὶ τῶν ἀγαθοποιῶν τις[6] ἀνατολὴν ἢ τὴν συναφὴν ποιοῖτο τῇ σελήνῃ, τῶν δὲ κακοποιῶν ὑπὸ δύσιν τις εἴη, ὑπ' αὐτῶν τῶν γονέων ἀναληφθήσεται. κατὰ τὸν αὐτὸν δὲ τὸν τρόπον[7] καὶ ἐπὶ τῶν πλειστο-

[1] ἢ VLDProc.; καὶ MNAECam.
[2] οἰκοδεσποτήσαντες VLDProc., -ων MNAECam.
[3] τυγχάνῃ libri, -οι Cam.   [4] ἑαυτῶν VLD.
[5] τῶν ἐγγυτέρων VLDProc.; τοῦ ἐγγυτέρω MNACam.; τῶν ἐγγυτέρω E.
[6] Post τις add. ἢ τὴν MNECam.Proc.
[7] κατὰ δὲ αὐτὸν τὸν τρόπον Cam.

TETRABIBLOS III. 9

places of the luminaries or of the horoscope. But if there chance to be two oppositions, when the luminaries are at the angles and the maleficent planets are in an isosceles configuration, then the infants are born dead or half-dead. And in such circumstances, if the luminaries should chance to be removing from conjunction with one of the beneficent planets, or are in some other aspect to them, but nevertheless cast their rays in the parts that precede them, the child that is born will live a number of months or days, or even hours, equal to the number of degrees between the prorogator [1] and the nearest rays of the maleficent planets, in proportion to the greatness of the affliction and the power of the planets ruling the cause. But if the rays of the maleficent planets fall before the luminaries, and those of the beneficent behind them, the child that has been exposed will be taken up and will live. And again, if the maleficent planets overcome [2] the beneficent ones that bear an aspect upon the geniture, they will live to affliction and subjection; but if the beneficent planets overcome, they will live but as supposititious children of other parents; and if one of the beneficent planets should either be rising or applying [3] to the moon, while one of the maleficent planets is setting, they will be reared by their own parents. And the same methods of judgement are to be used

---

[1] A luminary, planet, or portion of the zodiac which determines the length of life or the duration of some event. The prorogators are discussed in the next chapter.
[2] See on iii. 4 above (p. 245, n. 1).   [3] See i. 24.

127 γονούντων. ἐὰν μὲν ὑπὸ δύσιν τις ᾖ τῶν κατὰ δύο ἢ καὶ πλείους συνεσχηματισμένων ἀστέρων, ἡμιθανές τι[1] ἢ σάρκωμα καὶ ἀτελὲς τὸ γεννώμενον ἀποτεχθήσεται. ἐὰν δὲ ὑπὸ κακοποιῶν καθυπερτερῆται, ἄτροφον ἢ ἄχρονον ἔσται τὸ ὑπὸ τῆς κατ' αὐτὸν αἰτίας συγγεγενημένον.

⟨ι.⟩ Περὶ χρόνων ζωῆς

Τῶν δὲ μετὰ τὴν γένεσιν συμπτωμάτων ἡγεῖται μὲν ὁ περὶ χρόνων ζωῆς λόγος, ἐπειδήπερ κατὰ τὸν ἀρχαῖον γελοιόν ἐστι τὰ καθ' ἕκαστα τῶν ἀποτελουμένων ἐφαρμόζειν τῷ μηδ' ὅλως ἐκ τῆς τῶν βιωσίμων ἐτῶν ὑποστάσεως ἐπὶ τοὺς ἀποτελεστικοὺς αὐτῶν χρόνους ἥξοντι. θεωρεῖται δὲ οὗτος[2] οὐχ ἁπλῶς οὐδ' ἀπολελυμένως, ἀλλ' ἀπὸ τῆς τῶν κυριωτάτων τόπων ἐπικρατήσεως πολυμερῶς λαμβανόμενος. ἔστι δ' ὁ μάλιστά τε συμφωνῶν ἡμῖν καὶ ἄλλως ἐχόμενος φύσεως τρόπος τοιοῦτος. ἤρτηται μὲν γὰρ τὸ πᾶν ἔκ τε τῆς τῶν ἀφετικῶν τόπων[3] διαλήψεως καὶ ἐξ αὐτῶν τῶν τῆς[4] ἀφέσεως ἐπικρατούντων καὶ ἔτι ἐκ τῆς τῶν ἀναιρετικῶν τόπων ἢ ἀστέρων. διακρίνεται δὲ τούτων ἕκαστον οὕτως.

[1] τι VPLD; ἐστιν MNAECam.
[2] οὗτος MNAEProc.; οὕτως VPLD, om. Cam.
[3] τόπων PLAEProc., om. VMNDCam.
[4] αὐτῶν τῶν τῆς VPLD; τῶν τῆς αὐτῆς MNAECam.

---

[1] Perhaps a reference to Petosiris. The passage is included by E. Riess among the fragments of Nechepso and Petosiris, *Philologus*, Supplementband 6, p. 358.
[2] *Aphetic* is also used. *Hyleg* is the Arabic term.

also in cases of multiple births. But if one of the planets that two by two or in larger groups bear an aspect to the geniture is at setting, the child will be born half-dead, or a mere lump of flesh, and imperfect. But if the maleficent planets overcome them, the infant born subject to this influence will not be reared or will not survive.

10. *Of Length of Life.*

The consideration of the length of life takes the leading place among inquiries about events following birth, for, as the ancient [1] says, it is ridiculous to attach particular predictions to one who, by the constitution of the years of his life, will never attain at all to the time of the predicted events. This doctrine is no simple matter, nor unrelated to others, but in complex fashion derived from the domination of the places of greatest authority. The method most pleasing to us and, besides, in harmony with nature is the following. For it depends entirely upon the determination of the prorogative [2] places and the stars that rule the prorogation, and upon the determination of the destructive [3] places or stars.[4] Each of these is determined in the following fashion:

[3] Or *anaeretic.*

[4] Bouché-Leclercq's (p. 411) summary of Ptolemy's system of prorogations is helpful: " His theory rests essentially upon the likening of the zodiac to a wheel upon which the life of the individuals is cast with a greater or less force from a certain place of departure (τόπος ἀφετικός) and finds itself arrested, or in danger of being arrested, by barriers or destructive places (τόποι ἀναιρετικοί), without being able in any case to go beyond a quarter of the circle. The number of degrees traversed, converted into degrees of right ascension, gives the number of the years of life."

PTOLEMY

Τόπους¹ μὲν πρῶτον ἡγητέον ἀφετικοὺς ἐν οἷς εἶναι δεῖ πάντως τὸν μέλλοντα τὴν κυρίαν τῆς ἀφέσεως λαμβάνειν, τό τε περὶ τὸν ὡροσκόπον δωδεκατημόριον ἀπὸ πέντε μοιρῶν τῶν προαναφερομένων αὐτοῦ τοῦ ὁρίζοντος μέχρι τῶν λοιπῶν καὶ ἐπαναφερομένων εἴκοσι πέντε μοιρῶν, καὶ τὰς ταύταις ταῖς λ' μοίραις δεξιὰς ἑξαγώνους τε τοῦ ἀγαθοῦ δαίμονος, καὶ τετραγώνους τοῦ ὑπὲρ γῆν μεσουρανήματος, καὶ τριγώνους τοῦ καλουμένου θεοῦ, καὶ διαμέτρους τοῦ δύνοντος· προκρινομένων καὶ ἐν τούτοις εἰς δύναμιν ἐπικρατήσεως πρῶτον μὲν τῶν² κατὰ τὸ ὑπὲρ γῆν μεσουράνημα ἑστώτων,³ εἶτα τῶν κατὰ τὴν ἀνατολήν, εἶτα τῶν κατὰ τὴν ἐπαναφορὰν τοῦ μεσουρανήματος, εἶτα τῶν κατὰ τὸ δῦνον, εἶτα τῶν κατὰ τὸ προηγούμενον τοῦ μεσουρανήματος. τό τε γὰρ ὑπὸ γῆν πᾶν εἰκότως ἀθετητέον πρὸς τὴν τηλικαύτην κυρίαν, πλὴν μόνον τῶν παρ' αὐτὴν τὴν ἀναφορὰν εἰς φῶς ἐρχομένων, τοῦ τε ὑπὲρ γῆν οὔτε τὸ ἀσύνδετον τῷ ἀνατέλλοντι δωδεκατημόριον⁴ ἁρμόζει παρα-

¹ Hic titulum habent Περὶ τόπων ἀφετικῶν NCam.; om. VPLMADEProc.
² τῶν AE, om. PL; τῆς NCam., τὸ VMD.
³ ἑστώτων VPLD, om. MNAECam.
⁴ ὃ λέγεται τόπος ἀργός add. mg. N et Cam., om. libri omnes.

---

[1] Sc. degrees.
[2] Though he pays little attention to the system of "places" or "houses" so much used by the astrologers in

TETRABIBLOS III. 10

In the first place we must consider those places prorogative in which by all means the planet must be that is to receive the lordship of the prorogation; namely, the twelfth part of the zodiac surrounding the horoscope, from 5° above the actual horizon up to the 25° that remains, which is rising in succession to the horizon; the part sextile dexter to these thirty degrees, called the House of the Good Daemon; the part in quartile, the mid-heaven; the part in trine, called the House of the God; and the part opposite, the Occident. Among these there are to be preferred, with reference to power of domination, first those [1] which are in the mid-heaven, then those in the orient, then those in the sign succedent to the mid-heaven, then those in the occident,[2] then those in the sign rising before mid-heaven; for the whole region below the earth must, as is reasonable, be disregarded when a domination of such importance is concerned, except only those parts which in the ascendant sign itself are coming into the light. Of the part above the earth it is not fitting to consider either the sign that

---

the actual casting of nativities, Ptolemy here deals with four besides the horoscope itself. Their usual names are: I, Horoscope, ὡροσκόπος; II, Gate of Hades, Ἅιδου πύλη; III, Goddess, Θεά (i.e. moon); IV, lower mid-heaven, ὑπογεῖον; V, Good Fortune, ἀγαθὴ τύχη; VI, Bad Fortune, κακὴ τύχη; VII, Occident, δύσις; VIII, Beginning of Death, ἀρχὴ θανάτου; IX, God, Θεός (i.e. sun); X, mid-heaven, μεσουράνημα; XI, Good Daemon, ἀγαθὸς δαίμων; XII, Bad Daemon, κακὸς δαίμων. Cf. P. Mich. 149, col. ix, 13-19, where slightly different names are given. In this passage Ptolemy has mentioned numbers I, XI, X, IX, VII.

273

PTOLEMY

λαμβάνειν οὔτε τὸ προανατεῖλαν, ὃ καὶ καλεῖται κακοῦ δαίμονος, ἐπειδήπερ κακοῖ¹ τὴν ἐπὶ τὴν γῆν ἀπόρροιαν τῶν ἐν αὐτῷ ἀστέρων μετὰ τοῦ καὶ ἀποκεκλικέναι · θολοῖ τε² καὶ ὥσπερ ἀφανίζει τὸ ἀναθυμιώμενον ἐκ τῶν τῆς γῆς ὑγρῶν παχὺ καὶ ἀχλυῶδες παρ' ὃ καὶ τοῖς χρώμασι καὶ τοῖς μεγέθεσιν οὐ κατὰ φύσιν ἔχοντες φαίνονται.³

Μετὰ δὲ ταῦτα πάλιν ἀφέτας παραληπτέον τούς τε κυριωτάτους δ' τόπους ἥλιον, σελήνην, ὡροσκόπον, κλῆρον τύχης καὶ τοὺς τούτων οἰκοδεσποτήσαντας.⁴

Κλῆρον μέντοι τύχης τὸν συναγόμενον ἀπὸ τοῦ ἀριθμοῦ πάντοτε καὶ νυκτὸς καὶ ἡμέρας τοῦ τε ἀπὸ ἡλίου ἐπὶ σελήνην, καὶ τὰ ἴσα φέροντος⁵ ἀπὸ τοῦ ὡροσκόπου κατὰ τὰ ἑπόμενα τῶν ζῳδίων,⁶ ἵνα ὃν ἔχει λόγον καὶ σχηματισμὸν ὁ ἥλιος πρὸς τὸν

---

¹ κακοῖ V; κακοὶ D; cf. βλάπτει Proc.; ὑπερκακῇ (= ἐπειδήπερ κακοῖ) P; ὅπερ κἀκεῖ L; om. MNAECam.
² τε VD; μὲν PL; om. MNAECam.
³ κατὰ φύσιν ἔχοντες φαίνονται libri; καταφαίνονται Cam.
⁴ Post hoc verbum inser. titulum Περὶ τοῦ κλήρου τῆς τύχης NACam.; om. libri alii.
⁵ φέροντος VPLD; ἀφαιροῦντες MNAECam.; καὶ τὰ ἴσα ἔχοντος ἀπὸ τοῦ ιβ' κατὰ τὰ ἑπόμενα τῶν ζῳδίων Proc.
⁶ Hic add. NACam: ὅπου δ' ἂν ἐκπέσῃ ὁ ἀριθμὸς ἐκείνην τὴν μοῖραν τοῦ δωδεκατημορίου καὶ τὸν τόπον φαμὲν ἐπέχειν τὸν κλῆρον τῆς τύχης.

---

¹ The eighth house. "Sign," of course, in this passage means not the fixed signs of the zodiac, but the places or houses of the nativity. One MS. adds here, "which is

TETRABIBLOS III. 10

is disjunct from the ascendant,[1] nor that which rose before it, called the House of the Evil Daemon,[2] because it injures the emanation from the stars in it to the earth and is also declining, and the thick, misty exhalation from the moisture of the earth creates such a turbidity and, as it were, obscurity, that the stars do not appear in either their true colours or magnitudes.

After this again we must take as prorogatives the four regions of greatest authority, sun, moon, horoscope, the Lot of Fortune, and the rulers of these regions.

Take as the Lot of Fortune[3] always the amount of the number of degrees, both by night and by day, which is the distance from the sun to the moon, and which extends to an equal distance from the horoscope in the order of the following signs,[4] in order that, whatever relation and aspect the sun

---

called the Inactive Place," probably a scholion which has entered the text. See the critical note.

[2] The twelfth house.

[3] The directions given amount to this: Take the angular distance from sun to moon in the order of the following signs, *i.e.* in the direction in which the zodiac is graduated; then lay out the same distance, in the same sense, from the horoscope. The point reached is the Lot of Fortune, and it will be located with respect to the moon as the horoscope is with respect to the sun; hence it can be called a "lunar horoscope." With the older MSS. and Proclus we read φέροντος instead of ἀφαιροῦντες in this passage. On the various accounts of the Lot of Fortune see Bouché-Leclercq, pp. 289-296 (who, however, read ἀφαιροῦντες here).

[4] Here two MSS. and Camerarius (see the critical note) add: "and wherever the number falls, we may say that the Lot of Fortune falls upon that degree of the sign and occupies that place."

PTOLEMY

ὡροσκόπον[1] τοῦτον ἔχῃ καὶ ἡ σελήνη πρὸς τὸν κλῆρον τῆς τύχης καὶ ᾗ ὥσπερ σεληνιακὸς ὡροσκόπος.[2]

130 Προκριτέον δὲ καὶ ἐκ[3] τούτων ἡμέρας μὲν πρῶτον τὸν ἥλιον. ἐάνπερ ᾖ ἐν τοῖς ἀφετικοῖς τόποις· εἰ δὲ μή, τὴν σελήνην· εἰ δὲ μή, τὸν[4] πλείονας ἔχοντα λόγους οἰκοδεσποτίας πρός τε τὸν ἥλιον καὶ τὴν προγενομένην σύνοδον καὶ πρὸς[5] τὸν ὡροσκόπον, τουτέστιν ὅταν τῶν[6] οἰκοδεσποτικῶν τρόπων ε΄ ὄντων τρεῖς ἔχῃ πρὸς ἕνα ἢ καὶ πλείους τῶν εἰρημένων· εἰ δὲ μή, τελευταῖον τὸν ὡροσκόπον. νυκτὸς δὲ πρῶτον τὴν σελήνην, εἶτα τὸν

---

[1] ὡροσκόπον VDProc.; ἀνατολικὸν ὁρίζοντα PLMNECam.; τὴν ὡροσκοποῦσαν μοῖραν τοῦ ἀνατέλλοντος ιβ΄ τημορίου A.

[2] Hic add. NACam.: πλὴν ὀφείλομεν ὁρᾶν ποῖον τῶν φώτων ἐπὶ τὰ ἑπόμενα εὑρίσκεται τοῦ ἑτέρου. εἰ μὲν γὰρ ἡ σελήνη ὡς πρὸς τὰ ἑπόμενα μᾶλλον εὑρίσκεται τοῦ ἡλίου, τὸν ἐκβαλλόμενον ἀπὸ τοῦ ὡροσκόπου ἀριθμὸν ἐπὶ τὸν κλῆρον τῆς τύχης ὡς πρὸς τὰ ἑπόμενα τῶν ζῳδίων δεῖ ἡμᾶς τοῦτον διεκβάλλειν· εἰ δὲ ὡς πρὸς τὰ προηγούμενα τοῦ ἡλίου μᾶλλον εὑρίσκεται ἡ σελήνη, τὸν αὐτὸν ἀριθμὸν ὡς πρὸς τὰ προηγούμενα τοῦ ὡροσκόπου διεκβάλλειν. Om. VPLMDE Proc. Deinde pergunt VPLMNDCam.: ἴσως δὲ αὐτὸ τοῦτο θέλει, καὶ δύναται παρὰ τῷ συγγραφεῖ τὸ τοῖς νυκτὸς γεννωμένοις ἀπὸ σελήνης ἐπὶ ἥλιον ἀριθμεῖν καὶ ἀνάπαλιν ἀπὸ τοῦ ὡροσκόπου, τουτέστιν εἰς τὰ προηγούμενα, διεκβάλλειν. καὶ οὕτω γὰρ κἀκεῖνος ὁ αὐτὸς τόπος τοῦ κλήρου καὶ ὁ αὐτὸς τοῦ συσχηματισμοῦ λόγος ἐκβήσεται. Om. ἴσως δὲ ... διεκβάλλειν A, ἴσως δὲ ... ἐκβήσεται E; in mg. N scriptum est σχόλιον; habent ἐστί τε pro θέλει MNCam., εὑρεθήσεται pro ἐκβήσεται MNACam. Titulum capitis Πόσοι ἀφέται post haec add. NCam., om. VPLMADE.

[3] καὶ ἐκ VPLD, cf. Proc.; om. MNAECam.

[4] τὸν VD; τὴν PL, cf. Proc.; τοὺς MNAECam.

[5] πρὸς om. NDCam.   [6] τῶν om. MNECam.

TETRABIBLOS III. 10

bears to the horoscope, the moon also may bear to the Lot of Fortune, and that it may be as it were a lunar horoscope.[1]

Of these,[2] by day we must give first place to the sun, if it is in the prorogative places; if not, to the moon; and if the moon is not so placed, to the planet [3] that has most relations of domination to the sun, to the preceding conjunction, and to the horoscope; that is, when, of the five methods of domination [4] that exist, it has three to one, or even more; but if this cannot be, then finally we give preference to the horoscope. By night prefer the moon first,

---

[1] Camerarius and certain MSS. add here: "We ought, however, to observe which of the luminaries is found following the other. For if the moon is found following the sun, we must lay out the number which intervenes between the horoscope and the Lot of Fortune in the order of following signs; but if the moon is found preceding the sun, we must set forth this same number from the horoscope in the order of leading signs. Perhaps this is what he means, and the writer's intention is to count from moon to sun in the case of those born at night, and to make the interval in the other direction from the horoscope, that is in the order of leading signs; for thus it will turn out to be the same place for the Lot of Fortune and the same relation of aspect which he mentions." The first part of this passage can hardly be genuine because it is at variance with the general directions just given by Ptolemy; the introductory phrase of the last part clearly shows that it originated as a scholion.

[2] *I.e.* sun, moon, horoscope, Lot of Fortune, and the rulers (see above),

[3] In an aphetic (prorogative) place, says Cardanus (p. 469).

[4] See iii. 2 (p. 233).

277

PTOLEMY

ἥλιον, εἶτα τὸν πλείονας ἔχοντα[1] λόγους οἰκοδεσποτίας πρός τε τὴν σελήνην καὶ πρὸς τὴν προγενομένην πανσέληνον καὶ τὸν κλῆρον τῆς τύχης · εἰ δὲ μή, τελευταῖον, συνοδικῆς μὲν οὔσης τῆς προγενομένης συζυγίας, τὸν ὡροσκόπον, πανσεληνιακῆς δὲ τὸν κλῆρον τῆς τύχης.[2] εἰ δὲ καὶ ἀμφότερα τὰ φῶτα ἢ καὶ ὁ τῆς οἰκείας αἱρέσεως οἰκοδεσπότης ἐν τοῖς ἀφετικοῖς εἶεν τόποις, τὸν ἐν[3] τῷ κυριωτέρῳ τόπῳ[4] τῶν φώτων παραληπτέον· τότε δὲ μόνον τὸν οἰκοδεσπότην ἀμφοτέρων προκριτέον, ὅταν καὶ κυριώτερον ἐπέχῃ τόπον καὶ πρὸς ἀμφοτέρας τὰς αἱρέσεις οἰκοδεσποτίας λόγον ἔχῃ.[5]

Τοῦ δὲ ἀφέτου διακριθέντος, ἔτι καὶ τῶν ἀφέσεων δύο τρόπους παραληπτέον, τόν τε εἰς τὰ ἑπόμενα τῶν ζῳδίων μόνον ὑπὸ τὴν καλουμένην ἀκτινοβολίαν,

---

[1] τὸν ... ἔχοντα VP (ἔχωντα) LD ; cf. Proc. ; τοὺς ... ἔχοντας MNAECam.
[2] Hic add. MNECam.: εἰ δὲ μή, τελευταῖον ὁ ὡροσκόπος ἀφίησι τοὺς χρόνους ; om. VPLADProc.
[3] τὸν ἐν VMNDE, τὸν P, τῶν L, τῶν ἐν A, τὸ μὲν Cam.
[4] τόπῳ VMADEProc., om. PL, τρόπῳ NCam.
[5] Post ἔχῃ add. capitis titulum, Πόσοι τρόποι ἀφέσεως NCam.; om. VPLMADEProc.

---

[1] "But otherwise finally the horoscope is the prorogator" is added here in certain MSS.
[2] I.e. a planet which may be the prorogator. The "proper sect" will be diurnal in diurnal genitures, nocturnal in nocturnal.

next the sun, next the planets having the greater number of relations of domination to the moon, to the preceding full moon, and to the Lot of Fortune; otherwise, finally, if the preceding syzygy was a new moon, the horoscope, but if it was a full moon the Lot of Fortune.[1] But if both the luminaries or the ruler of the proper sect [2] should be in the prorogative places, we must take the one of the luminaries that is in the place of greatest authority. And we should prefer the ruling planet to both of the luminaries only when it both occupies a position of greater authority and bears a relation of domination to both the sects.

When the prorogator has been distinguished, we must still further adopt two methods of prorogation.[3] The one, that which follows the order of the following signs, must be used only in the case of what is called

---

[3] Bouché-Leclercq's (pp. 418-419) exposition may be quoted: "The prorogator once determined ... it is necessary to determine the sense in which it launches the life from its prorogative place; the direct sense, that is, in accordance with the proper movement of the planets, when it follows the series of [following] signs ...; retrograde ... when it follows the diurnal movement. ... At all events there is in both cases unity of measurement, the diurnal movement. In the sense here called direct the diurnal movement brings the anaeretic planet or 'following place' to meet the 'preceding place' where the prorogator is lodged. In the contrary sense it is the prorogator which is carried to the anaeretic place, which is always the occident. By either manner the length of life was equal to the number of degrees of right ascension between the prorogative place and the anaeretic place, at the rate of one year to a degree." He proceeds to point out that it therefore becomes necessary to convert degrees of the zodiac into degrees of right ascension measured on the equator.

PTOLEMY

ὅταν ἐν τοῖς ἀπηλιωτικοῖς τόποις, τουτέστι τοῖς ἀπὸ τοῦ μεσουρανήματος ἐπὶ τὸν ὡροσκόπον, ᾖ ὁ ἀφέτης· καὶ τὸν οὐ μόνον εἰς τὰ ἑπόμενα ἀλλὰ καὶ τὸν[1] εἰς τὰ προηγούμενα κατὰ τὴν λεγομένην ὡριμαίαν, ὅταν ἐν τοῖς ἀποκεκλικόσι τοῦ μεσουρανήματος τόποις ᾖ ὁ ἀφέτης.

Τούτων δὲ οὕτως ἐχόντων ἀναιρετικαὶ γίνονται μοῖραι κατὰ μὲν τὴν εἰς τὰ προηγούμενα τῶν ζῳδίων ἄφεσιν ἡ τοῦ δυτικοῦ ὁρίζοντος μόνη διὰ τὸ ἀφανίζειν τὸν κύριον τῆς ζωῆς· αἱ δὲ τῶν οὕτως ὑπαντώντων ἢ μαρτυρούντων ἀστέρων ἀφαιροῦσι μόνον καὶ προστιθέασιν ἔτη τοῖς[2] μέχρι τῆς καταδύσεως τοῦ ἀφέτου συναγομένοις καὶ οὐκ ἀναιροῦσι διὰ τὸ μὴ αὐτοὺς ἐπιφέρεσθαι τῷ ἀφετικῷ τόπῳ ἀλλ' ἐκεῖνον τοῖς αὐτῶν· καὶ προστιθέασι μὲν οἱ ἀγαθοποιοί, ἀφαιροῦσι δὲ οἱ κακοποιοί, τοῦ Ἑρμοῦ[3] πάλιν ὁποτέροις ἂν αὐτῶν συσχηματισθῇ προστιθεμένου.[4] ὁ δὲ ἀριθμὸς τῆς προσθέσεως ἢ ἀφαιρέσεως θεωρεῖται διὰ τῆς καθ' ἕκαστον μοιροθεσίας· ὅσοι γὰρ ἂν ὦσιν ὡριαῖοι χρόνοι τῆς ἑκάστου μοίρας, ἡμέρας μὲν οὔσης οἱ

[1] τὸν VAD, om. PLMNECam.
[2] Post τοῖς add. ὑπὸ τοῦ ἀφέτου συναγομένοις MNAE; haec omittunt et συναγομένοις post ἀφέτου inser. VPLD.
[3] τοῦ Ἑρμοῦ VD; τοῦ δὲ Ἑ. PL; τούτου Ἑ. A; ὁ δὲ τοῦ Ἑ. MNECam.
[4] προστιθεμένου VP (-τηθ-) LMADE, -ος NCam.

---

[1] On projection of rays (ἀκτινοβολία) see Bouché-Leclercq, pp. 247-250. The planets, by their rotation in their orbits moving, as the astrologers said, "from

TETRABIBLOS III. 10

the projection of rays,¹ when the prorogator is in the orient, that is, between mid-heaven and the horoscope. We must use not only the method that follows the order of following signs, but also that which follows the order of leading signs, in the so-called *horimaea*, when the prorogator is in places that decline from mid-heaven.²

This being the case, the destructive degrees in the prorogation that follows the order of leading signs are only the degree of the western horizon, because it causes the lord of life ³ to vanish ; and the degrees of the planets that thus approach or bear witness ⁴ merely take away and add years to the sum of those as far as the setting of the prorogator, and they do not destroy because they do not move toward the prorogative place, but it moves toward them.⁵ The beneficent stars add and the maleficent subtract. Mercury, again, is reckoned with the group to which he bears an aspect. The number of the addition or subtraction is calculated by means of the location in degrees in each case. For the entire number of years is the same as the number of hourly periods of each

---

right to left," " in the order of the following signs," " regard " those that precede them and " cast rays," like missiles, at those that follow them ; always, however, if the action is to be effective, at the angle of one of the recognized aspects (opposition, quartile, etc., these two having the greatest offensive force).

² That is, in such cases either method may be used.

³ The prorogator, which in this case moves toward the anaeretic place.

⁴ Planets in aspect to one another are said to " bear witness."

⁵ In this case the rays of the planets are cast away from the prorogator ; Bouché-Leclercq, p. 420.

της ημέρας, νυκτός δε οί της νυκτός, τοσούτον πλήθος ετών έσται το τέλειον, όπερ[1] επί[2] της ανατολής αυτών όντων[3] λογιστέον, είτα κατά το ανάλογον της αποχωρήσεως υφαιρετέον, έως αν προς τας δυσμάς εις το μηδέν καταντήση.

Κατά δε την εις τα επόμενα των ζωδίων άφεσιν αναιρούσιν οί τε των κακοποιών τόποι, Κρόνου και Άρεως, ήτοι σωματικώς υπαντώντων ή ακτίνα επιφερόντων οθενδήποτε τετράγωνον ή διάμετρον, ενίοτε δε και επί[4] των ακουόντων ή βλεπόντων κατ' ισοδυναμίαν εξαγώνων,[5] και αυτός δε ο τω αφετικώ τόπω τετράγωνος από των επομένων· ενίοτε δε και επί[6] των πολυχρονιούντων δωδεκατημορίων κακωθείς ο εξάγωνος,[7] επί δε των ολιγοχρονίων[8] ο τρίγωνος· σελήνης δε αφιείσης και ο του ηλίου τόπος.[9] ισχύουσι γαρ αι κατά την τοιαύτην άφεσιν απαντήσεις και αναιρείν και σώζειν, επειδή αύται τω του αφέτου τόπω επιφέρονται. ου πάντοτε μέντοι τούτους τους τόπους[10]

[1] όπερ VPLADE; όπως MNCam.
[2] επί VPLMADEProc.; εκ NCam.
[3] όλον post όντων add. MNAECam., om. VPLD.
[4] επί VPLADProc.; από MNECam.
[5] εξαγώνων VPDProc., -ον MLNAECam.
[6] επί VADEProc.; επί μεν PL; από MNCam.
[7] Post εξάγωνος ins. αναιρεί NACam.; om. VPLMDEProc.
[8] ολιγοχρονίων VPLDProc., -χρονιούντων MNAECam. πάλιν κακωθείς ins. post ολιγοχρονίων NAECam.; om. VPLMDProc.
[9] Post τόπος ins. αναιρεί MNAECam.; om. VPLDProc.
[10] τούτους τους τόπους VPLDA (add. και A); τοιούτους τους τόπους και M (cf. Proc.); τοιούτοις τοις τόποις και E, τους τοιούτους και Cam.

TETRABIBLOS III. 10

degree, hours of the day [1] when it is day and hours of the night when it is night; this must be our reckoning when they are in the orient, and subtraction must be made in proportion to their departure therefrom, until at their setting it becomes zero.

In the prorogation which follows the order of following signs, the places of the maleficent planets, Saturn and Mars, destroy, whether they are approaching bodily, or project their rays from any place whatever in quartile or in opposition, and sometimes too in sextile, upon the signs called " hearing " or " seeing " [2] on grounds of equality of power; and the sign that is quartile to the prorogative sign in the order of following signs likewise destroys. And sometimes, also, among the signs that ascend slowly the sextile aspect destroys, when it is afflicted,[3] and again among the signs that ascend rapidly the trine. When the moon is the prorogator, the place of the sun also destroys. For in a prorogation of this kind the approaches of planets avail both to destroy and to preserve, since these are

---

[1] " Hours " were merely twelfth parts of the day (sunrise to sunset) or of the night, and hence " hours of the day " are not of the same length as " hours of the night " except when day and night are equal.

[2] *Cf.* i. 15.

[3] See above, p. 267, concerning " affliction." Aries, Taurus, Gemini, Pisces, Aquarius, and Capricorn were classed as rapidly ascending signs; the others, as slowly ascending signs.

πάντως ἀναιρεῖν ἡγητέον, ἀλλὰ μόνον ὅταν ὦσι κεκακωμένοι. παραποδίζονται γὰρ ἐάν τε εἰς ἀγαθοποιοῦ ὅριον ἐμπέσωσιν, ἐάν τέ τις τῶν ἀγαθοποιῶν ἀκτῖνα συνεπιφέρῃ¹ τετράγωνον ἢ τρίγωνον ἢ διάμετρον ἤτοι πρὸς αὐτὴν τὴν ἀναιρετικὴν μοῖραν ἢ εἰς τὰ ἑπόμενα αὐτῆς, ἐπὶ μὲν Διὸς μὴ ὑπὲρ τὰς ιβ' μοίρας, ἐπὶ δὲ Ἀφροδίτης μὴ ὑπὲρ τὰς η'· ἐάν τε σωμάτων ὄντων ἀμφοτέρων τοῦ τε ἀφιέντος καὶ τοῦ ὑπαντῶντος, μὴ ταὐτὸ πλάτος ᾖ ἀμφοτέρων.² ὅταν οὖν δύο ᾖ καὶ πλείονα ᾖ ἑκατέρωθεν τά τε βοηθοῦντα καὶ τὰ κατὰ τὸ ἐναντίον ἀναιροῦντα, σκεπτέον τὴν ἐπικράτησιν ὁποτέρου τῶν εἰδῶν, κατά τε τὸ πλῆθος τῶν συλλαμβανομένων αὐτοῖς καὶ κατὰ τὴν δύναμιν· κατὰ μὲν τὸ πλῆθος, ὅταν αἰσθητῶς πλείονα ᾖ τὰ ἕτερα τῶν ἑτέρων, κατὰ δύναμιν δέ, ὅταν τῶν βοηθούντων ἢ ἀναιρούντων ἀστέρων οἱ μὲν ἐν οἰκείοις ὦσι τόποις, οἱ δὲ μή· μάλιστα δ' ὅταν οἱ μὲν ὦσιν ἀνατολικοί, οἱ δὲ δυτικοί. καθ' ὅλου γὰρ τῶν ὑπὸ τὰς αὐγὰς ὄντων οὐδένα παραληπτέον οὔτε πρὸς ἀναίρεσιν οὔτε πρὸς βοήθειαν, πλὴν εἰ μὴ σελήνης ἀφετίδος οὔσης αὐτὸς ὁ τοῦ ἡλίου τόπος ἀνέλῃ,³ συντετραμ-

---

¹ συνεπιφέρηται ECam.
² ἀμφοτέρων libri omnes; cf. Proc.; ἑκατέρων Cam.
³ ἀνέλῃ VMDE, -ει PL, -οι NCam., ἀναιρεῖ A.

---

[1] In this type of prorogation the diurnal movement of the heavens is carrying the planets toward the prorogative

in the direction of the prorogative place.[1] However, it must not be thought that these places always inevitably destroy, but only when they are afflicted. For they are prevented both if they fall within the term [2] of a beneficent planet and if one of the beneficent planets projects its ray from quartile, trine, or opposition either upon the destructive degree itself or upon the parts that follow it, in the case of Jupiter not more than 12°, and in that of Venus not over 8°; also if, when both the prorogator and the approaching planet are present bodily, the latitude of both is not the same.[3] Thus when there are two or more on each side, assisting and, *vice versa*, destroying, we must consider which of them prevails, both by the number of those that co-operate and by power; by number when one group is perceptibly more numerous than the other, and with regard to power when some of the assisting or of the destroying planets are in their own proper places, and some are not, and particularly when some are rising and others setting. For in general we must not admit any planet, either to destroy or to aid, that is under the rays of the sun, except that when the moon is prorogator the place of the sun itself is destructive, when it is changed about by the presence

---

place; *cf.* Bouché-Leclercq, pp. 420-421 (esp. 421). He points out the complexity of the calculation and the multitude of choices that lay open to an astrologer in his interpretation of a geniture.

[2] See i. 20-21.

[3] This would be true only in cases of the bodily approach of planets, not in aspect. The notion is that the ray will not hit its mark if the two bodies are not in the same latitude.

PTOLEMY

μένος μὲν ὑπὸ τοῦ συνόντος κακοποιοῦ, ὑπὸ μηδενὸς δὲ τῶν ἀγαθοποιῶν ἀναλελυμένος.¹

Ὁ μέντοι τῶν ἐτῶν ἀριθμὸς ὃν ποιοῦσιν οἱ τῶν μεταξὺ διαστάσεων τοῦ τε ἀφετικοῦ τόπου καὶ τοῦ ἀναιροῦντος οὐχ ἁπλῶς οὐδ' ὡς ἔτυχεν ὀφείλει λαμβάνεσθαι κατὰ τὰς τῶν πολλῶν παραδόσεις ἐκ τῶν ἀναφορικῶν πάντοτε χρόνων ² ἑκάστης μοίρας,³ εἰ μὴ μόνον ὅταν ἤτοι αὐτὸς ὁ ἀνατολικὸς ὁρίζων τὴν ἄφεσιν ᾖ εἰληφὼς ἤ τις τῶν κατ' αὐτὸν ποιουμένων ἀνατολήν. ἑνὸς γὰρ ἐκ παντὸς τρόπου τῷ φυσικῶς τοῦτο τὸ μέρος ἐπισκεπτομένῳ προκει-

¹ βοηθούμενος καὶ ἀναλελυμένος MACam., βο. ἢ ἀν. NE; βοηθούμενος καὶ om. VPLDProc.
² καὶ post χρόνων add. MCam.; om. alii.
³ ἑκάστης μοίρας Proc.; ἑκάστη μοῖρα VD; ἑκάστας μοίρας PLMNAECam.

---

[1] As the anonymous commentator says (p. 120, ed. Wolf), the sun is of a "middle temperature" (κρᾶσις), and takes the character, good or bad, of the planet associated with it; cf. i. 5 above.

[2] Some of the MSS. have βοηθούμενος καὶ (or ἢ) ἀναλελυμένος, "assisted or released"; probably an explanatory gloss which worked its way into the text. The anonymous commentator explains the word to mean that a beneficent planet does not permit the sun to retain the "affliction" attached by the evil planet, but "releases" it.

[3] The following general description is intended to apply to Ptolemy's lengthy account of this method. In each prorogation, two points on the ecliptic are concerned, the prorogator or precedent and the subsequent or anaeretic place, which we may call P and S respectively. S may or may not be occupied by a planet, but in this type of prorogation it always follows P, that is, lies east of it and comes to the horizon later. P, as a point on the ecliptic, may (a) lie at the intersection of the ecliptic and the equator or

TETRABIBLOS III. 10

of a maleficent planet [1] and is not released [2] by any of the beneficent ones.

However, the number of years, determined by the distances between the prorogative place and the destructive planet, ought not to be taken simply or offhand, in accordance with the usual traditions, from the times of ascension of each degree, except only when the eastern horizon itself is the prorogator, or some one of the planets that are rising in that region. For one method alone [3] is available for him who is

---

be (b) north of the equator or (c) south of it. The vernal and autumnal equinoxes, the beginnings of Aries and Libra, are the only points of the ecliptic which can occupy position (a); if, however, P is one of these, since it is also a point on the equator, it will pass, like all points on the equator, from horizon to meridian in 6 hours, at the rate of 15° in 1 hour (this is the hour called "equinoctial hour" by the Greeks). If P is to the north of the equator, in a north latitude, its ascension from horizon to meridian will be along a path parallel to the equator and longer than the distance from horizon to meridian on the equator; hence it takes longer than 6 equinoctial hours. Conversely, points south of the equator take a shorter course and ascend in times correspondingly shorter than 6 equinoctial hours. Nevertheless, since the Greeks defined "day" as the period from sunrise to sunset and divided it into 12 hours, similarly dividing the night, the ascension of P from rising to culmination, wherever it is situated on the ecliptic and whatever the latitude, takes place in 6 hours of the day, that is, ordinary or civil (καιρικαί) hours, which may be longer or shorter than equinoctial hours, and equal to them only when P occupies position (a), described above. The "horary magnitude" or "period" of a point on the ecliptic is the expression in terms of equinoctial times (see p. 95, n. 2) of the length of the civil hour when the sun is at that point; in north latitudes, horary magnitudes are greater than 15 for points north of the equator and less

[*For continuation of footnote, see pages* 288 *and* 289.

PTOLEMY

μένου, σκοπεῖν[1] μετὰ πόσους ἰσημερινοὺς χρόνους ὁ τοῦ ἑπομένου σώματος ἢ σχήματος τόπος ἐπὶ τὸν[2] τοῦ προηγουμένου κατ' αὐτὴν τὴν γένεσιν παραγίνεται, διὰ τὸ τοὺς ἰσημερινοὺς χρόνους ὁμαλῶς διέρχεσθαι καὶ τὸν ὁρίζοντα καὶ τὸν μεσημβρινόν, πρὸς οὓς ἀμφοτέρους αἱ τῶν τοπικῶν ἀποστάσεων[3] ὁμοιότητες λαμβάνονται, καὶ ἰσχύειν[4] δὲ ἕκαστον τῶν χρόνων ἐνιαυτὸν ἕνα ἡλιακὸν εἰκότως· ὅταν μὲν ἐπ' αὐτοῦ τοῦ ἀνατολικοῦ ὁρίζοντος ᾖ ὁ ἀφετικὸς καὶ προηγούμενος τόπος, τοὺς ἀναφορικοὺς χρόνους τῶν μέχρι τῆς ὑπαντήσεως μοιρῶν προσήκει λαμβάνειν· μετὰ τοσούτους γὰρ ἰσημερινοὺς χρόνους ὁ ἀναιρέτης ἐπὶ τὸν τοῦ ἀφέτου τόπον, τουτέστιν ἐπὶ τὸν ἀνατολικὸν ὁρίζοντα, παραγίνεται· ὅταν δὲ ἐπ' αὐτοῦ τοῦ μεσημβρινοῦ, τὰς ἐπ' ὀρθῆς τῆς σφαίρας ἀναφοράς, ἐν ὅσαις ἕκαστον τμῆμα διέρχεται τὸν μεσημβρινόν· ὅταν

---

[1] σκοπεῖν VPLD, τοῦ σκοπεῖν MNAECam.
[2] τὸν VDProc.; τὴν alii Cam.
[3] ἀποστάσεων VPMADEProc., ὑποστάσεων L, om. NCam.
[4] ἰσχύειν VPND, cf. Proc.; ἰσχύει LMAECam.

---

for points south, 15 being the horary magnitude of the two equinoctial points. All that has been said about P applies of course to S, which is another point on the ecliptic. The problem of prorogation is simply to discover after how many equinoctial periods or times S comes to the position originally occupied by P with relation to the meridian (or other centre, such as the western horizon). This position is defined as the one in which S is just as many civil hours removed from the meridian (or the point of reference) as was P in its original position.

considering this subject in a natural manner—to calculate after how many equinoctial periods [1] the place of the following body or aspect comes to the place of the one preceding at the actual time of birth, because the equinoctial periods pass evenly [2] through both the horizon and the mid-heaven, to both of which are referred the proportions of spatial distances, and, as is reasonable, each one of the periods has the value of one solar year.[3] Whenever the prorogative and preceding place is actually on the eastern horizon, we should take the times of ascension of the degrees up to the meeting-place; for after this number of equinoctial periods the destructive planet comes to the place of the prorogator, that is, to the eastern horizon. But when it [4] is actually at the mid-heaven, we should take the ascensions on the right sphere in which the segment [5] in each case passes mid-heaven; and when it is on

One therefore determines how far S was originally removed, how far it is removed when it comes to the position of P, and takes the difference, in equinoctial times, as the answer.

[1] An "equinoctial period" or "time" is the length of time which it takes one degree on the equator to pass a fixed point, *i.e.* 1/360 of 24 hours. An "equinoctial hour" is 15 "equinoctial times." For the definition *cf.* Heliodorus (?) in *CCAG*, vii. 122, 20 ff.

[2] At the rate of 15 per hour, in contrast to the varying horary periods of degrees on the ecliptic.

[3] In predicting the life of the subject of the horoscope. *Cf.* P. Mich. 149, col. xii. ll. 10-11.

[4] The prorogator.

[5] The "segment" is the arc (of the ecliptic) between the two places, but the ascension of the following body is to be measured on the right sphere; that is, it is right ascension, which is measured on the equator.

PTOLEMY

δὲ ἐπ' αὐτοῦ τοῦ δυτικοῦ ὁρίζοντος, ἐν ὅσαις ἑκάστη τῶν τῆς διαστάσεως μοιρῶν καταφέρεται, τουτέστιν ἐν ὅσαις αἱ διαμετροῦσαι ταύτας[1] ἀναφέρονται· τοῦ δὲ προηγουμένου τόπου μηκέτ' ὄντος ἐν τοῖς τρισὶ τούτοις ὅροις ἀλλ' ἐν ταῖς μεταξὺ διαστάσεσιν, οὐκ ἔτι τῶν προκειμένων ἀναφορῶν ἢ καταφορῶν ἢ μεσουρανήσεων[2] οἱ χρόνοι τοὺς ἑπομένους τόπους οἴσουσιν ἐπὶ τοὺς αὐτοὺς τοῖς προηγουμένοις, ἀλλὰ διάφοροι. ὅμοιος μὲν γὰρ καὶ ὁ αὐτὸς τόπος ἐστὶν ὁ τὴν ὁμοίαν καὶ ἐπὶ τὰ αὐτὰ μέρη θέσιν ἔχων ἅμα πρός τε τὸν ὁρίζοντα καὶ τὸν μεσημβρινόν. τοῦτο δὲ ἔγγιστα συμβέβηκε τοῖς ἐφ' ἑνὸς κειμένοις ἡμικυκλίου τῶν γραφομένων διὰ τῶν τομῶν τοῦ τε μεσημβρινοῦ καὶ τοῦ ὁρίζοντος, ὧν ἕκαστον κατὰ τὴν αὐτὴν θέσιν τὴν ἴσην ἔγγιστα καιρικὴν[3] ὥραν ποιεῖ. ὥσπερ δ',[4] ἂν περιάγηται περὶ τὰς εἰρημένας τομάς, ἔρχεται μὲν ἐπὶ τὴν αὐτὴν θέσιν καὶ τῷ ὁρίζοντι καὶ τῷ μεσημβρινῷ, τοὺς δὲ τῆς διελεύσεως τοῦ ζῳδιακοῦ χρόνους ἀνίσους ἐφ' ἑκάτερον[5] ποιεῖ, τὸν αὐτὸν τρόπον καὶ κατὰ τὰς τῶν ἄλλων ἀποστάσεων

---

[1] ταύτας VDMLE; cf. Proc.; ταύταις PNACam.
[2] συμμεσουρανήσεων NCam.
[3] καιρικὴν om. MNCam.   [4] δ(ὲ) om. MNCam.
[5] ἑκάτερον VD; -ου cett. Cam.; om. Proc.

---

[1] Comes to the meridian in the same time, and is on the same side of the equator (" in the same direction "). Ptolemy introduces this characterization of " same and

the western horizon, the number in which each of the degrees of the interval descends, that is, the number in which those directly opposite them ascend. But if the precedent place is not on these three limits but in the intervals between them, in that case the times of the aforesaid ascensions, descensions, or culminations will not carry the following places to the places of the preceding, but the periods will be different. For a place is similar and the same if it has the same position [1] in the same direction with reference both to the horizon and to the meridian. This is most nearly true of those which lie upon one of those semicircles [2] which are described through the sections of the meridian and the horizon, each of which at the same position makes nearly the same temporal hour. Even as, if the revolution is upon the aforesaid arcs, it reaches the same position with reference to both the meridian and horizon, but makes the periods of the passage of the zodiac unequal with respect to either, in the same way also at the positions of the other distances it makes their

---

similar places " because the whole system of prorogation depends on determining the period after which a subsequent body will come to the same place as, or a similar place to, that occupied by a precedent body. It cannot come to exactly the same place, because both bodies are on the ecliptic, oblique to the equator. Hence it is necessary to define " similar places."

[2] He refers to the arcs of circles, parallel to the equator, passing through the degree of the ecliptic in question, and cutting both horizon and meridian, which are intercepted between the horizon and the meridian.

PTOLEMY

θέσεις δι' ἀνίσων ἐκείνοις χρόνων τὰς παρόδους ἀπεργάζεται. μία δέ τις ἡμῖν ἔφοδος ἔστω[1] τοιαύτη, δι' ἧς, ἐάν τε ἀνατολικὴν ἐάν τε μεσημβρινὴν ἢ δυτικήν, ἐάν τε ἄλλην τινὰ ἔχῃ θέσιν ὁ προηγούμενος τόπος, τὸ ἀνάλογον τῶν ἐπ' αὐτὸν φερόντων χρόνων τὸν ἑπόμενον τόπον ληφθήσεται. προδιαλαβόντες γὰρ τὴν μεσουρανοῦσαν τοῦ ζῳδιακοῦ μοῖραν καὶ ἔτι τήν τε προηγουμένην καὶ τὴν ἐπερχομένην, πρῶτον σκεψόμεθα τὴν τῆς προηγουμένης θέσιν, πόσας καιρικὰς ὥρας ἀπέχει τοῦ μεσημβρινοῦ, ἀριθμήσαντες τὰς μεταξὺ αὐτῆς καὶ[2] τῆς μεσουρανούσης οἰκείως ἤτοι ὑπὲρ γῆν ἢ ὑπὸ γῆν μοίρας[3] ἐπ' ὀρθῆς τῆς σφαίρας ἀναφορὰς καὶ μερίσαντες εἰς τὸ πλῆθος τῶν αὐτῆς τῆς προηγουμένης μοίρας ὡριαίων χρόνων, εἰ μὲν ὑπὲρ

[1] ἔστω VDProc.; ἔσται PLMNAECam.
[2] καὶ om. LCam.
[3] μοίρας MAE, μοῖραν VPD, μοͬ N, μεσουρανοῖ Cam.

---

[1] This obscure sentence is thus explained by the anonymous commentator: "If you imagine a star moving either from the horoscope (sc. to mid-heaven), or from mid-heaven to the horoscope, you will discover the temporal periods of the distance; in the same way also when they are not upon the degrees of the angles."

[2] ὡριαῖοι χρόνοι; the expression ὡριαῖον μέγεθος, "horary magnitude," is used further on, when Ptolemy gives examples. In the *Almagest*, ii. 8, there is a table which gives the time, in degrees and minutes of the equator (*i.e.* equinoctial times), in which each arc of 10° of the ecliptic rises above the horizon in each of eleven latitudes beginning with the equator (right sphere); the table also gives the cumulative sums of these ascensions for each arc from the beginning of Aries. In the following chapter Ptolemy tells how the horary magnitude may be determined

TETRABIBLOS III. 10

passages in times unequal to the former.[1] We shall therefore adopt one method only, as follows, whereby, whether the preceding place occupies the orient, the mid-heaven, the occident, or any other position, the proportionate number of equinoctial times that bring the following place to it will be apprehended. For after we have first determined the culminating degree of the zodiac and furthermore the degree of the precedent and that of the subsequent, in the first place we shall investigate the position of the precedent, how many ordinary hours it is removed from the meridian, counting the ascensions that properly intervene up to the very degree of mid-heaven, whether over or under the earth, on the right sphere, and dividing them by the amount of the horary periods[2] of the precedent degree, diurnal if it is

by the use of this table. His directions are, in brief, to take the sum of the ascensions for the degree of the sun by day (or the opposite degree by night) both in the right sphere and in the given latitude; to ascertain the difference between the two and take $\frac{1}{6}$ of it; and then, if the degree was in the northern hemisphere, to add this fraction to the 15 "times" of one equinoctial hour, or, for a southern position, to subtract it. This will give the length of the ordinary or civil hour for the latitude and time of the year in question, in terms of the ascension of degrees of the equator, or "equinoctial times," or as Ptolemy puts it, "the number of (equinoctial) times of the civil hour under consideration." The civil day-time hour was $\frac{1}{12}$ of the period from sunrise to sunset, or, of course, $\frac{1}{6}$ of the time from sunrise to noon. In *Almagest*, ii. 9, Ptolemy gives the same directions for reducing periods expressed in equinoctial times to ordinary or civil hours; multiply the given equinoctial hours by 15 (in order to express them in "equinoctial times," as are the ascensions dealt with in the present passage) and divide by the horary period.

γῆν εἴη τῶν ἡμερησίων, εἰ δὲ ὑπὸ γῆν τῶν τῆς νυκτός. ἐπεὶ δὲ τὰ τὰς αὐτὰς καιρικὰς ὥρας ἀπέχοντα τοῦ μεσημβρινοῦ τμήματα τοῦ ζωδιακοῦ καθ' ἑνὸς καὶ τοῦ αὐτοῦ γίνεται τῶν προειρημένων ἡμικυκλίων, καὶ[1] δεήσει λαβεῖν μετὰ πόσους ἰσημερινοὺς χρόνους[2] καὶ τὸ ἑπόμενον τμῆμα τὰς ἴσας καιρικὰς ὥρας ἀφέξει τοῦ αὐτοῦ μεσημβρινοῦ τῇ προηγουμένῃ. ταύτας δὲ διειληφότες ἐπισκεψόμεθα πόσους τε κατὰ τὴν ἐξ ἀρχῆς θέσιν ἀπεῖχεν ἰσημερινοὺς χρόνους καὶ ἡ ἑπομένη μοῖρα τῆς κατὰ τὸ αὐτὸ μεσουράνημα διὰ τῶν ἐπ' ὀρθῆς πάλιν τῆς σφαίρας ἀναφορῶν, καὶ πόσους ὅτε τὰς ἴσας καιρικὰς ὥρας ἐποίει τῇ προηγουμένῃ · πολυπλασιάσαντές τε καὶ ταύτας ἐπὶ τὸ πλῆθος τῶν τῆς ἑπομένης μοίρας ὡριαίων χρόνων, εἰ μὲν πρὸς τὸ ὑπὲρ γῆν εἴη μεσουράνημα πάλιν ἡ σύγκρισις τῶν καιρικῶν ὡρῶν, τὸ[3] τῶν ἡμερησίων, εἰ δὲ πρὸς τὸ ὑπὸ γῆν τὸ τῶν τῆς νυκτός, καὶ τοὺς γινομένους ἐκ τῆς ὑπεροχῆς ἀμφοτέρων τῶν διαστάσεων λαβόντες ἕξομεν τὸ τῶν ζητουμένων ἐτῶν πλῆθος.[4]

Ἵνα δὲ φανερώτερον γένηται τὸ λεγόμενον, ὑποκείσθω προηγούμενος μὲν τόπος ἡ ἀρχὴ[5] τοῦ Κριοῦ λόγου ἕνεκεν, ἑπόμενος δὲ ὁ τῆς ἀρχῆς τῶν Διδύμων, κλίμα δὲ ὅπου ἡ μὲν μεγίστη ἡμέρα ὡρῶν ἐστι ιδ', τὸ δ' ὡριαῖον μέγεθος τῆς ἀρχῆς

[1] καὶ VPLD, om. MNAECam.
[2] χρόνους PLAProc., om. VMNDECam.
[3] τὸ (post ὡρῶν) ... τὸ (post γῆν) VPLD, om. MNAECam.
[4] Post πλῆθος ins. cap. Ὑπόδειγμα NCam., om. libri alii.
[5] ἡ ἀρχὴ VDProc., ὁ τῆς ἀρχῆς alii Cam.

TETRABIBLOS III. 10

above the earth and nocturnal if it is below. But since the sections of the zodiac which are an equal number of ordinary hours removed from the meridian lie upon one and the same of the aforesaid semicircles, it will also be necessary to find after how many equinoctial periods the subsequent section will be removed from the same meridian by the same number of ordinary hours as the precedent.[1] When we have determined these, we shall inquire how many equinoctial hours at its original position the degree of the subsequent was removed from the degree at mid-heaven, again by means of ascensions in the right sphere, and how many when it made the same number of ordinary hours as the precedent, multiplying these into the number of the horary periods[2] of the degree of the subsequent; if again the comparison of the ordinary hours relates to the mid-heaven above the earth, multiplying into the number of diurnal hours, but if it relates to that below the earth, the number of nocturnal hours. And taking the results from the difference of the two distances, we shall have the number of years for which the inquiry was made.

To make this clearer, suppose that the precedent place is the beginning of Aries, for example, and the subsequent the beginning of Gemini, and the latitude that where the longest day is fourteen hours long,[3] and the horary magnitude of the beginning of Gemini

---

[1] For it will then have " come to the same place " that the precedent originally occupied.

[2] Or, horary magnitude.

[3] This is the latitude of lower Egypt; *cf. Almagest*, ii. 6, p. 108, 15 ff. (Heiberg), and the table in ii. 8, pp. 134-141.

PTOLEMY

τῶν Διδύμων ἔγγιστα χρόνων ἰσημερινῶν ιζ',[1] καὶ ἀνατελλέτω πρῶτον ἡ ἀρχὴ τοῦ Κριοῦ, ἵνα μεσουρανῇ ἡ ἀρχὴ τοῦ Αἰγοκέρωτος, καὶ ἀπεχέτω [2] τοῦ ὑπὲρ γῆν μεσουρανήματος ἡ ἀρχὴ τῶν Διδύμων χρόνους ἰσημερινοὺς ρμη'.[3] ἐπεὶ οὖν ἡ τοῦ Κριοῦ ἀρχὴ ἀπέχει τοῦ μεσημβρινοῦ μεσουρανήματος καιρικὰς ὥρας ἕξ, ταύτας πολλαπλασιάσαντες ἐπὶ τοὺς ιζ' χρόνους, οἵπερ εἰσὶ τοῦ ὡριαίου μεγέθους τῆς ἀρχῆς τῶν Διδύμων, ἐπειδήπερ πρὸς τὸ ὑπὲρ γῆν μεσουράνημά ἐστιν ἡ τῶν ρμη' χρόνων ἀποχή, ἕξομεν καὶ ταύτης τῆς διαστάσεως χρόνους ρβ'.[4] μετὰ τοὺς τῆς ὑπεροχῆς ἄρα χρόνους μϛ'[5] ὁ ἑπόμενος τόπος ἐπὶ τὸν τοῦ προηγουμένου μεταβήσεται. τοσοῦτοι δ' εἰσὶν ἔγγιστα χρόνοι καὶ τῆς ἀναφορᾶς τοῦ τε Κριοῦ καὶ τοῦ Ταύρου, ἐπειδὴ ὁ ἀφετικὸς τόπος ὑπόκειται ὡροσκοπῶν.

Μεσουρανείτω δὲ ὁμοίως ἡ ἀρχὴ τοῦ Κριοῦ, ἵνα ἀπέχῃ κατὰ τὴν πρώτην θέσιν ἡ ἀρχὴ τῶν Διδύμων τοῦ ὑπὲρ γῆν μεσουρανήματος χρόνους ἰσημερινοὺς νή. ἐπειδὴ οὖν κατὰ τὴν δευτέραν θέσιν ὀφείλει μεσουρανεῖν ἡ ἀρχὴ τῶν Διδύμων,[6] ἕξομεν τὴν τῶν διαστάσεων ὑπεροχὴν [7] αὐτῶν τῶν[8] νη'[9] χρόνων, ἐν

[1] ιζ' VPLMDEProc., ιζ' η' NACam. Sic et infra.
[2] ἀπεχέτω VAD, ἔστω ἀπέχουσα Proc., ἀπέχει PL, ἀπέχῃ MNECam.
[3] ρμη' VPLMDEProc., ρμη' μζ' NACam.¹, ρμη' μη' Cam.²
[4] ρβ' VPLMDEProc., ρβ' μη' NACam.
[5] μϛ' libri omnes Proc. Cam.¹, με' Cam.²
[6] ἡ ἀρχὴ τῶν Διδύμων Proc.; Διδύμων om. VD; om. PLME; ὁ ἀφετικὸς τόπος NACam.
[7] τὴν τῶν διαστάσεων ὑπεροχὴν VPLD; ἡ ὑπεροχὴ τῆς διαστάσεως Proc., τὴν τῆς προτέρας διαστάσεως ὑπεροχὴν MNECam., τὴν τῆς τοιαύτης διαστ. ὑπ. A.

is approximately 17 equinoctial times.¹ Assume first that the beginning of Aries is rising, so that the beginning of Capricorn is at mid-heaven, and let the beginning of Gemini be removed from the mid-heaven above the earth 148 equinoctial times.² Now since the beginning of Aries is six ordinary hours³ removed from the diurnal mid-heaven, multiplying these into the 17 equinoctial times, which are the times of the horary magnitude of the beginning of Gemini, since the distance of 148 times relates to the mid-heaven above the earth, we shall have for this interval also 102 times. Hence, after 46 times, which is the difference, the subsequent place will pass to the position of the precedent. These are very nearly the equinoctial times of the ascension of Aries and Taurus, since it is assumed that the prorogative sign is the horoscope.

Similarly, let the beginning of Aries be at mid-heaven, so that at its original position the beginning of Gemini may be 58 equinoctial times⁴ removed from the mid-heaven above the earth. Therefore, since at its second position the beginning of Gemini should be at mid-heaven, we shall have for the difference of the distances precisely this amount of 58 times,

---

¹ The method described in *Almagest*, ii. 9, cited above, applied to data from the table in *Almagest*, ii. 8, gives 17 times 6 min. 30 sec.

² This is reckoned on the right sphere. The data from the table in the *Almagest* will give 147 times 44 min.

³ Likewise 6 equinoctial hours, since it is an equinoctial point.   ⁴ *I.e.* 148 minus 90.

---

⁸ αὐτῶν τῶν PE, τῶν τῶν VD, τῶν LProc., αὐτὴν τὴν τῶν MNACam.   ⁹ νζ´ μδ´ A.

PTOLEMY

ὅσοις πάλιν διὰ τὸ μεσουρανεῖν τὸν ἀφετικὸν τόπον διέρχεται τὸν μεσημβρινὸν ὅ τε Κριὸς καὶ ὁ Ταῦρος.
138 Δυνέτω δὲ τὸν αὐτὸν τρόπον ἡ ἀρχὴ τοῦ Κριοῦ, ἵνα μεσουρανῇ μὲν ἡ ἀρχὴ τοῦ Καρκίνου, ἀπέχῃ δὲ τοῦ ὑπὲρ γῆν μεσουρανήματος ἡ ἀρχὴ τῶν Διδύμων εἰς τὰ προηγούμενα χρόνους ἰσημερινοὺς λβ΄.[1] ἐπεὶ οὖν πάλιν ἐξ ὥρας καιρικὰς ἀπέχει τοῦ μεσημβρινοῦ ἡ ἀρχὴ τοῦ Κριοῦ πρὸς δυσμάς, ἐὰν ἑπτακαιδεκάκις ταύτας ποιήσωμεν, ἕξομεν ρβ΄ [2] χρόνους, οὓς ἀφέξει τοῦ μεσημβρινοῦ καὶ ἡ ἀρχὴ τῶν Διδύμων ὅταν δύνῃ. ἀπεῖχε δὲ καὶ κατὰ τὴν πρώτην θέσιν ἐπὶ τὰ αὐτὰ χρόνους λβ΄.[3] ἐν τοῖς τῆς ὑπεροχῆς ἄρα χρόνοις ἑβδομήκοντα[4] ἐπὶ τὸ δῦνον ἠνέχθη, ἐν οἷς καὶ καταφέρεται μὲν ὅ τε Κριὸς καὶ ὁ Ταῦρος, ἀναφέρεται δὲ τὰ διαμετροῦντα δωδεκατημόρια τό τε τῶν Χηλῶν καὶ τὸ τοῦ Σκορπίου.

Ὑποκείσθω τοίνυν ἐπὶ[5] μηδενὸς[6] μὲν οὖσα τῶν κέντρων ἡ ἀρχὴ τοῦ Κριοῦ, ἀπέχουσα δὲ λόγου ἕνεκεν εἰς τὰ προηγούμενα τῆς μεσημβρίας καιρικὰς ὥρας τρεῖς, ἵνα μεσουρανῇ μὲν ἡ τοῦ Ταύρου μοῖρα ὀκτωκαιδεκάτη, ἀπέχῃ δὲ κατὰ τὴν πρώτην θέσιν ἡ τῶν Διδύμων ἀρχὴ τοῦ ὑπὲρ γῆν μεσουρανήματος εἰς τὰ ἑπόμενα χρόνους ἰσημερινοὺς δεκατρεῖς. ἐὰν

---

[1] λβ΄ VPMDEProc., λη΄ L, λβ΄ ιϛ΄ NACam.¹, λβ΄ ιβ΄ Cam.²
[2] ρβ΄ VPLMDEProc., ρβ΄ μη΄ NACam.
[3] λβ΄ VPLMDEProc., λβ΄ ιϛ΄ NACam.¹, λβ΄ ιβ΄ Cam.²
[4] ἐν τοῖς τῆς ὑπεροχῆς ἄρα χρόνοις ἑβδομήκοντα VD, cf. Proc.; ἐν τοῖς τῆς ἄρα ὑπ. ὁ χρόν. P, ἐν ταύταις ἄρα ὑπ. ὁ χρόνος L, ἐν τοῖς (add. τῆς E) ὑπὲρ γῆν (γῆς E) ἄρα χρόν. ο΄ MNAECam., ο΄ λβ΄ A.
[5] ἐπὶ VPLDE, ὑπὸ MNACam., ἐν Proc.
[6] μηδενὸς VPLMDE, μηδὲν NACam.

in which again, because the prorogative sign is at mid-heaven, Aries and Taurus[1] pass through the meridian.

In the same way let the beginning of Aries be setting, so that the beginning of Cancer may be at mid-heaven and the beginning of Gemini may be removed from the mid-heaven above the earth in the direction of the leading signs[2] by 32 equinoctial periods. Since, then, again the beginning of Aries is six ordinary hours removed from the meridian in the direction of the occident, if we multiply this by 17 we shall have 102 times, which will be the distance of the beginning of Gemini from the meridian when it sets. At its first position also it was distant from the same point 32 times; hence it moved to the occident in the 70 times of the difference, in which period also Aries and Taurus descend and the opposite signs Libra and Scorpio ascend.[3]

Now let it be assumed that the beginning of Aries is not on any of the angles, but removed, for example, three ordinary hours from the meridian in the direction of the leading signs, so that the 18th degree of Taurus is at mid-heaven, and in its first position the beginning of Gemini is 13 equinoctial times removed from the mid-heaven above the earth in the order of

[1] The table of the *Almagest* gives 45 times 5 min. for the combined ascensions of these two signs in the latitude of lower Egypt.
[2] *I.e.* beyond the meridian and toward Aries.
[3] The table of the *Almagest* gives 70 times 23 min.

PTOLEMY

οὖν πάλιν τοὺς ιζ'[1] χρόνους ἐπὶ τὰς γ' ὥρας πολλαπλασιάσωμεν, ἀφέξει μὲν καὶ κατὰ τὴν δευτέραν θέσιν ἡ τῶν Διδύμων ἀρχὴ τῆς μεσημβρίας εἰς τὰ προηγούμενα χρόνους να',[2] τοὺς δὲ πάντας ποιήσει χρόνους ξδ,.[3] ἐποίει δὲ διὰ τῆς αὐτῆς ἀγωγῆς, ὅτε μὲν ἀνέτελλεν ὁ ἀφετικὸς τόπος, χρόνους μϚ',[4] ὅτε δὲ ἐμεσουράνει χρόνους νη', ὅτε δὲ ἔδυνε χρόνους ο'.[5] διήνεγκε μὲν ἄρα καὶ ὁ κατὰ τὴν μεταξὺ θέσιν τῆς τε μεσουρανήσεως καὶ τῆς δύσεως τῶν χρόνων ἀριθμὸς ἑκάστου τῶν ἄλλων. γέγονε γὰρ χρόνων ξδ', διήνεγκε δὲ κατὰ τὸ ἀνάλογον τῆς τῶν γ' ὡρῶν ὑπεροχῆς, ἐπειδήπερ αὕτη[6] ἐπὶ μὲν τῶν ἄλλων[7] κατὰ τὰ κέντρα τεταρτημορίων ιβ' χρόνων ἦν, ἐπὶ δὲ τῆς τῶν τριῶν ὡρῶν ἀποστάσεως ἐξ χρόνων. ἐπεὶ δὲ καὶ ἐπὶ πάντων ἡ αὐτὴ σχεδὸν ἀναλογία συντηρεῖται, δυνατὸν ἔσται καὶ κατὰ τοῦτον τὸν τρόπον ἁπλούστερον τῇ μεθόδῳ χρῆσθαι. πάλιν γὰρ ἀνατελλούσης μὲν τῆς προηγουμένης μοίρας ταῖς μέχρι τῆς ἑπομένης ἀναφοραῖς χρησόμεθα, μεσουρανούσης δὲ ταῖς ἐπ' ὀρθῆς τῆς σφαίρας, δυνούσης δὲ ταῖς καταφοραῖς. ὅταν δὲ μεταξὺ τούτων ᾖ, οἷον λόγου ἕνεκεν ἐπὶ τῆς ἐκκειμένης διαστάσεως τοῦ Κριοῦ, ληψόμεθα πρῶτον τοὺς

[1] ιζ' VPLMDEProc. ; ιζ' η' NACam.
[2] να' VPLMDEProc. ; να' κδ' ACam. ; να' δ' N.
[3] ξδ' VPLMDE ; ξδ' κδ' NACam.², ξδ' κζ' Cam.¹
[4] μϚ' libri Proc. Cam.¹ ; με' Cam.²
[5] ο' VPLMDEProc. ; ο' λβ' NACam.¹, λϚ' Cam.²
[6] αὕτη VAD, αὐτὴ PL, αὐτὸς MNECam.
[7] ἄλλων VPLADProc., ὅλων MNECam.

TETRABIBLOS III. 10

the following signs.¹ If, then, again we multiply 17 equinoctial times into the three hours, the beginning of Gemini will at its second position be distant from mid-heaven in the direction of the leading signs 51 equinoctial times, and it will make in all 64 times.² But it made 46 times by the same procedure when the prorogative place was rising, 58 when it was in mid-heaven, and 70 when it was setting. Hence the number of equinoctial times at the position between mid-heaven and the occident differs from each of the others. For it is 64, and the difference is proportional to the excess of three hours,³ since this was 12 equinoctial times in the case of the other quadrants at the centres, but 6 equinoctial times in the case of the distance of three hours. And inasmuch as in all cases approximately the same proportion is observed, it will be possible to use the method in this simpler way. For again, when the precedent degree is at rising, we shall employ the ascensions up to the subsequent; if it is at mid-heaven, the degrees on the right sphere; and if it is setting, the descensions. But when it is between these points, for example, at the aforesaid interval from Aries, we shall take

---

¹ Thus, the first of Aries is west of the meridian and the first of Gemini east of it.

² *I.e.* 13 times to reach the meridian, plus 51 times beyond it.

³ *I.e.* the centres are 6 hours removed from one another, and a difference of 12 times is observed when the movement of the subsequent place up to one of the centres is compared with its movement to the next centre in order. Hence when the prorogative place does not move between centre and centre, 6 hours, but only half of that time, this differential also will be only ½ of its full amount, 6 times instead of 12 times.

PTOLEMY

ἐπιβάλλοντας χρόνους ἑκατέρῳ[1] τῶν περιεχόντων[2] κέντρων, εὑρήσομεν δέ, ἐπειδὴ μετὰ τὸ μεσουράνημα τὸ ὑπὲρ γῆν ὑπέκειτο ἡ ἀρχὴ τοῦ Κριοῦ μεταξὺ τοῦ τε μεσουρανοῦντος κέντρου καὶ τοῦ δύνοντος, τοὺς ἐπιβάλλοντας χρόνους[3] μέχρι τῆς ἀρχῆς τῶν Διδύμων, τῶν μὲν συμμεσουρανήσεων νη΄, τῶν δὲ συγκαταδύσεων ο΄. ἔπειτα μαθόντες,[4] ὡς πρόκειται, πόσας καιρικὰς ὥρας ἀπέχει τὸ προηγούμενον τμῆμα ὁποτέρου τῶν κέντρων, ὅσον[5] ἂν ὦσι μέρος αὗται τῶν τοῦ τε τεταρτημορίου καιρικῶν ὡρῶν ἔξ, τοσοῦτον μέρος τῆς ἀμφοτέρων τῶν συναγωγῶν ὑπεροχῆς προσθήσομεν ἢ ἀφελοῦμεν τῶν συγκρινομένων κέντρων ·[6] οἷον ἐπεὶ τῶν προκειμένων ο΄ καὶ νη΄[7] ἡ ὑπεροχή ἐστι χρόνων ιβ΄, ὑπέκειτο δὲ τὰς ἴσας καιρικὰς ὥρας γ΄ ὁ προηγούμενος τόπος ἑκατέρου τῶν κέντρων ἀπέχων, αἵ εἰσι τῶν ἐξ ὡρῶν ἥμισυ μέρος, λαβόντες[8] καὶ τῶν ιβ΄ τὸ ἥμισυ καὶ ἤτοι τοῖς νη΄ προσθέντες ἢ τῶν ο΄ ἀφελόντες, εὑρήσομεν τὴν ἐπιβολὴν χρόνων ξδ΄.[9] εἰ δέ γε δύο καιρικὰς ὥρας ἀπεῖχεν ὁπότερον τῶν κέντρων, αἵ εἰσι τῶν Ϛ΄ ὡρῶν τρίτον μέρος,[10] τὸ τρίτον πάλιν τῶν τῆς ὑπεροχῆς ιβ΄ χρόνων, τουτέστι τοὺς δ΄, εἰ μὲν ἡ τῶν δύο ὡρῶν ἀποχὴ ἀπὸ τοῦ μεσουρανήματος

---

[1] ἑκατέρῳ VMADE, -ων PLNCam.
[2] περιεχόντων VP (-εχώντων) LD, -ομένων NMAECam.
[3] Post χρόνους add. ξδ΄ ἔγγιστα NACam.; om. VPLMDEProc.
[4] μαθόντες VPLMADEProc.; -ωμεν NCam.
[5] Post ὅσον add. δ᾽ Cam.; om. libri.
[6] τῶν συγκρινομένων κέντρων VLDProc., τῷ συγκρινομένῳ κέντρῳ PMNAECam.
[7] ο΄ καὶ νη΄ VPLDProc.; ἐτῶν add. VD.; ὡρῶν MNAECam.

TETRABIBLOS III. 10

first the equinoctial times corresponding to each of the surrounding angles, and we shall find, since the beginning of Aries was assumed to be beyond the mid-heaven above the earth, between mid-heaven and the occident, that the corresponding equinoctial times up to the first of Gemini from mid-heaven are 58 and from the occident 70. Next let us ascertain, as was set forth above,[1] how many ordinary hours the precedent section is removed from either of the angles, and whatever fraction they may be of the six ordinary hours of the quadrant, that fraction of the difference between both sums we shall add to or subtract from the angle with which comparison is made. For example, since the difference between the above mentioned 70 and 58 is 12 times, and it was assumed that the precedent place was removed by an equal number of ordinary hours, three, from each of the angles, which are one half of the six hours, then taking also one-half of the 12 equinoctial times and either adding them to the 58 or subtracting them from the 70, we shall find the result to be 64 times. But if it was removed two ordinary hours from either one of the angles, which are one-third of the six hours, again we shall take one-third of the 12 times of the excess, that is, 4, and if the removal by two hours had been assumed to be from the mid-heaven, we would have added

[1] See p. 297.

---

[8] δὲ post λαβόντες add. MNCam.
[9] ξα' NMCam.¹   [10] τρίτον μέρος om. MCam.

ὑπέκειτο,[1] προσεθήκαμεν ἂν τοῖς νη' χρόνοις · εἰ δ' ἀπὸ τοῦ δύνοντος, ἀφείλομεν ἂν ἀπὸ τῶν ο'.

Ὁ μὲν οὖν τρόπος τῆς τῶν χρονικῶν διαστάσεων[2] ποσότητος οὕτως ἡμῖν κατὰ τὸ ἀκόλουθον ὀφείλει λαμβάνεσθαι. διακρινοῦμεν δὲ λοιπὸν ἐφ' ἑκάστης τῶν προειρημένων ὑπαντήσεων ἢ καταδύσεων, κατὰ τὴν ἀπὸ τῶν ὀλιγοχρονιωτέρων τάξιν, τάς τε ἀναιρετικὰς καὶ τὰς κλιμακτηρικὰς καὶ τὰς ἄλλως παροδικάς, διά τε τοῦ ἢ κεκακῶσθαι τὴν ὑπάντησιν ἢ βοηθεῖσθαι κατὰ τὸν προειρημένον ἡμῖν τρόπον, καὶ διὰ τῶν καθ' ἕκαστον τῶν διασημαινομένων ἐκ τῆς ὑπαντήσεως χρονικῶν ἐπεμβάσεων. κεκακωμένων τε γὰρ ἅμα τῶν τόπων καὶ τῆς πρὸς τὴν ἐπέμβασιν τῶν ἐτῶν παρόδου τῶν ἀστέρων κακοποιούσης τοὺς κυριωτάτους τόπους, ἄντικρυς θανάτους ὑπονοητέον· τοῦ δ' ἑτέρου τούτων φιλανθρωποῦντος κλιμακτῆρας μεγάλους καὶ ἐπισφαλεῖς · ἀμφοτέρων δὲ[3] νωθρίας μόνον ἢ βλαβὰς καὶ καθαιρέσεις παροδικάς, τῆς καὶ ἐν τούτοις ἰδιότητος λαμβανομένης ἀπὸ τῆς τῶν ὑπαντικῶν[4] τόπων πρὸς τὰ τῆς γενέσεως πράγματα συνοικειώσεως. οὐδὲν δὲ ἐνίοτε κωλύει, διστάζομένων τῶν τὴν ἀναιρετικὴν κυρίαν λαμβάνειν ὀφειλόντων, τὰς καθ' ἕκαστον αὐτῶν ὑπαντήσεις ἐπιλογι-

[1] ἢ ... ἀποχὴ ... ὑπέκειτο VPLDProc.; αἱ ... ἀποχαὶ ... ὑπέκειντο MNAECam.
[2] διαστάσεων PLA, -εως VMNDECam.
[3] δὲ om. ECam.   [4] ὑπαντητικῶν MNECam.

---

[1] The prorogations, which are determined by the approach of the anaeretic place to that of the prorogator, or the setting of the prorogator.

them to the 58 times, but if it was measured from the occident we would have subtracted them from 70.

The method of ascertaining the amount of the temporal intervals ought in this way consistently to be followed. For the rest, we shall determine in each of the aforesaid cases of approach or setting,[1] in the order of those that ascend more rapidly, those which are destructive, climacteric, or otherwise transitional,[2] according as the meeting is afflicted or assisted in the way we have already explained,[3] and by means of the particular significance of the predictions made from the temporal ingresses of the meeting.[4] For when at the same time the places are afflicted and the transit of the stars relative to the ingress of the years of life afflicts the governing places, we must understand that death is definitely signified; if one of them is benignant, great and dangerous crises; if both are benignant, only sluggishness, injuries, or transitory disasters. In these matters the special quality is ascertained from the familiarity of the occurrent places with the circumstances of the nativity. Sometimes, when it is doubtful which ought to take over the destroying

[2] *I.e.* we shall discover whether the periods determined by such prorogations as have been described are terminated by actual death, some important crisis, or an event of less importance. *Cf.* Hephaestion ap. *CCAG*, viii. 2, p. 81, 1 ff.

[3] The reference is to what was said earlier in the chapter about the influence of the various planets; see pp. 281 ff.

[4] *Cf.* what is said about the chronocrators in the latter part of iv. 10.

PTOLEMY

ζομένους ἤτοι ταῖς μάλιστα πρὸς τὰ ἐκβάντα ἤδη τῶν συμπτωμάτων συμφωνούσαις καὶ πρὸς τὰ μέλλοντα κατακολουθεῖν, ἢ πρὸς ἁπάσας ὡς κατ' ἰσότητα τῆς δυνάμεως ἰσχυούσας παρατηρητικῶς ἔχειν, τὸ μᾶλλον καὶ ἧττον αὐτῶν κατὰ τὸν αὐτὸν τρόπον ἐπισκεπτομένους.

⟨ιᾱ.⟩ Περὶ μορφῆς καὶ κράσεως σωματικῆς

Ἐφοδευομένης δὲ καὶ τῆς τοῦ περὶ χρόνων ζωῆς λόγου πραγματείας, λέγομεν ἀρχὴν τὴν κατὰ μέρος λαβόντες κατὰ τὴν οἰκείαν τάξιν περί τε τῆς μορφῆς καὶ τῆς σωματικῆς διατυπώσεως, ἐπειδὴ καὶ τὰ τοῦ σώματος τῶν τῆς ψυχῆς[1] προτυποῦται κατὰ φύσιν, τοῦ μὲν σώματος διὰ τὸ ὑλικώτερον συγγεννωμένας ἔχοντος σχεδὸν τὰς τῶν ἰδιοσυγκράσεων φαντασίας, τῆς δὲ ψυχῆς μετὰ ταῦτα καὶ κατὰ μικρὸν τὰς ἀπὸ τῆς πρώτης αἰτίας ἐπιτηδειότητας ἀναδεικνυούσης, τῶν δ' ἐκτὸς ἔτι μᾶλλον ὕστερον[2] κατὰ τὸν ἐφεξῆς χρόνον ἐπισυμπιπτόντων.

Παρατηρητέον οὖν καθ' ὅλου μὲν τὸν ἀνατολικὸν ὁρίζοντα καὶ τοὺς ἐπόντας ἢ τοὺς τὴν οἰκοδεσποτίαν αὐτοῦ λαμβάνοντας τῶν πλανωμένων καθ' ὃν εἰρήκαμεν τρόπον, ἐπὶ μέρους δὲ καὶ τὴν σελήνην ὡσαύτως. διὰ γὰρ τῆς τῶν τόπων τούτων ἀμφοτέρων καὶ τῆς τῶν οἰκοδεσποτησάντων διαμορφωτικῆς φύσεως καὶ τῆς καθ' ἑκάτερον εἶδος συγκράσεως

---

[1] τῶν τῆς ψυχῆς VPL (τὸν ...) D, πρὸς τὴν ψυχὴν MNAEProc. Cam.
[2] ὕστερον VP (εἴστ-) LDProc.; om. MNAECam.

power, there is nothing to prevent our calculating the occourses of each and then either following, in predicting the future, the occourses which most agree with past events, or observing them all, as having equal power, determining as before the question of their degree.

11. *Of Bodily Form and Temperament.*

Now that the procedure in the matter of the length of life has been explained, we speak about the form and character of the body, beginning the detailed discussion in the proper order, inasmuch as naturally, too, the bodily parts are formed prior to the soul; for the body, because it is more material, carries almost from birth the outward appearances of its idiosyncrasies, while the soul shows forth the characters conferred upon it by the first cause only afterwards and little by little, and external accidental qualities come about still later in time.

We must, then, in general observe the eastern horizon and the planets that are upon it or assume its rulership in the way already explained;[1] and in particular also the moon as well; for it is through the formative power of these two places[2] and of their rulers and through the mixture of the two kinds,[3]

---

[1] See iii. 2 (p. 233).

[2] The eastern horizon and the place where the moon is found.

[3] Apparently, the influence of the places and that of their rulers are the two "kinds" to which reference is made.

PTOLEMY

καὶ ἔτι τῆς τῶν συνανατελλόντων αὐτοῖς ἀπλανῶν ἀστέρων σχηματογραφίας τὰ περὶ τὰς διατυπώσεις τῶν σωμάτων θεωρεῖται, πρωτευόντων μὲν τῇ δυνάμει τῶν τὴν οἰκοδεσποτίαν ἐχόντων ἀστέρων, ἐπισυνεργούσης δὲ καὶ τῆς τῶν τόπων αὐτῶν ἰδιοτροπίας.

Τὸ μέντοι καθ' ἕκαστον, καὶ ὡς ἄν τις ἁπλῶς οὕτως ἀποδοίη, τοῦτον ἔχει τὸν τρόπον. πρῶτον γὰρ ἐπὶ τῶν ἀστέρων ὁ μὲν τοῦ Κρόνου ἀνατολικὸς ὢν τὴν μὲν μορφὴν μελίχροας ποιεῖ καὶ εὐεκτικοὺς καὶ μελανότριχας καὶ οὐλοκεφάλους καὶ δασυστέρνους[1] καὶ μεσοφθάλμους[2] καὶ συμμέτρους τοῖς μεγέθεσι, τῇ δὲ κράσει τὸ μᾶλλον ἔχοντας ἐν τῷ ὑγρῷ καὶ ψυχρῷ· δυτικὸς δὲ ὑπάρχων τῇ μὲν μορφῇ μέλανας καὶ σπινώδεις καὶ μικροὺς καὶ ἁπλότριχας καὶ ὑποψίλους καὶ ὑπορρύθμους καὶ μελανοφθάλμους, τῇ δὲ κράσει τὸ[3] μᾶλλον ἔχοντας ἐν τῷ ξηρῷ καὶ ψυχρῷ.

Ὁ δὲ τοῦ Διὸς οἰκοδεσποτήσας τοὺς προκειμένους τόπους ἀνατολικὸς τῇ μὲν μορφῇ ποιεῖ λευκοὺς ἐπὶ τὸ εὔχρουν καὶ μεσότριχας καὶ μεγαλοφθάλμους[4] καὶ εὐμεγέθεις καὶ ἀξιωματικούς, τῇ δὲ κράσει τὸ πλέον ἔχοντας ἐν τῷ θερμῷ καὶ ὑγρῷ. δυτικὸς δὲ ὑπάρχων τῇ μὲν χρόᾳ λευκοὺς μέν, οὐκ ἐπὶ τὸ εὔχρουν δὲ ὁμοίως·[5] τετανότριχάς τε ἢ καὶ ἀναφαλάκρους[6] καὶ μεσοφαλάκρους καὶ μετρίους τοῖς

---

[1] καὶ δασυστέρνους VPLD, cf. Proc.; om. MNAECam.
[2] μεσοφθάλμους VPLDProc., μεγαλοφθάλμους MNAECam.
[3] τὸ om. MNECam.
[4] μεγαλοφθάλμους VP (-μας) LDE Proc., μελανοφθάλμους MNACam.

TETRABIBLOS III. 11

and furthermore through the forms of the fixed stars that are rising at the same time, that the conformation of the body is ascertained; the ruling planets have most power in this matter and the special characters of their places aid them.

The detailed account, then, as one might report it in simple terms, is this: First, among the planets, Saturn, if he is in the orient, makes his subjects in appearance dark-skinned, robust, black-haired, curly-haired, hairy-chested, with eyes of moderate size, of middling stature, and in temperament having an excess of the moist and cold. If Saturn is setting, in appearance he makes them dark, slender, small, straight-haired, with little hair on the body, rather graceful, and black-eyed; in temperament, sharing most in the cold and dry.

Jupiter, as the ruler of the aforesaid regions, when he is rising, makes his subjects in appearance light of skin, but in such a way as to have a good colour, with moderately curling hair and large eyes, tall, and commanding respect; in temperament they exceed in the hot and the moist. When Jupiter is setting, he makes his subjects light, to be sure, but not as before, in such a way as to give them a good colour, and with lank hair or even bald in front and on the

---

[5] δὲ post ὁμοίως add. MNECam.

[6] ἀναφαλάκρους Proc., ἀνωφαλάκρους Cam.², ἀναφαλανταίους VD, ἀναφαντολιακοὺς P, ἀναφανταλιαίους L, ἀναφαλάνδους MNAECam.¹.

μεγέθεσι, τῇ δὲ κράσει τὸ πλέον ἔχοντας ἐν τῷ ὑγρῷ.

Ὁ δὲ τοῦ Ἄρεως ὁμοίως[1] ἀνατολικὸς τῇ μὲν μορφῇ ποιεῖ λευκερύθρους καὶ εὐμεγέθεις καὶ εὐέκτας καὶ γλαυκοφθάλμους καὶ δασεῖς καὶ μεσότριχας, τῇ δὲ κράσει τὸ πλέον ἔχοντας ἐν τῷ θερμῷ καὶ ξηρῷ. δυτικὸς δὲ ὑπάρχων τῇ μὲν μορφῇ ἐρυθροὺς ἁπλῶς καὶ μετρίους τοῖς μεγέθεσι καὶ μικροφθάλμους[2] καὶ ὑποψίλους καὶ ξανθότριχας καὶ τετανούς, τῇ δὲ κράσει τὸ πλέον ἔχοντας ἐν τῷ ξηρῷ.

Ὁ δὲ τῆς Ἀφροδίτης τὰ παραπλήσια ποιεῖ τῷ τοῦ Διός, ἐπὶ μέντοι τὸ εὐμορφότερον καὶ ἐπιχαριτώτερον καὶ γυναικοπρεπωδέστερον καὶ θηλυμορφότερον[3] καὶ εὐχυμότερον καὶ τρυφερώτερον. ἰδίως δὲ τοὺς ὀφθαλμοὺς ποιεῖ μετὰ τοῦ εὐπρεποῦς ὑποχαροπούς.

Ὁ δὲ τοῦ Ἑρμοῦ ἀνατολικὸς τῇ μὲν μορφῇ ποιεῖ μελίχροας καὶ συμμέτρους τοῖς μεγέθεσι καὶ εὐρύθμους καὶ μικροφθάλμους καὶ μεσότριχας, τῇ δὲ κράσει τὸ πλέον ἔχοντας ἐν τῷ θερμῷ· δυτικὸς δὲ ὑπάρχων τῇ μὲν μορφῇ λευκοὺς μέν, οὐκ ἐπὶ τὸ εὔχρουν δὲ ὁμοίως, τετανότριχας,[4] μελανοχλώρους[5] καὶ σπινοὺς[6] καὶ ἰσχνοὺς καὶ λοξοφθάλμους τε[7] καὶ αἰγοποὺς[8] καὶ ὑπερύθρους, τῇ δὲ κράσει τὸ πλέον ἔχοντας ἐν τῷ ξηρῷ.

[1] ὁμοίως VPLD, om. MNAECam.
[2] μικροφθάλμους VPLDEProc., μικροκεφάλους MNACam.
[3] καὶ θηλυμορφότερον (or -φωτ-) VPLDProc., καὶ εὐσχημονέστερον MNAECam.
[4] λευκοὺς . . . τετανότριχας VPLDProc., om. MNAECam.

crown, and of average stature; in temperament they have an excess of the moist.

Similarly, Mars, when rising, makes his subjects in appearance red and white of complexion, tall and robust, gray-eyed, with thick hair, somewhat curly, and in temperament showing an excess of the warm and dry. When he is setting, he makes them in appearance simply ruddy, of middle height, with small eyes, not much hair on the body, and straight yellow hair; their temperament exceeds in the dry.

Venus has effects similar to Jupiter's, but is apt to make her subjects more shapely, graceful, womanish, effeminate in figure, plump, and luxurious. On her own proper account she makes the eyes bright as well as beautiful.

Mercury, in the orient, makes his subjects in appearance sallow, of moderate height, graceful, with small eyes and moderately curling hair; in temperament, showing an excess of the warm. In the occident he makes them, in appearance, of light but not of good colouring, with straight hair and olive complexion, lean and spare, with glancing, brilliant eyes,[1] and somewhat ruddy; in temperament they exceed in the dry.

---

[1] The text is perhaps corrupt; αἰγοπός seems to be otherwise unknown.

---

[5] μελανοχλώρους PLProc., μελαγχλώρους VD, μελίχροας MNAECam.

[6] σπινούς PLEProc., σπιρούς VD, σπανούς MNACam.

[7] λοξοφθάλμους τε PL, ληξοφθάλμους τε V, ξηροφθάλμους τε D, κοινοφθάλμους N, κυνοφθάλμους Cam.¹, κοιλοφθάλμους MAECam.²

[8] αἰγοπούς P (-ωπ-) LProc., αἰγόπλους VD, αἰγόποδας MNAECam.¹, αἰγίλοπας Cam.²

PTOLEMY

Συνεργοῦσι δ' ἑκάστῳ τούτων σχηματισθέντες, ὁ μὲν ἥλιος ἐπὶ τὸ μεγαλοπρεπέστερον καὶ εὐεκτικώτερον, ἡ δὲ σελήνη, καὶ μάλισθ' ὅταν τὴν ἀπόρροιαν αὐτῆς ἐπέχωσι, καθ' ὅλου μὲν ἐπὶ τὸ συμμετρώτερον καὶ ἰσχνότερον καὶ τῇ κράσει ὑγρότερον, κατὰ μέρος δ' ἀναλόγως τῇ τῶν φωτισμῶν ἰδιότητι κατὰ τὴν ἐν ἀρχῇ τῆς συντάξεως ἐκτεθειμένην κρᾶσιν.[1]

Πάλιν δὲ καθ' ὅλου ἑῷοι μὲν ὄντες καὶ φάσεις ποιησάμενοι μεγαλοποιοῦσι τὰ σώματα, στηρίζοντες δὲ τὸ πρῶτον ἰσχυρὰ καὶ εὔτονα, προηγούμενοι δὲ ἀσύμμετρα, τὸ δὲ δεύτερον στηρίζοντες ἀσθενέστερα, δύνοντες δὲ ἄδοξα μὲν παντελῶς, οἰστικὰ δὲ κακουχιῶν καὶ συνοχῶν.[2]

Καὶ τῶν τόπων δὲ αὐτῶν πρὸς τοὺς σχηματισμοὺς μάλιστα τῶν διατυπώσεων καὶ τὰς κράσεις, ὡς ἔφαμεν, συνεργούντων,[3] καθ' ὅλου δὲ πάλιν τὸ μὲν ἀπὸ ἐαρινῆς ἰσημερίας ἐπὶ θερινὴν τροπὴν τεταρτημόριον ποιεῖ εὔχροας εὐμεγέθεις εὐέκτας εὐοφθάλμους, τὸ πλέον ἔχοντας ἐν τῷ ὑγρῷ

[1] κατὰ ... κρᾶσιν VPLD, καθ' ὡς περὶ κράσεως ἐν ἀρχῇ τῆς συντάξεως ἔφαμεν Proc., καθάπερ ἐν ἀρχῇ τῆς συντάξεως ἐξεθέμεθα MNAECam.
[2] καὶ συνοχῶν libri, cf. Proc.; om. Cam.
[3] συνεργούντων VPLDProc., συνοικειούντων MNECam., συνοικειούντων καὶ συνεργούντων A.

---

[1] See i. 24.
[2] Probably a reference to the last paragraph of i. 10, but the anonymous commentator (p. 136, ed. Wolf) seems to think it refers to i. 8.
[3] The commentator's (*l.c.*) explanation of this phrase is " being oriental " (ἀνατολικοὶ τυχόντες). The φάσεις,

TETRABIBLOS III. 11

The luminaries assist each of these when they bear an aspect to them, the sun tending to a more impressive and robust effect, and the moon, especially when she is separating [1] from the planets, in general tending toward better proportion and greater slenderness, and toward a more moist temperament; but in particular cases her effect is proportioned to the special quality of her illumination, in accordance with the system of intermixture explained in the beginning of the treatise.[2]

Again, generally, when the planets are morning stars and make an appearance,[3] they make the body large; at their first station, powerful and muscular; when they are moving forward,[4] not well-proportioned; at their second station, rather weak; and at setting, entirely without repute but able to bear hardship and oppression.

Likewise their places, as we have said,[5] take an important part in the formation of the bodily characters and temperaments. In general terms, once more, the quadrant from the spring equinox to the summer solstice makes the subjects well-favoured in complexion, stature, robustness, and eyes, and exceeding

---

"appearances," "phases," are the positions of the planets with respect to the sun.

[4] Strangely enough, according to the ancient terminology, when the planets are "moving forward" (in the direction of the diurnal movement, "in the direction of the leading signs," or east to west) they are "retreating" (ἀναποδί-ζοντες) with respect to their (west to east) motion in their own orbits; cf. Bouché-Leclercq, p. 429, 1 (on this passage) and p. 117, 1. The commentator (l.c.) here says, τουτέστιν, ἀφετικοί (probably ἀφαιρετικοί should be read).

[5] He refers to places in the zodiac and to i. 10.

καὶ θερμῷ· τὸ δ' ἀπὸ θερινῆς τροπῆς μέχρι μετοπωρινῆς ἰσημερίας μεσόχροας συμμέτρους τοῖς μεγέθεσιν εὐέκτας μεγαλοφθάλμους[1] δασεῖς οὐλότριχας, τὸ πλέον ἔχοντας ἐν τῷ θερμῷ καὶ ξηρῷ· τὸ δ' ἀπὸ μετοπωρινῆς ἰσημερίας μέχρι χειμερινῆς τροπῆς μελίχροας ἰσχνοὺς σπινώδεις παθηνοὺς[2] μεσότριχας εὐοφθάλμους, τὸ πλέον ἔχοντας ἐν τῷ ξηρῷ καὶ ψυχρῷ. τὸ δ' ἀπὸ χειμερινῆς τροπῆς ἕως ἐαρινῆς ἰσημερίας μελανόχροας συμμέτρους τοῖς μεγέθεσι τετανότριχας ὑποψίλους ὑπορρύθμους,[3] τὸ πλέον ἔχοντας ἐν τῷ ὑγρῷ καὶ ψυχρῷ.

Κατὰ μέρος δὲ τὰ μὲν ἀνθρωποειδῆ τῶν ζῳδίων τῶν τε ἐν τῷ ζῳδιακῷ καὶ τῶν ἐκτὸς εὔρυθμα καὶ σύμμετρα τοῖς σχήμασι τὰ σώματα κατασκευάζει. τὰ δ' ἑτερόμορφα μετασχηματίζει πρὸς τὸ τῆς ἰδίας μορφώσεως οἰκεῖον τὰς τοῦ σώματος συμμετρίας καὶ κατά τινα λόγον ἀφομοιοῖ τὰ οἰκεῖα μέρη τοῖς ἑαυτῶν, ἤτοι ἐπὶ τὸ μεῖζον καὶ ἔλαττον ἢ ἐπὶ τὸ ἰσχυρότερον καὶ ἀσθενέστερον[4] ἢ ἐπὶ τὸ εὐρυθμώτερον καὶ ἀρρυθμώτερον·[5] ἐπὶ τὸ μεῖζον μὲν ὡς λόγου ἕνεκεν ὁ Λέων καὶ ἡ Παρθένος καὶ ὁ Τοξότης, ἐπὶ τὸ ἔλαττον δὲ ὡς οἱ Ἰχθῦς καὶ ὁ Καρκίνος καὶ ὁ Αἰγόκερως. καὶ πάλιν ὡς[6] τοῦ Κριοῦ καὶ τοῦ Ταύρου καὶ τοῦ Λέοντος τὰ μὲν ἄνω καὶ ἐμπρόσθια ἐπὶ τὸ εὐεκτικώτερον, τὰ δὲ κάτω καὶ ὀπίσθια ἐπὶ τὸ ἀσθενέστερον· τὸ δ' ἐναντίον ὡς τὸ

---

[1] μεγαλοφθάλμους VDProc., μελανοφθάλμους MNAECam., ὑοφθάλμους P, εὐθάλμους L.

[2] παθηνοὺς VD, παθινοὺς PL, νοσερούς Proc.; σπανοὺς NACam., σπανθινοὺς ME.

TETRABIBLOS III. 11

in the moist and warm. The quadrant from the summer solstice to the autumn equinox produces individuals with moderately good complexion and moderate height, robust, with large eyes and thick and curly hair, exceeding in the warm and dry. The quadrant from the autumn equinox to the winter solstice makes them sallow, spare, slender, sickly, with moderately curling hair and good eyes, exceeding in the dry and cold. The quadrant from the winter solstice to the spring equinox produces individuals of dark complexion, moderate height, straight hair, with little hair on their bodies, somewhat graceful, and exceeding in the cold and moist.

In particular, the constellations both within and outside of the zodiac which are of human shape produce bodies which are harmonious of movement and well-proportioned; those however which are of other than human shape modify the bodily proportions to correspond to their own peculiarities, and after a fashion make the corresponding parts like their own, larger and smaller, or stronger and weaker, or more and less graceful. For example, Leo, Virgo, and Sagittarius make them larger; others, as Pisces, Cancer, and Capricorn, smaller. And again, as in the case of Aries, Taurus, and Leo, the upper and fore parts make them more robust and the lower and hind parts weaker. Conversely the fore parts of

---

[3] ὑπορ(ρ)ύθμους VNMADE, ὑποερύθμους PL, εὐαρμόστους Proc., om. Cam.
[4] Post ἀσθενέστερον add. ἢ ἐπὶ τὸ VPLD, καὶ MNAECam.
[5] καὶ ἀρρυθμότερον E; ἀρυθμώτερον (ἀριθ- L) καὶ εὐρυθμώτερον PL; cf. Proc.; καὶ app. om. VMNADCam.
[6] ἐπὶ post ὡς add. MNAECam.

τοῦ Τοξότου καὶ τοῦ Σκορπίου καὶ τῶν Διδύμων τὰ μὲν ἐμπρόσθια ἐπὶ τὸ ἰσχνότερον,[1] τὰ δὲ ὀπίσθια ἐπὶ τὸ εὐεκτικώτερον· ὁμοίως δὲ ὡς ἡ μὲν Παρθένος καὶ αἱ Χηλαὶ καὶ ὁ Τοξότης ἐπὶ τὸ σύμμετρον καὶ εὔρυθμον, ὁ δὲ Σκορπίος καὶ οἱ Ἰχθῦς καὶ ὁ Ταῦρος ἐπὶ τὸ ἄρρυθμον καὶ ἀσύμμετρον, καὶ ἐπὶ τῶν ἄλλων ὁμοίως. ἅπερ ἅπαντα συνεφορῶντας καὶ συνεπικίρναντας[2] προσήκει τὴν ἐκ τῆς κράσεως συναγομένην ἰδιοτροπίαν περί τε τὰς μορφώσεις καὶ τὰς κράσεις τῶν σωμάτων καταστοχάζεσθαι.

⟨ιβ.⟩ Περὶ σινῶν καὶ παθῶν σωματικῶν

Ἑπομένου δὲ τούτοις τοῦ περὶ τὰ σωματικὰ σίνη τε καὶ πάθη λόγου, συνάψομεν αὐτοῖς κατὰ τὸ[3] ἑξῆς τὴν κατὰ τοῦτο τὸ εἶδος συνισταμένην ἐπίσκεψιν ἔχουσαν οὕτως· καὶ ἐνταῦθα γὰρ[4] πρὸς μὲν τὴν καθ' ὅλου διάληψιν ἀποβλέπειν δεῖ πρὸς τὰ τοῦ ὁρίζοντος δύο κέντρα, τουτέστι τὸ ἀνατέλλον καὶ τὸ δῦνον, μάλιστα δὲ πρός τε τὸ δῦνον αὐτὸ καὶ πρὸς τὸ προδῦνον,[5] ὅ ἐστιν ἀσύνδετον τῷ ἀνατολικῷ κέντρῳ, καὶ παρατηρεῖν τοὺς κακωτικοὺς τῶν ἀστέρων πῶς ἐσχηματισμένοι πρὸς αὐτὰ τυγχάνουσιν. ἐὰν γὰρ πρὸς τὰς ἐπαναφερομένας μοίρας τῶν εἰρημένων τόπων ὦσιν ἑστῶτες

[1] ἰσχνότερον VPA, τῶν ἰσχνοτέρων L, ἰσχυρότερον D, ἀσθενέστερον MNECam.Proc.
[2] συνεπικίρναντας VD; cf. Proc.; συνεπικρίνοντας PLMNAE Cam.

TETRABIBLOS III. 11-12

Sagittarius, Scorpio, and Gemini cause slenderness and the hind parts robustness. Similarly too Virgo, Libra, and Sagittarius tend to make them well-proportioned and graceful, while Scorpio, Pisces, and Taurus bring about awkwardness and disproportion. So it is with the rest, and it is fitting that we should observe and combine all these things and make a conjecture as to the character which results from the mixture, with regard both to the form and to the temperament of the body.

12. *Of Bodily Injuries and Diseases.*

Since the subject which comes next is that which treats of the injuries and diseases of the body, we shall attach here in regular order the method of investigation devised for this form of query. It is as follows. In this case also, to gain a general comprehension, it is necessary to look to the two angles of the horizon, that is, the orient and the occident, and especially to the occident itself and the sign preceding it, which is disjunct [1] from the oriental angle. We must also observe what aspect the maleficent planets bear to them. For if they, one or both of them, are stationed against the ascending degrees of the aforesaid

---

[1] See i. 16 ; this sign is the fifth from the ascendant and is the so-called sixth house.

---

[3] αὐτοῖς κατὰ τὸ VPL (καὶ τὸ) ADE ; cf. Proc. ; om. NCam.
[4] γὰρ VPLADE, ἐν M, om. NCam.
[5] προδύνον P, δύνον VMD, om. LE, τὸ πρὸ δύσεως Proc., ἡγούμενον NACam.

PTOLEMY

ἤτοι σωματικῶς ἢ τετραγωνικῶς ἢ καὶ κατὰ διάμετρον, ἤτοι ὁπότερος αὐτῶν ἢ καὶ ἀμφότεροι, σίνη καὶ πάθη σωματικὰ περὶ τοὺς γεννωμένους ὑπονοητέον, μάλιστα δ' ἂν καὶ τῶν φώτων ἤτοι τὸ ἕτερον ἢ καὶ ἀμφότερα κεκεντρωμένα καθ' ὃν εἰρήκαμεν τρόπον τυγχάνῃ ἢ ἅμα ἢ κατὰ διάμετρον. τότε γὰρ οὐ μόνον ἐὰν ἐπαναφέρηταί τις τῶν κακοποιῶν, ἀλλὰ κἂν προαναφέρηται τῶν φώτων, αὐτὸς κεκεντρωμένος, ἱκανός ἐστι διαθεῖναί τι τῶν ἐκκειμένων ὁποῖον ἂν οἵ τε τοῦ ὁρίζοντος τόποι καὶ οἱ τῶν ζῳδίων ὑποφαίνωσι σίνος ἢ πάθος, καὶ αἱ τῶν ἀστέρων φύσεις τῶν τε κακούντων καὶ τῶν κακουμένων καὶ ἔτι τῶν συσχηματιζομένων αὐτοῖς. τά τε γὰρ μέρη τῶν ζῳδίων ἑκάστου τὰ περιέχοντα τὸ ἀδικούμενον μέρος τοῦ ὁρίζοντος δηλώσει τὸ μέρος τοῦ σώματος περὶ ὃ ἔσται τὸ αἴτιον καὶ πότερον σίνος ἢ πάθος ἢ καὶ ἀμφότερα τὸ δηλούμενον μέρος ἐπιδέξασθαι δυνατόν, αἵ τε τῶν ἀστέρων φύσεις τὰ εἴδη καὶ τὰς αἰτίας τῶν συμπτωμάτων ποιοῦσιν,[1] ἐπειδὴ τῶν κυριωτάτων τοῦ ἀνθρώπου μερῶν ὁ μὲν τοῦ Κρόνου κύριός ἐστιν ἀκοῶν τε δεξιῶν καὶ σπληνὸς καὶ κύστεως καὶ φλέγματος καὶ ὀστῶν· ὁ δὲ τοῦ Διὸς ἁφῆς τε καὶ πνεύμονος καὶ ἀρτηριῶν καὶ σπέρματος· ὁ δὲ τοῦ Ἄρεως ἀκοῶν εὐωνύμων καὶ νεφρῶν καὶ φλεβῶν καὶ μορίων· ὁ δὲ ἥλιος ὁράσεως καὶ ἐγκεφάλου καὶ καρδίας καὶ νεύρων καὶ τῶν δεξιῶν πάντων· ὁ δὲ τῆς Ἀφροδίτης ὀσφρήσεώς τε καὶ ἥπατος καὶ

---

[1] ποιοῦσιν VPLADProc., om. MNECam.

places, either bodily on them or quartile or in opposition to them, we must conclude that the subjects born will suffer bodily injuries and disease, especially if either one or both of the luminaries as well chance to be angular in the manner described,[1] or in opposition. For in that case not only if one of the maleficent planets is rising after the luminaries, but even if it is rising before them and is itself angular, it has power to produce one of the aforesaid injuries or diseases of such kind as the places of the horizon and of the signs may indicate, likewise what is indicated by the natures of the afflicting and the afflicted[2] planets, and moreover by those that bear an aspect toward them. For the parts of the individual signs of the zodiac which surround the afflicted portion of the horizon will indicate the part of the body which the portent will concern, and whether the part indicated can suffer an injury or a disease or both, and the natures of the planets produce the kinds and causes of the events that are to occur. For, of the most important parts of the human body, Saturn is lord[3] of the right ear, the spleen, the bladder, the phlegm, and the bones; Jupiter is lord of touch, the lungs, arteries, and semen; Mars of the left ear, kidneys, veins, and genitals; the sun of the sight, the brain, heart, sinews and all the right-hand parts; Venus of

[1] *I.e.* in either the first or seventh house (orient or occident), and not at either of the other two angles.

[2] See on iii. 9 (p. 267).

[3] A planetary melothesia (distribution of parts of the body to the planets) follows. On such *cf.* Boll-Bezold-Gundel, p. 138, and P. Mich. 149, col. ii., 31 ff. (University of Michigan Studies, Humanistic Series, vol. xl.).

PTOLEMY

σαρκῶν· ὁ δὲ τοῦ Ἑρμοῦ λόγου καὶ διανοίας καὶ γλώσσης καὶ χολῆς καὶ ἕδρας· ἡ δὲ σελήνη γεύσεώς τε καὶ καταπόσεως καὶ στομάχου καὶ κοιλίας καὶ μήτρας καὶ τῶν εὐωνύμων πάντων.

Ἔστι δὲ τῶν καθ' ὅλου καὶ τὰ σίνη μὲν ὡς ἐπὶ τὸ πολὺ συμπίπτειν ἀνατολικῶν ὄντων τῶν τὸ αἴτιον ποιούντων κακοποιῶν, πάθη δὲ τοὐναντίον δυτικῶν αὐτῶν ὑπαρχόντων· ἐπειδήπερ καὶ διώρισται τούτων ἑκάτερον τῷ τὸ μὲν σίνος ἅπαξ διατιθέναι καὶ μὴ διατείνουσαν ἔχειν τὴν ἀλγηδόνα, τὸ δὲ πάθος ἤτοι συνεχῶς ἢ ἐπιληπτικῶς τοῖς πάσχουσιν ἐπισκήπτειν.

Πρὸς δὲ τὴν κατὰ μέρος ἐπιβολὴν ἤδη τινὰ παρατηρήσεως ἔτυχεν ἐξαιρέτου σινωτικά τε καὶ παθητικὰ σχήματα, διὰ τῶν ὡς ἐπὶ πᾶν κατὰ τὰς ὁμοιοσχήμονας θέσεις παρακολουθούντων συμπτωμάτων. πηρώσεις γὰρ ὄψεως ἀποτελοῦνται κατὰ μὲν τὸν ἕτερον τῶν ὀφθαλμῶν ὅταν τε ἡ σελήνη καθ' αὑτὴν[1] ἐπὶ τῶν προειρημένων οὖσα κέντρων ἢ συνοδεύουσα ἢ πανσεληνιάζουσα τύχῃ, καὶ ὅταν ἐφ' ἑτέρου[2] μὲν ᾖ πρὸς τὸν ἥλιον σχήματος τῶν λόγον[3] ἐχόντων, συνάπτῃ δέ[4] τινι τῶν νεφελοειδῶν ἐν τῷ ζωδιακῷ συστροφῶν, ὡς τῷ νεφελίῳ[5] τοῦ Καρκίνου καὶ τῇ Πλειάδι τοῦ Ταύρου[6] καὶ τῇ ἀκίδι τοῦ Τοξότου καὶ τῷ κέντρῳ τοῦ Σκορπίου καὶ τοῖς περὶ τὸν Πλόκαμον μέρεσι τοῦ Λέοντος ἢ τῇ καλπίδι τοῦ Ὑδροχόου· καὶ

---

[1] καθ' (ἑ)αυτὴν VPADEProc., καθ' ἑαυτοὺς L, κατ' αὐτὴν MNCam.; post haec verba add. ἐκτροπὴν Cam., om. libri Proc.

TETRABIBLOS III. 12

smell, the liver, and the flesh; Mercury of speech and thought, the tongue, the bile, and the buttocks; the moon of taste and drinking, the stomach, belly, womb, and all the left-hand parts.

For the most part it is a general principle that injuries occur when the significant maleficent planets are oriental, and diseases, conversely, when they are setting. The reason for this is that these two things are distinguished thus—an injury affects the subject once for all and does not involve lasting pain, while disease bears upon the patient either continuously or in sudden attacks.

For the purpose of ascertaining particulars, certain configurations significant of injury or sickness have been specially observed, by means of the events which generally accompany such positions of the stars. For blindness in one eye is brought about when the moon by itself is upon the aforesaid angles, or is in conjunction, or is full, and when it is in another aspect that bears a relation to the sun, but applies to one of the star clusters in the zodiac, as for example to the cluster in Cancer, and to the Pleiades of Taurus, to the arrow point of Sagittarius, to the sting of Scorpio, to the parts of Leo around the Coma Berenices, or to the pitcher of Aquarius;

---

[2] ἑτέρου VPLD, ἑκατέρου MNAECam.; sequitur in MNACam. τῶν, PL μέν, VD μὲν ᾖ, E μὲν τῶν.

[3] τῶν λόγον κτλ. ME, τῶν λόγων VD, τὸν λόγον PL, λόγον NACam.

[4] συνάπτῃ δὲ PEProc., συνάπτει δὲ VLMD, καὶ ὅταν συνάπτῃ NA (-ηιαι A).

[5] τῷ νεφελίῳ VMNADEProc., τῶν ἐφελίων P, τῶν νεφελίων L, om. Cam.

[6] τοῦ Ταύρου VADProc., om. PLMNECam.

PTOLEMY

ὅταν ὁ τοῦ Ἄρεως ᾖ καὶ ὁ τοῦ Κρόνου ἐπικέντρῳ οὔσῃ αὐτῇ καὶ ἀποκρουστικῇ ἀνατολικοὶ αὐτοὶ ὄντες ἐπιφέρωνται ἢ πάλιν τοῦ ἡλίου αὐτοὶ ἐπίκεντροι ὄντες προαναφέρωνται. ἐὰν δὲ ἀμφοτέροις ἅμα τοῖς φωσὶν ἤτοι κατὰ τὸ αὐτὸ ζῴδιον ᾖ καὶ κατὰ διάμετρον, ὡς εἴπομεν, συσχηματισθῶσιν, ἑῷοι μὲν τῷ ἡλίῳ ὄντες, τῇ δὲ σελήνῃ ἑσπέριοι, περὶ ἀμφοτέρους τοὺς ὀφθαλμοὺς τὸ αἴτιον ποιήσουσιν. ὁ μὲν γὰρ[1] τοῦ Ἄρεως ἀπὸ πληγῆς ἢ κρούσματος ἢ σιδήρου ἢ κατακαύματος ποιεῖ τὰς πηρώσεις, μετὰ δὲ Ἑρμοῦ συσχηματισθεὶς ἐν παλαίστραις καὶ γυμνασίοις ἢ κακουργῶν ἐφόδοις. ὁ δὲ τοῦ Κρόνου δι' ὑποχύσεων ἢ ψύξεων ἢ ἀπογλαυκώσεων καὶ τῶν τοιούτων· πάλιν ἐὰν ὁ τῆς Ἀφροδίτης ἐπί τινος ᾖ τῶν προειρημένων κέντρων, μάλιστα δὲ ἐπὶ τοῦ δύνοντος, τῷ μὲν τοῦ Κρόνου συνὼν ἢ καὶ συσχηματιζόμενος ἢ ἐνηλλαχὼς τοὺς τόπους, ὑπὸ δὲ τοῦ Ἄρεως καθυπερτερούμενος ἢ διαμετρούμενος, οἱ μὲν ἄνδρες ἄγονοι γίνονται, αἱ δὲ γυναῖκες ἐκτρωσμοῖς ἢ ὠμοτοκίαις ἢ καὶ ἐμβρυοτομίαις[2] περικυλίονται,[3] μάλιστα δὲ ἐν Καρκίνῳ καὶ Παρθένῳ καὶ Αἰγοκέρωτι.[4] κἂν ἡ σελήνη ἀπ' ἀνατολῆς τῷ τοῦ Ἄρεως συνάπτῃ, ἐὰν δὲ καὶ τῷ τοῦ Ἑρμοῦ κατὰ τὸ αὐτὸ συσχηματισθῇ σὺν τῷ τοῦ Κρόνου, τοῦ τοῦ Ἄρεως πάλιν καθυπερτεροῦντος ἢ διαμετροῦντος, εὐνοῦχοι ἢ ἑρμα-

[1] μὲν γὰρ VD, μὲν οὖν PLProc., μὲν MNAECam.
[2] ἐμβρυοτομίαις VNADECam.¹, ἐμβρυμοτομίαις M; cf. τὰ ἔμβρυα . . . κατακοπήσεται Proc.; ἐμβρυοτοκίαις Cam.², om. PL.

and whenever Mars or Saturn moves toward the moon, when it is angular and waning and they are rising, or again when they ascend before the sun, being themselves angular. But if they are in aspect with both luminaries at once, either in the same sign or in opposition, as we said, morning stars with respect to the sun and evening stars to the moon, they will affect both eyes; for Mars brings about blindness from a blow, a thrust, iron, or burning; when he has Mercury in aspect, in palaestras and gymnasiums or by felonious attack. Saturn causes it by suffusion, cold, glaucoma, and the like. Again if Venus is upon one of the aforesaid angles, particularly the occident, if she is joined with Saturn or is in aspect with him or has exchanged houses, and is inferior to Mars or has him in opposition, the men who are born are sterile, and the women are subject to miscarriages, premature births, or even to embryotomies, particularly in Cancer, Virgo, and Capricorn.[1] And if the moon at rising applies to Mars, and if she also bears the same aspect to Mercury that Saturn does, while Mars again is elevated above her or is in opposition, the children born are eunuchs or

[1] Certain MSS. here add, "when the moon applies to the star clusters she incapacitates the eyes," which, as Camerarius notes in the margin of the second edition, is redundant here.

---

[3] περικυλίονται VNMDECam.¹, περικηλύονται P, παρακηλύονται L, ἐπικυλίονται A, κηλοῦνται Cam.²

[4] Post Αἰγόκερωτι add. καὶ τοῖς νεφελοειδέσι συνάπτουσα ὀφθαλμὸν πηροῖ ἡ σελήνη VNADCam. (in mg. *notatum et haec redundant in hoc loco Cam.²); om. PLMEProc.

PTOLEMY

φρόδιτοι ἢ ἄτρωγλοι καὶ ἄτρητοι[1] γίνονται. τούτων δὲ οὕτως ἐχόντων, ἐπὰν καὶ ὁ ἥλιος συσχηματισθῇ, τῶν μὲν φωτῶν καὶ τοῦ τῆς Ἀφροδίτης ἠρρενωμένων, ἀποκρουστικῆς δὲ τῆς σελήνης οὔσης καὶ τῶν κακοποιῶν ἐν ταῖς ἐπαναφερομέναις[2] μοίραις ἐπιφερομένων, οἱ μὲν ἄνδρες ἀπόκοποι ἢ τὰ μόρια σεσινωμένοι γίνονται καὶ μάλιστα ἐν Κριῷ καὶ Δέοντι καὶ Σκορπίῳ καὶ Αἰγόκερῳ[3] καὶ Ὑδροχόῳ, αἱ δὲ γυναῖκες ἄτοκοι καὶ στεῖραι. ἐνίοτε δὲ οὐδ' ἀσινεῖς ταῖς ὄψεσιν οἱ τοιοῦτοι διαμένουσιν, ἐμποδίζονται δὲ τὴν γλῶτταν καὶ γίνονται τραυλοὶ ἢ μογιλάλοι ὅσοι τὸν τοῦ Κρόνου καὶ τὸν τοῦ Ἑρμοῦ συνόντας ἐπὶ τῶν εἰρημένων κέντρων ἔχουσι τῷ ἡλίῳ, μάλιστα δ' ἂν καὶ δυτικὸς ᾖ ὁ τοῦ Ἑρμοῦ καὶ συσχηματίζωνται ἀμφότεροι τῇ σελήνῃ· τούτοις δ' ὁ τοῦ Ἄρεως παρατυχὼν λύειν εἴωθεν ὡς ἐπὶ τὸ πολὺ τὸ τῆς γλώττης ἐμπόδιον ἀφ' οὗ ἂν ἡ σελήνη τὴν πρὸς αὐτὸν συνάντησιν[4] ποιήσηται. πάλιν ἐὰν ἤτοι τὰ φῶτα ἐπικέντροις τοῖς κακοποιοῖς ἐπιφέρηται[5] ἅμα ἢ κατὰ διάμετρον, ἢ ἐὰν τοῖς φωσὶν οἱ κακοποιοί, καὶ μάλιστα τῆς σελήνης ἐπὶ συνδέσμων ἢ ἐπὶ καμπίων οὔσης ἢ ἐπὶ τῶν ἐπαιτίων ζῳδίων, οἷον Κριοῦ, Ταύρου, Καρκίνου, Σκορπίου, Αἰγόκερῳ, γίνονται λωβήσεις τοῦ σώματος κυρτώσεων ἢ κυλλώσεων ἢ χωλώσεων

---

[1] ἄτρωγλοι καὶ ἄτρητοι VAD, ἄτρω. κ. ἀτροίτη P, ἀτρόγλοι κ. ἄτρωτοι L, ἄτρωγλοι καὶ om. MNECam., μὴ ἔχοντες τρυπήματα μηδὲ διέξοδον Proc.

[2] ἐν ταῖς μοίραις ταῖς ἐπαναφερομέναις Proc., ταῖς ἐπαναφ. μοίραις PVAD, τοῖς ἐπαναφερομένοις μοίραις L, κατὰ τὰς ἐπαναφερομένας μοίρας MNECam.

hermaphrodites or have no ducts and vents.¹ Since this is so, when the sun also is in aspect, if the luminaries and Venus are made masculine, the moon is waning, and the maleficent planets are approaching in the succeeding degrees, the males that are born will be deprived of their sexual organs or injured therein, particularly in Aries, Leo, Scorpio, Capricorn, and Aquarius, and the females will be childless and sterile. Sometimes those who have such genitures continue not without injury to the sight also; but those suffer impediment of speech, lisp, or have difficulty in enunciation who have Saturn and Mercury joined with the sun at the aforesaid angles, particularly if Mercury is also setting and both bear some aspect to the moon. When Mars is present with them he is generally apt to loosen the impediment to the tongue, after the moon meets him. Again, if the luminaries, together or in opposition, move toward the maleficent planets upon the angles, or if the maleficent planets move toward the luminaries, particularly when the moon is at the nodes² or her bendings, or in the injurious signs such as Aries, Taurus, Cancer, Scorpio, or Capricorn, there come about deformations of the body such as hunchback,

¹ Proclus paraphrases thus: ἢ μὴ ἔχοντες τρυπήματα μηδὲ διέξοδον.
² The points at which the moon's path intersects the ecliptic. The "bendings" are the points quartile to the nodes (cf. the anonymous commentator, p. 139, ed. Wolf).

---

³ καὶ Λέοντι . . . Αἰγόκερῳ VPLDProc., om. MNAECam.
⁴ συνάντησιν VPLADProc., ἀπάντησιν MNECam.
⁵ ἐπιφέρηται VPLDProc., ἐπαναφέρηται MNAECam.¹, ἐπαναφέρωνται Cam.²

ἢ παραλύσεων, ἐὰν μὲν σὺν τοῖς φωσὶν ὦσιν οἱ κακοποιοὶ ἀπὸ τῆς γενέσεως αὐτῆς, ἐὰν δὲ ἐν τοῖς μεσουρανήμασι καθυπερτεροῦντες τὰ φῶτα ἢ διαμηκίζοντες ἀλλήλους ὦσιν ἀπὸ κινδύνων μεγάλων, ὡς τῶν ἀποκρημνισμῶν ἢ συμπτώσεων ἢ ληστηρίων ἢ τετραπόδων· Ἄρεως μὲν ἐπικρατοῦντος, τῶν διὰ πυρὸς ἢ τραυμάτων ἢ χολικῶν[1] ἢ ληστηρίων· Κρόνου δὲ τῶν διὰ συμπτώσεων ἢ ναυαγίων ἢ σπασμῶν.

Ὡς ἐπὶ τὸ πολὺ δὲ γίνεται σίνη καὶ περὶ τὰ τροπικὰ καὶ ἰσημερινὰ σημεῖα τῆς σελήνης οὔσης, μάλιστα δὲ περὶ μὲν τὸ ἐαρινὸν τὰ δι' ἀλφῶν. περὶ δὲ τὸ θερινὸν τὰ διὰ λειχήνων· περὶ δὲ τὸ μετοπωρινὸν τὰ διὰ λεπρῶν· περὶ δὲ τὸ χειμερινὸν τὰ διὰ φακῶν καὶ τῶν ὁμοίων. πάθη δὲ συμβαίνειν εἴωθεν ὅταν ἐπὶ τῶν προκειμένων στάσεων οἱ κακοποιοὶ συσχηματισθῶσι, κατὰ τὸ ἐναντίον μέντοι, τουτέστιν ἑσπέριοι μὲν τῷ ἡλίῳ, τῇ δὲ σελήνῃ ἑῷοι. καθ' ὅλου γὰρ ὁ μὲν τοῦ Κρόνου ψυχροκοιλίους ποιεῖ καὶ πολυφλεγμάτους καὶ ῥευματώδεις, κατίσχνους τε καὶ ἀσθενικοὺς καὶ ἰκτερικοὺς[2] καὶ δυσεντερικοὺς καὶ βηχικοὺς καὶ ἀναφορικοὺς καὶ κωλικοὺς καὶ ἐλεφαντιῶντας· τὰς δὲ γυναῖκας ἔτι καὶ ὑστερικάς. ὁ δὲ τοῦ Ἄρεως αἱμαπτοϊκοὺς μελαγχολικοὺς[3] πνευμονικοὺς ψωριῶντας· ἔτι δὲ τοὺς διὰ τομῶν ἢ καύσεων[4] κρυπτῶν τόπων συνεχῶς ἐνοχλουμένους συρίγγων ἕνεκεν ἢ αἱμορροϊδῶν ἢ κονδυλωμάτων[5]

---

[1] ἢ χολικῶν VP (χωλοικ-) LADProc.; ὀχλικῶν MNECam.
[2] καὶ ἰκτερικοὺς om. Cam.
[3] μελαγχολικοὺς om. Cam.

crookedness, lameness, or paralysis, congenital if the maleficent planets are joined with the luminaries, but if they are at the mid-heaven points, elevated above the luminaries or in opposition one to the other, the deformations will result from serious dangers, such as falls from a height, the collapse of houses, or the attacks of robbers or animals. If Mars prevails, the danger is from fire, wounds, bilious attacks, or robberies; if it is Saturn, through collapse of buildings, shipwreck, or spasms.

For the most part injuries come about when the moon is near the solstitial or equinoctial signs, particularly at the spring equinox, injuries by white leprosy; at the summer solstice, by lichens; at the fall equinox, by leprosy; at the winter solstice, by moles and the like. Diseases are likely to result when at the positions already described the maleficent planets are in aspect, but in the opposite sense, that is, evening stars with respect to the sun and morning stars to the moon. For in general Saturn causes his subjects to have cold bellies, increases the phlegm, makes them rheumatic, meagre, weak, jaundiced, and prone to dysentery, coughing, raising, colic, and elephantiasis; the females he makes also subject to diseases of the womb. Mars causes men to spit blood, makes them melancholy, weakens their lungs, and causes the itch or scurvy; and furthermore he causes them to be constantly irritated by cutting or cautery of the secret parts because of fistulas, hæmorrhoids,

---

ᵃ Post καύσεων add. ἢ PLMNAECam; cf. Proc., διὰ καύσεως ἢ τομῆς εἰς κρυπτοὺς τόπους κτλ.
ᵇ ἢ κονδυλωμάτων VP (-λομ-) LDEProc., om. MNACam.; add. ἢ καὶ πυρωμάτων MNACam.

ἢ καὶ τῶν πυρωδῶν ἑλκώσεων ἢ νομῶν· τὰς δὲ γυναῖκας ἔτι καὶ ἐκτρωσμοῖς ἢ ἐμβρυοτομίαις[1] ἢ ἀναβρώσεσιν εἴωθε περικυλίειν. ἰδίως δὲ καὶ παρὰ[2] τὰς προειρημένας τῶν συσχηματιζομένων ἀστέρων φύσεις πρὸς τὰ μέρη τοῦ σώματος τὰ ἰδιώματα ποιοῦσι τῶν παθῶν.

Συνεργεῖ δ' αὐτοῖς μάλιστα πρὸς τὰς ἐπιτάσεις τῶν φαύλων ὁ τοῦ Ἑρμοῦ ἀστήρ, τῷ μὲν τοῦ Κρόνου πρὸς τὸ ψυχρὸν συνοικειούμενος καὶ μᾶλλον ἐν κινήσει συνεχεῖ ποιῶν τοὺς ῥευματισμοὺς καὶ τὰς τῶν ὑγρῶν ὀχλήσεις, ἐξαιρέτως δὲ τῶν περὶ θώρακα καὶ φάρυγγα καὶ στόμαχον· τῷ δὲ τοῦ Ἄρεως πρὸς τὸ ξηραντικώτερον συνεπισχύων, ὡς ἐπί τε τῶν ἑλκωδῶν πτιλώσεων[3] καὶ ἐσχαρῶν καὶ ἀποστημάτων καὶ ἐρυσιπελάτων καὶ λειχήνων ἀγρίων καὶ μελαίνης χολῆς ἢ μανίας[4] ἢ νόσου ἱερᾶς ἢ τῶν τοιούτων.

Καὶ παρὰ τὰς τῶν ζῳδίων ἐναλλαγὰς τῶν τοὺς προειρημένους ἐπὶ τῶν δύο κέντρων συσχηματισμοὺς περιεχόντων γίνονταί τινες ποιότητες παθῶν. ἰδίως γὰρ ὁ μὲν Καρκίνος καὶ ὁ Αἰγόκερως καὶ οἱ Ἰχθῦς καὶ ὅλως τὰ χερσαῖα καὶ τὰ ἰχθυϊκὰ ζῴδια τὰ διὰ τῶν νομῶν πάθη ποιεῖ καὶ λειχήνων ἢ λεπίδων[5] ἢ χοιράδων ἢ συρίγγων ἢ ἐλεφαντιάσεων καὶ τῶν τοιούτων. ὁ δὲ Τοξότης καὶ οἱ Δίδυμοι

---

[1] ἐμβρυοτοκίαις NCam.
[2] παρὰ VPLD, περὶ MNAECam.
[3] πτιλώσεων ego; πτηλώσεων PL, πιλλώσεων VD, ψιλώσεων MNAECam.
[4] ἢ μανίας VPLMADProc., om. NECam.

or tumours, or also burning ulcers, or eating sores; he is apt to afflict women furthermore with miscarriages, embryotomies, or corrosive diseases. Of themselves, they also bring about the properties of disease in agreement with the natures, which have been already discussed, of the planets in aspect, as they relate to the parts of the body.¹

Mercury assists them ² chiefly to prolong the evil effects, when he is allied with Saturn inclining toward cold and continually stirring into activity rheumatisms and gatherings of fluid, particularly about the chest, throat, and stomach. When he is allied with Mars he adds his force to produce greater dryness, as in cases of ulcerous sore eyes, eschars,³ abscesses, erysipelas, savage lichens or skin eruptions, black bile, insanity, the sacred disease,⁴ or the like.

Certain qualities of disease are determined by changes among the zodiacal signs which surround the aforesaid configurations on the two angles. For in particular Cancer, Capricorn, and Pisces, and in general the terrestrial and piscine signs, cause diseases involving eating sores, lichens, scales, scrofula, fistulas, elephantiasis, and the like. Sagittarius and Gemini are responsible for those that come

¹ The reference is to the planetary melothesia, earlier in the chapter (p. 319). Acting in their own proper characters (ἰδίως), the maleficent planets will affect those parts of the body of which, in the melothesia, they were said to be the "lords".
² Saturn and Mars, the maleficent planets.
³ Dry sloughs, crusts, or scabs.   ⁴ Epilepsy.

---

⁵ ἢ λεπίδων VD, ἢ λοιπίδων P, ὁ δὲ πίδων L, ἢ λεπρῶν MNAE, om. Cam.

τὰ διὰ πτωματισμῶν ἢ ἐπιλήψεων· καὶ ἐν ταῖς ἐσχάταις δὲ μοίραις παρατυγχάνοντες οἱ ἀστέρες τῶν δωδεκατημορίων περὶ τὰ ἄκρα μάλιστα τὰ πάθη[1] καὶ τὰ σίνη ποιοῦσι διὰ λωβήσεων ἢ ῥευματισμῶν, ἀφ' ὧν καὶ ἐλεφαντιάσεις τε καὶ ὡς ἐπὶ πᾶν χειράγραι καὶ ποδάγραι συμβαίνουσι. τούτων δὲ οὕτως ἐχόντων, ἐὰν μὲν μηδεὶς τῶν ἀγαθοποιῶν συσχηματίζηται τοῖς τὰ αἴτια ποιοῦσι κακοποιοῖς ἢ τοῖς κεκεντρωμένοις φωσίν, ἀνίατα καὶ ἐπαχθῆ τά τε σίνη καὶ τὰ πάθη γενήσεται· ὡσαύτως δὲ κἂν συσχηματίζωνται μέν, καθυπερτερῶνται δὲ ὑπὸ τῶν κακοποιῶν ἐν δυνάμει ὄντων. ἐὰν δὲ καὶ αὐτοὶ κατὰ κυρίων ὄντες σχημάτων καθυπερτερῶσι τοὺς τὸ αἴτιον ἐμποιοῦντας κακοποιούς, τότε τὰ σίνη εὐσχήμονα καὶ οὐκ ἐπονείδιστα γίνεται καὶ τὰ πάθη μέτρια καὶ εὐπαρηγόρητα, ἔσθ' ὅτε δὲ καὶ εὐαπάλλακτα, ἀνατολικῶν ὄντων τῶν ἀγαθοποιῶν. ὁ μὲν γὰρ τοῦ Διὸς βοηθείαις ἀνθρωπίναις διὰ πλούτων ἢ ἀξιωμάτων τά τε σίνη κρύπτειν εἴωθε καὶ τὰ πάθη παρηγορεῖν· σὺν δὲ τῷ τοῦ Ἑρμοῦ καὶ φαρμακείαις ἢ ἰατρῶν ἀγαθῶν ἐπικουρίαις. ὁ δὲ τῆς Ἀφροδίτης διὰ προφάσεως θεῶν καὶ χρησμῶν τὰ μὲν σίνη τρόπον τινὰ εὔμορφα καὶ ἐπιχαρῆ κατασκευάζει, τὰ δὲ πάθη ταῖς ἀπὸ θεῶν ἰατρείαις εὐπαρηγόρητα· τοῦ μέντοι Κρόνου προσόντος μετὰ παραδειγματισμῶν καὶ ἐξαγοριῶν[2] καὶ τῶν τοιού-

[1] ἄκρα μάλιστα τὰ πάθη VPLD, ἄγρια καὶ μάλιστα πάθη NCam.¹, ἄγρια μάλιστα πάθη MAE, ἔσχατα μέλη τὰ πάθη Cam.²
[2] ἐξαγοριῶν VD, -ειῶν A, ἐξαγωριῶν P, ἐξαγωνίων L, cf. ἐξαγορεύειν Proc.; ἐξαγορεύσεων MNECam.

about with falling fits or epileptic seizures. And when the planets are in the last degrees of the signs they cause diseases and injuries especially in the extremities, through lesions or rheumatism, from which elephantiasis and, in general, gout in the feet and hands result. Since this is the case, if no beneficent planet bears an aspect to the maleficent ones which furnish the cause, or to the luminaries on the centres, the injuries and diseases will be incurable and painful; so also, if they bear an aspect but the maleficent planets are in power and overcome them. But if the beneficent planets are themselves in the authoritative positions and overcome the maleficent planets that bear the responsibility for the evil, then the injuries are not disfiguring and do not entail reproach and the diseases are moderate and yield to treatment, and sometimes they may be easily cured, if the beneficent planets are rising. For Jupiter generally causes the injuries to be concealed by human aid through riches or honours, and the diseases to be mitigated; and in company with Mercury he brings this about by drugs and the aid of good physicians. And Venus contrives that through pronouncements of the gods and oracles the blemishes shall be, in a way, comely and attractive,[1] and that the diseases shall be readily moderated by divine healing; if however Saturn is by, the healing will be accompanied by exhibition and

[1] *Cf.* the famous passage of the *Republic* (474DE) in which Plato tells how lovers praise the irregular features and the complexions of their favourites.

των· τοῦ δὲ τοῦ Ἑρμοῦ μετ' ἐπικουρίας καὶ πορισμοῦ τινος δι' αὐτῶν τῶν σινῶν ἢ καὶ παθῶν τοῖς ἔχουσι περιγινομένου.

⟨ ιγ.⟩ Περὶ ποιότητος ψυχῆς

Περὶ μὲν οὖν τῶν σωματικῶν συμπτωμάτων ὁ τύπος τῆς ἐπισκέψεως τοιοῦτος ἄν τις εἴη. τῶν δὲ ψυχικῶν ποιοτήτων αἱ μὲν περὶ τὸ λογικὸν καὶ νοερὸν μέρος καταλαμβάνονται διὰ τῆς κατὰ τὸν τοῦ Ἑρμοῦ ἀστέρα θεωρουμένης ἑκάστοτε περιστάσεως· αἱ δὲ περὶ τὸ αἰσθητικὸν[1] καὶ ἄλογον ἀπὸ τοῦ σωματωδεστέρου τῶν φώτων,[2] τουτέστι τῆς σελήνης, καὶ τῶν πρὸς τὰς ἀπορροίας ἢ καὶ τὰς συναφὰς αὐτῆς συνεσχηματισμένων ἀστέρων. πολυτροπωτάτου δ' ὄντος τοῦ κατὰ τὰς ψυχικὰς ὁρμὰς εἴδους εἰκότως ἂν καὶ τὴν τοιαύτην ἐπίσκεψιν οὐχ ἁπλῶς οὐδ' ὡς ἔτυχε ποιοίμεθα, διὰ πλειόνων δὲ καὶ ποικίλων παρατηρήσεων. καὶ γὰρ αἱ τῶν ζωδίων τῶν περιεχόντων τόν τε τοῦ Ἑρμοῦ καὶ τὴν σελήνην ἢ τοὺς τὴν ἐπικράτησιν αὐτῶν εἰληφότας ἀστέρας διαφοραὶ πολὺ δύνανται συμβάλλεσθαι πρὸς τὰ τῶν ψυχικῶν[3] ἰδιώματα, καὶ οἱ τῶν λόγον ἐχόντων πρὸς τὸ προκείμενον εἶδος ἀστέρων σχηματισμοὶ πρὸς ἥλιόν τε καὶ τὰ κέντρα, καὶ ἔτι τὸ

[1] αἰσθητικὸν VDA (mg.: γρ. ἠθικόν), αἰσθητὸν PL ; cf. αἴσθησιν Proc. ; ἠθικὸν MNECam.
[2] τοῦ σωματοδεστέρου τῶν φώτων A ; similia habent VPLD ; τῶν σωματοδεστέρων φώτων MNCam., τῶν σ. τῶν φ. E.
[3] ψυχικῶν VP (-χη-) LDE, ψυχῶν MNACam.

confession of the disease,[1] and such like, but if Mercury [2] is joined with her it will be with the accrual of use and gain, through the injuries and diseases themselves, to those that have them.

13. *Of the Quality of the Soul.*

The character, then, of the inquiry into bodily affections would be of this sort. Of the qualities of the soul, those which concern the reason and the mind are apprehended by means of the condition of Mercury observed on the particular occasion; and the qualities of the sensory and irrational part are discovered from the one of the luminaries which is the more corporeal, that is, the moon, and from the planets which are configurated with her in her separations and applications.[3] But since the variety of the impulses of the soul is great, it stands to reason that we would make such an inquiry in no simple or offhand manner, but by means of many complicated observations. For indeed the differences between the signs which contain Mercury and the moon, or the planets that dominate them, can contribute much to the character of the soul; so likewise do the aspects to the sun and the angles shown by the planets that are related to the class of qualities under consideration, and, furthermore,

[1] The commentator (p. 141, ed. Wolf) says that this refers to the custom of taking the sick to temples for healing. So the disease would be openly exhibited and spoken of. Proclus indicates that the cure is through display and confession.
[2] Hermes (Mercury) was the god of commerce and gain.
[3] *Cf.* i. 24.

κατ' αὐτὴν τὴν ἑκάστου τῶν ἀστέρων φύσιν πρὸς τὰς ψυχικὰς κινήσεις ἰδιότροπον.

Τῶν μὲν οὖν ζῳδίων καθ' ὅλου τὰ μὲν τροπικὰ δημοτικωτέρας ποιεῖ τὰς ψυχὰς ὀχλικῶν τε καὶ πολιτικῶν πραγμάτων ἐπιθυμητικάς, ἔτι δὲ φιλοδόξους καὶ θεοπροσπλόκους[1] εὐφυεῖς τε καὶ εὐκινήτους, ζητητικάς τε καὶ εὑρετικάς, εὐεικάστους καὶ ἀστρολογικὰς[2] καὶ μαντικάς· τὰ δὲ δίσωμα ποικίλας, εὐμεταβόλους, δυσκαταλήπτους, κούφας, εὐμεταθέτους, διπλᾶς, ἐρωτικάς, πολυτρόπους, φιλομούσους, ῥαθύμους, εὐπορίστους, μεταμελητικάς· τὰ δὲ στερεὰ δικαίας, ἀκολακεύτους, ἐπιμόνους, βεβαίας, συνετάς, ὑπομονητικάς, φιλοπόνους, σκληράς, ἐγκρατεῖς, μνησικάκους, ἐκβιβαστικάς,[3] ἐριστικάς, φιλοτίμους, στασιώδεις, πλεονεκτικάς, ἀποκρότους, ἀμεταθέτους.

Τῶν δὲ σχηματισμῶν αἱ μὲν ἀνατολικαὶ καὶ ὡροσκοπίαι καὶ μάλιστα αἱ ἰδιοπροσωπίαι ἐλευθερίους καὶ ἁπλᾶς καὶ αὐθάδεις καὶ ἰσχυρὰς καὶ εὐφυεῖς καὶ ὀξείας καὶ ἀπαρακαλύπτους τὰς ψυχὰς ἀπεργάζονται· οἱ δὲ ἑῷοι στηριγμοὶ καὶ αἱ μεσουρανήσεις ἐπιλογιστικάς, ἐπιμόνους, μνημονευτικάς, βεβαίας, συνετάς, μεγαλόφρονας, ἀποτελεστικὰς ὧν βούλονται, ἀτρέπτους, ῥωμαλέας, ὠμάς, ἀνεξαπατήτους, κριτικάς, ἐμπράκτους, κολαστικάς, ἐπιστημονικάς· αἱ δὲ προηγήσεις καὶ αἱ δύσεις εὐμεταθέτους,

[1] θεοπροσπόλους NCam.
[2] ἀστρολογικὰς PLMAE, ἀστρολογίας VD; cf. Proc., ἀπολογιτικὰς N, -ητικὰς Cam.
[3] ἐκβιβαστικάς VP (-ηκας) L (ἐκβαβ-) MADEProc. Cam.¹; ἐκβιαστικάς NCam.²

TETRABIBLOS III. 13

that peculiar natural quality of each one of the planets which relates to the movements of the soul.

Of the signs of the zodiac in general, then, the solstitial signs produce souls fitted for dealing with the people, fond of turbulence and political activity, glory-seeking, moreover, and attentive to the gods, noble, mobile, inquisitive, inventive, good at conjecture, and fitted for astrology and divination. The bicorporeal signs make souls complex, changeable, hard to apprehend, light, unstable, fickle, amorous, versatile, fond of music, lazy, easily acquisitive, prone to change their minds. The solid signs make them just, unaffected by flattery, persistent, firm, intelligent, patient, industrious, stern, self-controlled, tenacious of grudges, extortionate, contentious, ambitious, factious, grasping, hard, inflexible.

Of configurations, positions in the orient and at the horoscope, and in particular those which are in proper face,[1] produce liberal, simple, self-willed, strong, noble, keen, open souls. Morning stations and culminations make them calculating, patient, of good memory, firm, intelligent, magnanimous, accomplishing what they desire, inflexible, robust, rough, not readily deceived, critical, practical, prone to inflict punishment, gifted with understanding. Precessions[2] and settings make them easily changed,

---

[1] See i. 23.
[2] The advances of a planet, as opposed to its retrograde movement (ἀναποδισμός) or its stations (στηριγμοί); cf. Bouché-Leclercq, p. 111. The term can be ambiguous; see on c. 11 above (p. 313).

ἀβεβαίους, ἀσθενεῖς, ἀφερεπόνους, ἐμπαθεῖς, ταπεινάς, δειλάς, ἀμφιβόλους, θρασυδείλους, ἀμβλείας, βλακώδεις, δυσκινήτους· οἱ δὲ ἑσπέριοι στηριγμοὶ καὶ αἱ ὑπὸ γῆν μεσουρανήσεις, ἔτι δὲ καὶ ἐφ' Ἑρμοῦ καὶ Ἀφροδίτης ἡμέρας μὲν αἱ ἑσπέριαι δύσεις, νυκτὸς δὲ αἱ ἑῷοι, εὐφυεῖς μὲν καὶ φρενήρεις,[1] οὐκ ἄγαν δὲ μνημονικὰς[2] οὐδ' ἐπιμόχθους καὶ φιλοπόνους, διερευνητικὰς δὲ τῶν ἀποκρύφων καὶ ζητητικὰς τῶν ἀθεωρήτων, οἷον μαγικάς, μυστηριακάς, μετεωρολογικάς, ὀργανικάς, μηχανικάς, θαυματοποιούς, ἀστρολογικάς, φιλοσόφους, οἰωνοσκοπικάς, ὀνειροκριτικὰς καὶ τὰς ὁμοίας.

Πρὸς τούτοις δὲ[3] ἐν ἰδίοις μὲν, ἢ καὶ οἰκείοις ὄντες τόποις καὶ αἱρήσεσιν οἱ τὴν κυρίαν ἔχοντες τῶν ψυχικῶν, καθ' ὃν ἐν ἀρχῇ διωρισάμεθα τρόπον, προφανῆ καὶ ἀπαραπόδιστα καὶ αὐθέκαστα καὶ ἐπιτευκτικὰ ποιοῦσι τὰ ἰδιώματα, καὶ μάλισθ' ὅταν οἱ αὐτοὶ τῶν δύο τόπων ἐπικρατήσωσιν ἅμα, τουτέστι[4] τῷ μὲν τοῦ Ἑρμοῦ ὁπωσδήποτε τυγχάνωσι[5] συνεσχηματισμένοι, τὴν δὲ τῆς σελήνης ἀπόρροιαν ἢ καὶ συναφὴν ἐπέχοντες· μὴ οὕτω δὲ διακείμενοι ἀλλ' ἐν ἀνοικείοις ὄντες τόποις, τὰ μὲν τῆς ἑαυτῶν φύσεως οἰκεῖα πρὸς τὴν ψυχικὴν ἐνέργειαν ἀνεπίφαντα καὶ ἀμαυρὰ καὶ ἀτελείωτα καὶ ἀπρόκοπα καθιστᾶσι. τὰ δὲ τῆς τῶν ἐπικρατησάντων ἢ καθυπερτερησάν-

---

[1] φρενήρεις] φρονίμους NCam.Proc.

[2] μνημονικὰς VP (-ηκὰς) LDE, cf. Proc.; μνημονευτικὰς MNACam.

[3] πρὸς τούτοις δὲ A, πρὸς τούτῳ δὲ P, πρὸς τούτοις L, πρὸ τούτοις δὲ VD, ἔτι δὲ Proc.; ὅτε δὴ MNECam. (τύχοιεν post ὄντες add. NCam.)

unstable, weak, unable to bear labour, emotional, humble, cowardly, deceitful, bullying, dull, slow-witted, hard to arouse. Evening stations and position at mid-heaven beneath the earth, and furthermore, in the case of Mercury and Venus, by day evening settings and by night morning settings, produce souls noble and wise, but with mediocre memory, not painstaking nor fond of labour, but investigators of hidden things and seekers after the unknown, as for example magicians, adepts in the mysteries, meteorologists, makers of instruments and machines, conjurors, astrologers, philosophers, readers of omens, interpreters of dreams, and the like.

When, in addition, the governors of the soul, as we explained at the beginning, are in their own or familiar houses or sects,[1] they make the characters of the soul open, unimpeded, spontaneous, and effective, especially when the same planets rule the two places at once, that is, when they are configurated to Mercury in any aspect whatever, and hold the separation or application of the moon;[2] if they are not so disposed, however, but are in places alien to them, it renders the properties of their own natures obscure, indistinct, imperfect, and ineffective with respect to the active quality of the soul. The powers, however, of the nature of the planets that dominate

---

[1] The governors of the soul are Mercury and the moon. For the houses, see i. 17, and for the sects, i. 7 and 12.
[2] That is, when the moon is separating from them or applying to them.

---

⁴ τουτέστι om. Cam.³   ⁵ τυγχάνωσι om. Cam.³

PTOLEMY

των ἰσχυρά τε καὶ ἐπιβλαβῆ τῶν ὑποκειμένων,[1] ὡς ὅταν οἵ τε διὰ κακοποιῶν οἰκείωσιν ἄδικοι καὶ πονηροί, κρατούντων μὲν αὐτῶν, εὐπροχώρητον ᾖ καὶ ἀνεμπόδιστον καὶ ἀκίνδυνον καὶ ἐπίδοξον ἔχουσι τὴν πρὸς τὸ κακῶς ἀλλήλους ποιεῖν ὁρμήν · κρατουμένων δὲ ὑπὸ τῆς ἐναντίας αἱρέσεως, κατάφοροι καὶ ἀνεπίτευκτοι καὶ εὐτιμώρητοι γίνονται. οἱ δ' αὖ πάλιν διὰ τὴν τῶν ἀγαθοποιούντων πρὸς τοὺς εἰρημένους ὅρους συνοικείωσιν ἀγαθοὶ καὶ δίκαιοι, ἀκαθυπερτερήτων μὲν ὄντων, αὐτοί τε χαίρουσι καὶ εὐφημοῦνται ἐπὶ ταῖς τῶν ἄλλων εὐποιΐαις καὶ ὑπὸ μηδενὸς ἀδικούμενοι ἀλλ' ὀνησιφόρον ἔχοντες τὴν δικαιοσύνην διατελοῦσι · κρατουμένων δὲ ὑπὸ τῶν ἐναντίων ἀνάπαλιν, δι' αὐτὸ τὸ πρᾶον καὶ φιλάνθρωπον καὶ ἐλεητικὸν[2] καὶ εὐκαταφρόνητοί τε καὶ ἐπίμεμπτοι ἢ καὶ ὑπὸ τῶν πλείστων εὐαδίκητοι τυγχάνουσιν.

Ὁ μὲν οὖν καθ' ὅλου τρόπος τῆς ἠθικῆς[3] ἐπισκέψεως τοιοῦτός τις ἂν εἴη · τὰς δὲ κατὰ μέρος ἀπ' αὐτῆς τῆς τῶν ἀστέρων φύσεως κατὰ τὴν τοιαύτην κυρίαν ἀποτελουμένας ἰδιοτροπίας ἑξῆς κατὰ τὸ κεφαλαιῶδες ἐπεξελευσόμεθα μέχρι τῆς καθ' ὁλοσχέρειαν θεωρουμένης συγκράσεως.

Ὁ μὲν οὖν τοῦ Κρόνου ἀστὴρ μόνος τὴν οἰκοδεσποτίαν τῆς ψυχῆς λαβὼν καὶ αὐθεντήσας τοῦ τε Ἑρμοῦ

---

[1] ὑποκειμένων VPLDE, προκειμένων MNACam.
[2] ἐλεητικὸν VP (-λαιη-) LMADE, ἐλεγκτικὸν NCam.
[3] ἠθικῆς VP (ἠθηκ-) MADE, cf. Proc.; εἰδικῆς MNCam., ἰδικῆς L.

TETRABIBLOS III. 13

or overcome[1] them are vigorous and injurious to the subjects. Thus men who, by reason of the familiarity of the maleficent planets, are unjust and evil, find their impulse to injure one another easy, unimpeded, secure, and honourable, if those planets are in power; but if they are overcome by planets of the opposite sect, the men are lethargic, ineffective, and easily punished. And those again that through the familiarity of the beneficent planets to the aforesaid boundaries are good and just, if these planets are not overcome, are themselves happy and bear a good repute for their kindness to others, and, injured by none, continue to benefit from their own justice; if, however, the good planets are dominated by opposites, simply because of their gentleness, kindness, and compassion, they suffer from contempt and reproach or even may easily be wronged by most people.

This, then, is the general method of inquiry as to character. We shall next briefly consider, in due order, the particular traits resulting from the very nature of the planets, in this kind of domination, until the theory of mixture has been treated in its most important aspects.

If Saturn alone is ruler of the soul and dominates Mercury and the moon, if he has a dignified position

---

[1] On the expression "overcome," see above, on iii. 4, p. 245. Planets would "dominate" the governors of the soul (Mercury and the moon) by exercising rulership (οἰκοδεσποτία) over the portion of the zodiac occupied by the governors; this could be done in any of the five ways specified by Ptolemy in iii. 2 (p. 233).

PTOLEMY

158 καὶ τῆς σελήνης, ἐὰν μὲν ἐνδόξως ἔχῃ πρός τε τὸ κοσμικὸν καὶ τὰ κέντρα, ποιεῖ φιλοσωμάτους, ἰσχυρογνώμονας, βαθύφρονας, αὐστηρούς, μονογνώμονας, ἐπιμόχθους, ἐπιτακτικούς, κολαστικούς, περιουσιαστικούς, φιλοχρημάτους, βιαίους, θησαυριστικούς, φθονερούς. ἐναντίως δὲ καὶ ἀδόξως κείμενος ῥυπαρούς, μικρολόγους, μικροψύχους,[1] ἀδιαφόρους, κακογνώμονας,[2] βασκάνους, δειλούς, ἀνακεχωρηκότας, κακολόγους, φιλερήμους, φιλοθρήνους, ἀναιδεῖς, δεισιδαίμονας, φιλομόχθους, ἀστόργους, ἐπιβουλευτικοὺς τῶν οἰκείων, ἀνευφράντους, μισοσωμάτους.

Τῷ δὲ τοῦ Διὸς κατὰ τὸν ἐκκείμενον τρόπον συνοικειωθεὶς ἐπὶ μὲν ἐνδόξων πάλιν διαθέσεων ποιεῖ ἀγαθούς, τιμητικοὺς τῶν πρεσβυτέρων, καθεστῶτας, καλογνώμονας, ἐπικούρους,[3] κριτικούς, φιλοκτήμονας, μεγαλοψύχους, μεταδοτικούς, εὐπροαιρέτους, φιλοικείους, πράους, συνετούς, ἀνεκτικούς, ἐμφιλοσόφους· ἐπὶ δὲ τῶν ἐναντίων ἀπειροκάλους, μανιώδεις, ψοφοδεεῖς, δεισιδαίμονας, ἱεροφοιτῶντας,

[1] μικροψύχους om. MECam.
[2] κακογνώμονας VPLDProc., μονογνώμονας MAECam.
[3] ἀπίκρους post ἐπικούρους add. MAE, om. VPLDProc.

---

[1] Bouché-Leclercq, p. 309, enumerates the conditions which should exist if a planet is to act effectively, classifying them as relations to the circles of the nativity, to the zodiac, to the other planets, and to the planet's own movement and the sun. With reference to the zodiac, the planet should be in a "solid" sign, in a quadrant and a sign of the same sex as itself, in one of its own proper domains (house, triangle, exaltation, terms, decans), and

TETRABIBLOS III. 13

with reference to the universe and the angles,[1] he makes his subjects lovers of the body,[2] strong-minded, deep thinkers, austere, of a single purpose, laborious, dictatorial, ready to punish, lovers of property, avaricious, violent, amassing treasure, and jealous; but if his position is the opposite and without dignity, he makes them sordid, petty, mean-spirited, indifferent, mean-minded, malignant, cowardly, diffident, evil-speakers, solitary, tearful, shameless, superstitious, fond of toil, unfeeling, devisers of plots against their friends, gloomy, taking no care of the body.

Saturn, allied with Jupiter in the way described, again in dignified positions, makes his subjects good, respectful to elders, sedate, noble-minded, helpful,[3] critical, fond of possessions, magnanimous, generous, of good intentions, lovers of their friends, gentle, wise, patient, philosophical; but in the opposite positions, he makes them uncultured, mad, easily frightened, superstitious, frequenters of shrines,

---

not in its place of depression. With regard to the circle of the nativity, the planet should be upon an angle (especially mid-heaven) or in a favourable aspect (trine or sextile) to an angle, and not in a place which bears no aspect to the horoscope (is disjunct). This will explain what, in general, are "dignified" or "honourable" positions, and their opposites.

[2] Ptolemy's lists of characters and qualities attaching to the various planets, which occupy the rest of this chapter, are remarkably useful in reconstructing a picture of life in Egypt under the Roman Empire. F. Cumont, *L'Égypte des astrologues* (Brussels, 1937), makes constant use of them for this purpose.

[3] Certain MSS. add "without sharpness" here; see the critical note.

ἐξαγορευτάς, ὑπόπτους, μισοτέκνους, ἀφίλους, ἐνδομύχους, ἀκρίτους, ἀπίστους, μωροκάκους,[1] ἰώδεις, ὑποκριτικούς, ἀδρανεῖς, ἀφιλοτίμους, μεταμελητικούς, αὐστηρούς, δυσεντεύκτους, δυσπροσίτους, εὐλαβητικούς,[2] εὐήθεις δ' ὁμοίως καὶ ἀνεξικάκους.

Τῷ δὲ τοῦ Ἄρεως συνοικειωθεὶς ἐπὶ μὲν ἐνδόξων διαθέσεων ποιεῖ ἀδιαφόρους, ἐπιπόνους, παρρησιαστικούς, ὀχληρούς, θρασυδείλους, αὐστηροπράξους, ἀνελεήμονας, καταφρονητικούς, τραχεῖς, πολεμικούς, ῥιψοκινδύνους, φιλοθορύβους, δολίους, ἐνεδρευτάς, δυσμηνίτας, ἀδήκτους,[3] ὀχλοκόπους, τυραννικούς, πλεονέκτας, μισοπολίτας, φιλέριδας, μνησικάκους, βαθυπονήρους, δράστας, ἀνυποίστους, σοβαρούς, φορτικούς, καυχηματίας, κακωτάς, ἀδίκους, ἀκαταφρονήτους,[4] μισανθρώπους, ἀτρέπτους, ἀμεταθέτους, πολυπράγμονας, εὐαναστρόφους μέντοι καὶ πρακτικοὺς καὶ ἀκαταγωνίστους καὶ ὅλως ἐπιτευκτικούς. ἐπὶ δὲ τῶν ἐναντίων ἅρπαγας, λῃστάς, νοθευτάς, κακοπαθεῖς, αἰσχροκερδεῖς, ἀθέους,[5] ἀστόργους, ὑβριστάς, ἐπιβουλευτικούς, κλέπτας, ἐπιόρκους, μιαιφόνους, ἀθεμιτοφάγους, κακούργους, ἀνδροφόνους, φαρμακευτάς, ἱεροσύλους, ἀσεβεῖς, τυμβωρύχους καὶ ὅλως [6] παγκάκους.

[1] μωροκάκους VADProc., ἀμωροκάκους PL, μωροκάλους MECam.
[2] αὐστηρούς .... εὐλαβητικούς om. PLMCam., habent VADEProc.
[3] ἀδήκτους codd. Cam.[1]; fortasse ἀδεήτους legendum est ut coniecit Cam.[2]; om. Proc.
[4] ἀκαταφρονήτους codd. et Proc., ἀκατακρίτους Cam.

TETRABIBLOS III. 13

public confessors of ailments, suspicious, hating their own children, friendless, hiding within doors, without judgement, faithless, knavishly foolish, venomous, hypocritical, ineffective, unambitious, prone to change their minds, stern, hard to speak with or to approach, cautious, but nevertheless foolish and submissive to abuse.

Saturn, allied with Mars, in honourable positions makes his subjects neither good nor bad, industrious, outspoken, nuisances, cowardly braggarts, harsh in conduct, without pity, contemptuous, rough, contentious, rash, disorderly, deceitful, layers of ambushes, tenacious of anger, unmoved by pleading, courting the mob, tyrannical, grasping, haters of the citizenry, fond of strife, malignant, evil through and through, active, impatient, blustering, vulgar, boastful, injurious, unjust, not to be despised, haters of mankind, inflexible, unchangeable, busy-bodies, but at the same time adroit and practical, not to be overborne by rivals, and in general successful in achieving their ends. In the opposite positions he makes his subjects robbers, pirates, adulterators, submissive to disgraceful treatment, takers of base profits, godless, without affection, insulting, crafty, thieves, perjurers, murderers, eaters of forbidden foods, evildoers, homicides, poisoners, impious, robbers of temples and of tombs, and utterly depraved.

---

⁵ ἀθέους VPLADProc., ἀθέτους MECam.¹, ἀθέσμους Cam.²
⁶ ὅλως om. Cam.

PTOLEMY

Τῷ δὲ τῆς Ἀφροδίτης συνοικειωθεὶς ἐπὶ μὲν ἐνδόξων διαθέσεων ποιεῖ μισογυναίους, φιλαρχαίους,[1] φιλερήμους, ἀηδεῖς πρὸς τὰς ἐντεύξεις, ἀφιλοτίμους, μισοκάλους, φθονερούς, αὐστηροὺς πρὸς συνουσίας, ἀσυμπεριφόρους, μονογνώμονας, φοιβαστικούς, θρησκευτάς, μυστηρίων καὶ τελετῶν ἐπιθυμητάς, ἱεροποιούς, ἐνθεαστικούς, θεοπροσπλόκους, σεμνοὺς δὲ καὶ εὐεντρέπτους, αἰδήμονας, 160 ἐμφιλοσόφους, πιστοὺς πρὸς συμβιώσεις,[2] ἐγκρατεῖς, ἐπιλογιστικούς, εὐλαβεῖς, ἀγανακτητάς τε καὶ πρὸς τὰς τῶν γυναικῶν ὑποψίας ζηλοτύπους· ἐπὶ δὲ τῶν ἐναντίων λάγνους, ἀσελγεῖς, αἰσχροποιούς, ἀδιαφόρους καὶ ἀκαθάρτους πρὸς τὰς συνουσίας, ἀνάγνους, ἐπιβουλευτικοὺς θηλυκῶν προσώπων καὶ μάλιστα τῶν οἰκειοτάτων, σαθρούς,[3] παμψόγους, καταφερεῖς, μισοκάλους, μωμητικούς, κακολόγους, μεθύσους, λατρευτικούς, ὑπονοθευτάς, ἀθεμίτους[4] πρὸς τὰς συνελεύσεις, διατιθέντας καὶ διατιθεμένους, οὐ μόνον πρὸς τὰ κατὰ φύσιν ἀλλὰ καὶ τὰ παρὰ φύσιν πρεσβυτέρων καὶ ἀτίμων καὶ παρανόμων καὶ θηριωδῶν μίξεων ἐπιθυμητάς, ἀσεβεῖς, θεῶν καταφρονητικούς, μυστηρίων καὶ ἱερῶν διασυρτικούς, πάμπαν ἀπίστους, διαβολικούς, φαρμακούς, παντοποιούς.

Τῷ δὲ τοῦ Ἑρμοῦ συνοικειωθεὶς ἐπὶ μὲν ἐνδόξων διαθέσεων ποιεῖ περιέργους, φιλοπεύστας, νομίμων

---

[1] φιλαρχαίους VPLDProc., -αρχίους E, -άρχους MACam.¹, -άνδρους Cam.²

[2] εὐσταθεῖς post συμβιώσεις add. MECam., om. VPLAD Proc.

TETRABIBLOS III. 13

Allied with Venus in honourable positions Saturn makes his subjects haters of women, lovers of antiquity, solitary, unpleasant to meet, unambitious, hating the beautiful, envious, stern in social relations, not companionable, of fixed opinions, prophetic, given to the practice of religious rites, lovers of mysteries and initiations, performers of sacrificial rites, mystics, religious addicts, but dignified and reverent, modest, philosophical, faithful in marriage,[1] self-controlled, calculating, cautious, quick to take offence, and easily led by jealousy to be suspicious of their wives. In positions of the opposite kind he makes them loose, lascivious, doers of base acts, undiscriminating and unclean in sexual relations, impure, deceivers of women and particularly their own kin, unsound, censorious, depraved, hating the beautiful, fault-finders, evil-speakers, drunken, servile, adulterators, lawless in sexual relations, both active and passive, both natural and unnatural, and willing to seek them with those barred by age, station, or law, or with animals, impious, contemptuous of the gods, deriding mysteries and sacred rites, entirely faithless, slanderous, poisoners, rogues who will stop at nothing.

Saturn, in familiarity with Mercury, in honourable positions makes his subjects meddlers, inquisitive,

[1] At this point some of the MSS. and Camerarius add "steadfast".

---

[3] σαθρούς VPDProc., καθρούς L, θρασεῖς MAECam.
[4] ἀθεμίτους VP (-μητ-) LADE, -τως MCam.; om. Proc.

PTOLEMY

ζητητικούς, φιλιάτρους, μυστικούς, μετόχους ἀποκρύφων καὶ ἀπορρήτων, τερατουργούς, παραλογιστάς, ἐφημεροβίους, ἐντρεχεῖς, διοικητικοὺς πραγμάτων καὶ ἀγχίφρονας, περιπίκρους καὶ ἀκριβεῖς, νήπτας, φιλόφρονας,[1] φιλοπράκτους, ἐπιτευκτικούς· ἐπὶ δὲ τῶν ἐναντίων ληρώδεις, μνησικάκους, νηλεεῖς
161 ταῖς ψυχαῖς, ἐπιμόχθους, μισοϊδίους, φιλοβασάνους,[2] ἀνευφράντους, νυκτερέμβους,[3] ἐνεδρευτάς, προδότας, ἀσυμπαθεῖς, κλέπτας, μαγικούς, φαρμακευτάς, πλαστογράφους, ῥᾳδιουργούς, ἀποτευκτικοὺς καὶ εὐεκπτώτους.

Ὁ δὲ τοῦ Διὸς ἀστὴρ μόνος τὴν οἰκοδεσποτίαν τῆς ψυχῆς λαβὼν ἐπὶ μὲν ἐνδόξων διαθέσεων ποιεῖ μεγαλοψύχους, χαριστικούς, θεοσεβεῖς, τιμητικούς, ἀπολαυστικούς, φιλανθρώπους, μεγαλοπρεπεῖς, ἐλευθέρους, δικαίους, μεγαλόφρονας, σεμνούς, ἰδιοπράγμονας, ἐλεήμονας, φιλολόγους, εὐεργετικούς,[4] φιλοστόργους, ἡγεμονικούς· ἐπὶ δὲ τῆς ἐναντίας διαθέσεως τυγχάνων τὰς ὁμοίας μὲν φαντασίας περιποιεῖ[5] ταῖς ψυχαῖς, ἐπὶ τὸ ταπεινότερον μέντοι καὶ ἀνεπιφαντότερον καὶ ἀκριτωτέρον· οἷον ἀντὶ μὲν μεγαλοψυχίας ἀσωτίαν, ἀντὶ δὲ θεοσεβείας δεισιδαι-

[1] φιλόφρονας PL, -ους VD, φιλοφρονητικούς Proc., φιλοπόνους MAECam.
[2] φιλοβασάνους VPLDEProc., φιλοβασκάνους MACam.
[3] νυκτερέμβους VPLD, νυκτιρρέμβους A, νυκτεριρέμβους MNECam., νυκτοβίους Proc.
[4] εὐεργετικούς VPLDProc., εὑρετικούς MNAECam.
[5] περιποιεῖται MNDCam.

inquirers into matters of law and custom, fond of the art of medicine, mystics, partakers in concealed and secret rites, miracle-workers, cheaters, living only for the day, facile, able to direct business, shrewd, bitter, accurate, sober, friendly, fond of practical affairs, capable of gaining their ends. In dishonourable positions he makes them frivolous talkers, malignant, with no pity in their souls, given to toil, hating their own kin, fond of torment, gloomy, night-prowlers, layers of ambushes, traitors, unsympathetic, thieves, magicians, poisoners, forgers, unscrupulous, unfortunate, and usually unsuccessful.

If Jupiter alone has the domination of the soul, in honourable positions he makes his subjects magnanimous, generous, god-fearing, honourable, pleasure-loving, kind, magnificent, liberal, just, high-minded, dignified, minding their own business, compassionate, fond of discussion, beneficent, affectionate, with qualities of leadership. If he chances to be in the opposite kind of position, he makes their souls seem similar, to be sure, but with a difference in the direction of greater humility, less conspicuousness, and poorer judgement.[1] For example, instead of magnanimity, he endows them with prodigality; instead

---

[1] Ptolemy probably has in mind Aristotle's famous doctrine that virtue is a mean (*Ethica Nicomachea*, 2, p. 1106b, 27) and the examples cited by Aristotle, but Ptolemy's instances are only similar to, not identical with, Aristotle's. Aristotle, for example, makes ἐλευθεριότης, "liberality," the virtue of which ἀσωτία, "prodigality" is an excess; contrasts μεγαλοψυχία, "magnanimity," with χαυνότης, "vanity," and μικροψυχία, "meanness of spirit"; αἰδήμων, "modest," with the excessive quality κατάπληξ, "shy," and with the deficiency ἀναίσχυντος, "shameless."

PTOLEMY

μονίαν, ἀντὶ δὲ αἰδοῦς δειλίαν, ἀντὶ δὲ σεμνότητος οἴησιν, ἀντὶ δὲ φιλανθρωπίας εὐήθειαν, ἀντὶ δὲ φιλοκαλίας φιληδονίαν, ἀντὶ δὲ μεγαλοφροσύνης βλακείαν, ἀντὶ δὲ ἐλευθεριότητος ἀδιαφορίαν, καὶ ὅσα τούτοις παραπλήσια.

Τῷ δὲ τοῦ Ἄρεως συνοικειωθεὶς ἐπὶ μὲν ἐνδόξων διαθέσεων ποιεῖ τραχεῖς, μαχίμους, στρατηγικούς,[1] διοικητικούς, κεκινημένους, ἀνυποτάκτους, θερμούς, παραβόλους, πρακτικούς, παρρησιαστικούς, ἐλεγκτικούς, ἀνυστικούς, φιλονείκους, ἀρχικούς, εὐεπιβούλους, ἐπιεικεῖς, ἐπάνδρους, νικητικούς, μεγαλοψύχους δὲ καὶ φιλοτίμους καὶ θυμικοὺς καὶ κριτικοὺς καὶ ἐπιτευκτικούς· ἐπὶ δὲ τῶν ἐναντίων ὑβριστάς, ἀδιαφόρους, ὠμούς, ἀνεξιλάστους, στασιαστάς, ἐριστικούς, μονοτόνους,[2] διαβόλους, οἰηματίας, πλεονέκτας, ἅρπαγας, ταχυμεταβόλους, κούφους, μεταμελητικούς, ἀστάτους, προπετεῖς, ἀπίστους, ἀκρίτους, ἀγνώμονας, ἐκστατικούς, ἐμπράκτους,[3] μεμψιμοίρους, ἀσώτους, ληρώδεις καὶ ὅλως ἀνωμάλους καὶ παρακεκινημένους.

Τῷ δὲ τῆς Ἀφροδίτης συνοικειωθεὶς ἐπὶ μὲν ἐνδόξων διαθέσεων ποιεῖ καθαρίους, ἀπολαυστικούς, φιλοκάλους, φιλοτέκνους, φιλοθεώρους, φιλομούσους, ᾠδικούς, φιλοτρόφους,[4] εὐήθεις, εὐεργετικούς,

---

[1] στρατηγικούς] στρατιωτικούς NCam.
[2] μονοτόνους PMEProc., μονοπόνους VLAD, μονοτρόπους NCam.
[3] ἐμπράκτους Proc., ἐμπατάκτους VPL, εὐπατάκτους MNADECam.
[4] φιλοτρόφους libri Cam.¹, -τρύφους Cam.²

TETRABIBLOS III. 13

of reverence for the gods, with superstition; instead of modesty, with cowardice; instead of dignity, with conceit; instead of kindness, with foolish simplicity; instead of the love of beauty, with love of pleasure; instead of high-mindedness, with stupidity; instead of liberality, with indifference, and the like.

Jupiter allied with Mars in honourable positions makes his subjects rough, pugnacious, military, managerial, restless, unruly, ardent, reckless, practical, outspoken, critical, effective, contentious, commanding, given to plotting, respectable, virile, fond of victory, but magnanimous, ambitious, passionate, judicious, successful. In the opposite position he makes then insolent, undiscriminating, savage, implacable, seditious, contentious, stubborn, slanderous, conceited, avaricious, rapacious, quickly changeable, light, readily changing their minds, unstable, headstrong, untrustworthy, of poor judgement, unfeeling, excitable, active, querulous, prodigal, gossipy, and in all ways uneven and easily excited.

Jupiter, allied with Venus, in honourable positions makes his subjects pure, pleasure-loving, lovers of the beautiful, of children, of spectacles, and of the domain of the Muses, singers, fond of those who reared them, of good character,[1] beneficent, com-

---

[1] εὐήθεια and the corresponding adjective, εὐήθης, have two distinct senses, the original, etymological one, "good character," and a derived meaning, "simplicity" or "guilelessness," which may amount to nothing more than downright folly. Plato, in *Republic*, 400 DE, uses εὐήθεια in the first sense, specifically saying that he does not mean the other kind of εὐήθεια. In the present passage, the context clearly shows that the first sense is intended; but in the very next paragraph εὐήθης occurs in its second meaning.

PTOLEMY

ἐλεητικούς,[1] ἀκάκους, φιλοθέους, ἀσκητάς, φιλαγωνιστάς, φρονίμους, φιλητικούς, ἐπαφροδίτους ἐν τῷ σεμνῷ, λαμπροψύχους, εὐγνώμονας, μεταδοτικούς, φιλογραμμάτους, κριτικούς, συμμέτρους καὶ εὐσχήμονας πρὸς τὰ ἀφροδίσια, φιλοικείους,[2] εὐσεβεῖς, φιλοδικαίους, φιλοτίμους, φιλοδόξους καὶ ὅλως καλούς τε καὶ ἀγαθούς· ἐπὶ δὲ τῶν ἐναντίων τρυφητάς, ἡδυβίους, θηλυψύχους, ὀρχηστικούς, γυναικοθύμους, δαπανηρούς,[3] κακογυναίους,[4] ἐρωτικούς, λάγνους, καταφερεῖς, λοιδόρους,[5] μοιχούς, φιλοκόσμους, ὑπομαλάκους,[6] ῥαθύμους, ἀσώτους, ἐπιμώμους,[7] ἐμπαθεῖς, καλλωπιστάς, γυναικονοήμονας, ἱερῶν ἐγκατόχους, προαγωγικούς, μυστηριακούς, πιστοὺς μέντοι καὶ ἀπονήρους καὶ ἐπιχαρίτους καὶ εὐπροσίτους[8] καὶ εὐδιαγώγους καὶ πρὸς τὰς συμφοράς[9] ἐλευθεριωτέρους.

Τῷ δὲ τοῦ Ἑρμοῦ συνοικειωθεὶς ἐπὶ μὲν ἐνδόξων διαθέσεων ποιεῖ πολυγραμμάτους,[10] φιλολόγους, γεωμέτρας,[11] μαθηματικούς, ποιητικούς, δημηγορικούς, εὐφυεῖς, σωφρονικούς, ἀγαθόφρονας, καλοσυμβούλους, πολιτικούς, εὐεργετικούς, ἐπιτροπικούς,

---

[1] ἐλεητικούς VD, ἐλεήμονας Proc., om. PL, ἐλεγκτικούς MNAECam.

[2] φιλοικείους E, φιλικείους VD, φιλοικίους P, φιλικίους L, φιλονείκους MNACam.

[3] δαπανηρούς PLProc., δαπάνους cett. Cam.

[4] κακογυναίους Proc., καταγυναίους VD, κατὰ γυναίων PL, καὶ γυναίους MNAECam.

[5] λοιδόρους μοιχούς Proc., om. λοιδόρους PLMNECam., om. μοιχούς VAD.

passionate, guileless, religious, prone to athletic training, fond of competition, wise, affectionate, charming in a dignified way, magnanimous, fair, charitable, fond of learning, of good judgement, moderate and decorous in matters of love, fond of their kinsfolk, pious, just, ambitious, seekers after glory, and in general gentlemanly. In the opposite positions he renders them luxurious, soft-livers, effeminate, fond of the dance, womanly in spirit, lavish in expenditure, evil in relations with women, erotic, lascivious, lecherous, slanderous, adulterous, lovers of ornament, rather soft, lazy, profligate, given to fault-finding, passionate, adorners of their persons, womanly minded, infatuated by religious rites, panderers, frequenters of the mysteries, trustworthy however and not rascally, but gracious, easy of approach, and cheerful, and inclined to liberality in misfortune.

Jupiter allied with Mercury in honourable positions makes his subjects learned, fond of discussion, geometricians, mathematicians, poets, orators, gifted, sober, of good intellect, good in counsel, statesmen, benefactors, managers, good-natured, generous, lovers

---

⁶ ὑπομαλάκους VP (-μαλλ-) LADE, φιλομαλάκους MNCam.

⁷ ἐπιμώμους VPLProc., ἐπιβώμους D, φιλομώμους MNECam., om. A; post hoc verbum add. ὑπομώρους MNECam., φιλομώρους A, om. cett. Proc.

⁸ Post εὐπροσίτους add. πιστούς MNCam., om. cett. Proc.

⁹ συμφοράς VDProc., περισυμφοράς P (-φωρ-) L, ἐπιφοράς MNAECam.

¹⁰ πολυγραμμάτους VADProc., φιλογραμμάτους MNECam., πολυπραγμάτους φιλοπράκτους PL.

¹¹ γεωμέτρας VPLDProc., φιλογεωμέτρας MNAECam.

PTOLEMY

χρηστοήθεις, φιλοδώρους, φιλόχλους, εὐεπηβόλους,[1] ἐπιτευκτικούς, ἡγεμονικούς, εὐσεβεῖς, φιλοθέους, εὐχρηματίστους, φιλοστόργους, φιλοικείους, εὐπαιδεύτους, ἐμφιλοσόφους, ἀξιωματικούς· ἐπὶ δὲ τῶν ἐναντίων εὐήθεις, ληρώδεις, σφαλλομένους, εὐκαταφρονήτους, ἐνθουσιαστικούς, θεοπροσπλόκους,[2] φληνάφους, ὑποπίκρους, προσποιησισόφους,[3] ἀνοήτους, ἀλαζονικούς, ἐπιτηδευτάς, μαγευτικούς, ὑποκεκινημένους, πολυΐστορας δὲ καὶ μνημονικοὺς καὶ[4] διδασκαλικοὺς καὶ καθαρίους ταῖς ἐπιθυμίαις.

Ὁ δὲ τοῦ Ἄρεως ἀστὴρ μόνος τὴν οἰκοδεσποτίαν τῆς ψυχῆς λαβὼν ἐπὶ μὲν ἐνδόξου διαθέσεως ποιεῖ γενναίους, ἀρχικούς, θυμικούς, φιλόπλους,[5] πολυτρόπους,[6] σθεναρούς, παραβόλους, ῥιψοκινδύνους, ἀνυποτάκτους, ἀδιαφόρους, μονοτόνους, ὀξεῖς, αὐθάδεις, καταφρονητικούς, τυραννικούς, δράστας, ὀργίλους, ἡγεμονικούς· ἐπὶ δὲ τῆς ἐναντίας ὠμούς· ὑβριστάς, φιλαίμους, φιλοθορύβους, δαπάνους, κραυγαστάς,[7] πλήκτας, προπετεῖς, μεθύσους, ἅρπαγας, κακούργους, ἀνελεήμονας, τεταραγμένους, μανιώδεις, μισοικείους, ἀθέους.

Τῷ δὲ τῆς Ἀφροδίτης συνοικειωθεὶς ἐπὶ μὲν ἐνδόξων διαθέσεων ποιεῖ ἐπιχάριτας, εὐδιαγώγους, φιλεταίρους, ἡδυβίους, εὐφροσύνους, παιγνιώδεις,

---

[1] εὐεπηβόλους ME, εὐεπιβούλους PLNCam., ἐπιβόλους VAD, om. Proc.

[2] θεοπροσπλόκους P (-πλωκ-) L (-πλωκ-) MAEProc., θεοπλόκους VD, θεοπροσπόλους NCam.

[3] προσποιησισόφους ME, προσποιήσει σοφούς PL, προσποιήσεις σοφούς VD, προσποιήτους σοφούς A, προσποιησόφους NCam.

[4] μνημονικοὺς καὶ om. Cam.[2]

of the mob, shrewd, successful, leaders, reverent, religious, skilful in business, affectionate, lovers of their own kin, well brought up, philosophical, dignified. In the opposite positions he makes them simple, garrulous, prone to make mistakes, contemptible, fanatical, religious enthusiasts, speakers of folly, inclined to bitterness, pretenders to wisdom, fools, boasters, students, magicians, somewhat deranged, but well informed, of good memory, teachers, and pure in their desires.

Mars alone, given the domination of the soul, in an honourable position makes his subjects noble, commanding, spirited, military, versatile,[1] powerful, venturesome, rash, unruly, indifferent, stubborn, keen, headstrong, contemptuous, tyrannical, active, easily angered, with the qualities of leadership. In a position of the opposite kind he makes them savage, insolent, bloodthirsty, makers of disturbances, spendthrifts, loud-mouthed, quick-fisted, impetuous, drunken, rapacious, evil-doers, pitiless, unsettled, mad, haters of their own kin, impious.

Allied with Venus, in honourable positions, Mars makes his subjects pleasing, cheerful, friendly, soft-living, happy, playful, artless, graceful, fond of

---

[1] The epithet constantly used to describe Odysseus by Homer.

---

[5] φιλόπλους VPLMADE, φιλοπολέμους Proc., φιλοπλούτους NCam.
[6] πολυτρόπους VP (πολλ-) LDProc., πολυτρόφους MNAECam.
[7] κραυγαστάς PL, κραυγάσους VD, κραυγαστικούς AProc., κραυγάζους MNECam.

PTOLEMY

ἀφελεῖς, εὐρύθμους, φιλορχηστάς,[1] ἐρωτικούς, φιλοτέχνους, μιμητικούς, ἀπολαυστικούς, διασκευαστάς, ἐπάνδρους καὶ εὐκαταφόρους μὲν πρὸς τὰς ἀφροδισιακὰς ἁμαρτίας, ἐπιτευκτικοὺς δὲ καὶ εὐπεριστόλους καὶ νουνεχεῖς καὶ δυσελέγκτους καὶ διακριτικούς,[2] ἔτι δὲ νέων ἐπιθυμητικοὺς ἀρρένων τε καὶ θηλειῶν, δαπανηρούς τε καὶ ὀξυθύμους καὶ ζηλοτύπους· ἐπὶ δὲ τῶν ἐναντίων ῥιψοφθάλμους, λάγνους, καταφερεῖς, ἀδιαφόρους, διασύρτας, μοιχικούς, ὑβριστάς, ψεύστας, δολοπλόκους, ὑπονοθευτὰς οἰκείων τε καὶ ἀλλοτρίων, ὀξεῖς ἅμα καὶ προσκορεῖς πρὸς τὰς ἐπιθυμίας, διαφθορέας γυναικῶν καὶ παρθένων, παραβόλους, θερμούς, ἀτάκτους,[3] ἐνεδρευτάς, ἐπιόρκους, εὐεμπτώτους τε καὶ φρενοβλαβεῖς, ἐνίοτε δὲ καὶ ἀσώτους,[4] φιλοκόσμους καὶ θρασεῖς καὶ διατιθεμένους καὶ ἀσελγαίνοντας.[5]

Τῷ δὲ τοῦ Ἑρμοῦ συνοικειωθεὶς ἐπὶ μὲν ἐνδόξων διαθέσεων ποιεῖ στρατηγικούς, δεινούς,[6] δράστας, 165 εὐκινήτους, ἀκαταφρονήτους, πολυτρόπους, εὑρετικούς,[7] σοφιστάς, ἐπιπόνους, πανούργους, προγλώσσους, ἐπιθετικούς, δολίους, ἀστάτους, μεθοδευτάς, κακοτέχνους, ὀξύφρονας, ἐξαπατητάς, ὑποκριτικούς, ἐνεδρευτάς, κακοτρόπους, πολυπράγμονας, φιλοπονήρους, ἐπιτευκτικοὺς δ' ἄλλως καὶ πρὸς τοὺς ὁμοίους εὐσυνθέτους καὶ εὐσυνδεξιάστους, καὶ ὅλως

---

[1] φιλοτέχνους PLProc.. φιλοτέκνους cett. Cam.
[2] διακριτικούς VPLADProc., ἀδιακρίτους MNECam.
[3] ἀτάκτους libri ; ἀτόπους Cam.
[4] ἀσώτους VADProc., αὐτῷ τοὺς PL, αὐτοὺς MNECam.
[5] Post ἀσελγαίνοντας add. ἀπεργάζεται MNAECam., om. VPLDProc.

dancing, erotic, artistic, imitative, pleasure-loving, able to secure themselves property,[1] masculine, and given to misconduct in matters of love, but still successful, circumspect, and sensible, difficult to convict and discreet, furthermore passionate for both young men and young women, spendthrifts, quick-tempered, and jealous. In contrary positions he makes them leering, lascivious, profligate, indifferent, slanderers, adulterers, insolent, liars, deceivers, seducers of those both in their own families and in those of others, at the same time keen and insatiate of pleasure, corrupters of women and maidens, venturesome, ardent, unruly, treacherous, perjurers, easily influenced and of unsound mind, but sometimes likewise profligate, fond of adornment, bold, disposed to base practices, and shameless.

Allied with Mercury, in honourable positions Mars makes his subjects leaders of armies, skilful, vigorous, active, not to be despised, resourceful, inventive, sophistic, painstaking, rascally, talkative, pugnacious, tricky, unstable, systematic workers, practising evil arts, keen-witted, deceitful, hypocritical, insidious, of bad character, meddlers, inclined to rascality but nevertheless successful and capable of keeping contract and faith with persons like themselves, and in

---

[1] διασκευαστής also means one who arranges a text, "editor," but here a less specialised meaning seems to be called for. The verb διασκευάζειν has, in general, the active meaning "set in order," and in the middle voice "equip one's self." Proclus omits this word in the *Paraphrase*.

---

[6] δεινούς VD, δειλούς MNAEProc.Cam.; δεινούς . . ἀκαταφρονήτους om. PL.
[7] εὑρετικούς] εὐεκτικούς NCam.

ἐχθρῶν μὲν βλαπτικούς, φίλων δὲ εὐποιητικούς· ἐπὶ δὲ τῶν ἐναντίων δαπανηρούς, πλεονέκτας, ὠμούς, παραβόλους, τολμηρούς, μεταμελητικούς, ἐμπαράκτους,[1] παρακεκινημένους, ψεύστας, κλέπτας, ἀθέους, ἐπιόρκους, ἐπιθέτας, στασιαστάς, ἐμπρηστάς, θεατροκόπους, ἐφυβρίστους,[2] λῃστρικούς, τοιχωρύχους,[3] μιαιφόνους, πλαστογράφους, ῥᾳδιουργούς, γόητας, μάγους, φαρμακούς, ἀνδροφόνους.

Ὁ δὲ τῆς Ἀφροδίτης μόνος τὴν οἰκοδεσποτίαν τῆς ψυχῆς[4] λαβὼν ἐπὶ μὲν ἐνδόξου διαθέσεως ποιεῖ προσηνεῖς, ἀγαθούς, τρυφητάς,[5] λογίους,[6] καθαρίους, εὐφροσύνους, φιλορχηστάς, καλοζήλους,[7] μισοπονήρους, φιλοτέχνους, φιλοθεωτάτους,[8] εὐσχήμονας, εὐεκτικούς, εὐονείρους, φιλοστόργους, εὐεργετικούς, ἐλεήμονας, σικχούς,[9] εὐσυναλλάκτους, ἐπιτευκτικοὺς καὶ ὅλως ἐπαφροδίτους· ἐπὶ δὲ τῆς ἐναντίας ῥᾳθύμους, ἐρωτικούς, τεθηλυσμένους, γυναικώδεις, ἀτόλμους, ἀδιαφόρους, καταφερεῖς, ἐπιψόγους, ἀνεπιφάντους, ἐπονειδίστους.[10]

Τῷ δὲ τοῦ Ἑρμοῦ συνοικειωθεὶς ἐπὶ μὲν ἐνδόξων διαθέσεων ποιεῖ φιλοτέχνους, ἐμφιλοσόφους, ἐπιστημονικούς, εὐφυεῖς, ποιητικούς, φιλομούσους, φιλοκάλους, χρηστοήθεις, ἀπολαυστικούς, τρυφερο-

---

[1] ἐμπαράκτους VD, ἐμπράκτους PLA, ἐμπατάκτους MNE Cam.; om. Proc. Fortasse legendum est εὐπαράκτους.
[2] ἐφυβρίστους VMNDE, om. PLProc., ἐφυβρίστας ACam.
[3] τοιχωρύχους VP (-ορ-) DProc., τυμβωρύχους MNAEL (-ορ-) Cam.
[4] τῆς ψυχῆς om. VDProc.
[5] κοινούς post τρυφητάς add. MNECam., om. VPLADProc.

TETRABIBLOS III. 13

general injurious to their enemies and helpful to their friends. In opposite positions he makes them spendthrifts, avaricious, savage, venturesome, daring, prone to change their minds, excitable, easily aroused, liars, thieves, impious, perjurers, ready to take the offensive, seditious, kindlers of fires, creators of disturbances in the theatre, insolent, piratical, burglars, murderers, forgers, villains, wizards, magicians, sorcerers, homicides.

If Venus alone takes the domination of the soul, in an honourable position she makes her subjects pleasant, good, luxurious,[1] eloquent, neat, cheerful, fond of dancing, eager for beauty, haters of evil, lovers of the arts, fond of spectacles, decorous, healthy, dreamers of pleasant dreams, affectionate, beneficent, compassionate, fastidious, easily conciliated, successful, and, in general, charming. In the opposite position she makes them careless, erotic, effeminate, womanish, timid, indifferent, depraved, censorious, insignificant, meriting reproach.

Joined with Mercury, in honourable positions Venus makes them artistic, philosophical, gifted with understanding, talented, poetic, lovers of the muses, lovers of beauty, of worthy character,

[1] Certain texts add here " affable " (κοινούς).

---

[6] λογίους VADProc., λογικούς PL, ἐλλογίμους MNECam.
[7] κακοζήλους MNEProc.Cam., καλοζήλους VPLAD.
[8] φιλοθεωτάτους libri Cam.¹, -θεώρους Cam.²
[9] σικχούς om. MNCam.   [10] ἐπονειδίστους om. Cam.

PTOLEMY

διαίτους,[1] εὐφροσύνους,[2] φιλοφίλους, εὐσεβεῖς, συνετούς, πολυμηχάνους, διανοητικούς, εὐεπιβόλους,[3] κατορθωτικούς, ταχυμαθεῖς,[4] αὐτοδιδάκτους, ζηλωτὰς τῶν ἀρίστων, μιμητὰς[5] τῶν καλῶν, εὐστόμους καὶ ἐπιχάριτας τῷ λόγῳ, ἐρασμίους, εὐαρμόστους τοῖς ἤθεσι, σπουδαίους, φιλάθλους, ὀρθούς,[6] κριτικούς, μεγαλόφρονας, τῶν δὲ ἀφροδισίων πρὸς μὲν τὰ γυναικεῖα φυλακτικούς, πρὸς δὲ τὰ παιδικὰ μᾶλλον κεκινημένους καὶ ζηλοτύπους· ἐπὶ δὲ τῆς ἐναντίας ἐπιθέτας, πολυμηχάνους, κακοστόμους, ἀλλοπροσάλλους, κακογνώμονας, ἐξαπατητάς, κυκητάς, ψεύστας, διαβόλους, ἐπιόρκους, βαθυπονήρους, ἐπιβουλευτικούς, ἀσυνθέτους, ἀδεξιάστους, νοθευτάς, γυναικῶν διαφθορέας καὶ παίδων, ἔτι δὲ καλλωπιστάς, ὑπομαλάκους, ἐπιψόγους,[7] κακοφήμους, πολυθρυλήτους, παντοπράξους,[8] καὶ ἐνίοτε μὲν ἐπὶ διαφθορᾷ τὰ τοιαῦτα ὑποκρινομένους, ἐνίοτε δὲ καὶ ταῖς ἀληθείαις, διατιθεμένους τε καὶ αἰσχροποιοῦντας καὶ ποικίλοις πάθεσιν ὑβριζομένους.

167 Ὁ δὲ τοῦ Ἑρμοῦ ἀστὴρ μόνος τὴν οἰκοδεσποτίαν τῆς ψυχῆς λαβὼν ἐπὶ μὲν ἐνδόξου διαθέσεως ποιεῖ τοὺς γεννωμένους συνετούς, ἀγχίνους, νοήμονας, πολυΐστορας, εὑρετικούς, ἐμπείρους, λογιστικούς,

---

[1] τρυφεροδιαίτους VP (τρυφαιροδιέτους) L (τριφεροδιέτους) AD, τρυφεροέτους ME, τρυφεροβίους Proc., τρυφερούς NCam.
[2] φιλοσόφους post εὐφροσύνους add. MNCam., om. cett. Proc.
[3] εὐεπιβόλους NACam., εὐεπηβόλους ME, εὐεπιβούλους VPLD; om. Proc.
[4] φιλομαθεῖς post ταχυμαθεῖς add. NCam., om. VPLADProc.; ταχυφιλομαθεῖς ME.

seekers after enjoyment, luxurious, happy,[1] fond of friends, pious, sagacious, resourceful, intellectual, intelligent, successful, quick to learn,[2] self-taught, seekers after the best, imitators of beauty, eloquent and pleasing in speech, commanding affection, of well-ordered character, earnest, fond of athletics, upright, of good judgement, magnanimous; in affairs of love, restrained in their relations with women but more passionate for boys, and jealous. In the contrary position she makes them pugnacious, resourceful, evil-speakers, unstable, of bad intentions, deceivers, agitators, liars, slanderers, perjurers, thorough rascals, plotters, faithless, unreliable, adulterators, corrupters of women and children; furthermore, adorners of their persons, rather effeminate, malicious in censure and in gossip, garrulous, villains, sometimes[3] feigning such acts with a view to corruption and sometimes performing them in earnest, lending themselves to base acts and performing them, and subjected to all sorts of base treatment.

Mercury, by himself taking the domination of the soul, in an honourable position makes those who are born under him wise, shrewd, thoughtful, learned, inventive, experienced, good calculators, inquirers

[1] "Fond of wisdom" (φιλοσόφους) is added here by certain MSS.
[2] Certain MSS. add "fond of learning" at this point.
[3] Proclus omits the rest of this paragraph.

---

[5] μιμητὰς VPLADE Proc., ζηλωτὰς MNCam.
[6] ὀρθούς VPLADProc.; om. MNECam.
[7] ἐπιψόγους VP (-ψωγ-) LADProc.; κακοψόγους MNECam.
[8] παντοπράξους VPLMD, -πράκτους A, -πράκτας NECam., πάντα ἐπιχειροῦντας Proc.

PTOLEMY

φυσιολόγους, θεωρητικούς, εὐφυεῖς, ζηλωτικούς, εὐεργετικούς, ἐπιλογιστικούς, εὐστόχους, μαθηματικούς, μυστηριακούς, ἐπιτευκτικούς· ἐπὶ δὲ τῆς ἐναντίας πανούργους, προπετεῖς, ἐπιλήσμονας, ὁρμηματίας,[1] κούφους, εὐμεταβόλους, μεταμελητικούς, μωροκάκους, ἄφρονας, ἁμαρτώλους, ψεύστας, ἀδιαφόρους, ἀστάτους, ἀπίστους, πλεονέκτας, ἀδίκους καὶ ὅλως σφαλερούς τε τῇ διανοίᾳ καὶ καταφόρους τοῖς ἁμαρτήμασι.

Τούτων δὲ οὕτως ἐχόντων συμβάλλεται μέντοι καὶ αὐτὴ ἡ τῆς σελήνης κατάστασις,[2] ἐπειδήπερ ἐν μὲν τοῖς ἐπικαμπίοις τυγχάνουσα τοῦ τε νοτίου καὶ τοῦ βορείου πέρατος συνεργεῖ τοῖς ψυχικοῖς ἰδιώμασιν ἐπὶ τὸ πολυτροπώτερον καὶ τὸ πολυμηχανώτερον καὶ εὐμεταβολώτερον· ἐπὶ δὲ τῶν συνδέσμων ἐπὶ τὸ ὀξύτερον καὶ πρακτικώτερον καὶ εὐκινητότερον· ἔτι δὲ ἐν μὲν ταῖς ἀνατολαῖς καὶ ταῖς τῶν φώτων αὐξήσεσιν ἐπὶ τὸ εὐφυέστερον καὶ προφανέστερον καὶ βεβαιότερον καὶ παρρησιαστικώτερον· ἐν δὲ ταῖς μειώσεσι[3] τῶν φώτων ἢ ταῖς κρύψεσιν ἐπὶ τὸ νωχελέστερον καὶ ἀμβλύτερον καὶ μεταμελητικώτερον καὶ εὐλαβέστερον καὶ ἀνεπιφανέστερον.

Συμβάλλεται δέ πως καὶ ὁ ἥλιος συνοικειωθεὶς τῷ τῆς ψυχικῆς κράσεως οἰκοδεσποτήσαντι, κατὰ μὲν τὸ ἔνδοξον πάλιν τῆς διαθέσεως ἐπὶ τὸ δικαιότερον

---

[1] ὁρμηματίας VPLD, ὁρμητάς MAE, ὁρμητικάς Cam.[1], ὁρμητικούς NCam.[2]

[2] αὐτὴ ἡ τῆς σελήνης κατάστασις VAD, ἡ αὐτῆς τῆς σελήνης PLMNECam.

[3] μειώσεσι(ν) P (μοι-) LMAEProc., βιώσεσιν VD, οἰκειώσεσι NCam.

TETRABIBLOS III. 13

into nature, speculative, gifted, emulous, beneficent, prudent, good at conjecture, mathematicians, partakers in mysteries, successful in attaining their ends. In the opposite position he makes them utter rascals, precipitate, forgetful, impetuous, light-minded, fickle, prone to change their minds, foolish rogues, witless, sinful, liars, undiscriminating, unstable, undependable, avaricious, unjust, and, in general, unsteady in judgement and inclined to evil deeds.

While the foregoing is true as stated, nevertheless the condition of the moon itself also makes a certain contribution. For when the moon happens to be at the bendings of its northern and southern limits,[1] it helps,[2] with respect to the character of the soul, in the direction of greater versatility, resourcefulness, and capacity for change; at the nodes, in the direction of greater keenness, activity, and excitability; again, at rising and in the increases of its illumination, towards greater natural endowments, renown, firmness, and frankness; and in the waning of its illumination, or its occultations, towards greater sluggishness and dullness, less fixity of purpose, greater cautiousness, and less renown.

The sun also aids, when it is familiar with the planet that governs the temperament of the soul, in an honourable position modifying it in the

---

[1] See the note on iii. 12 (p. 325) concerning the bendings and nodes of the moon's orbit.
[2] Here, as in the case of bodily form and temperament (iii. 11; *cf.* especially p. 313), the actual rulers are the five planets, and it is the rôle of the luminaries to assist, adding their influences to those of the former.

καὶ ἀνυστικώτερον καὶ τιμητικώτερον[1] καὶ σεμνότερον καὶ θεοσεβέστερον· κατὰ δὲ τὸ ἐναντίον καὶ ἀνοίκειον ἐπὶ τὸ ταπεινότερον καὶ ἐπιπονώτερον καὶ ἀσημότερον[2] καὶ ὠμότερον καὶ μονογνωμονέστερον καὶ αὐστηρότερον καὶ δυσδιαγωγότερον καὶ ὅλως ἐπὶ τὸ δυσκατορθώτερον.

⟨ιδ.⟩ Περὶ παθῶν ψυχικῶν

Ἐπεὶ δὲ τοῖς τῆς ψυχῆς ἰδιώμασιν ἀκολουθεῖ πως καὶ ὁ περὶ[3] τῶν ἐξαιρέτων αὐτῆς παθῶν λόγος, καθ' ὅλου μὲν πάλιν ἐπισημαίνεσθαι καὶ παρατηρεῖν προσήκει τόν τε τοῦ Ἑρμοῦ ἀστέρα καὶ τὴν σελήνην, πῶς ἔχουσι πρός τε ἀλλήλους καὶ τὰ κέντρα καὶ τοὺς πρὸς κάκωσιν οἰκείους τῶν ἀστέρων· ὡς ἐάν τε αὐτοὶ ἀσύνδετοι ὄντες πρὸς ἀλλήλους, ἐάν τε πρὸς τὸν ἀνατολικὸν ὁρίζοντα, καθυπερτερηθῶσιν ἢ ἐμπερισχεθῶσιν ἢ διαμηκισθῶσιν ὑπὸ τῶν ἀνοικείως καὶ βλαπτικῶς ἐσχηματισμένων, ποικίλων παθῶν περὶ τὰς ψυχικὰς ἰδιοτροπίας συμπιπτόντων εἰσὶ ποιητικοί, τῆς διακρίσεως[4] αὐτῶν πάλιν θεωρουμένης ἀπὸ τῆς προκατειλημμένης τῶν τοῖς τόποις συνοικειωθέντων ἀστέρων ἰδιοτροπίας.

Τὰ μὲν οὖν πλεῖστα τῶν μετριωτέρων παθῶν σχεδὸν καὶ ἐν τοῖς ἔμπροσθεν περὶ τῶν τῆς ψυχῆς ἰδιωμάτων ῥηθεῖσι διακέκριταί πως, τῆς ἐπιτάσεως αὐτῶν ἐκ τῆς τῶν κακούντων ὑπερβολῆς συνορᾶσθαι δυναμένης· ἐπειδήπερ ἤδη τις ἂν εἰκότως εἴποι

---

[1] ἀνυτικώτερον καὶ τιμητικώτερον VAD; πρακτικώτερον καὶ τιμητικώτερον Proc.; ἀνυτικώτερον MNECam.[1]; om. PL; ἠθικώτερον Cam.[2]

TETRABIBLOS III. 13-14

direction of justice, success, honour, dignity, and reverence for the gods, but in the contrary and alien position making it humbler, more industrious, less conspicuous, more savage, more obstinate, harsher, with a harder life, and in general less successful.

14. *Of Diseases of the Soul.*

Since the account of the principal diseases of the soul, in a sense, follows upon that of the soul's characteristics, it is in general needful to note and observe the positions of Mercury and the moon relative to each other, to the angles, and to the planets whose nature it is to do injury; for if, while they themselves are unrelated to each other, or to the eastern horizon, they are overcome, or surrounded, or held in opposition by unfamiliar stars in injurious aspect, they cause the incidence of various diseases which affect the soul's character. Their interpretation again is to be calculated from the previously described qualities of the planets which are familiar to the places [1] in the sky.

Indeed, most of the more moderate diseases have, in a way, already been distinguished in what has been said about the character of the soul, and their increase can be discerned from the excess of injurious influences; for one might now with propriety call

[1] *I.e.* of the moon and Mercury.

---

[2] ἀσημότερον] ἀσημώτερον VD, ἀσημ(ε)ιότερον PL; *cf.* ἀφανέστερον Proc.; ἀσεμνότερον MNAECam.

[3] ὁ περὶ] ὥσπερεὶ Cam.

[4] διακρίσεως VPLMADE, διακράσεως NCam.¹, δυσκρασίας Cam.²; *cf.* διάγνωσις Proc.

πάθη καὶ τὰ ἄκρα¹ τῶν ἠθῶν καὶ ἢ ἐλλείποντα ἢ πλεονάζοντα τῆς μεσότητος· τὰ δ' ἐξαίρετον² ἔχοντα τὴν ἀμετρίαν καὶ ὥσπερ νοσηματώδη καὶ παρ' ὅλην τὴν φύσιν καὶ περί τε αὐτὸ³ τὸ διανοητικὸν τῆς ψυχῆς μέρος καὶ περὶ τὸ παθητικόν, ὡς ἐν τύπῳ, τοιαύτης ἔτυχε παρατηρήσεως.

Ἐπιληπτικοὶ μὲν γὰρ ὡς ἐπὶ τὸ πολὺ γίνονται ὅσοι τῆς σελήνης καὶ τοῦ τοῦ Ἑρμοῦ, ὥσπερ εἴπομεν, ἢ ἀλλήλοις ἢ τῷ ἀνατολικῷ ὁρίζοντι ἀσυνδέτων ὄντων τὸν μὲν τοῦ Κρόνου ἡμέρας, τὸν δὲ τοῦ Ἄρεως νυκτὸς ἔχουσιν ἐπίκεντρον καὶ κατοπτεύοντα τὸ προκείμενον σχῆμα· μανιώδεις δ' ὅταν ἐπὶ τῶν αὐτῶν ἀνάπαλιν ὁ μὲν τοῦ Κρόνου νυκτός, ὁ δὲ τοῦ Ἄρεως ἡμέρας, κεκυριευκὼς ᾖ τοῦ σχήματος, καὶ μάλιστα ἐν Καρκίνῳ ἢ Παρθένῳ ἢ Ἰχθύσι· δαιμονιόπληκτοι δὲ καὶ ὑγροκέφαλοι ὅταν οὕτως ἔχοντες οἱ κακοποιοῦντες ἐπὶ φάσεως⁴ οὖσαν⁵ κατέχωσι τὴν σελήνην, ὁ μὲν τοῦ Κρόνου συνοδεύουσαν, ὁ δὲ τοῦ Ἄρεως πανσεληνιάζουσαν, μάλιστα δ' ἐν Τοξότῃ καὶ Ἰχθύσι. μόνοι μὲν οὖν οἱ κακοποιοὶ κατὰ τὸν προειρημένον τρόπον τὴν ἐπικράτησιν τοῦ σχήματος λαβόντες ἀνίατα μέν, ἀνεπίφαντα δὲ ὅμως καὶ ἀπαραδειγμάτιστα ποιοῦσι

---

¹ ἄκρα MNECam., ἄκρατα VADProc., ἀκράτητα P, ἀκρότατα L.

² ἐξαίρετον] ἐξαίροντα NCam.

³ περί τε αὐτὸ VD, περὶ αὐτὸ PL, περὶ τὸ διανοητικὸν κτλ. Proc.; παρ' ὅλον MNAECam.

⁴ ἐπὶ φάσεως] ἐπιφάσεως VPLDProc., οὕτω θέσεως E, ἐπὶ φῶς MNACam.

⁵ οὖσαν VPMD, οὓς ἂν L, ἔχουσαν E, ἰοῦσαν NACam.; οὖσα Proc.

TETRABIBLOS III. 14

" diseases " those extremes of character which either fall short of or exceed the mean. Those affections, however, which are utterly disproportionate and as it were pathological, which relate to the whole nature, and which concern both the intelligent part of the soul and its passive part, are, in brief, to be discerned as follows.

In most cases those are epileptic [1] in whose genitures the moon and Mercury are, as we said above, unrelated to each other or to the eastern horizon, while Saturn by day or Mars by night is angular and in the aspect previously described.[2] They are violently insane when, again under the same conditions, Saturn by night and Mars by day rules the position, particularly in Cancer, Virgo, or Pisces. They are afflicted by demons [3] and have water on the brain when the maleficent planets are in this position and control the moon in phase, Saturn when she is at conjunction, Mar when she is full, and particularly in Sagittarius and Pisces. When the maleficent planets are by themselves and rule the configuration in the manner stated, the diseases of the rational part of the soul which we have mentioned as being

---

[1] Epilepsy and insanity were also mentioned among the bodily diseases (c. 12 above, pp. 329, 331).

[2] Overcoming, surrounding, or opposing ; see above.

[3] On this superstition in Roman Egypt, cf. Cumont, L'Égypte des astrologues, 167-170. Ptolemy apparently identifies seizure by demons with " water on the brain."

PTOLEMY

τὰ προκείμενα[1] τοῦ διανοητικοῦ τῆς ψυχῆς νοσήματα. συνοικειωθέντων δὲ τῶν ἀγαθοποιῶν Διός τε καὶ Ἀφροδίτης ἐπὶ μὲν τῶν λιβυκῶν μερῶν ὄντες αὐτοί, τῶν ἀγαθοποιῶν ἐν τοῖς ἀπηλιωτικοῖς[2] κεκεντρωμένων, ἰάσιμα μέν, εὐπαραδειγμάτιστα[3] δὲ ποιοῦσι τὰ πάθη· ἐπὶ μὲν τοῦ τοῦ Διὸς διὰ θεραπειῶν ἰατρικῶν καὶ ἤτοι διαιτητικῆς[4] ἀγωγῆς ἢ φαρμακείας, ἐπὶ δὲ τοῦ τῆς Ἀφροδίτης διὰ χρησμῶν καὶ τῆς ἀπὸ θεῶν ἐπικουρίας. ἐπὶ δὲ τῶν ἀπηλιωτικῶν αὐτοὶ κεκεντρωμένοι, τῶν ἀγαθοποιῶν δυνόντων, ἀνίατά τε ἅμα καὶ πολυθρύλλητα καὶ ἐπιφανέστατα ποιοῦσι τὰ νοσήματα, κατὰ μὲν τὰς ἐπιληψίας συνεχείαις καὶ περιβοησίαις καὶ κινδύνοις θανατικοῖς τοὺς πάσχοντας περικυλίοντες· κατὰ δὲ τὰς μανίας καὶ ἐκστάσεις ἀκαταστασίαις[5] καὶ ἀπαλλοτριώσεσι τῶν οἰκείων καὶ γυμνητείαις καὶ βλασφημίαις καὶ τοῖς τοιούτοις· κατὰ δὲ τὰς δαιμονιοπληξίας ἢ τὰς τῶν ὑγρῶν ὀχλήσεις, ἐνθουσιασμοῖς καὶ ἐξαγορίαις καὶ αἰκίαις καὶ τοῖς ὁμοίοις τῶν παραδειγματισμῶν. ἰδίως δὲ καὶ τῶν τὸ σχῆμα περιεχόντων τόπων οἱ μὲν ἡλίου καὶ οἱ τοῦ Ἄρεως πρὸς τὰς μανίας μάλιστα συνεργοῦσιν, οἱ δὲ Διὸς καὶ Ἑρμοῦ πρὸς τὰς ἐπιληψίας, οἱ δὲ τῆς Ἀφροδίτης πρὸς τὰς θεοφορίας καὶ ἐξαγορίας, οἱ δὲ τοῦ Κρόνου καὶ σελήνης πρὸς τὰς τῶν ὑγρῶν ὀχλήσεις καὶ πρὸς τὰς δαιμονιοπληξίας.

[1] πάθη καὶ τὰ post προκείμενα add. MNAECam., om. VPLD.
[2] ἀπηλιωτικοῖς (ἀφηλ-, ἀπιλ-) VPLMADEProc., ἀγαθοποιοῖς NCam.[1], ἀνατολικοῖς Cam.[2]

caused by them are, to be sure, incurable, but latent and obscure. But if the beneficent planets Jupiter and Venus have some familiarity to them when they are themselves in the western parts and the beneficent planets are angular [1] in the east, they make the diseases curable, but noticeable; if it be Jupiter, curable by medical treatments, a diet, or drugs; if Venus, by oracles and the aid of the gods. When the maleficent planets themselves are angular in the east and the beneficent planets are setting, the diseases which they cause are both incurable, the subject of talk, and conspicuous; in epilepsy they involve the victims in continuous attacks, notoriety, and deadly peril; in madness and seizures, they cause instability, alienation of friends, tearing off clothes, abusive language, and the like; in demonic seizures, or water on the brain, possession, confession, torments, and similar manifestations. In detail, of the places that possess the configuration, those of the sun and Mars aid in causing madness, those of Jupiter and Mercury, epilepsy; those of Venus, divine possession and public confession; and those of Saturn and the moon, gatherings of water and demonic seizures.

[1] *I.e.* at the angle, in this case the orient.

---

³ εὐπαραδειγμάτιστα VPDE: ἐπιφανῆ Proc.; ἀπαραδειγμάτιστα MNACam.
⁴ διαιτητικῆς ego; διαιτικῆς VD, διαγητικῆς PL, ὑπὸ διαίτης Proc.; ἰατρικῆς MNAECam.
⁵ ἀκαταστασίαις VD, *cf.* ἀκαταστατοῦσι Proc.; ἀκατασχεσίαις cett. Cam.

PTOLEMY

Ἡ μὲν οὖν περὶ τὸ ποιητικοῦ τῆς ψυχῆς καθ' ὅλας τὰς φύσεις νοσηματικὴ παραλλαγὴ σχεδὸν ἔν τε τοῖς τοιούτοις[1] εἴδεσι καὶ διὰ τῶν τοιούτων ἀποτελεῖται σχηματισμῶν. ἡ δὲ περὶ τὸ παθητικόν, κατ' αὐτὸ πάλιν τὸ ἐξαίρετον θεωρουμένη, καταφαίνεται μάλιστα περὶ τὰς κατ' αὐτὸ τὸ γένος τοῦ ἄρρενος καὶ θήλεως ὑπερβολὰς καὶ ἐλλείψεις τοῦ κατὰ φύσιν, διαλαμβάνεται δὲ ἐπισκεπτικῶς κατὰ τὸν ὅμοιον τῷ προκειμένῳ τρόπον, τοῦ ἡλίου μέντοι μετὰ τῆς σελήνης ἀντὶ τοῦ Ἑρμοῦ παραλαμβανομένου καὶ τῆς τοῦ Ἄρεως σὺν τῷ τῆς Ἀφροδίτης πρὸς αὐτοὺς συνοικειώσεως· τούτων γὰρ οὕτως ὑπ' ὄψιν πιπτόντων, ἐὰν μὲν μόνα τὰ φῶτα ἐν ἀρρενικοῖς ᾖ ζῳδίοις, οἱ μὲν ἄνδρες ὑπερβάλλουσι τοῦ κατὰ φύσιν, αἱ δὲ γυναῖκες τοῦ παρὰ φύσιν πρὸς τὸ ἔπανδρον ἁπλῶς τῆς ψυχῆς καὶ δραστικώτερον· ἐὰν δὲ καὶ ὁ τοῦ Ἄρεως ᾖ καὶ ὁ τῆς Ἀφροδίτης ἤτοι ὁπότερος ἢ καὶ ἀμφότεροι[2] ὦσιν ἠρρενωμένοι, οἱ μὲν ἄνδρες πρὸς τὰς κατὰ φύσιν συνουσίας γίνονται καταφερεῖς καὶ μοιχικοὶ καὶ ἀκόρεστοι[3] καὶ ἐν παντὶ καιρῷ πρόχειροι πρός τε τὰ αἰσχρὰ καὶ τὰ παράνομα τῶν ἀφροδισίων· αἱ δὲ γυναῖκες πρὸς τὰς παρὰ φύσιν ὁμιλίας λάγναι καὶ ῥιψόφθαλμοι καὶ αἱ καλούμεναι τριβάδες· διατιθέασι δὲ θηλείας, ἀνδρῶν ἔργα ἐπιτελοῦσαι. κἂν μὲν μόνος ὁ τῆς Ἀφροδίτης ἠρρενωμένος ᾖ, λάθρα καὶ οὐκ ἀναφανδόν· ἐὰν δὲ καὶ ὁ τοῦ Ἄρεως, ἄντικρυς ὥστε

---

[1] Post τοιούτοις add. ἐστὶ(ν) PLMNECam., om. VADProc.
[2] ἀμφότεροι VADProc., ἑκάτερος PLMNCam., -οι E.
[3] ἀκόρεστοι VPL, ἀκόρεστι D, ἀκόλαστοι MNAECam.

TETRABIBLOS III. 14

The morbid perversion of the active part of the soul in its general nature, therefore, is produced in some such forms as these and is produced by these configurations of the planets. The corresponding perversion of the passive portion, as in the former instance viewed in its extreme cases, is most apparent in excesses and deficiencies in matters of sex, male and female, as compared with what is natural, and in inquiry is apprehended in the same fashion as before, though the sun is taken, together with the moon, instead of Mercury, and the relation to them of Mars, together with Venus, is observed. For when these thus fall under observation, if the luminaries are unattended in masculine signs, males exceed in the natural, and females exceed in the unnatural quality, so as merely to increase the virility and activity of the soul. But if likewise Mars or Venus as well, either one or both of them, is made masculine,[1] the males become addicted to natural sexual intercourse, and are adulterous, insatiate, and ready on every occasion for base and lawless acts of sexual passion, while the females are lustful for unnatural congresses, cast inviting glances of the eye, and are what we call *tribades*;[2] for they deal with females and perform the functions of males. If Venus alone is constituted in a masculine manner, they do these things secretly and not openly. But if Mars likewise is so constituted, without

[1] *Cf.* i. 6.   [2] *Cf.* p. 405, n. 1.

ἐνίοτε καὶ νομίμας ὥσπερ γυναῖκας τὰς[1] διατιθεμένας ἀναδεικνύειν.

Τὸ δ' ἐναντίον, τῶν φωτῶν κατὰ τὸν ἐκκείμενον σχηματισμὸν ἐν θηλυκοῖς ζῳδίοις ὑπαρχόντων μόνων, αἱ μὲν γυναῖκες ὑπερβάλλουσι τοῦ κατὰ φύσιν, οἱ δὲ ἄνδρες τοῦ παρὰ φύσιν, πρὸς τὸ εὔθρυπτον καὶ τεθηλυσμένον τῆς ψυχῆς· ἐὰν δὲ καὶ ὁ τῆς Ἀφροδίτης ᾖ τεθηλυσμένος, αἱ μὲν γυναῖκες καταφερεῖς τε καὶ μοιχάδες καὶ λάγναι γίνονται πρὸς τὸ διατίθεσθαι κατὰ[2] φύσιν ἐν παντί τε καιρῷ καὶ ὑπὸ παντὸς οὑτινοσοῦν, ὡς μηδενὸς ἁπλῶς, ἐάν τε αἰσχρὸν ᾖ, ἐάν τε παράνομον, ἀπέχεσθαι τῶν ἀφροδισίων· οἱ δὲ ἄνδρες μαλακοί τε καὶ σαθροί[3] πρὸς τὰς παρὰ φύσιν συνουσίας καὶ γυναικῶν ἔργα, διατιθέμενοι παθητικῶς, ἀποκρύφως μέντοι καὶ λεληθότως· ἐὰν δὲ καὶ ὁ τοῦ Ἄρεως ᾖ τεθηλυσμένος, ἄντικρυς καὶ μετὰ παρρησίας ἀναισχυντοῦσι, τὰ προκείμενα καθ' ἑκάτερον εἶδος ἀποτελοῦντες,[4] τὸ πορνικὸν καὶ πολύκοινον καὶ πολύψογον καὶ πάναισχρον σχῆμα περιβαλλόμενοι μέχρι τῆς κατά τε τὴν λοιδορίαν καὶ τὴν τῆς χρήσεως ὕβριν σημειώσεως.[5] συμβάλλονται δὲ καὶ οἱ μὲν ἀνατολικοὶ καὶ ἑῷοι σχηματισμοὶ τοῦ τε τοῦ Ἄρεως καὶ τοῦ τῆς Ἀφροδίτης πρός τε τὸ ἐπανδρότερον καὶ εὐδιαβοητότερον, οἱ δὲ δυτικοὶ καὶ ἑσπέριοι πρός τε τὸ θηλυκώτερον καὶ τὸ κατασταλτικώτερον· ὁμοίως δὲ καὶ ὁ μὲν τοῦ Κρόνου συμπροσγενόμενος ἐπὶ τὸ ἀσελγέστερον καὶ ἀκαθαρτότερον ἢ καὶ ἐπονειδιστότερον ἑκάστῳ τῶν ἐκκειμένων πέφυκε

---

[1] τὰς om. MNAECam. [2] κατὰ libri; παρὰ Cam.

reserve, so that sometimes they even designate the women with whom they are on such terms as their lawful " wives."

But on the other hand, when the luminaries in the aforesaid configuration are unattended in feminine signs, the females exceed in the natural, and the males in unnatural practice, with the result that their souls become soft and effeminate. If Venus too is made feminine, the women become depraved, adulterous, and lustful, with the result that they may be dealt with in the natural manner on any occasion and by any one soever, and so that they refuse absolutely no sexual act, though it be base or unlawful. The men, on the contrary, become effeminate and unsound with respect to unnatural congresses and the functions of women, and are dealt with as pathics, though privately and secretly. But if Mars also is constituted in a feminine manner, their shamelessness is outright and frank and they perform the aforesaid acts of either kind, assuming the guise of common bawds who submit to general abuse and to every baseness until they are stamped with the reproach and insult that attend such usages. And the rising and morning positions of both Mars and Venus have a contributory effect, to make them more virile and notorious, while setting and evening positions increase femininity and sedateness. Similarly, if Saturn is present, his influence joins with each of the foregoing to produce more licentiousness,

---

³ σαθροὶ VPLDProc.; θαρσεῖς NCam., θρασεῖς MAE.
⁴ ἀποτελοῦντες VD, -ουσι(ν) PL, ἐπιτελοῦσι MNAECam.
⁵ σημειώσεως MNACam.; δημιοσίως ἕως VD (διμ-) E, δημιοσίως ὡς PL.

συνεργεῖν, ὁ δὲ τοῦ Διὸς πρὸς τὸ εὐσχημονέστερον καὶ φυλακτικώτερον καὶ αἰδημονέστερον, ὁ δὲ τοῦ Ἑρμοῦ πρός τε τὸ περιβοητότερον καὶ τὸ τῶν παθῶν[1] εὐκινητότερον καὶ πολυτροπώτερον καὶ εὐπροσκοπώτερον.

ΒΙΒΛΙΟΝ Δ'

⟨ā. Προοίμιον⟩

Τὰ μὲν οὖν πρὸ τῆς γενέσεως καὶ τὰ κατ' αὐτὴν τὴν γένεσιν δυνάμενα θεωρεῖσθαι, καὶ ἔτι τῶν μετὰ τὴν γένεσιν ὅσα τῆς συστάσεως ἐστὶν ἴδια τὸ καθ' ὅλου ποιὸν τῶν συγκριμάτων ἐμφαίνοντα, σχεδὸν ταῦτ' ἂν εἴη. τῶν δὲ κατὰ τὸ ἐκτὸς συμβεβηκότων καὶ ἐφεξῆς ὀφειλόντων διαλαμβάνεσθαι προηγεῖται μὲν ὁ περὶ τύχης κτητικῆς τε καὶ ἀξιωματικῆς λόγος, συνῆπται δ' ὥσπερ ἡ μὲν κτητικὴ ταῖς τοῦ σώματος οἰκειώσεσιν, ἡ δ' ἀξιωματικὴ ταῖς τῆς ψυχῆς.

⟨β̄.⟩ Περὶ τύχης κτητικῆς

Τὰ μὲν οὖν τῆς κτήσεως ὁποῖά τινα ἔσται ληπτέον ἀπὸ τοῦ καλουμένου κλήρου τῆς τύχης, μόνου μέντοι καθ' ὃν πάντοτε τὴν ἀπὸ τοῦ ἡλίου ἐπὶ τὴν σελήνην διάστασιν ἐκβάλλομεν ἀπὸ τοῦ ὡροσκόπου καὶ ἐπὶ τῶν τῆς ἡμέρας καὶ ἐπὶ τῶν τῆς νυκτὸς γεννωμένων, δι' ἃς εἴπομεν ἐν τοῖς περὶ

---

[1] παθῶν VPLMADEProc., ἠθῶν NCam.

impurity, and disgrace, while Jupiter aids in the direction of greater decorum, restraint, and modesty, and Mercury tends to increase notoriety, instability of the emotions, versatility, and foresight.

BOOK IV.

[1. *Introduction.*]

THE foregoing may be taken as what can be learned by investigation of matters antecedent to the nativity and contemporary with it, together with such of those posterior to the nativity as properly apply to the constitution of the subject by disclosing the general quality of his temperament. Among external accidentals, which should be treated next in order, the discussion of the fortune of both riches and honour comes first; and as material fortune is associated with the properties of the body, so honour belongs to those of the soul.

2. *Of Material Fortune.*

What the subject's material acquisitions will be is to be gained from the so-called " Lot of Fortune ";[1] that one alone, however, to discover which we measure from the horoscope the distance from the sun to the moon, in both diurnal and nocturnal nativities, for the reasons which we stated in the

[1] See iii. 10, pp. 275-77. The authenticity of the following clause (to " nativities ") is doubtful, since it appears to refer to the sentence in iii. 10 (p. 277, n. 1) which is clearly an interpolation.

χρόνων ζωῆς αἰτίας. σκοπεῖν οὖν δεήσει τούτου¹ συνισταμένου² τὸν τρόπον τοῦτον, τοῦ³ δωδεκατημορίου λαβόντας τὴν οἰκοδεσποτίαν, καὶ πῶς ἔχουσιν οὗτοι δυνάμεως καὶ οἰκειότητος καθ' ὃν ἐν ἀρχῇ διωρισάμεθα τρόπον· ἔτι δὲ τοὺς συσχηματιζομένους αὐτοῖς⁴ ἢ τοὺς⁵ καθυπερτεροῦντας τῶν τῆς αὐτῆς ἢ τῆς ἐναντίας αἱρέσεως· ἐν δυνάμει μὲν γὰρ ὄντες οἱ τοῦ κλήρου τὴν οἰκοδεσποτίαν λαβόντες ποιοῦσι πολυκτήμονας, καὶ μάλισθ' ὅταν ὑπὸ τῶν φωτῶν οἰκείως τύχωσι μαρτυρηθέντες· ἀλλ' ὁ μὲν τοῦ Κρόνου διὰ θεμελίων ἢ γεωργιῶν ἢ ναυκληριῶν, ὁ δὲ τοῦ Διὸς διὰ πίστεως ἢ ἐπιτροπιῶν ἢ ἱερατειῶν, ὁ δὲ τοῦ Ἄρεως διὰ στρατειῶν καὶ ἡγεμονιῶν, ὁ δὲ τῆς Ἀφροδίτης διὰ φιλικῶν⁶ ἢ γυναικείων δωρεῶν, ὁ δὲ τοῦ Ἑρμοῦ διὰ λόγων καὶ ἐμποριῶν. ἰδίως δ' ὁ τοῦ Κρόνου τῇ κτητικῇ τύχῃ συνοικειούμενος, ἐὰν τῷ τοῦ Διὸς συσχηματισθῇ, κληρονομίας περιποιεῖ, καὶ μάλισθ' ὅταν ἐπὶ τῶν ἄνω κέντρων τοῦτο⁷ συμβῇ, τοῦ τοῦ Διὸς ἐν δισώμῳ ζῳδίῳ τυχόντος ἢ καὶ τὴν συναφὴν τῆς σελήνης ἐπέχοντος· τότε γὰρ καὶ εἰς παιδοποιίαν ἀναχθέντες ἀλλότρια κληρονομοῦσι· κἂν μὲν οἱ τῆς αὐτῆς αἱρέσεως τοῖς οἰκοδεσπόταις τὰς μαρτυρίας τῶν οἰκοδεσποτιῶν αὐτοὶ τύχωσι ποιούμενοι, τὰς κτήσεις ἀκαθαιρέτους διαφυλάττουσιν· ἐὰν δὲ οἱ τῆς ἐναντίας αἱρέσεως καθυπερτερήσωσι τοὺς κυρίους τόπους ἢ ἐπανενεχθῶσιν

¹ τούτου VD, τοῦ τοῦ P, τοῦ L, τοὺς τοῦ MNAECam.
² συνισταμένου libri Cam.¹, περιεχομένου Cam.² *Cf.* τούτου δὲ συσταθέντος Proc.
³ τοῦ om. MNAECam.
⁴ αὐτοῖς VADProc., -ῆς PL, -οὺς MNECam.

discussion of the length of life. As it is constituted in this way, we shall be obliged therefore to take the lordship of the sign, and observe what is the condition of these planets with regard to power and familiarity, in the way which we specified at the beginning.[1] Further, we must consider the planets in aspect with them, or those of their own or of the opposite sect that overcome them. For when the planets which govern the Lot of Fortune are in power, they make the subjects rich, particularly when they chance to have the proper testimony [2] of the luminaries; thus Saturn brings riches through building, or agriculture, or shipping ventures, Jupiter through fiduciary relationships, guardianships, or priesthoods, Mars through military operations and command, Venus through gifts from friends or women, and Mercury through eloquence and trade. And in a special way, when Saturn is associated with material fortune, if he is in aspect with Jupiter, he is the cause of inheritances, particularly when this comes about upon the upper angles and Jupiter is in a bicorporeal sign or holds the application of the moon. For in that case they are adopted and inherit the possessions of others; and if the planets of the same sect as the ruling planets happen themselves to witness to the rulership, they retain their possessions without loss; but if the planets of the opposite sect overcome the governing places or rise after them, they bring

[1] *Cf.* ii. 7 (pp. 169-71), and iii. 2 (p. 233).
[2] *Cf.* p. 379, n. 3.

---

[5] ἢ τοὺς VMADE, ἢ om. PL, ἢ τοὺς om. NCam.
[6] φιλικῶν VD, φυληκῶν P, φιλίων L, φίλων MNAECam.
[7] τοῦτο libri Proc., Cam.¹; αὐτός Cam.²

αὐτοῖς,[1] καθαιρέσεις ποιοῦνται τῶν ὑπαρχόντων, τοῦ καθολικοῦ καιροῦ λαμβανομένου διὰ τῆς τῶν τὸ αἴτιον ποιούντων πρὸς τὰ κέντρα καὶ τὰς ἐπαναφορὰς προσνεύσεως.

⟨γ̄.⟩ Περὶ τύχης ἀξιωματικῆς

Τὰ δὲ τῆς ἀξίας[2] καὶ τῆς τοιαύτης εὐδαιμονίας δεήσει σκοπεῖν ἀπό τε τῆς τῶν φώτων διαθέσεως καὶ τῆς τῶν δορυφορούντων ἀστέρων[3] οἰκειώσεως[4] αὐτοῖς·[5] ἐν ἀρρενικοῖς μὲν γὰρ ζῳδίοις ὄντων ἀμφοτέρων τῶν φώτων καὶ ἐπικέντρων ἤτοι ἀμφοτέρων πάλιν ἢ καὶ τοῦ ἑτέρου, μάλιστα δὲ τοῦ τῆς αἱρέσεως καὶ δορυφορουμένου ὑπὸ τῶν πέντε πλανωμένων, ἡλίου[6] μὲν ὑπὸ[7] ἑῴων, σελήνης δὲ ὑπὸ ἑσπερίων,[8] οἱ γεννώμενοι βασιλεῖς ἔσονται. κἂν μὲν οἱ δορυφοροῦντες ἀστέρες ἤτοι ἐπίκεντροι καὶ αὐτοὶ ὦσιν ἢ πρὸς τὸ ὑπὲρ γῆν κέντρον συσχηματίζωνται, μεγάλοι καὶ δυναμικοὶ καὶ κοσμοκράτορες διατελοῦσι· καὶ ἔτι μᾶλλον εὐδαίμονες ἐὰν οἱ δορυ-

---

[1] αὐτοῖς] ἐπ' αὐτοῖς MNCam.
[2] τῆς αὐτῆς ἀξίας NCam., τῆς τοιαύτης ἀξίας (corr. in τῆς αὐτῆς ἀ.) M.
[3] Post ἀστέρων add. συνορῶντα τὰς MNECam.
[4] οἰκειώσεις MNECam.
[5] αὐτῶν MNECam.
[6] ἡλίου VD, ἥλιον PLA, πρὸς ἥλιον MNECam.
[7] ὑπὸ om. MNECam.
[8] σελήνης . . . ἑσπερίων VPLAD; ἑσπερίων δὲ πρὸς σελήνην MNECam.

TETRABIBLOS IV. 2-3

about loss of possessions, and the general time [1] is discovered by means of the approach of the causative planets to the angles and the succedent signs.

3. *Of the Fortune of Dignity.*

It will be needful to determine the questions of dignity and happiness resulting therefrom from the position of the luminaries and the familiarity to them of their attendant planets.[2] For if both the luminaries are in masculine signs and either both of them, or even one of the two, angular, and particularly if the luminary of the sect [3] is also attended by the five planets, matutine to the sun and vespertine to the moon, the children will be kings. And if the attendant planets are either themselves angular or bear an aspect to the superior angle, the children born will continue to be great, powerful, and world-rulers,[4] and they will be even more fortunate if the

---

[1] When the inheritance falls due; Bouché-Leclercq, p. 437. Ashmand, p. 173, would have the expression refer to the duration of the wealth.

[2] "Attendance" is described by Porphyry, *Introduction*, pp. 190-191, ed. Wolf, whom Hephaestion i. 17, pp. 74-75, ed. Engelbrecht, follows. The second of the three varieties of attendance mentioned applies to the luminaries. If one of these is at the horoscope or mid-heaven, whether or not it is in its own house, it will have as attendant any planet of its own sect which projects its ray upon the luminary, those of the sun's (diurnal) sect in the direction of the diurnal movement of the heavens, those of the moon's sect in the other direction.

[3] The sect of the geniture, diurnal or nocturnal.

[4] Ptolemy doubtless meant Roman emperors, but the epithet was used of kings by the astrologers before it appeared in the inscriptions of the emperors (Cumont, *L'Égypte des astrologues*, p. 27).

φοροῦντες ἀστέρες δεξιοὶ τοῖς ὑπὲρ γῆν κέντροις συσχηματίζωνται. ἐὰν δὲ τῶν ἄλλων οὕτως ἐχόντων μόνος ὁ ἥλιος ᾖ ἐν ἀρρενικῷ, ἡ δὲ σελήνη ἐν θηλυκῷ, ἐπίκεντρον δὲ τὸ ἕτερον τῶν φωτῶν, ἡγεμόνες μόνον ἔσονται ζωῆς καὶ θανάτου κύριοι. ἐὰν δὲ πρὸς τούτοις μηδὲ οἱ δορυφοροῦντες ἀστέρες ἐπίκεντροι ὦσιν ἢ μαρτυρήσωσι τοῖς κέντροις, μεγάλοι μόνον ἔσονται καὶ ἐν ἀξιώμασι τοῖς ἀπὸ μέρους στεμματηφορικοῖς ἢ ἐπιτροπικοῖς ἢ στρατοπεδαρχικοῖς καὶ οὐχὶ τοῖς ἡγεμονικοῖς. ἐὰν δὲ τὰ φῶτα μὴ ᾖ ἐπίκεντρα, τῶν δὲ δορυφορούντων ἀστέρων οἱ πλεῖστοι ἤτοι ἐπίκεντροι ὦσιν ἢ συσχηματίζωνται τοῖς κέντροις, ἐν ἀξιώμασι μὲν ἐπιφανεστέροις οὐ γενήσονται, ἐν προαγωγαῖς δὲ πολιτικαῖς καὶ μετριότητι περὶ τὰς κατὰ τὸν βίον προλήψεις· μηδὲ τῶν δορυφορούντων μέντοι τοῖς κέντροις συνοικειωθέντων ἀνεπίφαντοι ταῖς πράξεσι καὶ ἀπρόκοποι καθίστανται· τέλειον δὲ ταπεινοὶ καὶ κακοδαίμονες γίνονται ταῖς τύχαις ὅταν μηδέτερον τῶν φωτῶν μήτε κεκεντρωμένον ᾖ μήτ' ἐν ἀρρενικῷ ζῳδίῳ τυγχάνῃ μήτε δορυφορῆται ὑπὸ τῶν ἀγαθοποιῶν. ὁ μὲν οὖν καθ' ὅλου τύπος τῆς προκειμένης ἐπισκέψεως τοιαύτην τινὰ τὴν αὐξομείωσιν ἔχει τῶν ἀξιωμάτων· τὰς δὲ μεταξὺ τούτων καταστάσεις

---

[1] Dexter, or on the right, is in the direction of the diurnal movement of the heavens.

[2] Certainly officers of very high rank in the imperial service are meant. Cumont, *op. cit.*, pp. 39-40, shows that ἡγεμών (Lat. *dux*) was commonly so understood in Egypt, and sometimes it is equivalent to *iudex*, " judge " (pp. 45-46).

attendant planets are in dexter aspect[1] to the superior angles. But if, while the others are in this position, the sun alone is in a masculine sign, and the moon is in a feminine one, and one of the luminaries is angular, they will merely be generals,[2] with power of life and death. If, however, besides this the attendant planets are neither angular nor witnessing[3] to the angles, they will be merely great and will enjoy partial dignities, those which involve the wearing of chaplets,[4] or those of superintendence[5] or of military command,[6] and not those of first rank. But if the luminaries are not angular, and most of the attendant planets are either angular or in aspect with the angles, they will not attain the more conspicuous honours but rather civil leadership and moderate advancement in their careers. If, however, the attendant planets are not associated with the angles, they are rendered obscure in their actions and without preferment, and they are entirely humble and miserable in their fortunes when neither of the luminaries is angular, or in a masculine sign, or attended by the beneficent planets. The general outline, then, of the investigation before us involves a gradation of dignities of this sort. Since there are very many

[3] In aspect.
[4] Connected with priestly dignities; *cf.* Cumont, *op. cit.*, p. 117.
[5] Probably referring to prominent positions at court or in the civil service.
[6] The word στρατοπεδάρχης primarily means "commander of a camp," as, in Latin, *praefectus castrorum*, but came to be used generally to mean "commander of troops"; *cf.* Cumont, *op. cit.*, pp. 40-41.

παμπληθεῖς οὔσας καταστοχαστέον ἀπὸ τῶν περὶ
αὐτὸ τὸ εἶδος τῶν τε φωτῶν καὶ τῆς δορυφορίας
αὐτῶν ἐπὶ μέρους ἐναλλοιώσεως καὶ τῆς κυρίας τῶν
δορυφορήσεων· ταύτης γὰρ περὶ μὲν τοὺς τὴν
αἵρεσιν ἔχοντας ἢ τοὺς ἀγαθοποιοὺς συνισταμένης
τὸ αὐθεντικώτερον καὶ ἀπταιστότερον τοῖς ἀξιώμασι
παρακολουθεῖ· περὶ δὲ τοὺς ἐναντίους ἢ τοὺς κακοποιούς, τὸ ὑποτεταγμένον καὶ ἐπισφαλέστερον. καὶ
τὸ τῆς ἀξίας δὲ τῆς ἐσομένης εἶδος ἀπὸ τῆς τῶν
δορυφορησάντων ἀστέρων ἰδιοτροπίας θεωρητέον·
ἐπειδήπερ ὁ μὲν τοῦ Κρόνου τὴν κυρίαν τῆς
δορυφορίας ἔχων ἐπὶ πολυκτημοσύνῃ καὶ συναγωγῇ
χρημάτων τὰς δυναστείας ποιεῖ, ὁ δὲ τοῦ Διὸς ἢ ὁ
τῆς Ἀφροδίτης ἐπὶ χάρισι καὶ δωρεαῖς καὶ τιμαῖς
καὶ μεγαλοψυχίαις· ὁ δὲ τοῦ Ἄρεως ἐπὶ στρατη-
λασίαις καὶ νίκαις καὶ φόβοις τῶν ὑποτεταγμένων·
ὁ δὲ τοῦ Ἑρμοῦ διὰ σύνεσιν ἢ παιδείαν καὶ ἐπιμέλειαν καὶ οἰκονομίαν τῶν πραγμάτων.

<δ.> Περὶ πράξεως[1] ποιότητος

Ὁ δὲ τῆς πράξεως τὴν κυρίαν ἐπέχων λαμβάνεται
κατὰ τρόπους δύο, ἀπὸ τοῦ τε ἡλίου καὶ τοῦ μεσουρανοῦντος ζῳδίου. σκοπεῖν γὰρ δεήσει τόν τε τὴν
φάσιν ἑῴαν ἔγγιστα πρὸς ἥλιον πεποιημένον καὶ
τὸν ἐπὶ τοῦ μεσουρανήματος, ὅταν μάλιστα τὴν
συναφὴν τῆς σελήνης ἐπέχῃ. κἂν μὲν ὁ[2] αὐτὸς ᾖ
ἀστὴρ ἀμφότερα ἔχων[3] τὰ εἰρημένα, τούτῳ μόνῳ

[1] πράξεων NCam.   [2] ὁ om. Cam.
[3] ᾖ ... ἔχων VPLD, ἔχῃ MNAECam.

conditions intermediate between these grades, one must estimate them from the specific qualities of the luminaries themselves, and the particular variations in the manner in which they are attended, and the government of the attendance. For if their attendance consists of planets of the same sect, or of the beneficent planets, greater independence and security will attend the dignities; but if it involves the opposite sect, or the maleficent planets, there will be dependency and less security. The kind of future honour is to be divined from the quality of the attending planets; for if Saturn governs the attendance, he brings about power based on wealth and the amassing of riches, but Jupiter or Venus that which rests upon favours, gifts, honours, and magnanimity; Mars brings power founded on generalships, victories, and the fears of subordinates, and Mercury that which depends upon intelligence, education, and the care and management of affairs.

4. *Of the Quality of Action.*

The lord of action is apprehended by two methods, from the sun and from the culminating sign. For it will be needful to look both for the planet that has made its morning appearance closest to the sun, and that which is at mid-heaven, particularly when it occupies the application of the moon; and if the same star occupies both the aforesaid positions, this alone must be employed, and similarly if none

προσχρηστέον· ὁμοίως δὲ κἂν τὸ ἕτερον μηδεὶς ἔχῃ, τῷ τὸ ἕτερον εἰληφότι μόνῳ. ἐὰν δὲ ἕτερος ᾖ ὁ τὴν[1] ἔγγιστα φάσιν πεποιημένος καὶ ἕτερος ὁ τῷ μεσουρανήματι καὶ τῇ σελήνῃ συνοικειούμενος, ἀμφοτέροις προσχρηστέον,[2] τὰ πρωτεῖα διδόντας τῷ κατὰ ἐπικράτησιν πλείους ἔχοντι ψήφους οἰκοδεσποτίας καθ' ὃν προεκτεθείμεθα τρόπον. ἐὰν δὲ μηδεὶς εὑρίσκηται μήτε φάσιν[3] πεποιημένος μήτε ἐπὶ τοῦ μεσουρανήματος, τὸν κύριον αὐτοῦ παραληπτέον, πρὸς ἐπιτηδεύσεις μέντοι τὰς κατὰ καιρούς· ἄπρακτοι γὰρ ὡς ἐπὶ πᾶν οἱ τοιοῦτοι γίνονται.

Ὁ μὲν οὖν τῆς πράξεως τὴν οἰκοδεσποτίαν λαβὼν ἀστὴρ οὕτως ἡμῖν διακριθήσεται· τὸ δὲ ποιὸν τῶν πράξεων ἔκ τε τῆς ἰδιοτροπίας τῶν τριῶν ἀστέρων Ἄρεως καὶ Ἀφροδίτης καὶ Ἑρμοῦ καὶ ἐκ τῆς τῶν ζῳδίων ἐν οἷς ἂν τύχωσι παραπορευόμενοι. ὁ μὲν γὰρ τοῦ Ἑρμοῦ τὸ πράττειν παρέχων, ὡς ἄν τις εἴποι τυπωδῶς, ποιεῖ γραμματέας, πραγματευτικούς,[4] λογιστάς, διδασκάλους, ἐμπόρους, τραπεζίτας, μάντεις, ἀστρολόγους, θύτας καὶ ὅλως τοὺς ἀπὸ γραμμάτων καὶ ἑρμηνείας καὶ δόσεως καὶ λήψεως ἐργαζομένους· κἂν μὲν ὁ τοῦ Κρόνου αὐτῷ μαρτυρήσῃ, ἀλλοτρίων οἰκονόμους ἢ ὀνειροκρίτας ἢ ἐν ἱεροῖς τὰς ἀναστροφὰς[5] ποιουμένους προφάσει μαντειῶν καὶ ἐνθουσιασμῶν· ἐὰν δὲ ὁ τοῦ Διός,

---

[1] τὴν om. MNCam.   [2] προχρηστέον NCam.²
[3] ἑῴαν post φάσιν add. MNAECam.; om. VPLDProc.
[4] πραγματευτικούς VP (-τηκ-) D, πραγματικούς L, πραγμάτων ἐπιμελητάς Proc., γραμματικούς MNAECam.
[5] ἀναστροφὰς] ἀνατροφὰς NMCam.¹; ἀναφορὰς E.

TETRABIBLOS IV. 4

occupies one of these places, we must use only the one which occupies the other of the places. And if one planet has made the nearest morning appearance and another is associated with the mid-heaven, and with the moon, we must employ them both, giving preference to the one which by reason of its strength has the greater number of claims to domination according to the scheme which we have already set forth.[1] But if not one is found which either has made an appearance[2] or is at mid-heaven, we must take the lord of the latter region, with reference however to the occasional pursuits of the subject, for persons with such genitures are for the most part inactive.

Thus, then, we shall determine the planet that governs action. The quality of the action, however, is to be discerned from the character of the three planets, Mars, Venus, and Mercury, and from that of the signs through which they happen to be passing. For if Mercury governs action, to speak generally, he makes his subjects scribes, men of business, calculators, teachers, merchants, bankers, soothsayers, astrologers, sacrificers, and in general those who perform their functions by means of documents, interpretation, and giving and taking. And if Saturn testifies to him, they will be managers of the property of others, interpreters of dreams, or frequenters of temples for the purpose of prophecies and inspiration. If it is Jupiter that witnesses, they will be law-makers,

---

[1] In iii. 2 (p. 233).
[2] Certain MSS. say " a morning appearance."

νομογράφους, ῥήτορας, σοφιστάς, μετὰ προσώπων μειζόνων ἔχοντας τὰς ἀναστροφάς.

Ὁ δὲ τῆς Ἀφροδίτης τὸ πράττειν παρέχων ποιεῖ τοὺς παρ' ὀσμαῖς ἀνθέων ἢ μύρων ἢ οἴνοις ἢ χρώμασιν ἢ βαφαῖς ἢ ἀρώμασιν ἢ κόσμοις τὰς πράξεις ἔχοντας, οἷον μυροπώλας, στεφανηπλόκους, ἐκδοχέας, οἰνεμπόρους,¹ φαρμακοπώλας, ὑφάντας, ἀρωματοπώλας, ζωγράφους, βαφέας,² ἱματιοπώλας· κἂν μὲν ὁ τοῦ Κρόνου αὐτῷ μαρτυρήσῃ, ἐμπόρους τῶν πρὸς ἀπόλαυσιν καὶ κόσμον, γόητας δὲ καὶ φαρμακοὺς καὶ προαγωγοὺς καὶ τοὺς ἐκ τῶν ὁμοίων τούτοις ποριζοντας· ἐὰν δὲ ὁ τοῦ Διός, ἀθλητὰς στεφανηφόρους, τιμῶν καταξιουμένους, ὑπὸ θηλυκῶν προσώπων προβιβαζομένους.

Ὁ δὲ τοῦ Ἄρεως μετὰ μὲν τοῦ ἡλίου συσχηματισθεὶς τοὺς διὰ πυρὸς ἐργαζομένους ποιεῖ, οἷον μαγείρους, χωνευτάς, καύστας, χαλκέας, μεταλλευτάς·³ χωρὶς δὲ τοῦ ἡλίου τυχών, τοὺς διὰ σιδήρου, οἷον ναυπηγούς, τέκτονας, γεωργούς, λατόμους, λιθοξόους,⁴ λιθουργούς, ξυλοσχίστας, ὑπουργούς· κἂν μὲν ὁ τοῦ Κρόνου αὐτῷ μαρτυρήσῃ, ναυτικούς, ἀντλητάς, ὑπονομευτάς, ζωγράφους, θηριοτρόφους,⁵ μαγείρους, παρασχιστάς·⁶ ἐὰν δὲ ὁ τοῦ Διός, στρα-

---

¹ οἰνεμπόρους VPAD; οἰνοπώλους Proc.; ἠνεαπόρους L; οἷον ἐμπόρους MNECam.

² βαφέας om. NECam.   ³ μεταλλευτάς om. Cam.

⁴ λιθοξόους Proc., λιθόξωας P, λιθόξοας L, λιθοξόους λαοξόους V, λιθ. λοξούς D, λαοξόους MNECam., om. A.

⁵ ζωογράφους θηριοτρόφους VDProc.; θηριοτρόφους P (θυρο-) LAE; στρατιώτας MNCam.

⁶ παρασχιστάς VDProc., παρασχηστάς PL; περιχύτας MNAECam.

orators, sophists, who enjoy familiarity with great persons.

If Venus rules action, she makes her subjects persons whose activities lie among the perfumes of flowers or of unguents, in wine, colours, dyes, spices, or adornments, as, for example, sellers of unguents, weavers of chaplets, innkeepers, wine-merchants, druggists, weavers, dealers in spices, painters, dyers, sellers of clothing. And if Saturn testifies to her, she makes them dealers in goods used for pleasure or adornment, sorcerers, poisoners, panders, and those who make their living from similar occupations. If Jupiter testifies, they will be athletes, wearers of the wreath, persons deemed worthy of honours, and men who derive advancement from women.

Mars, in aspect with the sun, makes his subjects those who use fire in their crafts, such as cooks, moulders, cauterizers, smiths, workers in mines; if he is not with the sun, those who work with iron, such as shipbuilders, carpenters, farmers, quarrymen, stone-dressers, jewellers, splitters of wood, and their subordinate workers. If Saturn testifies to him, he produces seamen, drawers of water, tunnelers, painters, gamekeepers,[1] cooks, embalmers.[2] If Jupiter testifies, he produces soldiers,

[1] The Egyptian kings and Roman emperors kept exotic animals and had servants to look after them; *cf.* Cumont, *op. cit.*, pp. 63-64.
[2] More accurately, those who opened the corpses for the purpose of embalming them; *cf.* Cumont, *op. cit.*, pp. 138 ff.

τιώτας, ὑπηρέτας, τελώνας, πανδοκέας, πορθμέας, θυσιουργούς.

Πάλιν δὲ δύο τῶν τὰς πράξεις παρεχομένων εὑρεθέντων, ἐὰν μὲν ὁ τοῦ Ἑρμοῦ καὶ ὁ τῆς Ἀφροδίτης λάβωσι τὴν οἰκοδεσποτίαν, ἀπὸ Μούσης καὶ ὀργάνων καὶ μελωδιῶν ἢ ποιημάτων καὶ ῥυθμῶν ποιοῦσι τὰς πράξεις, καὶ μάλισθ' ὅταν τοὺς τόπους ὦσιν 180 ἀμφιλελαχότες· ἀποτελοῦσι γὰρ θυμελικούς, ὑποκριτάς, σωματεμπόρους, ὀργανοποιούς, χορευτάς,[1] χορδοστρόφους,[2] ζωγράφους, ὀρχηστάς, ὑφάντας, κηροπλάστας· κἂν μὲν ὁ τοῦ Κρόνου πάλιν αὐτοῖς[3] μαρτυρήσῃ, ποιεῖ τοὺς περὶ[4] τὰ προειρημένα γένη καὶ τοὺς γυναικείους κόσμους ἐμπορευομένους· ἐὰν δὲ ὁ τοῦ Διός, δικολόγους, λογιστηρίων προισταμένους, ἐν δημοσίοις[5] ἀσχολουμένους, παίδων διδασκάλους, ὄχλων προεστῶτας.

Ἐὰν δὲ ὁ τοῦ Ἑρμοῦ καὶ ὁ τοῦ Ἄρεως ἅμα τὴν κυρίαν λάβωσι τῆς πράξεως, ποιοῦσιν ἀνδριαντοποιούς, ὁπλουργούς, ἱερογλύφους, ζῳοπλάστας,[6] παλαιστάς, ἰατρούς, χειρουργούς, κατηγόρους, μοιχικούς, κακοπράγμονας, πλαστογράφους· κἂν μὲν ὁ τοῦ Κρόνου αὐτοῖς μαρτυρήσῃ, φονέας, λωποδύτας, ἅρπαγας, λῃστάς, ἀπελάτας, ῥᾳδιούργους· ἐὰν δὲ ὁ τοῦ Διός, φιλόπλους ἢ φιλομονομάχους,[7] δράστας, δεινούς,

---

[1] χορευτάς Proc., χωρευτάς PL, om. VMNADECam.
[2] χορδοστρόφους VMADEProc., -τρόφας P, -τρόφους L; χονδροστρόφους NCam.
[3] αὑτοῖς VMDEProc., -ὁ P, -ὁς L, -ῷ NACam.
[4] τοὺς περὶ VAD, πρὸς τοὺς περὶ P, πρὸς τοὺς L; cf. ἐπὶ τοῖς εἰρημένοις Proc.; om. MNECam.
[5] ἐν δημοσίοις VPLDProc., δημοσίοις MAE, δημοσίους NCam.

servants, publicans, innkeepers, ferrymen, assistants at sacrifice.

Again, when two planets are found to rule action, if Mercury and Venus take the rulership, they bring about action expressed by the arts of the Muses, musical instruments, melodies, or poems, and rhythm, particularly when they have exchanged places. For they produce workers in the theatre, actors, dealers in slaves, makers of musical instruments, members of the chorus, makers of strings, painters, dancers, weavers, and wax-moulders. And again, if Saturn testifies to them, he produces those in the aforesaid callings, as well as dealers in feminine finery. If Jupiter testifies, he produces lawyers, supervisors of counting houses,[1] public officers, teachers of children, leaders of the populace.[2]

If Mercury and Mars together assume the lordship of action, they produce sculptors, armourers, makers of sacred monuments, modellers, wrestlers, physicians, surgeons, accusers, adulterers, evil-doers, forgers. If Saturn testifies to them, they produce murderers, sneak-thieves, burglars, pirates, cattle-thieves, villains. If Jupiter testifies, they produce men-at-arms, duellists, energetic, clever persons,

---

[1] Probably the public fiscal offices are meant; Cumont, p. 47, n. 1.

[2] *Cf.* Cumont, p. 71, n. 3, who remarks on the vagueness of astrological references to minor civil offices.

---

⁶ ζωοπλάστας VPLAD; *cf.* Proc.; πλαστάς MNECam.

⁷ φιλόπλους ἢ φιλομονομάχους VP (om. ἢ) L (om. ἢ) MADE; φιλοπόνους ἢ δράστας (om. φιλομονομάχους) NCam.

PTOLEMY

φιλοπράγμονας, ἀλλοτρίων ὑπεξερχομένους καὶ διὰ τῶν τοιούτων πορίζοντας.

Ἐὰν δὲ ὁ τῆς Ἀφροδίτης καὶ ὁ τοῦ Ἄρεως ἅμα τὴν οἰκοδεσποτίαν λάβωσι τῆς πράξεως, ποιοῦσι βαφέας, μυρεψούς, κασσιτεροποιούς, μολυβδουργούς, χρυσοχόους, ἀργυροκόπους, γεωργούς, ὁπλορχηστάς, φαρμακοποιούς, ἰατροὺς τοὺς διὰ τῶν φαρμάκων ταῖς θεραπείαις χρωμένους· κἂν μὲν ὁ τοῦ Κρόνου αὐτοῖς μαρτυρήσῃ, ἱερῶν ζῴων θεραπευτάς, ἀνθρώπων ἐνταφιαστάς, θρηνῳδούς, τυμβαύλας, ἐνθουσιαστάς, ὅπου μυστήρια καὶ θρῆνοι καὶ αἱμαγμοὶ τὰς ἀναστροφὰς ποιουμένους· ἐὰν δὲ ὁ τοῦ Διός, ἱεροπροσπλόκους,[1] οἰωνιστάς, ἱεροφόρους, γυναικῶν προϊσταμένους, γάμων καὶ συνεπιπλοκῶν ἑρμηνέας καὶ διὰ τῶν τοιούτων ζῶντας, ἀπολαυστικῶς ἅμα καὶ ῥιψοκινδύνως.[2]

Καὶ τῶν ζῳδίων δὲ ἐν οἷς ἂν ὦσιν οἱ τὸ πράττειν παρέχοντες αἱ κατ᾽ εἶδος ἰδιοτροπίαι συμβάλλονταί τι πρὸς τὸ ποικίλον τῶν πράξεων. τὰ μὲν γὰρ ἀνθρωπόμορφα συνεργεῖ πως πρὸς πάσας τὰς ἐπιστημονικὰς καὶ περὶ[3] τὴν ἀνθρωπίνην χρείαν καταγινομένας· τὰ δὲ τετράποδα πρὸς τὰς μεταλλικὰς καὶ ἐμπορικὰς καὶ οἰκοδομικὰς καὶ τεκτονικάς· τὰ δὲ τροπικὰ καὶ ἰσημερινὰ πρὸς τὰς ἑρμηνευτικὰς καὶ μεταβολικὰς καὶ μετρητικὰς[4] καὶ γεωργικὰς

---

[1] ἱεροπροσπλόκους VADProc., ἱεροπροσπόλους cett. Cam.

[2] ἀπολαυστικῶς ... ῥιψοκινδύνως VMDE, -ους ... -ους cett. Cam.; om. Proc.

[3] περὶ VADProc., πρὸς cett. Cam.

[4] μετρητικὰς VLD (-ιτι-) Proc., μετρικὰς P; γεωμετρικὰς cett. Cam.

TETRABIBLOS IV. 4

busybodies, who meddle in others' affairs and thereby gain their living.

But if Venus and Mars together dominate action, they produce dyers, perfumers, workers in tin, lead, gold, and silver, farmers, dancers in armour, druggists, physicians who employ drugs in their treatments. If Saturn testifies to them, they produce attendants of sacred animals, those who bury men, mourners, pipers at funerals, fanatics, who resort to wherever there are mysteries, laments, and bloody rites. But if Jupiter testifies, frequenters of temples, interpreters of omens, bearers of the sacred instruments, supervisors of women, interpreters of marriages [1] and matches, making their living by such occupations, and at the same time devoted to pleasure, and reckless.

Likewise the specific natures of the signs in which are the rulers of action contribute to the variety of the action. For anthropomorphic signs [2] are of some assistance to all scientific pursuits or those useful to man; the quadrupedal [3] assist in those that concern mines, commerce, building, and carpentry; the solstitial and equinoctial,[4] those that are interpretative, involve barter, or concern measuring,

---

[1] Perhaps, "matrimonial agents"; cf. Cumont, p. 177, n. 3.
[2] Gemini, Virgo, Sagittarius (partly), Libra. This and the following notes depend upon Hephaestion's characterisations.
[3] Leo, Sagittarius.
[4] Cancer, Capricorn, Aries, Libra.

καὶ ἱερατικάς· τὰ δὲ χερσαῖα καὶ τὰ κάθυγρα πρὸς τὰς ἐν ὑγροῖς ἢ δι' ὑγρῶν καὶ τὰς βοτανικὰς καὶ ναυπηγικάς· ἔτι τε περὶ ταφὰς ἢ ταριχείας ἢ ἁλείας.

Ἰδίως δὲ πάλιν ἡ σελήνη ἐὰν τὸν πρακτικὸν τόπον[1] ἐπισχῇ, τὸν ἀπὸ συνόδου δρόμον ποιουμένη σὺν τῷ τοῦ Ἑρμοῦ, ἐν μὲν Ταύρῳ καὶ Αἰγόκερῳ καὶ Καρκίνῳ ποιεῖ μάντεις, θύτας, λεκανομάντεις. ἐν δὲ Τοξότῃ καὶ Ἰχθύσι νεκρομάντεις καὶ δαιμόνων κινητικούς· ἐν δὲ Παρθένῳ καὶ Σκορπίῳ μάγους, ἀστρολόγους, ἀποφθεγγομένους, προγνώσεις ἔχοντας· ἐν δὲ Ζυγῷ καὶ Κριῷ καὶ Λέοντι θεολήπτους, ὀνειροκρίτας, ἐξορκιστάς.[2]

Τὸ μὲν οὖν αὐτῶν τῶν πράξεων εἶδος διὰ τῶν τοιούτων κατὰ τὸ συγκρατικὸν εἶδος δεήσει καταστοχάζεσθαι· τὸ δὲ μέγεθος αὐτῶν ἐκ τῆς τῶν οἰκοδεσποτησάντων ἀστέρων δυνάμεως. ἀνατολικοὶ μὲν γὰρ ὄντες ἢ ἐπίκεντροι ποιοῦσι τὰς πράξεις αὐθεντικάς· δυτικοὶ δὲ ἢ ἀποκεκλικότες τῶν κέντρων, ὑποτακτικάς·[3] καὶ ὑπὸ μὲν ἀγαθοποιῶν καθυπερτερούμενοι μεγάλας καὶ ἐπιδόξους καὶ ἐπικερδεῖς καὶ ἀπταίστους καὶ ἐπαφροδίτας, ὑπὸ δὲ κακοποιῶν ταπεινὰς καὶ ἀδόξους καὶ ἀπερικτήτους καὶ ἐπισφαλεῖς· Κρόνου μὲν ἐναντιουμένου καταψύξεις καὶ

---

[1] τὸν πρακτικὸν τόπον VADE, τῶν πρακτικῶν τόπων PL, cf. τὸν τῆς πράξεως τόπον Proc.; τὸν προσθετικὸν τόπον MNCam.

[2] ἐξορκιστάς MNAECam., ἐφορκιστάς VPLD, ἐπ- Proc.

[3] ὑποτακτικάς Proc.; ὑποπρακτικάς VPLD, -καί A; ὑπὸ τὰς πρακτικάς MNECam.

agriculture, and religion; the terrestrial[1] and aquatic,[2] activities in or with liquids, or those that are botanical, or concern shipbuilding, and furthermore burial, or pickling, or salting.[3]

In a special way, again, if the moon holds the place of action, and is moving away from conjunction, together with Mercury, in Taurus, Capricornus, and Cancer, she produces soothsayers, makers of sacrifices, and adepts in lekanomancy;[4] in Sagittarius and Pisces necromancers and those who can arouse daemons; in Virgo and Scorpio magicians, astrologers, prophets, those who have second sight; in Libra, Aries, and Leo persons inspired by the gods, interpreters of dreams, and exorcists.

So, then, the particular species of action will have to be conjectured by such means, through combinations; its amplitude must be discovered from the power of the dominating planets. For when they are rising or angular the actions which they cause are independent, but if they are setting or declining from the angles, subordinate; when beneficent planets overcome them, great, glorious, profitable, unerring, and gracious; but if maleficent planets overcome them, mean, inglorious, profitless, and fallible. With Saturn in opposition, they bring

---

[1] Aries, Taurus, Scorpio, Sagittarius.
[2] Pisces; Cancer and Capricorn are amphibious.
[3] Preserved fish were an important article of commerce in Egypt; Cumont, p. 112. ταριχευτής (cf. ταριχείας in the text) means also one who embalms corpses; Cumont, p. 139.
[4] Divination by the inspection of liquids in vessels.

PTOLEMY

χρωματοκρασίας, Ἄρεως δὲ καταρριψοκινδυνίας καὶ περιβοησίας, ἀμφοτέρων δὲ κατὰ τὰς τελείας ἀναστασίας, τοῦ καθολικοῦ χρόνου τῆς αὐξήσεως ἢ τῆς ταπεινώσεως πάλιν θεωρουμένου διὰ τῆς τῶν αἰτίων τοῦ ἀποτελέσματος ἀστέρων πρὸς τὰ ἑῷα καὶ τὰ ἑσπέρια κέντρα ἀεὶ[1] διαθέσεως.

⟨ē.⟩ Περὶ συναρμογῶν

Ἑξῆς δὲ τούτοις ὄντος τοῦ περὶ συναρμογῶν λόγου, περὶ μὲν τῶν[2] κατὰ νόμους ἀνδρὸς καὶ γυναικὸς συμβιώσεων οὕτω σκεπτέον. ἐπὶ μὲν τῶν ἀνδρῶν ἀφορᾶν[3] δεῖ τὴν σελήνην αὐτῶν[4] πῶς διάκειται. πρῶτον μὲν γὰρ ἐν τοῖς ἀπηλιωτικοῖς τυχοῦσα τεταρτημορίοις νεογάμους ποιεῖ τοὺς ἄνδρας ἢ νεωτέραις παρ' ἡλικίαν συμβάλλοντας· ἐν δὲ τοῖς λιβυκοῖς, βραδυγάμους ἢ πρεσβυτέραις συνιόντας· εἰ δὲ ὑπὸ τὰς αὐγὰς εἴη καὶ τῷ τοῦ Κρόνου συσχηματιζομένη, τέλεον ἀγάμους. ἔπειτα ἐὰν μὲν ἐν μονοειδεῖ ζῳδίῳ ᾖ καὶ ἑνὶ τῶν ἀστέρων

---

[1] ἀεὶ VPLAD, om. MNECam.
[2] τῶν . . . συμβιώσεων VADE, τῆς . . . συμβιώσεως PLProc., τῆς . . . συμβιβάσεως MNCam.
[3] ἀφορᾶν VPMNADE, ἐφορᾶν Cam., ἐμφοράν L.
[4] αὐτῶν VD, αὐτὴν MNAECam., om. PL.

cold and mixtures of colours;[1] with Mars, temerity and notoriety; with both together, utter ruin of action. In general the period of increase or diminution, again, is calculated by means of the position, from time to time, of the planets responsible for the effect relative to the eastern and western angles.[2]

5. *Of Marriage.*

As the subject of marriage comes next in order to these matters, the following is the method whereby the lawful association of man and wife must be investigated. For men it is necessary to observe the position of the moon in their genitures.[3] For, in the first place, if she chances to be in the eastern quadrants, she makes men marry young or marry women younger than themselves; but if she is in the western quadrants they marry late or marry older women. And if she is under the rays of the sun [4] and in aspect with Saturn, they do not marry at all. Then again, if the moon is in a sign of a single

---

[1] The anonymous commentator (p. 152, ed. Wolf) explains: τουτέστιν ἀσχημοσύνας, "that is, deformities." Proclus paraphrases, "Saturn brings opposition in cold and in the mixtures of colours."

[2] *Cf.* the directions for computation of the time involved which were given at the end of iv. 2 (p. 377).

[3] The text has, literally, "their moon," but this, of course, means the moon as found in the genitures of the subjects. *Cf.* P. Mich. 149, vi. 31-32, τούτων Ἀφροδείτη εὑρεθήσεται κτλ., "Venus in the genitures of these men will be found," etc.

[4] Within 15° of the sun; *cf.* Bouché-Leclercq, p. 309.

συνάπτουσα τύχῃ, μονογάμους ἀποτελεῖ· ἐὰν δὲ ἐν δισώμῳ ᾖ καὶ πολυμόρφῳ ᾖ καὶ πλείοσιν ἐν τῷ αὐτῷ ζῳδίῳ τὴν συναφὴν ἔχουσα, πολυγάμους. κἂν μὲν οἱ τὰς συναφὰς ἐπέχοντες τῶν ἀστέρων ἤτοι κατὰ κολλήσεις ἢ κατὰ μαρτυρίας[1] ἀγαθοποιοὶ[2] τυγχάνωσι, λαμβάνουσι γυναῖκας ἀγαθάς· ἐὰν δὲ κακοποιοί, τὰς ἐναντίας. Κρόνος μὲν γὰρ ἐπισχὼν τὴν συναφὴν περιποιεῖ γυναῖκας ἐπιπόνους καὶ αὐστηράς· Ζεὺς δέ, σεμνὰς καὶ οἰκονομικάς· Ἄρης δέ, θρασείας καὶ ἀνυποτάκτους· Ἀφροδίτη δέ, ἱλαρὰς καὶ εὐμόρφους καὶ ἐπιχάριτας· Ἑρμῆς δέ, συνετὰς καὶ ὀξείας. ἔτι δὲ Ἀφροδίτη μετὰ μὲν Διὸς ἢ Κρόνου ἢ[3] μεθ' Ἑρμοῦ βιωφελεῖς καὶ φιλάνδρους καὶ φιλοτέκνους· μετὰ δὲ Ἄρεως θυμικὰς καὶ ἀστάτους καὶ ἀγνώμονας.

Ἐπὶ δὲ τῶν γυναικῶν ἀφορᾶν[4] δεῖ τὸν ἥλιον αὐτῶν,[5] ἐπειδήπερ καὶ αὐτὸς ἐν μὲν τοῖς ἀπηλιωτικοῖς πάλιν τυχὼν τεταρτημορίοις ποιεῖ τὰς ἐχούσας αὐτὸν οὕτω διακείμενον ἤτοι νεογάμους ἢ νεωτέροις συμβαλλούσας, ἐν δὲ τοῖς λιβυκοῖς βραδυγάμους ἢ πρεσβυτέροις παρ' ἡλικίαν ζευγνυμένας· καὶ ἐν μὲν μονοειδεῖ ζῳδίῳ τυχὼν ἢ ἑνὶ

---

[1] μαρτυρίας VPLAD; cf. μαρτυρίαν Proc.; μαρτυροποιίας MNECam.
[2] ἀγαθοποιοί] ἀγαθοί NCam.
[3] ἢ (post Κρόνου) VPLAD, om. MNECam.
[4] ἐφορᾶν Cam.   [5] αὐτῶν VPD, αὐτόν cett. Cam.

---

[1] The "bicorporeal" signs (δίσωμα) precede the solstitial and equinoctial signs and follow the "solid" signs; see i. 11. Ptolemy explains the name on the ground that they

figure, or is applying to one of the planets,[1] she makes them men of one marriage; but if she is in a bicorporeal or multiform sign, or applies to several planets in the same sign, she makes them marry more than once. And if the planets to which she applies, either by propinquity, or by testimony,[2] are beneficent, the men get good wives; but if they are maleficent planets, the opposite. If she applies to Saturn, he makes the wives hardworking and stern; Jupiter, dignified and good managers; Mars, bold and unruly; Venus, cheerful, beautiful, and charming; Mercury, intelligent and keen. Further, Venus with Jupiter, Saturn, or Mercury makes them thrifty and affectionate to their husbands and children, but with Mars, easily roused to wrath, unstable, and unfeeling.

In the case of the wives one must observe the sun in their genitures; for if he, again, chances to be in the eastern quadrants, he makes those who have him in this position in their genitures either marry young or marry men younger than themselves, but in the western quadrants, he makes them marry late or marry husbands older than themselves. And if the sun is in a sign of a single figure, or applies to one of

---

share in two kinds of weather, rather than that the constellations represent more than one figure (*e.g.* Gemini, Pisces), or a figure of a mixed nature (διφυής; *e.g.* Sagittarius, Capricorn); it is characteristic of him to prefer scientific explanations to those based on mythology or fancy. The anonymous commentator says that he means by " signs of a single figure " the tropical and solid signs, with the exception of the fecund (πολύσπερμα), which are akin to the bicorporeal. For " application," *cf.* i. 24.

[2] Synonymous with " aspect."

PTOLEMY

τῶν ἑῴων ἀστέρων συνάπτων,[1] μονογάμους· ἐν δισώμῳ δὲ ἢ πολυμόρφῳ πάλιν ἢ καὶ πλείοσιν ἑῴοις συσχηματισθείς, πολυγάμους. Κρόνου μὲν οὖν ὡσαύτως τῷ ἡλίῳ συσχηματισθέντος, λαμβάνουσιν ἄνδρας καθεστῶτας καὶ χρησίμους καὶ φιλοπόνους· Διὸς δέ, σεμνοὺς καὶ μεγαλοψύχους· Ἄρεως δέ, δράστας καὶ ἀστόργους καὶ ἀνυποτάκτους· Ἀφροδίτης δέ, καθαρίους καὶ εὐμόρφους· Ἑρμοῦ δέ, βιωφελεῖς καὶ ἐμπράκτους· Ἀφροδίτης δὲ μετὰ μὲν Κρόνου, νωχελεῖς καὶ ἀσθενεστέρους ἐν τοῖς ἀφροδισίοις· μετὰ δὲ Ἄρεως, θερμοὺς καὶ καταφερεῖς καὶ μοιχώδεις· μετὰ δὲ Ἑρμοῦ, περὶ παῖδας ἐπτοημένους. λέγομεν δὲ νῦν ἀπηλιωτικὰ τεταρτημόρια ἐπὶ μὲν τοῦ ἡλίου τὰ προηγούμενα τοῦ τε ἀνατέλλοντος σημείου τοῦ ζῳδιακοῦ καὶ τοῦ δύνοντος· ἐπὶ δὲ τῆς σελήνης τὰ ἀπὸ συνόδου καὶ πανσελήνου μέχρι τῶν διχοτόμων·[2] λιβυκὰ δὲ τὰ τοῖς εἰρημένοις ἀντικείμενα.

Διαμένουσιν μὲν οὖν ὡς ἐπὶ πᾶν αἱ συμβιώσεις ὅταν ἀμφοτέρων τῶν γενέσεων τὰ φῶτα συσχηματιζόμενα τύχῃ συμφώνως, τουτέστιν ὅταν ᾖ τρίγωνα ἢ ἀλλήλοις ἢ ἑξάγωνα, καὶ μάλισθ' ὅταν ἐναλλὰξ τοῦτο συμβαίνῃ· πολὺ δὲ πλέον

[1] ἑνὶ τῶν (τῶν om. A) ἑῴων ἀστέρων συνάπτων VAD, ἑνὶ ἑῴῳ ὄντων (ὄντες L) ἀστέρων PL, ἑνὸς ἑῴου τῶν ἀστέρων (om. συνάπτων) MNECam.
[2] τῶν διχοτόμων VP (-χω-) LADProc., τῆς διχοτόμου MNECam.

---

[1] The anonymous commentator (p. 154, ed. Wolf) says, on this passage: "And if (sc. the aspects) are harmonious,

the oriental planets, he makes them marry but once; but, again, if he is in a bicorporeal or multiform sign, or in aspect with several planets in the east, they marry more than once. If Saturn is similarly in aspect with the sun, they marry sedate, useful, industrious husbands; if Jupiter is in aspect, dignified and magnanimous; Mars, men of action, lacking in affection, and unruly; Venus, neat and handsome; Mercury, thrifty and practical; Venus with Saturn, sluggish and rather weak in sexual relations; Venus with Mars, ardent, impetuous, and adulterous; Venus with Mercury, infatuated with boys. In this connection we mean by eastern quadrants, in the case of the sun, the signs which precede the rising sign of the zodiac, and those which precede the setting sign; with reference to the moon, the signs from new and full moon to the quarters; and by western quadrants the signs opposite these.

Marriages for the most part are lasting when in both the genitures the luminaries happen to be in harmonious aspect, that is, in trine or in sextile with one another, and particularly when this comes about by exchange;[1] and even more when the

---

either both the luminaries (*sc.* are in aspect), or in both the genitures, or one with the other; and if one (*sc.* with the other), either sun with sun, or moon with moon, or alternately (ἐνηλλαγμένα) the sun with the moon and the moon with the sun." By the expression "one with the other" he seems to mean "the luminaries in one geniture with those in the other," and this would be his interpretation of Ptolemy's ἐναλλάξ (Proclus, κατ' ἐναλλαγήν). This is more likely to be correct than Bouché-Leclercq's assumption (p. 449) of an exchange of houses, especially as the houses of the sun and moon, Leo and Cancer, are disjunct (ἀσύνδετα).

ὅταν ἡ τοῦ ἀνδρὸς σελήνη τῷ τῆς γυναικὸς ἡλίῳ. διαλύονται δ' ἐκ τῶν τυχόντων καὶ ἀπαλλοτριοῦνται τέλεον ὅταν αἱ προειρημέναι τῶν φωτῶν στάσεις ἐν ἀσυνδέτοις ζῳδίοις τύχωσιν ἢ ἐν διαμέτροις ἢ τετραγώνοις. κἂν μὲν τοὺς συμφώνους τῶν φωτῶν συσχηματισμοὺς οἱ ἀγαθοποιοὶ τῶν ἀστέρων ἐπιθεωρῶσιν, ἡδείας καὶ προσηνεῖς καὶ ὀνησιφόρους τὰς διαμονὰς συντηροῦσιν· ἐὰν δ' οἱ κακοποιοί, μαχίμους καὶ ἀηδεῖς[1] καὶ ἐπιζημίους. ὁμοίως δὲ καὶ ἐπὶ τῶν ἀσυμφώνων στάσεων οἱ μὲν ἀγαθοποιοὶ τοῖς φωσὶ μαρτυρήσαντες οὐ τέλεον ἀποκόπτουσι τὰς συμβιώσεις, ἀλλὰ ποιοῦσιν ἐπανόδους καὶ ἀναμνήσεις συντηρούσας τό τε προσηνὲς καὶ τὸ φιλόστοργον· οἱ δὲ κακοποιοὶ μετά τινος ἐπηρείας καὶ ὕβρεως[2] ποιοῦσι τὰς διαλύσεις. τοῦ μὲν οὖν[3] τοῦ Ἑρμοῦ μόνου σὺν αὐτοῖς γενομένου, ἐν[4] περιβοησίαις καὶ ἐγκλήμασι περικυλίονται·[5] μετὰ δὲ τοῦ τῆς Ἀφροδίτης ἐπὶ[6] μοιχείαις ἢ φαρμακείαις ἢ τοῖς τοιούτοις. τὰς δὲ κατ' ἄλλον οἱονδήποτε τρόπον γενομένας συναρμογὰς διακριτέον ἀφορῶντας[7] εἴς τε τὸν τῆς Ἀφροδίτης ἀστέρα καὶ τὸν τοῦ Ἄρεως καὶ τὸν τοῦ Κρόνου. συνόντων γὰρ αὐτῶν τοῖς φωσὶν οἰκείως[8] καὶ τὰς συμβιώσεις[9] οἰκείας καὶ νομίμους τὰς συγγενείας· συγγένειαν[10] γὰρ ὥσπερ ἔχει πρὸς ἑκάτερον τῶν εἰρημένων ἀστέρων ὁ τῆς Ἀφροδίτης, καὶ πρὸς μὲν τὸν τοῦ

---

[1] ἀηδεῖς VLDE, ἀειδεῖς P, cf. ἀηδής Proc.; ἀναιδεῖς MNACam.
[2] ὕβρεως VLADEProc., ὕβριος P, ὕρας MN, ἄρυς Cam.

husband's moon is in such aspect with the wife's sun. Divorces on slight pretexts and complete alienations occur when the aforesaid positions of the luminaries are in disjunct signs, or in opposition or in quartile. And if the beneficent planets regard the luminaries when the latter are in harmonious aspect, they keep the marriage pleasant, agreeable, and profitable, but if the maleficent planets so regard the luminaries, the marriage will be quarrelsome, unpleasant, and unprofitable. Similarly, when the luminaries are in inharmonious positions, the beneficent planets testifying to the luminaries do not completely terminate the marriages, but bring about renewals and recollections, which preserve kindness and affection; but the maleficent planets cause divorces with abuse and violence. If Mercury alone is with them, they are involved in notoriety and recriminations; and along with Venus, in adultery, poisonings, and the like. Marriages which come about in any other manner whatsoever must be judged by looking to Venus, Mars, and Saturn. For if they are with the luminaries in familiarity, we must decide that the marriages also will be domestic and the relationship lawful. For the marriage relationship will follow the relation which Venus holds to each of the planets mentioned,

---

³ μὲν οὖν VPLD, μὲν MNAECam.
⁴ ἐν PL, om. cett. Cam. ⁵ περικυλίοντες VD.
⁶ ἐπὶ VPLDEProc., om. MNACam.
⁷ ἀφορῶντας VP (-ορουτ-) LADE, ἀμφοτέρας MNCam.
⁸ οἰκείως VP (οἰκί-) MADE, οἰκείοις L, om. NCam.
⁹ καὶ τὰς συμβιώσεις PLMA, om. καὶ VD; om. NCam.
¹⁰ συγγένειαν PLMA, συγγένειαν VD, συγγένεια NECam.

Ἄρεως κατὰ τὸ συνακμάζον πρόσωπον, ἐπειδήπερ ἐν τοῖς τριγωνικοῖς ἀλλήλων ζῳδίοις ἔχουσι τὰ ὑψώματα, πρὸς δὲ τὸν τοῦ Κρόνου κατὰ τὸ πρεσβύτερον πρόσωπον, ἐπειδὴ πάλιν ἐν τοῖς τριγωνικοῖς ἀλλήλων ἔχουσι τοὺς οἴκους.

Ὅθεν ὁ τῆς Ἀφροδίτης μετὰ μὲν τοῦ τοῦ Ἄρεως ἁπλῶς ἐρωτικὰς διαθέσεις ποιεῖ· προσόντος δὲ τοῦ τοῦ Ἑρμοῦ, καὶ περιβοησίας· ἐν δὲ τοῖς ἐπικοίνοις καὶ συνοικειουμένοις ζῳδίοις Αἰγόκερῳ, Ἰχθύσιν, ἀδελφῶν ἢ συγγενῶν ἐπιπλοκάς· κἂν μὲν ἐπὶ τῶν ἀνδρῶν τῇ σελήνῃ συμπάρῃ, ποιεῖ δυσὶν ἀδελφαῖς ἢ συγγενέσι συνερχομένους· ἐὰν δὲ ἐπὶ τῶν γυναικῶν τῷ τοῦ Διός, δυσὶν ἀδελφοῖς ἢ συγγενέσιν.

Μετὰ δὲ τοῦ τοῦ Κρόνου πάλιν ὁ τῆς Ἀφροδίτης τυχὼν ἁπλῶς μὲν ἡδείας καὶ εὐσταθεῖς ποιεῖ τὰς συμβιώσεις· προσόντος δὲ τοῦ τοῦ Ἑρμοῦ, καὶ ὠφελίμους· συμπροσγενομένου δὲ καὶ τοῦ τοῦ Ἄρεως, ἀστάτους καὶ βλαβερὰς καὶ ἐπιζήλους. κἂν μὲν ὁμοιοσχημονῇ[1] αὐτοῖς, πρὸς ὁμήλικας ποιεῖ τὰς ἐπιπλοκάς· ἂν δ' ἀνατολικώτερος αὐτῶν, πρὸς νεωτέρους ἢ νεωτέρας· ἐὰν δὲ δυτικώτερος, πρὸς πρεσβυτέρας ἢ πρεσβυτέρους. ἐὰν δὲ καὶ ἐν τοῖς ἐπικοίνοις ζῳδίοις ὦσιν ὁ τῆς Ἀφροδίτης καὶ ὁ τοῦ Κρόνου, τουτέστιν Αἰγόκερῳ καὶ Ζυγῷ,

---

[1] ὁμοιοσχημονῇ VAD, ὁμοιοσχήμων ᾖ PL, ὁμοιοσχήμων αὐτοῖς ᾖ NCam.

---

[1] More properly, their exaltations are in trine with their houses; for the exaltation of Mars (Capricorn) is in trine

TETRABIBLOS IV. 5

toward Mars, that of persons of the same age, since they have their exaltations in signs that are in trine to one another;[1] toward Saturn, that of the older person, since again they have their houses in signs which are in trine to each other.[2]

Therefore Venus, with Mars, produces merely amorous dispositions, but if Mercury is present, notoriety also; in the common and familiar signs,[3] Capricorn and Pisces, unions with brethren or kindred. If in the case of men Venus is with the moon, she makes them unite with two sisters or kinsfolk, and if in the case of women Venus is with Jupiter, with two brothers, or kinsfolk.

Again, if Venus happens to be with Saturn, she produces merely pleasant and firm unions, but if Mercury is present, they are also beneficial. But if Mars also is present the marriage will be unstable, harmful, and full of jealousy. And if she is in the same aspect to them, she brings about marriages with equals in age; but if she is further to the east than they, marriages with younger men or women, and if she is further to the west, with older women or men. But if Venus and Saturn are also in the common signs, that is, in Capricorn or Libra,[4] they

---

with the house of Venus (Taurus), not with her exaltation (Pisces). The latter is in trine with Scorpio, the house of Mars.

[2] This is literally so; Taurus, the house of Venus, and Capricorn, the house of Saturn, both belong to the second or south-eastern triangle.

[3] Capricorn is the house of Saturn and Pisces the exaltation of Venus.

[4] Capricorn is the house of Saturn; Libra the house of Venus and the exaltation of Saturn.

PTOLEMY

συγγενικὰς ποιοῦσι¹ τὰς συνελεύσεις. ὡροσκοπήσαντι δὲ ἢ μεσουρανήσαντι τῷ προειρημένῳ σχήματι ἡ σελήνη μὲν συμπροσγενομένη ποιεῖ τοὺς μὲν ἄρρενας μητράσιν ἢ μητέρων ἀδελφαῖς² ἢ μητρυιαῖς συνέρχεσθαι, τὰς δὲ θηλείας υἱοῖς ἢ υἱοῖς ἀδελφῶν³ ἢ θυγατέρων ἀνδράσιν· ἥλιος δὲ δυτικῶν μάλιστα ὄντων τῶν ἀστέρων τοὺς μὲν ἄρρενας θυγατράσιν ἢ θυγατέρων ἀδελφαῖς ἢ γυναιξὶν υἱῶν, τὰς δὲ θηλείας πατράσιν ἢ πατέρων ἀδελφοῖς ἢ πατρωοῖς.⁴ ἐὰν δ' οἱ προκείμενοι σχηματισμοὶ τῶν μὲν συγγενικῶν ζῳδίων μὴ τύχωσιν, ἐν θηλυκοῖς δὲ ὦσι τόποις,⁵ ποιοῦσι καὶ οὕτως καταφερεῖς καὶ πρὸς τὸ διαθεῖναί τε καὶ διατεθῆναι⁶ πάντα τρόπον προχείρους, ἐπ' ἐνίων δὲ μορφώσεων καὶ ἀσελγεῖς, ὡς ἐπί τε τῶν ἐμπροσθίων καὶ ὀπισθίων τοῦ Κριοῦ καὶ τῆς Ὑάδος καὶ τῆς Καλπίδος⁷ καὶ τῶν ὀπισθίων τοῦ Λέοντος καὶ τοῦ προσώπου τοῦ Αἰγόκερω. κεντρωθέντες⁸ δὲ κατὰ μὲν τῶν πρώτων δύο κέντρων τοῦ τε ἀπηλιωτικοῦ καὶ τοῦ μεσημβρινοῦ, παντελῶς ἀποδεικνύουσι τὰ πάθη καὶ ἐπὶ δημοσίων τόπων προάγουσι· κατὰ δὲ τῶν ἐσχάτων δύο τοῦ τε λιβυκοῦ καὶ τοῦ βορείου σπάδοντας ποιοῦσι καὶ

---

¹ ποιοῦσι] ποιοῦνται MNCam.
² ἀδελφαῖς VPADE, -οῖς cott. Cam.; (πρὸς) ἀδελφάς Proc.
³ υἱοῖς ἀδελφῶν VMDE, πρὸς υἱοὺς ἀδελφῶν Proc., υἱῶν ἀδελφοῖς PLNCam., om. A.
⁴ θυγατέρων ἀνδράσιν PLProc.; πατρωοῖς cett. Cam.
⁵ καὶ προσώποις add. MNAECam., om. VPLDProc.
⁶ διατεθῆναι] desinit N.
⁷ καὶ τῆς Καλπίδος om. MECam.

TETRABIBLOS IV. 5

portend marriages of kin. If the moon is present with this aforesaid combination when it is at the horoscope or at mid-heaven, she makes men wed their mothers, or with their mother's sisters, or their stepmothers, and women wed their sons, their brothers' sons, or their daughters' husbands. The sun, particularly if the planets are setting, makes men wed their daughters, daughters' sisters, or sons' wives, and the women wed their fathers, fathers' brothers, or stepfathers. But if the aforesaid aspects chance not to be composed of signs of the same gender, but are in feminine places,[1] thus they produce depraved individuals, ready in every way for both active and passive participation, and in some formations utterly obscene, as for instance in the forward and hinder parts of Aries, the Hyades, and the Pitcher, and the hind parts of Leo, and the face of Capricorn. But if the configuration is angular, on the first two angles, the eastern and mid-heaven, they make a complete display of their abnormalities and bring them forward even in public places; on the last two, that is, the western and northern, they produce spades and eunuchs or sterile women and

---

[1] *Cf.* i. 6, according to which positions following the sun, or in the two quadrants from mid-heaven to occident and from lower mid-heaven to orient are feminine. The anonymous commentator in his explanation (p. 157, ed. Wolf) apparently has i. 6 in mind, but his account seems somewhat confused.

---

⁸ κεντρωθέντες VD, *cf.* Proc.; -θέντος PEACam., -θὲν L, -θέντα M.

PTOLEMY

αὐλικοὺς[1] ἢ στείρας[2] ἢ ἀτρήτους· Ἄρεως δὲ προσόντος, ἀποκόπους ἢ τριβάδας.

Καὶ καθ' ὅλου δὲ ποδαπήν[3] τινα διάθεσιν[4] πρὸς τὰ ἀφροδίσια ἕξουσιν ἐπὶ μὲν τῶν ἀνδρῶν ἀπὸ τοῦ τοῦ Ἄρεως ἐπισκεψόμεθα. τοῦ μὲν γὰρ τῆς Ἀφροδίτης καὶ τοῦ τοῦ Κρόνου χωρισθείς, μαρτυρηθεὶς δὲ ὑπὸ Διός, καθαρίους καὶ σεμνοὺς περὶ τὰ ἀφροδίσια ποιεῖ καὶ μόνης τῆς φυσικῆς χρείας στοχαζομένους· μετὰ Κρόνου δὲ μόνου μὲν τυχών, εὐλαβεῖς καὶ ὀκνηροὺς καὶ καταψύχρους ἀπεργάζεται· συσχηματιζομένων δ' Ἀφροδίτης καὶ Διός, 188 εὐκινήτους μὲν καὶ ἐπιθυμητικούς, ἐγκρατεῖς δὲ καὶ ἀντιληπτικοὺς καὶ τὸ αἰσχρὸν φυλαττομένους· μετὰ μόνης δ' Ἀφροδίτης ἢ καὶ τοῦ Διὸς σὺν αὐτῇ τυχόντος, ἀπόντος τοῦ τοῦ Κρόνου, λάγνους καὶ ῥαθύμους καὶ πανταχόθεν ἑαυτοῖς τὰς ἡδονὰς ποριζομένους. κἂν ὁ μὲν ἑσπέριος ᾖ τῶν ἀστέρων, ὁ δὲ ἑῷος, καὶ πρὸς ἄρρενας καὶ πρὸς θηλείας οἰκείως ἔχοντας, οὐχ ὑπερπαθῶς[5] μέντοιγε πρὸς οὐδέτερα τὰ πρόσωπα· ἐὰν δ' ἀμφότεροι ἑσπέριοι, πρὸς τὰ θηλυκὰ μόνα καταφερεῖς· θηλυκῶν δ' ὄντων τῶν ζῳδίων, καὶ αὐτοὺς διατιθεμένους· ἐὰν δ' ἀμφότεροι ἑῷοι, πρὸς τὰ παιδικὰ μόνα[6] νοσηματώδεις· ἀρρενικῶν δ' ὄντων τῶν ζῳδίων, καὶ πρὸς πᾶσαν ἀρρένων ἡλικίαν. κἂν μὲν ὁ τῆς Ἀφροδίτης δυτικώτερος ᾖ, ταπειναῖς ἢ δούλαις ἢ

---

[1] αὐλικοὺς VMADECam.¹, αὐλίσκους PL, εὐνούχους Cam.²
[2] στείρους Cam.²
[3] ποδαπήν Cam.¹, ποταπήν ME, παντοδαπήν VPAD, παντοδαπεῖς L, om. Cam.²
[4] διάθεσιν libri, ποιότητα Cam.², om. Cam.¹

those without passages; if Mars is present, men who have lost their genitals, or the so-called *tribades*.¹

In general we shall, in the case of men, investigate through Mars what will be their disposition with respect to matters of love. For if Mars is separated from Venus and Saturn, but has the testimony of Jupiter, he produces men who are cleanly and decorous in love and who aim only at its natural use. But if he is accompanied by Saturn alone, he produces men cautious, hesitant, and frigid. If Venus and Jupiter are in aspect with him, he will produce men easily roused and passionate, who are, however, continent, hold themselves in check, and avoid unseemliness. With Venus alone, or if Jupiter also is with her, but Saturn is not present, he produces lustful, careless men, who seek their pleasures from every quarter; and if one of the planets is an evening and the other a morning star, men who have relations with both males and females, but no more than moderately inclined to either. But if both are evening stars, they will be inclined toward the females alone, and if the signs of the zodiac are feminine, they themselves will be pathics. If both are morning stars, they will be infected only with love of boys, and if the signs of the zodiac are masculine, with males of any age. If Venus is further to the west, they will have to do with women of low degree, slaves, or

¹ Female perverts; see Cumont, pp. 182-183.

---

⁵ ὑπερπαθῶς VD, ὑπὲρ παθ PL, ὑπὲρ παθῶν MECam.¹, ὑπερπάσχοντας Cum.², ὑπὲρ παθ/// (lacuna) A; ὑπερβολικῶς Proc.
⁶ μόνα VAD, -ον cett. Cam.

PTOLEMY

ἀλλοφύλοις συνερχομένους· ἐὰν δὲ ὁ τοῦ Ἄρεως, ὑπερεχούσαις ἢ ὑπάνδροις ἢ δεσποίναις.

Ἐπὶ δὲ τῶν γυναικῶν τὸν τῆς Ἀφροδίτης ἐπισκεπτέον. συσχηματιζόμενος γὰρ τῷ τοῦ Διὸς ἢ καὶ τῷ τοῦ Ἑρμοῦ, σώφρονας καὶ καθαρίους ποιεῖ περὶ τὰ ἀφροδίσια· καὶ τοῦ τοῦ Κρόνου[1] δὲ ἀπόντος, τῷ τοῦ Ἑρμοῦ συνοικειωθείς, κεκινημένας μὲν καὶ ὀρεκτικάς, εὐλαβεῖς δὲ καὶ ὀκνηρὰς τὰ πολλὰ καὶ τὸ αἰσχρὸν φυλαττομένας. Ἄρει δὲ μόνῳ μὲν συνὼν ἢ καὶ συσχηματισθεὶς ὁ τῆς Ἀφροδίτης ποιεῖ λάγνους καὶ καταφερεῖς καὶ μᾶλλον ῥαθύμους· ἐὰν δὲ καὶ ὁ τοῦ Διὸς αὐτοῖς προσγένηται, κἂν μὲν ὁ τοῦ Ἄρεως ὑπὸ τὰς αὐγὰς ᾖ τοῦ ἡλίου,[2] συνέρχονται δούλοις ἢ ταπεινοτέροις ἢ ἀλλοφύλοις· ἐὰν δὲ ὁ τῆς Ἀφροδίτης, ὑπερέχουσιν ἢ δεσπόταις, ἑταιρῶν[3] ἢ μοιχάδων ἐπέχουσαι τρόπον· κἂν μὲν τεθηλυσμένοι ὦσι τοῖς τόποις ἢ τοῖς σχήμασιν οἱ ἀστέρες, πρὸς τὸ διατίθεσθαι μόνον καταφερεῖς· ἐὰν δὲ ἠρρενωμένοι, καὶ πρὸς τὸ διατιθέναι γυναῖκας. ὁ μέντοι τοῦ Κρόνου τοῖς προκειμένοις σχήμασι συνοικειωθείς, ἐὰν μὲν καὶ αὐτὸς ᾖ τεθηλυσμένος, ἀσελγειῶν μόνος[4] γίνεται αἴτιος· ἐὰν δὲ ἀνατολικὸς καὶ ἠρρενωμένος, ἐπιψόγους ἵστησιν ἢ τῶν ἐπιψόγων ἐραστὰς ἀπεργάζε-

---

[1] *Κρόνου* VPLDProc., *Διὸς* MAECam.
[2] *τοῦ ἡλίου* PLProc.; om. cett. Cam.
[3] *ἑαυτῶν* post *δεσπόταις* add. MECam.
[4] *μόνος* VPLMAE, *μόνον* DCam.

---

[1] The reading of the better MSS. and Proclus is restored here. Camerarius (see the cr. n.) read "Jupiter" with

foreigners; if Mars is further west, with superiors, or married women, or ladies of high station.

In the genitures of women one must examine Venus. For if Venus is in aspect with Jupiter or likewise with Mercury, she makes them temperate and pure in love. If Saturn [1] is not present, but she is associated with Mercury, she makes them easily aroused and full of desire, but generally cautious, hesitant, and avoiding turpitude. But if Venus is together with Mars only, or is in some aspect to him, she makes them lustful and depraved and more heedless. If Jupiter too is present with them, and if Mars is under the sun's rays, they have commerce with slaves, men of lower classes, or foreigners; but if Venus is in this position, they consort with men of superior rank or masters, playing the part of mistresses or adulteresses; if the planets are made feminine by their places or aspects,[2] they are inclined only to take the passive part, but if the planets are made masculine they are so depraved as actively to have commerce with women. However, when Saturn is brought into association with the aforesaid configurations, if he is himself made feminine, he is by himself the cause of licentiousness, but if he is rising and is in a masculine position, he makes them the objects of censure or lovers of such; but combination with

---

some plausibility, to be sure, because Jupiter and Mercury have been associated with Venus in the preceding sentence; but this very plausibility would have been a good reason for substituting "Jupiter" for an original "Saturn." Furthermore, the effect of the absence of Saturn, in this sentence, is not unlike what it is said to be in the preceding paragraph, that is, to make the subjects more lustful.

[2] *Cf.* i. 6.

ται, τοῦ μὲν τοῦ Διὸς πάλιν ἀεὶ πρὸς τὸ εὐσχημονέστερον τῶν παθῶν συλλαμβανομένου, τοῦ δὲ τοῦ Ἑρμοῦ πρὸς τὸ διαβοητότερον καὶ εὐπταιστότερον.

⟨ϛ.⟩ Περὶ τέκνων

Ἐπειδὴ δὲ τῷ περὶ γάμου τόπῳ καὶ ὁ περὶ τέκνων ἀκολουθεῖ, σκοπεῖν δεήσει τοὺς τῷ κατὰ κορυφὴν τόπῳ ἢ τῷ ἐπιφερομένῳ, τουτέστι τῷ τοῦ ἀγαθοῦ δαίμονος, προσόντας ἢ συσχηματιζομένους· εἰ δὲ μή, τοὺς τοῖς διαμέτροις αὐτῶν· καὶ σελήνην μὲν καὶ Δία καὶ Ἀφροδίτην πρὸς δόσιν τέκνων λαμβάνειν, ἥλιον δὲ καὶ Ἄρη καὶ Κρόνον πρὸς ἀτεκνίαν ἢ ὀλιγοτεκνίαν· τὸν δὲ τοῦ Ἑρμοῦ, πρὸς ὁποτέρους ἂν αὐτῶν τύχῃ συσχηματισθείς, ἐπίκοινον καὶ ἐπιδοτῆρα μὲν ὅταν ἀνατολικὸς ᾖ, ἀφαιρέτην δ' ὅταν δυτικός.

190 Οἱ μὲν οὖν δοτῆρες ἁπλῶς μὲν οὕτω κείμενοι καὶ κατὰ μόνας ὄντες μοναχὰ διδόασι τέκνα· ἐν δισώμοις δὲ καὶ ἐν θηλυκοῖς ζῳδίοις, ὁμοίως δὲ καὶ ἐν τοῖς πολυσπέρμοις, οἷον Ἰχθύσι καὶ Σκορπίῳ καὶ Καρκίνῳ, δισσὰ ἢ καὶ πλείονα· καὶ ἠρρενωμένοι μὲν τοῖς τε ἀρρενικοῖς[1] ζῳδίοις καὶ τοῖς πρὸς ἥλιον σχηματισμοῖς ἄρρενα· τεθηλυσμένοι δὲ θήλεα· καθυπερτερηθέντες δὲ ὑπὸ τῶν κακοποιῶν ἢ καὶ ἐν στειρώδεσι τόποις[2] τυχόντες, οἷόν ἐστι[3]

[1] ἀρρενικοῖς PL; cf. Proc.; om. cett. Cam.
[2] τόποις VD; τόποις ἢ ζῳδίοις PLProc.; ζῳδίοις MAECam.
[3] ἐστι VDProc., om. cett. Cam.

---

[1] The eleventh place, or house.
[2] Some of the MSS. at this point read "places," some "signs," and some (with Proclus) "places or signs"; see

Jupiter, again, always gives a more seemly appearance to these faults, and with Mercury makes them more notorious and unsafe.

6. *Of Children.*

As the topic of children follows upon that of marriage, we shall have to observe the planets that are in the mid-heaven or in aspect with it or with its succedant, that is, the house of the Good Daemon,[1] or, in default of such planets, those connected with the diametrically opposite places; and we must take the moon, Jupiter, and Venus to portend the giving of children, the sun, Mars, and Saturn to indicate few or no children. Mercury must be taken as common, with whichever group of planets he chances to be in aspect, and to give children when he is a morning star, and to take them away when he is an evening star.

Now, the donative planets, when they are merely in such a position and are by themselves, give single offspring, but if they are in bicorporeal and feminine signs, and similarly if they are in the fecund signs, such as Pisces, Scorpio, and Cancer, they give two or even more. If they are of a masculine nature, because they are in masculine signs or in aspect to the sun, they give male children; but female, if they are of a feminine nature. If the maleficent planets overcome them, or if they are found in sterile places,[2] such as Leo or Virgo,

the critical note. Probably the less usual term, "places" (τόποις), is the more original; "signs" (ζῳδίοις) was added as a gloss, and thus came into the text.

PTOLEMY

Λέων ἢ Παρθένος, διδόασι μέν, οὐκ ἐπὶ καλῷ δέ, οὐδ' ἐπὶ διαμονῇ. ἥλιος δὲ καὶ οἱ κακοποιοὶ διακατασχόντες τοὺς εἰρημένους τόπους, ἐὰν μὲν ἐν ἀρρενικοῖς ὦσιν ἢ στειρώδεσι ζῳδίοις καὶ ὑπὸ τῶν ἀγαθοποιῶν ἀκαθυπερτέρητοι,[1] τελείας εἰσὶν ἀτεκνίας δηλωτικοί, ἐπὶ θηλυκῶν δὲ ἢ πολυσπέρμων ζῳδίων τυχόντες ἢ ὑπὸ τῶν ἀγαθοποιῶν μαρτυρηθέντες διδόασι μέν, ἐπισινῆ δὲ καὶ ὀλιγοχρόνια. τῶν δὲ αἱρέσεων ἀμφοτέρων λόγον ἐχουσῶν πρὸς τὰ τεκνοποιὰ ζῴδια, τῶν δοθέντων τέκνων ἀποβολαὶ γενήσονται ἢ πάντων ἢ ὀλίγων, πρὸς τὰς ὑπεροχὰς[2] τῶν καθ' ἑκατέραν αἵρεσιν μαρτυρησάντων, ὁποτέρους ἂν εὑρίσκωμεν ἤτοι πλείους ἢ δυνατωτέρους[3] ἐν τῷ ἀνατολικωτέρους ὑπάρχειν ἢ ἐπικεντροτέρους ἢ καθυπερτερεῖν ἢ ἐπαναφέρεσθαι. ἐὰν μὲν οὖν οἱ κυριεύσαντες τῶν εἰρημένων ζῳδίων ἀνατολικοὶ τυγχάνωσι, δοτῆρες ὄντες[4] τέκνων, εἰ[5] ἐν ἰδίοις ὦσι[6] τόποις, ἔνδοξα καὶ ἐπιφανῆ ποιοῦσι τὰ δοθέντα τέκνα· ἐὰν δὲ δυτικοὶ καὶ ἐν τοῖς τῆς ἀλλοτρίας αἱρέσεως τόποις, ταπεινὰ καὶ ἀνεπίφαντα. κἂν μὲν σύμφωνοι τῇ ὥρᾳ καὶ τῷ κλήρῳ τῆς τύχης καταλαμβάνωνται, προσφιλῆ τοῖς γονεῦσι καὶ ἐπαφρόδιτα καὶ κληρονομοῦντα τὰς οὐσίας αὐτῶν· ἂν δ' ἀσύνδετοι ἢ ἀντικείμενοι, μάχιμα

---

[1] ἀκαθυπερτέρητοι . . . ἀγαθοποιῶν om. MECam.; habent libri reliqui et Proclus.
[2] ὑπεροχὰς VPLAD ; cf. Proc. ; ὑπερεχούσας δὲ MECam.
[3] δυνατωτέρους ἢ MAE.
[4] ὄντες VPLDProc.; ἔσονται MAECam.
[5] εἰ δὲ MACam., εἰ E, ἢ VPLD.
[6] ὦσι(ν) VPLMAD, εἰσὶ E, εἶεν Cam.

they give children, but for no good nor for any length of time. When the sun and the maleficent planets govern the aforesaid regions, if they are in masculine signs or in sterile signs, and if they are not overcome by the beneficent planets, they signify complete childlessness, but if they are in feminine or fecund signs or have the testimony of the beneficent planets, they give offspring, but it will suffer injury and be short-lived. If both the sects [1] bear some relation to the signs which signify the begetting of children, there will be losses among the children given, either of all of them or of a few, depending upon the superiority of the planets of either sect that bear witness, whichever we find to be more in number, or greater in power, because they are further to the east, or are closer to the angles, or are superior, or are succedant. If, then, the planets which rule the aforesaid signs are rising, and are givers of children, if they are in their own places, they will make famous and illustrious the children which are given; but if they are setting and are in places belonging to the other sect, the children will be humble and obscure. And if they are found to be in harmony with the horoscope and with the Lot of Fortune, the children will be dear to their parents, they will be attractive, and will inherit their parents' estates; if however they are disjunct or opposed, they will be

[1] The Anonymous (p. 159, Wolf) says that Ptolemy here does not mean the ordinary sects, diurnal and nocturnal, but the donative and destructive planets.

PTOLEMY

καὶ ἐχθροποιούμενα καὶ ἐπιβλαβῆ καὶ μὴ[1] παραλαμβάνοντα τὰς τῶν γονέων οὐσίας. ὁμοίως δὲ κἂν μὲν ἀλλήλοις ὦσι συνεσχηματισμένοι συμφώνως[2] οἱ τὰ τέκνα διδόντες,[3] διαμένουσιν οἱ δοθέντες φιλάδελφοι καὶ τιμητικοὶ[4] πρὸς ἀλλήλους· ἂν δ' ἀσύνδετοι ἢ διάμετροι, φιλέχθρως καὶ ἐπιβουλευτικῶς διακείμενοι. τὰ δὲ κατὰ μέρος πάλιν ἄν τις καταστοχάζοιτο χρησάμενος ἐφ'[5] ἑκάστου[6] τῷ τὴν δόσιν πεποιημένῳ τῶν ἀστέρων ὡροσκοπίῳ καὶ ἀπὸ τῆς λοιπῆς διαθέσεως ὡς ἐπὶ γενέσεως τὴν περὶ τῶν ὁλοσχερεστέρων ἐπίσκεψιν ποιούμενος.

⟨ζ̄.⟩ Περὶ φίλων καὶ ἐχθρῶν

Τῶν δὲ φιλικῶν διαθέσεων καὶ τῶν ἐναντίων, ὧν τὰς μὲν μείζους καὶ πολυχρονίους καλοῦμεν συμπαθείας καὶ ἔχθρας, τὰς δὲ ἐλάττους καὶ προσκαίρους συναστρίας[7] καὶ ἀντιδικίας, ἡ ἐπίσκεψις ἡμῖν ἔσται τὸν τρόπον τοῦτον. ἐπὶ μὲν γὰρ τῶν κατὰ μεγάλα[8] συμπτώματα θεωρουμένων παρατηρεῖν δεῖ τοὺς ἀμφοτέρων τῶν γενέσεων κυριωτάτους τόπους, τουτέστι τόν τε ἡλιακὸν καὶ τὸν σεληνιακὸν καὶ τὸν ὡροσκοπικὸν καὶ τὸν τοῦ κλήρου τῆς τύχης, ἐπειδήπερ κατὰ μὲν τῶν αὐτῶν τυχόντες δωδεκατημορίων ἢ ἐναλλάξαντες τοὺς τόπους ἤτοι πάντες ἢ

[1] μὴ VPLADECam.¹, cf. Proc.; om. MCam.²
[2] συμφώνως L, -ος P, ἢ συμφώνως VD, ἢ σύμφωνα A, σύμφωνα MECam., οἰκείως Proc., οἱ om. MAECam.
[3] διδόντες libri Cam.¹, διδόασι καὶ Cam.²
[4] τιμητικοὶ libri Proc., μιμητικοὶ Cam.
[5] ἐφ' libri Proc., ἀφ' Cam.

quarrelsome, trouble-makers, and injurious, and will not succeed to their patrimony. And similarly, if also the planets which give children are in harmonious aspect one to another, the children which they give continue in brotherly affection and mutual respect; but if they are disjunct or in opposition to one another, the disposition of the children will be quarrelsome and scheming. Particular details, again, one could conjecture by using in each case as a horoscope the planet which gives children, and making his investigation of the more important questions from the rest of the configuration, as in a geniture.

7. *Of Friends and Enemies.*

With regard to friendly dispositions and the opposite, the deeper and more lasting of which we call sympathies and hostilities, and the lesser and occasional acquaintances [1] and quarrels, our investigation will follow this course. In inquiries regarding matters of importance we must observe the places in both nativities which have the greatest authority, that is, those of the sun, the moon, the horoscope, and the Lot of Fortune; for if they chance to fall in the same signs of the zodiac, or if they exchange

[1] συναστρία is an uncommon word. The anonymous commentator says that Ptolemy uses it of the "second and moderate" type of friendship.

---

[6] ἑκάστου VPADEProc., -ῳ cett. Cam.
[7] συναστρίας libri Proc. Cam.¹, *συναφείας Cam.²
[8] μεγάλα libri, τὰ μεγάλα Cam.

PTOLEMY

οἱ πλείους, καὶ μάλισθ' ὅταν οἱ ὡροσκοποῦντες περὶ τὰς ιζ' μοίρας ἀλλήλων ἀπέχωσι, ποιοῦσι συμπαθείας ἀπταίστους καὶ ἀδιαλύτους καὶ ἀνεπηρεάστους· κατὰ δὲ τῶν ἀσυνδέτων ἢ τῶν διαμετρούντων σταθέντες ἔχθρας μεγίστας καὶ ἐναντιώσεις πολυχρονίους· μηδετέρως δὲ τυχόντες ἀλλὰ μόνον ἐν τοῖς συσχηματιζομένοις, εἰ μὲν ἐν τοῖς τριγώνοις εἶεν ἢ ἐν ἑξαγώνοις,[1] ἥττονας ποιοῦσι τὰς συμπαθείας· εἰ δ' ἐν τοῖς τετραγώνοις, ἥττονας τὰς ἀντιπαθείας, ὡς[2] γίνεσθαί τινας κατὰ καιροὺς ἐν μὲν ταῖς φιλίαις ἀποσιωπήσεις καὶ μικρολογίας[3] ὅταν οἱ κακοποιοὶ τὸν συσχηματισμὸν[4] παροδεύωσιν· ἐν δὲ ταῖς ἔχθραις σπονδὰς καὶ ἀποκαταστάσεις κατὰ τὰς τῶν ἀγαθοποιῶν τοῖς σχηματισμοῖς[5] ἐπεμβάσεις. ἐπεὶ δὲ φιλίας καὶ ἔχθρας εἴδη τρία· ἢ γὰρ διὰ προαίρεσιν οὕτως ἔχουσι πρὸς ἀλλήλους ἢ διὰ χρείαν ἢ δι' ἡδονὴν καὶ λύπην· ὅταν μὲν[6] πάντες[7] ἢ οἱ πλείους τῶν εἰρημένων τόπων οἰκειωθῶσι πρὸς ἀλλήλους, ἐκ πάντων ἡ φιλία συνάγεται τῶν εἰδῶν, ὥσπερ ὅταν ἀνοικείως[8] ἡ ἔχθρα. ὅταν δὲ οἱ τῶν φώτων μόνον, διὰ προαίρεσιν, ἥτις ἐστὶ φιλία καὶ βελτίστη καὶ ἀσφαλεστάτη καὶ[9] ἔχθρα[10] χειρίστη καὶ ἄπιστος· ὁμοίως δ' ὅταν μὲν οἱ τῶν

[1] ἐν ἑξαγώνοις VD, ἐν τοῖς ἑξ. A, ἐν om. PLMECam. Proc.
[2] ὡς VPLAD, ὥστε Proc., οἷα MECam.
[3] μικρολογίας VP (μηκρο-) MADECam.¹, -αις L, μακρολογίας Cam.²
[4] τὸν σχηματισμὸν VLAD, τοῦ συσχηματισμοῦ PProc., τῶν συσχηματισμῶν MECam.
[5] τοῖς (συ)σχηματισμοῖς VPLAD, συσχηματισμοὺς ME, -ῶν Cam.

places,[1] either all or most of them, and particularly if the horoscopic regions are about 17° apart, they bring about secure and indissoluble sympathy, unbroken by any quarrel. However, if they are in disjunct signs or opposite signs, they produce the deepest enmities and lasting contentions. If they chance to be situated in neither of these ways, but merely in signs which bear an aspect to one another, if they are in trine or in sextile, they make the sympathies less, and in quartile, the antipathies less. Thus there come about occasional spells of silence and of disparaging talk in friendships, whenever the maleficent planets are passing through these configurations, and truces and reconciliations in enmities at the ingress of the beneficent planets upon them. For there are three classes of friendship and enmity, since men are so disposed to one another either by preference or by need or through pleasure and pain; when all or most of the aforesaid places have familiarity with each other, the friendship is compounded of all three kinds, even as the enmity is, when they are dissociated. But when the places of the luminaries only are in familiarity, the friendship will result from choice, which is the best and surest kind, and in the case of enmity the worst and faithless; similarly, when the places of the

---

[1] See Bouché-Leclercq, p. 241, n. 1.

---

[6] μέν] μὲν γὰρ Cam.   [7] οἱ πάντες MCam.
[8] ἀνοικείως VAD, ἂν οἰκείως PL, ἀνοίκειος MECam.
[9] καὶ (post ἀσφαλεστάτη) VPLD, ἥτις ME, ἣ ἥτις A, ἣ Cam.
[10] ἔχθρα om. MECam.

κλήρων¹ τῆς τύχης, διὰ χρείας· ὅταν δὲ οἱ τῶν ὡροσκόπων, δι' ἡδονὰς ἢ λύπας.

Παρατηρητέον δὲ τῶν συσχηματιζομένων τόπων τάς τε καθυπερτερήσεις καὶ τὰς² τῶν ἀστέρων ἐπιθεωρήσεις·³ ἐφ' ὧν μὲν γὰρ⁴ ἂν γενέσεων ᾖ ἡ τοῦ σχηματισμοῦ καθυπερτέρησις, ἢ ἐὰν τὸ αὐτὸ ᾖ τὸ ἔγγιστα ᾖ ζῴδιον τῇ ἐπαναφορᾷ, ἐκείνῃ τὸ αὐθεντικώτερον καὶ ἐπιστατικώτερον⁵ τῆς φιλίας ἢ τῆς ἔχθρας προσνεμητέον· ἐφ' ὧν δὲ ἡ ἐπιθεώρησις τῶν ἀστέρων βελτίων πρὸς ἀγαθοποιίαν καὶ δύναμιν, ἐκείναις⁶ τό τε ἐκ τῆς φιλίας ὠφελιμώτερον καὶ τὸ ἐκ τῆς ἔχθρας κατορθωτικώτερον ἀποδοτέον.⁷

Ἐπὶ δὲ τῶν κατὰ χρόνους τισὶ συνισταμένων προσκαίρων συναστριῶν τε καὶ ἐναντιώσεων προσεκτέον ταῖς καθ' ἑκατέραν γένεσιν κινήσεσι τῶν ἀστέρων, τουτέστι κατὰ ποίους χρόνους αἱ τῶν τῆς ἑτέρας γενέσεως ἀστέρων ἀφέσεις ἐπέρχονται⁸

¹ οἱ τῶν κλήρων] cf. οἱ τόποι τῶν κλήρων Proc.; οἱ κλῆροι MEACam., τὸν κλῆρον VPD, τῶν κλήρων L.
² τὰς om. Cam.
³ ἐπιθεωρήσεις libri Cam.¹ (cf. Proc.); ὑποθεωρήσεις Cam.²
⁴ γὰρ om. MECam.
⁵ καὶ ἐπιστατικώτερον om. MECam.
⁶ ἐκείναις VPAD, -ας L, -ης MECam.
⁷ κατορθωτικώτερον (κατορθοκώτερον VD) ἀποδοτέον VDAE; om. ἀποδοτέον PL; ἀποδοτικώτερον κατορθωτέον MECam.
⁸ ἐπέρχονται VPDEProc., ὑπέρχ. L, ἐπιφέρωνται Cam., ἀφέσεις ... ἀστέρων om. MA.

---

¹ A star to the right is elevated above, or "overcomes," a star to the left, that is, one which follows it in the diurnal motion. Cf. Porphyry, Introd., pp. 188-189, Wolf.

TETRABIBLOS IV. 7

Lots of Fortune are familiar, through need; and when the places of the horoscopes are familiar, through pleasure or pain.

One must observe, of the places in aspect, their elevations[1] and how the planets regard them. To the nativity in which an elevation of the configuration occurs, whether it is the same sign as the succedant place or the one closest to it,[2] must be assigned the greater authority and direction over friendship or enmity; and to those nativities in which the regard of the planets is more favourable[2] for benevolence and power, we must allot the greater benefit from the friendship and the greater success in the enmity.

In the occasional acquaintances and oppositions that arise from time to time between individuals, we must pay attention to the movements of the planets in each of the nativities, that is, at what times the prorogations of the planets of one nativity reach the

---

[2] Rather obscure, but apparently he means whether the preceding and the succeeding places, which might be, *e.g.* the horoscopes of the two genitures, are in the same sign or in successive ones. The latter is possible, for in unbroken friendships, as he said above, the horoscopes should be within 17° of each other, and hence could be in successive signs. Proclus paraphrases thus: "For that place will have the greater authority over the friendship or the enmity to which the elevation or the succedant place is near, either in the same sign or closest by" (ἐκεῖνος γὰρ ὁ τόπος ἕξει· τὸ δυνατώτερον τῆς φιλίας ἢ τῆς ἔχθρας πρὸς ὃν ἐγγίζει ἡ καθυπερτέρησις ἢ ἐπαναφορὰ, ἢ κατὰ τὸ αὐτὸ ζῴδιον ἢ ἔγγιστα).

[3] As, for example, trine is generally more favourable than quartile.

τοῖς τόποις τῶν τῆς ἑτέρας γενέσεως ἀστέρων.¹ γίνονται γὰρ κατὰ τούτους φιλίαι καὶ ἔχθραι μερικαὶ καὶ² διακρατοῦσαι³ χρόνον ὀλίγιστον μὲν τὸν μέχρι τῆς διαλύσεως αὐτῆς, πλεῖστον δὲ τὸν μέχρι τῆς ἑτέρου τινὸς τῶν ἐπιφερομένων ἀστέρων καταλήψεως. Κρόνος μὲν οὖν καὶ Ζεὺς ἐπελθόντες τοῖς ἀλλήλων τόποις ποιοῦσι φιλίας διὰ συστάσεις⁴ ἢ γεωργίας ἢ κληρονομίας· Κρόνος δὲ καὶ Ἄρης μάχας καὶ ἐπιβουλὰς τὰς κατὰ προαίρεσιν· Κρόνος δὲ καὶ Ἀφροδίτη συνεπιπλοκὰς διὰ συγγενικῶν προσώπων, ταχὺ μέντοι ψυχούσας· Κρόνος δὲ καὶ Ἑρμῆς συμβιώσεις καὶ κοινωνίας⁵ διὰ δόσιν καὶ λῆψιν καὶ ἐμπορίαν ἢ μυστήρια· Ζεὺς δὲ καὶ Ἄρης ἑταιρίας δι' ἀξιωματικῶν ἢ οἰκονομικῶν· Ζεὺς δὲ καὶ Ἀφροδίτη φιλίας τὰς διὰ θηλυκῶν⁶ προσώπων ἢ⁷ τῶν ἐν ἱεροῖς θρησκειῶν ἢ χρησμῶν ἢ τῶν τοιούτων· Ζεὺς δὲ καὶ Ἑρμῆς συναναστροφὰς διὰ λόγους καὶ ἐπιστήμας καὶ προαίρεσιν φιλόσοφον·⁸ Ἄρης δὲ καὶ Ἀφροδίτη συνεπιπλοκὰς τὰς δι' ἔρωτας καὶ μοιχείας ἢ νοθείας,⁹ ἐπισφαλεῖς δὲ καὶ οὐκ ἐπὶ πολὺ διευθηνούσας· Ἄρης δὲ καὶ Ἑρμῆς ἔχθρας καὶ περιβοησίας καὶ δίκας διὰ πραγμάτων¹⁰ ἢ φαρμάκων ἀφορμάς· Ἀφροδίτη δὲ καὶ Ἑρμῆς

---

[1] τοῖς τόποις ... ἀστέρων VDE (τὸν pro τῶν VD); τοῖς τόποις PL, τοῖς τῆς ἑτέρας τόποις Cam.

[2] καὶ (post μερικαὶ) MAEProc.Cam., om. VD, αἱ PL.

[3] διακρατοῦσαι VPLAD, -οῦσι MECam., cf. διαμένουσαι Proc.

[4] συστάσεις VDProc., -ης P, -εως cett. Cam.

[5] συμβιώσεις καὶ κοινωνίας VP (κυνον-) L (κοινον-) ADE, συμβ. κ. συγγενείας M, συγγενείας καὶ συμβιώσεις Cam.; post haec verba add. διδόασι καὶ PLMAECam., om. VDProc.

places of the other.¹ For partial friendships and enmities take place in these times, prevailing at the shortest up to the completion of the prorogation, and at the longest until some other of the approaching planets reaches the place. Now if Saturn and Jupiter approach each other's places they produce friendships through introductions, agriculture, or inheritance; Saturn and Mars make intentional quarrels and schemings; Saturn and Venus, associations through kinsfolk, which, however, quickly cool; Saturn and Mercury make marriage and partnerships for the sake of giving and receiving, trade, or the mysteries. Jupiter and Mars cause associations through dignities or the management of property; Jupiter and Venus friendships through women, religious rites, oracles, or the like; Jupiter and Mercury associations for learned discussion, based upon philosophic inclination. Mars and Venus cause associations through love, adultery, or illegitimate relations, but they are unsure and flourish only briefly; Mars and Mercury produce enmities, noisy disputes, and lawsuits which arise through business or poisonings. Venus and

¹ The method of prorogation explained at length in iii. 10 is used, with a point of departure in one nativity and point of arrival in the other.

---

⁶ θηλυκῶν VP (θυλη-) LDEProc., καθολικῶν MACam.
⁷ ἦ (post προσώπων) om. Cam.
⁸ φιλόσοφον VPLDProc.Cam.¹, -ων MAECam.²
⁹ νωθείας AECam.
¹⁰ πραγμάτων VADProc., γραμμάτων PLMECam.

συμβιώσεις τὰς διὰ τέχνην τινὰ ἢ μοῦσαν ἢ σύστασιν ἀπὸ γραμμάτων ἢ θηλυκῶν προσώπων.

Τὴν μὲν οὖν ἐπὶ τὸ μᾶλλον καὶ ἧττον ἐπίτασιν καὶ ἄνεσιν τῶν συναστριῶν ἢ τῶν ἐναντιώσεων διακριτέον ἐκ τῆς τῶν ἐπιλαμβανομένων τόπων πρὸς τοὺς πρώτους καὶ[1] κυριωτάτους τέτταρας τόπους διαθέσεως· ἐπειδήπερ κατὰ κέντρων[2] μὲν ἢ κλήρων ἢ τῶν φώτων τυχόντες ἐπιφανεστέρας ποιοῦσι τὰς ἐπισημασίας· ἀλλοτριωθέντες δὲ αὐτῶν ἀνεπιφάντους. τὴν δὲ ἐπὶ τὸ βλαβερώτερον ἢ ὠφελιμώτερον τοῖς ἑταίροις ἐκ τῆς τῶν ἐπιθεωρούντων ἀστέρων τοὺς εἰρημένους τόπους ἐπὶ τὸ ἀγαθὸν ἢ κακὸν ἰδιοτροπίας.

Ἰδίως δὲ ὁ περὶ δούλων τόπος ἢ λόγος καὶ τῆς τῶν δεσποτῶν πρὸς αὐτοὺς συμπαθείας ἢ ἀντιπαθείας ἐκ τοῦ κακοδαιμονοῦντος ζῳδίου λαμβάνεται, καὶ τῆς τῶν ἐπιθεωρούντων τὸν τόπον[3] ἀστέρων[4] κατά τε τὴν γένεσιν αὐτὴν καὶ κατὰ τὰς ἐπεμβάσεις ἢ διαμετρήσεις φυσικῆς ἐπιτηδειότητος, καὶ μάλισθ᾽ ὅταν[5] οἱ τοῦ δωδεκατημορίου κυριεύσαντες ἤτοι συμφωνῶσι[6] τοῖς αὐθεντικοῖς τόποις τῆς γενέσεως ἢ ἐναντίους ποιῶνται τοὺς συσχηματισμούς.

[1] πρώτους καὶ libri, om. Cam.
[2] κέντρον VD; cf. πρὸς τοὺς τόπους τῶν κλήρων ἢ τῶν φώτων κεντρωθέντες, Proc.
[3] τὸν τοιοῦτον τόπον Cam.
[4] ἀστέρων VPLDProc., τοῦ τοιούτου ζῳδίου ἀστέρων A, ζῳδίου ME, τοῦ ζῳδίου Cam.
[5] ὅταν VPLADE, ὅτε MCam.
[6] συμφωνῶσι VD, συμφώνως PMECam., -ους A, -ήσεως L.

TETRABIBLOS IV. 7

Mercury give associations based upon some art or domain of the Muses, or an introduction by letter or through women.

Now then we must determine the degree of the intensity or relaxation of acquaintances and oppositions from the relation between the places which they assume and the four principal and most authoritative places,[1] for if they are upon the angles or the Lots of Fortune or the houses of the luminaries, their portent is the more conspicuous, but if they are removed from them, they are insignificant. Whether the association will be more injurious or more beneficial to the associates is to be determined from the character for good or bad of the planets which regard the places named.

The special topic or account of slaves[2] and the sympathy or antipathy of their masters to them is elucidated from the house of the Evil Daemon[3] and from the natural suitability of the planets which regard this place both in the nativity itself and in their ingresses and oppositions to it, particularly when the lords of the sign are either in harmonious aspect to the principal places of the nativity, or the opposite.[4]

---

[1] *I.e.* those named at the beginning of the chapter: horoscope, Lot of Fortune, sun, and moon.

[2] Camerarius and one or two of the MSS. here insert the heading of a new chapter, Περὶ δούλων ("Of Slaves"). The prominence given to the subject reflects the importance of slavery in ancient society.

[3] The twelfth house, immediately preceding the horoscope.

[4] This passage has difficulties, as Bouché-Leclercq points out (p. 454, esp. n. 4). Apparently we are to observe, as

[For continuation of footnote see pages 422 and 423.

PTOLEMY

⟨η.⟩ Περὶ ξενιτείας

Ὁ δὲ περὶ ξενιτείας τόπος καταλαμβάνεται διὰ τῆς τῶν φωτῶν πρὸς τὰ κέντρα στάσεως, ἀμφοτέρων μέν, μάλιστα δὲ τῆς σελήνης. δύνουσα γὰρ ἢ ἀποκεκλικυῖα τῶν κέντρων ξενιτείας καὶ τόπων μεταβολὰς ποιεῖ. δύναται δὲ τὸ παραπλήσιον ἐνίοτε καὶ ὁ τοῦ Ἄρεως ἤτοι δύνων ἢ[1] καὶ αὐτὸς[2] ἀποκεκλικὼς τοῦ κατὰ κορυφήν, ὅταν τοῖς φωσὶ διάμετρον ἢ τετράγωνον ἔχῃ στάσιν. ἐὰν δὲ καὶ ὁ κλῆρος τῆς τύχης ἐν τοῖς ποιήσασι τὴν ἀποδημίαν ζῳδίοις ἐκπέσῃ,[3] καὶ τοὺς βίους ὅλους καὶ τὰς ἀναστροφὰς καὶ τὰς πράξεις ἐπὶ τῆς ξένης ἔχοντες διατελοῦσιν. ἀγαθοποιῶν μὲν οὖν ἐπιθεωρούντων τοὺς εἰρημένους τόπους ἢ ἐπιφερομένων αὐτοῖς, ἐνδόξους ἔξουσι καὶ ἐπικερδεῖς τὰς ἐπὶ ξένης πράξεις καὶ τὰς ἐπανόδους ταχείας καὶ ἀνεμποδίστους· κακοποιῶν δέ, ἐπιπόνους καὶ ἐπιβλαβεῖς καὶ ἐπικινδύνους καὶ δυσανακομίστους,[4] τῆς συγκρατικῆς ἐπισκέψεως πανταχῆ συμπαραλαμβανομένης κατ' ἐπικράτησιν τῶν τοῖς

[1] ἢ VD, εἴη PL, om. cett. Cam.
[2] Post αὐτός add. ἢ MAECam., καὶ PL.
[3] ἐκπέσῃ VPLADEProc., ἐμπέσῃ MCam.
[4] δυσανακομίστους libri, *ἐπανόδους βραδείας Cam.

---

he says, whether the planets that are actually in the twelfth house, or are in aspect to it, or in opposition to it, are of the same natural temperament; but in the following clause Bouché-Leclercq confesses himself not to be sure of the meaning of αὐθεντικοῖς, rendered *praecipuis* by Cardanus,

8. *Of Foreign Travel.*

The topic of foreign travel[1] receives treatment by observing the position of the luminaries to the angles, both of them, but particularly the moon. For when the moon is setting or declining from the angles,[2] she portends journeys abroad or changes of place. Mars too sometimes has a similar force, either when he is setting or when he himself also has declined from mid-heaven, when he is in opposition or quartile to the luminaries. If the Lot of Fortune also falls among the signs that cause travel, the subjects spend their whole lives abroad and will have all their personal relations and business there. If beneficent planets regard the aforesaid places or succeed them, their activities abroad will be honourable and profitable and their return quick and unimpeded; but if the maleficent planets regard them, their journeys will be laborious, injurious, and dangerous, and the return difficult, although in every case the mixture of influences is taken into consideration, determined

---

locis dominii et potestatis eorum by Junctinus, and *cum dominatore nativitatis* by Melanchthon. It may be noted that Proclus has πρὸς τοὺς κυρίους τόπους τῆς γενέσεως. The anonymous commentator gives no help.

[1] The insecurity and uncertainty of travel in ancient times made it a much more serious undertaking than nowadays, and consequently the astrologers devoted much attention to it.

[2] *I.e.* when she is in the Occident (seventh house) or the so-called ἀποκλίματα (third, sixth, ninth, and twelfth houses). These and the zodiacal signs that fall upon them are the " signs that cause travel." The moon is the greatest traveller among the celestial objects. *Cf.* Bouché-Leclercq, p. 455.

αὐτοῖς τόποις συσχηματιζομένων, καθάπερ ἐν τοῖς πρώτοις διωρισάμεθα.

Ὡς ἐπὶ πᾶν δὲ ἐν μὲν τοῖς τῶν ἑῴων τεταρτημορίων ἀποκλίμασιν ἐκπεσόντων τῶν φώτων, εἰς τὰ πρὸς ἀνατολὰς καὶ μεσημβρίαν μέρη τῶν οἰκήσεων τὰς ἀποδημίας γίνεσθαι συμβαίνει· ἐν δὲ τοῖς τῶν λιβυκῶν ἢ καὶ ἐν αὐτῷ τῷ δύνοντι, εἰς τὰ πρὸς ἄρκτους[1] καὶ δυσμάς.[2] κἂν μὲν μονοειδῆ τύχῃ τὰ τὴν ξενιτείαν ποιήσαντα ζῴδια, ἤτοι αὐτὰ ἢ οἱ οἰκοδεσποτήσαντες αὐτῶν ἀστέρες, διὰ μακροῦ καὶ κατὰ καιροὺς ποιήσονται τὰς ἀποδημίας· ἐὰν δὲ δίσωμα ἢ δίμορφα, συνεχῶς καὶ ἐπὶ πλεῖστον χρόνον. Ζεὺς μὲν οὖν καὶ Ἀφροδίτη κύριοι γενόμενοι τῶν τὴν ξενιτείαν ποιούντων τόπων καὶ φώτων οὐ μόνον ἀκινδύνους ἀλλὰ καὶ θυμήρεις ποιοῦσι τὰς ὁδοιπορίας·[3] ἤτοι γὰρ ὑπὸ τῶν προεστώτων ἐν ταῖς χώραις ἢ διὰ φίλων ἀφορμὰς[4] παραπέμπονται, συνεργούσης αὐτοῖς τῆς τε τῶν καταστημάτων εὐαερίας καὶ τῆς τῶν ἐπιτηδείων ἀφθονίας· προσγενομένου δὲ αὐτοῖς καὶ τοῦ τοῦ Ἑρμοῦ πολλάκις καὶ δι' αὐτῆς τῆς εἰρημένης συντυχίας ὠφέλειαι καὶ προκοπαὶ καὶ δωρεαὶ καὶ τιμαὶ[5] προσγίνονται. Κρόνος δὲ καὶ Ἄρης ἐπιλαβόντες τὰ φῶτα, κἂν μάλιστα διαμηκίζωσιν ἀλλήλους, τὰ περιγενόμενα ποιοῦσιν ἄχρηστα καὶ κινδύνοις περικυλίουσι μεγάλοις, ἐν μὲν τοῖς καθύγροις τυχόντες ζῳδίοις, διὰ δυσπλοιῶν καὶ ναυαγίων ἢ πάλιν δυσοδιῶν καὶ

---

[1] τὰ πρὸς ἄρκτους VADE, τὰς π. ἄ. cett. Cam.
[2] δυσμάς VPLAD, ἐν δυσμαῖς MECam.
[3] ὁδοιπορίας VMADEProc., ἀποδημίας PLCam.

TETRABIBLOS IV. 8

by the dominance of the planets that bear an aspect to these same places, as we explained at first.[1]

In general, it happens that, if the luminaries fall in the lower parts of the eastern quadrants, the travel is to the eastern and southern parts of the world, but if in the western quadrants or in the occident itself, to the north and the west; and if the zodiacal signs which caused the travel chance to be those of a single figure, either themselves or the planets that rule them, the journeys will be made at long intervals and upon occasion; but if they are bicorporeal signs, or of double form, they will travel continuously and for a very long time. If Jupiter and Venus are the rulers of the places which govern travel, and of the luminaries, they make the journeys not only safe but also pleasant; for the subjects will be sent on their way either by the chief men of the country or by the resources of their friends, and favourable conditions of weather and abundance of supplies will also aid them. Often, too, if Mercury is added to these, profit, gain, gifts, and honour result from this good fortune of which we have spoken. If Saturn and Mars control the luminaries, however, and particularly if they are in opposition to each other, they will make the results useless and will involve the subject in great dangers, through unfortunate voyages and shipwreck if they are in watery signs, or

[1] *Cf.* iii. 4 *ad fin.*

---

[4] ἀφορμὰς VPLAD (ἐνεργείας supra scr. A), ἐνεργείας MECam.
[5] καὶ τιμαὶ VPLADProc., om. MECam. (καὶ habet M).

ἐρήμων τόπων· ἐν δὲ τοῖς στερεοῖς, διὰ κρημνισμῶν καὶ ἐμβολῶν πνευμάτων· ἐν δὲ τοῖς τροπικοῖς καὶ ἰσημερινοῖς δι' ἔνδειαν τῶν ἐπιτηδείων καὶ νοσώδεις καταστάσεις· ἐν δὲ τοῖς ἀνθρωποειδέσι διὰ ληστήρια καὶ ἐπιβουλὰς καὶ συλήσεις·[1] ἐν δὲ τοῖς χερσαίοις διὰ θηρίων ἐφόδους ἢ σεισμούς, Ἑρμοῦ δὲ συμπροσόντος διὰ μετέωρα καὶ κατηγορίας ἐπισφαλεῖς, ἔτι δὲ καὶ διὰ τὰς τῶν ἑρπετῶν καὶ τῶν ἄλλων ἰοβόλων πληγάς, παρατηρουμένης ἔτι μὲν τῆς τῶν συμπτωμάτων, ἐάν τε ὠφέλιμα[2] ἐάν τε βλαβερὰ ᾖ, ἰδιοτροπίας, τουτέστι[3] τῆς περὶ τὸ αἴτιον[4] διαφορᾶς, καὶ ἐκ τῆς τῶν αἰτιατικῶν τόπων πράξεως ἢ κτήσεως ἢ σώματος ἢ ἀξιώματος κατὰ τὴν ἐξ ἀρχῆς διάθεσιν κυρίας,[5] τῶν δὲ τὰς ἐπισημασίας μάλιστα ποιησόντων καιρῶν ἐκ τῆς τῶν ε' πλανωμένων[6] κατὰ χρόνους ἐπεμβάσεων ποιότητος. καὶ ταῦτα μὲν ἡμῖν μέχρι τοσούτων ὑποτετυπώσθω.

⟨θ.⟩ Περὶ θανάτου ποιότητος

Καταλειπομένης δ' ἐπὶ πᾶσι τῆς περὶ τὸ ποιὸν τῶν θανάτων ἐπισκέψεως, προδιαληψόμεθα διὰ τῶν ἐν τοῖς περὶ τῶν χρόνων τῆς ζωῆς ἐφωδευμένων πότερον κατὰ ἄφεσιν ἀκτῖνος ἢ ἀναίρεσις ἀποτελεσθήσεται ἢ κατὰ τὴν ἐπὶ[7] τὸ δυτικὸν τοῦ

---

[1] συλήσεις VAD, συλλείσης P, συλλήσεις L, τυραννήσεις cett. Cam.
[2] ὠφέλιμος MECam.
[3] τουτέστι(ν) VPLD, ἐκ MAECam.
[4] Post αἴτιον add. ἔσται VPLD.
[5] κυρίας VPLD, κυρ(ε)ίαν MECam., καὶ κυρείαν A.

again through hard going and desert places; and if they are in solid signs, through falling from heights and assaults of winds; in the solstitial and equinoctial signs, through lack of provisions and unhealthy conditions; in the signs of human form, through piracy, plots, and robberies; in the terrestrial signs, through the attacks of beasts, or earthquakes, and if Mercury is present at the same time, through the weather, dangerous accusations, and, furthermore, through the bites of reptiles and other poisonous creatures. The peculiar quality of the events, whether they be beneficial or harmful—that is, the differentiation in the cause—is observed from the government of the places significant of action, property, body, or dignity, according to our original disposition of them,[1] and the occasions which will to the greatest degree bring about these portended events are judged from the time of the ingresses [2] of the five planets. Such be our general account of the matter.

9. *Of the Quality of Death.*

Since after all the others the inquiry concerning the quality of death remains, we shall first determine, through the means furnished by the discussion of the length of life, whether the destruction will be accomplished by the projection of a ray or by the descent

[1] *Cf.* iv. 4, iv. 2, iii. 11, and iv. 3 respectively.
[2] Presumably into the "signs that cause travel."

---

[6] ἐ' πλανωμένων VDProc., om. cett. Cam.
[7] τὴν ἐπὶ VPAD, om. cett. Cam.

PTOLEMY

ἐπικρατήτορος[1] καταφοράν.[2] εἰ μὲν γὰρ κατὰ ἄφεσιν καὶ ὑπάντησιν ἡ ἀναίρεσις γίνοιτο, τὸν τῆς ὑπαντήσεως τόπον εἰς τὴν τοῦ θανάτου ποιότητα προσήκει παρατηρεῖν· εἰ δὲ κατὰ τὴν ἐπὶ τὸ δῦνον καταφοράν, αὐτὸν τὸν δυτικὸν τόπον. ὁποῖοι γὰρ ἂν ὦσιν ἤτοι οἱ ἐπόντες τοῖς εἰρημένοις τόποις, ἢ ἐὰν μὴ ἐπῶσιν, οἱ πρῶτοι τῶν ἄλλων αὐτοῖς ἐπιφερόμενοι, τοιούτους καὶ τοὺς θανάτους ἔσεσθαι διαληπτέον, συμβαλλομένων ταῖς φύσεσιν αὐτῶν πρὸς τὸ ποικίλον τῶν συμπτωμάτων τῶν τε συσχηματιζομένων ἀστέρων καὶ τῆς αὐτῶν τῶν εἰρημένων ἀναιρετικῶν τόπων ἰδιοτροπίας ζῳδιακῶς τε καὶ κατὰ τὴν τῶν ὁρίων φύσιν.

Ὁ μὲν οὖν τοῦ Κρόνου τὴν κυρίαν τοῦ θανάτου λαβὼν ποιεῖ τὰ τέλη διὰ νόσων πολυχρονίων καὶ φθίσεων καὶ ῥευματισμῶν καὶ συντήξεων[3] καὶ ῥιγοπυρέτων καὶ σπληνικῶν καὶ ὑδρωπικῶν καὶ κοιλιακῶν[4] καὶ ὑστερικῶν διαθέσεων καὶ ὅσαι κατὰ πλεονασμὸν τοῦ ψυχροῦ συνίστανται. ὁ δὲ τοῦ Διὸς ποιεῖ τοὺς θανάτους ἀπὸ συνάγχης καὶ περιπνευμονίας καὶ ἀποπληξίας καὶ σπασμῶν καὶ κεφαλαλγίας καὶ τῶν καρδιακῶν διαθέσεων καὶ ὅσαι κατὰ πνεύματος ἀμετρίαν ἢ δυσωδίαν ἐπισυνάπτουσιν.[5] ὁ δὲ τοῦ Ἄρεως ἀπὸ πυρετῶν συνεχῶν καὶ ἡμιτριταϊκῶν καὶ αἰφνιδίων πληγῶν καὶ νεφριτικῶν καὶ αἱμοπτυϊκῶν διαθέσεων καὶ

---

[1] ἐπικρατήτορος P, ἐπικράτηρος VLAD, κρατήτορος MECam.
[2] καταφοράν VPADE, δι' ἀφοράν L, καταφορά MCam.
[3] καὶ συντήξεων om. MCam.

of the significator to the occident.¹ For if the destruction should come about through the projection of rays and occourse, it is fitting to observe the place of the occourse in order to determine the quality of the death, but if it occurs by the descent of the significator to the occident, we must observe the occident itself. For of whatever quality are the planets that are upon the aforesaid places, or, if they are not upon them, the first planets to approach them, such we must understand that the deaths will be, while at the same time the planets in aspect by their natures contribute to the complexity of the events, as do also the peculiar characters of the aforesaid destructive places themselves, both through the signs of the zodiac and through the nature of the terms.²

Now then, if Saturn holds the lordship of death, he brings about the end through long illness, phthisis, rheumatism, colliquations, chills and fever, and splenic, dropsical, enteric, or hysteric conditions, and such as arise through excesses of cold. Jupiter causes death through strangulation, pneumonia, apoplexy, spasms, headaches, and cardiac affections, and such conditions as are accompanied by irregularity or foulness of breath. Mars kills by means of fevers, continued or intermittent at intervals of one and a half days, sudden strokes, nephritic con-

---

¹ *Cf.* iii. 10, especially p. 279. The "significator," as the anonymous commentator points out, is the prorogator (ἀφέτης).
² For the "terms," *cf.* i. 21-22.

---

⁴ κοιλιακῶν VLDProc., κυληακῶν P. κωλυκῶν ME, κωλικῶν ACam.
⁵ ἐπισυνάπτουσιν VPLD, ἐπισυμπίπτουσιν MAECam

αἱμορραγιῶν[1] καὶ ἐκτρωσμῶν καὶ τοκετῶν καὶ ἐρυσιπελατῶν καὶ ὀλέθρων καὶ ὅσα τῶν νοσημάτων κατ' ἐκπύρωσιν καὶ ἀμετρίαν τοῦ θερμοῦ τοὺς θανάτους ἐπιφέρει. ὁ δὲ τῆς Ἀφροδίτης διὰ στομαχικῶν καὶ ἡπατικῶν καὶ δυσεντερικῶν διαθέσεων ποιεῖ τοὺς θανάτους, ἔτι δὲ διὰ νομῶν καὶ συρίγγων καὶ λειχήνων καὶ φαρμάκων δόσεως καὶ ὅσα τοῦ ὑγροῦ πλεονάσαντος ἢ φθαρέντος ἀποτελεῖται συμπτώματα. ὁ δὲ τοῦ Ἑρμοῦ διὰ μανιῶν καὶ ἐκστάσεων καὶ μελαγχολιῶν[2] καὶ πτωματισμῶν καὶ ἐπιλήψεων καὶ βηχικῶν καὶ ἀναφορικῶν νοσημάτων καὶ ὅσα τοῦ ξηροῦ πλεονάσαντος ἢ φθαρέντος συνίσταται.

Ἰδίοις μὲν οὖν τελευτῶσι θανάτοις οἱ κατὰ τὸν εἰρημένον τρόπον μεταστάντες τοῦ ζῆν, ὅταν οἱ τὴν κυρίαν τοῦ θανάτου λαβόντες ἐπὶ τῆς ἰδίας ἢ τῆς οἰκείας φυσικῆς ἰδιοτροπίας τύχωσιν ὄντες, ὑπὸ μηδενὸς καθυπερτερηθέντες τῶν κακῶσαι καὶ ἐπιφανέστερον ποιῆσαι τὸ τέλος δυναμένων· βιαίοις δὲ καὶ ἐπισήμοις ὅταν ἢ ἀμφότεροι κυριεύσωσιν οἱ κακοποιοὶ τῶν ἀναιρετικῶν τόπων ἤτοι συνόντες ἢ τετραγωνίζοντες ἢ διαμηκίζοντες ἢ ὁπότερος αὐτῶν ἢ καὶ ἀμφότεροι τὸν ἥλιον ἢ τὴν σελήνην ἢ καὶ ἀμφότερα τὰ φῶτα καταλάβωσι,[3] τῆς μὲν τοῦ θανάτου κακώσεως ἀπὸ τῆς αὐτῶν συνελεύσεως συνισταμένης, τοῦ δὲ μεγέθους ἀπὸ

[1] αἱμορραγιῶν VADProc., αἱμορηγιῶν P, αἱμογγιῶν L, αἱμορροϊκῶν MECam.
[2] μελαγχολικῶν ACam.; καὶ (post hoc verbum) om. AECam.

ditions and those that involve the spitting of blood, hæmorrhages, miscarriages, childbirth, erysipelas, and pestilences, and such diseases as induce death by fever and immoderate heat. Venus causes death by stomachic, hepatic, and intestinal conditions, and furthermore through cancers, fistulas, lichens, taking poisons, and such misfortunes as come about from excess or deficiency of moisture. Mercury portends death by madness, distraction, melancholy, the falling sickness, epilepsy, diseases accompanied by coughing and raising, and all such ailments as arise from the excess or deficiency of dryness.

Thus, then, those who depart from life in the way described die natural deaths,[1] whenever the lords of death happen to be in their own or in kindred natural characters,[2] and if no planet that is able to do injury and to make the end more remarkable overcomes them. They die, however, by violent and conspicuous means whenever both the evil planets dominate the destructive places, either in conjunction, or in quartile, or in opposition, or also if one of the two, or both, seize upon [3] the sun, or the moon, or both the luminaries. The affliction of the death in this case arises from their junction, its magnitude

---

[1] Literally, "by their own deaths," contrasted with violent (βίαιοι) deaths caused by some external agency. The anonymous commentator thus explains.

[2] When they are in the houses of members of their own sect, says the Anonymous.

[3] Apparently the word is used in the sense of "affliction" (see iii. 9, p. 267).

---

[3] καταλάβωσι VA (mg.: γρ. κακωθῶσιν) DProc., λάβωσι(ν) PL, κακωθῶσι MECam.

PTOLEMY

τῆς τῶν φωτῶν ἐπιμαρτυρήσεως, τῆς δὲ ποιότητος πάλιν ἀπὸ τῆς τῶν λοιπῶν ἀστέρων συνεπιθεωρήσεως καὶ τῶν τοὺς κακοποιοὺς περιεχόντων[1] ζῳδίων.

Ὁ μὲν γὰρ τοῦ Κρόνου τὸν ἥλιον παρὰ τὴν αἵρεσιν τετραγωνίσας ἢ διαμηκίσας ἐν μὲν τοῖς στερεοῖς ποιεῖ τοὺς κατὰ θλίψιν[2] ὄχλων ἢ ἀγχόναις ἢ στραγγαλιαῖς ἀπολλυμένους· ὁμοίως δὲ κἂν δύνῃ τῆς σελήνης ἐπιφερομένης· ἐν δὲ τοῖς θηριώδεσι ζῳδίοις, ὑπὸ θηρίων διαφθειρομένους· κἂν ὁ τοῦ Διὸς ἐπιμαρτυρήσῃ κεκακωμένος καὶ αὐτός, ἐν δημοσίοις τόποις ἢ ἐπισήμοις ἡμέραις[3] θηριομαχοῦντας· ἀνθωροσκοπήσας δὲ ὁποτέρῳ τῶν φωτῶν, ἐν εἱρκταῖς ἀπολλυμένους· τῷ δὲ τοῦ Ἑρμοῦ συσχηματισθεὶς καὶ μάλιστα περὶ τοὺς ἐν τῇ σφαίρᾳ ὄφεις ἢ τὰ χερσαῖα τῶν ζῳδίων,[4] ἀπὸ δακέτων ἰοβόλων ἀποθνήσκοντας· Ἀφροδίτης δὲ αὐτοῖς προσγενομένης, ὑπὸ φαρμακειῶν καὶ γυναικείων ἐπιβουλῶν· ἐν Παρθένῳ δὲ καὶ Ἰχθύσιν ἢ τοῖς καθύγροις ζῳδίοις τῆς σελήνης συσχηματισθείσης, ὑποβρυχίους καὶ ἐν ὕδασιν ἀποπνιγομένους· περὶ δὲ τὴν Ἀργώ, καὶ ναυαγίοις περιπίπτοντας· ἐν δὲ τοῖς τροπικοῖς ἢ τετραπόδοις[5] ἡλίῳ[6] συνὼν ἢ διαμηκίσας ἢ ἀντὶ

---

[1] περιεχόντων Proc., -εχόντων VMADECam., ὑπερεχόντων P (-εχώντ-) L.

[2] κατὰ θλίψιν VLAD, κατὰ θλύψιν P, κατὰ λῆψιν ME, διὰ καταλῆψιν Cam.

[3] ἡμέραις APL (ἢ μέραις) Proc., ἡμέρας cett. Cam.

[4] ζῳδίων VProc., ζῴων cett. Cam.

[5] ἢ τετραπόδοις VProc., τετραπόδοις PL, om. cett. Cam.

[6] ἡλίῳ VMD, cf. Proc.; -ος PLAECam.

TETRABIBLOS IV. 9

from the testimony of the luminaries, and its quality, again, from the way in which the other planets regard them, and from the signs in which the evil planets are found.

For if Saturn is in quartile to the sun from a sign of the opposite sect, or is in opposition, in the solid signs he causes death by trampling in a mob, or by the noose, or by indurations, and similarly if he is setting and the moon is approaching him; in the signs that have the form of animals, he causes death by wild beasts, and if Jupiter, who is himself afflicted, bears witness to him, death in public places, or on days of celebration, in fighting with the beasts; but in the ascendant, in opposition[1] to either of the luminaries, death in prison. If he is in aspect to Mercury, and particularly in the neighbourhood of the serpents[2] in the sphere, or in the terrestrial signs, he makes men die from the bites of poisonous creatures, and if Venus is present with them, by poisoning and by feminine plots; but in Virgo and Pisces, or the watery signs, if the moon is in aspect, by drowning and suffocation in water; in the neighbourhood of Argo, as the victims of shipwreck; in the tropical or four-footed signs, when [Saturn] is with the sun or is in opposition to him, or if he is

[1] The Anonymous, p. 165, Wolf, explains the rare word ἀνθωροσκοπήσας thus. Melanchthon, however, took it in the opposite sense, "in the occident and opposing the luminaries."

[2] The Anonymous says that he means the constellations, such as Draco and Hydra, of serpent-like form.

PTOLEMY

τοῦ ἡλίου τῷ τοῦ Ἄρεως, ὑπὸ συμπτώσεων κατα-
λαμβανομένους· ἐὰν δὲ καὶ μεσουρανῶσιν ἢ ἀντιμεσουρανῶσιν,[1] ἀπὸ ὕψους κατακρημνιζομένους.

Ὁ δὲ τοῦ Ἄρεως τῷ ἡλίῳ παρ' αἵρεσιν ἢ τῇ
σελήνῃ τετράγωνος ἢ διάμετρος σταθεὶς ἐν μὲν
τοῖς ἀνθρωποείδεσι ζῳδίοις ἐν στάσεσιν ἐμφυλίοις
ἢ ὑπὸ πολεμίων ποιεῖ σφαζομένους ἢ αὐτόχειρας
ἑαυτῶν γινομένους, διὰ γυναῖκας δὲ ἢ καὶ γυναικῶν
φονέας,[2] ἐπὰν καὶ ὁ τῆς Ἀφροδίτης αὐτοῖς[3] μαρ-
τυρήσῃ· κἂν ὁ τοῦ Ἑρμοῦ δὲ τούτοις[4] συσχηματισθῇ, ὑπὸ πειρατῶν ἢ ληστηρίων ἢ κακούργων
ἀπολλυμένους· ἐπὶ δὲ τῶν μελοκοπουμένων καὶ
ἀτελῶν ζῳδίων ἢ κατὰ τὸ γοργόνιον τοῦ Περσέως,
ἀποκεφαλιζομένους ἢ μελοκοπουμένους· ἐν δὲ
Σκορπίῳ καὶ Ταύρῳ[5] καύσεσιν ἢ τομαῖς ἢ ἀποτο-
μαῖς ἰατρῶν ἢ σπασμοῖς ἀποθνήσκοντας· ἐπὶ δὲ
τοῦ μεσουρανήματος ἢ ἀντιμεσουρανήματος, σταυ-
ροῖς ἀνορθουμένους, καὶ μάλιστα περὶ τὸν Κηφέα
καὶ τὴν Ἀνδρομέδαν· ἐπὶ δὲ τοῦ δύνοντος ἢ ἀνθω-
ροσκοποῦντος, ζῶντας καιομένους· ἐν δὲ τοῖς
τετράποσιν, ἀπὸ συμπτώσεων καὶ συνθραύσεων καὶ
συμπτωμάτων[6] ἀποθνήσκοντας. τοῦ δὲ τοῦ Διὸς
καὶ τούτῳ μαρτυρήσαντος καὶ συγκακωθέντος

[1] ἢ ἀντιμεσουρανῶσιν (aut -ήσωσιν) codd.; om. Cam.
[2] φονέας VP (φων-) LMDEProc., φονευομένους ACam.
[3] αὐτοῖς VDProc., -ῆς PL, -ὸν MAECam.
[4] τούτοις VPLADProc., αὐτῷ MECam.
[5] Ταύρῳ VPLDProc., Κενταύρῳ MAECam.
[6] καὶ συνθραύσεων καὶ συμπτωμάτων VPLD (cf. ἀπὸ συμπτωμάτων καὶ κλασμάτων Proc.); καὶ συνθ. ἢ συμπ. A, ἢ συρμάτων
MECam.

TETRABIBLOS IV. 9

with Mars instead of the sun, by being caught in the collapse of a house; and if they are in mid-heaven, above or below the earth, by a fall from a height.

If Mars is quartile or in opposition to the sun or the moon, from a sign of the other sect, in the signs of human form, he causes the subjects to be slaughtered in civil factions or by the enemy, or to commit suicide, and to die because of women or as murderers of women, whenever Venus testifies to them;[1] and if Mercury also is in aspect to these, he causes death at the hands of pirates, robbers, or criminals; in the mutilated and imperfect signs,[2] or in the Gorgon of Perseus, death by decapitation or mutilation; in Scorpio and Taurus, death through cautery, cutting,[3] or amputation by physicians, or death in convulsions; at mid-heaven or the opposite point, by being set up on stakes,[4] and particularly in Cepheus and Andromeda; at the occident or in opposition to the horoscope, by being burned alive; in the quadrupedal signs, death by the collapse of houses, by breaking, or by crushing; if Jupiter also bears witness to him and is afflicted at the same time, again the subjects perish

---

[1] *I.e.* Mars and the luminaries.
[2] Such as Taurus, the blind Cancer, Scorpio, Sagittarius; *cf.* Bouché-Leclercq, p. 151.
[3] καῦσις and τομή were the two principal methods of ancient surgery, were often applied together, and so are frequently mentioned together, as in Plato, *Rep.* 406D (see Adam *ad loc.*).
[4] *I.e.* crucifixion.

ἐπισήμοις πάλιν ἀπόλλυνται κατακρίσεσι καὶ χόλοις ἡγεμόνων ἢ βασιλέων.

Συγγενόμενοι δὲ ἀλλήλοις οἱ κακοποιοὶ καὶ οὕτω διαμηκίσαντες ἐπί τινος τῶν εἰρημένων αἰτιατικῶν διαθέσεων συνεργοῦσιν ἔτι μᾶλλον πρὸς τὴν τοῦ θανάτου κάκωσιν, τῆς κατὰ τὸ ποιὸν κυρίας περὶ τὸν [1] αὐτοῦ τοῦ ἀναιρετικοῦ τόπου τυχόντα [2] γινομένης, ἢ καὶ πολλῶν τῶν θανατικῶν συμπτωμάτων ἢ δισσῶν ἤτοι κατὰ τὸ ποιὸν ἢ κατὰ τὸ ποσὸν ἀποτελουμένων, ὅταν ἀμφότεροι λόγον ἔχωσι πρὸς τοὺς ἀναιρετικοὺς τόπους. οἱ τοιοῦτοι δὲ καὶ ταφῆς ἄμοιροι καταλείπονται· δαπανῶνται δὲ ὑπὸ θηρίων ἢ οἰωνῶν, ὅταν περὶ τὰ ὁμοειδῆ τῶν ζῳδίων οἱ κακοποιοὶ τύχωσι, μηδενὸς τῶν ἀγαθοποιῶν [3] τῷ ὑπὸ γῆν [4] ἢ τοῖς ἀναιρετικοῖς τόποις μαρτυρήσαντος. ἐπὶ ξένης δὲ οἱ θάνατοι γίνονται τῶν τοὺς ἀναιρετικοὺς τόπους κατασχόντων ἀστέρων ἐν τοῖς ἀποκλίμασιν [5] ἐκπεσόντων, καὶ μάλισθ' ὅταν καὶ ἡ σελήνη παροῦσα ἢ τετραγωνίζουσα ἢ διαμηκίζουσα τύχῃ τοὺς εἰρημένους τόπους.

⟨ῑ.⟩ Περὶ χρόνων διαιρέσεως

Ἐφωδευμένου δὲ ἡμῖν κεφαλαιωδῶς τοῦ τύπου τῆς καθ' ἕκαστον εἶδος ἐπισκέψεως μέχρι μόνων

---

[1] τυγχάνοντα post περὶ τὸν add. MECam.
[2] Post τόπου add. τυχόντα VPLMADE, *αἰτίας Cam.
[3] ἀγαθοποιῶν τινα PL.
[4] τῷ ὑπὸ γῆν VADE, ὑπὸ γῆν PL, τῷ ὑπὸ τη//////// (lac.) M, *ἐν τῷ ὑπὲρ γῆν ἡμισφαιρίῳ ὄντος Cam.[2]; om. Cam.[1]; cf. Proc.
[5] ἀποκλίμασιν VDEProc., ἀποκλήμασιν PL, ἀποτελέσμασιν MACam.

conspicuously by condemnation and through the anger of generals or kings.

If the maleficent planets are together and in this state are in opposition in some one of the aforesaid significant positions, they work together all the more for the affliction of the death. In this case the signification of the quality of the death lies with the one that chances to occupy the destructive place, or else the fatal occurrences are multiplied, or doubled, either in quality or in quantity, whenever both have some relation to the destructive places. Persons with such genitures are even left without burial, and are consumed by wild beasts or birds, whenever the maleficent planets chance to be in signs of such form,[1] if none of the beneficent planets is witnessing to the lower mid-heaven or to the destructive places. Deaths occur in foreign lands if the planets that occupy the destructive places fall in the declining places,[2] and particularly whenever the moon happens to be in, or quartile to, or in opposition to, the aforesaid regions.

10. *Of the Division of Times.*

As we have treated systematically under its several heads the outline of each kind of inquiry only so

[1] That is, constellations that have the form of wild beasts or birds. The anonymous commentator cites as an instance "if the dog star (κύων) or Corvus (κόραξ) were rising at the same time," *i.e.* were παρανατέλλοντα (*cf.* Bouché-Leclercq, p. 125, n. 1).

[2] The " places " (twelfths of the zodiac) may be classified as κέντρα, the angles; ἐπαναφοραί, succedants, the signs rising immediately after the angles; and ἀποκλίματα, the declining places, which follow the succedants.

αὐτῶν, ὥσπερ ἐν ἀρχῇ προεθέμεθα, τῶν καθ' ὅλα μέρη λαμβανομένων πραγματειῶν, λοιπὸν ἂν εἴη προσθεῖναι κατὰ τὸν αὐτὸν τρόπον ὅσα καὶ περὶ τὰς τῶν χρόνων διαιρέσεις ὀφείλει θεωρηθῆναι φυσικῶς καὶ ἀκολούθως ταῖς ἐπὶ μέρους ἐκτεθειμέναις πραγματείαις. ὥσπερ τοίνυν καὶ ἐπὶ πάντων ἁπλῶς τῶν γενεθλιαλογικῶν τόπων προυφέστηκέ τις τῶν ἐπὶ μέρους εἱμαρμένη μείζων, ἢ τῆς τῶν χωρῶν αὐτῶν, ᾗ τὰ καθ' ἕκαστον ὁλοσχερῶς θεωρούμενα περὶ τὰς γενέσεις ὑποπίπτειν πέφυκεν, ὥς τά τε περὶ τὰς τῶν σωμάτων μορφὰς καὶ τὰς τῶν ψυχῶν ἰδιοτροπίας καὶ τὰς τῶν ἐθῶν καὶ νομίμων ἐναλλαγάς, καὶ δεῖ τὸν φυσικῶς ἐπισκεπτόμενον ἀεὶ τῆς πρώτης καὶ κυριωτέρας αἰτίας κρατεῖν, ὅπως μὴ κατὰ τὸ τῶν γενέσεων παρόμοιον λάθῃ[1] ποτέ, τὸν μὲν ἐν Αἰθιοπίᾳ γενόμενον,[2] φέρε εἰπεῖν, λευκόχρουν ἢ τετανὸν τὰς τρίχας εἰπών, τὸν δὲ Γερμανὸν ἢ τὸν Γαλάτην μελάγχροα[3] καὶ οὐλοκέφαλον· ἢ τούτους μὲν ἡμέρους τοῖς ἤθεσιν ἢ φιλολόγους ἢ φιλοθεώρους, τοὺς δ' ἐν τῇ Ἑλλάδι τὰς ψυχὰς ἀγρίους καὶ τὸν λόγον ἀπαιδεύτους· ἢ πάλιν κατὰ τὸ τῶν ἐθῶν καὶ νομίμων ἴδιον ἐπὶ τῶν συμβιώσεων, λόγου χάριν, τῷ μὲν Ἰταλῷ τὸ γένος ἀδελφικὸν γάμον προθέμενος, δέον τῷ Αἰγυπτίῳ, τούτῳ δὲ μητρικόν, δέον τῷ Πέρσῃ· καὶ ὅλως προδιαλαμβάνειν τὰς καθ' ὅλου τῆς εἱμαρμένης περιστάσεις, εἶτα τὰς κατὰ μέρος πρὸς τὸ μᾶλλον

[1] λάθῃ VPLADE, λάθοι M, πάθῃ Cam.
[2] τὸν ... γενόμενον] τὸν μὲν Αἰθίοπα Cam.

far as to explain the general doctrine, which was our original intention, it would remain to add in the same manner any observations that should be made about the division of times, in such manner as to agree with nature and to be consistent with the specific doctrines which have already been set forth. So then, as, among all genethlialogical inquiries whatsoever, a more general destiny takes precedence of all particular considerations, namely, that of country of birth, to which the major details of a geniture are naturally subordinate, such as the topics of the form of the body, the character of the soul and the variations of manners and customs, it is also necessary that he who makes his inquiry naturally should always hold first to the primary and more authoritative cause, lest, misled by the similarity of genitures, he should unwittingly call, let us say, the Ethiopian white or straight-haired, and the German or Gaul black-skinned and woolly-haired, or the latter gentle in character, fond of discussion, or fond of contemplation, and the Greeks savage of soul and untutored of mind; or, again, on the subject of marriage, lest he mistake the appropriate customs and manners by assigning, for example, marriage with a sister to one who is Italian by race, instead of to the Egyptian as he should, and a marriage with his mother to this latter, though it suits the Persian. Thus in general it is needful first to apprehend universal conditions of destiny, and then to attach to them the particular conditions which relate to

---

[3] μελάγχροα VD, μελανόχρουν Proc., μελίχρουν MAECam., om. PL.

ἢ ἧττον ἐφαρμόζειν· τὸν αὐτὸν τρόπον καὶ ἐπὶ τῶν χρονικῶν[1] διαιρέσεων τὰς τῶν χρονικῶν ἡλικιῶν διαφορὰς καὶ ἐπιτηδειότητας πρὸς ἕκαστα τῶν ἀποτελεσμάτων ἀναγκαῖον προϋποτίθεσθαι, καὶ σκοπεῖν ὅπως μὴ κατὰ τὸ κοινὸν καὶ ἁπλοῦν τῶν πρὸς τὴν ἐπίσκεψιν θεωρουμένων συμβατικῶν[2] λάθωμεν αὐτούς ποτε τῷ μὲν βρέφει πρᾶξιν ἢ γάμον ἤ τι τῶν τελειοτέρων εἰπόντες, τῷ δὲ πάνυ γέροντι τεκνοποιΐαν ἤ τι τῶν νεανικωτέρων· ἀλλὰ καθάπαξ τὰ διὰ τῶν ἐφόδων τῶν χρονικῶν θεωρούμενα κατὰ τὸ παρόμοιον καὶ ἐνδεχόμενον τῶν ταῖς ἡλικίαις συμφύλων ἐφαρμόζωμεν.[3] ἔστι γὰρ ἐπιβολὴ μία καὶ ἡ αὐτὴ πάντων ἐπὶ τῶν χρονικῶν τῆς καθ' ὅλου φύσεως τῶν ἀνθρώπων, ἐχομένη καθ' ὁμοιότητα καὶ παραβολὴν τῆς τάξεως τῶν ἑπτὰ πλανωμένων, ἀρχομένη μὲν ἀπὸ τῆς πρώτης ἡλικίας καὶ τῆς πρώτης ἀφ' ἡμῶν σφαίρας, τουτέστι τῆς σεληνιακῆς, λήγουσα δὲ ἐπὶ τὴν πυμάτην τῶν ἡλικιῶν καὶ τῶν πλανωμένων σφαιρῶν τὴν ὑστάτην, Κρόνου δὲ προσαγορευομένην. καὶ συμβέβηκεν ὡς ἀληθῶς ἑκάστῃ τῶν ἡλικιῶν τὰ οἰκεῖα τῇ φύσει τοῦ παραβεβλημένου τῶν πλανωμένων, ἃ δεήσει παρατηρεῖν, ὅπως τὰ μὲν καθ' ὅλου

---

[1] ἐπὶ τῶν χρονικῶν MAECam., χρονικῶν om. VPLD.
[2] συμβατικῶν VA, συμβαντικῶν PLD, συμβαματικῶν MECam.
[3] ἐφαρμόζωμεν ACam., -ειν VP (-μωζ-) LD, -ομεν ME.

---

[1] Boll, *Studien*, p. 123, points out that this chapter, with its account of the seven ages of man, does not properly belong to the plan adopted for the *Tetrabiblos* and is in certain details at variance with what has preceded; *e.g.*

degree. In the same fashion likewise, dealing with the division of time, one must take as a basis in each single prediction the differences and special proprieties of the temporal ages, and see to it that we do not, in the ordinary, simple treatment of matters incident to the inquiry, carelessly assign to a babe action or marriage, or anything that belongs to adults, or to an extremely old man the begetting of children or anything else that fits younger men; but once and for all let us harmonize those details which are contemplated in temporal terms with that which is suitable and possible for persons in the various age-classes. For in the matter of the age-divisions of mankind [1] in general there is one and the same approach, which for likeness and comparison depends upon the order of the seven planets; it begins with the first age of man and with the first sphere from us, that is, the moon's, and ends with the last of the ages and the outermost of the planetary spheres, which is called that of Saturn. And in truth the accidental qualities of each of the ages are those which are naturally proper to the planet compared with it, and these it will be needful to observe, in order that by this means we may investigate the

there are seven ages instead of four, as in i. 10, and "seven planets," though elsewhere the two luminaries are kept distinct from the five planets. We may, however, agree with his conclusion that the style of the chapter is unquestionably Ptolemaic and that it is more probably an addition by the author than an interpolation by another hand. Nevertheless, Ptolemy has probably borrowed much of this material from others, and the differences in his sources will account for apparent discrepancies. The ages of man, most familiar to us through *As You Like It*, II. vii, are found in many ancient writers.

τῶν χρονικῶν ἐντεῦθεν σκοπῶμεν, τὰς δὲ τῶν κατὰ μέρος διαφορὰς ἀπὸ τῶν ἐν ταῖς γενέσεσιν εὑρισκομένων ἰδιωμάτων.

Μέχρι μὲν γὰρ τῶν πρώτων σχεδόν που τεττάρων ἐτῶν κατὰ τὸν οἰκεῖον ἀριθμὸν τῆς τετραετηρίδος τὴν τοῦ βρέφους ἡλικίαν ἡ σελήνη λαχοῦσα[1] τήν τε ὑγρότητα καὶ ἀπηξίαν τοῦ σώματος καὶ τὸ τῆς αὐξήσεως ὀξὺ καὶ τὸ τῶν τροφῶν ὡς ἐπὶ πᾶν ὑδατῶδες καὶ τὸ τῆς ἕξεως εὐμετάβολον καὶ τὸ τῆς ψυχῆς ἀτελὲς καὶ ἀδιάρθρωτον[2] ἀπειργάσατο τοῖς περὶ τὸ ποιητικὸν αὐτῆς συμβεβηκόσιν οἰκείως.

Ἐπὶ δὲ τὴν ἑξῆς δεκαετίαν τὴν παιδικὴν ἡλικίαν δεύτερος καὶ δευτέραν λαχὼν ὁ τοῦ Ἑρμοῦ ἀστὴρ[3] τοῦ καθ' ἥμισυ μέρους[4] τοῦ τῆς εἰκοσαετηρίδος ἀριθμοῦ τό τε διανοητικὸν καὶ λογικὸν τῆς ψυχῆς ἄρχεται διαρθροῦν καὶ διαπλάττειν, καὶ μαθημάτων ἐντιθέναι σπέρματά τινα καὶ στοιχεῖα, τῶν τε ἠθῶν καὶ τῶν ἐπιτηδειοτήτων[5] ἐμφαίνειν[6] τὰς ἰδιοτροπίας, διδασκαλίαις ἤδη καὶ παιδαγωγίαις καὶ τοῖς πρώτοις γυμνασίοις[7] ἐγείρων τὰς ψυχάς

Ὁ δὲ τῆς Ἀφροδίτης τὴν μειρακιώδη καὶ τρίτην ἡλικίαν παραλαβὼν ἐπὶ τὴν ἑξῆς ὀκταετίαν[8] κατὰ τὸν ἴσον ἀριθμὸν τῆς ἰδίας περιόδου κίνησιν εἰκότως

---

[1] λαχοῦσα VPLAD, λαβοῦσα E, παραλαβοῦσα MCam.
[2] ἀδιάρθρωτον PLA, ἀρθρωτὸν VD, ἀδιόρθωτον MECam.
[3] ἀστὴρ libri, om. Cam.; post hoc verbum add. τοῦ VD, τὸ AE, τὴν PLMCam.
[4] μέρους VPLD, μέρος cett. Cam.
[5] ἐπιτηδειοτήτων VADProc., -τάτων L, ἐπιτηδι ... (?) P, ἐπιτηδευμάτων MECam.
[6] ἐμφαίνειν PLMAE, -ει VD, ἐκφαίνειν Cam., ἐμφανίζει Proc.

general questions of the temporal divisions, while we determine particular differences from the special qualities which are discovered in the nativities.

For up to about the fourth year, following the number which belongs to the quadrennium,[1] the moon takes over the age of infancy and produces the suppleness and lack of fixity in its body, its quick growth and the moist nature, as a rule, of its food, the changeability of its condition, and the imperfection and inarticulate state of its soul, suitably to her own active qualities.

In the following period of ten years, Mercury, to whom falls the second place and the second age, that of childhood, for the period which is half of the space of twenty years,[2] begins to articulate and fashion the intelligent and logical part of the soul, to implant certain seeds and rudiments of learning, and to bring to light individual peculiarities of character and faculties, awaking the soul at this stage by instruction, tutelage, and the first gymnastic exercises.

Venus, taking in charge the third age, that of youth, for the next eight years, corresponding in number to her own period, begins, as is natural, to

---

[1] The Anonymous says that four years is assigned to the moon because after a period of that length its phases again occur in the same degrees.

[2] Only half the period is assigned to Mercury because of the latter's double nature, according to the Anonymous.

---

[7] τοῖς πρώτοις γυμνασίοις PProc., τ. π. γενεσίοις L, τῆς πρώτης γυμνασίοις VD, ταῖς πρώταις γυμνασίαις MAECam.

[8] ὀκταετίαν VPADEProc., ὀκτωετίαν MCam., ὀκταετησίας L.

τῶν σπερματικῶν πόρων ἐμποιεῖν ἄρχεται κατὰ[1] τὴν πλήρωσιν αὐτῶν καὶ ὁρμὴν ἐπὶ τὴν τῶν ἀφροδισίων συνέλευσιν, ὅτε μάλιστα λύσσα τις ἐγγίνεται ταῖς ψυχαῖς[2] καὶ ἀκρασία καὶ πρὸς τὰ τυχόντα τῶν ἀφροδισίων ἔρως καὶ φλεγμονὴ καὶ ἀπάτη καὶ τοῦ προπετοῦς[3] ἀβλεψία.

Τὴν δὲ τετάρτην καὶ τάξει μέσην ἡλικίαν τὴν νεανικὴν λαβὼν ὁ τῆς μέσης σφαίρας κύριος[4] ὁ ἥλιος[5] ἐπὶ τὰ τῆς ἐννεακαιδεκαετηρίδος ἔτη τὸ δεσποτικὸν ἤδη καὶ αὐθεντικὸν τῶν πράξεων ἐμποιεῖ τῇ ψυχῇ, βίου τε καὶ δόξης καὶ καταστάσεως ἐπιθυμίαν καὶ μετάβασιν ἀπὸ τῶν παιγνιωδῶν καὶ ἀνεπιπλάστων[6] ἁμαρτημάτων ἐπὶ τὸ προσεκτικὸν καὶ αἰδημονικὸν καὶ φιλότιμον.

Μετὰ δὲ τὸν ἥλιον ὁ τοῦ Ἄρεως πέμπτος, ἐπιλαβὼν τὸ τῆς ἡλικίας ἀνδρῶδες ἐπὶ τὰ ἴσα τῆς ἰδίας περιόδου πεντεκαίδεκα ἔτη, τὸ αὐστηρὸν καὶ κακόπαθον εἰσάγει τοῦ βίου, μερίμνας τε καὶ σκυλμοὺς ἐμποιεῖ τῇ ψυχῇ καὶ τῷ σώματι, καθάπερ αἴσθησίν τινα ἤδη καὶ ἔννοιαν ἐνδιδοὺς τῆς παρακμῆς καὶ ἐπιστρέφων πρὸς τὸ πρὶν ἐγγὺς ἐλθεῖν

---

[1] κατὰ VPLAD, καὶ MECam.
[2] ἐγγίνεται ταῖς ψυχαῖς VPLAD, γίνεται MECam.
[3] προπετοῦς VP (πρω-) LAD; cf. τὸ προπετές Proc.; πρέποντος ME; βλέποντος Cam.
[4] κύριος om. Cam.   [5] ὁ ἥλιος PL, ὁ om. cett. Cam.
[6] ἀνεπιπλάστων VPLAD, ἀνεπιστήτων πλάστων ME, ἀκαταστήτων καὶ πλαστῶν Cam.

inspire, at their maturity, an activity of the seminal passages and to implant an impulse toward the embrace of love. At this time particularly a kind of frenzy enters the soul, incontinence, desire for any chance sexual gratification, burning passion, guile, and the blindness of the impetuous lover.

The lord of the middle sphere, the sun, takes over the fourth age, which is the middle one in order, young manhood, for the period of nineteen years, wherein he implants in the soul at length the mastery and direction of its actions, desire for substance, glory, and position, and a change from playful, ingenuous error to seriousness, decorum, and ambition.

After the sun, Mars, fifth in order, assumes command of manhood for the space of fifteen years, equal to his own period.[1] He introduces severity and misery into life, and implants cares and troubles in the soul and in the body, giving it, as it were, some sense and notion of passing its prime and urging it, before it approaches its end, by labour to accomplish

[1] As Bouché-Leclercq (p. 409) remarks, why fifteen years should be given as the " period " of Mars is a mystery. The synodic period of this planet is 780 days and its sidereal period 687 days. In the next paragraph twelve years, stated to be the period of Jupiter, is not far from the actual sidereal period of this planet (11.86 years) and is the measurement ordinarily given by ancient astronomers. For this astrological, not astronomical, statement about Mars cf. P. Mich. 149, col. v, 18 ff., which speaks of the " period of Mars, who returns to his original position in fifteen years " (ἐν τῷ Ἄρεως κύκλῳ, ὃς ἐν ἔτεσιν ιε΄ τὴν ἀποκατάστασιν ἔχει). In the Michigan astrological treatise, however, the length of the period of Mars is associated with the age of boys at puberty rather than with the length of a division of the life of man, as in the *Tetrabiblos*.

τοῦ τέλους ἀνύσαι τι λόγου ἄξιον μετὰ πόνου τῶν μεταχειριζομένων.

Ἕκτος δ' ὁ τοῦ Διὸς τὴν πρεσβυτικὴν ἡλικίαν λαχὼν ἐπὶ τὴν τῆς ἰδίας περιόδου πάλιν δωδεκαετίαν τὸ μὲν αὐτουργὸν καὶ ἐπίπονον καὶ ταραχῶδες καὶ παρακεκινδυνευμένον τῶν πράξεων ἀποστρέφεσθαι ποιεῖ, τὸ δὲ εὔσχημον καὶ προνοητικὸν καὶ ἀνακεχωρηκός, ἔτι δὲ ἐπιλογιστικὸν πάντων καὶ νουθετικὸν καὶ παραμυθητικὸν ἀντεισάγει, τιμῆς τότε μάλιστα καὶ ἐπαίνου καὶ ἐλευθεριότητος ἀντιποιεῖσθαι παρασκευάζων μετ' αἰδοῦς καὶ σεμνοπρεπείας.[1]

Τελευταῖος δὲ ὁ τοῦ Κρόνου τὴν ἐσχάτην καὶ γεροντικὴν ἡλικίαν ἐκληρώθη μέχρι τῶν ἐπιλοίπων τῆς ζωῆς χρόνων, καταψυχομένων ἤδη καὶ ἐμποδιζομένων τῶν τε σωματικῶν καὶ τῶν ψυχικῶν κινήσεων ἐν ταῖς ὁρμαῖς καὶ ἀπολαύσεσι καὶ ἐπιθυμίαις καὶ ταχείαις, τῆς ἐπὶ τὴν φύσιν[2] παρακμῆς ἐπιγινομένης τῷ βίῳ κατεσκληκότι καὶ ἀθύμῳ καὶ ἀσθενικῷ καὶ εὐπροσκόπῳ καὶ πρὸς πάντα[3] δυσαρέστῳ[4] κατὰ τὸ οἰκεῖον τῆς τῶν κινήσεων νωχελείας.

Αἱ μὲν οὖν κατὰ τὸ κοινὸν καὶ καθ' ὅλου τῆς φύσεως θεωρούμεναι τῶν χρόνων ἰδιοτροπίαι τοῦτον τὸν τρόπον προϋποτετυπώσθωσαν. τῶν δὲ ἐπὶ μέρους κατὰ τὸ τῶν γενέσεων ἴδιον

[1] σεμνοπρεπείας VPADE, -τρεπείας L, -τροπίας MCam.
[2] τῆς ἐπὶ τὴν φύσιν VD, ταῖς ἐ. τ. φ. PL, τῇ φύσει MAECam.
[3] πάντα VD, ἅπαντα PL, πάντας MAECam.; om. Proc.
[4] καὶ post δυσαρέστῳ add. MECam.

something among its undertakings that is worthy of note.

Sixth, Jupiter, taking as his lot the elderly age, again for the space of his own period, twelve years, brings about the renunciation of manual labour, toil, turmoil, and dangerous activity, and in their place brings decorum, foresight, retirement, together with all-embracing deliberation, admonition, and consolation; now especially he brings men to set store by honour, praise, and independence, accompanied by modesty and dignity.

Finally to Saturn falls as his lot old age, the latest period, which lasts for the rest of life. Now the movements both of body and of soul are cooled and impeded in their impulses, enjoyments, desires, and speed; for the natural decline supervenes upon life, which has become worn down with age, dispirited, weak, easily offended, and hard to please in all situations, in keeping with the sluggishness of his movements.

The foregoing, then, may be taken as a preliminary description of the characteristics of the ages of life, viewed generally and in accordance with the ordinary course of nature. But as for particulars,[1] which are

---

[1] Bouché-Leclercq, pp. 502 ff., discusses the following sections of this chapter, which present Ptolemy's treatment of the subject of καταρχαί, " initiatives "—the prediction of the success or failure of individual enterprises—insofar as he recognizes the theme. The general method is the same as that of iii. 10, but five places are taken simultaneously as prorogatives, and the planets that influence by their occourse (ὑπάντησις), which may be either bodily or by aspect, need not be merely the destructive ones, as in the prorogation discussed in iii. 10, but also the beneficent stars.

ὀφειλουσῶν λαμβάνεσθαι, τὰς μὲν κατὰ τὸ προϋποτιθέμενον πάλιν καὶ ὁλοσχερέστερον ἀπὸ τῶν κυριωτάτων πάλιν ἀφέσεων ποιησόμεθα, πασῶν μέντοι καὶ οὐκ ἀπὸ μιᾶς, ὥσπερ ἐπὶ τῶν τῆς ζωῆς χρόνων, ἀλλὰ τὴν μὲν ἀπὸ τοῦ ὡροσκόπου πρὸς τὰ σωματικὰ τῶν συμπτωμάτων καὶ τὰς ξενιτείας, τὴν δὲ ἀπὸ τοῦ κλήρου τῆς τύχης πρὸς τὰ τῆς κτήσεως, τὴν δὲ ἀπὸ τῆς σελήνης πρὸς τὰ τῆς ψυχῆς πάθη καὶ τὰς συμβιώσεις, τὴν δὲ ἀπὸ τοῦ ἡλίου πρὸς τὰ¹ κατ' ἀξίαν καὶ δόξαν, τὴν δ' ἀπὸ τοῦ μεσουρανήματος πρὸς τὰς λοιπὰς καὶ κατὰ μέρος τοῦ βίου διαγωγάς, οἷον πράξεις, φιλίας, τεκνοποιίας. οὕτω γὰρ² ἐν τοῖς αὐτοῖς καιροῖς οὐχ εἷς ἔσται ἤτοι ἀγαθοποιὸς ἢ κακοποιὸς³ κύριος αὐτῶν, πολλῶν ὡς ἐπὶ τὸ πολὺ συμβαινόντων ὑπὸ τοὺς αὐτοὺς χρόνους ἐναντίων συμπτωμάτων, ὡς ὅταν τις ἀποβαλὼν πρόσωπον οἰκεῖον λάβῃ κληρονομίαν, ἢ νόσῳ κατακλιθῇ κατὰ τὸ αὐτὸ καὶ τύχῃ τινὸς ἀξίας καὶ προκοπῆς, ἢ ἐν ἀπραγίᾳ τυγχάνων τέκνων γένηται πατήρ, καὶ ὅσα τοιαῦτα συμβαίνειν εἴωθεν. οὐ γὰρ τὸ αὐτὸ σώματος καὶ ψυχῆς καὶ κτήματος καὶ ἀξιώματος καὶ τῶν συμβιούντων, ἀγαθῶν ἢ κακῶν, ὡς ἐξ ἀνάγκης ἐν ἅπασι τούτοις εὐτυχεῖν τινα ἢ πάλιν ἀτυχεῖν, ἀλλὰ συμβαίνοι μὲν ἂν ἴσως καὶ τὸ τοιοῦτο ἐπὶ τῶν τέλεον εὐδαιμονιζομένων ἢ ταλανιζομένων καιρῶν, ὅταν ἐν πάσαις ἢ ταῖς πλείσταις ἀφέσεσι συνδράμωσιν αἱ ὑπαντήσεις ἀγαθοποιῶν πάντων ἢ κακοποιῶν,

---

¹ πρὸς τά] in his verbis desinit V.
² ἂν post γὰρ add. MADECam., om. PLProc.

to be discovered from the peculiarities of the nativities, some of them again we shall base upon the general considerations already set forth, that is, upon the prorogations of greatest authority, all of them, however, and not one, as in the case of the space of life. We shall apply the prorogation from the horoscope to events relating to the body and to journeys abroad; that from the Lot of Fortune to matters of property; that from the moon to affections of the soul and to marriage; that from the sun to dignities and glory; that from the mid-heaven to the other details of the conduct of life, such as actions, friendships, and the begetting of children. For thus it will come about that one beneficent or maleficent star will not be the ruler of all of them on the same occasion, for usually many contradictory events take place at the same time. One may, for example, lose a relative and receive an inheritance, or at once be prostrated by illness and gain some dignity and promotion, or in the midst of misfortune become the father of children, or have other experiences of this sort which are apt to occur. For it is not usual that alike in goodness or badness of body, soul, property, dignity, and companions, one must by very necessity be either fortunate or, again, unfortunate in all these particulars. This, to be sure, might perhaps happen upon occasions that are completely blessed or completely unhappy, when the occourses of all the beneficent planets, or of all the maleficent planets, converge upon all or the majority of the prorogations. Rarely would this take place, however, because

---

³ ἢ κακοποιός om. Cam.

PTOLEMY

σπανίως δὲ διὰ τὸ τῆς ἀνθρωπίνης φύσεως ἀτελὲς μὲν πρὸς ἑκατέραν τῶν ἀκροτήτων,[1] εὐκατάφορον δὲ πρὸς τὴν ἐκ τῆς ἐναλλαγῆς τῶν ἀγαθῶν καὶ κακῶν συμμετρίαν. τοὺς μὲν οὖν ἀφετικοὺς τόπους κατὰ τὸν εἰρημένον τρόπον διακρινοῦμεν, τοὺς δὲ ἐν ταῖς ἀφέσεσιν ὑπαντῶντας οὐ μόνον πάλιν τοὺς ἀναιρέτας, ὥσπερ ἐπὶ τῶν τῆς ζωῆς χρόνων, ἀλλὰ πάντας ἁπλῶς παραληπτέον, καὶ ὁμοίως οὐ τοὺς σωματικῶς μόνον ἢ κατὰ διάμετρον ἢ τετράγωνον στάσιν συναντῶντας ἀλλὰ καὶ τοὺς κατὰ τρίγωνον καὶ ἑξάγωνον σχηματισμόν.

Καὶ πρῶτον μὲν δοτέον τοὺς χρόνους καθ' ἑκάστην ἄφεσιν τῷ κατ' αὐτῆς τῆς ἀφετικῆς μοίρας τυχόντι ἢ συσχηματισθέντι, ἐὰν δὲ μὴ οὕτως ἔχῃ, τῷ τὴν ἔγγιστα προήγησιν ἐπιλαβόντι μέχρι τοῦ τὴν ἑξῆς εἰς τὰ ἑπόμενα μοῖραν ἐπιθεωρήσαντος, εἶτα τούτῳ μέχρι τοῦ ἑξῆς καὶ ἐπὶ τῶν ἄλλων ὁμοίως, παραλαμβανομένων εἰς οἰκοδεσποτίαν καὶ τῶν τὰ ὅρια ἐπεχόντων ἀστέρων. δοτέον δὲ πάλιν ταῖς τῶν διαστάσεων μοίραις ἔτη· κατὰ μὲν τὴν ἀπὸ τοῦ ὡροσκόπου ἄφεσιν ἰσάριθμα τοῖς τοῦ οἰκείου κλίματος χρόνοις ἀναφορικοῖς, κατὰ δὲ τὴν ἀπὸ τοῦ μεσουρανήματος ἰσάριθμα τοῖς χρόνοις τῶν μεσουρανήσεων, κατὰ δὲ τὰς ἀπὸ τῶν λοιπῶν ἀνάλογον ἢ κατὰ τὸν [2] πρὸς τὰ κέντρα συνεγγισμὸν [3] τῶν ἀναφορῶν ἢ καταφορῶν ἢ συμ-

---

[1] ἀκροτήτων PL (-κρι-) ADE ; cf. ἀκρότητα Proc. ; ἀκρωτάτων MCam.², ἀκροτάτων Cam.¹

[2] ἢ καιὰ τὸν PL, cf. Proc., om. MADECam.

[3] συνεγγισμὸν] cf. κατὰ τὴν ἐγγύτητα Proc. ; συνεγγισμῶν P, συνεγγὺς L, συνεγγισμῷ MADECam.

human nature is imperfectly adapted to either one of the extremes, but is inclined toward the balance of good and evil arising from their alternation. We shall, then, make distinctions among the prorogatory places in the manner described, and as for the stars whose occourses take place in the prorogations, we must take into account not only the destructive ones, as in the case of the length of life, but absolutely all of them, and similarly not those alone that meet the prorogation only bodily, or by opposition, or in quartile,[1] but also those that are in the trine and sextile aspects.

In the first place, we must give the rulership of the times in each prorogation to the star that is actually upon the prorogatory degree or in aspect to it, or, if this condition does not exist, to the one that most nearly precedes, until we come to another which is in aspect with the next following degree in the order of the signs; then to this as far as the next following, and so on; and the planets which govern the terms are to be given a part of the rulership. And again we must assign years to the degrees of the intervals : in the prorogation from the horoscope a number equal to the times of ascension in the latitude concerned; in the prorogation from midheaven, as many as the times of the culminations; and in the prorogations from all the others, in proportion to or in accordance with the nearness of the

---

[1] That is, not only in the harmful aspects but also in the favourable ones.

μεσουρανήσεων, καθάπερ καὶ ἐπὶ τῶν τῆς ζωῆς χρόνων διωρισάμεθα.

Τοὺς μὲν οὖν καθολικοὺς χρονοκράτορας ληψόμεθα τὸν εἰρημένον τρόπον, τοὺς δ' ἐνιαυσιαίους ἐκβάλλοντες[1] τὸ πλῆθος τῶν ἀπὸ τῆς γενέσεως ἐτῶν ἀφ' ἑκάστου τῶν ἀφετικῶν τόπων εἰς τὰ ἑπόμενα κατὰ ζῴδιον,[2] καὶ τοῦ συντελειουμένου ζῳδίου τὸν οἰκοδεσπότην συμπαραλαμβάνοντες. τὸ δ' αὐτὸ καὶ ἐπὶ τῶν μηνῶν ποιήσομεν, ἐκβάλλοντες[3] πάλιν καὶ τούτων τὸ[4] ἀπὸ τοῦ γενεθλιακοῦ μηνὸς πλῆθος ἀπὸ τῶν τὴν κυρίαν τοῦ ἔτους λαβόντων τόπων, κατὰ ζῴδιον μέντοι ἡμέρας κη'. ὁμοίως δὲ καὶ ἐπὶ τῶν ἡμερῶν· τὰς γὰρ ἀπὸ τῆς γενεθλιακῆς ἡμέρας ἐκβαλοῦμεν ἀπὸ τῶν μηνιαίων τόπων, κατὰ ζῴδιον ἡμέρας $\bar{β}$ γ'.[5]

Προσεκτέον δὲ καὶ ταῖς ἐπεμβάσεσι πρὸς τοὺς τῶν χρόνων[6] τόπους γινομέναις, ὡς οὐ τὰ τυχόντα καὶ αὐταῖς συμβαλλομέναις πρὸς τὰ τῶν καιρῶν

---

[1] ἐκβάλλοντες] cf. ἐκβαλοῦμεν Proc.; ἐκβαλλόντων L, ἐμβάλλοντες PMADECam.
[2] ἐν post ζῴδιον add. MADECam., om. PLProc.
[3] ἐκβάλλοντες] ἐκβαλόντες P; cf. ἐκβαλοῦμεν Proc.; ἐμβάλλοντες cett. Cam.
[4] τὸ ego; cf. τὸν ἀριθμὸν τὸν . . . εὑρισκόμενον Proc.; τὰ MADECam.; om. PL.
[5] $\bar{β}$ γ' ME; cf. ἡμέρας δύο καὶ τρεῖς Proc.; β' καὶ ἥμισυ AD; β' ἥμισυ Cam.
[6] τῶν χρόνων PEProc., χρόνων L, καθολικοὺς μάλιστα MADCam.

---

[1] Literally, "masters of the times." The Anonymous (p. 173, Wolf) says that there are three " general chronocrators " (i.e. in each of the five general prorogations), the

TETRABIBLOS IV. 10

risings, or settings, or culminations, to the angles, as we explained in the discussion of the length of life.

We shall discover the general chronocrators,[1] then, in the manner described, and the annual chronocrators by setting out from each of the prorogatory places, in the order of the signs, the number of years from birth, one year to each sign,[2] and taking the ruler of the last sign. We shall do the same thing for the months, setting out, again, the number of months from the month of birth, starting from the places that govern the year, twenty-eight days to a sign; and similarly for the days, we shall set out the number of the days from the day of birth, starting with the places which govern the months, two and a third days to a sign.[3]

We must also pay attention to the ingresses [4] which are made to the places of the times, for they play no small part in the prediction of the times of

---

ἀφέτης (prorogator), ὑπαντήτωρ ("the one which comes to meet" the prorogator), and ὁριοκράτωρ ("master of the term").

[2] This is evidently the meaning of the text and it is so taken by the Anonymous, Proclus' *Paraphrase*, Gogava, and Cardanus, yet Bouché-Leclercq (p. 504) and Melanchthon's translation would count one year to each degree.

[3] There is dispute over the readings in this passage; the text reports what is best attested by the MSS. Bouché-Leclercq (p. 505, n. 1) would assign 30 days to a sign in laying out the number of months (so too Cardanus, but without any manuscript support), and 2½ days to a sign in the calculation of days (this reading is found in two MSS.). If "28 days" is correct, it represents roughly the length of the lunar month.

[4] ἐπέμβασις, "ingress," is the time taken by a planet to pass through one sign of the zodiac; *cf.* Bouché-Leclercq, p. 506; Cardanus, p. 364.

ἀποτελέσματα, καὶ μάλιστα ταῖς μὲν τοῦ Κρόνου πρὸς τοὺς καθολικοὺς τῶν χρόνων τόπους, ταῖς δὲ τοῦ Διὸς πρὸς τοὺς τῶν ἐνιαυσιαίων, ταῖς δὲ τοῦ ἡλίου καὶ Ἄρεως καὶ Ἀφροδίτης καὶ Ἑρμοῦ πρὸς τοὺς τῶν μηνιαίων, ταῖς δὲ τῆς σελήνης παρόδοις πρὸς τοὺς τῶν ἡμερησίων, καὶ ὡς τῶν μὲν καθολικῶν χρονοκρατόρων κυριωτέρων ὄντων πρὸς τὴν τοῦ ἀποτελέσματος τελείωσιν, τῶν δ' ἐπὶ μέρους συνεργούντων ἢ ἀποσυνεργούντων κατὰ τὸ οἰκεῖον ἢ ἀνοικεῖον τῶν φύσεων, τῶν δ' ἐπεμβάσεων τὰς ἐπιτάσεις καὶ τὰς ἀνέσεις τῶν συμπτωμάτων ἀπεργαζομένων. τὸ μὲν γὰρ καθ' ὅλου τῆς ποιότητος ἴδιον καὶ τὴν τοῦ χρόνου παράτασιν ὅ τε τῆς ἀφέσεως τόπος καὶ ὁ τῶν καθολικῶν χρόνων κύριος μετὰ τοῦ τῶν ὁρίων διασημαίνει, διὰ τὸ συνοικειοῦσθαι τῶν ἀστέρων ἕκαστον ἐπ' αὐτῆς τῆς γενέσεως τοῖς τόποις ὧν[1] ἀπ' ἀρχῆς ἔτυχον λαβόντες τὴν οἰκοδεσποτίαν.

Τὸ δὲ πότερον ἀγαθὸν ἢ τοὐναντίον ἔσται τὸ σύμπτωμα καταλαμβάνεται διὰ τῆς τῶν χρονοκρατόρων φυσικῆς τε καὶ συγκρατικῆς ἰδιοτροπίας, εὐποιητικῆς ἢ κακωτικῆς, καὶ τῆς ἀπ' ἀρχῆς πρὸς τὸν ἐπικρατούμενον τόπον συνοικειώσεως ἢ ἀντιπαθείας. τὸ δ' ἐν ποίοις χρόνοις μᾶλλον ἐπισημανθήσεται τὸ ἀποτέλεσμα δείκνυται διὰ τῶν ἐνιαυσιαίων καὶ μηνιαίων ζῳδίων πρὸς τοὺς αἰτιατικοὺς τόπους συσχηματισμῶν καὶ τῶν κατὰ τὰς ἐπεμβάσεις τῶν ἀστέρων καὶ τὰς φάσεις ἡλίου καὶ σελήνης πρὸς τὰ ἐνιαύσια καὶ μηνιαῖα τῶν ζῳδίων. οἱ μὲν γὰρ συμφώνως ἔχοντες πρὸς τοὺς διατιθε-

TETRABIBLOS IV. 10

events; particularly to the ingresses of Saturn to the general places of the times, and to those of Jupiter to the places of the years; to those of the sun, Mars, Venus, and Mercury to those of the months, and to the transits of the moon to those of the days. The reason for this is that the general chronocrators have greater authority to realize the prediction, while the partial chronocrators assist or deter, in accordance with the familiarity or unfamiliarity of their natures, and the ingresses influence the degree of increase or diminution in the event. For in general the special quality and the length of time are signified by the prorogatory place and the lord of the general times together with the lord of the terms, because each one of the planets at the very time of the nativity is made familiar with the places which they happened at first to govern.

Whether the event will be good or bad is discovered from the natural and composite properties of the chronocrators, whether they are beneficent or maleficent, and from their original familiarity with or antipathy to the places which they possess. At what time the predicted event will be evidenced is shown by the aspects of the annual and monthly signs to the places which furnish the causes, and by the aspects of the signs into which the planets are making ingress and in which the phases of the sun and moon occur to the annual and monthly signs. For those whose relation to the affected places under

---

[1] ἄν post ὧν add. MADECam.; om. PLProc.

μένους τόπους ἀπὸ τῆς ἐν τῇ γενέσει καταρχῆς καὶ κατὰ τὰς ἐπεμβάσεις συμφώνως αὐτοῖς συσχηματισθέντες ἀγαθῶν εἰσι[1] περὶ τὸ ὑποκείμενον εἶδος ἀπεργαστικοί, καθάπερ ἐὰν ἐναντιωθῶσι φαύλων· οἱ δὲ ἀσυμφώνως καὶ παρ' αἵρεσιν διαμηκίσαντες μὲν ἢ τετραγωνίσαντες ταῖς παρόδοις κακῶν εἰσιν αἴτιοι, κατὰ δὲ τοὺς ἄλλους σχηματισμοὺς οὐκέτι.

Κἂν μὲν οἱ αὐτοὶ καὶ τῶν χρόνων καὶ τῶν ἐπεμβάσεων κυριεύσωσιν ἀστέρες, ὑπερβάλλουσα καὶ ἄκρατος γίνεται ἡ τοῦ ἀποτελέσματος φύσις, ἐάν τε ἐπὶ τὸ ἀγαθὸν ἐάν τε ἐπὶ τὸ φαῦλον ῥέπῃ·[2] καὶ πολὺ πλέον[3] ἐὰν μὴ μόνον[4] διὰ τὸ χρονοκράτορας εἶναι κυριεύσωσι τοῦ τῆς αἰτίας εἴδους, ἀλλὰ καὶ διὰ τὸ κατ' αὐτὴν τὴν ἀρχὴν τῆς γενέσεως τὴν οἰκοδεσποτίαν αὐτοῦ τετυχηκέναι. κατὰ πάντα δ' ὁμοῦ δυστυχοῦσιν ἢ εὐτυχοῦσιν, ὅταν ἤτοι τόπος εἷς καὶ ὁ αὐτὸς ὑπὸ πασῶν ἢ τῶν πλείστων ἀφέσεων τύχῃ καταληφθείς, ἢ τούτων διαφόρων οὐσῶν οἱ αὐτοὶ χρόνοι πάσας ἢ τὰς πλείστας ὑπαντήσεις ὁμοίως ἀγαθοποιοὺς ἢ κακοποιοὺς τύχωσιν ἐσχηκότες. ὁ μὲν οὖν τύπος[5] τῆς τῶν καιρῶν ἐπισκέψεως τοιοῦτός[6] τις ἂν γίγνοιτο,

---

[1] εἰσι PLAD, εἰς τὸ MECam.
[2] ῥέπῃ MEACam.¹, -ει D, om. PLCam.²
[3] καὶ πολ(λ)ὺ πλέον PL, πολὺ δὲ πλέον MAD, ὡς ἐπὶ πολὺ δὲ πλέον ECam.
[4] ἐὰν μὴ μόνον PL, εἰ μὲν οὐ μόνον Cam.², om. MADECam.¹

TETRABIBLOS IV. 10

consideration is harmonious from the beginning made in the nativity, and which in their ingresses are in favourable aspect to them, exert a good effect upon the species of the matter concerned, even as they cause evil if they oppose. And those which are inharmoniously related and of opposite sect cause evil if they are in opposition or in quartile to the transits, but not in the other aspects.

And if the same planets are lords of both the times and the ingresses, the nature of the predicted event is made excessive and unalloyed, whether it incline to the good or to the bad; all the more so if they govern the species of the cause [1] not only because they are chronocrators, but also because they ruled it originally in the nativity. The subjects are unfortunate or fortunate in all respects at once, whenever either all or most of the prorogations are found in one and the same place, or if these are different, whenever all or most of the occourses occurring at the same times are similarly fortunate or unfortunate. The character of the investigation of the times, then, is of this fashion,[2]

---

[1] *I.e.* determine the quality (good or bad) of the causation.
[2] The original ending of the treatise is in doubt; see the Introduction, pp. xviii-xx.

---

[b] τύπος libri, τόπος Cam.
[c] τοιοῦτος PL, τοσοῦτος cett. Cam.

PTOLEMY

Conclusion according to Parisinus 2425:
κατὰ τὸν ἁρμόζοντα ταῖς φυσικαῖς[1] χρηματείαις[2] τύπον· τὰς δὲ κατὰ μέρος ἐπιβολὰς τῆς ποιότητος τῶν χρονικῶν ἀποτελεσμάτων πολυχόως[3] καὶ δυσερμηνεύτως ἐχούσας ἐνθάδε μάλιστα ⟨κατὰ⟩[4] τὸ διεξοδικὸν τῶν ἀποβησομένων ὑπολειπτέον,[5] διὰ τὴν ἐξ ἀρχῆς ἡμῶν πρόθεσιν, τῇ τοῦ μαθηματικοῦ πρὸς τὸ συγκρατικὸν εἶδος εὐστοχίᾳ,[6] τὸ τῆς καθ' ὅλου φύσεως τῶν ἀστέρων ποιητικὸν ἔτι καὶ τοῖς ἐπὶ μέρους ὁμοίως κατὰ τὸ ἀκόλουθον ἐφαρμόζειν δυναμένου. διοδευομένου δὲ καὶ τοῦ γενεθλιαλογικοῦ τόπου κεφαλαιωδῶς ⟨καλῶς⟩ ἂν ἔχοι[7] καὶ τῇδε τῇ πραγματείᾳ τὸ προσῆκον ἐπιθεῖναι τέλος.

Conclusion according to MADProc.Cam.:
τὰ δὲ εἴδη[8] τῶν ἀποτελεσμάτων τῶν συμβαινόντων κατὰ χρόνους συνάπτειν ἐνταῦθα κατὰ διέξοδον παραλείψομεν, δι' ὃν ἔφην σκοπὸν ἐξ ἀρχῆς, ὅτι[9] τῶν ἀστέρων ἡ ποιητικὴ δύναμις, ἣν ἔχουσιν ἐπὶ τοῖς καθ' ὅλου, ὁμοίως καὶ ἐν τοῖς μερικοῖς κατὰ τὸ ἀκόλουθον ἐφαρμόζεσθαι δύναται, συναπτομένων εὐστόχως τῆς τε αἰτίας τοῦ μαθηματικοῦ καὶ τῆς αἰτίας τῆς ἐκ τῆς συγκράσεως.

---

[1] φυσικαῖς] δυσικαῖς PL.
[2] χρηματείαις] χριμαντείαις P, χρωματίαις L.
[3] πολυχόως] πολύχρουν P, πολύχροαν L; cf. πολύχουν τε ὄντα καὶ σχεδὸν ἄπειρον p. 107, 5 Cam.²
[4] ⟨κατὰ⟩ addidi; cf. infra κατὰ διέξοδον et iii. 1, p. 226, κατὰ τὴν διέξοδον.
[5] ὑπολυπτέον P, ὑπoληπτέον L.
[6] εὐστοχίαν PL. [7] ἂν ἔχοι] ἀνέχῃ P, ἀνέχει L.

TETRABIBLOS IV. 10

Conclusion according to Parisinus 2425:
by the style which agrees with the natural procedures.¹ At this point, however, the method of attacking, in particular cases, the problem of the quality of temporal predictions, with a complete account of the results, which is a complicated matter difficult of explanation, must, in accordance with our original programme, be left to the astrologer's good judgement of the matter of temperaments, for thereby he is able correctly to accommodate to specific instances the effective force of the stars' general nature. Now since the topic of nativities has been summarily reviewed, it would be well to bring this procedure also to a fitting close.

Conclusion according to MADProc.Cam.:
We shall, however, omit adding at this point ² a detailed account of the kinds of predicted events that happen at the times, on account of the plan which I stated at the outset, namely that the effective power which the planets exercise in general situations can be made to apply similarly and consistently in particular cases also, if the cause furnished by the astrologer and the cause arising from the mixture are combined with due skill.

¹ Parallels to many of the words and expressions used in the conclusion which appears in PL can be found in iii. 1; see the Introduction, p. xx, n. 1.

² This concluding paragraph, found in MAD among the MSS. studied, seems to have been borrowed bodily from the *Paraphrase* of Proclus. Camerarius used it in both his editions.

---

⁸ τὰ δὲ εἴδη . . . ἐκ τῆς συγκράσεως scr. m. altera M: ipsissima haec verba ap. Vat. gr. 1453 (Procli Paraphrasin continentem) leguntur.   ⁹ ὅτι] ὅτε Cam.

INDEX TO PTOLEMY.

Action, prediction of the quality of, 381 ff.
Adonis, 147.
Affliction, 267 n., 285, 431 n.
Ages of man, 61, 223, 437 ff.
Allatius, Leo, xv.
Almagest, vi ff., 3, 60 n., 95 n., 171 n., 292 n., 295 n., 297 n., 299 n.
Amazons, 149.
Ammon, 153.
Anaeretic, *see* Destructive.
Andromeda, 57, 435.
Angles, 61, 121 ; of a nativity, 165, 191 n., 207, 235.
Anonymous Commentator on the *Tetrabiblos*, xiv, 105 n., 107 n., 113 n., 114 n., 125 n., 170 n., 178 n., 199 n., 245 n., 249 n., 286 n., 333 n., 395 n., 396 n., 403 n., 411 n., 427 n., 433 n., 437 n., 443 n., 453 n.
Antares, 51.
Apeliotes, 63.
Aphetic, *see* Prorogation.
Apoclimata, 423 n., 437.
Apparition, *see* Appearance.
Appearance, 209, 211, 313, 381.
Application, 113, 169, 209.
Approach, 9.
Aquarius, effect of, 53, 175, 205, 325 ; solid, 67 ; house of Saturn, 81 ; N.E. triangle, 87.
Aquila, 57, 173.
Ara, 59.
Arcturus, 55.
Argo, 57, 175, 433.
Aries, 47, 201, 315, 325, 391 ; starting point of zodiac, 61 ; equinoctial, 67 ; masculine, 69 ; diurnal, 69 ; house of Mars, 81 ; N.W. triangle, 83 ; exaltation of sun and depression of Saturn, 89.

Aristotle, vii, 4 n., 5 n., 34 n., 161 n., 347 n.
Ascensions, 75, 95, 233 ; use of, in prorogation, explained, 286 n.
Ashmand, J. M., xiii, xv, 377 n.
Aspects, 9, 72 f. ; of the fixed stars, 171.
Asses, 49, 217.
Astrolabe, 229.
Astrology distinguished from astronomy, 3 f. ; possibility of, 5 ff. ; false practitioners of, 13 ; difficulty of, 15 ; value of, 21 ff. ; universal *vs.* particular, 25 n., 117 f., 221.
Attendance, 241, 377 n.
Auriga, 55.

" Beams," 193.
" Beholding " signs, 77.
Bicorporeal signs, 67, 175, 253, 257, 335, 394 n., 409.
Bodily conjunction, 114 n.
Bodily form, prediction of, 307 ff.
Body, parts of, governed by planets, 319.
Boll, Franz, xii.
Boötes, 55.
Boreas, 63.
Brothers and sisters, predictions about, 251 ff.

Camerarius, Joachim, xi *et passim*.
Cancer, 49, 173, 203, 315, 323, 325, 329, 365, 391, 409 ; solstitial, 67 ; house of moon, 79 ; S.W. triangle, 87 ; exaltation of Jupiter and depression of Mars, 91.
Canis, 57.
Capricorn, 53, 173, 205, 311, 323, 325, 329, 391 ; solstitial, 67 ; house of Saturn, 81 ; S.E. triangle, 85 ; exaltation of

INDEX

Mars and depression of Jupiter, 91.
Cardanus, Hieronymus, xiii, xv, 13 n., 40 n., 41 n., 129 n., 133 n., 178 n., 206 n., 209 n., 259 n., 261 n., 266 n., 422 n., 453 n.
Cassiopeia, 55.
Castor and Pollux, 49.
Centaurus, 57.
Cepheus, 55, 435.
Cetus, 57.
Chaldaean system of terms, 91, 99; observations, 14 n.
Chariots, 111.
Children, predictions about, 409 ff.
Children that are not reared, genitures of, 265 ff.
Chronocrators or rulers of times, 451 ff., 452 n.
Cities, nativities of, 161.
Clepsydra, 231.
Climes, 231 n.
Coma Berenices, 55, 321.
Comets, 193, 217.
Commanding and obeying signs, 75.
Conception *vs.* birth as the starting-point of life, 223 ff.
Conjunctions, 207.
Corona Australis, 59.
Corona Septentrionalis, 55.
Corvus, 57, 437 n.
Cosmic position *vs.* position in a nativity, 239, 253.
Countries, characteristics of the inhabitants of, 133 ff.
Crater, 57.
Culmination, 239; *see* Mid-heaven.
Cygnus, 55.

Day and night, 287 n.
Day, prediction of weather for, 211.
Death, predictions of quality of, 427 ff.
Delphinus, 57, 173.
Demeter and Korê, geniture of, 259.
Demons, affliction by, 365 f.
Demophilus, xiv.
Depressions and exaltations, 89.
Destructive places and bodies, 271, 283 ff.
Dignities, prediction of, 377 ff.
Dioscuri, geniture of the, 259.

Diseases of the body, prediction of, 317 ff.; of the soul, prediction of, 363 ff.
Disjunct signs, 77, 275, 317.
Division of times, *see* Ages of man.
Domination, 233, 238, 339 n.
Draco, 55, 433 n.

Eclipses in predictions about countries and cities, 161 ff.; colours of, 191.
Ecliptic, 47 n.; obliquity of, 209.
Effluence or emanation, 7, 275.
Egyptians, 197; combination of astrology and medicine by, 31 ff.; terms according to, 91 ff.
Elevation, 417; *see* Overcoming.
Epicycles, 115 n.
Equal power, signs of, 77.
Equinoctial signs, 67, 175, 427; times or periods, 287 n., 289 n.
Equinoxes, 197; as beginnings of signs, 109.
Epilepsy, 365 f.
Eridanus, 57.
Ethiopians, 123.
Ethnography, astrological, 121 ff.
Exaltations and depressions, 89.
Exchange, 396 n., 413, 415 n.
Exhalations, 37, 275.
Exposing of children, 264 n.

"Face" (or "proper face"), 111.
Familiarity, 65 n.
Fate, 23 f.
Fathers, predictions about, 241 ff.
Feminine, *see* Masculine.
"Following" and "preceding," 105 n., 112 n., 201 n.
Fortune, Lot of, 243, 255, 373 ff., 411, 413, 417, 421, 423, 449; how determined, 275 f.; as prorogator, 275 ff.
Fortune, material, predictions about, 373 ff.
Friends and enemies, predictions about, 413 ff.

Gemini, 49, 203, 317, 329; bicorporeal, 67; house of Mercury, 83; N.E. triangle, 87.
Genethlialogy, 119, 221; subdivisions of, 235 f.
Geniculator, 55.
Geniture, *see* Nativity, Horoscope.

INDEX

Gnomon, 231.
Gogava, Antonius, xiii, 453 n.
Good Daemon, house of, in predictions about children, 409.
Graces, geniture of the, 259.

Halos, 193, 215, 217.
Harpocratiacs, 263.
Heliacal rising, *see* Rising.
Hemispheres, summer and winter, 77.
Hephaestion, 193 n., 217 n, 305 n.
Hermaphrodites, 263.
Horary magnitude or period, 287 n., 292 n.
Horoscope, 69, 163, 190 n, 253; determination of, 229 ff ; in prediction of sex, 255; in prediction of twins, 257; in genitures of monsters, 261 ff ; defined, 273; as prorogator, 275 ff., 449.
Hourly prediction of weather, 211.
Hours, ordinary or civil, 77, 165, 287 n., 293 n.; equinoctial, 167.
Houses or the planets, 79; of a nativity, 190 n., 272 n.
Hyades, 47, 203, 403.
Hydra, 57, 433 n.

Iatromathematica, 31 ff.
Inclination, 9 n.
Increasing and diminishing motion of planets, 115 n., 239.
Ingress, 427, 453 n.
Initiatives, 447 n.
Injuries of the body, prediction of, 317 ff.
Insanity, 365 f.
Isis, 139.
Isosceles configuration, 267, 269.

"Jars," 193.
Junctinus, Fr , xii, 423 n.
Jupiter, 37, 183, 263, 309, 331, 373, 375, 381, 383 ff., 395, 397; beneficent, 39; masculine, 41; diurnal, 43; houses of, 81; governs N.W. triangle, 83, parts of body, 319, elderly age, 447; exaltation of, 89; as ruler of soul, 347 ff. ; in predictions about children, 409 ff., friendship, 419, travel, 425, death, 429.

Kings, geniture of the, 259.

Latitude, 207.
" Leading," *see* Following.
Leo, 49, 203, 315, 325, 391, 409; solid, 67; house of sun, 79; N.W. triangle, 83.
Lepus, 57.
Libra (or " Claws "), 51, 205, 317, 391; equinoctial, 67; masculine, 69; diurnal, 69; house of Venus, 81; N.E. triangle, 87; exaltation of Saturn and depression of sun, 89.
Life, years of, assigned by planets, 93; length of, predictions about, 271 ff.
Lucian (pseudo-), 12 n.
Luminaries and planets, table of, xxv; in predictions of sex, 255; in prediction of twins, 257; in genitures of monsters, 261 ff.
Luminaries in predictions of dignities, 377 ff. ; in predictions about travel, 423 ff.
Lupus, 59.
Lyra, 55.

Magnets, 27.
Males and females, predictions about the birth of, 255 ff.
Manger (Praesepe), 49, 203, 217.
Marriage, predictions about, 393 ff.
Mars, 37, 183, 311, 321 ff., 375, 381, 395, 397, 399; maleficent, 39; masculine, 41; nocturnal, 43; houses of, 81; governs S.W. triangle, 87, parts of body, 319, manhood, 445; exaltation of, 91; as ruler of soul, 353 ff.; in predictions about sexual passion and perversion, 369 ff., action, 383, 385 ff., love and marriage, 405 ff., children, 409 ff., friendship, 419, travel, 425, death, 427, 435.
Masculine and feminine planets, 41, 176 n., 369 n.; signs, 69.
Matutine stars, 40 n. ; appearances, 211.
Melanchthon, Philip, xi, xiii, 423 n.
Melothesia, 310, 329 n.
Mercury, 39, 187, 263, 311, 329, 373, 375, 381, 395, 397, 399; common, 39, 41, 43; houses of,

463

INDEX

83; governs N.E. triangle, 87 parts of body, 321, childhood, 443; exaltation of, 91; in prorogation, 281; in predictions about qualities of mind, 333 ff. diseases of the soul, 363 ff., action, 383 ff., children, 409 ff., friendship, 419, travel, 425, death, 431; as ruler of the soul, 359 f.
Meteors, 217 f.
Michigan astrological papyrus, 111 n., 319 n., 393 n., 445 n.
Mid-heaven, 165, 449; in predictions about action, 237, about children, 409.
Mithras, 139.
Mixture, *see* Temperament.
Monsters, birth of, 261 ff.
Month, prediction of weather for, 209.
Moon, 7 ff., 35, 71, 361; feminine, 41; nocturnal, 43; effect of phases of, 45; house of, 79; governs S.E. triangle, 85, S.W. triangle, 87, parts of body, 321, infancy, 443; exaltation of, 89; new and full, 207, 231; in predictions about weather, 215, mothers, 241, 247 ff., blood-brethren, 251 ff., bodily form, 307, 313, quality of soul, 333 ff., diseases of soul, 363 ff., sexual passion and perversion, 369 ff., action, 391, marriage, 393 ff., children, 409 ff., friendship, 413 ff., travel, 423 ff; as prorogator, 275 ff.; nodes and bendings of, 325.
Mother of the Gods, 147.
Mothers, predictions about, 247 ff.
Multiple births. 259.

Nativity (geniture, horoscope), 190 n.
Nechepso and Petosiris, 91 n., 227 n., 270 n.
New moon of the year, 195.
Nicomachus of Gerasa, 33 n., 73 n., 83 n.
Nile, 175, 197.
Non-signifying places, 267 n.
Notus, 63.

Obeying, 75.
Occident, in predictions of injury or disease, 317 ff.
Occidental, defined, 241.
Occourse, 447 n.
Occultations, 9.
Ophiuchus, 55.
Opposition, 73, 245, 283; disharmonious, 75.
Orient in predictions of bodily form, 307, of injuries and disease, 317 ff.
Oriental and occidental defined, 241.
Orion, 57.
Overcoming, 189 n., 245 n., 253, 339 n., 416 n.; *see* Elevation.

Paranatellonta, 159 n.
Parents, predictions about, 241 ff.
Parheliac clouds, 215.
Pegasus, 57.
Perseus, 55, 435.
Petosiris, *see* Nechepso.
Pisces, 53, 175, 205, 315, 329, 365, 391, 409; bicorporeal, 67; house of Jupiter, 81; S.W. triangle, 87; exaltation of Venus and depression of Mercury, 91.
Piscis Australis, 53 n., 57.
Pitcher (constellation), 403.
" Places " (in theory of terms), 109.
Planets, table of, xxv; effects of, 7 f.; names of, 35 n.; order of, 37 n.; beneficent and maleficent, 39; masculine and feminine, 41, 176 n.; effect of aspects of, to sun, 45; houses of, 79; triangles governed by, 67, 83 ff.; exaltations and depressions of, 89; strength and weakness of, 239; maleficent, in genitures of monsters, 261 ff., of children that are not reared, 265 ff., in prorogation, 281 ff., in predictions of injury and disease, 317 ff., in predictions of death, 437; beneficent, in genitures of exposed children, 269, in prorogation, 281 ff.; parts of body governed by, 319 f.; *see also* Stations.
Pleiades, 47, 201, 321.
Porphyry, *Introduction to the Tetrabiblos*, xiv, 377 n., 416 n.

INDEX

Posidonius, vii, 121 n.
Praesepe, *see* Manger.
"Preceding," or "leading"; *see* "Following."
Precessions, 335.
Proclus, *Paraphrase of the Tetrabiblos* ascribed to, xiv f., 5 n. 30 n., 61 n., 98 n., 199 n., 235 n., 251 n., 325 n., 355 n., 393 n., 406 n., 408 n., 417 n., 423 n., 453 n., 459 n.
Procyon, 57.
Prorogation, 269, 271 ff., 449; two methods of, 279 ff.; examples of, 295 ff.
Ptolemy, Claudius, life of, v ff.; works of, vii f.; literary style of, xxii.

Quadrants (of ecliptic), 71, 313.
Quarters of the world, 129 ff.; of the year or zodiac, 207.
Quartile, 73; disharmonious, 75, 245, 283, 417 n., 451.

Rays, projection of, 114 n., 115, 269, 281, 427 ff.; of the sun, under the, 285, 303 n.
Regulus, 49.
Rejoicing of planets, 113.
Release, 286 n.
Return of heavenly bodies to their original positions (ἀποκατάστασις), 15.
Right and left, 378 n.
Rising and setting, 45, 169.
Rods, 193.

Sagitta, 55.
Sagittarius, 51, 173, 205, 315 f., 329, 365, 391; bicorporeal, 67; house of Jupiter, 81; N.W. triangle, 83.
Saturn, 35, 179, 309, 321 ff., 375, 381, 383 ff., 393, 395, 397, 399; maleficent, 39; masculine, 41; diurnal, 43; houses of, 81; governs N.E. triangle, 87, parts of body, 319, old age, 447; exaltation of, 89; in predictions about fathers, 241 ff., children, 409 ff., friendship, 419, travel, 425, death, 429, 433; as ruler of soul, 339 ff.

Scorpio, 51, 205, 317, 325, 391, 409; solid, 67; house of Mars, 81; S.W. triangle, 87; depression of moon, 89.
Scythians, 123.
Seasons, 59, 199.
Sects, 43 n.
Separation, 113, 169.
Serpents produced from snowstorms, 181.
Sex, *see* Males and females; Masculine and feminine planets.
Sextile, 73, 283; harmonious, 75.
Sexual passion and perversion, predictions about, 369 ff.
Significator, 429 n.
Signs, table of, xxv; classification of, by shapes, etc., 71, 171 ff.; sympathetic to cities, 161; human and animal, 261 ff., 389, 427, 433; terrestrial and aquatic, 391, 427, 433; simple and multiform, 395; fecund and sterile, 409 ff.; watery, 425, 433; mutilated, 435; *see also* "Beholding"; Bicorporeal; Commanding; Disjunct; Equinoctial; Equinoxes; Masculine; Obeying; Solid; Solstices; Solstitial.
Sirius, 57, 197, 437 n.
Slaves, predictions about, 421 ff.
Solid signs, 67, 175, 335, 425.
Solstices, 197; as beginnings of signs, 109.
Solstitial signs, 67, 175, 335, 427.
Soul, quality of, predictions about, 333 ff.; diseases of, predictions about, 363 ff.
Spica, 51.
Stars, fixed, effects of, 7 f.
Stations of planets, 45, 163, 169, 313.
Sun, 7 ff., 35, 313, 361; common, 39, 286 n.; diurnal, 43; house of, 79; governs N.W. triangle, 83, parts of body, 319, young manhood, 445; exaltation of, 89; in predictions about weather, 213, fathers, 237, 241 ff., sexual passion, 369 ff., action, 381 ff., marriage, 395 ff., friendship, 413 ff.; as prorogator, 275 ff., 449.
Syrus, addressed in *Tetrabiblos*, ix, 3.
Syzygy, 231 n., 261, 279.

465

INDEX

Taurus, 47, 201, 315 f., 325, 391; solid, 67; house of Venus, 81; S.E. triangle, 85; exaltation of moon, 89.
Temperament, 64 n., 223.
Terms, 91 ff., 429; according to the Egyptians, 91 ff.; according to the Chaldaeans, 99; according to Ptolemy, 103 ff.
Testimony, 395 n.
Tetrabiblos of Claudius Ptolemy, name of, viii f.; genuineness of, ix f.; text editions of, xi f.; translations of, xii ff.; commentaries on, xiv f.; manuscripts of, xv ff.; ending of, xix f.
Thrones, 111.
Torch, 47.
Transits, 121.
Travel, predictions about, 423 ff.
Triangles or triplicities, 83 ff.; familiarity of, with countries, 129 ff.
Triangulum, 57.
Trine, 73, 283; harmonious, 75, 417 n.
Triplets, birth of, 259.
"Trumpets," 193.
Twins, predictions about the birth of, 257 ff.

Ursa Major, 55, 123.
Ursa Minor, 55, 123.

Venus, 37, 185, 263, 311, 331, 375, 381, 395, 397, 399; beneficent, 39; feminine, 41; nocturnal, 43; houses of, 81; governs S.E. triangle, 85, S.W. triangle, 87, parts of body, 319 f., youth, 443; exaltation of, 91; in predictions about mothers, 241, 247 ff., blood-brethren, 251 ff., sexual passion and perversion, 369 ff., action, 383, 385 ff., marriage, 401, 407, children, 409 ff., friendship, 419, travel, 425, death, 431; as ruler of soul, 357 f.
Vespertine stars, 40 n.; appearances, 211.
Vindemiator, 51.
Virgo, 49, 173, 203, 315 f., 323, 365, 391, 409; bicorporeal, 67; house of Mercury, 83; S.E. triangle, 85; exaltation of Mercury and depression of Venus, 91.

Weather, 201 ff.
Whalley, John, vi n., xlii, 261 n.
Winds, 63, 199, 209, 219.
Witnessing, 261.

Zephyrus, 63.
Zodiac, 47 n.; table of signs of, xxv; starting-point of, 59, 109 n., 195; quarters of, 207.

www.ingramcontent.com/pod-product-compliance
Lightning Source LLC
Chambersburg PA
CBHW040212020526
44111CB00050B/2936